NETWORKING ESSENTIALS: FOURTH EDITION

A COMPTIA NETWORK+ N10-006 TEXTBOOK

JEFFREY S. BEASLEY AND PIYASAT NILKAEW

Pearson
800 East 96th Street
Indianapolis, Indiana 46240 USA

NETWORKING ESSENTIALS: FOURTH EDITION

Networking Essentials, Fourth Edition

ISBN-13: 978-0-7897-5819-4
ISBN-10: 0-7897-5819-9

Library of Congress Control Number: 2015955285

Printed in the United States of America

Second Printing: June 2017

Trademarks

All terms mentioned in this book that are known to be trademarks or service marks have been appropriately capitalized. Pearson IT Certification cannot attest to the accuracy of this information. Use of a term in this book should not be regarded as affecting the validity of any trademark or service mark.

Warning and Disclaimer

Every effort has been made to make this book as complete and as accurate as possible, but no warranty or fitness is implied. The information provided is on an "as is" basis. The authors and the publisher shall have neither liability nor responsibility to any person or entity with respect to any loss or damages arising from the information contained in this book or from the use of the CD or programs accompanying it.

Special Sales

For information about buying this title in bulk quantities, or for special sales opportunities (which may include electronic versions; custom cover designs; and content particular to your business, training goals, marketing focus, or branding interests), please contact our corporate sales department at corpsales@pearsoned.com or (800) 382-3419.

For government sales inquiries, please contact governmentsales@pearsoned.com.

For questions about sales outside the U.S., please contact international@pearsoned.com.

ASSOCIATE PUBLISHER
Dave Dusthimer

EXECUTIVE EDITOR
Brett Bartow

SENIOR DEVELOPMENT EDITOR
Chris Cleveland

MANAGING EDITOR
Sandra Schroeder

PROJECT EDITOR
Mandie Frank

COPY EDITOR
Bart Reed

INDEXER
Ken Johnson

PROOFREADER
Jess DeGabriele

TECHNICAL EDITORS
Anthony Sequeria
Dr. Kenneth L Hawkins
Douglas E. Maume

PEER REVIEWERS
DeAnnia Clements
Osman GuzideGene Carwile
Dr. Theodor Richardson

PUBLISHING COORDINATOR
Vanessa Evans

DESIGNERS
Mark Shirar
Alan Clements

COMPOSITOR
Tricia Bronkella

CONTENTS AT A GLANCE

TABLE OF CONTENTS

CHAPTER 2   Physical Layer Cabling: Twisted Pair   **64**

CHAPTER 11 **Troubleshooting** **514**

ABOUT THE AUTHORS

Jeffrey S. Beasley is a professor in the Information and Communications Technology program at New Mexico State University, where he teaches computer networking and many related topics. He is the author of *Networking, Second Edition,* as well as coauthor of *Modern Electronic Communication*, Ninth Edition, *Networking Essentials 3e,* and *A Practical Guide to Advance Networking.*

Piyasat Nilkaew is the director of Telecommunications and Networking at New Mexico State University, with more than 15 years of experience in network management and consulting. He has extensive expertise in deploying and integrating multiprotocol and multivendor data, voice, and video network solutions. He is coauthor of *Networking Essentials 3e* and *A Practical Guide to Advance Networking.*

DEDICATIONS

This book is dedicated to my family: Kim, Damon, and Dana. —Jeff Beasley

This book is dedicated to my family: June, Ariya, and Atisat. —Piyasat Nilkaew

ACKNOWLEDGMENTS

I am grateful to the many people who have helped with this text. My sincere thanks go to the following technical consultants:

- Danny Bosch and Matthew Peralta for sharing their expertise with optical networks and unshielded twisted-pair cabling, Don Yates for his help with the initial Net-Challenge software, and Abel Sanchez for his assistance the newest version of Net-Challenge.

I would also like to thank my many past and present students for their help with this book.

- Kathryn Sager and Joshua Cook for their work on the Net-Challenge software; Adam Segura for his help with taking pictures of the steps for CAT6 termination; Marc Montez, Carine George-Morris, Brian Morales, Michael Thomas, Jacob Ulibarri, Scott Leppelman, and Aarin Buskirk for their help with laboratory development; and Josiah Jones and Raul Marquez Jr. for their help with the Wireshark material.

- Aaron Shapiro and Aaron Jackson for their help in testing the many network connections presented in the text.

- Paul Bueno and Anthony Bueno for reading through the early draft of the text.

Your efforts are greatly appreciated.

We appreciate the excellent feedback of the following reviewers: Phillip Davis, DelMar College, TX; Thomas D. Edwards, Carteret Community College, NC; William Hessmiller, Editors & Training Associates; Bill Liu, DeVry University, CA; and Timothy Staley, DeVry University, TX.

Our thanks to the people at Pearson for making this project possible: Dave Dusthimer, for providing us with the opportunity to work on the fourth edition of this text, and Vanessa Evans, for helping make this process enjoyable. Thanks to Christopher Cleveland, and the all the people at Pearson IT Certification, and also to the many technical editors for their help with editing the manuscript.

Special thanks to our families for their continued support and patience.

—Jeffrey S. Beasley and Piyasat Nilkaew

ABOUT THE TECHNICAL REVIEWERS

Anthony Sequeria began his IT career in 1994 with IBM in Tampa, Florida. He quickly formed his own computer consultancy, Computer Solutions, and then discovered his true passion—teaching and writing about Microsoft and Cisco technologies. Anthony has lectured to massive audiences around the world while working for Mastering Computers. Anthony has never been happier in his career than he is now as a full-time trainer for CBT Nuggets. He is an avid tennis player, a private pilot, and a semi-professional poker player, and he enjoys getting beaten up by women and children at the martial arts school he attends with his daughter.

Dr. Kenneth L. Hawkins is the Program Director of Information Technology at the Hampton campus of Bryant and Stratton College. He earned his doctorate in Education from Nova Southeastern University, a master's degree in Computer Science from Boston University, a master's degree in Education from Old Dominion University, a master's degree in Management from Troy State University, and his undergraduate degree in Mathematics from Michigan Technological University. Dr. Hawkins, a retired military officer, has worked in post-secondary education for the past 14 years as department head, campus dean, and faculty for undergraduate and graduate business and information technology courses at six Tidewater universities. A graduate of the Leadership Institute of the Virginia Peninsula, he is actively involved both professionally and socially in the community, having served as district chairman for the Boy Scouts of America, educational administration consultant for a local private school, board member of two area businesses, member of the international professional society Phi Gamma Sigma, and member of the Old Point Comfort Yacht Club.

Douglas E. Maume is currently the Lead Instructor for the Computer Networking program at Centura College Online. He has been conducting new and annual course reviews for both the CN and IT programs since 2006. He is also an adjunct professor for Centura College, teaching Computer Networking, Information Technology, and Business Management courses since 2001. Mr. Maume owned his own business called Wish You Were Here, Personal Postcards, creating digital postcards on location at the Virginia Beach oceanfront. He earned a Bachelor's degree in Graphic Design from Old Dominion University, and an Associate's in Applied Science degree in Graphic Design from Tidewater Community College. Mr. Maume is currently Esquire to the District Deputy Grand Exalted Ruler for Southeast Virginia in the Benevolent and Protective Order of Elks. He has been actively involved with the Elks since 1999, serving the veterans and youth of the Norfolk community. He is also the Registrar for the adult men's league Shipps Corner Soccer Club, and has been playing competitively since 1972.

WE WANT TO HEAR FROM YOU!

As the reader of this book, you are our most important critic and commentator. We value your opinion and want to know what we're doing right, what we could do better, what areas you'd like to see us publish in, and any other words of wisdom you're willing to pass our way.

We welcome your comments. You can email or write to let us know what you did or didn't like about this book—as well as what we can do to make our books better.

Please note that we cannot help you with technical problems related to the topic of this book.

When you write, please be sure to include this book's title and author as well as your name and email address. We will carefully review your comments and share them with the author and editors who worked on the book.

Email: feedback@pearsonitcertification.com

Mail: Pearson IT Certification
         ATTN: Reader Feedback
         800 East 96th Street
         Indianapolis, IN 46240 USA

READER SERVICES

Register your copy of *Networking Essentials* at www.pearsonitcertification.com for convenient access to downloads, updates, and corrections as they become available. To start the registration process, go to www.pearsonitcertification.com/register and log in or create an account*. Enter the product ISBN, 9780789758194, and click Submit. Once the process is complete, you will find any available bonus content under Registered Products.

*Be sure to check the box that you would like to hear from us in order to receive exclusive discounts on future editions of this product.

INTRODUCTION

This book provides a look at computer networking from the point of view of the network administrator. It guides readers from an entry-level knowledge in computer networks to advanced concepts in Ethernet networks; router configuration; TCP/IP networks; routing protocols; local, campus, and wide area network configuration; network security; wireless networking; optical networks; Voice over IP; the network server; and Linux networking. After covering the entire text, readers will have gained a solid knowledge base in computer networks.

In our years of teaching, we have observed that technology students prefer to learn "how to swim" after they have gotten wet and taken in a little water. Then they are ready for more challenges. Show the students the technology, how it is used, and why, and they will take the applications of the technology to the next level. Allowing them to experiment with the technology helps them to develop a greater understanding. This book does just that.

ORGANIZATION OF THE TEXT

Thoroughly updated to reflect the latest version of CompTIA's Network+ exam, *Networking Essentials*, **4th Edition,** is a practical, up-to-date, and hands-on guide to the basics of networking. Written from the viewpoint of a working network administrator, it requires absolutely no experience with either network concepts or day-to-day network management. This first volume has been revised and reorganized around the needs of introductory networking students, and assumes no previous knowledge. Throughout the text, the students will gain an appreciation of how basic computer networks and related hardware are interconnected to form a network. This involves understanding the concepts of twisted-pair cable, fiber optics, interconnecting LANs, configuring TCP/IP, subnet masking, basic router configuration, switch configuration and management, wireless networking, and network security.

Key Pedagogical Features

- *Chapter Outline, Network+ Objectives, Key Terms,* and *Introduction* at the beginning of each chapter clearly outline specific goals for the reader. An example of these features is shown in Figure P-1.

Chapter Outline   **Chapter Objectives**   **Introduction: Chapter openers clearly outline specific goals**

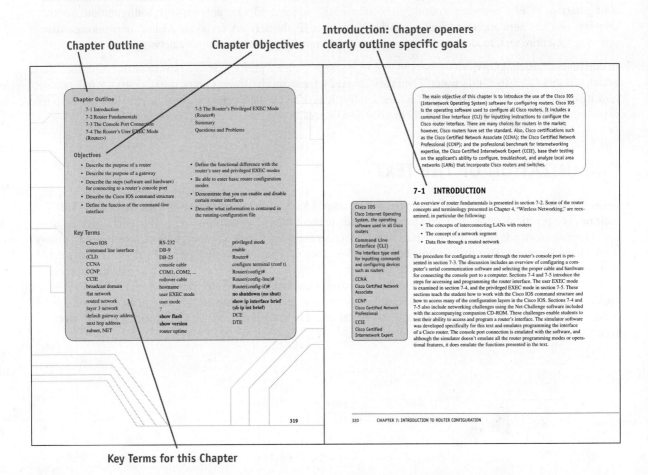

Key Terms for this Chapter

- *Net-Challenge Software* provides a simulated, hands-on experience in configuring routers and switches. Exercises provided in the text (see Figure P-2) and on the CD-ROM challenge readers to undertake certain router/network configuration tasks. The challenges check the students' ability to enter basic networking commands and to set up router functions, such as configuring the interface (Ethernet and Serial) and routing protocols (that is, RIP and static). The software has the look and feel of actually being connected to the router's console port.

Net-Challenge exercises are found throughout the text where applicable

Exercises challenge readers to undertake certain tasks

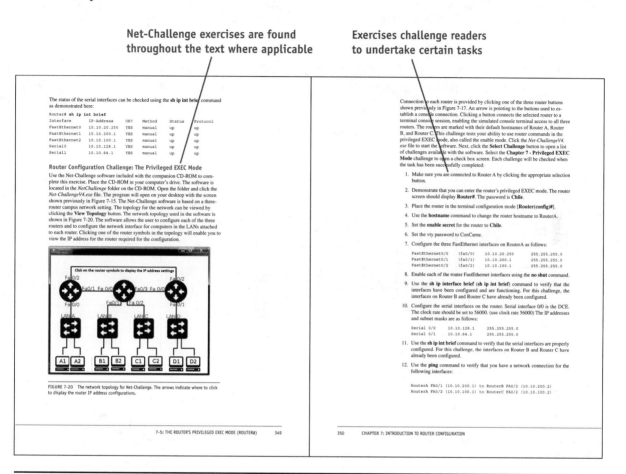

The status of the serial interfaces can be checked using the **sh ip int brief** command as demonstrated here:

```
Router# sh ip int brief
Interface      IP-Address    OK?   Method   Status   Protocol
FastEthernet0  10.10.20.250  YES   manual   up       up
FastEthernet1  10.10.200.1   YES   manual   up       up
FastEthernet2  10.10.100.1   YES   manual   up       up
Serial0        10.10.128.1   YES   manual   up       up
Serial1        10.10.64.1    YES   manual   up       up
```

Router Configuration Challenge: The Privileged EXEC Mode

Use the Net-Challenge software included with the companion CD-ROM to complete this exercise. Place the CD-ROM in your computer's drive. The software is located in the *NetChallenge* folder on the CD-ROM. Open the folder and click the *Net-ChallengeV4.exe* file. The program will open on your desktop with the screen shown previously in Figure 7-15. The Net-Challenge software is based on a three-router campus network setting. The topology for the network can be viewed by clicking the **View Topology** button. The network topology used in the software is shown in Figure 7-20. The software allows the user to configure each of the three routers and to configure the network interface for computers in the LANs attached to each router. Clicking one of the router symbols in the topology will enable you to view the IP address for the router required for the configuration.

FIGURE 7-20   The network topology for Net-Challenge. The arrows indicate where to click to display the router IP address configurations.

Connection to each router is provided by clicking one of the three router buttons shown previously in Figure 7-17. An arrow is pointing to the buttons used to establish a console connection. Clicking a button connects the selected router to a terminal console session, enabling the simulated console terminal access to all three routers. The routers are marked with their default hostnames of Router A, Router B, and Router C. This challenge tests your ability to use router commands in the privileged EXEC mode, also called the enable mode. Click the *Net-ChallengeV4.exe* file to start the software. Next, click the **Select Challenge** button to open a list of challenges available with the software. Select the **Chapter 7 - Privileged EXEC Mode** challenge to open a check box screen. Each challenge will be checked when the task has been successfully completed:

1. Make sure you are connected to Router A by clicking the appropriate selection button.

2. Demonstrate that you can enter the router's privileged EXEC mode. The router screen should display **Router#**. The password is **Chile**.

3. Place the router in the terminal configuration mode [**Router(config)#**].

4. Use the **hostname** command to change the router hostname to RouterA.

5. Set the **enable secret** for the router to **Chile**.

6. Set the vty password to ConCarne.

7. Configure the three FastEthernet interfaces on RouterA as follows:

```
FastEthernet0/0   (fa0/0)   10.10.20.250   255.255.255.0
FastEthernet0/1   (fa0/1)   10.10.200.1    255.255.255.0
FastEthernet0/2   (fa0/2)   10.10.100.1    255.255.255.0
```

8. Enable each of the router FastEthernet interfaces using the **no shut** command.

9. Use the **sh ip interface brief (sh ip int brief)** command to verify that the interfaces have been configured and are functioning. For this challenge, the interfaces on Router B and Router C have already been configured.

10. Configure the serial interfaces on the router. Serial interface 0/0 is the DCE. The clock rate should be set to 56000. (use clock rate 56000) The IP addresses and subnet masks are as follows:

```
Serial 0/0   10.10.128.1   255.255.255.0
Serial 0/1   10.10.64.1    255.255.255.0
```

11. Use the **sh ip int brief** command to verify that the serial interfaces are properly configured. For this challenge, the interfaces on Router B and Router C have already been configured.

12. Use the **ping** command to verify that you have a network connection for the following interfaces:

```
RouterA FA0/1 (10.10.200.1) to RouterB FA0/2 (10.10.200.2)
RouterA FA0/2 (10.10.100.1) to RouterC FA0/2 (10.10.100.2)
```

FIGURE P-2

- The textbook features and introduces how to use the *Wireshark Network Protocol Analyzer*. Examples of using the software to analyze data traffic are included throughout the text. *Numerous worked-out examples* are included in every chapter to reinforce key concepts and aid in subject mastery, as shown in Figure P-3.

Examples using the Wireshark protocol analyzer are included throughout the text where applicable

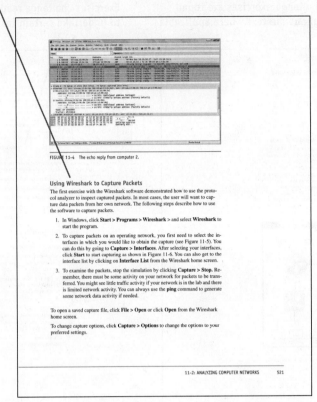

FIGURE P-3

- *Key Terms* and their definitions are highlighted in the margins to foster inquisitiveness and ensure retention. Illustrations and photos are used throughout to aid in understanding the concepts discussed. This is illustrated in Figure P-4.

Key terms are highlighted in the text and defined in the margin

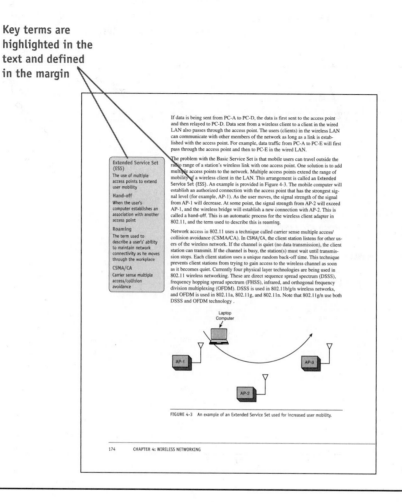

FIGURE P-4

- *Extensive Summaries, Questions and Problems, Critical Thinking*, as well as *Network+-specific Certification Questions* are found at the end of each chapter, as shown in Figure P-5

Summary of key concepts   Questions and problems are organized by section   Critical Thinking questions and problems further develop analytical skills

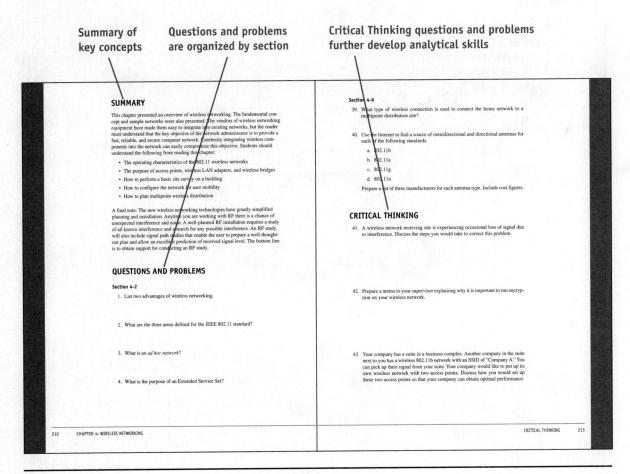

SUMMARY

This chapter presented an overview of wireless networking. The fundamental concept and sample networks were also presented. The vendors of wireless networking equipment have made them easy to integrate into existing networks, but the reader must understand that the key objective of the network administrator is to provide a fast, reliable, and secure computer network. Carelessly integrating wireless components into the network can easily compromise this objective. Students should understand the following from reading this chapter:

- The operating characteristics of the 802.11 wireless networks
- The purpose of access points, wireless LAN adapters, and wireless bridges
- How to perform a basic site survey on a building
- How to configure the network for user mobility
- How to plan multipoint wireless distribution

A final note: The new wireless networking technologies have greatly simplified planning and installation. Anytime you are working with RF there is a chance of unexpected interference and noise. A well-planned RF installation requires a study of all known interference and a search for any possible interference. An RF study will also include signal path studies that enable the user to prepare a well-thought-out plan and allow an excellent prediction of received signal level. The bottom line is to obtain support for conducting an RF study.

QUESTIONS AND PROBLEMS

Section 4-2

1. List two advantages of wireless networking.

2. What are the three areas defined for the IEEE 802.11 standard?

3. What is an *ad hoc network*?

4. What is the purpose of an Extended Service Set?

Section 4-6

39. What type of wireless connection is used to connect the home network to a multipoint distribution site?

40. Use the Internet to find a source of omnidirectional and directional antennas for each of the following standards.
   a. 802.11b
   b. 802.11a
   c. 802.11g
   d. 802.11n

Prepare a list of three manufacturers for each antenna type. Include cost figures.

CRITICAL THINKING

41. A wireless network receiving site is experiencing occasional loss of signal due to interference. Discuss the steps you would take to correct this problem.

42. Prepare a memo to your supervisor explaining why it is important to run encryption on your wireless network.

43. Your company has a suite in a business complex. Another company in the suite next to you has a wireless 802.11b network with an SSID of "Company A." You can pick up their signal from your suite. Your company would like to put up its own wireless network with two access points. Discuss how you would set up these two access points so that your company can obtain optimal performance.

FIGURE P-5

- An extensive *Glossary* is found at the end of the book and offers quick, accessible definitions to key terms and acronyms, as well as an exhaustive *Index* (see Figure P-6).

Complete Glossary of terms and acronyms provide quick reference

Exhaustive Index provides quick reference

FIGURE P-6

Accompanying CD-ROM

The CD-ROM packaged with the text includes the captured data packets used in the text. It also includes the Net-Challenge Software, which was developed specifically for this text. The CD-ROM also includes sample videos on the topic of network virtualization from the CompTIA Network+ N10-006 Complete Video Course. See the special offer for a discount on the full version of this product in the sleeve in the back of the book.

1
CHAPTER

INTRODUCTION TO COMPUTER NETWORKS

Chapter Outline

Objectives

- Explain the various LAN topologies
- Define the function of a networking protocol
- Describe CSMA/CD for the Ethernet protocol
- Describe the structure of the Ethernet frame
- Define the function of the network interface card

- Describe the purpose of the MAC address on a networking device
- Discuss how to determine the MAC address for a computer
- Discuss the fundamentals of IP addressing
- Discuss the issues of configuring a home network
- Discuss the issue of assembling an office LAN

Key Terms

local area network (LAN)
protocol
topology
Token Ring topology
token passing
IEEE
deterministic
Token Ring hub
bus topology
ThinNet
star topology
hub
multiport repeater
broadcast
switch
ports
mesh topology
OSI
OSI model
physical layer
data link layer

network layer
transport layer
session layer
presentation layer
application layer
CSMA/CD
frame
network interface card (NIC)
MAC address
organizationally unique identifier (OUI)
Ethernet, physical, hardware, or adapter address
ipconfig /all
IANA
IP address
network number
host number
host address
ISP

private addresses
intranet
IP internetwork
TCP/IP
wired network
wireless network
Wi-Fi
wireless router
range extender
hotspots
Service Set Identifier (SSID)
firewall protection
Stateful Packet Inspection (SPI)
virtual private network (VPN)
Network Address Translation (NAT)
overloading

Port Address Translation (PAT)
CAT6 (category 6)
RJ-45
Mbps
numerics

ports
crossover
straight-through
uplink port
link light
link integrity test

link pulses
ping
Internet Control Message Protocol (ICMP)
ipconfig

1-1 INTRODUCTION

Each day, computer users use their computers for browsing the Internet, sending and retrieving email, scheduling meetings, sharing files, preparing reports, exchanging images, downloading music, and maybe checking the current price of an auction item on the Internet. All this requires computers to access multiple networks and share their resources. The multiple networks required to accomplish this are the local area network (LAN), the enterprise network, the campus area network (CAN), the metropolitan area network (MAN), Metro Ethernet, the personal area network (PAN), and the wide area network (WAN).

This text introduces the essentials for implementing modern computer networks. Each chapter steps you through the various modern networking technologies. The accompanying CD-ROM comes with the Net-Challenge simulator software developed specifically for this text. This software provides the reader with invaluable insight into the inner workings of computer networking and with the experience of configuring the router and switch for use in the computer networks.

The ease of connecting to the Internet and the dramatic decrease in computer systems' cost has led to an explosion in their usage. Organizations such as corporations, colleges, and government agencies have acquired large numbers of single-user computer systems. These systems might be dedicated to word processing, scientific computation, process control, or might be general-purpose computers that perform many tasks. This has generated a need to interconnect these locally distributed computer networks. Interconnection allows users to exchange information (data) with other network members. It also allows resource sharing of expensive equipment such as file servers and high-quality graphics printers or access to more powerful computers for tasks too complicated for the local computer to process. The network commonly used to accomplish this interconnection is called a **local area network (LAN)**, which is a network of users that share computer resources in a limited area.

> **Local Area Network (LAN)**
> Network of users that share computer resources in a limited area

Table 1-1 outlines the CompTIA Network+ objectives and identifies the chapter section that covers each objective. At the end of each chapter section you will find a review with comments of the Network+ objectives presented in that section. These comments are provided to help reinforce the reader's understanding of a particular Network+ objective. The chapter review also includes "Test Your Knowledge" questions to aid in the understanding of key concepts before the reader advances to the next section of the chapter. The end of the chapter includes a complete set of questions as well as sample certification type questions.

TABLE 1-1 Chapter 1 CompTIA Network+ Objectives

Domain/ Objective Number	Domain/Objective Description	Section Where Objective Is Covered
1.0	*Networking Architecture*	
1.1	Explain the functions and applications of various network devices	1-5
1.2	Compare and contrast the use of networking services and applications	1-5
1.3	Install and configure the following networking services/applications	1-5
1.4	Explain the characteristics and benefits of various WAN technologies	1-1
1.5	Install and properly terminate various cable types and connectors using appropriate tools	1-6
1.6	Differentiate between common network topologies	1-2
1.7	Differentiate between network infrastructure implementations	1-1, 1-5, 1-6
1.8	Given a scenario, implement and configure the appropriate networking addressing schema	1-4, 1-5
1.12	Given a set of requirements, implement a basic network	1-1, 1-2
2.0	*Network Operations*	
2.4	Explain the importance of implementing network segmentation	1-5
2.6	Given a scenario, configure a switch using proper features	1-4, 1-5
2.7	Install and configure a wireless LAN infrastructure and implement the appropriate technologies in support of wireless-capable devices	1-5
3.0	*Network Media and Topologies*	
3.2	Compare and contrast network vulnerabilities and threats	1-5
3.3	Given a scenario, implement network-hardening techniques	1,4 1-5
4.0	*Troubleshooting*	
4.1	Given a scenario, implement the following network troubleshooting methodology	1-3, 1-5, 1-7
4.2	Given a scenario, analyze and interpret the output of troubleshooting tools	1-4, 1-7

Domain/ Objective Number	Domain/Objective Description	Section Where Objective Is Covered
5.0	**Industry Standards, Practices, and Network Theory**	
5.1	Analyze a scenario and determine the corresponding OSI layers	1-3
5.2	Explain the basics of network theory and concepts	1-4
5.3	Given a scenario, deploy the appropriate wireless standard	1-5
5.4	Given a scenario, deploy the appropriate wired connectivity standard	1-5, 1-6
5.8	Explain the basics of change management procedures	1-6
5.9	Compare and contrast the following ports and protocols	1-3

1-2 NETWORK TOPOLOGIES

Local area networks are defined in terms of the **protocol** and the **topology** used for accessing the network. The networking protocol is the set of rules established for users to exchange information. The topology is the network architecture used to interconnect the networking equipment. The most common architectures for LANs are the ring, bus, and star, as illustrated in Figure 1-1.

Figure 1-2 shows an example of a LAN configured using the **Token Ring topology**. In this topology, a "token" (shown as a T) is placed in the data channel and circulates around the ring, hence the name *Token Ring*. If a user wants to transmit, the computer waits until it has control of the token. This technique is called **token passing** and is based on the **IEEE** 802.5 Token-Ring Network standard. A Token Ring network is a **deterministic** network, meaning each station connected to the network is ensured access for transmission of its messages at regular or fixed time intervals.

> **Protocol**
> Set of rules established for users to exchange information
>
> **Topology**
> Architecture of a network
>
> **Token Ring Topology**
> A network topology configured in a logical ring that complements the token passing protocol
>
> **Token Passing**
> A technique where an electrical token circulates around a network—control of the token enables the user to gain access to the network
>
> **IEEE**
> Institute of Electrical and Electronics Engineers, one of the major standards-setting bodies for technological development
>
> **Deterministic**
> Access to the network is provided at fixed time intervals

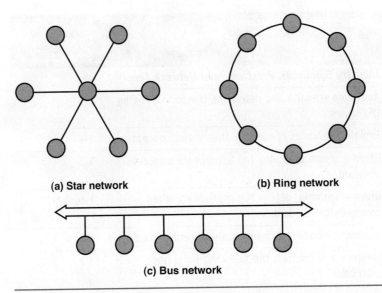

(a) Star network (b) Ring network

(c) Bus network

FIGURE 1-1 Network topologies. (From Modern Electronic Communication 9/e, by G. M. Miller & J. S. Beasley, 2008 Copyright © 2008 Pearson Education, Inc. Reprinted by permission of Pearson Education, Inc., Upper Saddle River, NJ.)

FIGURE 1-2 The Token Ring network topology.

One disadvantage of the Token Ring system is that if an error changes the token pattern, it can cause the token to stop circulating. Additionally, ring networks rely on each system to relay the data to the next user. A failed station can cause data traffic to cease. Another disadvantage of the Token Ring network is from the troubleshooting and maintenance point of view. The Token Ring path must be temporarily broken (path interrupted) if a computer or any device connected to the network is to be removed or added to the network. This results in downtime for the network. A fix to this is to attach all the computers to a central **Token Ring hub**. Such a device manages the passing of the token rather than relying on individual computers to pass it, which improves the reliability of the network. It is important to note that the Token Ring network has become a "legacy" now in computer networking. Ethernet technology has replaced this in almost all modern computer networks.

Figure 1-3 illustrates a **bus topology.** In a bus system, the computers share the media (coaxial cable) for data transmission. In this topology, a coaxial cable (called **ThinNet**) is looped through each networking device to facilitate data transfer.

FIGURE 1-3   The bus topology.

In a bus topology, all LAN data traffic is carried over a common coaxial cable link. Referring to Figure 1-3, if computer 1 is printing a large file, the line of communications will be between computer 1 and the printer. However, in a bus system, all networking devices will see computer 1's data traffic to the printer and the other devices will have to wait for pauses in transmission or until it is complete before they can initiate their own transmission. If more than one computer's data is placed on the network at the same time, the data will be corrupted and will have to be retransmitted. This means that the use of a shared coaxial cable in a bus topology prevents data transmission from being very bandwidth-efficient. This is one reason, but not the only reason, why bus topologies are seldom used in modern computer networks.

The **star topology**, shown in Figure 1-4, is the most common networking topology in today's LANs. Twisted-pair cables (see Chapter 2, "Physical Layer Cabling: Twisted Pair") with modular plugs are used to connect the computers and other networking devices. At the center of a star network is either a switch or a hub. This connects the network devices and facilitates the transfer of data. For example, if computer 1 wants to send data to the network laser printer, the **hub** or switch provides the network connection. If a hub is used, computer 1's data is sent to the hub, which then forwards it to the printer. However, a hub is a **multiport repeater**, meaning the data it receives is **broadcast** and seen by all devices connected to its ports. Therefore, the hub will broadcast computer 1's data traffic to all networking devices interconnected in the star network. The data traffic path for this is shown in the solid black arrowed lines going to all networking devices in Figure 1-4. This is similar to the bus topology in that all data traffic on the LAN is being seen by all computers. The fact that the hub broadcasts all data traffic to the devices connected to its network ports makes these devices of limited use in large networks.

- – – –▶ **Hub traffic from computer 1 to the printer**
- ▪▪▪▪▪▪▪▪ **Switch traffic from computer 1 to the printer**
- ⋯⋯⋯⋯▶ **Switch traffic from computer 5 to computer 6**

FIGURE 1-4   The star topology.

To minimize unnecessary data traffic and isolate sections of the network, a **switch** can be used at the center of a star network, as shown in Figure 1-4. Networking devices such as computers each has a hardware or physical address. (This concept is fully detailed in section 1-4.) A switch stores the hardware or physical address for each device connected to its ports. The storage of the address enables the switch to directly connect two communicating devices without broadcasting the data to all devices connected to its **ports**.

For example, if a switch is used instead of a hub, the data from computer 1 is transmitted directly to the printer and the other computers do not see the data traffic. The traffic path for the switched network is shown in the dotted lines in Figure 1-4. The use of a switched connection greatly improves the efficiency of the available bandwidth. It also permits additional devices in the LAN to simultaneously communicate with each other without tying up network resources. For example, while computer 1 is printing a large file, computers 5 and 6 can communicate with each other, as shown in the dashed line in Figure 1-4. For troubleshooting and maintenance, individual computers can be removed without negatively affecting the network in a star or extended star topology. Also the upgrade from a hub to a switched topology can be accomplished without requiring a change in the cable infrastructure and therefore at minimal downtime and expense.

Another topology is the **mesh topology**, shown in Figure 1-5. In this topology, all networking devices are directly connected to each other. This provides for full redundancy in the network data paths but at a cost. The additional data paths increase the cabling costs and the networking hardware cost (for example, expense of multiple network ports for each device connected to the network). Not only that, but the mesh design adds more complexity. This topology can be suitable for high-reliability applications but can be too costly for general networking applications.

> **Ports**
> The physical input/output interfaces to the networking hardware

> **Mesh Topology**
> All networking devices are directly connected to each other

FIGURE 1-5   The mesh topology.

Section 1-2 Review

This section has covered the following **Network+** Exam objectives.

1.6 Differentiate between common network topologies

This section presented the star, ring, bus, and mesh network topologies. You should be able to identify each topology and understand how data travels in each network topology. You should also have a basic understanding of the difference between a topology and protocol.

1.12 Given a set of requirements, implement a basic network

This section also introduced some basic networking hardware, such as the hub and switch. Make sure you have a basic understanding of each device. You should also have developed an understanding that data from a hub is replicated out all ports. This means that the information is seen by all networking devices connected to its ports. You should also know that a switch will filter unicast frames out of the appropriate ports, unlike a hub.

Test Your Knowledge

1. What is the most common network topology today?

    a. Star

    b. Hub

    c. Ring

    d. Mesh

2. A hub is also called a multiport repeater.

    a. True

    b. False

3. The term deterministic means

    a. Access to the network is provided at random time intervals.

    b. Access to the network is provided using CSMA/CD.

    c. Access to the network is provided at fixed time intervals.

    d. None of these answers is correct.

4. A protocol defines the network architecture used to interconnect the networking equipment.

    a. True

    b. False

1-3 THE OSI MODEL

An open systems interconnect (**OSI**) reference model was developed by the International Organization for Standardization in 1984 to enable different types of networks to be linked together. The model contains seven layers, as shown in Figure 1-6. These layers describe networking functions from the physical network interface to the software applications interfaces. The intent of the **OSI model** is to provide a framework for networking that ensures compatibility in the network hardware and software and to accelerate the development of new networking technologies. A discussion of the OSI model follows as well as a summary of the seven layers outlined in Table 1-2.

> **OSI**
> Open system interconnect
>
> **OSI Model**
> The seven layers describing network functions

7. Application
6. Presentation
5. Session
4.Transport
3. Network
2. Data link
1. Physical

FIGURE 1-6   The seven layers of the OSI reference model.

TABLE 1-2   **Summary of the OSI Layers**

Layer	Function	Examples
7. Application	Support for applications	HTTP, FTP, SMTP (email)
6. Presentation	Protocol conversion, data translation	ASCII, JPEG
5. Session	Establishes, manages, and terminates sessions	NFS, SQL
4. Transport	Ensures error-free packets	TCP, UDP
3. Network	Provides routing decisions	IP, IPX
2. Data link	Provides for the flow of data	MAC addresses
1. Physical	Signals and media	NICs, twisted-pair cable, fiber

Physical Layer

Provides the electrical and mechanical connection to the network

Data Link Layer

Handles error recovery, flow control (synchronization), and sequencing

Network Layer

Accepts outgoing messages and combines messages or segments into packets, adding a header that includes routing information

Transport Layer

Is concerned with message integrity between source and destination

Session Layer

Provides the control functions necessary to establish, manage, and terminate the connections

Presentation Layer

Accepts and structures the messages for the application

Application Layer

Interacts with application programs that incorporate a communication component such as your Internet browser and email

1. **Physical layer:** Provides the electrical and mechanical connection to the network. Examples of technologies working in this layer are Electronic Industries Alliance/Telecommunications Industry Association (EIA/TIA) related technologies, UTP, fiber, and network interface cards (NICs).

2. **Data link layer:** Handles error recovery, flow control (synchronization), and sequencing (which terminals are sending and which are receiving). It is considered the "media access control layer" and is where Media Access Control (MAC) addressing is defined. The Ethernet 802.3 standard is defined in this area, which is why the MAC address is sometimes called the Ethernet address.

3. **Network layer:** Accepts outgoing messages and combines messages or segments into packets, adding a header that includes routing information. It acts as the network controller. Examples of protocols working in this layer are Internet Protocol (IP) and Internetwork Packet Exchange (IPX).

4. **Transport layer:** Is concerned with message integrity between source and destination. It also segments/reassembles (the packets) and handles flow control. Examples of protocols working in this layer are Transmission Control Protocol (TCP) and User Datagram Protocol (UDP).

5. **Session layer:** Provides the control functions necessary to establish, manage, and terminate the connections as required to satisfy the user request. Examples of technologies working in this layer are Network File System (NFS) and Structured Query Language (SQL).

6. **Presentation layer:** Accepts and structures the messages for the application. It translates the message from one code to another if necessary. This layer is responsible for data compression and encryption. Examples of technologies working in this layer are American Standard Code for Information Interchange (ASCII) and Joint Photographic Experts Group (JPEG).

7. **Application layer:** Interacts with application programs that incorporate a communication component such as your Internet browser and email. This layer is responsible for logging the message in, interpreting the request, and determining what information is needed to support the request. Examples are Hypertext Transfer Protocol (HTTP) for web browsing, File Transfer Protocol (FTP) for transferring files, and Simple Mail Transfer Protocol (SMTP) for email transmission.

Note

Network administrators often describe networking problems by layer number. For example, a physical link problem is described as a layer 1 problem; a router problem is layer 3; and so on.

The network administrator needs to have a good understanding of all seven layers of the OSI model. Knowledge of the layers can help to isolate the network problem. There are three basic steps in the process of isolating the network problem:

- Is the connection to the machine down? (layer 1)
- Is the network down? (layer 3)
- Is a service on a specific machine down? (layer 7)

The network administrator uses the OSI model to troubleshoot network problems by verifying functionality of each layer. In many cases, troubleshooting the network problem requires the network administrator to isolate at which layer the network problem occurs.

For example, assume that a network is having problems accessing an email server that uses SMTP—a layer 7 application. The first troubleshooting step for the network administrator is to ping the IP address of the email server (layer 3 test). A "ping" to an IP address can be used to check quickly that there is a network connection. (Note: The **ping** command is discussed in detail in section 1-7, "Testing and Troubleshooting a LAN.") A "reply from" response for the ping indicates the connection to the server is up. A "request timed out" response indicates the network connection is down. This could be due to a cabling problem (layer 1) or a problem with a switch (layer 2) or a router (layer 3), or the email server could be completely down (layer 7). In the case of "request timed out," the network administrator will have to go directly to the telecommunications closet or the machine to troubleshoot the problem. In this case, the administrator should first check for layer 1 (physical layer) problems. Many times this just requires verifying that a network cable is connected. Cables do get knocked loose or break.

Section 1-3 Review

This section has covered the following **Network+** Exam objectives.

4.1 Given a scenario, implement the following network troubleshooting methodology

The network administrator needs to have a good understanding of all seven layers of the OSI model. Knowledge of the layers can help to isolate the network problem. Remember, there are three basic steps in the process of isolating the network problem:

1. *Is the connection to the machine down? (layer 1)*

2. *Is the network down? (layer 3)*

3. *Is a service on a specific machine down? (layer 7)*

5.1 Analyze a scenario and determine the corresponding OSI layers

The OSI layers have been presented in this section. Develop some method to remember the name, the function, and examples of the seven layers of the OSI model. A good overview of this is presented in Table 1-2. This provides a good start for understanding how the OSI model relates to applications, devices, and protocols.

5.9 Compare and contrast the following ports and protocols

This chapter presented several protocols such as HTTP, TCP, and UDP and how they fit into the OSI model.

Test Your Knowledge

1. TCP functions at which layer of the OSI model?

   a. Layer 4

   b. Layer 2

   c. Layer 3

   d. Layer 5

   e. Layer 7

2. HTTP functions at which layer of the OSI model?

   a. Layer 6

   b. Layer 5

   c. Layer 4

   d. Layer 7

   e. All of these answers are correct.

3. IP is an example of a protocol that operates in which layer of the OSI model?

   a. Layer 7

   b. Layer 6

   c. Layer 5

   d. Layer 2

   e. None of these answers is correct.

4. The NIC operates at which layer of the OSI model?

   a. Layer 1

   b. Layer 3

   c. Layer 5

   d. Layer 7

   e. All of these answers are correct.

5. The network address is another name for a layer 4 address.

   a. True

   b. False

1-4 THE ETHERNET LAN

The networking protocol used in most modern computer networks is Ethernet, a carrier sense multiple access with collision detection (**CSMA/CD**) protocol for local area networks. It originated in 1972, and the full specification for the protocol was provided in 1980 via a joint effort among Xerox, Digital Equipment Corporation, and Intel. Basically, for a computer to "talk" on the Ethernet network, it first "listens" to see whether there is any data traffic (carrier sense). This means that any computer connected to the LAN can be "listening" for data traffic, and any of the computers on the LAN can access the network (multiple access). There is a chance that two or more computers will attempt to broadcast a message at the same time; therefore, Ethernet systems must have the capability to detect data collisions (collision detection).

> **CSMA/CD**
> The Ethernet LAN media-access method, carrier sense multiple access with collision detection

The information in an Ethernet network is exchanged in a frame format. The frame provides grouping of the information for transmission that includes the header, data, and trailer. The header consists of the preamble, start frame delimiter, destination and source addresses, and length/type field. Next is the actual data being transmitted, followed by the pad used to bring the total number of bytes up to the minimum of 46 if the data field is less than 46 bytes. The last part of the frame is a 4-byte cyclic redundancy check (CRC) value used for error checking. The structure of the Ethernet packet frame is shown in Figure 1-7 and described in Table 1-3.

> **Frame**
> Provides grouping of the information for transmission

Preamble	Start frame delimiter	Destination MAC address	Source MAC address	Length type	Data	Pad	Frame check sequence

FIGURE 1-7 The data structure for the Ethernet frame. (From Modern Electronic Communication 9/e, by G. M. Miller & J. S. Beasley, 2008. Copyright © 2008 Pearson Education, Inc. Reprinted by permission of Pearson Education, Inc., Upper Saddle River, NJ.)

TABLE 1-3 **Components of the Ethernet Packet Frame**

Preamble	An alternating pattern of 1s and 0s used for synchronization.
Start frame delimiter	A binary 8-bit sequence of 1 0 1 0 1 0 1 1 that indicates the start of the frame.
Destination MAC address and source	Each computer has an Ethernet network interface card (NIC) or network adapter that has a unique media access control.
MAC address	MAC address associated with it. The MAC address is 6 bytes (12 hex characters) in length.

Length/type	An indication of the number of bytes in the data field if this value is less than 1500. If this number is greater than 1500, it indicates the type of data format—for example, IP and IPX.
Data	The variable length of data being transferred from the source to the destination.
Pad	A field used to bring the total number of bytes up to the minimum of 64 if the data field is less than 64 bytes.
Frame check sequence	A 4-byte CRC value used for error detection. The CRC is performed on the bits from the destination MAC address through the Pad fields. If an error is detected, the frame is discarded.

The minimum length of the Ethernet frame is 64 bytes from the destination MAC address through the frame check sequence. The maximum Ethernet frame length is 1,518 bytes; 6 bytes for the destination MAC address; 6 bytes for the source MAC address; 2 bytes for length/type; and 1,500 bytes for the data.

Source: Adapted from *Modern Electronic Communication 9/e*, by G. M. Miller & J. S. Beasley, 2008. Copyright © 2008 Pearson Education, Inc. Adapted by permission of Pearson Education, Inc., Upper Saddle River, NJ.

Network Interface Card (NIC)

The electronic hardware used to interface the computer to the network

MAC Address

A unique 6-byte address assigned by the vendor of the network interface card

Organizationally Unique Identifier (OUI)

The first 3 bytes of the MAC address that identifies the manufacturer of the network hardware

How are the destination and source addresses for the data determined within a LAN? Networked devices, such as computers and network printers, each have an electronic hardware interface to the LAN called a **network interface card (NIC)** (see Figure 1-8) or integrated network port. The NIC contains a unique network address called the **MAC address**. MAC stands for "media access control." The MAC address is 6 bytes, or 48 bits, in length. The address is displayed in 12 hexadecimal digits. The first 6 digits are used to indicate the vendor of the network interface, also called the **organizationally unique identifier (OUI)**, and the last 6 numbers form a unique value for each NIC assigned by the vendor. IEEE is the worldwide source of registered OUIs.

FIGURE 1-8　A 3COM network interface card (courtesy of 3Com Corporation).

The MAC address, also called the **Ethernet, physical, hardware,** or **adapter address,** can be obtained from computers operating under Microsoft Windows by typing the **ipconfig /all** command while in the command mode or at the MS-DOS prompt. The following is an example of obtaining the MAC address for a computer operating under Windows 7, Windows Vista, or XP.

In Windows XP and Vista, the first step is to enter the command window by selecting **Start** and then **Run**. The Run window, shown in Figure 1-9, displays. Enter **cmd** as shown and click **OK** to open the command prompt. In Windows 7, you can the **cmd** at the search field of the **Start** menu or find it by selecting **Start > Programs > Accessories > cmd**.

Ethernet, Physical, Hardware, or Adapter Address
Other names for the MAC address

ipconfig /all
Enables the MAC address information to be displayed from the command prompt

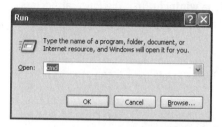

FIGURE 1-9   The Run window used to enter the command prompt in Windows 7.

In the command prompt, enter the **ipconfig /all** command as shown in Figure 1-10. The **/all** switch on the command enables the MAC address information to be displayed—for this example, the information for computer 1. Note that the Host Name for the computer is Computer-1. This information is typically established when the computer's operating system is installed, but it can be changed as needed. The MAC address is listed under **Ethernet adapter Local Area Connection** as shown in Figure 1-10. The **Media State—Media disconnected** text indicates that no active Ethernet device, such as a hub or switch, is connected to the computer. The **Description** lists the manufacturer and model of the network interface, and the **Physical Address** of **00-10-A4-13-99-2E** is the actual MAC address for the computer.

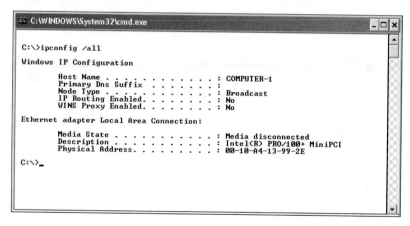

FIGURE 1-10   A typical text screen result when entering the ipconfig /all command in the command window.

Table 1-4 lists how the MAC address can be obtained for various computer operating systems.

TABLE 1-4 Commands for Obtaining the MAC Address for Various Operating Systems

Operating System	Command Sequence	Comments
Windows 98	Click **Start > Run**, type **winipcfg**, and press **Enter**.	The Adapter Address is the MAC address.
Windows NT	Click **Start > Run** and type **winipcfg**. In the command prompt, type **ipconfig/all** **and** press **Enter**.	The Physical Address is the MAC address.
Windows 2000	Click **Start > Run** and type **cmd**. In the command prompt, type **ipconfig/all**, and then press **Enter**.	The Physical Address is the MAC address.
Windows Vista/XP	In Windows XP and Vista, enter the command window by selecting **Start** and then **Run**. In the command prompt, type **ipconfig/all**, and then press **Enter**.	The Physical Address is the MAC address.
Windows 7, 8, 10	In Windows 7, 8, 10 the text **cmd** can be entered at the search field of the **Start** menu. In the command prompt, type **ipconfig/all**, and then press **Enter**.	The Physical Address is the MAC address.
Linux	At the command prompt, type **ifconfig**.	The HWaddr line contains the MAC address.
Mac OS (9.x and older)	Click the **Apple**, and then select **Control Panels > AppleTalk** and click the **Info** button.	The Hardware Address is the MAC address.
Mac OS X	Click **Apple > About this MAC > more info > Network > Built-in Ethernet**.	The Hardware Address is the MAC address.

In summary, the MAC address provides the information that ultimately enables the data to reach a destination in a LAN. This is also how computer 1 and the printer communicated directly in the star topology example using the switch (refer to Figure 1-4). The switch stored the MAC addresses of all devices connected to its ports and used this information to forward the data from computer 1 directly to the printer. The switch also used the MAC address information to forward the data from computer 5 to computer 6 (refer to Figure 1-4).

MAC addresses are listed in hexadecimal (base-16). The complete MAC address consists of 12 hexadecimal digits. The first 6 digits identify the vendor. The last 6 form a serial number assigned by the manufacturer of the network interface card. A searchable database of IEEE OUI and company ID assignments is available at http://standards-oui.ieee.org/oui.txt. Table 1-5 lists a few examples of MAC addresses. Also large companies may have many OUI numbers assigned to them. For example, the OUI 00-AA-00 is only one of Intel's many OUIs.

TABLE 1-5   A Sample of MAC Addresses

Company ID-Vendor Serial #	Manufacturer (Company ID)
00-AA-00-B6-7A-57	Intel Corporation (00-AA-00)
00-00-86-15-9E-7A	Megahertz Corporation (00-00-86)
00-50-73-6C-32-11	Cisco Systems, Inc. (00-50-73)
00-04-76-B6-9D-06	3COM (00-04-76)
00-0A-27-B7-3E-F8	Apple Computer, Inc. (00-0A-27)

IP Addressing

The MAC address provides the physical address for the network interface card but provides no information as to its network location or even on what LAN or in which building, city, or country the network resides. Internet Protocol (IP) addressing provides a solution to worldwide addressing through incorporating a unique address that identifies the computer's local network. IP network numbers are assigned by **Internet Assigned Numbers Authority (IANA)**, the agency that assigns IP addresses to computer networks and makes sure no two different networks are assigned the same IP network address. The web address for IANA is http://www.iana.org/.

IANA
The agency that assigns IP addresses to computer networks

IP addresses are classified as either IPv4 or IPv6. IP version 4 (IPv4) is the current TCP/IP addressing technique being used on the Internet. Address space for IPv4 is quickly running out due to the rapid growth of the Internet and the development of new Internet-compatible technologies. However, both IPv4 and IPv6 are being supported by manufacturers of networking equipment and the latest computer operating systems. The details about IPv6 are addressed in Chapter 6, "TCP/IP." IPv4 is currently the most common method for assigning IP addresses. This text refers to IPv4 addressing as "IP addressing." The **IP address** is a 32-bit address that identifies on which network the computer is located and differentiates the computer from all other devices on the same network. The address is divided into four 8-bit parts. The format for the IP address is:

IP Address
Unique 32-bit address that identifies on which network the computer is located as well as differentiates the computer from all other devices on the same network

A.B.C.D

where the A.B.C.D values are written as the decimal equivalent of the 8-bit binary value. The range for each of the decimal values is 0–255. IP addresses can be categorized by class. Table 1-6 provides examples of the classes of IP networks, and Table 1-7 provides the address range for each class.

TABLE 1-6   The Classes of IPv4 Networks

Class	Description	Example IP Numbers	Maximum Number of Hosts
Class A	Governments, very large networks	44.x.x.x.	2^{24}=16,777,214
Class B	Midsize companies, universities, and so on	128.123.x.x	2^{16}=65,534
Class C	Small networks	192.168.1.x	2^{8}=254
Class D	Reserved for multicast groups	224.x.x.x	not applicable

TABLE 1-7   The Address Range for Each Class of Network

Class A	0.0.0.0 to 127.255.255.255
Class B	128.0.0.0 to 191.255.255.255
Class C	192.0.0.0 to 223.255.255.255
Class D	224.0.0.0 to 239.255.255.255

Network Number
The portion of the IP address that defines which network the IP packet is originating from or being delivered to

Host Number
The portion of the IP address that defines the location of the networking device connected to the network; also called the host address

Host Address
Same as host number

ISP
Internet service provider

Private Addresses
IP addresses set aside for use in private intranets

Intranet
An internal network that provides file and resource sharing but is not accessed from the Internet

Examples of network addresses also are shown in Table 1-6. The decimal numbers indicate the **network number**, which is the portion of the IP address that defines which network the IP packet is originating from or being delivered to. The x entries for each class represent the **host number**, which is the portion of the IP address that defines the address of the networking device connected to the network. The host number is also called the **host address**. The network number provides sufficient information for routing the data to the appropriate destination network. A device on the destination network then uses the remaining information (the x portion) to direct the packet to the destination computer or host. The x portion of the address is typically assigned by the local network system administrator or is dynamically assigned when users need access outside their local networks. For example, your Internet service provider (**ISP**) dynamically assigns an IP address to your computer when you log on to the Internet. Remember, you can check the IP address assigned to your computer by your ISP using the **ipconfig** command in the command prompt.

For this chapter and the rest of the text, a group of IP addresses called **private addresses** will be used for assigning IP addresses to networks. Private addresses are IP addresses set aside for use in private **intranets**. An intranet is an internal internetwork that provides file and resource sharing. Private addresses are not valid addresses for Internet use because they have been reserved for internal use and are not routable on the Internet. However, these addresses can be used within a private

LAN (intranet) to create an **IP internetwork**. An IP internetwork uses IP addressing for identifying devices connected to the network and is also the addressing scheme used in **TCP/IP** networks. TCP/IP stands for Transmission Control Protocol/Internet Protocol and is the protocol suite used for internetworks such as the Internet. The three address blocks for the private IP addresses are as follows:

10.0.0.0–10.255.255.255
172.16.0.0–172.31.255.255
192.168.0.0–192.168.255.255

The topic of IP addressing will be examined in greater detail throughout the text. For Chapter 1, the objective is to use the IP addresses for configuring the address of the computers for operation in a TCP/IP network.

> **IP Internetwork**
> A network that uses IP addressing for identifying devices connected to the network
>
> **TCP/IP**
> Transmission Control Protocol/Internet Protocol, the protocol suite used for internetworks such as the Internet

Section 1-4 Review

This section has covered the following **Network+** Exam objectives:

1.8 Given a scenario, implement and configure the appropriate addressing schema

It is important that you understand the structure of the IPv4 address and what bits define the network address and which bits are the host bits. Make sure you understand the structure of both the MAC address and the IPv4 address and know how to get this information from many types of computers.

4.2 Given a scenario, analyze and interpret the output of troubleshooting tools

Remember, you can check the IP address assigned to your computer by your ISP using the **ipconfig** command in the command prompt. *Issuing the **ipconfig /all** command enables the network administrator to determine whether the network interface card is connected to a network and to determine the MAC and IP address of a networking device.*

5.2 Explain the basics of network theory and concepts

The most common networking protocol, CSMA/CD, has been introduced in this section. Make sure you understand how this protocol manages network access from multiple devices.

Test Your Knowledge

1. How do the IP address and MAC address differ? (Select one.)

    a. They are the same.

    b. The MAC address defines the network location.

    c. The IP address is only used as part of the ARP request.

    d. The MAC address provides the physical address of the network interface card.

2. The MAC address on a Windows computer can be accessed by typing **ipconfig /all** from the command prompt.

    a. True

    b. False

3. The OUI for the MAC address 00-10-A4-13-99-2E is 13992E.

    a. True

    b. False

4. Define the acronym NIC.

    a. Network Interface Card

    b. National Integrated Communicator

    c. Network Integration Card

    d. National Integration Communicator

    e. None of these answers is correct

1-5 HOME NETWORKING

Wired Network

Uses cables and connectors to establish the network connection

Wireless Network

Uses radio signals to establish the network connection

Setting up a home network is probably one of the first networks that the student sets up. This is an exciting opportunity for the student to demonstrate his/her knowledge of computer networks, but setting up the home network can also be quite a challenge. One of the first questions asked is, "Do I want to set up a wired or wireless home network?" A **wired network** uses cabling and connectors to establish the network connections. A **wireless network** uses radio signals to establish the network connection.

Section 1-6, "Assembling an Office LAN," introduces setting up wired networks for both office and home networks; however, the home networking technologies are presented in this section.

A wireless home network is probably the most common home network configuration in use today.

Table 1-8 lists the advantages and disadvantages of both wired and wireless networks.

TABLE 1-8 **Wired and Wireless Network Advantages and Disadvantages**

	Advantages	Disadvantages
Wired network	Faster network data transfer speeds (within the LAN).	The cable connections typically require the use of specialized tools.
	Relatively inexpensive to set up.	The cable installation can be labor-intensive and expensive.
	The network is not susceptible to outside interference.	

	Advantages	Disadvantages
Wireless network	User mobility.	Security issues.
	Simple installations.	The data transfer speed within the LAN can be slower than wired networks.
	No cables.	

Wireless networks also go by the name **Wi-Fi**, which is the abbreviated name for the Wi-Fi Alliance (Wi-Fi stands for wireless fidelity). The Wi-Fi Alliance is an organization whose function is to test and certify wireless equipment for compliance with the 802.11x standards, which is the group of wireless standards developed under IEEE 802.11. IEEE is the Institute of Electrical and Electronics Engineers. The most common IEEE wireless standards include

- **802.11a (Wireless-A)**: This standard can provide data transfer rates up to 54Mbps and an operating range up to 75 feet. It operates at 5GHz.

- **802.11b (Wireless-B)**: This standard can provide data transfer rates up to 11Mbps with ranges of 100–150 feet. It operates at 2.4GHz.

- **802.11g (Wireless-G)**: This standard can provide data transfer rates up to 54Mbps up to 150 feet. It operates at 2.4GHz.

- **802.11n (Wireless-N)**: This standard provides data transfer rates up to 4 × 802.11g speeds (200+Mbps). It operates either at 2.4GHz or 5GHz.

- **802.11ac (Wireless-AC):** This is the latest wireless standard. It provides single-station data transfer rates of 500Mbps and operates in the 5GHz frequency band.

Figure 1-11 illustrates the placement and type of equipment found in a typical wired or wireless home network. Figure 1-11 (a) shows a wired LAN that is using cabling to interconnect the networking devices. A router is being used to make the connection to the ISP. The router can also contain a switch and a broadband modem. The switch is used to interconnect other networking devices, and the broadband modem is used to make the data connection to the ISP. The most common broadband connections to the ISP are via a cable modem and DSL. In some cases the router, switch, and broadband modem will be separate devices, but most often they will be integrated into one device. One of the computers may also have the configuration settings for managing the router, which can include the settings for connecting to the ISP.

Figure 1-11 (b) shows a wireless LAN that is being used to interconnect the networking devices. A **wireless router** is being used to make the data connection to the ISP, which is typically via a cable or DSL modem. The wireless router also has a wireless access point and will typically have a switch to facilitate wired network connections. Sometimes the broadband modem is integrated into the wireless router. The access point is used to establish the wireless network connection to each of the wireless computers.

to ISP

Router + Switch +
Broadband Modem

(a)

to ISP

Wireless Router
(Access Point/Switch/
Broadband Modem)

(b)

FIGURE 1-11 Examples of (a) wired and (b) wireless Wi-Fi home networks.

The components of a home network can include the following:

- **Hub**: This is used to interconnect networking devices. A drawback to the hub is that it broadcasts the data it receives to all devices connected to its ports. The hub has been replaced by the network switch in most modern networks. Figure 1-12 provides an image of a hub.

- **Switch**: This is the best choice for interconnecting networking devices. It can establish a direct connection from the sender to the destination without passing the data traffic to other networking devices. Figure 1-13 provides an image of a switch.

- **Network adapter**: Wired and wireless network adapters are available. The type of network adapter used in desktop computers is called the network interface card (NIC). Figure 1-14 provides an image of a wired network adapter. This type of NIC is inserted into an expansion slot on the computer's motherboard and is a wired-only adapter.

FIGURE 1-12 Linksys EtherFast ® 8-Port 10/100 Auto-Sensing Hub (courtesy of Linksys).

FIGURE 1-13 Linksys 24-Port 10/100/1000 Gigabit Switch (courtesy of Linksys).

FIGURE 1-14 Linksys Instant Gigabit Network Adapter (courtesy of Linksys).

The PC Card adapter connects to notebook computers and provides an RJ-45 jack for connecting to wired networks. RJ stands for registered jack. This device supports connections to both 10Mbps and 100Mbps networks. Figure 1-15 provides an image of a PC card adapter.

FIGURE 1-15   Linksys EtherFast® 10/100 32-Bit Integrated CardBus PC Card (courtesy of Linksys).

The Wireless-N adapter inserts into a notebook or laptop computer PC Card slot. The Wireless-N technology offers a data transfer speed that is faster than Wireless-G and is also compatible with both Wireless-B and Wireless-G technologies. Figure 1-16 provides an image of a Wireless-N adapter.

FIGURE 1-16   Linksys Wireless-N Notebook Adapter (courtesy of Linksys).

Another option for connecting to networks is to use a network adapter that attaches to a USB port on the computer. This device has the USB type A connector on one end and an RJ-45 jack on the other and will support connections to both 10Mbps, 100Mbps, and 1000Mbps data networks. Figure 1-17 provides an image of a USB network adapter.

FIGURE 1-17 Linksys Compact USB 2.0 10/100 Network Adapter (courtesy of Linksys).

- **Router**: A networking device used to connect two or more networks (for example, your LAN and the Internet) using a single connection to your ISP. A modern home networking router can also contain a switch and a broadband modem. Figure 1-18 provides an image of a router.

FIGURE 1-18 Linksys EtherFast® Cable/DSL Firewall Router with 4-Port Switch (courtesy of Linksys).

- **Access point**: Used to interconnect wireless devices and provide a connection to the wired LAN. The data transfer speeds for access points are dictated by the choice of wireless technology for the clients, but this device will support Wireless-N. Figure 1-19 provides an image of an access point.

- **Wireless router**: This device uses RF to connect to the networking devices. A wireless router typically contains a router, switch, and wireless access point and is probably the most common way to interconnect wireless LANs to the ISP's access device. Note that these devices also have wired network connections available on the system. Figure 1-20 provides an image of a wireless router.

FIGURE 1-19 The Linksys Wireless-N access point.

- **Broadband modem/gateway**: This describes the device used to provide high-speed data access via your cable connection or via a telephone company's DSL connection. A gateway combines a modem and a router into one network box. Figure 1-21 provides an image of a broadband modem/gateway.

- **Cable modem**: This device is used to make a broadband network connection from your home network to the ISP using your cable connection. This setup requires a splitter to separate the cable TV from the home network. Access to the Internet is typically provided by the cable TV service provider. Figure 1-22 provides an image of a cable modem.

FIGURE 1-20   Linksys Wireless-G Broadband Router (courtesy of Linksys).

FIGURE 1-21   Linksys Wireless-G Cable Gateway (courtesy of Linksys).

FIGURE 1-22   Linksys Cable Modem with USB and Ethernet connections (courtesy of Linksys).

- **DSL modem**: This device is used to make a broadband network connection from your home network to the ISP using the telephone line. Broadband access to the Internet is provided via the phone company or a separate ISP. The DSL connection requires the placement of filters on all telephone lines except the one going into the modem to prevent interference. Figure 1-23 provides an image of a DSL modem.

FIGURE 1-23   D-Link ADSL2 Modem (courtesy of D-Link).

Several issues should be considered when planning for a home network, including the following:

- **Data speed**: This will be determined by whether you chose to implement a wired or wireless home network. Wired networks offer the best data transfer rate inside the home network, up to 10Gbps. The best data transfer rates for a wireless home network can be obtained using 802.11n (Wireless-N) technology. This is the next generation of high-speed wireless connectivity providing data transfer rates up to 4×802.11g speeds (200+Mbps).

- **Cost**: Implementing a high-speed wired network can be quite expensive. With the networking hardware, cabling, and related hardware, you can incur an unexpected additional cost for implementing the high-speed wired home network. The cost of switching to or implementing an 802.11n Wireless-N network is minimal and is a suitable alternative to a wired network. But remember, the maximum data rate for a Wireless-N network is still much lower than that possible with a wired LAN.

- **Ease of implementation**: A wireless home network is probably the easiest to implement if the cabling and connectors for a wired network are not already installed. The time required to install the wireless home network is usually minimal as long as unexpected problems do not surface.

- **Appearance**: A wireless home network offers the best choice in regards to appearance because there won't be cables and networking hardware scattered around the house. The wireless home network will require a wireless router and an external wired connection to the ISP (refer to Figure 1-11(b)).

- **Home access**: The choice of wired or wireless technology will not affect home access. However, the wired network will offer the best data transfer speed internal to the network, but the wireless network offers the best choice for mobility.

- **Public access**: The choice of wired or wireless technology will not impact public access. The data rate for the connection to/from the ISP will be the limiting factor for the data transfer rate for public access.

It is not uncommon for a wired or wireless home network to stop functioning, although the downtime is usually minimal. The steps for troubleshooting wired and wireless home networks include the following:

Step 1 Check to ensure that the proper lights for your networking device that connects you to your ISP are properly displayed. Incorrect lights can indicate a connection problem with your cable modem, DSL modem, or telephone connection. Your ISP might also be having a problem, and you might need to call them to verify your connection.

Step 2 Next, to fix basic connection problems to the ISP, you should reboot the host computer (the computer connected to the router) and reboot the router. This usually will fix the problem, and the correct lights should be displayed. In some cases, you might also have to power down/up your broadband modem. (Note that the broadband modem might be integrated with the router.) Once again, check to see whether the correct lights are being displayed.

Step 3 You should always verify your hardware cable or phone connection is in place and has not been pulled loose. Make corrections as needed. You should also verify that all wireless units have a network connection. The following are steps to verify wireless connectivity for Windows 10/8/7, Windows XP, and Mac OS X:

- Windows 10/8/7, Windows Vista: Go to Control Panel > Network and Sharing Center. The wireless connection will show enabled if there is a wireless connection.

  - **Windows XP**: Right-click **My Network Places**. The computer will indicate whether there is a wireless network connection.

  - **Mac OS X**: Click the **Apple icon > System Preferences > Network**. If you are connected:

    - If you are connected, the Wi-Fi status will display "Connected" with green indicator.

    - If the wireless Wi-Fi is on but is not connected to a network, the Wi-Fi status will display "On" with amber indicator.

    - If the Wi-Fi is off, the Wi-Fi status will display "Off" with red indicator.

  Also note that if you are connected to a wireless network, a radio wave icon will appear at the top of the screen in the menu bar to indicate you are connected to a wireless network.

Step 4 Sometimes you might need to verify your network settings. This can happen if your computer has lost the data for the settings. In this case, follow the steps provided by the manufacturer of your broadband modem or your ISP.

The following are the basic steps for establishing the wireless connection for a wireless notebook computer running Windows 10/8/7, Windows Vista, XP, or Mac OS X: Windows Vista, XP, or Mac OS X:

- **Windows 10/8: Go to Control Panel > Network and Sharing Center—Set up a new connection or network**. You need to choose the **Connect to the Internet** option and then select **Wireless** to establish a wireless connection.

- **Windows 7**: Click **Start > Control Panel > Network and Sharing Center— Set up a new connection or network**. You need to choose **Connect to the Internet** option; then select **Wireless** to establish a wireless connection.

- **Windows Vista**: Click **Start > Settings > Network Connections** and then right-click **Wireless Network Connection**. You might need to click **Enable** and/or **Connect/Disconnect** to establish a wireless connection. A red X indicates a wireless connection is not established.

- **Windows XP**: This can vary depending on your wireless card. Click **Start > Programs** and select the setup program for your wireless card. Follow the steps displayed on the screen to establish a wireless network connection. You will need to know the name of the network you want to join as well as the SSID. The SSID is the Service Set Identifier and is used to identify which wireless devices are allowed to connect to the network.

- **Mac OS X**: Click the **Apple icon > System Preferences > Network**, select the **Wi-Fi** connection then click the **Turn Wi-Fi On** button. The available wireless networks will appear under the **Network Name** drop down menu. Select a desired wireless network and enter password for WEP/WPA/WPA2 when prompted. If connected, a radio wave should now appear at the top of the screen in the menu bar, which indicates the network is connected.

There are many choices of wireless technologies for configuring a wireless network. The 802.11b, g, and n (Wireless-B, -G, and -N) technologies are compatible even though they offer different data speeds. If compatible but different wireless technologies are being used, the data transfer speeds will be negotiated at the rate specified by the slowest technology. For example, the 802.11n (Wireless-N) standard offers a faster data rate (comparable to Wireless-G), but when devices of both technologies are present, the data transfer rate will be negotiated at the Wireless-G data rate.

In some cases, the wireless signal might not be reaching all the areas that need coverage. In this case, a device called a **range extender** can be used. This device relays the wireless signals from an access point or wireless router into areas with a weak signal or no signal at all. This improves the wireless remote access from all points in the home. This same technology can also be used to improve connectivity in stores and warehouses and can also be used to provide excellent connectivity in public places such as **hotspots**. Hotspots are defined as a limited geographic area that provides wireless access for the public. Hotspots are typically found in airports, restaurants, libraries, and schools.

Range Extender
Device that relays the wireless signals from an access point or wireless router into areas with a weak signal or no signal at all

Hotspots
A limited geographic area that provides wireless access for the public

Securing the Home Network

Many potential security issues are associated with a wireless network. Securing the home wireless network is extremely important because a wireless signal can be intercepted by the wrong person, and they can possibly connect to your network. The following are some basic steps that can be used to help protect the home network.

1. **Change the default factory passwords.** Wireless equipment is shipped with default passwords that are set at the factory. These default settings are known by the public, including people who would like to gain access into your network and possibly change your settings. It is best that you select your own password that is a combination of alphanumeric characters.

2. **Change the default SSID.** The SSID is the name used to identify your network and is used by your access point or wireless router to establish an association. Establishing an association means that a wireless client can join the network. The SSID can be up to 32 characters and should be changed often so hackers who have figured out your SSID will no longer have access to your home network.

Service Set Identifier (SSID)
Name that is used to identify your wireless network and is used by your access point or wireless router to establish an association

3. **Turn encryption on.** Probably the most important thing to do is turn on the security features that include data encryption. These options include Wired Equivalent Privacy (WEP), Wi-Fi Protected Access (WPA), and WPA2. WPA2 is a product certification issued by the Wi-Fi Alliance. It uses a stronger encryption than WPA and is also backward compatible with adapters using WPA. **WPS** is the Wi-Fi Protected setup. WPS simplifies the configuration process, enabling the user to set up WPA PSK without having to enter a long string of symbols, random numbers, or letters. This provides a feature to protect wireless networks, but it is susceptible to brute force attacks.

4. **Turn off the SSID broadcast.** Wireless systems broadcast the SSID so that the network can be easily identified as an available network. Hackers can use this information to possibly gain access to your network, so you should turn off the SSID broadcast. The exception to this is in hotspots where public access is

available. Please note, hotspots make it easy for the user to gain wireless access but hackers can also be on the same network, so it is important to have encryption turned on.

5. **Enable MAC address filtering.** All computer devices use a unique MAC address for identifying the device. This can be used to select which devices can be allowed access to the network. When MAC address filtering is turned on, only wireless devices that have specific MAC addresses will be allowed access to the network.

Another important security concern is limiting outside access to your home network via your connection to the ISP. The following are some things that can be done to protect the home network from outside threats:

- **Network Address Translation:** The outsider sees only the router IP address because the IP addresses of the internal networking devices are not provided on the Internet. Only the ISP-assigned IP address of the router is provided. The home network typically uses a private address that is not routable on the Internet. (Private IP addresses are blocked by the ISP.)

- **Firewall protection:** A common practice is to turn on the **firewall protection**. The purpose of a firewall is to prevent unauthorized access to your network. Firewall protection is available in both the Windows and MAC operating environments. A type of firewall protection is **Stateful Packet Inspection (SPI)**. This type of firewall inspects incoming data packets to make sure they correspond to an outgoing request. For example, you might be exchanging information with a website. Data packets that are not requested are rejected. The topic of firewalls is covered in more detail in Chapter 12, "Network Security."

- **Establish a VPN connection when transferring sensitive information:** A **virtual private network (VPN)** establishes a secure network connection and is a way to protect your LAN's data from being observed by outsiders. The VPN connection capability is available with Windows 10, Windows 8, Windows 7, Windows Vista, Windows XP, and Mac OS X. A VPN connection enables a remote or mobile user to access the network as if they were actually physically at the network. Additionally, the VPN connection is encrypted, providing privacy for the data packets being transmitted.

> **Firewall Protection**
> Used to prevent unauthorized access to your network
>
> **Stateful Packet Inspection (SPI)**
> Type of firewall that inspects incoming data packets to make sure they correspond to an outgoing request
>
> **Virtual Private Network (VPN)**
> Establishes a secure network connection and is a way to protect your LAN's data from being observed by outsiders

IP Addressing in the Home Network

A common question asked about home networks is, "How is IP addressing handled for all the computers connected to the Internet?" The home network typically has only one connection to the ISP, but multiple computers can be connected to the Internet at the same time. The answer is that IP addressing for the home network is managed by the router or wireless router that connects to the ISP. The ISP will issue an IP address to the router from an available pool of IP addresses managed by the ISP. The computers in the home network should be issued private IP addresses (applicable ranges are 10.0.0.0–10.255.255.255; 172.16.0.0–172.31.255.255; 192.168.0.0–192.168.255.255) using a technique called **Network Address Translation (NAT)**.

Network Address Translation (NAT)
Translates the private IP address to a public address for routing over the Internet

Figure 1-24 provides an example. A routable public IP address is issued by the ISP for the wireless router. This public IP address enables all computers in the home network access to the Internet. The wireless router issues private addresses to all computers connected to the network.

The wireless computers (1 and 2) will use private IP address that are assigned by the wireless router.

to ISP

Wireless Router
(Access Point/Switch/
Broadband Modem)

FIGURE 1-24   A home network using a wireless router connected to the ISP.

NAT translates the private IP address to a public address for routing over the Internet. For example, computer 1 in the home network (see Figure 1-24) might establish a connection to an Internet website. The wireless router uses NAT to translate computer 1's private IP address to the public IP address assigned to the router. The router uses a technique called **overloading**, where NAT translates the home network's private IP addresses to the single public IP address assigned by the ISP. In addition, the NAT process tracks a port number for the connection. This technique is called **Port Address Translation (PAT)**. The router stores the home network's IP address and port number in a NAT lookup table. The port number differentiates the computer that is establishing a connection to the Internet because the router uses the same address for all computers. This port number is used when a data packet is returned to the home network. The port number identifies the computer that established the Internet connection, and the router can deliver the data packet to the correct computer.

Overloading
Where NAT translates the home network's private IP addresses to a single public IP address

Port Address Translation (PAT)
A port number is tracked with the client computer's private address when translating to a public address

For example, if computer 1 establishes a connection to a website on the Internet, the data packets from the website are sent back to computer 1 using the home network's routable public IP address. This first step enables the data packet to be routed back to the home network. Next, the router uses the NAT lookup table and port number to translate the destination for the data packet back to the computer 1 private IP address and original port number, which might be different. Figure 1-25 demonstrates an example of the NAT translation process for a home network. The home network has been assigned Class C private IP addresses (192.168.0.x) by the router. The x is a unique number (from 1 to 254) assigned to each computer. The router translates the private IP addresses to the public routable IP address assigned by the ISP. Additionally, the router tracks a port number with the public IP address to identify the computer. For example, the computer with the private IP address of 192.168.0.64 is assigned the public IP address 128.123.246.55:1962, where 1962 is the port number tracked by the router.

FIGURE 1-25   The NAT translation using PAT.

Section 1-5 Review

This section covered the following **Network+** Exam objectives:

1.1 Explain the functions and applications of various network devices

This section has presented a look at the wireless router, switch, access point, and the firewall. All of these devices are key for providing wireless network access. The purpose of a firewall is to prevent unauthorized access to your network.

1.2 Compare and contrast the use of networking services and applications

The benefit of incorporating a VPN connection for your wireless network is presented. A virtual private network (VPN) establishes a secure network connection and is a way to protect your LAN's data from being observed by outsiders.

1.3 Install and configure the following networking services/applications

This section presents an overview of both NAT (Network Address Translation) and PAT (Port Address Translation).

1.7 Differentiate between network infrastructure implementations

Hotspots are introduced in this section. Hotspots are defined as limited geographic areas that provide wireless access for the public.

1.8 Given a scenario, implement and configure the appropriate networking addressing schema

This section presents an overview of both NAT (Network Address Translation) and PAT (Port *Address Translation*).

2.4 Explain the importance of implementing network segmentation

This section includes many discussions on the various wireless standards available today. There are many choices of wireless technologies for configuring a wireless network. It is very important that you understand the advantages and limitations of each wireless standard.

2.6 Given a scenario, configure a switch using proper features

This section introduces MAC address filtering. When MAC address filtering is turned on, only wireless devices that have specific MAC addresses will be allowed to access the network.

2.7 Install and configure wireless LAN infrastructure and implement the appropriate technologies in support of wireless-capable devices

A wireless router typically contains a router, switch, and wireless access point and is probably the most common way to interconnect wireless LANs to the ISP's access device.

3.2 Compare and contrast network vulnerabilities and threats

WPS is the Wi-Fi Protected setup. WPS simplifies the configuration process enabling the user to set up WPA PSK without having to enter a long string of symbols, random numbers, or letters. This provides a feature to protect wireless networks, but it is susceptible to brute force attacks.

3.3 Given a scenario, implement network-hardening techniques

Probably the most important thing to do is turn on the security features that include data encryption. These options include Wired Equivalent Privacy (WEP), Wi-Fi Protected Access (WPA), and WPA2.

4.1 Given a scenario, implement the following network troubleshooting methodology

The basic steps for troubleshooting the wireless network were discussed in this section. Step 1 is to verify that the proper lights are being displayed on your modem connection.

5.3 Given a scenario, deploy the appropriate wireless standard

This section includes many discussions on the various wireless standards available today. There are many choices of wireless technologies for configuring a wireless network. It is very important that you understand the advantages and limitations of each wireless standard.

5.4 Given a scenario, deploy the appropriate wired connectivity standard

The cable modem is used to make a broadband network connection from your home network to the ISP using your cable connection.

Test Your Knowledge

1. Which of the following issues should be considered when planning for a home network?

    a. Data speed

    b. Public access

    c. Cost

    d. All of these answers are correct.

2. How does MAC address filtering help to secure a wireless network?

    a. This is used to help prevent the theft of network interface cards.

    b. This requires an additional login step requiring the user to enter his MAC address.

    c. MAC address filtering is seldom used anymore because of NIC restrictions.

    d. This can be used to select which networking devices can be allowed access to the network.

3. Which of the following are examples of wireless technologies?

    a. 802.11a

    b. 802.11g

    c. 802.11n

    d. All of these answers are correct.

4. What is NAT?

    a. Network Asynchronous Transfer

    b. Network Address Translation

    c. Network Address Transfer

    d. None of these answers is correct.

1-6 ASSEMBLING AN OFFICE LAN

An example of assembling an office-type LAN is presented in this section. The Ethernet protocol will be used for managing the exchange of data in the network, and the networking devices will be interconnected in a star topology. There are many options for assembling and configuring a LAN, but this example presents a networking approach that is simple and consistent with modern computer networking. It will also provide a good introduction to the networking topics presented in the text.

For this example, three computers and one printer are to be configured in the star topology. Each device in the network will be assigned an IP address from the private address space. The following step-by-step discussion guides you through the process of assembling, configuring, and testing an office LAN:

Step 1 The first step in assembling an office LAN is to document the devices to be connected in the network and prepare a simple sketch of the proposed network. Each device's MAC and IP addresses should be included in the network drawing documentation.

Figure 1-26 provides an example of a small office LAN. The desired IP addresses and the actual MAC addresses for each computer and printer are listed. Remember, each NIC contains a unique MAC address and the IP addresses are locally assigned by the network administrator. The MAC addresses were obtained by entering the **ipconfig /all** command from the command prompt in Windows 7. Repeat this step for all computing devices connected to the LAN. Table 1-9 provides the results of the MAC address inquiries. Each networking device will be assigned an IP address. Table 1-9 also lists the planned IP addresses of the devices used in this office LAN.

FIGURE 1-26 An example of a small office LAN star topology

TABLE 1-9 **The MAC and Assigned IP Address for the Devices in the Office LAN**

Device (Hostname)	MAC Address	IP Address
Computer 1	00-10-A4-13-99-2E	10.10.10.1
Computer 2	00-10-A4-13-6C-6E	10.10.10.2
Computer 3	00-B0-D0-25-BF-48	10.10.10.3
Laser Printer	00-10-83-0B-A6-2F	10.10.10.20

Note

In this text, you will function as the network administrator. The network administrator must know how to obtain all IP and MAC address information for devices connected to the network. This requires that the network administrator keep good documentation of the network.

Step 2   Connect all the networking devices using the star topology shown in Figure 1-26.

At the center of this star topology network will be a switch or hub. Recall that either can be used to connect the networking devices. The switch is the best choice because the hub broadcasts data it receives to all devices connected to its ports, and the switch enables the devices to communicate directly. Although hubs are not as sophisticated as switches and are not reflective of modern computer networking, the hub is still suitable for use in small networks.

The connections from the switch to the computers and the printer will be made using premade twisted-pair patch cables. The cable type used here is **CAT6 (category 6)** twisted-pair cable. CAT6 twisted-pair cables have **RJ-45** modular connectors on each end, as shown in Figure 1-27, and are capable of carrying 1000**Mbps** (1 gigabit) or more of data up to a length of 100 meters. Chapter 2 covers the twisted-pair media and its various category specifications. If the network hardware and software are properly set up, all computers will be able to access the printer and other computers. Chapter 2 addresses issues associated with the proper cabling including CAT 6/5e.

> **CAT6 (category 6)**
>
> Twisted-pair cables capable of carrying up to 1000Mbps (1 gigabit) of data up to a length of 100 meters
>
> **RJ-45**
>
> The 8-pin modular connector used with CAT6/5e/5 cable
>
> **Mbps**
>
> Megabits per second

FIGURE 1-27   The RJ-45 twisted-pair patch cables (courtesy of StarTech.com).

> **Numerics**
>
> A numerical representation

The media used for transporting data in a modern computer network are either wireless, twisted-pair, or fiber-optic cables. The principles behind selecting, installing, and testing twisted-pair cabling are presented in Chapter 2. Table 1-10 lists the common **numerics** used to describe the data rates for the twisted-pair media and the older style copper coaxial cable used in a LAN. Common numerics for fiber-optic LANs are also listed. Numerics are an alphanumeric description of a technology. For example, 100BaseT means that this is a 100-Mbps, baseband, twisted-pair technology.

TABLE 1-10 **Common Numerics for Ethernet LAN Cabling**

Numeric	Description
10Base2	10Mbps over coaxial cable up to 185 m, also called ThinNet (seldom used anymore)
10Base5	10Mbps over coaxial cable up to 500 m, also called ThickNet (seldom used anymore)
10BaseT	10Mbps over twisted-pair
10BaseF	10Mbps over multimode fiber-optic cable
10BaseFL	10Mbps over 850 nm multimode fiber-optic cable
100BaseT	100Mbps over twisted-pair (also called Fast Ethernet)
100BaseFX	100Mbps over fiber
1000BaseT	1000Mbps over twisted-pair
1000BaseFX	1000Mbps over fiber
10GE	10GB Ethernet

The RJ-45 plugs connect to the switch inputs via the RJ-45 jacks. Figure 1-28 shows a simple 8-port switch. The inputs to the switch are also called the input **ports**, which are the interfaces for the networking devices. The switch inputs marked with an "x" or uplink port [Figure 1-28(b)] indicate that these devices are cross-connected, meaning the transmit and receive pairs on the twisted-pair cable are crossed to properly align each for data communication. The term for a cable that has cross-connected TX/RX data lines is **crossover**. Some of the switches might have the port labeled "Uplink," which indicates the cross-connect capability. Furthermore, some of the newer switches nowadays are equipped with automatic crossover detection, so the users don't have to worry about whether to use a straight-through cable or a crossover cable. Examples of straight-through and crossover cables are presented in Chapter 2.

> **Ports**
> The interface for the networking devices
>
> **Crossover**
> Transmit and receive signal pairs are crossed to properly align the transmit signal on one device with the receive signal on the other device

The switch used to connect the networking devices
(a)

RJ-45 Jack

X
(cross-connected input)
(b)

FIGURE 1-28 (a) The switch used to connect the networking devices; (b) close-up view of "x" input indicating an uplink port (courtesy of Anixter, Inc.).

Figure 1-29(a) provides an example of this cross-connected concept. Switches usually have at least one port that can be switched or selected for use as either a cross-connected or **straight-through** input. A straight-through port is also called an **uplink port**. The uplink port allows for the connection of a switch to a switch or hub without having to use a special cable. Devices requiring the cross-connected input port are computers, printers, and routers. Devices requiring a straight-through connection are uplink connections to other switches or hubs. Figure 1-29(b) provides a block diagram explaining the concept of a straight-through input.

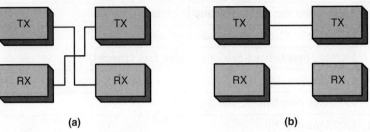

(a)   (b)

FIGURE 1-29   (a) An example of the wiring on an "x" type input on a hub; (b) an example of straight-through wiring.

A networking connection can be verified by examining the **link light** on the switch or hub. The presence of a link light indicates that the transmit and receive pairs are properly aligned and the connected devices are communicating. Absence of the light indicates a possible cabling or hardware problem. The Ethernet protocol uses the **link integrity test** to verify that a communication link between two Ethernet devices has been established. The link light remains lit when communication is established and remains lit as long as there is a periodic exchange of link pulses from the attached devices. **Link pulses** are sent by each of the connected devices via the twisted-pair cables to indicate that the link is up, but the link pulses are not part of the Ethernet packet and are sent at regular intervals when data is not being transmitted.

Step 3   Configure the IP address settings on each computer according to the assigned addresses provided in Table 1-7.

The following describes how the network administrator configures the computers to operate on the LAN. This requires that each computing device be assigned an IP address. The assigned IP addresses for this LAN are provided in Table 1-7. Examples of configuring the computers in the office LAN using Windows 10/8/7, Windows Vista, Windows XP, and Mac OS X follow. A printer is also attached to the network and setup for printers is discussed later in the text.

- **Windows 10/8 Go to Control Panel > Network and Internet—Network and Sharing Center. Click Local Area Connection** and select **Properties**, and then click **Continue**. This opens the Local Area Connection Properties menu. Double-click **Internet Protocol Version 4 (TCP/IPv4)**. This opens the Properties menu. Now select **Use the following IP address**, enter the IP address and subnet mask, and click **OK**.

- **Windows 7**: **Click Start > Control Panel > Network and Internet—Network and Sharing Center. Click Local Area Connection** and select **Properties**, and then click **Continue**. This opens the Local Area Connection Properties menu. Double-click **Internet Protocol Version 4 (TCP/IPv4)**. This opens the Properties menu. Now select **Use the following IP address**, enter the IP address and subnet mask, and click **OK**.

- **Windows Vista**: Click **Start > Network Connection** or click **Start > Control Panel > Network and Sharing Center**. Right-click **Local Area Connection** and select **Properties**, and then click **Continue**. This opens the Local Area Connection Properties menu. Double-click **Internet Protocol Version 4 (TCP/IPv4)**. This opens the Properties menu. Now select **Use the following IP address**, enter the IP address and subnet mask, and click **OK**.

- **Windows XP**: To set the IP address in Windows XP, click **Start > Settings > Control Panel** and click **Network Connections**. Right-click **Local Area Connection**, and then click **Properties**. You should see the Local Area Connection Properties menu. Make sure the **TCP/IP** box is checked and the words **Internet Protocol TCP/IP** are highlighted (selected). Click the **Properties** button. You should now see the **Internet Protocol (TCP/IP) Properties** menu. At this point you must specify whether the IP address is to be obtained automatically or if you are to use a specified (static) address. For this example, click **Use the following IP address**. Type the desired IP address and subnet mask and select **OK**.

- **Mac OS X**: Click the **Apple icon > System Preferences > Network** and select the **Ethernet** or **USB Ethernet** connection. Under the Configure IPv4 drop down menu, select **Manually**. This option lets you manually set the IP address and subnet mask. Fields should now be displayed for inputting both the IP address and subnet mask. Enter the desired IP address and subnet mask, and select **Apply**.

The IP addresses and subnet mask being used in the office LAN example are listed in Table 1-7. The IP address for computer 1 is 10.10.10.1, and in this example, a subnet mask of 255.255.0.0 is being used. Chapter 6 examines subnet masking in detail. For now, leave the remaining fields empty; their purpose will be discussed later in the text. Your network configuration for computer 1 should now be complete. These steps are repeated for computers 2 and 3 in this LAN example.

Section 1-6 Review

This section has covered the following Network+ Exam objectives.

1.5 Install and properly terminate various cable types and connectors using appropriate tools

The popular RJ-45 plugs and jacks are introduced in this section. You will find this type of connector on all computer networks. Table 1-10 provides a good description of the common networking cable types.

1.7 Differentiate between network infrastructure implementations

This section introduces the basic steps for implementing a LAN (local area network).

5.3 Given a scenario, deploy the appropriate wired connectivity standard

The common numerics for Ethernet LAN cabling are listed in Table 1-10. This provides a good start for understanding the different types of cable used in Ethernet LANs.

5.4 Given a scenario, deploy the appropriate wired connectivity standard

Table 1-10 provides a good description of the common networking cable types.

5.8 Explain the basics of change management procedures

The first step in assembling an office LAN is to document the devices being connected to the network. It is easy to skip this step, but it is critical that good documentation be a priority.

Test Your Knowledge

1. The "X" on the input to a switch represents a router-only port.

   a. True

   b. False

2. A cross-connected input port indicates that

   a. The transmit and receive pairs are crossed.

   b. Is only used on connections to routers.

   c. The cable is wired incorrectly.

   d. Must be avoided on hub and switch port inputs.

3. A lit link light indicates that (select all that apply)

   a. The Link Integrity Test is operational.

   b. Link pulses are being shared by all devices in the LAN.

   c. A 10Mbps data link has been established.

   d. A 100Mbps data link has been established.

   e. All of these answers are correct.

1-7 TESTING AND TROUBLESHOOTING A LAN

When the network configurations on the computers are completed and the cable connections are in place, you will need to test and possibly troubleshoot the network.
First, verify that the computers are properly connected on the network. Do this by
verifying that you have link lights on each switch port that is connected to a computer
or other networking device. Link verification will typically appear as a lit link light.
An example of a switch with the link light activated is shown in Figure 1-30.

FIGURE 1-30   An example of the link light on a hub.

After you have verified that the networking devices are physically connected, use
the **ping** command to verify that the networking devices are communicating. **Ping**
uses **Internet Control Message Protocol (ICMP)** echo requests and replies to test that
a device on the network is reachable. The ICMP protocol verifies that messages are
being delivered. The **ping** command is available in the command window of Windows to verify the networking devices are communicating. The command structure
for the **ping** command is as follows:

```
Usage ping[-t] [-a] [-n count) [-1 size] [-f -i TTL] [-v TOS]  [-r count] [-s
count]
[[-j host-list]:[-k host-list] [-w timeout] destination-list
Options
-t              Ping the specified host until stopped
                To see statistics and continue, type Control-Break
                To stop, type Control-C
```

> **Ping**
> Command used to test
> that a device on the
> network is reachable
>
> **ICMP**
> Internet Control Message
> Protocol

```
-a              Resolve addresses to host-names
-n count        Number of echo requests to send
-1 size         Send buffer size
-f              Set Don't Fragment flag in packet
-I
TTL             Time To Live v
TOS             Type Of Service
r count         Record route for count hops
s count         Timestamp for count hops
j host-list     Loose source route along host-list
k host-list     Strict source route along host-list
w timeout       Timeout in milliseconds to wait for each reply
```

For example, the command **ping 10.10.10.1** is used to ping the IP address for computer 1. The IP address 10.10.10.1 is the destination address. Another example would be the destination IP address for computer 3; in this case **ping 10.10.10.3** would be used. (Refer to Table 1-9 and Figure 1-26 for the IP addresses of the computers in our sample network.)

The following is an example of pinging another computer on the network to verify that the computers are communicating. In this example, computer 1 is used to ping computer 2. Remember, the **ping** command is executed from the command window.

```
ping 10.10.10.2
Pinging 10.10.10.2 with 32 bytes of data:
Reply from 10.10.10.2: bytes 32 time<1ms TTL 128
Reply from 10.10.10.2: bytes 32 time<1ms TTL 128
Reply from 10.10.10.2: bytes 32 time<1ms TTL 128
Reply from 10.10.10.2: bytes 32 time<1ms TTL 128
Ping statistics for 10.10.10.2:
     Packets: Sent = 4, Received = 4, Lost = 0 (0% loss),
Approximate round trip times in milli-seconds:
     Minimum = 0ms, Maximum = 0ms, Average = 0ms
```

The text shows that 32 bytes of data are being sent to the computer with the IP address of 10.10.10.2. The "Reply from 10.10.10.2" indicates that computer 2 received the message. If the computer at IP address 10.10.10.2 did not respond, the message **"Request timed out."** is displayed:

```
ping 10.10.10.2
Pinging 10.10.10.2 with 32 bytes of data:
Request timed out.
Request timed out.
Request timed out.
Request timed out.

Ping statistics for 10.10.10.2:
     Packets: Sent = 4, Received = 0, Lost= 4
(100% loss),
```

At times you might want to verify the IP address of the computer you are working on. Remember, a method of obtaining the IP address is to enter the command **ipconfig** at the command prompt. You don't need to include the **/all switch** after the **ipconfig** command unless you also want the MAC address information displayed. Figure 1-31 shows an example of displaying the IP address for computer 1.

Windows IP Configuration
Ethernet adapter Local Area Connection:
    Connection-specific DNS Suffix .:
    IP Address.............: 10.10.10.1
    Subnet Mask...........: 255.255.0.0
    Default Gateway ....:

(a)

10/2/07 2:26 PM

Configuration Name	Interface	Type	IP Address
AirPort	en1	AirPort	128.123.244.53
Bluetooth	Bluetooth-Modem	PPP (PPPSerial)	
Built-in Ethernet	en0	Ethernet	10.10.20.1
Internal Modem	modem	PPP (PPPSerial)	

Built-in Ethernet:

Interface:	en0
Type:	Ethernet
IP Address:	10.10.20.1
Subnet Mask:	255.255.255.0
Broadcast Address:	10.10.20.255
Ethernet Address:	00:0d:93:c2:d8:74

(b)

FIGURE 1-31   (a) An example of displaying the IP address for computer 1 using the ipconfig command in Windows and (b) an example of the displayed IP address in Mac OS X for the built-in Ethernet connection.

Section 1-7 Review

This section has covered the following **Network+** Exam objectives.

> 4.1 Given a scenario, implement the following network troubleshooting methodology

*This section introduces the important step for verifying network connectivity using the **ping** command. Several examples of using **ping** to troubleshoot the network are presented.*

> 4.2 Given a scenario, analyze and interpret the output of troubleshooting tools

An important step in verifying connectivity between two networking devices is to issue the ping command using the destination IP address for the other. The ping command is available from the command window in Windows. Make sure you know how to issue the command and the options available with the command such as implementing continuous pinging and setting the buffer size.

Test Your Knowledge

1. The network administrator needs to verify a network connection. Which of the following steps should be taken? (Select two.)

   a. Verify the link lights.

   b. Use the **ping** command to verify network connectivity.

   c. Perform an ARP request.

   d. Ping the MAC address.

2. The **ping -t** *ip address* command (select all that apply)

   a. Pings the host at the specified IP address until it is stopped.

   b. Pings the MAC address of the host at the specified IP address.

   c. Allows the **ping** to pass through routers.

   d. Allows the **ping** command to be executed from the command prompt.

SUMMARY

This chapter introduced the basic concepts of computer networking. The technologies and techniques for assembling a computer network using the Ethernet protocol have been presented. The student should now understand the following major topics:

- The various LAN topologies
- The concept of CSMA/CD in the Ethernet protocol
- The structure of the Ethernet frame
- The purpose of the network interface card
- The purpose of the MAC address
- How to determine the MAC address for a computer
- The purpose and structure of the IP address
- The concept of private IP addresses
- The OSI Model
- The network topologies and technologies used to implement twisted-pair computer networks
- How to configure and verify a computer's IP address
- How to configure a home network and an office LAN
- The purpose of the link light
- The purpose of using *ping* to test a network connection

QUESTIONS AND PROBLEMS

Section 1-1

1. State whether the following network descriptions are describing a MAN, WAN, or LAN:

    a. A network of users that share computer resources in a limited area

    b. A network of users that share computer resources across a metropolitan area

    c. A network that connects local area networks across a large geographic area

2. Expand the acronym *NIC*.

3. Expand the acronym *MAC*.

4. Expand the acronym *LAN*.

5. Expand the acronym *WAN*.

Section 1-2

6. Define the term *protocol*.

7. Define the term *topology*.

8. Define the term *deterministic*.

9. A disadvantage of the Token Ring system is that if an error changes the token pattern, it can cause the token to stop circulating. This can be eliminated by adding which of the following?

    a. Router

    b. Multiport repeater

    c. Token passer

    d. Token Ring hub

10. State the network topology being used in Figure 1-32 (Bus, Star, Ring, or Mesh).

    a. Mesh

    b. Bus

    c. Ring

    d. Star

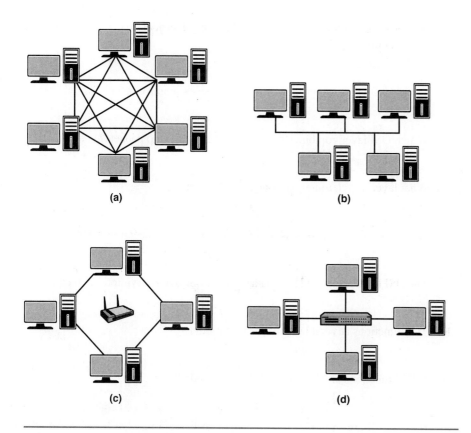

FIGURE 1-32 The networks for question 10.

11. What is the difference between a *hub* and a *switch*?

Section 1-3

12. What are the seven layers of the OSI model?

13. Which OSI layer is responsible for adding a header that includes routing information?

14. Which OSI layer is considered the media access control layer?

15. Which OSI layer combines messages or segments into packets?

16. What layer does a router work at?

17. Which OSI layer is responsible for the mechanical connection to the network?

18. The OSI layer responsible for data compression and encryption is which layer?

19. TCP functions at what layer of the OSI model?

20. HTTP functions at what layer of the OSI model?

21. IP and IPX are examples of protocols that operate in what layer of the OSI model?

22. The network interface card operates at what layer of the OSI model?

23. Why are the layers of the OSI model important to the network administrator?

Section 1-4

24. Define the acronym *CSMA/CD* and the protocol that uses CSMA/CD.

25. What information is not included in an Ethernet frame?

    a. Frame size

    b. Source MAC address

    c. Pad

    d. Frame check sequence

26. What is the minimum size of the data payload in an Ethernet frame?

27. What is the minimum and maximum size of an Ethernet frame?

28. Define the acronym *OUI*. Where is the OUI used?

29. What does the *OUI* represent?

30. In Windows Vista or Windows XP, how would you find the Ethernet (MAC) address?

31. INTERNET SEARCH: Find the device manufacturer for the following Ethernet devices:

    a. 00-C0-4F-49-68-AB

    b. 00-0A-27-B7-3E-F8

    c. 00-04-76-B6-9D-06

    d. 00-00-36-69-42-27

32. State the class of address (A, B, or C) for the following IP addresses:

    a. 46.39.42.05_____
    b. 220.244.38.168_____
    c. 198.1.0.4_____
    d. 126.87.12.34_____
    e. 99.150.200.251_____
    f. 128.64.32.16_____

33. Expand the acronym *TCP/IP.*

Section 1-5

34. Cite the three advantages of a wired network.

35. Cite three advantages of a wireless network.

36. What does it mean for a wireless networking device to be Wi-Fi compliant?

37. What are the most common types of equipment that are used to establish a broadband connection to the ISP?

38. Name six issues that should be considered when planning a home network?

39. Why is checking the lights of the networking device that connects to the ISP important?

40. What is the purpose of a range expander?

41. What is a hotspot?

42. List five steps that can be used to protect the home network.

43. You have the choice of selecting a networking device with WEP and another with WPA. Which offers better security and why?

44. What are the potential problems of using the default factory passwords?

45. What is the purpose of the SSID, and what can the network administrator do to protect the network from hackers who might have learned the SSID?

46. What is the purpose of MAC filtering on a wireless network?

47. How does NAT (Network Address Translation) help protect outsider access to computers in the home network?

48. What is Stateful Packet Inspection?

49. What is a VPN, and how does it protect the data transferred over a wireless network?

50. How is IP addressing typically handled in a home network?

51. What is Port Address Translation (PAT)?

52. A router on a home network is assigned an IP address of 128.123.45.67. A computer in the home network is assigned a private IP address of 192.168.10.62. This computer is assigned the public IP address 128.123.45.67:1922. Which IP address is used for routing data packets on the Internet? Is overloading being used?

Section 1-6

53. Which of the following is not a step in building an office LAN?

    a. Obtaining proper government permits

    b. Configuring the network settings

    c. Connecting the devices together

    d. Network documentation

54. What does *RJ-45* represent?

    a. A 45-pin connector for CAT6

    b. An IEEE standard for data speed

    c. An 8-pin modular connector for twisted pair Ethernet

    d. Protocol used to verify a communications link

55. What is an *uplink port*?

56. What is the maximum speed and length for Category 6 cabling?

57. What do the link lights on a hub represent?

58. What does *cross-connected* mean?

59. Documentation: Draw a network diagram similar to Fig 1-33 consisting of three computers, a switch, and a printer. Use the MAC addresses given in Table 1-9. Assign each network device an IP address from the private address space 192.168.5.x network. You are the network administrator and may choose the host address for each device.

MAC Address: 00-10-A4-13-99-2E
IP Address: 192.168.5.1

- CAT6 cable

CAT6 cable

CAT6 cable

Switch

MAC Address: 00-10-A4-13-6C-6E
IP Address: 192.168.5.2

- CAT6 cable

MAC Address: 00-B0-D0-25-BF-48
IP Address: 192.168.5.3

FIGURE 1-33 The sample network diagram for question 59.

Section 1-7

60. What command would you use to ping 10.3.9.42 indefinitely?

61. What command would you use to ping 192.168.5.36 20 times with 1024 bytes of data?

62. Expand the acronym *TTL*.

CERTIFICATION QUESTIONS

63. In terms of computer security, a switch offers better security than a hub. Why is this?

    a. A hub requires a special pin to activate the connection.

    b. A hub forwards the data it receives to every device connected to the hub. It is possible for network devices to pick up data intended for a different device. A switch eliminates this by only forwarding data packets to the correct device whenever possible.

    c. A switch forwards the data it receives to every device connected to the switch. It is possible for network devices to pick up data intended for a different device. A hub eliminates this by only forwarding data packets to the correct device whenever possible.

    d. The use of the switch guarantees that all devices connected to it will share link integrity pulses. This sharing of the pulses strengthens the security of the connection.

64. What networking protocol does Ethernet use?

    a. Ethernet uses a token ring passing scheme. The computer devices must possess the ring to be able to pass a token.

    b. Ethernet uses Carrier Access – Multiple Sensing / Collision Detection

    c. Ethernet uses Carrier Sense – Multiple Access / Collision Detection

    d. Ethernet uses Collision Sense – Carrier Access / Multiple Pairing

65. Network interface card has a MAC address of 00-00-86-15-7A. From this information, specify the OUI.

    a. There is not sufficient information to specify the OUI.

    b. The OUI is 86-15-7A.

    c. The OUI is 86-00-00

    d. The OUI is 00-00-86

66. An IP address for an internal computer is assigned by

    a. the Internet Assigned Numbers Authority

    b. the local network administrator

    c. the user of the computer

    d. Internet Address Numbers Authority

67. The topology shown is which of the following?

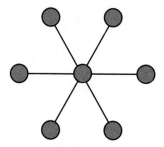

    a. star

    b. token-ring

    c. bus

    d. mesh

    d. None of these answers is correct.

68. The topology shown is which of the following?

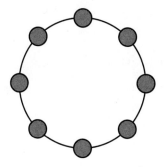

    a. star

    b. token-ring

    c. bus

    d. mesh

    d. None of these answers is correct.

69. The topology shown is which of the following?

    a. star

    b. token-ring

    c. bus

    d. mesh

    d. None of these answers is correct.

70. The pad field in an Ethernet packet

    a. is used to bring the total number of bytes up to 46 if the data file is less than 46 bytes.

    b. is used to bring the total number of bytes up to 64 if the data file is less than 64 bytes.

    c. is not required with CSMA/CD.

    d. provides grouping of the information for transmission.

71. The IP address 10.10.20.250 is an example of (select all that apply)

    a. class A address.

    b. class B address.

    c. a private IP address.

    d. a routable IP address.

    e. a nonroutable Internet IP address.

72. An Intranet is (select all that apply)

    a. uses class E addressing.

    b. used in high speed (gigabit) Ethernet.

    c. an internal network that provides file and resource sharing.

    d. enables Fast Ethernet connections.

    e. not typically accessed from the Internet

PHYSICAL LAYER CABLING: TWISTED PAIR

CHAPTER OUTLINE

OBJECTIVES

- Describe the six subsystems of a structured cabling system
- Define horizontal cabling
- Define UTP and STP
- Define the categories of UTP cable
- Describe the difference in the T568A and T568B wire color order
- Describe the procedure for placing RJ-45 plugs and jacks on twisted-pair cable

- Describe how to terminate twisted-pair cable for computer networks
- Define the basic concepts for planning a cable installation for an office LAN
- Describe the procedure for certifying a twisted-pair cable for CAT6 and CAT5e
- Describe the issues of running 10 gigabit Ethernet over copper
- Describe the basic steps for troubleshooting cable problems

KEY TERMS

physical layer
EIA
TIA
campus network
EIA/TIA 568-B
building entrance
entrance facilities (EF)
equipment room (ER)
telecommunications closet
TR
backbone cabling
horizontal cabling
TCO
work area
main cross-connect (MC)
intermediate cross-connect (IC)
cross-connect
horizontal cross-connect (HC)

MDF (Main Distribution Frame or Main Equipment Room)
CD (Campus Distributor)
BD (Building Distributor)
FD (Floor Distributors)
workstation or work area outlet (WO)
TO (telecommunications outlet)
terminated
8P8C
patch cable
UTP
CAT6/6a
CAT5/e
balanced mode
FastEthernet
network congestion
bottlenecking

full duplex
gigabit Ethernet
CAT7/7a and CAT6a
10GBASE-T
STP
EMI
T568A
T568B
color map
TX
continues
RX
straight-through cable
wire-map
crossover cable
link
full channel
attenuation (insertion loss)

near-end crosstalk (NEXT)
crosstalk
power sum NEXT (PSNEXT)
equal level FEXT (ELFEXT)
PSELFEXT
ACR
PSACR
return loss
propagation delay
nominal velocity of propagation (NVP)
delay skew
IEEE 802.3an-2006
10GBASE-T

10GBASE-T
pair data
Alien Crosstalk (AXT)
PSANEXT
PSAACRF
F/UTP
TCL
ELTCTL
LCL
TCTL
PSANEXT
PSAACRF
multilevel encoding
hybrid echo cancellation circuit

This chapter examines the twisted-pair media used to link computers together to form a local area network (LAN). This is called **physical layer** cabling. The term *physical layer* describes the media that interconnects networking devices. The objective of this chapter is for the reader to gain an introductory understanding of the cable media including the category types, the steps for terminating cables, cable testing, certification, and troubleshooting. The main focus is on the use of UTP cable in computer networks, although an overview of shielded twisted-pair (STP) is presented. Fiber-optic cables are playing an important role in modern computer networks and are not overlooked in this text. This media is thoroughly examined in Chapter 3, "Physical Layer Cabling: Fiber Optics."

Other types of cabling you might encounter in computer networking are RG-6 and possibly RG-59. These types of cables are called *coaxial cables* and are primarily used to connect satellite systems or cable television and modems. Cable terminations for these types of cable include "F-type" and BNC connectors.

2-1   INTRODUCTION

This chapter begins with an overview of the concept of structured cabling. This section defines the six subsystems of a structured cabling system and focuses on the basic issues associated with horizontal cabling or wiring a LAN. Next, the basic operational characteristics of UTP cable are examined. The discussion includes an examination of the various categories of UTP cable currently available. Following that is an overview of constructing twisted-pair patch and horizontal link cabling. The tools and techniques for properly terminating UTP cabling for both CAT6 and CAT5e are presented. An introduction to testing and certifying CAT6 and CAT5e cables follows. This section includes several examples of cable test data and how to interpret the test results. The chapter concludes with a section on troubleshooting computer networks, with a focus on cable or physical failures.

> **Physical Layer**
> Describes the media that interconnects networking devices

Table 2-1 lists and identifies, by chapter section, where each of the CompTIA Network+ objectives is presented in this chapter. At the end of each chapter section is a review with comments of the Network+ objectives presented in that section. These comments are provided to help reinforce the reader's understanding of a particular Network+ objective. The chapter review also includes "Test Your Knowledge" questions to aid in the understanding of key concepts before the reader advances to the next section of the chapter. The end of the chapter includes a complete set of question plus sample certification type questions.

TABLE 2-1 Chapter 2 CompTIA Network+ Objectives

Domain/Objective Number	Domain/Objective Description	Section Where Objective Is Covered
1.0	*Network Architecture*	
1.5	Install and properly terminate various cable types and connectors using the appropriate tools	2-1, 2-2, 2-3, 2-4, 2-7
2.2	Given a scenario, analyze metrics and reports from monitoring and tracking performance tools	2-3
3.4	Compare and contrast physical security controls	2.2, 2-3
4.2	Given a scenario, analyze and interpret the output of troubleshooting tools	2-5
4.4	Given a scenario, troubleshoot and resolve common copper cable issues	2-4, 2-5, 2-7
5.4	Given a scenario, deploy the appropriate wired connectivity standard	2-2, 2-4

2-2 STRUCTURED CABLING

EIA
Electronic Industries Alliance

TIA
Telecommunications Industry Association

The first major standard describing a structured cabling system for computer networks was the TIA/EIA 568-A in 1995. EIA is the Electronics Industries Alliance, a trade organization that lobbies for the interests of manufacturers of electronics-related equipment. TIA stands for the Telecommunications Industry Association, which is a trade organization that represents the interests of the telecommunications industry. The most important addendum to the EIA/TIA 568-A standard was Addendum 5, published in 1999. This addendum defined the transmission performance specifications for 4-pair 100-ohm category 5e twisted-pair cabling. TIA/EIA adopted new category 6 (CAT6) cable specifications in June 2002. This is the type of cabling recommended for use in today's computer networks, although CAT7 twisted-pair cabling might soon become the recommended standard.

The EIA/TIA 568-A standard defined the minimum requirements for the internal telecommunications wiring in buildings and between structures in a **campus network**. A campus network consists of interconnected LANs within a limited geographic area such as a college campus, military base, or group of commercial buildings. The EIA/TIA 568-A was revised and updated many times, and in 2000 a new standard—the **EIA/TIA 568-B**—was published. The three parts of the EIA/TIA 568-B are as follows:

- **EIA/TIA-568-B.1:** Commercial Cabling Standard, Master Document
- **IA/TIA-568-B.2:** Twisted-pair Media
- **EIA/TIA-568-B.3:** Optical Fiber Cabling Standard

Within the EIA/TIA 569B Commercial Standard for Telecommunication Pathways and Spaces are guidelines defining the six subsystems of a structured cabling system:

1. **Building entrance:** The point where the external cabling and wireless services interconnect with the internal building cabling in the equipment room. This is used by both public and private access (for example, Telco, satellite, cable TV, security, and so on). The building entrance is also called the **entrance facilities (EF)**. Both public and private network cables enter the building at this point, and typically each has separate facilities for the different access providers.

2. **Equipment room (ER):** A room set aside for complex electronic equipment such as the network servers and telephone equipment.

3. **Telecommunications closet:** The location of the cabling termination points that includes the mechanical terminations and the distribution frames. The connection of the horizontal cabling to the backbone wiring is made at this point. This is also called the telecommunications room (**TR**) or telecommunications enclosure (**TE**). In some older systems, the network administrator might encounter two of the following types of punchdown blocks in the telecommunications closet: a **66** block and a **110** block. These types of terminations use insulation-displacement connectors (IDC) to terminate twisted-pair cables and are commonly used in telephone systems but not computer networks.

Note

One room can serve as the entrance facility, equipment room, and the telecommunications closet.

---

4. **Backbone cabling:** Cabling that interconnects telecommunication closets, equipment rooms, and cabling entrances in the same building and between buildings.

5. **Horizontal cabling:** Cabling that extends out from the telecommunications closet into the LAN work area. Typically, the horizontal wiring is structured in a star configuration running to each area telecommunications outlet (**TCO**). This is the wall plate where the fiber or twisted-pair cable terminates in the room. In some cases, the TCO terminates telephone, fiber, and video in addition to data into the same wall plate.

6. **Work area:** The location of the computers and printers, patch cables, jacks, computer adapter cables, and fiber jumpers.

Figure 2-1 provides a drawing of the structure for a telecommunications–cabling system. In the figure, it shows the connection of the carriers (Telco, ISP, and so on) coming into the ER. The ER is the space set aside for the carrier's equipment contained in the **main cross-connect (MC)** or **intermediate cross—connect (IC)**. The EF consists of the cabling, connector hardware, protection devices that are used as the interface between any external building cabling, and wireless services with the equipment room. This area is used by both public and private access providers (for example, Telco, satellite, cable TV, security, and so on). The ER and EF space is typically combined with the MC equipment room.

FIGURE 2-1   The telecommunications Cabling System Architecture.

Between the MC and the IC are the campus backbone cabling (listed as the inter-building backbone cabling). This defines the connections between the MC and IC. A definition of a **cross-connect** is a space where you are going to take one or multiple cables and connect them to one or more cables or equipment. For example, you could be bringing in 60 UTP cables, with 50 that are cross-connected to a switch and 10 that are cross-connected to a backbone cable going to another location. Typical connections between the MC and IC are single-mode and multimode fibers and possibly coax for cable TV, although most installations are migrating to fiber. The building backbone cabling (intrabuilding backbone cabling) makes the connection between the IC and the TC/HC. TC is the telecommunications closet, and HC is the **horizontal cross-connect (HC)**. Usually this connection is CAT5 UTP or better, or possibly single- or multimode fiber or some combination. Fiber is the best choice for making these connections, although copper is sometimes used. The horizontal cabling is the cabling between the HC and the work area. It is usually CAT5 UTP or better or fiber. The standard currently specifies CAT6. Fiber is gaining acceptance for connecting to the **work area outlets (WO)**.

Figure 2-2 provides a more detailed view of the cabling from the MC to the IC and the HC. This drawing shows the three layers of the recommended backbone hierarchy cabling for a computer network. The first level of the hierarchy is the MC. The MC connects to the second level of the hierarchy, the IC. The backbone cabling connects the MC to the IC and the IC to the TC/HC. The HC connects the horizontal cabling to the work area and to the WO.

Cross-connect

A space where you are going to take one or multiple cables and connect them to one or more cables or equipment

Horizontal Cross-connect (HC)

The connection between the building distributors and the horizontal cabling to the work area or workstation outlet—another term used for the HC is the floor distributors (FD)

Workstation or Work Area Outlet (WO)

Also called the TO (telecommunications outlet), it's used to connect devices to the cable plant. The cable type typically used is CAT3, CAT5, CAT5e, CAT6, CAT6A, and various coaxial cables. Devices typically connected to these outlets are PCs, printers, servers, phones, televisions, and wireless access points.

Legend

MC Main Cross-Connect
IC Intermediate Cross-Connect
HC Horizontal Cross-Connect
WO Workstation Outlet

FIGURE 2-2   The Campus Network Hierarchical topology.

The focus of this chapter is on the issues associated with the horizontal cabling and the work area (LAN) subsystems. The text addresses all six subsystems of a structured cabling system, but at the point when the networking concepts and related hardware are introduced. Many of the concepts covered in each structured cabling subsystem require that the reader have a firm grasp of basic networking to gain a full appreciation of how each network piece fits into a structured cabled system.

Horizontal Cabling

Permanent network cabling within a building is considered to be *horizontal cabling*, defined as the cabling that extends out from the telecommunications closet into the LAN work area. Take time to plan for your horizontal cabling installation because this is where your network interfaces with the users. There is always a substantial installation cost associated with horizontal cabling, and there is an even greater cost of having to replace or upgrade a cable installation. You don't want to have to re-cable your system very often. Careful attention should be given to planning for the horizontal cabling of a LAN. Make sure you fully understand your current networking needs and that your proposed plan meets the needs. Also make sure your plan addresses the future needs and growth of your network.

Figure 2-3 illustrates the basic blocks of a horizontal cabling system from the telecommunications closet to the computer in the LAN. The following components are typically found in the telecommunications closet:

A. Backbone cabling interconnecting this closet with other closets

B. Switch or hub

C. Patch panels

D. Patch cables

E. Cabling to the LAN (horizontal cabling)

F. Wall plate

G. Patch cable connecting the computer to the wall plate

FIGURE 2-3   Block diagram of a horizontal cabling system.

Item E in Figure 2-3 shows the cabling leaving the telecommunications closet. The cable extends to where it is **terminated** at the wall plate (item F) in the LAN or work area. The term *terminated* describes where the cable connects to a jack in a wall plate, a patch panel, or an RJ-45 modular plug. In this case, the cable terminates into an RJ-45 jack in the wall plate. Figure 2-4 provides an example of the RJ-45 wall plate and patch panel.

Note

The proper term for the RJ-45 modular plug used in computer systems is actually **8P8C** for both male and female connectors. 8P8C stands for 8-pin 8-conductors and is defined by ANSI/TIA-968-A and B but is commonly called RJ-45 by both professionals and end users.

An individual cable is used to connect each connector in the outlet to the patch panel in the telecommunications closet (F to E). RJ-45 (8P8C) plugs and jacks are defined in section 2-4. Another 8-pin connector using the 8P8C modular connector is the RJ-48. This type of connector is commonly used in T1 data lines. This type of connector typically uses shielded twisted-pair cabling. Although the RJ-45 and RJ-48 connectors look similar, they do not use the same wiring scheme and are intended for different data-transmission applications.

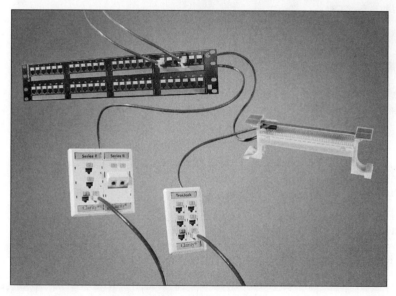

FIGURE 2-4   The Ortronics clarity twisted-pair system (courtesy of Ortronics).

In a star topology, there is an individual cable run for each outlet in the wall plate. This means that you assign one computer to each terminated outlet. A **patch cable** (item G) is used to make the physical connection from the computer to the wall plate, as shown in Figure 2-3. A patch cable is a short cable used to make the physical connection between networking equipment. There is a 100-meter overall length limitation of the cable run from the telecommunications closet to the networking device in the work area. This includes the length of the patch cables at each end (items D and G) plus the cable run (item E). A general rule of thumb is to allow

90 meters for the cable run from the telecommunications closet to the work area (item E). This allows 5 meters of cable length for the work area and 5 meters for the patch cables in the telecommunications closet (item D) and the work area (item G). Figure 2-5 shows an example of the insides of a telecommunications closet.

FIGURE 2-5   Inside a telecommunications closet.

Section 2-2 Review

This section has covered the following **Network+** Exam objectives:

> 1.5 Install and properly terminate various cable types and connectors using the appropriate tools

The termination of computer cabling associated with a horizontal cabling systems has been presented.

> 3.4 Compare and contrast physical security controls

This section has provided a through overview of the purpose and function of the telecommunications closet. Figure 2-5 shows an example of the interior of a telecommunications closet.

5.4 Given a scenario, deploy the appropriate wired connectivity standard

The standard that defines structure cabling, the EIA/TIA 568 standard, has been introduced. This is an important standard defining cabling for computer networks.

Test Your Knowledge

1. What is the overall length limitation of a UTP cable run from the telecommunications closet to a networking device in the work area?

    a. 10 meters

    b. 100 meters

    c. 10K meters

    d. 100K meters

2. The six subsystems of a structured cabling system are the following:

    Building Entrance

    Equipment Room

    Backbone Cabling

    Telecommunications Closet

    Vertical Cabling

    Work Area

    True or False?

3. Horizontal cabling consists of which of the following basic blocks? (Select two.)

    a. Switch or hub

    b. Routers

    c. Backbone cabling

    d. Patch panel

2-3 UNSHIELDED TWISTED-PAIR CABLE

Unshielded twisted-pair (**UTP**) cable plays an important role in computer networking. The most common twisted-pair standards used for computer networking today are category 6 (**CAT6**), category 6a (**CAT6a**), and category 5e (**CAT5e**). CAT6 cable is tested to provide the transmission of data rates up to 1000Mbps for a maximum length of 100 meters. CAT6a is an improved version of CAT6 and will support 10GB Ethernet.

CAT5e cable is an enhanced version of CAT5 and provides improved performance requirements of the cable. CAT6 provides improved performance and a bandwidth of 250MHz. CAT5/5e twisted-pair cable contains four color-coded pairs of 24-gauge wires terminated with an RJ-45 (8P8C) connector. Figure 2-6 provides an example of a CAT5e cable terminated with an RJ-45 (8P8C) modular plug. CAT6 twisted-pair cable also contains four color-coded wires, but the wire gauge is 23AWG. CAT6 cable has a stiffer feel compared to CAT5e.

The precise manner in which the twist of CAT6/5e/5 cable is maintained, even at the terminations, provides a significant increase in signal transmission performance. CAT5/5e standards allow 0.5 inches of untwisted cable pair at the termination. CAT6 has an even tighter requirement that allows for only 3/8-inch of untwisted cable at the termination. The termination is the point where the cable is connected to terminals in a modular plug, jack, or patch panel.

Balanced Mode
Neither wire in the wire pairs connects to ground

CAT6/5e/5 twisted-pair cable contains four twisted wire pairs for a total of eight wires. In twisted-pair cable, none of the wires in the wire pairs are connected to ground. The signals on the wires are set up for a high (+) and low (-) signal line. The (+) indicates that the phase relationship of the signal on the wire is positive, and the (-) indicates that the phase of the signal on the wire is negative; both signals are relative to a virtual ground. This is called a **balanced mode** of operation—the balance of the two wire pairs helps maintain the required level of performance in terms of crosstalk and noise rejection.

FIGURE 2-6   An example of an RJ-45 modular plug (courtesy of Cyberguys.com).

Table 2-2 lists the various categories of twisted-pair cable defined by the EIA/TIA 568B standard. The table includes an application description and minimum bandwidth for each category. Notice that there is not a listing for CAT1 and CAT2.

TABLE 2-2   Different Categories for Twisted-pair Cable, Based on TIA568B

Category	Description	Bandwidth/Data Rate
Category 3 (CAT3)	Telephone installations Class C	Up to 16Mbps
Category 5 (CAT5)	Computer networks Class D	Up to 100MHz/100Mbps 100-m length
Enhanced CAT5 (CAT5e)	Computer networks	100MHz/1000Mbps applications with improved noise performance in a full duplex mode
Category 6 (CAT6)	Higher-speed computer	Up to 250MHz networks Class E/1000Mbps CAT6 supports 10Gbps but at distances fewer than 100 meters
Category 6a (CAT6a)	Increased bandwidth	Up to 500MHz networks Class Ea/10Gbps
Category 7 (CAT7)	International Organization for Standardization (ISO) standard, not an EIA/TIA standard	Up to 600MHz speed computer networks Class F/10Gbps
Category 7a (CAT7a)	ISO standard, not an EIA/ TIA standard	Up to 1000MHz speed computer networks Class FA/10Gbps

CAT1 and CAT2 cable specifications are not defined in the EIA/TIA 568B standard. The first CAT or category specification is for CAT3. CAT3 is being replaced with CAT5e or better. CAT4 is not listed in the table because the category was removed from the TIA568B standard as its data capacity specification was outdated. The category 5 cable standard was established in 1991, and many computer networks are still using the older CAT5 cables. Certified CAT5 cabling works well in both Ethernet and FastEthernet networking environments that run 10Mbps Ethernet and 100Mbps FastEthernet data rates. Note that the term **FastEthernet** is used to describe the 100Mbps data rate for FastEthernet networks.

In some cases, users on networks are experiencing **network congestion** or **bottlenecking** of the data due to the increased file transfer sizes and the limited bandwidth of their network. These terms describe excessive data traffic that is slowing down computer communications even in FastEthernet networks. Basically, the demands on the network exceeded the performance capabilities of the CAT5 cable. The slowdown of the data is of major concern in computer networks. File access time is delayed, productivity is affected, and the time required to complete a task is increased. A slowdown in your network could be costing your company money. Can you imagine the consequences if a slowdown in your network causes a delay in the company's billing?

TIA/EIA ratified the CAT5e cabling specification in 1999 to address this continuing need for greater data handling capacity in the computer networks. The enhanced CAT5 cable (CAT5e) provides an improvement in cable performance, and if all components of the cable installation are done according to specification, then CAT5e will support **full duplex gigabit Ethernet** (1000Mbps Ethernet) using all four wire pairs. Full duplex means that the computer system can transmit and receive at the same time. TIA/EIA ratified the CAT6 cabling specification in June 2002. This cable provides an even better performance specification and 250MHz of bandwidth, and maintains backward compatibility with CAT5/5e. CAT6 can support 10Gbps data rates but over a distance less than 100 meters. The **CAT6a** standard supports 10GBGB data rates up to 100 meters, and **CAT7** will also support 10Gbps up to 100 meters with improved bandwidth. The 10GBGB standard over copper is called **10GBASE-T**.

Shielded Twisted-Pair Cable

In some applications, a wire screen or metal foil shield is placed around the twisted-pair cable. Cable with the addition of a shield is called **STP** cable. The addition of this shield reduces the potential for electromagnetic interference (**EMI**) as long as the shield is grounded. EMI originates from devices such as motors and power lines and from some lighting devices such as fluorescent lights.

The shield on the twisted-pair cable does not reject all potentially interfering noise (EMI), but it does greatly reduce noise interference. There is an active debate in the networking community as to which product is superior, UTP or STP. It is important to note that the objective of both cables is to successfully transport data from the telecommunications closet to the work area. Industry testing on STP cable has shown that the addition of a shield does increase the usable bandwidth of the cable by increasing the noise rejection between each of the wire pairs. However, the tests have shown that there is not a significant advantage of placing a shield over a properly installed 4-pair 100-ohm UTP cable. Additionally, STP is more expensive and the increased costs may not justify the benefits. For now, most manufacturers are recommending the use of UTP cable for cabling computer networks except for very noisy environments.

Section 2-3 Review

This section has covered the following **Network+** Exam objectives:

1.5 Install and properly terminate various cable types and connectors using the appropriate tools

The RJ-45 modular plug used in most computer networks has been presented. The RJ-45 plug is also called 8P8C. Table 2-2 lists the different categories for twisted-pair cable, based on TIA568B. Make sure you know the different category types. You should also understand that the precise manner in which the twist of the wire pairs is managed provides for a significant increase in signal transmission performance.

2.2 Given a scenario, analyze metrics and supports from monitoring and tracking performance tools

This section introduced the concept of network congestion or bottlenecking of the data due to the increased file transfer sizes and the limited bandwidth of the network. Selecting the proper UTP cable can help minimized this problem.

Test Your Knowledge

1. What is the data rate for FastEthernet?

    a. 10Mbps

    b. 100Mbps

    c. 1000Mbps

    d. 10Kbps

    e. None of these answers is correct.

2. What type of cable is currently recommended for LAN work areas?

    a. Shielded twisted-pair

    b. CAT6 shielded twisted-pair

    c. CAT 5e UTP

    d. CAT6 UTP

    e. CAT7 UTP

3. What is the benefit of shielded twisted-pair cable?

    a. Ease of installation

    b. Excellent EMI protection

    c. Less expensive

    d. Preferred by industry for all installations

    e. None of these answers is correct.

2-4 TERMINATING CAT6/5E/5 UTP CABLES

This section introduces the techniques for terminating high-performance UTP cables. Terminating the RJ-45 (8P8C) connector for CAT6/5e/5 cable is defined by the EIA/TIA standard EIA/TIA568-B.2 and B.2-1. This portion of the standard defines the specifications of the copper cabling hardware. The standard specifies cabling components, transmission, system models, and the measurement procedures needed for verification of the balanced twisted-pair cabling.

Within the EIA/TIA568B standard are the wiring guidelines **T568A** and **T568B**. These wiring guidelines specify the color of wire that connects to which pin on the connector. The specification of the wire color that connects to which pin is called a **color map**. Table 2-3 provides the color maps specified by the T568A and T568B wiring guidelines.

TABLE 2-3 **The Wiring Color Schemes for T568A and T568B**

Pin #	568A Wire Color	568B Wire Color
1	White-Green	White-Orange
2	Green	Orange
3	White-Orange	White-Green
4	Blue	Blue
5	White-Blue	White-Blue
6	Orange	Green
7	White-Brown	White-Brown
8	Brown	Brown

Figure 2-7(a) shows the placement of the wire pairs in the RJ-45 (8P8C) modular plug for the T568A standard; Figure 2-7(b) shows the placement of the wire pairs in the RJ-45 (8P8C) modular plug for the T568B standard. The pin numbers for the RJ-45 (8P8C) modular plug are shown at the top of the figure, and a wire color table is provided for reference. In the T568A wire color scheme (Figure 2-7[a]), a white-green wire connects to pin 1, the wire color green connects to pin 2, the wire color connected to pin 3 is white-orange, and so on. Similar information is provided in Figure 2-7(b) for the T568B wiring standard. The color of the wire connected to pin 1 is white-orange, pin 2 is orange, pin 3 is white-green, and so on. This information also agrees with Table 2-2.

A common question is, "What is the difference between T568A and T568B?" Basically, these are just two different manufacturer standards used to wire the modular connector hardware. There is not a performance improvement with either, just a color order choice. Industry tends to favor the T568A wiring order; however, either order can be used as long as the order is maintained throughout the network.

This material has defined the wire color order for terminating the RJ-45 (8P8C) plugs and jacks onto the CAT6/5e twisted-pair cables. Be able to describe the difference between the T568A and T568B wire color order. Also make sure you know what wire color configuration you are using in a network, T568A or T568B, and that you specify hardware that is compatible with your selected color scheme.

Connector Head
Bottom Side Up

#	T568A COLOR
1	White-Green
2	Green
3	White-Orange
4	Blue
5	White-Blue
6	Orange
7	White-Brown
8	Brown

(a)

Connector Head
Bottom Side Up

#	T568B COLOR
1	White-Orange
2	Orange
3	White-Green
4	Blue
5	White-Blue
6	Green
7	White-Brown
8	Brown

(b)

FIGURE 2-7 (a) The wiring of the RJ-45 (8P8C) connector and the wire color codes for the T568A standard; (b) the wiring of the RJ-45 connector for the T568B standard (courtesy of StarTech.com).

Computer Communication

As mentioned in section 2-2, the CAT6/5e cable contains four twisted wire pairs. Figure 2-8 provides a picture of the four wire pairs. Figure 2-9 shows the signals and pin number assignments for the RJ-45 (8P8C) plug for CAT5e. Notice in Figure 2-9 that the Transmit Out signals are marked with a (+) and (-). The Receive In (+) and (-) signals are also marked in the same way. The (+) and (-) symbols are typical ways of indicating the positive and negative sides of a balanced wire pair. Recall from section 2-3, "Unshielded Twisted-Pair Cable," that in a balanced mode of operation, neither signal line is at ground.

FIGURE 2-8   The four wire pairs of the CAT6/CAT5e.

Pin No.	Function
Pin 1	Transmit Out +
Pin 2	Transmit Out −
Pin 3	Receive In +
Pin 4	No Connection
Pin 5	No Connection
Pin 6	Receive In −
Pin 7	No Connection
Pin 8	No Connection

Front View

RJ-45 Modular Plug
Pin Assignments

FIGURE 2-9   The pin assignments and signal names for the RJ-45 (8P8C) modular plug (CAT5e).

TX
Abbreviation for transmit

RX
Abbreviation for receive

For computers to communicate in a LAN, the transmit and receive pairs must be properly aligned. This means the transmit (TX) (+) and (-) signals must connect to the receive (RX) (+) and (-), as shown in Figure 2-10. Notice in Figure 2-10 that pins 1–2 of device A connect to pins 3–6 of device B. Pins 1–2 of device B connect to pins 3–6 of device A. This configuration is always valid when the data rates are 10Mbps or 100Mbps.

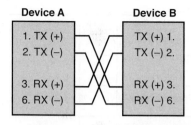

FIGURE 2-10 The proper alignment of the transmit and receive pairs in a CAT6/5e data link operating 10Mbps or 100Mbps.

In a LAN, the proper alignment of the transmit and receive pairs is managed by a switch or hub, not typically in the cable. Remember, in a star topology, all network communication travels through a switch or hub. You will see an "X" or "Uplink" on many of the switch and hub input ports, indicating that this is a cross-connected input. This means that transmit and receive pairs are internally swapped to maintain proper signal alignment of the TX and RX pairs. Even if the "X" or "Uplink" is missing, the switch or hub still properly aligns the TX and RX wire pairs. There is an exception to this on many switches and hubs. Some switches and hubs have an input port that can be selected to be "straight" or "crossed." These ports are typically used in uplink applications when you connect a switch or hub to another switch or hub. If a device has a cross-connected port, then a straight-through cable is used because the device is providing the alignment. Just remember, proper alignment of the transmit and receive pair must be maintained for the computers to communicate. And a final note, if the wires are not properly connected, there won't be a link light.

There is a difference with the signal names for the UTP cable when operating at 1Gbps and 10Gbps. At these higher data rates, the use of all four wire pairs is required and the data is bidirectional, which means the same wire pairs are being used for both transmitting and receiving data. Figure 2-11 shows the pin assignments and signal names.

Pin	1000 Mbps and 10 Gbps Color (T568A)	10/100 Mbps	1000 Mbps and 10 Gbps
1	green/white	TX+	BI_DA+
2	Green	TX–	BI_DA–
3	orange/white	RX+	
4	blue	–	BI_DC+
5	blue/white	–	BI_DC–
6	orange	RX–	BI_DB–
7	brown/white	–	BI_DD+
8	brown		BI_DD–

(a) The pin assignments and signal names for 1 Gbps and 10 Gbps (T568A).

Pin	1000 Mbps and 10 Gbps Color (T568B)	10/100 Mbps Signal	1000 Mbps Signal
1	orange/white	TX+	BI_DA+
2	Orange	TX–	BI_DA–
3	green/white	RX+	BI_DB+
4	blue	–	BI_DC+
5	blue/white	–	BI_DC–
6	green	RX–	BI_DB–
7	brown/white	–	BI_DD+
8	brown	–	BI_DD–

(b) The pin assignments and signal names for 1 Gbps and 10 Gbps (T568B).

FIGURE 2-11   The pin assignments and signal names for 1Gbps and 10Gbps (T568A and T568B).

Straight-through and Crossover Patch Cables

Category 6/5e twisted-pair cables are used to connect networking components to each other in the network. These cables are commonly called *patch cables*. In this section, a technique for terminating CAT6/5e cables with RJ-45 (8P8C) modular plugs is demonstrated for two different configurations of patch cables, a straight-through and a crossover cable. In a **straight-through cable** the four wire pairs connect to the same pin numbers on each end of the cable. For example, pin 1 on one end connects to pin 1 on the other end. Figure 2-12 shows an example of the **wire-map** for a straight-through cable. A wire-map is a graphical or text description of the wire connections from pin to pin for a cable under test. Notice that in Figure 2-12 the transmit and receive pairs connect to the same connector pin numbers at each end of the cable, hence the name *straight* or *straight-through* cable.

FIGURE 2-12   The wire-map for a straight-through cable.

In some applications in 10/100Mbps data links, it is necessary to construct a cable where the transmit and receive wire pairs are reversed in the cable rather than by the switch or the hub. This cable configuration is called a **crossover cable**, which means the transmit pair of device A connects to the receive pair of device B, and the transmit pair of B connects to the receive pair of A. Figure 2-13 shows the wire-map for a crossover cable.

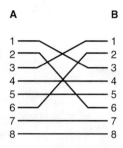

FIGURE 2-13   The wire-map for crossover cable 10/100Mbps links.

Note

The crossover cable diagram shown in Figure 2-13 is for 10/100Mbps. A gigabit crossover cable requires that all four wire-pairs be crossed. Although this is possible, it is not practical to make a gigabit crossover cable because of the limit on untwisted wire.

Terminating the CAT6 Horizontal Link Cable

This section presents the steps required for terminating a CAT6 cable using the AMP SL series termination procedure, AMP SL tool, CAT6 cable, and AMP SL Series AMP-TWIST-6S Category 6 modular jacks. In this example, an RJ-45 (8P8C) jack is used to terminate each end of the cable. One end connects to a wall plate in the network work area. The other end will terminate into a CAT6 RJ-45 (8P8C) patch panel, which is typically located in the LAN network closet.

The technical specifications and assembly requirements are more stringent with CAT6. This means that more care must be taken when terminating a CAT6 cable. However, advancements in the tools and connectors have actually made it easier to terminate CAT6 than it was with the old punch-down tools. The steps for terminating the CAT6 horizontal link cables are as follows:

1. Before terminating the cable, inspect the cable for any damage that might have occurred in installation. Examples of damage to look for include nicked or cut wires and possible stretching of the cable.

2. At the work area outlet end, add about one foot extra and cut the wire. Then coil the extra cable and insert it in the receptacle box. It is good to leave a little extra in case you make an error in installation and have to redo the termination. Remember, you can't splice a CAT6 cable. At the distribution end, you must route the cable and create a slack loop. A slack loop is simply extra cable looped at the distribution end that is used if the equipment must be moved. In

cases where you are having the cable pulled through ductwork or conduit by an installer, make sure you specify that extra cable length will be run. This will vary for each installation. Remember to allow for 5 meters in the telecommunications closet and allow for 5 meters in the work area.

3. Place a bend limiting strain relief boot on the cable, as shown in Figure 2-14(a). This is used in the last step to secure the RJ-45 (8P8C) jack. After placing the boot on the cable, you will need to strip approximately 3 inches of cable jacket from the UTP cable as shown in Figure 2-14(b). Be careful not to nick or cut the wires.

(a)   (b)

FIGURE 2-14   (a)Placing the bend-limiting strain relief boot on the cable and (b) stripping off 3 inches of jacket from the UTP cable.

4. Remove the jacket from the UTP cable. Bend the cable at the cut, as shown in Figure 2-15(a), and remove the jacket and expose the four wire pairs, as shown in Figure 2-15(b).

(a)   (b)

FIGURE 2-15   (a) Separating the cut jacket from the wire pairs and (b) removing of the jacket and exposing the four wire pairs.

5. Cut the plastic pull line and the string as shown in Figure 2-16(a). The plastic line adds strength to cable for pulling, and the string is used to remove extra cable jacket as needed. Place a lacing fixture on the cable, as shown in Figure 2-16(b), and sort the wires in either T568A or T668B color order.

(a)   (b)

FIGURE 2-16 (a) Removing the plastic pull line and (b) placing the lacing tool on the cable with the color sorted cable pairs.

The sorted wire pairs are matched up with colors provided on the lacing fixture for 568A and 568B as shown in Figure 2-17.

6. Place the wires in the slots of the lacing tool as shown in Figure 2-18. The wire colors are matched to the proper order (T568A/T568B) displayed on the sides of the lacing tool.

(a)   (b)

FIGURE 2-17 The sides of the lacing tool showing the T568A and T568B wire color connections.

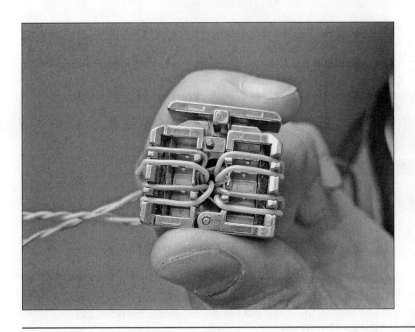

FIGURE 2-18 The routed cable wires on the lacing tool. The wire order shown is T568B.

7. Align an RJ-45 (8P8C) jack with the lacing fixture as shown in Figure 2-19(a). The RJ-45 jack must be properly aligned with the wires on the lacing fixture to maintain proper color order. Figure 2-19(b) provides a close-up picture of the AMP SL series AMP-TWIST-6S modular jack. This picture shows the locations of the displacement connectors on the modulator jack.

8. Insert the RJ-45 (8P8C) modular jack into the AMP SL tool as shown in Figure 2-20(a), and then insert the RJ-45 (8P8C) jack into the AMP SL tool as shown in Figure 2-20(b). Press the wires into the eight displacement connectors on the RJ-45 (8P8C) jack using the AMP SL tool as shown in Figure 2-20(c). This technique enables the pair twist to be maintained right up to the point of termination. In fact, the untwisted-pair length is less than or equal to 1/4 inch.

(a)

Displacement Connectors   Displacement Connectors

AMP SL Series AMP-TWIST-6S
Category 6 Modular Jack

(b)

FIGURE 2-19 (a) Aligning the RJ-45 (8P8C) jack and the lacing fixture and (b) a close-up view of the AMP-TWIST-6S CAT6 modular jack.

(a)   (b)   (c)

FIGURE 2-20 (a) Aligning the RJ-45 (8P8C) jack with the lacing tool; (b) inserting the RJ-45 (8P8C) jack and the lacing tool into the AMP SL tool; and (c) using the AMP SL tool to crimp the RJ-45 (8P8C) jack onto the eight displacement connectors and to cut the wires.

9. Connect the bend-limiting strain relief boot to the RJ-45 (8P8C) jack as shown in Figure 2-21(a). Figure 2-21(b) shows the completed termination.

(a) Connecting the bend-limiting strain relief boot to the RJ-45 jack.   (b) The finished RJ-45 jack termination.

FIGURE 2-21 Connecting the bend-limiting strain relief boot to the RJ-45 (8P8C) jack.

Assembling the Straight-through CAT5e/5 Patch Cable

This section presents a technique for assembling a straight-through CAT5e/5 patch cable. In a straight-through patch cable, the wire pairs in the cable connect to the same pin numbers on each end of the CAT5e/5 patch cable. Figure 2-22 shows a CAT5e patch cable with RJ-45 (8P8C) modular plugs.

FIGURE 2-22   CAT5e patch cable with RJ-45 (8P8C) modular plugs (courtesy of StarTech.com).

The steps for making straight-through patch cables are as follows:

1. Before terminating the cable, inspect the cable for any damage that might have occurred in installation, such as nicked or cut wires and possible stretching of the cable.

2. Measure the cable to length, add about 6 inches extra, and cut the wire. It is good to have a little extra in case you make an error in installation and have to redo the termination. You can't splice CAT5e/5 twisted-pair cable!

3. Strip approximately 3/4 of an inch of the cable jacket from the end of the cable using a cable stripper. Figure 2-23 illustrates how to use a cable stripper. Notice that the stripper is positioned about 3/4 of an inch from the end of the cable. The cable insulation is removed by rotating the insulation stripper around the wire until the wire jacket is loose and easily removable. (Note: These tools must be periodically adjusted so that the blade cuts through the outer insulation only. If the blades are set too deep, they will nick the wires and the process must be repeated. The damaged portion of the cable must be cut away. Nicking the insulation of the twisted-pair wires is *not permitted*!)

FIGURE 2-23   An example of using the cable jacket stripper to remove the insulation.

4. Sort the wire pairs so that they fit into the connector and orient the wire in the proper order for either T568A or T568B as shown in Figures 2-24(a) and 2-24(b). Be careful to avoid creating a split pair connection. This happens when

a wire from one pair and a wire from another pair are used to make a connection. This potentially creates interference and crosstalk problems, thus preventing the cable to pass a certification test. This is discussed in section 2-5.

(a)

(b)

FIGURE 2-24   (a) Separating wire pairs; (b) orienting the wires.

5. Clip the wires so that they are even and insert the wires onto the RJ-45 (8P8C) modular plug as shown in Figure 2-25.

FIGURE 2-25   The clipped wires ready for insertion into the RJ-45 (8P8C) plug.

6. Push the wires into the connector until the ends of each wire can be seen through the clear end of the connector. (Note: Now is the time to verify that the wire order is correct.) The wires are visible through the plastic connector, as shown in Figure 2-26.

FIGURE 2-26   Wires pushed into the RJ-45 (8P8C) plug.

7. Use a crimping tool to crimp the wires onto the RJ-45 (8P8C) plug. The RJ-45 plug is inserted into the crimping tool until it stops as shown in Figure 2-27(a). Next, squeeze the handle on the crimping tool all the way until it clicks and releases (see Figure 2-27[b]). This step crimps the wire onto the insulation displacement connector pins on the RJ-45 (8P8C) jack.

(a)

(b)

FIGURE 2-27   (a) Inserting the connector; (b) crimping the connector.

8. Repeat these steps for the other end of the twisted-pair cable.

The next step is to test the cable. These techniques and procedures are discussed in section 2-5.

Section 2-4 Review

This section has covered the following **Network+** Exam objectives.

> 1.5 Install and properly terminate various cable types and connectors using the appropriate tools

The steps for terminating CAT5 and CAT6 UTP cables have been presented. Make sure you understand the procedure and the purpose of the various tools required to terminate cables and a jack.

> 4.4 Given a scenario, troubleshoot and resolve common copper cable issues

The pin assignments and the signal names for wiring UTP cables have been presented. The proper alignment of the transmit and receive pairs was presented in Figure 2-10. This is an important concept. The concept of a split pair was also introduced.

> 5.4 Given a scenario, deploy the appropriate wired connectivity standard

This section has presented the T568A and T568B wiring schemes. It is very important that you know the wire colors and associated pin assignments.

Test Your Knowledge

1. The following is the color map and pin numbers for T568A:

Pin#	Wirecolor
1	White-Green
2	Blue
3	White-Orange
4	Green
5	White-Blue
6	Orange
7	White-Brown
8	Brown

True or False?

2. The following is the color map and pin numbers for T568B:

Pin#	Wirecolor
1	White-Orange
2	Orange
3	White-Green
4	Blue
5	White-Blue
6	Green
7	White-Brown
8	Brown

True or False?

3. How many wires are in a CAT5e/6 twisted-pair cable?

    a. 12 wires

    b. 8 wires

    c. 4 wires

    d. 6 wires

2-5 CABLE TESTING AND CERTIFICATION

The need for increased data rates is pushing the technology of twisted-pair cable to even greater performance requirements and placing even greater demands on accurate testing of the cable infrastructure. The data speeds over twisted-pair copper cable are now at 10Gbps. The EIA/TIA 568B standard defines the minimum cable specifications for twisted-pair categories operating over bandwidths of 100MHz and at data rates up to 10Gbps.

The CAT6/5e designations are simply minimum performance measurements of the cables and the attached terminating hardware such as RJ-45 (8P8C) plugs, jacks, and patch panels. The **link** (the point from one cable termination to another) and the **full channel** (which consists of all the link elements from the hub or switch to the wall plate) must satisfy minimum **attenuation** loss and **near-end crosstalk (NEXT)** for a minimum frequency of 100MHz. Figure 2-28 shows a graphical representation of the link and the full channel. Table 2-4 lists the CAT5e, CAT6, CAT6A, CAT7, and CAT7A EIA/TIA 568B channel specifications.

Link

Point from one cable termination to another

Full Channel

Consists of all the link elements from the wall plate to the hub or switch

Attenuation (Insertion Loss)

The amount of loss in the signal strength as it propagates down a wire or fiber strand

Near-end Crosstalk (NEXT)

A measure of the level of crosstalk or signal coupling within the cable, with a high NEXT (dB) value being desirable

FIGURE 2-28   The link and channel areas for cable testing.

TABLE 2-4   **EIA/TIA 568B CAT5e, CAT6, CAT6A, CAT7 and CAT7A Channel Specifications**

Parameter	Category 5e	Category 6	Category 6A	Category 7/7A
Class	Class D	Class E	Class E_A	Class F/F_A
Bandwidth	100MHz	250MHz	500MHz	600MHz/1000MHz
Insertion Loss (dB)	24.0	21.3	20.9	20.8/20.3
NEXT Loss (dB)	30.1	39.9	39.9	62.9/65.0
PSNEXT Loss (dB)	27.1	37.1	37.1	59.9/62.0

Parameter	Category 5e	Category 6	Category 6A	Category 7/7A
ACR (dB)	6.1	18.6	18.6	42.1/46.1
PSACR (dB)	3.1	15.8	15.8	39.1/41.7
ACRF1 (ELFEXT) (dB)	17.4	23.3	23.3	44.4/47.4
(PSELFEXT) (dB)	14.4	20.3	20.3	41.1/44.4
Return Loss (dB)	10.0	12.0	12.0	12.0/12.0
* PANEXT Loss (dB)	n/s	n/s	60.0	n/s / 67.0
* PSAACRF (dB)	n/s	n/s	37.0	n/s / 52.0
* TCL (dB)	n/s	n/s	20.3	20.3/20.3
*ELTCTL (dB)	n/s	n/s	0.5	0/0
Propagation Delay (ns)	548	548	548	548/548
Delay Skew (ns)	50	50	50	30/30

*These parameters are discussed in section 2-6, "10 Gigabit Ethernet over Copper."

The list that follows describes some of the parameters listed in Table 2-4:

- **Attenuation (insertion loss):** This parameter defines the amount of loss in signal strength as it propagates down the wire. This is caused by the resistance of the twisted-pair cable, the connectors, and leakage of the electrical signal through the cable insulation. Attenuation also will increase with an increase in frequencies due to the inductance and capacitance of the cable. The cable test results will report a margin. Margin for attenuation (insertion loss) is defined as the difference between the measured value and the limit for the test. If the margin shows a negative value, the test has failed. A negative value is produced when the measured value is less than the limit. The limit for attenuation (insertion loss) for CAT6 is 21.3 dB, CAT6A is 20.9, CAT7 is 20.8, and CAT7a is 20.3. It is also important to note that UTP cables have a limit on how much the cable can be bent (bend radius). The limit on the bend radius is four times the outer jacket diameter. The reason for this is bends exceeding the limit can introduce attenuation loss.

- **NEXT:** When current travels in a wire, an electromagnetic field is created. This field can induce a voltage in adjacent wires resulting in crosstalk. **Crosstalk** is what you occasionally hear on the telephone when you can faintly hear another conversation. Near-end crosstalk, or NEXT, is a measure of the level of crosstalk, or signal coupling within the cable. The measurement is called *near-end testing* because the receiver is more likely to pick up the crosstalk from the transmit to the receiver wire pairs at the ends. The transmit signal levels at each end are strong, and the cable is more susceptible to crosstalk at this point. Additionally, the receive signal levels have been attenuated due to normal cable path loss and are significantly weaker than the transmit signal. A high NEXT (dB) value is desirable.

> **Crosstalk**
> Signal coupling in a cable

Figure 2-29 graphically depicts NEXT. The dark gray area shows where the near-end crosstalk occurs. The margin is the difference between the measured value and the limit. A negative number means the measured value is less than the limit, and therefore the measurement fails. Crosstalk is more problematic at higher data rates (for example, 1Gbps, 10Gbps). Figure 2-30 shows how CAT6 cable has a built-in separator to help minimize crosstalk among wire pairs. This separator is used to keep each wire pair at a minimum distance from other wire pairs. This addition reduces crosstalk at higher frequencies and helps provide improved signal bandwidth, and therefore it will support faster data rates. This addition also helps improve the far-end cross-talk. Note that not all cable manufacturers use the separator.

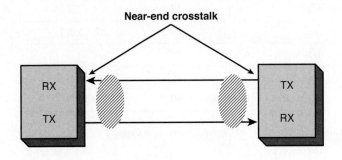

FIGURE 2-29   A graphical depiction of near-end crosstalk.

FIGURE 2-30   The cross-section of a CAT6 cable showing the separator used to minimize crosstalk problems.

- **Power Sum NEXT (PSNEXT):** The enhanced twisted-pair cable must meet four-pair NEXT requirements, called PSNEXT testing. Basically, power sum testing measures the total crosstalk of all cable pairs. This test ensures that the cable can carry data traffic on all four pairs at the same time with minimal interference. A higher PSNEXT value is desirable because it indicates better cable performance.

- **Equal Level FEXT (ELFEXT):** This measurement differs from NEXT in that the measurement is for the far end of the cable. Additionally, the ELFEXT measurement does not depend on the length of the cable. This is because ELFEXT is obtained by subtracting the attenuation value from the far-end crosstalk (**FEXT**) loss. Higher ELFEXT values (dB) indicate the signals at the far end of the cable are larger than the cross-talk measured at the far end. A larger ELFEXT (dB) value is desirable. A poor ELFEXT can result in data loss.

- **PSELFEXT:** Power sum ELFEXT that uses all four wire pairs to obtain a combined ELFEXT performance measurement. This value is the difference between the test signal level and the cross-talk measured at the far end of the cable. A higher PSELFEXT value indicates better cable performance.

- **ACR:** This measurement compares the signal level from a transmitter at the far end to the crosstalk measured at the near end. A larger ACR indicates that the cable has a greater data capacity and also indicates the cable's ability to handle a greater bandwidth. Essentially, it is a combined measurement of the quality of the cable. A higher ACR value (dB) is desirable.

- **PSACR:** Power sum ACR uses all four wire pairs to obtain the measure of the attenuation–crosstalk ratio. This is a measurement of the difference between PSNEXT and attenuation (insertion loss). The difference is measured in dB, and higher PSACR dB values indicate better cable performance.

- **Return loss:** An equally important twisted-pair cable measurement is return loss. This measurement provides a measure of the ratio of power transmitted into a cable to the amount of power returned or reflected. The signal reflection is due to impedance changes in the cable link and the impedance changes contributing to cable loss. Cables are not perfect, so there will always be some reflection. Examples of the causes for impedance changes are non-uniformity in impedance throughout the cable, the diameter of the copper, cable handling, and dielectric differences. A low return loss value (dB) is desirable.

- **Propagation delay:** This is a measure of the amount of time it takes for a signal to propagate from one end of the cable to the other. The delay of the signal is affected by the **nominal velocity of propagation (NVP)** of the cable. NVP is some percentage of the velocity of light and is dependent on the type of cable being tested. The typical delay value for CAT5/5e UTP cable is about 5.7 nsec per meter. The EIA/TIA specification allows for 548 nsec for the maximum 100-meter run for CAT5e, CAT6, CAT6a, CAT7, and CAT7A

- **Delay skew:** This is a measure of the difference in arrival time between the fastest and the slowest signal in a UTP wire pair. It is critical in high-speed data transmission that the data on the wire pair arrive at the other end at the same time. If the wire lengths of different wire pairs are significantly different, then the data on one wire will take longer to propagate along the wire, hence arriving at the receiver at a different time and potentially creating distortion of the data and data packet loss. The wire pair with the shortest length will typically have the least delay skew.

Note

The power sum measurements are critical for high-speed data communication over UTP. It has also been shown that twisted-pair cable can handle gigabit data rates over a distance up to 100 meters. However, the gigabit data rate capability of twisted-pair requires the use of all four wire pairs in the cable, with each pair handling 250Mbps of data. The total bit rate is 4 X 250Mbps, or 1Gbps, hence the need to obtain the combined performance measurements of all four wire pairs.

Section 2-5 Review

This section has covered the following **Network+** Exam objectives.

4.2 Given a scenario, analyze and interpret the output of troubleshooting tools

This chapter presented an overview of testing the installed UTP cable. In this section, you learned the details of the EIA/TIA UTP specifications for many category types. You were also introduced to what the test parameters mean. Make sure you develop an understanding of each test parameter.

4.4 Given a scenario, troubleshoot and resolve common copper cable issues

This section has introduced some very important cable issue concepts. Make sure you have a good understanding of near-end, far-end crosstalk, attenuation, and distance limitation.

Test Your Knowledge

1. A full channel test tests all the link elements from the computer through the patch panel to the wall plate. True or False?

2. NEXT stands for Near End Cross Talk and a low dB value is desirable. True or False?

3. Signals travel in a cable at some percentage of the velocity of light. The term for this is called the nominal velocity of propagation. True or False?

2-6 10 GIGABIT ETHERNET OVER COPPER

Ethernet over copper is available for 10Mbps (Ethernet), 100Mbps (FastEthernet), 1000Mbps (gigabit Ethernet), and now 10Gbps (ten gigabit Ethernet). (Note that Mbps is "megabits per second." Some literature writes this as Mb/s.) The increase in the required bandwidth for transporting a 10GB data transfer rate is placing increased demands on the copper cable as well as the hardware used for terminating the cable ends and for connecting to the networking equipment. There are three improvements required for transmitting the higher data bit rates over the copper cabling:

1. Improve the cable so it can carry greater bandwidth.

2. Improve the electronics used to transmit and receive (recover) the data.

3. Utilize improvements in both the cable and electronics to facilitate greater bandwidths and distance.

This section examines the changes in technology that are required to enable the transportation of ten gigabit data (**10GBASE-T**) over copper. The first part presents an overview of ten gigabit GB Ethernet over copper. The second part examines the modifications required to the technical specs (CAT6A and CAT7/7A) that are necessary for testing and certifying twisted-pair copper cable transporting ten gigabit data rates. The last section examines the issues of how the ten gigabit data is actually transmitted.

> **10GBASE-T**
> 10Gbps over twisted-pair copper cable

Overview

The standard for 10Gbps is **IEEE 802.3an-2006 10GBASE-T**. This standard was developed to support running 10Gbps data over twisted-pair cabling. The newer standard requires the bandwidth to be increased from 250MHz to 500MHz. Additionally, the new standard supports 10GB Ethernet up to 100 meters in cable length. At one time, most people assumed that higher data rates would be limited to fiber optics. While this is still true for lengthy runs (more than 100 meters) twisted-pair copper is finding its place in the horizontal runs from the telecommunications closet to the work area.

> **IEEE 802.3an-2006 10GBASE-T**
> The standard for 10Gbps

Alien Crosstalk

Alien Crosstalk is an important issue at higher data rates such as with 10GBASE-T. **Alien Crosstalk (AXT)** is unwanted signal coupling from one permanent link to another. Basically, this is the coupling of a signal from one 4-pair cable to another 4-pair cable. Figure 2-31 depicts the AXT from one 4-pair cable to another 4-pair cable. The other key measurements for 10GBASE-T are **NEXT (PSANEXT), FEXT (PSAACRF)**, and Return Loss. PSANEXT (Power Sum Alien Near-End Crosstalk) and PSAACRF (Power Sum Alien Attenuation to Crosstalk Ratio) are new measurements for NEXT and FEXT that incorporate measures for Alien Crosstalk. Alien Crosstalk is considered to be the main electrical limiting parameter for 10G Ethernet. Alien Crosstalk causes disturbances in the neighboring cable. It is difficult for the electronics to cancel the AXT noise created; therefore, new cables have been developed to support the 10Gbps data rates. The newer cables have improved the cable separation, and new connectors have also been developed to help meet the required specifications to support 10G.

FIGURE 2-31   Alien Crosstalk from a neighboring 4-pair cable.

Cable manufacturers are starting to offer CAT6 and higher grades of twisted-pair cable with foil over each of the four wire-pairs. The designation for this type of cable is **F/UTP**. There are several advantages to using a shielded cable:

- A shielded cable offers better security because there is less chance that the data will radiate outside the cable.

- The foil shield helps improve noise immunity from EMI, radio frequency interference (RFI), and (most importantly) AXT.

Transmission of data over twisted-pair cabling relies on the signals being "balanced" over the wire pairs. The balance or symmetry of the signal over the wire pairs helps minimize unwanted leakage of the signal. There are two parameters now defined for CAT6 and better cabling that address the issue of balanced data. The first is **TCL (Transverse Conversion Loss)** and the other is **ELTCTL (Equal Level Transverse Conversion Transfer Loss)**. The TCL measurement is obtained by applying a common-mode signal to the input and measuring the differential signal level on the output. TCL is sometimes called **LCL (Longitudinal Conversion Loss)**. The ELTCTL value (expressed in dB) is the difference between the **TCTL (Transverse Conversion Transfer Loss)** and the differential mode insertion loss of the pair being measured. TCTL is the loss from a balanced signal at the near-end to the unbalanced signal at the far end.

The newer tests also require additional Power-Sum tests. These are **PSANEXT (Power-Sum Alien Near-End Cross-Talk)** and **PSAACRF (Power-Sum Alien Attenuation Cross-talk Ratio Far-end)**. These tests have been developed to help ensure cable compatibility with data transmission and reception that requires the use of all four wire-pairs. Both gigabit and ten gigabit require the use of all four wire pairs.

Signal Transmission

The 10GBASE-T system requires the use of all four wire pairs as shown in Figure 2-32. This system splits the 10Gbps of data into four 2.5Gbps data channels. This same technique is also used for 1000Mbps (1GB) data rates, except the 1000Mbps signal is split into four 250Mbps data channels. The system requires the use of signal conditioners and digital signal processing (DSP) circuits for both transmission and reception. The data transmission for ten gigabit uses a **multilevel encoding** technique as shown in Figure 2-33. The advantage of this type of encoding is the reduction in the required bandwidth required to transport the data.

TCL
Transverse Conversion Loss

ELTCTL
Equal Level Transverse Conversion Transfer Loss

LCL
Longitudinal Conversion Loss

TCTL
Transverse Conversion Transfer Loss

PSANEXT
Power-Sum Alien Near-End Crosstalk

PSAACRF
Power-Sum Alien Attenuation Cross-talk Ratio Far-End

Multilevel Encoding
Technique used to reduce in the required bandwidth required to transport the data

FIGURE 2-32 The four wire-pairs in UTP cabling required for transporting 10GBASE-T data. This same technique is used for 1000Mbps except the data rate for each of the four channels is 250Mbps.

2- level

4- level

FIGURE 2-33 An example of multilevel encoding of the data streams to reduce the required bandwidth.

10GBASE-T data transmission also requires the use of DSP Compensation Techniques. The DSP circuitry provides many functions, such as signal conditioning and echo cancellation. Anytime a signal is transmitted down a cable, part of the signal will be reflected. This reflection adds to overall signal degradation and limits the performance of the system. In 10GBASE-T, the transmit and receive signals are sharing the same wire pair. This is called full duplex transmission and requires the use of a device called a **hybrid echo cancellation circuit**. The hybrid circuit removes the transmitted signal from the receive signal.

The final issue with 10GBASE-T signal transmission is the performance of the cable. As mentioned previously, return loss, insertion loss, and crosstalk are all key limiting issues for 10GBASE-T. Crosstalk is the most important factor. The types of crosstalk observed are AXT, NEXT, FEXT, and ELFEXT. The cabling systems that will support 10GBASE-T operation with links up to 100 meters are CAT6 with the foil screen, augmented CAT6 (CAT6a), CAT7, and CAT7a.

Section 2-6 Review

This section has covered the following **Network+** Exam objectives.

5.4 Given a scenario, deploy the appropriate wired connectivity standard

This section has presented a look at the issue of running 10Gbps of data over UTP cable. This is based on the 10GBASE-T Ethernet standard. Probably one of the most important concepts associated with 10Gbps over twisted-pair is Alien Crosstalk, which is unwanted signal coupling from one permanent link to another.

Test Your Knowledge

1. The term for unwanted signal coupling from one permanent link to another is

    a. Near-end crosstalk

    b. Alien Crosstalk

    c. Far-end crosstalk

    d. None of these answers is correct.

2. 10GBASE-T requires the use of which of the following in the transmission of data over UTP?

   a. The high data lines

   b. Pins 4/5 7/8 only

   c. All four wire pairs

   d. 10G is not possible at 10G.

2-7   TROUBLESHOOTING CABLING SYSTEMS

This section examines some of the issues that the network administrator can have with both CAT6 and CAT5e cables tests. It is important that the network administrator monitor all parts of the cable installation, from pulling to terminating the cable ends. The reasons a cable fails a certification test can be due to multiple types of problems, such as with installation, cable stretching, and the cable failing to meet manufacturer specifications. These types of problems are discussed next, followed by a look at the certification reports for failures of both CAT6 and CAT5e.

Installation

If you obtain bad PowerSum measurements or NEXT or FEXT, there might be a problem with the installation. The certification report provided in Figure 2-34 indicates this cable does not pass CAT6 certification, as shown by the X in the upper-right corner of the certification report. This test indicates a "NEXT" failure, which is most likely due to a problem at the terminations. The most common error is the installer has allowed too much untwisted cable at the termination point. Remember, the twist on UTP cable must be maintained to less than 3/8 inch. At this point, the best thing is to go and inspect the terminations to see whether any terminations have too much untwisted cable and verify whether there is a procedure problem with the installation.

FIGURE 2-34 The DTX-1800 certification report: Failure due to termination problem.

Cable Stretching

It is important to avoid stretching of the UTP cable. Stretching of the cable is bad because it changes the electrical characteristics of the cable, increasing the attenuation and crosstalk. The maximum pulling tension is specified by the manufacturer data sheets, and the datasheet will list the maximum pulling tension put on a cable. The units for the pulling tension are expressed in lb-ft.

Cable Failing to Meet Manufacturer Specifications

Occasionally, manufacturers do experience problems with the cable failing to meet specifications. This could be due to a bad production run, and the result is that the cable does not meet minimum specifications. Repeated test failures with no apparent reason for the failure could indicate that the problem is with the cable. This rarely happens, but there is a possibility that there was a bad cable production run. As the manager, you need to isolate the source of the problem.

Figure 2-35 provides another CAT6 certification report, which indicates that the cable failed due to excessive insertion loss. Examination of the certification report shows that the cable length for pairs 7–8 is 311 ft. The maximum cable length for a permanent link is 295 ft. This cable run is too long for it to be certifiable.

FIGURE 2-35 The DTX-1800 certification report: Failure due to excessive insertion loss.

CAT5e Cable Test Examples

The next section presents some test results for several CAT5e cable tests. There are still many CAT5e horizontal cable runs already in place, and these runs support 100-Mbps data rates. Therefore, it is important for the network administrator to have a good understanding of certifying CAT5e links. The objective of this section is to acquaint the reader with possible CAT5e test results and problems they might encounter on the job. The procedures presented are the same for CAT6 except that the test mode of the cable analyzer must be set to CAT5e performance specifications. The testers used for conducting the CAT5e certification reports are the Fluke OMNIscanner and OMNIremote.

Test 1

The first example presented is the test on a short patch cable. This shows that short patch cables can and should be tested. UTP cable testing is not restricted to long cables. The length of the wire pairs is about 3 feet. You also have a record that this cable meets CAT5e requirements. The test was conducted using the OMNIscanner.

The OMNIscanner certification report verifies that the cable passes the CAT5e link test. Figure 2-36 shows the certification report, which indicates that the cable passed the test. This report shows that the cable length is 3 feet.

FIGURE 2-36 The certification report for Test 1 showing that the short jumper cable passes CAT5e link test.

Test 2
This shows the test on the same 3-foot cable used in Test 1; however, the cable no longer meets CAT5e requirements, as shown in Figure 2-37. The test results indicate

FAIL. In fact, careful inspection of the cable showed that it had been cut or nicked. This underscores the importance of documenting the network installation and having a record that the cable link was certified. Test 1 showed that the cable met specifications, but damage to the cable no longer enables it to meet CAT5e link specifications.

Inspection of the wire-map test results (see Figure 2-37) shows the cable failed, highlighted by the FAIL symbol in the upper-right corner of the certification report. In this test, the cable has failed a wire-map test. Not only is the text highlighted, but there is an exclamation preceding the text that indicates a failure. A quick check of the wire-map test shows that the number 4 wire was not detected at the remote.

FIGURE 2-37 The results for Test 2 showing that the cable failed the CAT5e link test.

Test 3

This cable test (Figure 2-38) also generated a test result of FAIL. Examination of the attenuation and return-loss menu shows that the cable failed to meet CAT5e attenuation and return-loss specifications. The permitted attenuation in CAT5e cable is 24 dB. However, the 1–2 and 3–6 pairs have attenuation losses of 38.0 dB and 41.1 dB. Both cases greatly exceed the permitted maximum. An arrow points to these attenuation loss scores.

This cable also fails return loss for pairs 1–2 and 3–6. CAT5e cable permits 10 dB of return-loss. The tests show that the pairs fail the return-loss test at both the OMNIscanner and the remote test unit. This cable will fail a CAT5e certification based solely on attenuation or return loss. In fact, this cable also fails NEXT, ELFEXT, and PSELFEXT tests. Any of these failures are sufficient to not certify this cable.

Test 4

Figure 2-39 shows the certification report for the cable tested in Test 4. This cable test generated a test result of FAIL. Examination of the certification report shows the cable failed the delay skew. This cable exceeds the maximum allowed by EIA/TIA 568B. Additionally, this cable fails attenuation, ELFEXT, and PSELFEXT tests. No, the cable should not be certified.

The measured delay skew of 47 ns exceeds the tester setting of 45 ns. The EIA/TIA 568B standard permits a delay skew of 50 ns, so actually this cable meets delay skew requirements for CAT5e cable. The specification set on the tester actually exceeds the CAT5e requirements. Should the cable have been certified? Look at the length measurement for the 3–6 pair length. The cable is 1040 feet in length. Remember, the maximum cable length for a CAT5e cable run is 100 meters.

OMNI *Scanner* ™

OMNIScanner2 Certification Report

FAIL

Circuit ID:	Split Pairs	**OMNIScanner**		**OMNIRemote**	
Project:	TIA Project	50D99L00377	**SW:** V06.00	50E99L00037	
Owner:	OMNISCANNER 2	**Adapter**		**Adapter**	
Autotest:	*Cat 5E Link*	CHAN 5/5E/6		CHAN 5/5E/6	
Cable:	Cat 5E UTP				
NVP:	72				

		Limit	**12**	**36**	**45**	**78**
Site:	Las Cruces					
Building:	Manufacturing	**Length** ft	(308)	45	45	47	47
Floor:	3rd	**Delay (ns):**	(518)	64	64	66	67
Closet:	315A	**Resistance (Ohms):**	(—)	—	—	—	—

Wiremap	**Expected**	**Actual**		
OMNI:	12345678	! 12345678	**Skew (ns):**	(45) 3
Remote:	12345678	! 12345678	**Bandwidth (MHz):**	—

Attenuation — Overall Margin (dB)[1] -19.5

Pairs	dB	Margin	MHz
12	! 38.0	-16.4	99.4
36	! 41.1	-19.5	99.9
45	2.9	18.6	99.2
78	2.9	18.7	99.9

Return Loss — Overall Margin (dB)[1] -5.4

	OMNIScanner			OMNIRemote		
Pairs	dB	Margin	MHz	dB	Margin	MHz
12	! 10.6	-5.3	29.3	! 10.5	-5.3	29.5
36	! 10.4	-5.4	29.8	! 10.6	-5.2	29.3
45	19.4	6.1	68.0	20.8	3.8	1.4
78	20.3	3.3	1.4	21.3	4.3	1.6

NEXT — Overall Margin (dB)[1] -37.7

	OMNIScanner			OMNIRemote		
Pairs	dB	Margin	MHz	dB	Margin	MHz
12/36	! 22.3	-37.7	1.6	! 11.0	-36.4	11.8
12/45	56.6	5.4	6.8	54.2	3.5	7.3
12/78	69.8	9.9	1.9	70.2	10.9	2.1
36/45	39.4	4.9	74.1	56.1	3.9	5.9
36/78	68.2	9.6	2.3	68.7	9.4	2.1
45/78	59.5	15.5	19.0	57.3	13.2	19.0

ACR — Overall Margin (dB)[1] —

	OMNIScanner			OMNIRemote		
Pairs	dB	Margin	MHz	dB	Margin	MHz
12/36	—	—	—	—	—	—
12/45	—	—	—	—	—	—
12/78	—	—	—	—	—	—
36/45	—	—	—	—	—	—
36/78	—	—	—	—	—	—
45/78	—	—	—	—	—	—

ELFEXT — Overall Margin (dB)[1] -30.1

	OMNIScanner			OMNIRemote		
Pairs	dB	Margin	MHz	dB	Margin	MHz
12/36	! 26.4	-30.1	1.6	! 26.6	-29.9	1.6
12/45	67.8	16.6	2.8	37.2	16.6	93.8
12/78	80.0	22.3	1.4	80.1	22.3	1.4
36/12	! 26.6	-29.9	1.6	! 26.4	-30.1	1.6
36/45	60.8	14.7	5.0	35.4	13.0	76.3
36/78	79.9	22.2	1.4	57.9	21.2	14.7
45/12	! 8.6	-11.4	99.4	! 10.4	-9.6	99.4
45/36	! 1.9	-18.2	99.4	! 5.8	-14.2	99.9
45/78	50.3	15.5	18.3	49.8	15.2	18.7
78/12	! 14.4	-5.6	99.4	! 9.2	-10.9	99.4
78/36	! 10.4	-9.7	99.9	23.3	3.3	99.9
78/45	49.9	15.3	18.7	50.4	15.6	18.3

PSNEXT — Overall Margin (dB)[1] -34.7

	OMNIScanner			OMNIRemote		
Pairs	dB	Margin	MHz	dB	Margin	MHz
12	! 22.2	-34.7	2.1	! 11.0	-33.4	11.8
36	! 22.2	-34.7	2.1	! 11.0	-33.4	11.8
45	53.1	5.3	7.3	52.0	3.7	6.8
78	66.1	9.2	2.1	66.3	9.4	2.1

PSELFEXT — Overall Margin (dB)[1] -27.1

	OMNIScanner			OMNIRemote		
Pairs	dB	Margin	MHz	dB	Margin	MHz
12	! 26.6	-26.8	1.6	! 26.4	-27.0	1.6
36	! 26.4	-27.1	1.6	! 26.6	-26.9	1.6
45	68.9	14.2	1.4	33.6	14.2	76.3
78	72.0	17.3	1.4	72.1	17.4	1.4

PSACR — Overall Margin (dB)[1] —

	OMNIScanner			OMNIRemote		
Pairs	dB	Margin	MHz	dB	Margin	MHz
12	—	—	—	—	—	—
36	—	—	—	—	—	—
45	—	—	—	—	—	—
78	—	—	—	—	—	—

[1] Overall margin value is the worst margin for OMNI and Remote.

⩔MICROTEST®

Date: **Page 1**

FIGURE 2-38 The Test 3 CAT5e link test showing failures with attenuation.

FAIL

OMNIScanner2 Certification Report

Circuit ID:	Long Box	**OMNIScanner**		**OMNIRemote**	
Project:	TIA Project	50D99L00377	SW: V06.00	50E99L00037	
Owner:	OMNISCANNER 2	**Adapter**		**Adapter**	
Autotest:	*Cat 5E Link*	CHAN 5/5E/6		CHAN 5/5E/6	
Cable:	Cat 5E UTP				
NVP:	72				

		Limit	12	36	45	78
Site:	Las Cruces					
Building:	Manufacturing	Length ft	(308)	1068	! 1040	1050	1074
Floor:	3rd	Delay (ns):	(518)	1508	! 1469	1482	1516
Closet:	315	Resistance (Ohms):	(—)	—	—	—	—

Wiremap	Expected	Actual		
OMNI:	12345678	12345678	Skew (ns):	(45) ! 47
Remote:	12345678	12345678	Bandwidth (MHz):	——

Attenuation

Overall Margin (dB)¹ -62.1

Pairs	dB	Margin	MHz
12	! 72.7	-52.8	86.4
36	! 74.5	-54.1	89.8
45	! 80.4	-61.5	78.3
78	! 82.4	-62.1	89.1

Return Loss

Overall Margin (dB)¹ 4.9

	OMNIScanner			OMNIRemote		
Pairs	dB	Margin	MHz	dB	Margin	MHz
12	23.2	7.0	26.4	27.4	10.4	2.1
36	25.2	8.2	1.4	23.3	9.1	50.7
45	20.9	4.9	27.5	24.6	7.6	12.9
78	25.4	8.4	2.3	24.6	8.6	28.0

NEXT

Overall Margin (dB)¹ 7.6

	OMNIScanner			OMNIRemote		
Pairs	dB	Margin	MHz	dB	Margin	MHz
12/36	60.3	13.8	13.6	63.6	13.8	8.4
12/45	44.1	10.1	78.5	53.8	15.7	44.1
12/78	48.4	8.6	34.9	59.6	8.2	6.6
36/45	66.1	8.1	2.5	62.6	7.6	3.9
36/78	45.4	13.0	99.2	69.3	12.4	3.0
45/78	63.8	13.0	7.3	69.4	16.9	5.7

ACR

Overall Margin (dB)¹ ——

	OMNIScanner			OMNIRemote		
Pairs	dB	Margin	MHz	dB	Margin	MHz
12/36	——	——	——	——	——	——
12/45	——	——	——	——	——	——
12/78	——	——	——	——	——	——
36/45	——	——	——	——	——	——
36/78	——	——	——	——	——	——
45/78	——	——	——	——	——	——

ELFEXT

Overall Margin (dB)¹ -21.1

	OMNIScanner			OMNIRemote		
Pairs	dB	Margin	MHz	dB	Margin	MHz
12/36	! 5.1	-15.7	91.6	! 7.5	-13.5	89.8
12/45	! 9.6	-11.1	92.5	! 4.4	-17.8	78.3
12/78	! 3.0	-18.0	89.1	! 0.6	-20.4	89.1
36/12	! 13.0	-8.7	83.0	! 11.2	-9.1	96.1
36/45	! 1.4	-20.8	78.3	! 5.6	-16.1	82.8
36/78	! 8.3	-12.6	90.4	! 1.7	-19.4	89.1
45/12	! 7.7	-13.6	86.4	! 8.3	-13.0	86.4
45/36	! 5.4	-16.3	82.8	! 8.1	-13.5	82.8
45/78	! 1.3	-19.0	96.7	! 1.3	-19.7	89.1
78/12	! 8.6	-13.1	83.0	! 6.7	-14.9	83.0
78/36	! 4.7	-16.2	89.8	! 7.6	-13.4	89.8
78/45	! 1.1	-21.1	78.3	! 4.9	-17.2	78.3

PSNEXT

Overall Margin (dB)¹ 9.4

	OMNIScanner			OMNIRemote		
Pairs	dB	Margin	MHz	dB	Margin	MHz
12	47.9	11.1	34.9	59.3	10.8	6.6
36	64.3	10.2	3.0	62.2	10.0	3.9
45	64.7	9.4	2.5	62.1	9.9	3.9
78	58.5	10.7	7.3	59.5	11.0	6.6

PSELFEXT

Overall Margin (dB)¹ -18.4

	OMNIScanner			OMNIRemote		
Pairs	dB	Margin	MHz	dB	Margin	MHz
12	! 5.0	-13.3	86.4	! 6.2	-12.4	83.0
36	! 1.3	-16.5	91.6	! 3.4	-14.6	89.8
45	! 4.3	-14.9	78.3	! 0.7	-18.4	78.3
78	! 0.3	-17.7	89.1	! 0.8	-17.2	90.4

PSACR

Overall Margin (dB)¹ ——

	OMNIScanner			OMNIRemote		
Pairs	dB	Margin	MHz	dB	Margin	MHz
12	——	——	——	——	——	——
36	——	——	——	——	——	——
45	——	——	——	——	——	——
78	——	——	——	——	——	——

¹ Overall margin value is the worst margin for OMNI and Remote.

MICROTEST®

Date: Page 1

FIGURE 2-39   A CAT5e link test showing failures with delay skew (Test 4).

Summary of CAT5e Cable Test Examples

This section has provided a few examples of CAT5e link tests. The objective has been to provide actual test data for various cable problems that might occur on the job. In the tests where a failure was detected, the tester displayed a failed screen, and the certification report identified the problem. The following is a summary of the tests:

- **Test 1**: The certification report shows a test result of PASS.

- **Test 2:** The certification report shows a test result of FAIL. The report shows the cable failed the wire-map test.

- **Test 3:** This cable test generated a test result of FAIL. Examination of the attenuation and return-loss shows that the cable failed to meet CAT5e attenuation and return-loss specifications. The cable also failed NEXT, ELFEXT, PSNEXT, and PSELFEXT tests.

- **Test 4**: The certification report shows the cable fails the CAT5e link test. Examination of the report shows the cable failed the delay skew measurement because the cable length exceeded the 100-meter maximum. The cable also fails attenuation, ELFEXT, and PSELFEXT tests.

The reasons for examining the test results is to find out why a cable fails a test. You need to know whether the problem is with your terminations, cable layout, or the way the cable is installed. Keeping a record of the cable tests will help you isolate recurring problems.

Tests 1 and 2 demonstrate the importance of keeping a record of tests. In this case, the cable was certified but later failed. The documentation provided by the certification report provides evidence that the cable was functioning properly and did meet CAT5e specifications.

Section 2-7 Review

This section has covered the following **Network+** Exam objectives.

> 1.5 Install and properly terminate various cable types and connectors using the appropriate tools

The certification exams require the use of sophisticated test gear to conduct the many tests needed to certify a cable.

> 4.4 Given a scenario, troubleshoot and resolve common cable issues

This section presents several examples of tests and possible problems that might be encountered. Some problems could be a result of poor installation, bad connectors, or bad cable, and the network administrator needs to have good documentation that each cable has been certified if possible.

Test Your Knowledge

1. Patch cables are too short to be tested. True or False?

2. A UTP certification report lists the following.

Pairs	12	36	45	78
Length	285	288	284	283

What do these results indicate?

   a. The test must be repeated.

   b. Insufficient information to obtain an answer.

   c. The cable length is too long.

   d. The cable passes the length test.

3. A data problem is reported to the network administrator. The problem is found to be with the UTP network connection. Which steps could the network administrator have taken to isolate the problem? (Select two.)

   a. Visually inspect all UTP terminations.

   b. Run a cable test using a cable tester.

   c. Use the **ping** command to verify network connectivity.

   d. Use pairs 4/5 7/8 to repair the connection.

   e. Contact the installer of the UTP cable to obtain a certification report.

SUMMARY

This chapter introduced the basics of horizontal cabling and unshielded twisted-pair cable. The major topics the student should now understand include the following:

- Six subsystems of a structured cabling system
- The purpose of the telecommunication closet and the LAN work area
- The performance capabilities of CAT6/5e UTP
- The wiring color schemes for T568A and T568B
- The pin assignments for the RJ-45 (8P8C) modular plug
- The technical issues of copper over 10G Ethernet
- The procedures for testing a CAT6/5e link
- The procedures for troubleshooting a CAT6/5e link
- How to examine and use the test results provided by a CAT6/5e link certification report

QUESTIONS AND PROBLEMS

Section 2-2

1. What is an 8P8C connector?

   a. Another term for an RJ-11 connector

   b. Another term for an RJ-6 connector

   c. Another term for an RJ-45 connector

   d. Another term for RS-232

2. What do EIA and TIA stand for?

3. What are the three parts of the EIA/TIA 568B standard?

4. Identify the six subsystems of a structured cabling system.

5. Which subsystem does permanent networking cabling within a building belong to?

6. What is a cross-connect?

7. What is the main cross-connect?

8. The Telco and the ISP usually connect to what room in the campus network hierarchy?

9. What is the WO, and what is its purpose?

10. The patch cable from a computer typically terminates into which of the following?

    a. Jack in a wall plate

    b. BNC connector

    c. Thin net

    d. RJ-11 modular plug

    e. RG-59

11. What is the over all length limitation of an individual cable run from the telecommunications closet to a networking device in the work area?

12. A general rule of thumb is to allow how many meters for the cable run from the telecommunications closet to the work area?

Section 2-3

13. How many pins does an RJ-45 modular plug have?

14. What is the difference in CAT 5 and CAT 5e?

15. What is the data rate for Ethernet?

16. What is the data rate for FastEthernet?

17. What improvements will CAT6 and CAT7 cable provide?

18. What is the data rate for gigabit Ethernet?

19. What is a benefit of using shielded twisted-pair cabling?

20. Which cable, UTP or STP, is preferred by the industry?

Section 2-4

21. What are the color maps and pin number assignments for T568A and T568B?

22. What is the difference between T568A and T568B?

23. How many wires are in a CAT6 twisted-pair cable?

24. How many wire pairs are in a CAT6 twisted-pair cable?

25. In regards to a CAT6 cable, what pin numbers in an RJ-45 connecter are used to carry data in a FastEthernet network?

26. What does an "X" on the input to a hub represent?

27. Define the term cross-connected input.

28. Draw a picture of properly aligned transmit and receive signal of a computer's data link that is running Ethernet data rates.

29. What is the difference between "straight" and "cross-connected" input ports?

30. Draw the wire-map for a "cross-over" CAT6 UTP cable running FastEthernet.

31. Define a UTP link test.

32. Define a UTP full channel test.

33. Define the term NEXT and what it measures.

34. A NEXT measurement of 59.5 dB is made on wire pairs 1–2/3–6. A next measurement of 51.8 dB is made on wire pairs 3–6/7–8. Which cable pairs have the best measure NEXT performance?

35. Define Power-Sum measurements.

36. Define propagation delay.

37. Signals travel in a cable at some percentage of the velocity of light. What is the term for this?

38. Why is delay skew critical?

39. Why are power-sum measurements critical for high-speed data communication over UTP?

40. The expected + loss of a 20m UTP cable should be (greater than or less than) a 90m UTP cable?

41. What is 8P8C, and what connector type is most associated with this?

42. What are the pin assignments for 1/10 Gbps?

43. What is the purpose of a lacing tool?

Section 2-5

44. What is the limit on the bend radius for a UTP cable, and why is this important?

45. Is a high PSNEXT measurement desirable?

46. Define margin (dB) relative to cable measurements. What does it mean if the margin lists a negative value?

Section 2-6

47. Define Alien Crosstalk and draw a picture of how this can happen.

48. What is F/UTP, and what is its purpose?

49. Why is balance an issue in UTP cables, and what is TCL?

50. Answer the following questions for the certification report displayed here.

a. What is the length of pair 7–8?

b. What is the length of pair 4–5?

c. Why did this cable fail the test?

51. Answer the following questions for the certification report displayed here.

a. What is the length of wire pair 7–8?

b. What is the delay skew for pair 4–5?

c. Why did this cable fail the wire-map test?

52. Answer the following questions for the certification report displayed here.

OMNI Scanner™

OMNIScanner2 Certification Report

FAIL

Circuit ID:	Grey 1	**OMNIScanner**	**OMNIRemote**
Project:	TIA Project	50D99L00377	50E99L00037
Owner:	OMNISCANNER 2	SW: V06.00	
		Adapter	**Adapter**
Autotest:	*Cat 5E Link*	CHAN 5/5E/6	CHAN 5/5E/6
Cable:	Cat 5E UTP		
NVP:	72		
Site:	Las Cruces		
Building:	Manufacturing		
Floor:	3rd		
Closet:	315		

	Limit	12	36	45	78
Length ft	(308)	21	0	22	! 21
Delay (ns):	(518)	30	0	31	30
Resistance (Ohms):	(—)	—	—	—	—

Wiremap	Expected	Actual			
OMNI:	12345678	! 12345678	Skew (ns):	(45)	31
Remote:	12345678	! 12547683	Bandwidth (MHz):		—

Attenuation — Overall Margin (dB)* 19.7

Pairs	dB	Margin	MHz
12	1.5	19.7	96.1
36	—	—	—
45	—	—	—
78	—	—	—

Return Loss — Overall Margin (dB)* —

	OMNIScanner			OMNIRemote		
Pairs	dB	Margin	MHz	dB	Margin	MHz
12	19.2	6.9	94.3	19.0	6.7	95.6
36	—	—	—	—	—	—
45	—	—	—	—	—	—
78	—	—	—	—	—	—

NEXT — Overall Margin (dB)* —

	OMNIScanner			OMNIRemote		
Pairs	dB	Margin	MHz	dB	Margin	MHz
12/36	—	—	—	—	—	—
12/45	—	—	—	—	—	—
12/78	—	—	—	—	—	—
36/45	—	—	—	—	—	—
36/78	—	—	—	—	—	—
45/78	—	—	—	—	—	—

ACR — Overall Margin (dB)* —

	OMNIScanner			OMNIRemote		
Pairs	dB	Margin	MHz	dB	Margin	MHz
12/36	—	—	—	—	—	—
12/45	—	—	—	—	—	—
12/78	—	—	—	—	—	—
36/45	—	—	—	—	—	—
36/78	—	—	—	—	—	—
45/78	—	—	—	—	—	—

ELFEXT — Overall Margin (dB)* —

	OMNIScanner			OMNIRemote		
Pairs	dB	Margin	MHz	dB	Margin	MHz
12/36	—	—	—	—	—	—
12/45	—	—	—	—	—	—
12/78	—	—	—	—	—	—
36/12	—	—	—	—	—	—
36/45	—	—	—	—	—	—
36/78	—	—	—	—	—	—
45/12	—	—	—	—	—	—
45/36	—	—	—	—	—	—
45/78	—	—	—	—	—	—
78/12	—	—	—	—	—	—
78/36	—	—	—	—	—	—
78/45	—	—	—	—	—	—

PSNEXT — Overall Margin (dB)* 8.7

	OMNIScanner			OMNIRemote		
Pairs	dB	Margin	MHz	dB	Margin	MHz
12	—	—	—	—	—	—
36	—	—	—	—	—	—
45	—	—	—	—	—	—
78	—	—	—	—	—	—

PSELFEXT — Overall Margin (dB)* 10.3

	OMNIScanner			OMNIRemote		
Pairs	dB	Margin	MHz	dB	Margin	MHz
12	—	—	—	—	—	—
36	—	—	—	—	—	—
45	—	—	—	—	—	—
78	—	—	—	—	—	—

PSACR — Overall Margin (dB)* —

	OMNIScanner			OMNIRemote		
Pairs	dB	Margin	MHz	dB	Margin	MHz
12	—	—	—	—	—	—
36	—	—	—	—	—	—
45	—	—	—	—	—	—
78	—	—	—	—	—	—

* Overall margin value is the worst margin for OMNI and Remote.

M MICROTEST®   Page 1

a. Why did the cable fail the test?

b. Draw the wire-map diagram for this cable.

Section 2-7

53. A UTP Certification report lists the following.

Pairs	12	36	45	78
Length	285	288	284	283

What do these results indicate? Select the correct answer.

   a. The test must be repeated.

   b. Insufficient information to obtain an answer.

   c. The cable length is too long.

   d. The cable passes the length test.

54. A data problem is reported to the network administrator. The problem is found to be with the UTP network connection. What steps could the network administrator have taken to isolate the problem? (Select two.)

   a. Visually inspect all UTP terminations.

   b. Run a cable test using a cable tester.

   c. Use the **ping** command to verify network connectivity.

   d. Use pairs 4/5 7/8 to repair the connection.

   e. Contact the installer of the UTP cable to obtain a certification report.

CERTIFICATION QUESTIONS

55. A NEXT measurement of 59.5 dB is made on wire pairs 1-2/3-6. A NEXT measurement of 51.8 dB is made on wire pairs 3-6/7-8. Pairs 3-6/7-8 have the best NEXT performance measurement.

   a. True

   b. False

56. In regards to CAT5e / CAT6 cable operating at half-duplex mode for Ethernet or FastEthernet, pins 1/2 3/6 are used to carry the data.

   a. True

   b. False

57. A CAT5e / 6 link test, tests from one termination to another.

   a. True

   b. False

58. Only two wire-pairs are used to obtain a proper Power Sum measurement.

    a. True

    b. False

59. Delay skew is critical because if the wire lengths of different wire pairs are significantly different, the data will arrive at the receiver at a different time potentially creating distortion of the data.

    a. True

    b. False

60. Which does permanent networking cabling within a building belong to?

    a. Vertical Cabling

    b. Work Area

    c. Equipment Room

    d. None of these answers is correct.

61. How many pins does an RJ-45 modular plug have?

    a. 4

    b. 6

    c. 8

    d. 16

    e. None of these answers is correct.

62. Which of the following best defines horizontal cabling?

    a. Cabling that extends out from the telecommunications closet into the LAN work area.

    b. Cabling that extends out from the work area into the LAN.

    c. Cabling that extends out from the backbone into the LAN work area.

    d. Cabling that extends out from the equipment room into the LAN work area.

    e. None of these answers is correct.

63. A UTP Certification report lists the following.

Pairs	12	36	45	78
Length	! 310	308	! 311	307

What do these results indicate? Select the correct answer.

   a. The cable fails the certification test.

   b. Pairs 36 78 will be certified.

   c. Pairs 1245 will be certified.

   d. The cable has passed the certification test.

   e. The ! sign indicates the cable pair meets or exceeds Power Sum test criteria.

64. The length difference in wire pairs for UTP

   a. indicate the cable should not be certified.

   b. indicate the cable should be certified.

   c. is due to the difference in the cable twists for each wire pair.

   d. is due to poorly manufactured cable.

3 CHAPTER

PHYSICAL LAYER CABLING: FIBER OPTICS

Chapter Outline

Objectives

- Describe the advantages of glass fiber over copper conductors

- Describe the differences in how light travels in single- and multimode fiber

- Define *attenuation* and *dispersion* in fiber–optic cabling

- Describe the components of a fiber-optic system

- Describe the issues of optical networking, including fiber-to-the-business and fiber to-the-home

- Describe the new networking developments associated with optical Ethernet

- Understand the safety issues when working with fiber optics

Key Terms

refractive index

infrared light

optical spectrum

cladding

numerical aperture

multimode fiber

pulse dispersion

graded-index fiber

single-mode fiber

step-index fiber

long haul

mode field diameter

scattering

absorption

macrobending

microbending

dispersion

modal dispersion

chromatic dispersion

polarization mode–dispersion

zero-dispersion–wavelength

dispersion compensating fiber

fiber Bragg grating

DL

LED

distributed feedback (DFB) laser

dense wavelength division multiplex (DWDM)

vertical cavity surface emitting lasers (VCSELs)

tunable laser

fiber, light pipe, glass

isolator

received signal level (RSL)

fusion splicing

mechanical splices

index-matching gel

SC, ST, FC, LC, MT-RJ

SONET/SDH

STS

FTTC

FTTH

FTTB

FTTD

optical Ethernet

fiber cross-connect

GBIC

SFP

XENPAK

XPAK

X2

XFP

SFP+

IDC

IC

logical fiber map

physical fiber map

mm

sm

backbone

Recent advances in the development and manufacture of fiber-optic systems have made them the latest frontier in the field of optical networking. They are being used extensively for both private and commercial data links and have replaced a lot of copper wire. The latest networking technologies to benefit from the development in optical networking are gigabit Ethernet and 10 gigabit Ethernet.

3-1 INTRODUCTION

A fiber-optic network is surprisingly simple, as shown in Figure 3-1. It is comprised of the following elements:

1. A fiber-optic transmission strand can carry the signal (in the form of a modulated light beam) a few feet or even hundreds or thousands of miles. A cable may contain three or four hair-like fibers or a bundle of hundreds of such fibers.

2. A source of invisible infrared radiation—usually a light-emitting diode (LED) or a solid-state laser—that can be modulated to impress digital data or an analog signal on the light beam.

3. A photosensitive detector to convert the optical signal back into an electrical signal at the receiver.

4. Efficient optical connectors at the light source-to-cable interface and at the cable-to-photo detector interface. These connectors are also critical when splicing the optical cable due to excessive loss that can occur at connections.

The advantages of optical communication links compared to copper conductors are enormous and include the following:

1. **Extremely wide system bandwidth:** The intelligence is impressed on the light by varying the light's amplitude. Because the best LEDs have a 5 ns response time, they provide a maximum bandwidth of about 100MHz. With laser light sources, however, data rates over 10Gbps are possible with a single-mode fiber. The amount of information multiplexed on such a system, in the hundreds of Gbps, is indeed staggering.

2. **Immunity to electrostatic interference:** External electrical noise and lightning do not affect energy in a fiber-optic strand. However, this is true only for the optical strands, not the metallic cable components or connecting electronics.

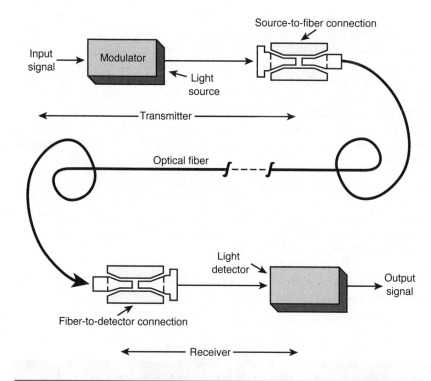

FIGURE 3-1 Fiber-optic communication system. (From Modern Electronic Communication 9/e, by J.S. Beasley & G. M. Miller, 2008, p. 781. Copyright ©2002 Pearson Education, Inc. Reprinted by permission of Pearson Education, Inc., Upper Saddle River, NJ.)

3. **Elimination of crosstalk:** The light in one glass fiber does not interfere with, nor is it susceptible to, the light in an adjacent fiber. Recall that crosstalk results from the electromagnetic coupling between two adjacent copper wires.

4. **Lower signal attenuation than other propagation systems:** Typical attenuation of a 1GHz bandwidth signal for optical fibers is 0.03 dB per 100 ft., compared to 4.0 dB for RG-58U coaxial.

5. **Lower costs:** Optical fiber costs are continuing to decline. The costs of many systems are declining with the use of fiber, and that trend is accelerating.

6. **Safety:** In many wired systems, the potential hazard of short circuits requires precautionary designs. Additionally, the dielectric nature of optic fibers eliminates the spark hazard.

7. **Corrosion:** Given that glass is basically inert, the corrosive effects of certain environments are not a problem.

8. **Security:** Due to its immunity to and from electromagnetic coupling and radiation, optical fiber can be used in most secure environments. Although it can be intercepted or tapped, it is very difficult to do so.

This chapter examines the issues of optical networking. Section 3-2 presents an overview of optical fiber fundamentals including a discussion on wavelengths and type of optical fibers. Section 3-3 examines the two distance-limiting parameters in fiber-optic transmission, attenuation, and dispersion. Optical components are presented in section 3-4. This includes the various types of connectors currently used on fiber. Optical networking is presented in section 3-5. An overview of SONET and FDDI are presented, followed by optical Ethernet. This section includes a discussion on setting up the building and campus distribution for fiber. Safety is extremely important when working with fiber. A brief overview of safety is presented in section 3-6.

Table 3-1 lists and identifies, by chapter section, where each of the CompTIA Network+ objectives are presented in this chapter. At the end of each chapter section is a review with comments of the Network+ objectives presented in that section. These comments are provided to help reinforce the reader's understanding of a particular Network+ objective. The chapter review also includes "Test Your Knowledge" questions to aid in the understanding of key concepts before the reader advances to the next section of the chapter. The end of the chapter includes a complete set of question plus sample certification type questions.

TABLE 3-1 **Chapter 3 CompTIA Network+ Objectives**

Domain/Objective Number	Domain/Objective Description	Section Where Objective Is Covered
1.0	*Network Architecture*	
1.4	Explain the characteristics and benefits of various WAN technologies	3-4, 3-5
1.5	Install and properly terminate various cable types and connectors using the appropriate tools	3-4, 3-5
1.7	Differentiate between network infrastructure implementations	3-2
4.0	*Troubleshooting*	
4.5	Given a scenario, troubleshoot and resolve common fiber cable issues	3-3, 3-4, 3-5
5.0	*Industry standards, practices, and network theory*	
5.2	Explain the basics of network theory and concepts	3-2, 3-4, 3-5
5.6	Summarize safety practices	3-6

3-2 THE NATURE OF LIGHT

Before you can understand the propagation of light in a glass fiber, it is necessary to review some basics of light refraction and reflection. The speed of light in free space is 3×10^8 m/s but is reduced in other media, including fiber-optic cables. The reduction as light passes into denser material results in refraction of the light. Refraction causes the light wave to be bent, as shown in Figure 3-2. The speed reduction and subsequent refraction is different for each wavelength, as shown in Figure 3-2(b). The visible light striking the prism causes refraction at both air/glass interfaces and separates the light into its various frequencies (colors) as shown. This same effect produces a rainbow, with water droplets acting as prisms to split the sunlight into the visible spectrum of colors (the various frequencies).

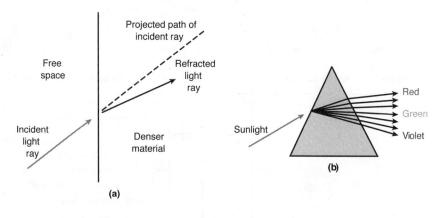

FIGURE 3-2 Refraction of light. (From Modern Electronic Communication 9/e, by J.S. Beasley & G. M. Miller, 2008, p. 782. Copyright ©2002 Pearson Education, Inc. Reprinted by permission of Pearson Education, Inc., Upper Saddle River, NJ.)

The amount of bend provided by refraction depends on the **refractive index** of the two materials involved. The refractive index, *n,* is the ratio of the speed of light in free space to the speed in a given material. It is slightly variable for different frequencies of light, but for most purposes a single value is accurate enough.

> **Refractive Index**
> Ratio of the speed of light in free space to its speed in a given material

In the fiber-optics industry, spectrum notation is stated in nanometers (nm) rather than in frequency (Hz) simply because it is easier to use, particularly in spectral-width calculations. A convenient point of commonality is that 3×10^{14} Hz, or 300THz, is equivalent to 1 μm, or 1000 nm. This relationship is shown in Figure 3-3. The one exception to this naming convention is when discussing dense wavelength division multiplexing (DWDM), which is the transmission of several optical channels, or wavelengths, in the 1550-nm range, all on the same fiber. For DWDM systems, notations, and particularly channel separations, are stated in terahertz (THz). Wavelength division multiplexing (WDM) systems are discussed in section 3-5. An electromagnetic wavelength spectrum chart is provided in Figure 3-3. The electromagnetic light waves just below the frequencies in the visible spectrum extending from 680 nm up are called **infrared light** waves. Whereas visible light has a wavelength from approximately 430 nm up to 680 nm, infrared light extends from 680 nm up to the microwaves. The frequencies from the infrared on up are termed the **optical spectrum**.

FIGURE 3-3 The electromagnetic wavelength spectrum. (From Modern Electronic Communication 9/e, by J.S. Beasley & G. M. Miller, 2008, p. 784. Copyright ©2008 Pearson Education, Inc. Reprinted by permission of Pearson Education, Inc., Upper Saddle River, NJ.)

The commonly used wavelengths in today's fiber-optic systems are

- **Multimode fiber**: (850 and 1310) nm
- **Single mode fiber**: (1310 and 1550) nm
- **Fiber to the home/business**: 1600–1625 nm

Figure 3-4 shows the typical construction of an optical fiber. The *core* is the portion of the fiber strand that carries the transmitted light. The **cladding** is the material surrounding the core. It is almost always glass, although plastic cladding of a glass fiber is available but rarely used. In any event, the refraction index for the core and the cladding are different. The cladding must have a lower index of refraction to keep the light in the core. A plastic coating surrounds the cladding to provide protection. Figure 3-5 shows examples of fiber strands from a fiber bundle.

Protective
jacket

Cladding

Core

FIGURE 3-4 Single-fiber construction. (From Modern Electronic Communication 9/e, by J.S. Beasley & G. M. Miller, 2008, p. 785. Copyright ©2008 Pearson Education, Inc. Reprinted by permission of Pearson Education, Inc., Upper Saddle River, NJ.)

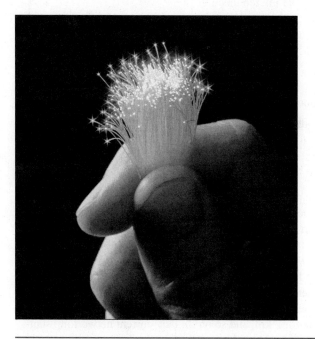

FIGURE 3-5 Fiber strands (courtesy of Anixter, Inc.).

Another measure of a fiber's light acceptance is **numerical aperture**. The numerical aperture is a basic specification provided by the manufacturer that indicates the fiber's ability to accept light and shows how much light can be off-axis and still propagate.

> **Numerical Aperture**
> A measure of a fiber's ability to accept light

Several types of optical fibers are available, with significant differences in their characteristics. The first communication-grade fibers (early 1970s) had light-carrying core diameters about equal to the wavelength of light. They could carry light in just a single waveguide mode.

The difficulty of coupling significant light into such a small fiber led to development of fibers with cores of about 20 to 100 μm. These fibers support many waveguide modes and are called **multimode fibers**. The first commercial fiber-optic systems used multimode fibers with light at 800–900 nm wavelengths. A variation of the multimode fiber was subsequently developed, termed graded-index fiber. This afforded greater bandwidth capability.

As the technology became more mature, the single-mode fibers were found to provide lower losses and even higher bandwidth. This has led to their use at 1300 nm, 1550 nm, up to 1625 nm in many telecommunication and fiber-to-the home applications. The new developments have not made old types of fiber obsolete. The application now determines the type used. The following major criteria affect the choice of fiber type:

1. Signal losses

2. Ease of light coupling and interconnection

3. Bandwidth

Figure 3-6 presents a graphic of a fiber showing three modes (that is, multimode) of propagation:

- The lowest-order mode is seen traveling along the axis of the fiber.

- The middle-order mode is reflected twice at the interface.

- The highest-order mode is reflected many times and makes many trips across the fiber.

As a result of these variable path lengths, the light entering the fiber takes a variable length of time to reach the detector. This results in a pulse-broadening or dispersion characteristic, as shown in Figure 3-6. This effect is termed **pulse dispersion** and limits the maximum distance and rate at which data (pulses of light) can be practically transmitted. You will also note that the output pulse has reduced amplitude as well as increased width. The greater the fiber length, the worse this effect will be. As a result, manufacturers rate their fiber in bandwidth per length, such as 400MHz/km. This means the fiber can successfully transmit pulses at the rate of 400MHz for 1 km, 200MHz for 2 km, and so on. In fact, current networking standards limit multimode fiber distances to 2 km. Of course, longer transmission paths are attained by locating regenerators at appropriate locations. Step-index multimode fibers are rarely used in networking due to their very high amounts of pulse dispersion and minimal bandwidth capability.

FIGURE 3-6 Modes of propagation for step-index fiber. (From Modern Electronic Communication 9/e, by J.S. Beasley & G. M. Miller, 2008, p. 787. Copyright ©2008 Pearson Education, Inc. Reprinted by permission of Pearson Education, Inc., Upper Saddle River, NJ.)

Graded-Index Fiber

In an effort to overcome the pulse-dispersion problem, the **graded-index fiber** was developed. In the manufacturing process for this fiber, the index of refraction is tailored to follow the parabolic profile shown in Figure 3-7. This results in low-order modes traveling through the constant-density material in the center. High-order modes see a lower index of refraction material farther from the core, and thus the velocity of propagation increases away from the center. Therefore, all modes, even though they take various paths and travel different distances, tend to traverse the fiber length in about the same amount of time. These fibers can therefore handle higher bandwidths and/or provide longer lengths of transmission before pulse dispersion effects destroy intelligibility and introduce bit errors.

FIGURE 3-7   Modes of propagation for graded-index fiber. (From Modern Electronic Communication 9/e, by J.S. Beasley & G. M. Miller, 2008, p. 788. Copyright ©2008 Pearson Education, Inc. Reprinted by permission of Pearson Education, Inc., Upper Saddle River, NJ.)

Graded-index multimode fibers with 50 μm-diameter cores and 125 μm cladding are used in many telecommunication systems at up to 300 megabits per second (Mbps) over 50-km ranges without repeaters. Graded-index fiber with up to a 100 μm core is used in short-distance applications that require easy coupling from the source and high data rates, such as for video and high-speed local area networks (LANs). The larger core affords better light coupling than the 50 μm core and does not significantly degrade the bandwidth capabilities. In the telecommunications industry, there are two commonly used core sizes for graded-index fiber, these being 50 μm and 62.5 μm. Both have 125 μm cladding. The large core diameter and the high NA (numerical aperture) of these fibers simplify input cabling and allow the use of relatively inexpensive connectors. Fibers are specified by the diameters of their core and cladding. For example, the fibers just described would be called 50/125 fiber and 62.5/125 fiber.

Single-Mode Fibers

A technique used to minimize pulse dispersion effects is to make the core extremely small—on the order of a few micrometers. This type accepts only a low-order mode, thereby allowing operation in high-data-rate, long-distance systems. This fiber is typically used with high-power, highly directional modulated light sources such as a laser. Fibers of this variety are called **single-mode** (or monomode) **fibers.**

Core diameters of only 7–10 μm are typical. The various types of optical fibers are shown in Figure 3-8.

FIGURE 3-8 Types of optical fiber. (From Modern Electronic Communication 9/e, by J.S. Beasley & G. M. Miller, 2008, p. 789. Copyright ©2008 Pearson Education, Inc. Reprinted by permission of Pearson Education, Inc., Upper Saddle River, NJ.)

Single-mode fibers are widely used in **long-haul** and wide area network (WAN) applications. They permit transmission of about 10Gbps and a repeater spacing of up to 80 km. These bandwidth and repeater spacing capabilities are constantly being upgraded by new developments.

When describing the core size of single-mode fibers, the term **mode field diameter** is the term more commonly used. Mode field diameter is the actual guided optical power distribution diameter. In a typical single-mode fiber, the mode field diameter is 1 μm or so larger than the core diameter. The actual value depends on the wavelength being transmitted. In fiber specification sheets, the core diameter is stated for multimode fibers, but the mode field diameter is typically stated for single-mode fibers.

Figure 3-8 provides a graphical summary of the three types of fiber discussed, including typical dimensions, refractive index profiles, and pulse-dispersion effects.

Section 3-2 Review

This section has covered the following **Network+** Exam objectives.

1.7 Differentiate between network infrastructure implementations

This chapter introduced infrared light waves. Infrared light extends from 680 nm up to the microwaves. The frequencies from the infrared on up are termed the "optical spectrum."

5.2 Explain the basics of network theory and concepts

This section has introduced the reader to the nature of light and fiber-optics; in particular, single-mode and multimode fiber. Figure 3-4 provides a good graphical view of the composition of a fiber-optic cable. The concept of how light travels in an optical waveguide such as fiber was also presented.

Test Your Knowledge

1. What are the light waves just below the frequencies in the visible spectrum?

    a. Sub-light waves

    b. Infrared light waves

    c. Refractive waves

    d. Multimode waves

    e. Polar waves

2. What is the material surrounding the core of an optical waveguide called?

    a. Cladding

    b. Aperture

    c. Mode field

    d. Step-index

    e. Graded-index

3. Single-mode fiber cables have a core diameter of about 7–10 micrometers. True or False?

3-3 FIBER ATTENUATION AND DISPERSION

There are two key distance-limiting parameters in fiber-optic transmissions: attenuation and dispersion.

Attenuation

Attenuation is the loss of power introduced by the fiber. This loss accumulates as the light is propagated through the fiber strand. The loss is expressed in dB/km (decibels per kilometer) of length. The loss, or attenuation, of the signal is due to the combination of four factors: scattering, absorption, macrobending, and microbending. Two other terms for attenuation are intrinsic and extrinsic.

Scattering is the primary loss factor over the three wavelength ranges. Scattering in telecommunication systems accounts for 96 percent of the loss and is the basis of the attenuation curves and values, such as that shown in Figure 3-9, and industry data sheets. The scattering is known as *Rayleigh scattering* and is caused by refractive index fluctuations. Rayleigh scattering decreases as wavelength increases, as shown in Figure 3-9.

Absorption is the second loss factor, a composite of light interaction with the atomic structure of the glass. It involves the conversion of optical power to heat. One portion of the absorption loss is due to the presence of OH hydroxol ions dissolved in the glass during manufacture. These cause the water attenuation or OH peaks, shown in Figure 3-9, and other attenuation curves.

Macrobending is the loss caused by the light mode breaking up and escaping into the cladding when the fiber bend becomes too tight. As the wavelength increases, the loss in a bend increases. Although losses are in fractions of dB, the bend radius in small splicing trays and patching enclosures should be minimal.

Microbending is a type of loss caused by mechanical stress placed on the fiber strand, usually in terms of deformation resulting from too much pressure being applied to the cable. For example, excessively tight tie wraps or clamps will contribute to this loss. This loss is noted in fractions of a dB.

> **Scattering**
> Caused by refractive index fluctuations; accounts for 96 percent of attenuation loss

> **Absorption**
> Light interaction with the atomic structure of the fiber material; also involves the conversion of optical power to heat

> **Macrobending**
> Loss due to light breaking up and escaping into the cladding

> **Microbending**
> Loss caused by very small mechanical deflections and stress on the fiber

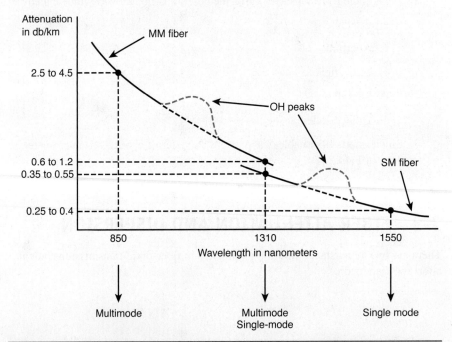

FIGURE 3-9 Typical attenuation of cabled fiber strands. (From Modern Electronic Communication 9/e, by J.S. Beasley & G. M. Miller, 2008, p. 792. Copyright ©2008 Pearson Education, Inc. Reprinted by permission of Pearson Education, Inc., Upper Saddle River, NJ.)

Dispersion

Dispersion, or pulse broadening, is the second of the two key distance-limiting parameters in a fiber-optic transmission system. It is a phenomenon in which the light pulse spreads out in time as it propagates along the fiber strand. This results in a broadening of the pulse. If the pulse broadens excessively, it can blend into the adjacent digital time slots and cause bit errors. Figure 3-10 illustrates the effects of dispersion on a light pulse.

> **Dispersion**
> Broadening of a light pulse as it propagates through a fiber strand

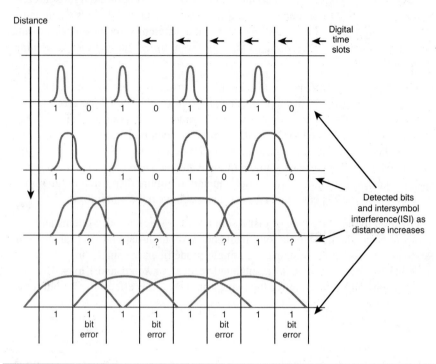

FIGURE 3-10 Pulse broadening or dispersion in optical fibers. (Adapted from Modern Electronic Communication 9/e, by J.S. Beasley & G. M. Miller, 2008, p. 793. Copyright ©2008 Pearson Education, Inc. Adapted by permission of Pearson Education, Inc., Upper Saddle River, NJ.)

There are three types of dispersion:

- **Modal dispersion:** The broadening of a pulse due to different path lengths taken through the fiber by different modes.

- **Chromatic dispersion:** The broadening of a pulse due to different propagation velocities of the spectral components of the light pulse.

- **Polarization mode dispersion:** The broadening of a pulse due to the different propagation velocities of the X and Y polarization components of the light pulse.

Modal dispersion occurs predominantly in multimode fiber. From a light source, the light rays can take many paths as they propagate along the fiber. Some light rays do travel in a straight line, but most take variable-length routes. As a result, the rays arrive at the detector at different times, and the result is pulse broadening. This was shown in Figures 3-6 and 3-7. The use of graded-index fiber greatly reduces the effects of modal dispersion and therefore increases the bandwidth to about 1GHz/km. On the other hand, single-mode fiber does not exhibit modal dispersion, given that only a single mode is transmitted.

A second equally important type of dispersion is chromatic. Chromatic dispersion is present in both single-mode and multimode fibers. Basically, the light source, both lasers and LEDs, produce several different wavelength light rays when generating the light pulse. Each light ray travels at a different velocity, and as a result, these rays arrive at the receiver detector at different times, causing the broadening of the pulse.

There is a point where dispersion is actually at zero, this being determined by the refractive index profile. This happens near 1310 nm and is called the **zero dispersion wavelength**. By altering the refractive index profile, this zero dispersion wavelength can be shifted to the 1550-nm region. Such fibers are called *dispersion-shifted*. This is significant because the 1550-nm region exhibits a lower attenuation than at 1310 nm. This becomes an operational advantage, particularly to long-haul carriers because with minimum attenuation and minimum dispersion in the same wavelength region, repeater and regenerator spacing can be maximized.

Polarization mode is the type of dispersion found in single-mode systems and becomes of particular concern in long-haul and WAN high-data-rate digital and high-bandwidth analog video systems. In a single-mode fiber, the single propagating mode has two polarizations, horizontal and vertical, or X axis and Y axis. The index of refraction can be different for the two components; this affects their relative velocity as shown in Figure 3-11.

FIGURE 3-11 Polarization mode dispersion in single-mode fiber. (From Modern Electronic Communication 9/e, by J.S. Beasley & G. M. Miller, 2008, p. 794. Copyright ©2008 Pearson Education, Inc. Reprinted by permission of Pearson Education, Inc., Upper Saddle River, NJ.)

Dispersion Compensation

A considerable amount of fiber in use today was installed in the 1980s and early 1990s. This cable was called the class IVa variety. These cables were optimized to operate in the 1310-nm region, which means their zero-dispersion point was in the 1310-nm wavelength. Due to continuous network expansion needs in recent years, it is often desired to add transmission capacity to the older fiber cables by using the 1550-nm region, particularly because the attenuation at 1550 nm is less than at

1310 nm. One major problem arises at this point. The dispersion value is higher at 1550 nm, which severely limits its distance capability.

To overcome this problem, a fiber called **dispersion compensating fiber** was developed. This fiber acts as an equalizer, negative dispersion canceling positive dispersion. The fiber consists of a small coil normally placed in the equipment rack just prior to the optical receiver input. This does introduce some insertion loss (3–10 dB) and may require the addition of an optical-line amplifier.

A new device is a **fiber Bragg grating**. This technology involves etching irregularities onto a short strand of fiber, which changes the index of refraction and, in turn, reflects slower wavelengths to the output before the faster ones. This results in a compressed, or narrower, light pulse, minimizing intersymbol interference (ISI).

> **Dispersion Compensating Fiber**
> Acts as an equalizer, canceling dispersion effects and yielding close to zero dispersion in the 1550-nm region
>
> **Fiber Bragg Grating**
> A short strand of modified fiber that changes the index of refraction and minimizes intersymbol interference

Section 3-3 Review

This section has covered the following **Network+** Exam objectives.

4.5 Given a scenario, troubleshoot and resolve common fiber cable issue

This section introduced the concepts of attenuation and macrobending. Attenuation is the loss of power introduced by the fiber. This loss accumulates as the light is propagated through the fiber strand. Macrobending is the loss caused by the light mode breaking up and escaping into the cladding when the fiber bend becomes too tight. As the wavelength increases, the loss in a bend increases. Although losses are in fractions of dB, the bend radius in small splicing trays and patching enclosures should be minimal.

5.2 Explain the basics of network theory and concepts

There are two key distance-limiting parameters in a fiber-optic transmission system. These are attenuation and dispersion, and these concepts were presented. Knowledge of the properties of fiber-optics is critical for planning a network installation or upgrade.

Test Your Knowledge

1. Which of the following terms refers to broadening of a light pulse as it propagates through a fiber strand?

   a. Pulse shaping

   b. Diffusion

   c. Absorption

   d. Dispersion

2. Which of the following terms is caused by refractive index fluctuations and accounts for 96% of attenuation loss?

a. Scattering

b. Absorption

c. Dispersion

d. Diffusion

3. Which of the following terms refers to loss due to light breaking up and escaping into the cladding?

a. Microbending

b. Scattering

c. Macrobending

d. Absorption

3-4 OPTICAL COMPONENTS

DL
Diode laser

LED
Light-emitting diode

Two kinds of light sources are used in fiber-optic communication systems: the diode laser (**DL**) and the high-radiance light-emitting diode (**LED**). In designing the optimum system, the special qualities of each light source should be considered. Diode lasers and LEDs bring to systems different characteristics:

1. Power levels

2. Temperature sensitivities

3. Response times

4. Lifetimes

5. Characteristics of failure

The diode laser is a preferred source for moderate-band to wideband systems. It offers a fast response time (typically less than 1 ns) and can couple high levels of useful optical power (usually several mW) into an optical fiber with a small core and a small numerical aperture. The DL is usually used as the source for single-mode fiber because LEDs have a low input coupling efficiency.

Some systems operate at a slower bit rate and require more modest levels of fiber-coupled optical power (50–250 µW). These applications allow the use of high-radiance LEDs. The LED is cheaper, requires less complex driving circuitry than a DL, and needs no thermal or optical stabilizations.

The light output wavelength spread, or spectrum, of the DL is much narrower than that of LEDs: about 1 nm compared with about 40 nm for an LED. Narrow spectra are advantageous in systems with high bit rates since the dispersion effects of the fiber on pulse width are reduced, and thus pulse degradation over long distances is minimized.

Another laser device, called a **distributed feedback (DFB) laser**, uses techniques that provide optical feedback in the laser cavity. This enhances output stability, which produces a narrow and more stable spectral width. Widths are in the range of 0.01–0.1 nm. This allows the use of more channels in **dense wavelength division multiplex (DWDM)** systems. Another even more recent development is an entirely new class of laser semiconductors called **vertical cavity surface emitting lasers (VCSELs)**. These lasers can support a much faster signal rate than LEDs, including gigabit networks. They do not have some of the operational and stability problems of conventional lasers, however.

VCSELs have the simplicity of LEDs with the performance of lasers. Their primary wavelength of operation is in the 750–850-nm region, although development work is underway in the 1310-nm region. Reliabilities approaching 10^7 hours are projected.

Most lasers emit a fixed wavelength, but there is a class called **tunable lasers** in which the fundamental wavelength can be shifted a few nanometers, but not from a modulation point of view as in frequency modulation. Figure 3-12 shows an example of a tunable laser diode module. The primary market for these devices is in a network operations environment where DWDM is involved. Traffic routing is often made by wavelength, and, as such, wavelengths or transmitters must be assigned and reassigned to accommodate dynamic routing or networking, bandwidth on demand, seamless restoration (serviceability), optical packet switching, and so on. Tunable lasers are used along with either passive or tunable WDM filters.

Distributed Feedback (DFB) Laser
A more stable laser suitable for use in DWDM systems

Dense Wavelength Division Multiplex (DWDM)
Incorporates the propagation of several wavelengths in the 1550-nm range for a single fiber

Vertical Cavity Surface Emitting Lasers (VCSELs)
Lasers with the simplicity of LEDs and the performance of lasers

Tunable Laser
Laser in which the fundamental wavelength can be shifted a few nanometers, ideal for traffic routing in DWDM systems

FIGURE 3-12 A tunable laser diode module (courtesy of Fujitsu Compound Semiconductor, Inc.).

Intermediate Components

The typical fiber-optic telecommunication link (as shown previously in Figure 3-1) is a light source or transmitter and light detector or receiver interconnected by a strand of optical **fiber**, **light pipe**, or **glass**. An increasing number of specialized networks and system applications have various intermediate components along the span between the transmitter and the receiver. A brief review of these devices and their uses is provided in the list that follows.

Fiber, Light Pipe, Glass

Terms used to describe a fiber-optic strand

Isolator

An inline passive device that allows optical power to flow only in one direction

Received Signal Level (RSL)

The input signal level to an optical receiver

- **Isolators**: An **isolator** is an inline passive device that allows optical power to flow in one direction only.

- **Attenuators**: Attenuators are used to reduce the **received signal level (RSL)**. They are available in fixed and variable configurations.

- **Branching devices**: Branching devices are used in simplex systems where a single optical signal is divided and sent to several receivers, such as point-to-multipoint data or a CATV distribution system.

- **Splitters**: Splitters are used to split, or divide, the optical signal for distribution to any number of places.

- **Wavelength division multiplexers**: Wavelength division multiplexers combine or divide two or more optical signals, each having a different wavelength. They are sometimes called optical beam splitters.

- **Optical-line amplifiers**: Optical-line amplifiers are analog amplifiers. Placement can be at the optical transmitter output, midspan, or near the optical receiver.

Detectors

The devices used to convert the transmitted light back into an electrical signal are a vital link in a fiber-optic system. This important link is often overlooked in favor of the light source and fibers. However, simply changing from one photodetector to another can increase the capacity of a system by an order of magnitude.

The important characteristics of light detectors are as follows:

- **Responsivity:** This is a measure of output current for a given light power launched into the diode.

- **Response speed:** This determines the maximum data rate capability of the detector.

- **Spectral response:** This determines the responsivity that is achieved relative to the wavelength at which responsivity is specified.

Optical fibers are joined either in a permanent fusion splice or with a mechanical splice (for example, connectors and camsplices). The connector allows repeated matings and unmatings. Above all, these connections must lose as little light as possible. Low loss depends on correct alignment of the core of one fiber to another, or to a source or detector. Losses for properly terminated fusion and mechanical splices is typically 0.2 dB or less. Signal loss in fibers occurs when two fibers are not perfectly aligned within a connector. Axial misalignment typically causes the greatest loss—about 0.5 dB for a 10 percent displacement. Figure 3-13 illustrates this condition as well as other loss sources.

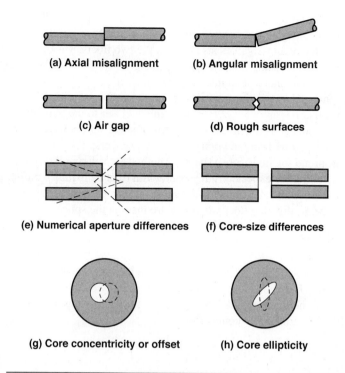

(a) Axial misalignment (b) Angular misalignment

(c) Air gap (d) Rough surfaces

(e) Numerical aperture differences (f) Core-size differences

(g) Core concentricity or offset (h) Core ellipticity

FIGURE 3-13 Sources of connection loss. (From Modern Electronic Communication 9/e, by J.S. Beasley & G. M. Miller, 2008, p. 806. Copyright ©2008 Pearson Education, Inc. Reprinted by permission of Pearson Education, Inc., Upper Saddle River, NJ.)

Angular misalignment [Figure 3-13(b)] can usually be well controlled in a connector. Most connectors leave an air gap, as shown in Figure 3-13(c). The amount of gap affects loss since light leaving the transmitting fiber spreads conically.

The losses due to rough end surfaces shown in Figure 3-13(d) are often caused by a poor cut, or "cleave," but can be minimized by polishing or using pre-polished connectors. Polishing typically takes place after a fiber has been placed in a connector. The source of connection losses shown in Figure 3-13(d) can, for the most part, be controlled by a skillful cable splicer. There are four other situations that can cause additional connector or splice loss, although in smaller values. These are shown in Figure 3-13(e), (f), (g), and (h). These are related to the nature of the fiber strand at the point of connection and are beyond the control of the cable splicer. The effect of these losses can be minimized somewhat by the use of a rotary mechanical splice, which by the joint rotation will get a better core alignment.

With regard to connectorization and splicing, there are two techniques to consider for splicing. **Fusion splicing** is a long-term method, in which two fibers are fused or welded together. The two ends are stripped of their coating, cut or cleaved, and inserted into the splicer. The ends of the fiber are aligned, and an electric arc is fired across the ends, melting the glass and fusing the two ends together. There are both manual and automatic fusion splicers; the choice usually depends on the number of splices to be done on a given job, technician skill levels available, and of course the budget. Typical insertion losses of less than 0.1 dB—frequently in the 0.05 dB range—can be consistently achieved.

Fusion Splicing
A long-term method where two fibers are fused or welded together

Mechanical splices can be permanent and an economical choice for certain fiber-splicing applications. Mechanical splices also join two fibers together, but they differ from fusion splices in that an air gap exists between the two fibers. This results in a glass-air-glass interface, causing a severe double change in the index of refraction. This change results in an increase in insertion loss and reflected power. The condition can be minimized by applying an **index-matching gel** to the joint. The gel is a jellylike substance that has an index of refraction much closer to the glass than air. Therefore, the index change is much less severe. Mechanical splices have been universally popular for repair and for temporary or laboratory work. They are quick, cheap, easy, and appropriate for small jobs. The best method for splicing depends on the application, including the expected future bandwidth (that is, gigabit), traffic, the job size, and economics. The loss in a mechanical splice can be minimized by using an OTDR to properly align the fiber when you are making the splice.

Fiber Connectorization

For fiber connectorization, there are several choices on the market such as **SC, ST, FC, LC, MT-RJ**, and others. The choice of the connector is typically dictated by the hardware being used and the fiber application. Figure 3-14(a–e) provides some examples of SC, ST, FC, LC, and MTRJ connectors

(a) SC connector

(b) ST connector

(c) MT-RJ connector

(d) LC Connector

(e) FC Connector

FIGURE 3-14   Typical fiber connections. [(a), (b), and (c) From Modern Electronic Communication 9/e, by J.S. Beasley & G. M. Miller, 2008, p. 808. Copyright ©2008 Pearson Education, Inc. Reprinted by permission of Pearson Education, Inc., Upper Saddle River, NJ. (d) and (e) from Black Box Corporation.]

Some general requirements for fiber connectors are as follows:

- Easy and quick to install
- Low insertion loss—a properly installed connector will have as little as 0.25 dB insertion loss
- High return loss greater than 50 dB—this is increasingly important in gigabit networks, DWDM systems, high-bandwidth video, and so on
- Repeatability
- Economical

In preparing the fiber for splicing or connectorization, only the coating is removed from the fiber strand. The core and the cladding are not separable. The 125μm cladding diameter is the portion that fits into the splice or connector, and therefore most devices can handle both single and multimode fiber.

Sometimes the issue arises as to the advisability of splicing together fibers of different core sizes. The one absolute rule is do *not* splice single- and multimode fiber together! Similarly, good professional work does not allow different sizes of multimode fiber to be spliced together. However, in an emergency, different sizes can be spliced together if the following is considered:

When transmitting from a small- to large-core diameter, there will be minimal, if any, increase in insertion loss. However, when the transmission is from a larger to a smaller core size, there will be added insertion loss and a considerable increase in reflected power should be expected.

Industrial practice has confirmed the acceptability of different core size interchangeability for emergency repairs in the field, mainly as the result of tests with 50 m and 62.5 m multimode fiber for a local area network.

Section 3-4 Review

This section has covered the following **Network+** Exam objectives.

1.4 Explain the characteristics and benefits of various WAN technologies

This section introduced DWDM (Dense Wave Division Multiplexing), which incorporates the propagation of several wavelengths in the 1550nm range for a single fiber.

1.5 Install and properly terminate various cable types and connectors using the appropriate tools

This section presented a look at optical components. Issues with connection loss are shown in Figure 3-13, and the different types of connectors are shown in Figure 3-14.

3-5   OPTICAL NETWORKING

The need for increased bandwidth is pushing the fiber-optic community into optical networking solutions that are almost beyond the imagination of even the most advanced networking person. Optical solutions for long-haul, wide area, metropolitan, campus, and local area networks are available. Cable companies are already using the high-bandwidth capability of fiber to distribute cable programming as well as data throughout their service areas.

The capital cost differences between a fiber system and a copper-based system are diminishing, and the choice of networking technology for new networks is no longer just budgetary. Fiber has the capacity to carry more bandwidth, and because the fiber infrastructure cost decreases, fiber will be chosen to carry the data. Of course, the copper infrastructure is already in place, and new developments are providing increases in data speed over copper (for example, CAT6 and CAT7). However, optical fiber is smaller and easier to install in already crowded ducts and conduits. Additionally, security is enhanced because it is difficult to tap optical fiber without detection. Will fiber replace copper in computer networks? For many years, a hybrid solution of fiber and copper is expected.

Defining Optical Networking

Optical networks are becoming a major part of data delivery in homes, in businesses, and for long-haul carriers. The telecommunications industry has been using fiber to carry long-haul traffic for many years. Some major carriers are merging with cable companies so that they are poised to provide high-bandwidth capabilities to the home. Developments in optical technologies are reshaping the way we will use fiber in future optical networks.

But there is a new slant with optical networks. Dense wave division multiplexing and tunable lasers have changed the way optical networks can be implemented. It is now possible to transport many wavelengths over a single fiber. Lab tests at AT&T have successfully demonstrated the transmission of 1,022 wavelengths over a single fiber. Such transport of multiple wavelengths opens up the possibilities to routing or switching many different data protocols over the same fiber but on different wavelengths. The development of cross-connects that allow data to arrive on one wavelength and leave on another opens other possibilities.

Synchronous optical network (**SONET**) and **SDH** were the North American and international standards for the long-haul optical transport of telecommunication for many years. SONET/SDH defined a standard for the following:

- Increase in network reliability

- Network management

- Defining methods for the synchronous multiplexing of digital signals such as DS-1 (1.544Mbps) and DS-3 (44.736Mbps)

- Defining a set of generic operating/equipment standards

- Flexible architecture

SONET/SDH specifies the various optical carrier (OC) levels and the equivalent electrical synchronous transport signals (**STS**) used for transporting data in a fiber-optic transmission system. Optical network data rates are typically specified in terms of the SONET hierarchy. When a digital signal is carried over SONET, the signal is essentially enveloped or encapsulated within the optical carrier. Table 3-2 lists the more common data rates. The table shows the capacity, not equivalence. It merely states that OC-1 is capable of carrying 28 DS-1s or 1 DS-3. With the conversion overhead, it yields a bit rate of 51.84Mbps when carrying one DS-3 signal.

SONET/SDH
Synchronous optical network; protocol standard for optical transmission in long-haul communication/synchronous digital hierarchy

STS
Synchronous transport signals

TABLE 3-2 SONET Hierarchy Data Rates

Signal	Bit Rate	Capacity
OC-1 (STS-1)	51.840Mbps	28DS-Is or 1 DS-3
OC-3 (STS-3)	155.52Mbps	84DS-Is or 3 DS-3s
OC-12 (STS-12)	622.080Mbps	336 DS-1s or 12 DS-3s
OC-48 (STS-48)	2.48832Gbps	1344 DS-1s or 48 DS-3s
OC-192 (STS-192)	9.95328Gbps	5376 DS-Is or 192 DS-3s

OC: Optical carrier—DS-1: 1.544Mbps

STS: Synchronous transport signal—DS-3: 44.736Mbps

FTTC
Fiber to the curb

FTTH
Fiber to the home

The architectures of fiber networks for the home include providing fiber to the curb (**FTTC**) and fiber to the home (**FTTH**). FTTC is being deployed today. It provides high bandwidth to a location with proximity to the home and provides a high-speed data link, via copper (twisted-pair), using VDSL (very high-data digital subscriber line). This is a cost-effective way to provide large-bandwidth capabilities to a home. FTTH will provide unlimited bandwidth to the home; however, the key to its success is the development of a low-cost optical-to-electronic converter in the home and laser transmitters that are tunable to any desired channel.

FTTB
Fiber to the business

FTTD
Fiber to the desktop

Another architecture in place is fiber to the business (**FTTB**). A fiber connection to a business provides for the delivery of all current communication technologies including data, voice, video, conferencing, and so on. An additional type is fiber to the desktop (**FTTD**). This setup requires that the computer has a fiber network interface card (NIC). FTTD is useful in applications such as computer animation work that has high-bandwidth requirements.

Optical Ethernet
Ethernet data running over a fiber link

Conventional high-speed Ethernet networks are operating over fiber. This is called **optical Ethernet** and uses the numerics listed in Table 3-3 for describing the type of network configuration. Fiber helps to eliminate the 100-m distance limit associated with unshielded twisted-pair (UTP) copper cable. This is possible because fiber has a lower attenuation loss. In a star network, the computer and the switch are directly connected. If the fiber is used in a star network, an internal or external media converter is required. The media converter converts the electronic signal to an optical signal, and vice versa. A media converter is required at both ends, as shown in Figure 3-15. The media converter is typically built in to the network interface card.

TABLE 3-3 Optical Ethernet Numerics

Numeric	Description
10BASE-F	10Mbps Ethernet over fiber—generic specification for fiber
10BASE-FB	10Mbps Ethernet over fiber—part of the IEEE 10BASE-F specification; segments can be up to 2 km in length
10BASE-FL	10Mbps Ethernet over fiber—segments can be up to 2 km in length; it replaces the FOIRL specification.

Numeric	Description
10BASE-FP	A passive fiber star network; segments can be up to 500 m in length
100BASE-FX	A 100Mbps fast Ethernet standard that uses two fiber strands
1000BASE-LX	Gigabit Ethernet standard that uses fiber strands using long-wavelength transmitters
1000BASE-SX	Gigabit Ethernet standard using short-wavelength transmitters
10GBASE-R	10 gigabit (10.325Gbps) Ethernet for LANs
10GBASE-W	10 gigabit (9.95328Gbps) Ethernet for WANs using OC-192 and SONET Framing

Multimode fiber—2 km length single mode—10 km length

FIGURE 3-15 An example of connecting a PC to an Ethernet hub or switch via fiber. (From Modern Electronic Communication 9/e, by J.S. Beasley & G. M. Miller, 2008, p. 820. Copyright ©2008 Pearson Education, Inc. Reprinted by permission of Pearson Education, Inc., Upper Saddle River, NJ.)

Two important issues to be considered when designing a fiber network are the guidelines for the following:

Building distribution

Campus distribution

The following subsections discuss techniques for planning the fiber plant, the distribution of the fiber, and the equipment and connections used to interconnect the fiber. The first example is for a building distribution, the second for a campus distribution.

Building Distribution

Figure 3-16 shows an example of a simple fiber network for a building. Fiber lines consist of a minimum of two fibers, one for transmitting and one for receiving. Fiber networks work in the full-duplex mode, meaning that the links must be able to simultaneously transmit and receive; hence, the need for two fibers on each link.

FIGURE 3-16 A simple fiber distribution in a building.

Fiber Cross-connect

Optical patch panel used to interconnect fiber cables

Item A is the main fiber feed for the building. This is called a *building distribution (BD)* fiber. The two fibers for the BD link terminate into a main fiber cross-connect (item B). A **fiber cross-connect** is the optical patch panel used to connect the fiber cables to the next link. The fiber cross-connect typically uses mechanical splices to make the fiber connections.

Items C and E represent the active equipment in the main distribution closet in the building. The active equipment could be a router, switch, or telephone PBX (private branch exchange). Item D shows the jumpers connecting the main fiber cross-connect (item B) to the active equipment (item C).

GBIC

Gigabit interface converter

The active equipment will need some type of optical interface for the optical-electrical signal conversion, such as a **GBIC** (pronounced "gee-bick"). GBIC, or the Gigabit Interface Converter, is a hot-swappable transceiver that is used for transmitting and receiving higher-speed signals over fiber-optic lines. This is shown in Figure 3-17(a).

SFP

Small Form Pluggable

To increase port density on the active network equipment, the industry has been moving toward using a mini-GBIC or **SFP** (Small Form factor Pluggable). This is shown in Figure 3-17(b) The SFP is more than half the size of the GBIC shown in Figure 3-17(a). These modules are used to connect to other fiber-optic systems such as 1000Base-SX, which operates with multimode fiber in a short wavelength, and 1000Base-LX, which operates with the single-mode fiber in a longer wavelength. GBIC and SFP modules are designed to plug into interfaces such as routers and switches.

FIGURE 3-17 The Cisco (a) GBIC, (b) SFP, (c) XENPAK, (d) X2, and (e) XFP optical-to-fiber transceivers (courtesy of Cisco).

In the ten gigabits (10G) Ethernet world, several versions of optical-to-fiber transceivers have been developed. It all started with the **XENPAK**, shown in Figure 3-17(c), transceivers which were followed by the **XPAK** and the **X2,** shown in Figure 3-17(d). These later transceiver modules are smaller than the XENPAK. Then, an even smaller size module called XFP was developed. The **XFP,** shown in Figure 3-17(e), has lower power consumption than the XENPAK, XPAK, and X2, but it still can deliver up to 80 km in distance, which is the same as the older modules. With its small size, its lower power consumption, and its reachability, the XFP was thought to be the future of the 10G transceiver. Recently, a new type of 10G transceiver has emerged, and it is a **SFP+**. Its look and size are identical to a 1000Base SFP transceiver. To be able to deliver 10G speed in its small form factor, the working distance that the SFP+ can deliver is reduced to 40 km. So, if the distance is not of the concern, then SFP+ might be the 10G transceiver of choice. These modules support 850, 1310, and 1550 fiber wavelengths. Figure 3-17 collectively shows examples of 1000Base and 10GBASE transceivers.

Referring to Figure 3-16, items F and G show the two fiber pairs patched into the main fiber cross-connect connecting to the **IDC**. These fibers (F and G) are called the interconnect (**IC**) fibers. The fibers terminate into the IDC fiber cross-connects (items H and I).

Items J and K in Figure 3-16 are fiber jumpers that connect the fiber cross-connect to the IDC active equipment. Once again, the active equipment must have a GBIC or some other interface for the optical-electrical signal conversion.

> **XENPAK, XPAK, X2, XFP, SFP+**
> The ten gigabit interface adapter

> **IDC**
> Intermediate distribution closet
>
> **IC**
> Interconnect fibers branch exchange—item D shows the jumpers connecting the main fiber cross-connect (item B) to the active equipment (item C)

A general rule for fiber is that the distribution in a building should be limited to "2 deep." This means that a building should have only the main distribution and the intermediate distribution that feeds the horizontal distribution to the work area.

Figure 3-18(a) and (b) illustrate an example of the "2-deep" rule. Figure 3-18(a) shows an example of a building distribution that meets the "2-deep" rule. The IDC is at the first layer, and the horizontal distribution (HD) is at the second layer. Figure 3-18(b) illustrates an example of a fiber distribution that does not meet the "2-deep" rule. In this example, the HD and work area are 3-deep, or 3 layers from the building's main distribution.

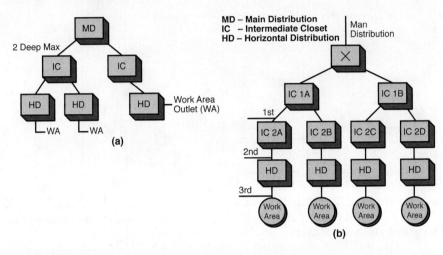

FIGURE 3-18 Examples of the "2-deep" rule: (a) the distribution meeting the requirement; (b) the distribution not meeting the requirement.

Campus Distribution

Figure 3-19 shows a map of the fiber distribution for a campus network. This map shows how the fiber is interconnected and data is distributed throughout the campus and is called a **logical fiber map.** Another style of map often used to show the fiber distribution is a **physical fiber map,** as shown in Figure 3-20. This map shows the routing of the fiber but also shows detail about the terrain, underground conduit, and entries into buildings. Both map styles are important and necessary for documentation and planning of the fiber network. This material focuses on the documentation provided in the logical fiber map.

Logical Fiber Map

Shows how the fiber is interconnected and data is distributed throughout a campus

Physical Fiber Map

Shows the routing of the fiber but also shows detail about the terrain, underground conduit, and entries into buildings

FIGURE 3-19 A logical fiber map.

Referring to the logical fiber map in Figure 3-19, this campus network has two connections to the Telco: the primary Telco demarcation (item A) in building 1 and the secondary Telco demarcation (item B) in building 2. These two Telco connections provide for redundant Internet and wide area network data services. If something happens in building 1 that shuts down the external data services, Internet and WAN data traffic can be switched to building 2. Also data traffic can be distributed over both connections to prevent bottlenecking. Buildings 1 and 2 are interconnected with 36 multimode (**mm**) and 48 single-mode (**sm**) fibers. This is documented on the line interconnecting buildings 1 and 2 (item C) and written as 36/48 (item D). The dotted line between buildings 1 and 2 indicates the **backbone** or main fiber distribution for the campus network. The bulk of the campus network data traffic travels over these fibers. The campus backbone (green dotted line) also extends from building 2 to building 4 and from building 3 to building 5.

This setup enables the data to be distributed over the campus. For example, data traffic from the primary Telco demarcation (item A) reaches building 12 by traveling via fiber through buildings 1-3-5-11-12. If the building 3 connection is down, then data traffic from the primary Telco demarcation can be routed through buildings 1-2-4-7-6-5-11-12. What happens to the data traffic for building 12 if building 5 is out of operation? In this case, data traffic to/from buildings 11 and 12 is lost.

Item E shows a fiber connection to/from buildings 4 and 10. This fiber bundle provides an alternative data path from the primary Telco demarcation to the other side of the campus network.

mm
Multimode

sm
Single mode

Backbone
Main fiber distribution

FIGURE 3-20 An example of a physical fiber map (courtesy of Palo Alto Utilities).

The cabling between buildings is a mix of multimode and single-mode fiber. The older fiber runs a 12/12 cable (12 multimode/12 single-mode). Fiber cables are bundled in groups of 12 fibers. For example, a 12/12 fiber will have two bundles: one bundle of multimode and one bundle of single-mode fiber. A 36/48 cable will have 3 bundles of multimode and 4 bundles of single-mode fiber. Each bundle of fibers is color-coded as listed in Table 3-4. For example, in a 36/48 fiber cable, the 3 bundles of multimode are in loose tubes that are color-coded blue/orange/green. The four bundles of single mode are in loose tubes that are color-coded brown/slate/white/red.

TABLE 3-4   The Fiber Color-code for the Twelve Fibers in a Bundle

Pair	Color
1/2	Blue/Orange
3/4	Green/Brown
5/6	Slate/White
7/8	Red/Black
9/10	Yellow/Violet
11/12	Rose/Aqua Marine

In this example, the newer fiber cabling installations were run with a 36/48 and 24/48 mix. Why the difference? The main reason is economics. The cost per foot (meter) of the new fiber is cheaper, so more fiber can be placed in a cable for the same cost per foot.

The fiber connecting the buildings is typically run either in PVC conduit, which makes it easy to add or remove fiber cables, or in trenches or tunnels. Running fiber in trenches is very expensive and significantly increases the installation cost. (*Note:* Network administrators need to be aware of any trenches being dug on campus.) Even if the budget doesn't allow for buying fiber at the time, at least have a conduit and pull line installed.

Fiber provides substantially increased bandwidth for building and campus networks and can easily handle the combined traffic of PCs, switches, routers, video, and voice services. Fiber has greater capacity, which enables faster transfer of data, minimizes congestion problems, and provides tremendous growth potential for each of the fiber runs.

Another important application of optical Ethernet is extending the reach of the Ethernet network from the local and campus network out to the metropolitan and wide area networks. Essentially, optical networking is introducing Ethernet as a viable WAN technology. Extending Ethernet into a WAN is a seamless integration of the technologies. The Ethernet extension into the WAN simply requires optical adapters such as a GBIC (gigabit interface converter) and two fiber strands, one for transmitting and one for receiving. Conventional high-speed Ethernet LANs operating over fiber use the numerics listed in Table 3-4 for describing the network configuration.

Section 3-5 Review

This section has covered the following **Network+** Exam objectives.

   1.4 Explain the characteristics and benefits of various WAN technologies

This section has introduced SONET, OC3, and OC12.

1.5 Install and properly terminate various cable types and connectors using the appropriate tools

The active equipment will need some type of optical interface for the optical-electrical signal conversion from fiber to Ethernet. One device is a GBIC, or the Gigabit Interface Converter. In the 10 gigabits (10G) Ethernet world, several versions of optical-to-fiber transceivers have been developed: the XENPAK, the XPAK, and the X2 are shown in Figure 3-17(d).

4.5 Given a scenario, troubleshoot and resolve common fiber issue

This section introduce the SFP/GBIC transceiver. Industry has made this move to increase port density on the active network equipment.

5.1 Explain the basics of change management procedures

Documenting a fiber-optic network becomes extremely important when trying to keep track of how the data is routed and which fibers are being used. Equally important are which fibers are available for future expansion.

5.2 Explain the basics of network theory and concepts

A block diagram for fiber distribution in a building is provided in Figure 3-18. A logical fiber map that shows how the fiber is interconnected in a network is provided in Figure 3-19. An example of a physical fiber map showing detail such as terrain and entries into a building is provided in Figure 3-20.

Test Your Knowledge

1. What does the logical fiber map show? (Select all that apply.)

    a. How data is distributed throughout a campus

    b. The routing of the fiber

    c. Terrain and underground conduits

    d. How the fiber is interconnected

2. What does the physical fiber map show? (Select all that apply.)

    a. The routing of the fiber

    b. The LAN connections

    c. Terrain issues

    d. Router placement

3. What is the name of the optical-to-fiber interface used at 10 gigabits?

    a. GBIC

    b. 10GBIC

    c. XENPAK

    d. ZENPAK

3-6 SAFETY

Any discussion of fiber-optics or optical networking is not complete unless it addresses safety issues, even if only briefly. As the light propagates through a fiber, two factors will further attenuate the light if there is an open circuit:

1. A light beam will disperse or fan out from an open connector.

2. If a damaged fiber is exposed on a broken cable, the end will likely be shattered, which will considerably disperse the light. In addition, there would be a small amount of attenuation from the strand within the cable, plus any connections or splices along the way.

However, there are two factors that can increase the optical power at an exposed fiber end.

1. There could be a lens in a pigtail that could focus more optical rays down the cable.

2. In the newer DWDM systems, there will be several optical signals in the same fiber; although separate, they will be relatively close together in wavelength. The optical power incident on the eye will then be multiplied.

There are two factors to be aware of:

1. The eye can't see fiber-optic communication wavelength, so there is no pain or awareness of exposure. However, the retina can still be exposed and damaged. (Refer to Figure 3-3, the electromagnetic spectrum.)

2. Eye damage is a function of the optical power, wavelengths, source or spot diameter, and duration of exposure.

So for those working on fiber-optic equipment:

1. *DO NOT EVER* look into the output connector of energized test equipment. Such equipment can have higher powers than the communication equipment itself, particularly OTDRs.

2. If you need to view the end of a fiber, *ALWAYS turn off the transmitter,* particularly if you don't know whether the transmitter is a laser or LED, given that lasers are higher-power sources. If you are using a microscope to inspect a fiber, the optical power will be multiplied.

From a mechanical point of view:

1. Good work practices are detailed in safety, training, and installation manuals. READ AND HEED.

2. Be careful with machinery, cutters, chemical solvents, and epoxies.

3. Fiber ends are brittle and will break off easily, including the ends cut off from splicing and connectorization. These ends are extremely difficult to see and can become "lost" and/or easily embedded in your finger. You won't know until your finger becomes infected. Always account for all scraps.

4. Use safety glasses specifically designed to protect the eye when working with fiber-optic systems.

5. Obtain and *USE* an optical safety kit.

6. Keep a *CLEAN* and orderly work area.

In all cases, be sure the craft personnel have the proper training for the job!

Section 3-6 Review

This section has covered the following **Network+** Exam objectives.

5.6 Summarize safety practices

Any time you are working with fiber, you need to be careful. This section presents an overview of safety.

Test Your Knowledge

1. The eye cannot see fiber-optic communication wavelengths, so never look into the end of a fiber. True or False?

2. It is important to be very careful working with fiber ends. These ends are extremely difficult to see and can become "lost" and/or easily embedded in your finger. True or False?

SUMMARY

This chapter introduced the field of fiber-optics and optical networking. The chapter has provided examples using fiber to interconnect LANs in both a building and a campus network. The major topics that the student should understand include the following:

- The advantages offered by optical networking
- The properties of light waves
- The physical and optical characteristics of optical fibers
- Attenuation and dispersion effects in fiber
- The description of the common techniques used to connect fiber
- The usage of fiber-optics in LANs, campus networks, and WANs
- System design of optical networks
- Safety considerations when working with fiber
- Analysis of OTDR waveforms

QUESTIONS AND PROBLEMS

Section 3-1

1. List the basic elements of a fiber optic communication system.

2. List five advantages of an optical communications link.

Section 3-2

3. Define refractive index.

4. What are the commonly used wavelengths in fiber optic systems?

5. What part of an optical fiber carries the light?

6. What is a measure of a fiber's light acceptance?

7. Define pulse dispersion.

8. What are the typical core/cladding sizes (in microns) for multimode fiber?

9. What is the typical core size for single-mode fiber?

10. Define mode field diameter.

Section 3-3

11. What are the two key distance-limiting parameters in fiber optic transmissions?

12. What are the four factors that contribute to attenuation?

13. Define *dispersion*.

14. What are three types of dispersion?

15. What is meant by the *zero-dispersion wavelength*?

16. What is a dispersion compensating fiber?

Section 3-4

17. What are the two kinds of light sources used in fiber-optic communication systems?

18. Why is a narrower spectra advantageous in optical systems?

19. Why is a tunable laser of importance in optical networking?

20. What is the purpose of an optical attenuator?

21. List two purposes of optical detectors.

22. What is the advantage of fusion splicing over mechanical splicing?

Section 3-5

23. Define: (a) FTTC; (b) FTTH; (c) FTTB; (d) FTTD.

24. What is the purpose of a GBIC?

25. What is the "2-deep" rule?

26. What is the purpose of a logical fiber map?

27. What are the typical maximum lengths for (a) multimode and (b) single-mode fiber?

28. What is FDDI?

Section 3-6

29. Why is safety an important issue in optical networking?

30. A campus network is planning to put fiber-optic cables in to replace outdated coaxial cables. They have the choice of putting in single-mode, multimode, or a combination of single–multimode fibers in the ground. Which fiber type should they select? Why?

31. The networking cables for a new building are being installed. You are asked to prepare a study about which cable type(s) should be used. Discuss the issues related to the cable selection.

CERTIFICATION QUESTIONS

32. Which of the following are advantages of optical communication links. (Select three.)

    a. Extremely wide bandwidth

    b. Elimination of crosstalk

    c. Elimination of attenuation

    d. Security

33. The stretching of a received pulse is due to (select two)

    a. Multiple paths taken by the light waves

    b. Misaligned connectors

    c. Pulse-dispersion

    d. OTDR testing

34. The broadening of a pulse due to the different path lengths taken through the fiber by different modes is called:

   a. chromatic dispersion

   b. polarization mode dispersion

   c. modal dispersion

   d. diffusion

35. The broadening of a pulse due to different propagation of the spectral components of the light pulse is called:

   a. chromatic dispersion

   b. modal dispersion

   c. polarization mode dispersion

   d. diffusion

36. The broadening of a light pulse due to the different propagation velocities of the X and Y polarization components of the light pulse is called:

   a. modal dispersion

   b. chromatic dispersion

   c. diffusion

   d. polarization mode dispersion

37. What is the data rate for OC-192?

   a. 1.522 Mbps

   b. 155.52 Mbps

   c. 9.95 Gbps

   d. 2.488 Gbps

38. What is the name of the optical-to-fiber interface used at 1 gigabit?

   a. XENPAK

   b. GBIC

   c. 10GBIC

   d. ZENPAK

39. What is the "two deep" rule relative to optical networking?

    a. This means the horizontal distribution to the work floor can only have two 8P8C connections.

    b. This means the horizontal distribution to the work floor can only have two ST connections to the fiber patch panel.

    c. This is not longer an issue with high-speed single-mode fiber and wave division multiplexing equipment.

    d. This means that a building should only have the main distribution and the intermediate distribution that feeds the horizontal distribution to the work area.

40. Which type of fiber is used is preferred for use in modern computer networks?

    a. Multimode

    b. Polarsized mode

    c. Single-mode

    d. All of these answers are correct.

41. What is the material surrounding the core of an optical waveguide called?

    a. Aperture

    b. Mode field

    c. Step-index

    d. Cladding

    e. Graded-index

4 CHAPTER

WIRELESS NETWORKING

Chapter Outline

Objectives

- Define the features of the 802.11 wireless LAN standard

- Understand the components of the wireless LAN

- Explore how wireless LANs are configured

- Examine how site surveys are done for wireless LANs

- Investigate the issues of securing a wireless LAN

- Explore how to configure a point-to-multipoint wireless LAN

Key Terms

WLAN

Basic Service Set (BSS)

ad hoc

access point

transceiver

Extended Service Set (ESS)

hand-off

roaming

CSMA/CA

DSSS

ISM

FHSS

pseudorandom

hopping sequence

OFDM

U-NII

MIMO

multiuser MIMO (MUMIMO)

beamforming

Wi-Fi

SSID

site survey

inquiry procedure

paging procedure

piconet

pairing

Passkey

WiMAX

BWA

NLOS

last mile

Radio Frequency Identification (RFID)

backscatter

Slotted Aloha

war driving

beacon

WPA

EAP

RADIUS

This chapter examines the features and technologies used in the wireless local area network (**WLAN**). Wireless networking is an extension of computer networks into the radio frequency (RF) world. The WLAN provides increased flexibility and mobility for connecting to a network. A properly designed WLAN for a building provides mobile access for a user from virtually any location in the building. The user doesn't have to look for a connection to plug into; also, the expense of pulling cables and installing wall plates required for wired networks can be avoided. However, a network administrator must carefully plan the wireless LAN installation and have a good understanding of the issues of using WLAN technologies to ensure the installation of a reliable and secure network.

This chapter addresses the basic issues of incorporating WLAN technologies into a network. The fundamentals of the IEEE 802.11 WLAN standard are examined in section 4-2. This includes an overview of WLAN concepts and terminology, frequency allocations, and spread spectrum communication. The applications of WLANs are presented in section 4-3. This includes a look at various types of WLAN configurations, such as point-to-point and point-to-multipoint. Other wireless networking technologies are examined in section 4-4. This section looks at Bluetooth, WiMAX, and RFID. Anytime a signal is transmitted over the air or even through a cable, there is some chance that the signal can be intercepted. Transmitting data over a wireless network introduces new security issues. Section 4-5 examines the basic issues of securing WLAN communications. The last section (4-6) presents an example of configuring a WLAN to provide access for users in a metropolitan area.

4-1 INTRODUCTION

WLAN
Wireless local area network

Table 4-1 lists and identifies, by chapter section, where each of the CompTIA Network+ objectives are presented in this chapter. At the end of each chapter section is a review with comments of the Network+ objectives presented in that section. These comments are provided to help reinforce the reader's understanding of a particular Network+ objective. The chapter review also includes "Test Your Knowledge" questions to aid in the understanding of key concepts before the reader advances to the next section of the chapter. The end of the chapter includes a complete set of question plus sample certification type questions.

TABLE 4-1 Chapter 4 CompTIA Network+ Objectives

Domain/ Objective Number	Domain/Objective Description Is Covered	Section Where Objective Is Covered
1.1	Explain the functions and applications of various network devices	4-2
1.4	Explain the characteristics and benefits of various WAN technologies	4-4
1.7	Differentiate between network infrastructure and implementations	4-4
2.1	Given a scenario, use the appropriate monitoring tools	4-3
2.2	Given a scenario, analyze metrics and reports from monitoring and tracking performance tools	4-3
2.6	Given a scenario, configure a switch using the proper features	4-3
2.7	Install and configure a wireless LAN infrastructure and implement the appropriate technologies in support of wireless-capable devices	4-2, 4-3, 4-4, 4-6
3.2	Compare and contrast common network vulnerabilities and threats	4-5
3.3	Given a scenario, implement network-hardening techniques	4-2, 4-3, 4-5
3.6	Explain the purpose of various network access control models	4-5
4.2	Given a scenario, analyze and interpret the output of troubleshooting tools	4-3
4.3	Given a scenario, troubleshoot and resolve common wireless issues	4-2, 4-3, 4-6
5.2	Explain the basics of network theory and concepts	4-2, 4-4

4-2 THE IEEE 802.11 WIRELESS LAN STANDARD

A typical computer network uses twisted-pair and fiber-optic cable to interconnect LANs. Another media competing for use in higher data-rate LANs is wireless, based on the IEEE 802.11 wireless standard. The advantages of wireless include

- A cost-effective networking media for use in areas that are difficult or too costly to wire

- User mobility in the workplace

Wireless networks have become more and more the network of choice in environments such as home, small offices, and public places. Being able to connect to the network without a wire is convenient for users, not to mention the cost is much lower. In the age of laptops and mobile devices, wireless opens the door to user mobility in the workplace. User mobility provides flexibility. Workers can potentially access the network or wireless data services from virtually any location within the workplace. Accessing information from the network is as easy as if the information were on a USB drive.

The benefits of wireless networks in the workplace are numerous. To provide wireless connectivity, the network administrator must be sure the network services are reliable and secure. Providing reliable network services means the administrator must have a good understanding of WLAN configurations and technologies. This and the following sections examine the fundamentals of wireless networking; the 802.11 standard and its family, 802.11a, 802.11b, 802.11g, 802.11n, and 802.11ac; and how WLANs are configured.

The IEEE 802.11 WLAN standard defines the physical (PHY) layer, the medium access control (MAC) layer, and the media access control (MAC) management protocols and services.

The PHY (physical) layer defines the following:

- The method of transmitting the data, which can be either RF or infrared (although infrared is rarely used)

- The MAC layer defined

- The reliability of the data service

- Access control to the shared wireless medium

- Protecting the privacy of the transmitted data

The wireless management protocols and services are authentication, association, data delivery, and privacy.

The fundamental topology of the WLAN is the **Basic Service Set (BSS)**. This is also called the independent Basic Service Set, or **ad hoc** network. Figure 4-1 provides an example of an ad hoc network. In this network, the wireless clients (stations) communicate directly with each other. This means the clients have recognized the other stations in the WLAN and have established a wireless data link.

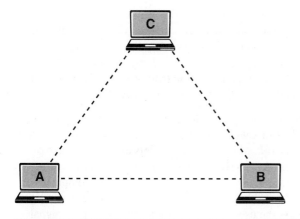

FIGURE 4-1   An example of the independent Basic Service Set or "ad hoc" network.

The performance of the Basic Service Set can be improved by including an **access point**. The access point is a transmit/receive unit (**transceiver**) that interconnects data from the wireless LAN to the wired network. Additionally, the access point provides 802.11 MAC layer functions and supports bridge protocols. The access point typically uses an RJ-45 jack for connecting to the wired network. If an access point is being used, users establish a wireless communications link through it to communicate with other users in the WLAN or the wired network, as shown in Figure 4-2.

> **Access Point**
> A transceiver used to interconnect a wireless and a wired LAN
>
> **Transceiver**
> A transmit/receive unit

FIGURE 4-2   Adding an access point to the Basic Service Set.

If data is being sent from PC-A to PC-D, the data is first sent to the access point and then relayed to PC-D. Data sent from a wireless client to a client in the wired LAN also passes through the access point. The users (clients) in the wireless LAN can communicate with other members of the network as long as a link is established with the access point. For example, data traffic from PC-A to PC-E will first pass through the access point and then to PC-E in the wired LAN.

The problem with the Basic Service Set is that mobile users can travel outside the radio range of a station's wireless link with one access point. One solution is to add multiple access points to the network. Multiple access points extend the range of mobility of a wireless client in the LAN. This arrangement is called an **Extended Service Set (ESS)**. An example is provided in Figure 4-3. The mobile computer will establish an authorized connection with the access point that has the strongest signal level (for example, AP-1). As the user moves, the signal strength of the signal from AP-1 will decrease. At some point, the signal strength from AP-2 will exceed AP-1, and the wireless bridge will establish a new connection with AP-2. This is called a **hand-off**. This is an automatic process for the wireless client adapter in 802.11, and the term used to describe this is **roaming**.

Network access in 802.11 uses a technique called carrier sense multiple access/collision avoidance (CSMA/CA). In **CSMA/CA**, the client station listens for other users of the wireless network. If the channel is quiet (no data transmission), the client station can transmit. If the channel is busy, the station(s) must wait until transmission stops. Each client station uses a unique random back-off time. This technique prevents client stations from trying to gain access to the wireless channel as soon as it becomes quiet. Currently four physical layer technologies are being used in 802.11 wireless networking. These are direct sequence spread spectrum (DSSS), frequency hopping spread spectrum (FHSS), infrared, and orthogonal frequency division multiplexing (OFDM). DSSS is used in 802.11b/g/n wireless networks, and OFDM is used in 802.11a, 802.11g, and 802.11n. Note that 802.11g/n use both DSSS and OFDM technology .

Extended Service Set (ESS)

The use of multiple access points to extend user mobility

Hand-off

When the user's computer establishes an association with another access point

Roaming

The term used to describe a user's' ability to maintain network connectivity as he moves through the workplace

CSMA/CA

Carrier sense multiple access/collision avoidance

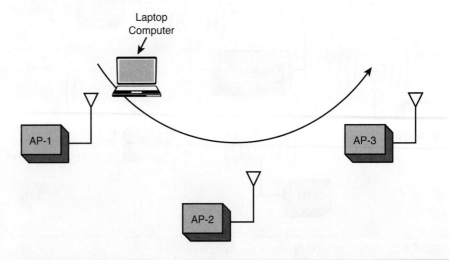

FIGURE 4-3   An example of an Extended Service Set used for increased user mobility.

802.11 **DSSS** implements 14 channels (each consuming 22MHz) over approximately 90MHz of RF spectrum in the 2.4GHz **ISM** (industrial, scientific, and medical) band. DSSS is a technique used to spread the transmitted data over a wide bandwidth; in this case it is a 22MHz bandwidth channel. Table 4-2 lists the frequency channels used in North America. Note that only 11 channels out of 14 channels are made available in North America. Figure 4-4 shows an example of the frequency spectrum for 3-channel DSSS.

TABLE 4-2 **North American DSSS Channels**

Channel Number	Frequency (GHz)
1	2.412
2	2.417
3	2.422
4	2.427
5	2.432
6	2.437
7	2.442
8	2.447
9	2.452
10	2.457
11	2.462

FIGURE 4-4 An example of the three channels in the DSSS spectrum.

In frequency hopping spread spectrum (**FHSS**), the transmit signal frequency changes based on a pseudorandom sequence. **Pseudorandom** means the sequence appears to be random but in fact does repeat, typically after some lengthy period of time. FHSS uses 79 channels (each 1MHz wide) in the ISM 2.4GHz band. FHSS requires that the transmitting and receiving units know the **hopping sequence** (the order of frequency changes) so that a communication link can be established and synchronized. FHSS data rates are typically 1Mbps and 2Mbps. FHSS is not commonly used anymore for wireless LANs. It's still part of the standard, but very few (if any) FHSS wireless LAN products are sold.

The maximum transmit power of 802.11b wireless devices is 1000 mW; however, the nominal transmit power level is 100 mW. The 2.4GHz frequency range used by 802.11b/g is shared by many technologies, including Bluetooth, cordless telephones, and microwave ovens.

LANs emit significant RF noise in the 2.4GHz range that can affect wireless data. A significant improvement in wireless performance is available with the IEEE 802.11a standards. The 802.11a equipment operates in the 5GHz range and provides significant improvement over 802.11b with respect to RF interference.

Another technique used in the 802.11 standard is **orthogonal frequency division multiplexing (OFDM)**. The basic idea behind this technique is to divide the signal bandwidth into smaller subchannels and to transmit the data over these subchannels in parallel. These subchannels can be overlapping, but they will not interfere with each other. The subchannels are mathematically orthogonal, which yields uncorrelated or independent signals.

The 802.11a standard transports the data over 12 possible channels in the Unlicensed National Information Infrastructure (**U-NII**). U-NII was set aside by the FCC to support short-range, high-speed wireless data communications. Table 4-3 lists the operating frequencies for 802.11a; Table 4-4 lists the transmit power levels for 802.11a.

TABLE 4-3   **IEEE 802.11a Channels and Operating Frequencies**

Channel	Center Frequency (GHz)	
36	5.180	
40	5.20	Lower band
44	5.22	
48	5.24	
52	5.26	
56	5.28	Middle band
60	5.30	
64	5.32	
149	5.745	
153	5.765	Upper band
157	5.785	
161	5.805	

TABLE 4-4   Maximum Transmit Power Levels for 802.11a with a 6dBi Antenna Gain

Band	Power Level
Lower	40 mW
Middle	200 mW
Upper	800 mW

IEEE 802.11a equipment is not compatible with 802.11b, 802.11g, or 802.11n. The good aspect of this is that 802.11a equipment will not interfere with 802.11b, g, or n; therefore, 802.11a and 802.11b/g/n links can run next to each other without causing any interference. Figure 4-5 illustrates an example of the two links operating together.

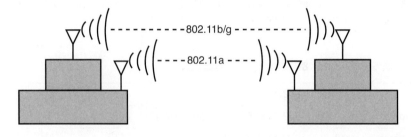

FIGURE 4-5   An example of an 802.11a installation and an 802.11b link running alongside each other.

The downside of 802.11a is the increased cost of the equipment and increased power consumption because of the OFDM technology. This is of particular concern with mobile users because of the effect it can have on battery life. However, the maximum usable distance (RF range) for 802.11a is about the same or even greater than that of 802.11b/g/n.

Another IEEE 802.11 wireless standard is IEEE 802.11g. The 802.11g standard supports the higher data transmission rates of 54Mbps but operates in the same 2.4GHz range as 802.11b. The 802.11g equipment is also backward compatible with 802.11b equipment. This means that 802.11b wireless clients will be able to communicate with the 802.11g access points and the 802.11g wireless client equipment will communicate with the 802.11b access points.

The obvious advantage of this is that a company with an existing 802.11b wireless network will be able to migrate to the higher data rates provided by 802.11g without having to sacrifice network compatibility. In fact, new wireless equipment support both the 2.4GHz and 5GHz standards, giving it the flexibility of high speed, compatibility, and noninterference.

Another entry into wireless networks is the 802.11n. This wireless technology operates in the same ISM frequency as 802.11b/g (2.4GHz) and can also operate in the 5GHz band. A significant improvement with 802.11n is Multiple Input Multiple Output (MIMO). MIMO uses a technique called space-division multiplexing, where

MIMO
A space-division multiplexing technique where the data stream is split into multiple parts called spatial streams

the data stream is split into multiple parts called *spatial streams*. The different spatial streams are transmitted using separate antennas. With MIMO, doubling the spatial streams doubles the effective data rate. The downside of this is the possibility of increased power consumption. The 802.11n specification includes a MIMO power-save mode. With this, 802.11n only uses multiple data paths when faster data transmission is required—thus saving power.

The latest addition to the 802.11 family is 802.11ac. The 802.11ac technology operates in the 5GHz band. It uses a new version of MIMO technology with eight spatial streams and has channels up to 80MHz wide. This is called **Multiuser MIMO (MUMIMO)**. 802.11ac incorporates standardized **beamforming**. Beamforming is a technique that is used to direct transmission of the radio signal to a specific device. The benefit of this is increasing data throughput while reducing power consumption. 802.11n used beamforming, but it was not standardized. The transmit range for 802.11ac is similar to or better than 802.11n.

Table 4-5 provides a summary of 802.11n and 802.11ac in terms of their compatibility with other Wi-Fi technologies and frequencies supported.

TABLE 4-5   **A Summary of 802.11ac and 802.11n**

	802.11n	802.11ac
Backward-compatible with	802.11g, 802.11b, and 802.11a	802.11n
Frequencies supported	2.4GHz and 5GHz	5GHz

Wireless networks also go by the name **Wi-Fi**, which is the abbreviated name for the Wi-Fi Alliance (Wi-Fi stands for wireless fidelity). The Wi-Fi Alliance is an organization whose function is to test and certify wireless equipment for compliance with the 802.11x standards, the group of wireless standards developed under the IEEE 802.11 standard. The following list provides a summary of the most common wireless standards:

- **802.11a (Wireless-A):** This standard can provide data transfer rates up to 54Mbps and an operating range up to 75 feet. It operates at 5GHz. (Modulation—OFDM)

- **802.11b (Wireless-B):** This standard can provide data transfer rates up to 11Mbps with ranges of 100–150 feet. It operates at 2.4GHz. (Modulation—DSSS)

- **802.11g (Wireless-G):** This standard can provide data transfer rates up to 54Mbps up to 150 feet. It operates at 2.4GHz. (Modulation—DSSS or OFDM)

- **802.11n (Wireless-N):** This high-speed wireless connectivity promises data transfer rates over 200+ Mbps. It operates at 2.4GHz and 5GHz. (Modulation—DSSS or OFDM)

- **802.11i:** This standard for WLANs provides improved data encryption for networks that use the 802.11a, 802.11b, and 802.11g standards

Multiuser MIMO (MUMIMO)
Use of MIMO technology with eight spatial streams

Beamforming
A technique used to direct transmission of the radio signal to a specific device

Wi-Fi
Wi-Fi Alliance—an organization that tests and certifies wireless equipment for compliance with the 802.11x standards

- **802.11r:** This standard is designed to speed hand-offs between access points or cells in a WLAN. This standard is a critical addition to 802.11 WLANs if voice traffic is to become widely deployed

- **802.11ac:** This is the next generation of high-speed wireless connectivity. This technology promises data rates up to 1Gbps and operates over the 5GHz band.

Section 4-2 Review

This section has covered the following **Network+** Exam objectives:

1.1 Explain the functions and applications of various network devices

This section introduced the access point, a transmit/receive unit (transceiver) that interconnects data from the wireless LAN to the wired network.

2.7 Install and configure a wireless LAN infrastructure and implement the appropriate technologies in support of wireless-capable devices

This section examined the 802.11a/b/g/n/ac standards and the issues of transmit distance, data speed, and frequencies. This section also introduced the concept of MIMO, which is used to increase the effective transmit data rate.

3.3 Given a scenario, implement network-hardening techniques

This section introduced the concept of authentication for accessing a wireless network.

4.3 Given a scenario, troubleshoot and resolve common wireless issues

This section discussed the many wireless standards, including compatibility issues. Tables 4-2, 4-3, and 4-5 provide a list of the frequencies used in 802.11 wireless networks.

5.2 Explain the basics of network theory and concepts

802.11 wireless systems use CSMA/CA for managing network access. You should make sure you understand the difference between CSMA/CA and CSMA/CD.

Test Your Knowledge

1. 802.11ac networking equipment is compatible with 802.11b. True or False?

2. 802.11g networking equipment is compatible with 802.11b. True or False?

3. 802.11a and 802.11b wireless networks can run side-by-side. True or False?

4. 802.11ac networking equipment is compatible with 802.11n. True or False?

4-3 802.11 WIRELESS NETWORKING

A wireless LAN can be configured in many ways to meet the needs of an organization. Figure 4-6 provides an example of a basic 802.11b/g/n WLAN configuration. Each PC is outfitted with a wireless LAN adapter card. The PC cards come in many styles, such as PCI, ISA, PCMCIA, and USB, and some units are external to the computer. Today, most computer desktops and especially computer laptops are equipped with a wireless adapter. The wireless adapter (wireless LAN adapter) is the device that connects the client to the wireless medium. The medium is typically a radio wave channel in the 2.4GHz or 5GHz ISM band. The wireless medium can also be infrared, although this is not used very often. The following services are provided by the wireless LAN adapter:

- Delivery of the data
- Authentication
- Privacy

FIGURE 4-6 The setup for a basic WLAN.

One of the biggest misconceptions about wireless is that it does not require a wired connection. This is not quite correct. The connection to a wired LAN is provided by a wireless access point, which provides a bridge between the wireless LAN and the wired network. A physical cable connection (typically CAT6/5e) ties the access point to the wired network's switch or hub (typically Ethernet).

For example, computer PC-A shown in Figure 4-6 sends a data packet to PC-D, a destination in the wired LAN. PC-A first sends a data packet over the wireless link. The access point recognizes the sender of the data packet as a host in the wireless LAN-X and allows the wireless data to enter the access point. At this time, the data is sent out the physical Ethernet connection to the wired LAN. The data packet is then delivered to PC-D in the wired LAN.

A question should come up at this point: "How does the access point know that the wireless data packet is being sent from a client in the wireless LAN?"

The answer is the 802.11 wireless LAN devices use an **SSID** to identify what wireless data traffic is allowed to connect to the network. The SSID is the wireless *service set identifier*, basically a password that enables the client to join the wireless network.

The access point uses the SSID to determine whether the client is to become a member of the wireless network. The term *association* is used to describe that a wireless connection has been obtained.

Another common question is "Why does the access point have two antennas?" The answer is that the two antennas implement what is called *spatial diversity*. This antenna arrangement improves received signal gain and performance.

Figure 4-7 provides an example of the information displayed on the wireless adapter's console port when an association is made. The text indicates that a connection has been made to a parent (access point) whose MAC address is 00-40-96-25-9d-14. The text indicates this MAC address has been "added" to the list of associations. This type of information is typically available via the wireless management software that comes with the wireless PC or PCMCIA adapter.

> **SSID**
> Service set identifier

FIGURE 4-7 An example of the information displayed when an association is made by a client with an access point.

Access points use the association to build a table of users (clients) on the wireless network. Figure 4-8 provides an example of an association table. The association table lists the MAC addresses for each networking device connected to the wireless network. The access point then uses this table to forward data packets between the access point and the wireless network. The wireless client adapter will also notify the user if the client has lost an association with the access point. An example of this also is provided in Figure 4-8.

A wireless bridge is a popular choice for connecting LANs (running similar network protocols) even if the LANs are miles apart. Examples are provided in Figure 4-9(a) and 4-9(b). Figure 4-9(a) shows a point-to-point wireless bridge. Each building shown in Figure 4-9(a) has a connection from the wireless bridge to the building's LAN, as shown in Figure 4-10. The wireless bridge then connects to an antenna placed on the roof. A clear (line-of-sight) transmission path must exist between the two buildings; otherwise, signal *attenuation* (loss) or signal disruption can result. Antenna selection is also critical when configuring the connection. This issue is addressed in section 4-5. The antenna must be selected so that the signal strength at the receiving site is sufficient to meet the required received signal level.

FIGURE 4-8　An example of a "lost" association.

Figure 4-9(b) shows how a wireless bridge can be used to connect multiple remote sites to the main transmitting facility. Each building uses a bridge setup similar to that shown in Figure 4-10. The bridge connects to its respective LAN. In this case, Bld-A uses an antenna that has a wide coverage area (radiation pattern). The key objective with antenna selection is that the antenna must provide coverage for all receiving sites (in this case, Bld-B and Bld-C).

Wireless LANs have a maximum distance the signal can be transmitted. This is a critical issue inside buildings when user mobility is required. Many obstacles can reflect and attenuate the signal, causing reception to suffer. Also, the signal level for mobile users is hampered by the increased distance from the access point. Distance is also a critical issue in outdoor point-to-multipoint wireless networks.

A solution is to place multiple wireless access points within the facility, as shown in Figure 4-11. Mobile clients will be able to maintain a connection as they travel through the workplace because the wireless client will automatically select the access point that provides the strongest signal level. The access points can be arranged so that overlapping coverage of the workplace is provided, thus enabling seamless roaming for the client. The signal coverage is shown in the shape of circles in Figure 4-11. In actual practice, the radiation patterns are highly irregular due to reflections of the transmitted signal.

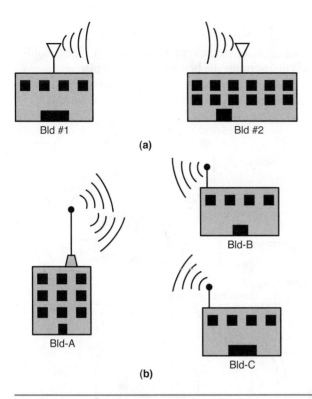

FIGURE 4-9   Examples of (a) point-to-point and (b) point-to-multipoint wireless bridge configurations.

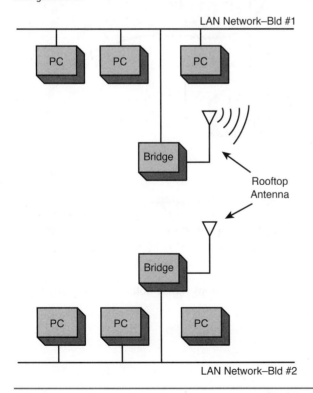

FIGURE 4-10   The wireless bridge connection to the wired network inside the building.

Site Survey
Performed to determine
the best location(s)
for placing the access
point(s) to provide
maximum RF coverage for
the wireless clients

It is important to verify that sufficient RF signal level is available for the users in the WLAN. This is best accomplished by performing a **site survey**. Inside a building, a site survey is performed to determine the best location(s) for placing the access point(s) for providing maximum RF coverage for the wireless clients. Site surveys are also done with outside installations to determine the coverage area.

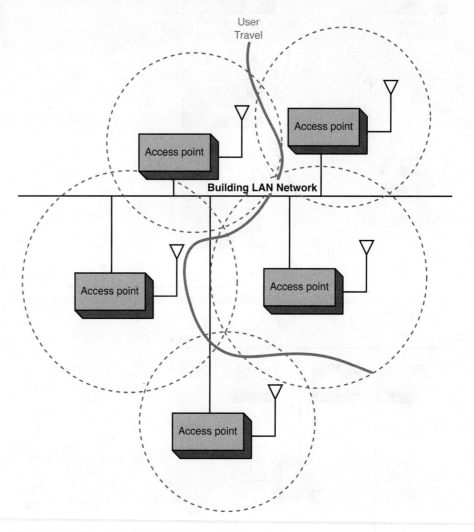

FIGURE 4-11   An example of configuring multiple access points to extend the range for wireless connectivity.

A site survey for indoor and outdoor installations should obtain the following key information:

- **Indoor**
    - Electrical power
    - Wired network connection point(s)
    - Access point placement

- RF coverage—user mobility
- Bandwidth supported
- Identify any significant RF interference

- **Outdoor**
    - Electrical power (base access point)
    - Connection back to the home network
    - Antenna selection
    - Bandwidth supported
    - RF coverage
    - Identify any significant RF interference

For example, a site survey was conducted to determine access point placement to provide wireless network connectivity for a building. The objective was to provide mobile client access throughout the building. The building already had two wired connections available for placing an access point. Figure 4-12 provides the floor plan for the building.

▶ = Ethernet CAT5e

FIGURE 4-12   The floor plan of the building being surveyed for a wireless LAN.

The available wired network connections are indicated in the drawing. The site survey began with placing an access point at position 1. A wireless mobile client was used to check the signal throughout the building. This used to be performed by a laptop with a WLAN adapter. Today, many more options are available. Handheld devices, such as tablets and smartphones, can be conveniently used for wireless suite survey. Their form factor and mobility are perfect for this purpose. Most of these devices are already equipped with a built-in wireless chip. All they need is the appropriate wireless software or app, and there are many of them out there. The following example shows the test results gathered from an Android tablet with a free Wi-Fi Analyzer app installed.

Figure 4-13 shows the snapshot of the wireless environment within the area. The graph shows the signal strength of all wireless SSIDs found. The signal strength is the wireless signal power level and it is represented in –dBm format, from 0 to –100. This is the power ratio in dB of the measured power referenced to one milliwatt. The closer the value is to 0, the stronger the signal. The stronger the signal, the more reliable the wireless connection is. Wireless is everywhere today, so do not be too surprise to see more SSIDs than just yours. For this example, the site survey is intended for the wireless SSID "ET377." As the graph shows, it has the strongest signal of all SSIDs.

FIGURE 4-13 The snapshot of the RF signal environment.

The first measurement was taken at point A, as shown in Figure 4-14. Notice that the signal strength is at –43 dBm, which is an excellent connection. This will change if the signal level decreases significantly.

The next observation was made at point B. The signal strength is measured at –52 dBm. The signal has decreased somewhat, but it is still in the green zone, which indicates that a connection is still good. Figure 4-15 shows the observation made at point B. The signal level drops to –67 dBm, which is in the yellow zone, at point C, as shown in Figure 4-16. This connection is fair.

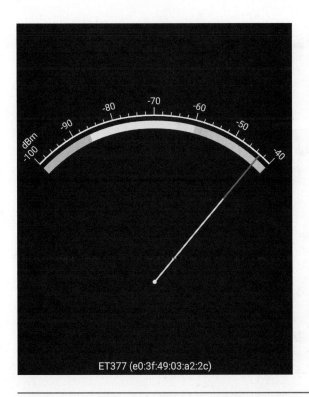

FIGURE 4-14 The RF signal strength observed at point A.

FIGURE 4-15 The RF signal strength at point B.

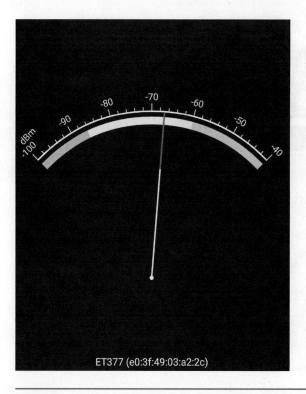

FIGURE 4-16   The drop in the signal quality to "Fair" at point C.

The mobile client was moved to point D in the building, and a signal quality of "Out of range" was observed. This is also called a *loss of association* with the access point. Figure 4-17 shows the observed signal level.

The site survey shows that one access point placed at point 1 in the building is not sufficient to cover the building's floor plan. The survey shows that the additional cost of another access point is easily justified for providing full building wireless LAN coverage. The building has two wired network connections available for placing an access point (points 1 and 2). It was decided to place another access point at point 2. The site survey was repeated, and it showed that "Excellent" signal strength was obtained throughout the building. In some cases, a *range extender* can be used to provide additional wireless coverage. This device basically extends the reach of the wireless network.

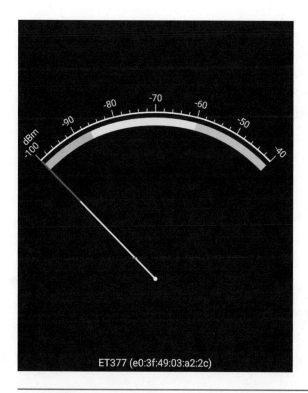

ET377 (e0:3f:49:03:a2:2c)

FIGURE 4-17   The "Out of range" measurement for point D.

Section 4-3 Review

This section has covered the following **Network+** Exam objectives:

> 2.1 Given a scenario, use appropriate monitoring tools

This section has presented techniques for preparing a site survey and developing an understanding of signal strength.

> 2.2 Given a scenario, analyze metrics and reports from monitoring and tracking performance tools

This section demonstrated the use of monitoring tools to perform a site survey.

> 2.7 Install and configure a wireless LAN infrastructure and implement the appropriate technologies in support of wireless capable devices

This section presented a look a configuring a WLAN for a building. The discussions includes examples of measurements taken at various locations within the building.

> 3.3 Given a scenario, implement network-hardening techniques

The authentication services provided by the wireless LAN adapter are introduced in this section.

4.2 Given a scenario, analyze and interpret the output of troubleshooting tools

This section demonstrates the use of a site survey for a wireless facility. Various RF measurements are presented.

4.3 Given a scenario, troubleshoot and resolve common wireless issues

This section addresses preparing a site to support access point placement and the changes in signal strength as a result of environmental factors.

Test Your Knowledge

1. The term *association* is characterized by which of the following?

    a. Describe that a wireless connection has been obtained.

    b. Describe the MAC address of the client.

    c. Prevent unauthorized network access.

    d. Prevent excessive routing.

2. Site Surveys provide the following:

    Best location for placing access points

    Power connection

    RF coverage

    Antenna selection

    IP address selection

    True or False?

4-4   BLUETOOTH, WIMAX, RFID, AND MOBILE COMMUNICATIONS

This section looks at four wireless technologies: Bluetooth, WiMAX, RFID, and Mobile. Each of these technologies plays an important role in the wireless networks. The sections that follow examine each of these wireless technologies, including a look at configuration and examples of the hardware being used.

Bluetooth

This section examines another wireless technology called *Bluetooth*, based on the 802.15 standard. Bluetooth was developed to replace the cable connecting computers, mobile phones, handheld devices, portable computers, and fixed electronic devices. The information normally carried by a cable is transmitted over the 2.4GHz ISM frequency band, which is the same frequency band used by 802.11b/g/n. There are three output power classes for Bluetooth. Table 4-6 lists the maximum output power and the operating distance for each class.

TABLE 4-6   Bluetooth Output Power Classes

Power Class	Maximum Output Power	Operating Distance
1	20 dBm	~ 100 m
2	4 dBm	~ 10 m
3	0 dBm	~ 1 m

When a Bluetooth device is enabled, it uses an inquiry procedure to determine whether any other Bluetooth devices are available. This procedure is also used to allow itself to be discovered.

If a Bluetooth device is discovered, it sends an inquiry reply back to the Bluetooth device initiating the inquiry. Next, the Bluetooth devices enter the paging procedure. The paging procedure is used to establish and synchronize a connection between two Bluetooth devices. When the procedure for establishing the connection has been completed, the Bluetooth devices will have established a piconet. A piconet is an ad hoc network of up to eight Bluetooth devices such as a computer, mouse, headset, earpiece, and so on. In a piconet, one Bluetooth device (the master) is responsible for providing the synchronization clock reference. All other Bluetooth devices are called slaves.

The following is an example of setting up a Bluetooth network linking a Mac OS X computer to another Bluetooth-enabled device. To enable Bluetooth on the Mac OS X, click the **Apple icon > System Preferences > Bluetooth** and then click **Turn Bluetooth On**. The Mac will automatically discover other Bluetooth devices nearby.

In the next step you will select the device with which you will be establishing a Bluetooth connection. When Bluetooth is turned on, the Mac will search for another Bluetooth device. When a Bluetooth device is found, it will appear in the **Devices** window. To connect the desired Bluetooth device, select **Pair** button next to the device. This is called paring when another Bluetooth device is set up to connect to another Bluetooth device. You will be asked for a Passkey. The Passkey is used in Bluetooth Security to limit outsider access to the pairing. Only people with the Passkey will be able to pair with your Bluetooth device.

Paging Procedure
Used to establish and synchronize a connection between two Bluetooth devices

Piconet
An ad hoc network of up to eight Bluetooth devices

Pairing
When a Bluetooth device is set up to connect to another Bluetooth device

Passkey
Used in Bluetooth Security to limit outsider access to the pairing

FIGURE 4-18   The window for configuring the Bluetooth settings.

At this point, you are now able to transfer files between the paired devices. This requires that the Bluetooth Sharing settings for the device have been set to allow files to come in. Click the **Apple icon > System Preferences > Sharing** and select **Bluetooth Sharing**. Figure 4-19 shows an example of the setup for the file transfer.

FIGURE 4-19   The window showing the settings for a file transfer.

The screen shown in Figure 4-20 shows an incoming text file. The File Transfer menu enables the user to select where received files are saved. In this case, the incoming files are being saved to the desktop.

FIGURE 4-20   The window showing that a text file is coming in from another Bluetooth device.

This example has demonstrated setting up Bluetooth on a Mac OS X. The steps for setting up Bluetooth on Windows 10, Windows 8, or even a Blackberry differ slightly, but the basic steps are the same. The following are the basic steps you need to complete to pair with another Bluetooth device:

1. Enable the Bluetooth radio.

2. Enable Discoverability (this enables other Bluetooth devices to find you).

3. Select the device for pairing.

WiMAX

WiMAX (**W**orldwide **I**nteroperability for **M**icrowave **Acc**ess) is a broadband wireless system that has been developed for use as broadband wireless access (**BWA**) for fixed and mobile stations and can provide a wireless alternative for last mile broadband access in the 2GHz–66GHz frequency range. BWA access for fixed stations can be up to 30 miles, whereas mobile BWA access is 3–10 miles. Internationally, the WiMAX frequency standard is 3.5GHz, while the United States uses both the unlicensed 5.8GHz and the licensed 2.5GHz spectrum. There are also investigations with adapting WiMAX for use in the 700MHz frequency range. Information transmitted at this frequency is less susceptible to signal blockage due to trees. The disadvantage of the lower frequency range is the reduction in the bandwidth.

WiMAX uses Orthogonal Frequency Division Multiplexing (OFDM) as its signaling format. This signaling format was selected for the WiMAX standard IEEE 802.16a standard because of its improved **NLOS** (non-line-of-sight) characteristics in the 2GHz–11GHz frequency range. An OFDM system uses multiple frequencies for transporting the data, which helps minimize multipath interference problems. Some frequencies may be experiencing interference problems, but the system can select the best frequencies for transporting the data.

WiMAX also provides flexible channel sizes (for example, 3.5MHz, 5MHz, and 10MHz), which provides adaptability to standards for WiMAX worldwide. This also helps ensure that the maximum data transfer rate is being supported. For

WiMAX
A broadband wireless system based on the IEEE 802.16e standard

BWA
Broadband wireless access

NLOS
Non-line-of-sight

example, the allocated channel bandwidth could be 6MHz, and the adaptability of the WiMAX channel size allows it to adjust to use the entire allocated bandwidth.

Additionally, the WiMAX (IEEE 802.16e) media access control (MAC) layer differs from the IEEE 802.11 Wi-Fi MAC layer in that the WiMAX system has to compete only once to gain entry into the network. When a WiMAX unit has gained access, it is allocated a time slot by the base station, thereby providing the WiMAX with scheduled access to the network. The WiMAX system uses time division multiplexing (TDM) data streams on the downlink and time-division multiple access (TDMA) on the uplink and centralized channel management to ensure time-sensitive data is delivered on time. Additionally, WiMAX operates in a collision-free environment, which improves channel throughput.

Last Mile

The last part of the connection from the telecommunications provider to the customer

WiMAX has a range of up to 30 miles, and it operates in both point-to-point and point-to-multipoint configurations. This can be useful in situations where DSL or cable network connectivity is not available. WiMAX is also useful for providing the last mile connection. The **last mile** is basically the last part of the connection from the telecommunications provider to the customer. The cost of the last mile connection can be expensive, which makes a wireless alternative attractive to the customer.

The 802.16e WiMAX standard holds a lot of promise for use as a mobile air interface. Another standard, 802.20, is a mobile air interface being developed for consumer use. This standard plans to support data rates over 1Mbps, which is comparable to DSL and cable connections. Additional 802.20 is being developed to support high-speed mobility. In other words, the user could be in a fast car or train and still have network connectivity.

Radio Frequency Identification

Radio Frequency Identification (RFID)

A technique that uses radio waves to track and identify people, animals, objects, and shipments

Backscatter

Refers to the reflection of the radio waves striking the RFID tag and reflecting back to the transmitter source

Radio frequency identification (RFID) is a technique that uses radio waves to track and identify people, animal, objects, and shipments. This is done by the principle of modulated **backscatter**. The term "backscatter" is referring to the reflection of the radio waves striking the RFID tag and reflecting back to the transmitter source with its stored unique identification information.

Figure 4-21 illustrates the basic block for an RFID system.

FIGURE 4-21   Basic block diagram of an RFID system.

The RFID system consists of two things:

- An RFID tag (also called the RF transponder) includes an integrated antenna and radio electronics.

- A reader (also called a transceiver) consists of a transceiver and an antenna. A transceiver is the combination of a transmitter and receiver.

The reader (transceiver) transmits radio waves, which activates (turns on) an RFID tag. The tag then transmits modulated data, containing its unique identification information stored in the tag, back to the reader. The reader then extracts the data stored on the RFID tag.

The RFID idea dates back to 1948, when the concept of using reflected power as a means of communication was first proposed. The 1970s saw further development in RFID technology—in particular, a UHF scheme that incorporates rectification of the RF signal for providing power to the tag. Development of RFID technology significantly increased in the 1990s. Applications included toll collection that allowed vehicles to pass through tollbooths at highway speeds while still being able to record data from the tag.

Today, RFID technology is being used to track inventory shipments for major commercial retailers, the transportation industries, and the Department of Defense. Additionally, RFID applications are being used in Homeland Security in tracking container shipments at border crossings. Additionally, RFID is being incorporated into WLAN computer networks to keep better track of inventory. Wireless technologies are becoming more important for the enterprise. RFID technology is being used as a wireless means for asset tracking and as a result is placing more importance on its role in the network. The tracking technology is even being extended to tracking Wi-Fi devices within the WLAN infrastructure.

There are three parameters that define an RFID system. These include the following:

- Means of powering the tag

- Frequency of operation

- Communications protocol (also called the air interface protocol)

Powering the Tag

RFID tags are classified in three ways based on how they obtain their operating power. The three classifications are passive, semi-active, and active:

- **Passive:** Power is provided to the tag by rectifying the RF energy, transmitted from the reader, that strikes the RF tag antenna. The rectified power level is sufficient to power the ICs on the tags and also provides sufficient power for the tag to transmit a signal back to the reader. Figure 4-22 shows an example of a passive RFID tag (also called an inlay).

  The tag inlays include both the RFID chip and the antenna mounted on a substrate.

- **Semi-active:** The tags use a battery to power the electronics on the tag but use the property of backscatter to transmit information back to the reader.

- **Active:** Use a battery to power the tag and transmit a signal back to the reader. Basically this is a radio transmitter. New active RFID tags are incorporating wireless Ethernet, the 802.11b–Wi-Fi connectivity. An example is the G2C501 Active RFID tag from G2 Microsystems shown in Figure 4-23. The power consumption of the G2C501 is 10µA in the sleep mode and uses two AA batteries with an expected lifetime of five years. The G2C501 also works in the standard 915MHz range. The G2C501 also has location capability. This is accomplished by making Receive Signal Strength Indicator (RSSI) measurements from three separate access points. The three measurements provide sufficient information to make a triangulation measurement for use in locating the object.

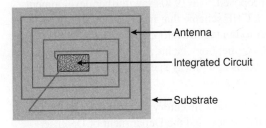

FIGURE 4-22   Examples of an RFID inlay.

FIGURE 4-23   The G2C501 Active RFID tag from G2Microsystems (courtesy of G2Microsystems).

Frequency of Operation

The RFID tags must be tuned to the reader's transmit frequency to turn on. RFID systems typically use three frequency bands for operation, LF, HF, and UHF as shown in Figure 4-24:

- **Low-frequency (LF)** tags typically use frequency-shift keying (FSK) between the 125/134KHz frequencies. The data rates from these tags is low (~12Kbps), and they are not appropriate for any applications requiring fast data transfers. However, the low-frequency tags are suitable for animal identification, such as dairy cattle and other livestock. The RFID tag information is typically obtained when the livestock are being fed. The read range for low-frequency tags is approximately .33 meters.

- **High-frequency (HF)** tags operate in the 13.56MHz industrial band. High-frequency tags have been available commercially since 1995. It is known that the longer wavelengths of the HF radio signal are less susceptible to absorption by water or other liquids. Therefore, these tags are better suited for tagging liquids. The read range for high-frequency tags is approximately 1 meter. The short read range provides for better defined read ranges. The applications for tags in this frequency range include access control, smart cards, and shelf inventory. The data rate for high-frequency (HF) tags is 26Kbps.

- **Ultra-high frequency (UHF)** tags work at 860–960MHz and at 2.4GHz. The data rates for these tags can be from 50–150Kbps and greater. These tags are popular for tracking inventory. The read range for passive UHF tags is 10–20 feet, which make it a better choice for reading pallet tags. However, if an active tag is used, a read range up to 100 meters is possible.

LF	HF	UHF
125/134 kHz	13.56 MHz	860 - 960 MHz
		2.4 GHz

FIGURE 4-24   The frequency bands used by RFID tags.

Communications (Air Interface) Protocol

The air interface protocol adopted for RFID tags is **Slotted Aloha**, a network communications protocol technique similar to the Ethernet protocol. In a Slotted Aloha protocol, the tags are only allowed to transmit at predetermined times after being energized. This technique reduces the chance of data collisions between RFID tag transmissions and allows for the reading of up to 1000 tags per second. (Note: This is for high-frequency tags.) The operating range for RFID tags can be up to 30 meters. This means that multiple tags can be energized at the same time, and a possible RF data collision can occur. If a collision occurs, the tag will transmit again after a random back-off time. The readers transmit continuously until there is no tag collision.

Slotted Aloha
A wireless network communications protocol technique similar to the Ethernet protocol

Mobile Communications

Today, many additional types of mobile devices can be used to access computer networks. Examples include smartphones, laptops, tablets, and gaming devices. All of these devices are extremely powerful and utilize wireless technology to connect to the network. This chapter has provided an overview of many of the wireless technologies being used today. These include the 802.11 family of Wi-Fi technologies, Bluetooth, WiMAX, and RFID. This section provides a brief summary of the some of the other wireless technologies currently available.

CDMA (Code Division Multiple Access)

This is a communications system in which spread-spectrum techniques are used to multiplex more than one signal within a single channel. In this case, each device uses a different binary sequence to modulate the carrier, spreading the spectrum of the waveform (spread-spectrum). The signals are separated at the receiver by using a "correlator" that accepts only the signal from the selected binary sequence.

LTE/4G

LTE, or Long Tem Evolution, is a 4G Wireless communications standard. It has been designed to provide up to 10 times 3G network speeds.

HSPA+

HSPA+ (Evolved High-Speed Packet Access) has been developed to provide network speeds comparable to LTE networks. Theoretical speeds for download are said to be 168Mbps and uplink 22Mbps.

3G/4G

3G (third generation) was developed to provide broadband network wireless services. The standard defining 3G wireless is called international mobile communications, or IMT 2000.

4G (fourth generation) is the successor to 3G technology and provides download speeds of 100Mbps.

Edge

EDGE (Enhanced Data GSM Evolution) provides download speeds of 384Kbps.

Section 4-4 Review

This section has covered the following **Network+** Exam objectives:

1.4 Explain the characteristics and benefits of various WAN technologies

This section has introduced WiMAX, GSM/CDMA, LTE/4G/ 3G/ HSPA+, and Edge technologies. WiMAX can support links up to 36 miles and is a possible alternative to provide the last-mile connection.

1.7 Differentiate between network infrastructure implementations

This section introduced the use of Bluetooth for implementing a PAN (personal area network).

2-7 Install and configure a wireless LAN infrastructure and implement the appropriate technologies in support of wireless-capable devices

This section has introduced various mobile devices that are now common additions to wireless networks.

5.2 Explain the basics of network theory and concepts

This section has introduced TDM in the WiMAX system. WiMAX uses (TDM) data streams on the downlink, time-division multiple access (TDMA) on the uplink, and centralized channel management to ensure time-sensitive data is delivered on time.

Test Your Knowledge

1. WiMAX operates at which frequencies in the United States?

   a. Both the unlicensed 5.2GHz and the licensed 2.4GHz

   b. Both the unlicensed 5.3GHz and the licensed 2.6GHz

   c. Both the unlicensed 13.2GHz and the licensed 5.6GHz

   d. Both the unlicensed 5.8GHz and the licensed 2.5GHz

2. The range of WiMAX is up to what distance?

   a. 30 kilometers

   b. 30 miles

   c. 30 meters

   d. None of these answers is correct.

3. Bluetooth operates at which frequency?

   a. 5GHz

   b. 100MHz

   c. 2.4GHz

   d. None of these answers is correct.

4-5 SECURING WIRELESS LANS

This section provides an overview of securing 802.11 wireless LANs. The network administrator must be aware of the security issues when configuring a wireless LAN. The fact is, RFs will pass through walls, ceilings, and floors of a building even with low signal power. Therefore, the assumption should never be made that the wireless data is confined to only the user's area. The network administrator must assume that the wireless data can be received by an unintended user. In other words, the use of an unsecured wireless LAN is opening a potential threat to network security.

In fact, a threat to wireless devices includes war driving. **War driving** is a term that applies to driving with an antenna out the door connected to a mobile device running Windows or Linux. A wireless card in a PC and a software application are used to detect management packets that come from the wireless access points. Some access points allow the management packets to be turned off. All 11 channels must be cycled through to check for data (management packets). The software can also determine if wireless security is turned on, the type of access points, and so on. If wireless security is not enabled, the attacker can attempt to break into the network. If the wireless security features are not enabled, the packets that come from the access points can be viewed.

To address this threat to WLAN security, the network administrator must ensure that the WLAN is protected by firewalls and intrusion detection (see Chapter 10, Inernet Technologies: Out to the Internet"), and most importantly the network administrator must make sure that the wireless security features are enabled.

This might seem to be a bold statement, but surprisingly enough, many WLANs are placed on a network without turning on available wireless security features. Many times the user in the WLAN assumes that no one would break into her computer because nothing important exists on the system. This may be true, but to an attacker, the user has one very important item—access to the wired network through an unsecured client.

WLANs use an SSID (service set identifier) to authenticate users, but the problem is that the SSID is broadcast in radio link beacons about 10 times per second. In WLAN equipment, the **beacons** are transmitted so that a wireless user can identify an access point to connect to. The SSID can be turned off so it isn't transmitted with a beacon, but it is still possible for the SSID to be obtained by packet sniffing. As noted previously, *packet sniffing* is a technique used to scan through unencrypted data packets to extract information. In this case, an attacker uses packet sniffing to extract the SSID from data packets. Disabling SSID broadcasting will make it so that most client devices (such as Windows PCs and laptops) won't notice that the wireless LAN is present. This at least keeps "casual snoopers" off the network. Enterprise-grade access points implement multiple SSIDs, with each configured SSID having its own VLAN and wireless configuration. This allows the deployment of a common wireless LAN infrastructure that supports multiple levels of security, which is important for some venues such as airports and hospitals (where there are both public and private users).

IEEE 802.11 supports two ways to authenticate clients: open and sharekey. *Open* authentication basically means that the correct SSID is being used. In *sharekey* authentication, a packet of text is sent by the access point to the client with the instruction to encrypt the text and return it to the access point. This requires that wired equivalent privacy (WEP) be turned on. WEP is used to encrypt and decrypt wireless data packets. The exchange and the return of the encrypted text verifies that the client has the proper WEP key and is authorized to be a member of the wireless network. It is important to note that shared key authentication is extremely vulnerable. As a result, it's standard practice to avoid the use of shared key authentication. An example of the setting for WEP encryption is provided in Figure 4-25 (a and b). In Figure 4-25(a), the user has the WEP options of disabled (No Privacy), 64-bit WEP (Privacy), and 128-bit WEP (More Privacy). Figure 4-25(b) shows the wireless security settings in Windows Vista. There are clearly more options, and these newer wireless security settings are discussed next.

(a)

(b)

FIGURE 4-25   An example of setting WEP encryption on a wireless client.

There is some concern that WEP isn't a strong enough encryption to secure a wireless network. There is published information about WEP vulnerabilities, but even with this, WEP does provide some basic security and is certainly better than operating the network with no security.

An improvement with wireless security is provided with WPA and WPA2. **WPA** stands for Wi-Fi Protected Access, and it supports the user authentication provided by 802.1x and replaces WEP as the primary way for securing wireless transfers. WPA2 is an improved version of WPA. The 802.1x standard enhances wireless security by incorporating authentication of the user. Cisco Systems uses an 802.1x authentication system called LEAP. In Cisco LEAP, the user must enter a password to access the network. This means that if the wireless client is being used by an unauthorized user, the password requirement will keep the unauthorized user out of the network.

> **WPA**
> Wi-Fi Protected Access

WPA is considered to be a higher level of security for wireless systems. In the 802.1x system, a user requests access to the wireless network via an access point. The next step is for the user to be authenticated. At this point, the user can only send EAP messages. **EAP** is the Extensible Authentication Protocol and is used in both WPA and WPA2 by the client computer and the access point. The access point sends an EAP message requesting the user's identity. The user (client computer) returns the identity information that is sent by the access point to an authentication

> **EAP**
> Extensible Authentication Protocol

server. The server will then accept or reject the user's request to join the network. If the client is authorized, the access point will change the user's (client's) state to authorized. A Remote Authentication Dial-In User Service (**RADIUS**) service is sometimes used to provide authentication. This type of authentication helps prevent unauthorized users from connecting to the network. Additionally, this authentication helps to keep authorized users from connecting to rogue or unauthorized access points.

Another way to further protect data transmitted over a WLAN is to establish a VPN connection (see Chapter 12, Network Security"). In this way, the data is protected from an attacker. The following are basic guidelines for wireless security:

- Make sure the wireless security features are turned on.
- Use firewalls and intrusion detection on your WLAN.
- Improve authentication of the WLAN by incorporating 802.1x features.
- Consider using third-party end-to-end encryption software to protect the data that might be intercepted by an unauthorized user.
- Whenever possible, use encrypted services such as SSH and Secure FTP.

The bottom line is that the choice of the level of security will be based on multiple factors within the network. For example, what is the cost benefit ratio of increased security? How will incorporating or not incorporating increased wireless security affect users? The network administrator and the overall management will have to make the final decision regarding wireless security before it is installed and the network becomes operational.

Section 4-5 Review

This section has covered the following **Network+** Exam objectives:

3.2 Compare and contrast common network vulnerabilities and threats

The network administrator must assume that the wireless data can be received by an unintended user. In other words, the use of an unsecured wireless LAN is opening a potential threat to network security. To address this threat to WLAN security, the network administrator must ensure that the WLAN is protected by firewalls and intrusion detection, and most importantly the network administrator must make sure that the wireless security features are enabled.

3.3 Given a scenario, implement network-hardening techniques

This section has provided an overview of WEP, WPA, and the WPA2 wireless encryption protocols. Information for each protocol has been discussed as well as possible weaknesses. It is important to understand that these protocols provide some support of security and are much better than not running any security protocol.

3.6 Explain the purpose of various network access control models

The 802.1x standard is introduced in this section. This standard enhances wireless security by incorporating authentication of the user.

4-6 CONFIGURING A POINT-TO-MULTIPOINT WIRELESS LAN: A CASE STUDY

This section presents an example of preparing a proposal for providing a point-to-multipoint wireless network for a company. The administrators for the company have decided that it would be beneficial to provide a wireless network connection for their employees back to the company's network (home network). This example addresses the following issues:

1. Conducting an initial antenna site survey

2. Establishing a link from the home network to the distribution point

3. Configuring the multipoint distribution

4. Conducting an RF site survey for establishing a baseline signal level for the remote wireless user

5. Configuring the remote user's installation

The objective is to establish a point-to-multipoint wireless network that provides remote users with a wireless network connection. The remote users are to be at fixed locations within the proposed coverage area. A simple terrain profile of the proposed area is shown in Figure 4-26. The data rate for the wireless connection to remote users needs to be at least 2 Mbps.

FIGURE 4-26 The terrain profile of the area to be supported by the proposed point-to-multipoint wireless network.

1. Antenna Site Survey

The proposed antenna site (see Figure 4-26) is on top of a hill approximately 1 kilometer (km) from the home network. A site survey provides the following information:

- The site has a tower that can be used to mount the wireless antenna.
- The site has a small building and available rack space for setting up the wireless networking equipment.
- There is a clear view of the surrounding area for 6 km in every direction.
- There is not an available wired network connection back to the home network. The decision is made to use the proposed antenna site and set up an 11Mbps wireless link back to the home network.

2. Establishing a Point-to-Point Wireless Link to the Home Network

The cost is too high to install a wired connection back to the home network; therefore, it is decided to use a point-to-point 802.11 wireless link for the interconnection. This requires that antennas be placed at both the home network and the antenna site. A wireless bridge is used at each end of the point-to-point wireless link to interconnect the networks. The bridge will connect to the wired home network and to the multipoint distribution on the antenna site. Also each antenna will be outfitted with lightning arrestors to protect the electronics from any possible lightning strikes. Figure 4-27 shows the proposed wireless connection.

FIGURE 4-27 The proposed point-to-point wireless link from the home network to the antenna site.

Many manufacturers of antennas support wireless networking, and many types of antenna can be used. Antenna types from many manufacturers were investigated for possible use in the interconnection. Three possible antennas were selected for the wireless network, as outlined in Table 4-7.

TABLE 4-7   Sample of 802.11b Wireless Antennas

Antenna	Type	Radiation Pattern	Range in km at 2Mbps	Range in km at 11Mbps	Costs
A.	Omni	Omnidirectional	7	2	Moderate
B.	Yagi	Directional	12	7.5	Moderate
C.	Dish	Highly directional	38	18	High

Antenna A has an omnidirectional radiation pattern. This means the antenna can receive and transmit signals in a 360-degree pattern. Figure 4-28(a) shows the radiation pattern for an omnidirectional antenna. Antenna A supports a 2Mbps data rate up to 7 km from the antenna and supports an 11Mbps data rate at a maximum distance of 2 km. Table 4-7 also indicates that this antenna has a moderate cost.

Antenna B is a Yagi antenna with a directional radiation pattern as shown in Figure 4-28(b). The Yagi antenna supports a 2Mbps data rate for a maximum of 12 km.

Antenna C is a "dish" antenna or parabolic reflector. These antennas provide extremely high directional gain. In this example, the dish antenna supports 11Mbps up to 18 km away and 2Mbps up to 38 km away. The cost of the dish antenna can be quite high relative to the cost of the Yagi or omnidirectional antenna.

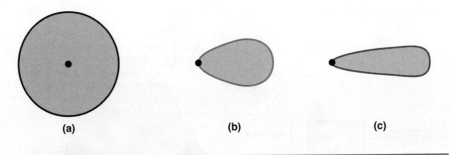

| (a) | (b) | (c) |

FIGURE 4-28   Antenna radiation patterns for (a) omnidirectional, (b) Yagi, and (c) dish [parabolic reflector] antenna, and supports 11Mbps up to 7.5 km from the antenna. The cost of the Yagi antenna is comparable to the omnidirectional antenna.

Antenna B, the directional Yagi, is selected for the point-to-point link. The antenna meets the distance requirement and also meets the 11Mbps data rate requirement. Antennas A and C were not selected for the following reasons:

- **Antenna A**: The omnidirectional radiation pattern is not appropriate.
- **Antenna C**: The cost of a high gain dish antenna is not justified for the short distance.

3–4. Configuring the Multipoint Distribution/Conducting an RF Site Survey

At this point, an 11Mbps wireless data link has been established with the home network. The next task is to configure the antenna site for multipoint distribution. It was previously decided that a 2Mbps link would be adequate for the remote users, based on the data rate to be supported for the planned coverage area.

The site survey in step 1 showed that there is a clear view of the surrounding area for 6 km in each direction. Antenna A (see Table 4-7) provides an omnidirectional radiation pattern for 7 km. This satisfies the coverage area and 2Mbps data rate. Antenna A is mounted on the antenna site tower, connected to a lightning arrestor and then connected to the output of a wireless bridge. Next, an RF site survey of the planned coverage area is done to verify the signal quality provided by the antenna selected. Measurements are made from multiple locations within the planned coverage area. All remote sites within 4 km of the distribution show a signal strength of "Excellent," as shown in Figure 4-29.

The signal quality drops to "Good" at 6 km at all surveyed remote locations except for one area that shows a "Poor." Figure 4-30 provides the measurement for this site. Apparently the signal is being affected by multipath distortion off a small lake area. A fix to this might be to move the antenna to a different height to minimize reflection problems. An antenna at a different height will receive different reflections and possibly less interference. In some cases antenna alignment can be changed to decrease the interference. A more costly solution is to add antenna "diversity." Basically, this means that multiple antennas are placed on the receiving tower and the best signal is used for the connection.

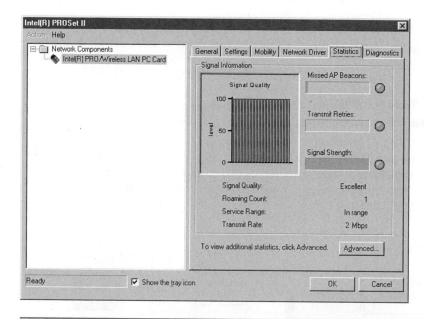

FIGURE 4-29   The signal quality of "Excellent" measured for the multipoint distribution.

FIGURE 4-30   The signal quality of "Poor" measured at the remote site near the lake.

5. Configuring the Remote Installations

The last task is to develop a configuration for the remote users. The antenna for each remote user needs to be able to see only the multipoint distribution antenna site. The requirements for the remote client are as follows:

- 2Mbps data rate connection
- Directional antenna (Yagi) plus mount, lightning arrestor, wireless bridge

Antenna B (see Table 4-7) is selected for the directional antenna. This antenna will provide sufficient RF signal level for the remote user. Each remote user will need a wireless bridge and a switch to connect multiple users. (Note that the bridge is set for a 2Mbps data rate.) Figure 4-31 shows the setup for the remote user.

FIGURE 4-31 The setup for the remote user in the proposed point-to-multipoint wireless network.

Section 4-6 Review

This section has covered the following **Network+** Exam objectives:

> 2.7 Install and configure a wireless LAN infrastructure and implement the appropriate technologies in support of wireless-capable devices

This section presents a look at a case study for installing a point-to-multipoint wireless LAN. The study addresses the issue of antenna selection, establishing a data link, configuring the multipoint distribution, conducting an RF site survey, and configuring the remote user's installation. Make sure you have a good understanding of each step and understand the steps for configuring such a site.

> 4.3 Given a scenario, troubleshoot and resolve common wireless issues

This section provides an overview of selecting the appropriate antenna type.

Test Your Knowledge

1. The antennae typically used at receive sites from a multipoint distribution system include which of the following? (Select all that apply.)

    a. Yagi

    b. Omnidirectional

    c. Parabolic

    d. Hydroxyl

2. When configuring remote installations for wireless networks, the receive site needs to be able to see the multipoint distribution antenna site. True or False?

SUMMARY

This chapter presented an overview of wireless networking. The fundamental concept and sample networks were also presented. The vendors of wireless networking equipment have made them easy to integrate into existing networks, but the reader must understand that the key objective of the network administrator is to provide a fast, reliable, and secure computer network. Carelessly integrating wireless components into the network can easily compromise this objective. Students should understand the following from reading this chapter:

- The operating characteristics of the 802.11 wireless networks
- The purpose of access points, wireless LAN adapters, and wireless bridges
- How to perform a basic site survey on a building
- How to configure the network for user mobility
- How to plan multipoint wireless distribution

A final note: The new wireless networking technologies have greatly simplified planning and installation. Anytime you are working with RF there is a chance of unexpected interference and noise. A well-planned RF installation requires a study of all known interference and a search for any possible interference. An RF study will also include signal path studies that enable the user to prepare a well-thought-out plan and allow an excellent prediction of received signal level. The bottom line is to obtain support for conducting an RF study.

QUESTIONS AND PROBLEMS

Section 4-2

1. List two advantages of wireless networking.

2. What are the three areas defined for the IEEE 802.11 standard?

3. What is an *ad hoc network*?

4. What is the purpose of an Extended Service Set?

5. What are the four physical layer technologies being used in 802.11 wireless networking?

6. Describe the frequency spectrum for the DSSS channels in 802.11b wireless networking.

7. Define a *pseudorandom sequence* as it applies to FHSS.

8. What must the FHSS transmitting and receiving units know to communicate?

9. What is the frequency range used by 802.11a, and what modulation technique is used?

10. What is the maximum data rate for the following?

    a. 802.11b

    b. 802.11a

    c. 802.11g

    d. 802.11n

    e. 802.11ac

11. Define MIMO as it applies to 802.11n.

12. What is the purpose of the power-save mode in 802.11n?

Section 4-3

13. What is the purpose of an access point?

14. How does the access point know if a wireless data packet is intended for its network?

15. What is an *association*, and what is its purpose?

16. Draw a picture of a point-to-point wireless connection.

17. Draw a picture of a point-to-multipoint wireless network.

18. What are the key issues to be obtained from conducting a site survey for each of the following?

    a. Indoor

    b. Outdoor

Section 4-4

19. In what frequency band does Bluetooth operate?

20. How many output power classes does Bluetooth have? List the power level and the operating range for each class.

21. What is a piconet?

22. What is the purpose of the inquiry procedure in Bluetooth?

23. What is the purpose of the paging procedure in Bluetooth?

24. Define the term *backscatter*.

25. What are the three parameters that define an RFID system?

26. Explain how power is provided to a passive RFID tag.

27. Cite three advantages for using an active RFID tag.

28. What are the three frequency bands typically used for RFID tags?

29. What is the WiMAX frequency standard for the United States?

30. Why was OFDM selected for WiMAX?

31. How does WiMAX differ from Wi-Fi?

Section 4-5

32. What is the most important thing to do if using a wireless network?

33. What is the purpose of wireless beacons?

34. What information can be obtained from a wireless beacon?

35. What is the purpose of WEP?

36. List four guidelines for wireless security.

37. Describe the steps used by WPA2 to authenticate a user.

38. What is a RADIUS server?

39. What type of wireless connection is used to connect the home network to a multipoint distribution site?

40. Use the Internet to find a source of omnidirectional and directional antennas for each of the following standards.

    a. 802.11b

    b. 802.11a

    c. 802.11g

    d. 802.11n

    Prepare a list of three manufacturers for each antenna type. Include cost figures.

CRITICAL THINKING

41. A wireless network receiving site is experiencing occasional loss of signal due to interference. Discuss the steps you would take to correct this problem.

42. Prepare a memo to your supervisor explaining why it is important to run encryption on your wireless network.

43. Your company has a suite in a business complex. Another company in the suite next to you has a wireless 802.11b network with an SSID of "Company A." You can pick up their signal from your suite. Your company would like to put up its own wireless network with two access points. Discuss how you would set up these two access points so that your company can obtain optimal performance.

CERTIFICATION QUESTIONS

44. If the signal quality drops from excellent to good, the antenna or access point should be replaced. True or False?

45. The network administrator is setting up a wireless network. There is a chance of radio interference. How can the network administrator avoid or minimize potential interference problems?

    a. An RF study should be performed prior to the installation of the wireless network.

    b. Contact all owners of equipment that may cause interference and ask them to uses different systems.

    c. Contact the FCC to have the interfering sources shut down.

    d. All of these answers are correct

46. Define MIMO relative to 802.11n.

    a. A multiplexing technique where the power is split into multiple parts called spatial currents

    b. A frequency-division multiplexing technique where the data stream is split into multiple parts called spectral streams

    c. An OFDM multiplexing technique where the digital data is portioned into multiple parts called filtered streams

    d. A space-division multiplexing technique where the data stream is split into multiple parts called spatial streams

47. Which of the following best characterizes CSMA/CA?

    a. Replaces CSMA/CD

    b. Provides carrier sense / collision avoidance

    c. Provides carrier sense / congestion avoidance

    d. Provides congestion sensing / collision avoidance

48. An advantage of the 802.11g is (select all that apply)

    a. compatibility with 802.11b

    b. compatibility with 802.11a

    c. using infrared instead of radio

    d. high speed

49. This is used in wireless LANs to identify if a client is to become a member of the wireless network.

    a. SSID

    b. MAC address

    c. IP address

    d. echo

50. What does the term "last mile" mean relative to telecommunications?

    a. The distance from the RF transmitter to the receiver in WiMAX.

    b. A measurement of signal coverage for WiMAX and for Wi-Fi

    c. A term for the last connection prior to linking to the RF transmitter

    d. The last part of the connection from the telecommunications provider to the customer

51. A solution to extend the radio range of a station's wireless link with one access point is to add (select the best answer)

    a. multiple access points

    b. additional wiring

    c. 87BZS encoding

    d. B8ZS encoding

52. Wi-Fi is which of the following?

    a. The Wi-Fi Alliance, which is an organization that assembles and tests wireless equipment before it is shipped to the vendors

    b. The Wi-Fi Alliance, which is an organization that tests and certifies wireless equipment for compliance with the 803.1 standards

    c. The Wi-Fi Alliance, which is an organization that tests and certifies wireless equipment for compliance with the 802.11x standards

    d. None of these answers is correct.

53. Which of the following are current wireless networking standards?

    a. 802.12n

    b. 802.11g

    c. 803.11g

    d. 802.11a

    e. 802.11b

    f. 802.55a

    g. 802.11n

    h. 802.1a

    i. 802.11ac

5 CHAPTER

INTERCONNECTING THE LANS

Chapter Outline

Objectives

- Describe how a bridge is used to interconnect LANs
- Describe how a switch is used to interconnect LANs
- Discuss the advantages of using a switch instead of a hub
- Describe the function of a router when used to interconnect LANs
- Describe the interface associated with a router
- Describe the function of a gateway in a computer network
- Describe the concept of a network segment
- Describe the concept of auto-negotiation

Key Terms

campus network
bridge
bridging table
association
broadcast
ARP
broadcast storm
network slowdown
ARP cache
ARP table
transparent bridge
translation bridge
layer 2 switch
multiport bridge
multicast
managed switch
Cisco Network Assistant (CNA)
dynamic assignment
static assignment

secure addresses
aging time
isolating the collision-domain
content addressable memory (CAM)
flooding
broadcast domain
store-and-forward
cut-through
switch latency
error threshold
multilayer switch (MLS)
wire speed routing
network address
logical address
router interface
power on/off
auxiliary input
console input

serial ports
AUI port
media converter
enterprise network
FastEthernet port (FA0/0, FA0/1, FA0/2, …)
serial port (S0/0, S0/1, S0/2, …)
routing table
gateway
auto-negotiation
fast link pulse (FLP)
half-duplex

The utility of LANs led to the desire to connect two (or more) networks together. For example, a large corporation might have had separate networks for research and engineering and another for its manufacturing units. These network systems probably used totally different networking technologies and specifications for communicating and were located in different cities, states, or even countries, but it was deemed necessary to "tie" them together. The objective of this and subsequent chapters is to introduce the concepts and issues behind interconnecting LANs. Interconnecting LANs in a **campus network** or even interconnecting LANs in wide area networks (WANs) incorporate similar concepts and issues. The campus network is a collection of two or more interconnected LANs, either within a building or housed externally in multiple buildings.

5-1   INTRODUCTION

Campus Network

A collection of two or more interconnected LANs in a limited geographic area

The framework defining the network layers for linking networks together is defined by the OSI model and was introduced in Chapter 1, "Introduction to Computer Networks," section 1-3. The OSI model provides a framework for networking that ensures compatibility in the network hardware and software. The concepts behind the hardware technologies used to interconnect LANs are presented in sections 5-2 to 5-5. The properties of a networking bridge are defined in section 5-2. The layer 2 switch is examined in section 5-3, and the router is introduced in section 5-4. An example of interconnecting LANs is provided in section 5-5. The chapter concludes with a section on the concept of auto-negotiation, examining the advantages and disadvantages of this network configuration option.

Table 5-1 lists and identifies, by chapter section, where each of the CompTIA Network+ objectives are presented in this chapter. The chapter sections where each objective is presented are identified. At the end of each chapter section is a review with comments of the Network+ objectives presented in that section. These comments are provided to help reinforce the reader's understanding of a particular Network+ objective. The chapter review also includes "Test Your Knowledge" questions to aid in the understanding of key concepts before the reader advances to the next section of the chapter. The end of the chapter includes a complete set of question plus sample certification type questions.

TABLE 5-1   Chapter 5 CompTIA Network+ Objectives

Domain/ Objective Number	Domain/Objective Description	Section Where Objective Is Covered
1.0	**Network Architecture**	
1.1	Explain the functions and applications of various network devices	5-3, 5-4
1.3	Install and configure the following networking services/applications	5-4
1.4	Explain the characteristics and benefits of various WAN technologies	5-4
1.7	Differentiate between network infrastructure implementations	5-2
1.8	Given a scenario, implement and configure the appropriate addressing schema	5-2, 5-3
1.9	Explain the basics of routing concepts and protocols	5-3, 5-5
2.0	**Network Operations**	
2.6	Given a scenario, configure a switch using proper features	5-4
4.0	**Troubleshooting**	
4.2	Given a scenario, analyze and interpret the output of troubleshooting tools	5-3
4.6	Given a scenario, troubleshoot and resolve common network issues	5-5
5.0	**Industry standards, practices, and network theory**	
5.2	Explain the basics of network theory and concepts	5-2, 5-4, 5-6

5-2 THE NETWORK BRIDGE

A bridge can be used in computer networks to interconnect two LANs together and separate network segments. Recall that a *segment* is a section of a network separated by bridges, switches, and routers. The **bridge** is a layer 2 device in the OSI model, meaning that it uses the MAC address information to make decisions regarding forwarding data packets. Only the data that needs to be sent across the bridge to the adjacent network segment is forwarded. This makes it possible to

> **Bridge**
> A networking device that uses the MAC address to forward data and interconnect two LANs

isolate or segment the network data traffic. An example of using a bridge to segment two Ethernet LANs is shown in Figure 5-1. The picture shows that LAN A connects to port 1 of the bridge and LAN B connects to port 2 on the bridge, creating two segments, as shown. There are four computers in LAN A and three computers in LAN B. It is important to note that bridges are now legacy networking devices, but studying these will help you better understand the functionality of switches, especially how data traffic is sent to connected LANs.

Bridges monitor all data traffic in each of the LAN segments connected to its ports. Recall that a *port* is an input/output connection on a networking device. The bridges use the MAC addresses to build a **bridging table** of MAC addresses and port locations for hosts connected to the bridge ports. A sample bridging table is provided in Table 5-2. The table shows the stored MAC address and the port where the address was obtained.

Bridging Table

List of MAC addresses and port locations for hosts connected to the bridge ports

TABLE 5-2 **Bridging Table**

MAC Address	Port
00-40-96-25-85-BB	1
00-40-96-25-8E-BC	1
00-60-97-61-78-5B	2
00-C0-4F-27-20-C7	2

The source MAC address is stored in the bridge table as soon as a host talks (transmits a data packet) on the LAN. For example, if computer 1 in LAN A sends a message to computer 2 (see Figure 5-1), the bridge will store the MAC addresses of both computers and record that both of these computers are connected to port 1. If computers 5 or 6 are placing data packets on the network, then the source MAC addresses for 5 and 6 are stored in the bridge table and it is recorded that these computers connect to port 2 on the bridge. The MAC addresses for computers 3 and 4 will not be added to the bridging table until each transmits a data packet.

FIGURE 5-1 Using a bridge to interconnect two Ethernet LANs.

The bridge monitors the data on its ports to check for an **association** between the destination MAC address of the Ethernet frames to any of the hosts connected to its ports. An association indicates that the destination MAC address for a host is connected to one of the ports on the bridge. If an association is found, the data is forwarded to that port. For example, assume that computer 1 sends a message to computer 5 (see Figure 5-1). The bridge detects an association between the destination MAC address for computer 5 and port 2. The bridge then forwards the data from computer 1 to computer 5 in LAN B via port 2.

The capability of a bridge to forward data packets only when there is an association is used to isolate data traffic in each segment. For example, assume that computer 1 and computer 2 in LAN A generate a lot of data traffic. The computers in LAN B will not see any of the data traffic as long as there is not an association between the destination MAC addresses of the Ethernet packets and any of the hosts in LAN B (computers 5, 6, and 7).

A potential problem with bridges has to do with the way broadcasts are handled. A **broadcast** means the message is being sent to all computers on the network; therefore, all broadcasts in a LAN will be forwarded to all hosts connected within the bridged LANs. For example, the broadcast associated with an ARP will appear on all hosts. **ARP** stands for Address Resolution Protocol, which is a protocol used to map an IP address to its MAC address. In the address resolution protocol, a broadcast is sent to all hosts in a LAN connected to the bridge. This is graphically shown in Figure 5-2. The bridge forwards all broadcasts; therefore, an ARP request broadcasting the message "Who has this IP address?" is sent to all hosts on the LAN. The data packets associated with ARP requests are small, but it requires computer time to process each request. Excessive amounts of broadcasts being forwarded by the bridge can lead to a **broadcast storm**, resulting in degraded network performance, called a **network slowdown**.

The MAC address entries stored in a bridge table are temporary. Each MAC address entry to the bridge table remains active as long as there is periodic data traffic activity from that host on its port. However, an entry into the table is deleted if the port becomes inactive. In other words, the entries stored into the table have a limited lifetime. An expiration timer will commence once the MAC address is entered into the bridge table. The lifetime for the entry is renewed by new data traffic by the computer, and the MAC address is reentered.

In a similar manner, all networking devices (for example, computers) contain an **ARP cache**, a temporary storage of MAC addresses recently contacted. This is also called the **ARP table**. The ARP cache holds the MAC address of a host, and this enables the message to be sent directly to the destination MAC address without the computer having to issue an ARP request for a MAC address. The following list outlines typical steps of a communication process between computer 1 and computer 2.

Association
Indicates that the destination address is for a networking device connected to one of the ports on the bridge

Broadcast
Transmission of the data to all connected devices

ARP
Address Resolution Protocol

Broadcast Storm
Excessive amounts of broadcasts

Network Slowdown
Degraded network performance

ARP Cache
Temporary storage of MAC addresses recently contacted

ARP Table
Another name for the ARP cache

Data Traffic
- - - - **Broadcast Traffic**

FIGURE 5-2 An example of using a bridge to isolate data traffic.

1. Computer 1 checks its ARP cache to determine if it already has the MAC address of computer 2. If it does, it will skip to the final step; otherwise, it proceeds to the next step.

2. Computer 1 generates an ARP request message for computer 2 with its own MAC and IP information included.

3. Computer 1 then broadcasts the ARP request message on its local network.

4. Every local network device processes the ARP request message. Those computers that are not computer 2 will discard the message.

5. Only a match, which is computer 2, generates an ARP reply message and updates its ARP cache with computer 1 MAC and IP information.

6. Computer 2 sends an ARP reply message directly to computer 1.

7. Computer 1 receives the ARP reply message and updates its ARP cache with the MAC and IP of computer 2.

The ARP cache contents on a Windows computer can be viewed using the **arp -a** command while in the command prompt, as shown here:

Windows			Mac OS X
C:\arp –a			jmac:~mymac$ **arp –a**
Interface: 10.10.20.2 on Interface x1000002			C1.salsa.org (192.168.12.1) at
Internet Address	Physical Address	Type	00-08-a3-a7-78-0c on en1
10.10.20.3	00-08-a3-a7-78-0c	dynamic	[ethernet]
10.10.20.4	00-03-ba-04-ba-ef	dynamic	C3.salsa.org (192.168.12.1) at
			00-08-a3-a7-78-0c on en1
			[ethernet]

The ARP cache contents on a Mac OS X computer can be viewed using the **arp -a** command while in the terminal mode.

The following message is generated if all the ARP entries have expired:

```
c:\arp -a
No ARP Entries Found
```

The name for the type of bridge used to interconnect two LANs running the same type of protocol (for example, Ethernet) is a **transparent bridge**. Bridges are also used to interconnect two LANs that are operating two different networking protocols. For example, LAN A could be an Ethernet LAN and LAN B could be a token ring. This type of bridge is called a **translation bridge**. An example is provided in Figure 5-3. The bridge allows data from one LAN to be transferred to another. Also the MAC addressing information is standardized so the same address information is used regardless of the protocol.

Transparent Bridge
Interconnects two LANs running the same type of protocol

Translation Bridge
Used to interconnect two LANs that are operating two different networking protocols

Ethernet   **Token ring**

FIGURE 5-3   Using a translation bridge to interconnect an Ethernet and token-ring LAN.

A common application today using a bridge is interconnecting LANs using wireless technology. The use of wireless bridges in LANs is a popular choice for interconnecting the LANs when the cost of physically connecting them is prohibitive. Wireless technology and its LAN applications were presented in Chapter 4, "Wireless Networking."

The use of a bridge is not as common as it used to be except for wireless network applications. New networking technologies are available that provide similar capabilities to the bridge but that are much more powerful. However, the bridge still is useful and has several advantages. Table 5-3 provides a summary of the advantages and disadvantages of a networking bridge.

TABLE 5-3 **Summary of the Advantages and Disadvantages of a Bridge for Interconnecting LANs**

Advantages	Disadvantages
Easy to install	Works best in low-traffic areas
Does an excellent job of isolating the data traffic in two segments	Forwards broadcasts and is susceptible to broadcast storms
Relatively inexpensive	
Can be used to interconnect two LANs with different protocols and hardware	
Reduces collision domains (remember how the CSMA/CD protocol works)	

Section 5-2 Review

This section has covered the following **Network+** Exam objectives.

1.7 Differentiate between network infrastructure implementations

This section presents a look at the network bridge. The advantages and disadvantages of the network bridge are presented in Table 5-3. A key concept presented in this section is an "association" that indicates that the destination address for a networking device has been obtained.

1.8 Given a scenario, implement and configure the appropriate addressing schema

Another important concept presented in this section is that a bridge will pass a broadcast to all devices connected to its ports. Excessive broadcast can potentially have a negative impact on data traffic and result in a network slowdown. The purpose of the bridging table for storing the MAC addresses of connected devices was also presented. Each MAC address entry to the bridge table remains active as long as there is periodic data traffic activity from that host on its port. However, an entry into the table is deleted if the port becomes inactive.

5.2 Explain the basics of network theory and concepts

An important concept presented in this section is that a bridge will pass a broadcast to all devices connected to its ports. Excessive broadcast can potentially have a negative impact on data traffic and result in a network slowdown.

Test Your Knowledge

1. Which command is used on a computer to view the contents of the ARP cache?

   a. **arp -c**

   b. **arp -l**

   c. **arp -a**

   d. **arp -b**

   e. **arp**

2. An association indicates which of the following?

   a. That the destination address for a networking device is connected to one of its ports

   b. That the source address is for a networking device connected to one of the ports on the bridge

   c. That the destination address is for a networking device connected to one of the ports on the hub

   d. That the source address is for a networking device connected to one of the ports on the hub

3. An ARP cache is which of the following?

   a. A temporary storage of IP addresses for networking devices recently contacted

   b. A temporary storage of MAC addresses for networking devices to be contacted

   c. A temporary storage of IP addresses for networking devices to be contacted

   d. A temporary storage of MAC addresses for networking devices recently contacted

5-3 THE NETWORK SWITCH

The bridge provides a method for isolating the collision domains for interconnected LANs but lacks the capability to provide a direct data connection for the hosts. The bridge forwards the data traffic to all computers connected to its port. This was shown in Figure 5-2. The networking hub provides a technology for sharing access to the network with all computers connected to its ports in the LAN but lacks the capability to isolate the data traffic and provide a direct data connection from the source to the destination computer. The increase in the number of computers being used in LANs and the increased data traffic are making bridges and hubs of limited use in larger LANs. Basically, there is too much data traffic to be shared by the entire network. What is needed is a networking device that provides a direct data connection between communicating devices. Neither the bridge nor the hub provides a direct data connection for the hosts. A technology developed to improve the efficiency of the data networks and address the need for direct data connections is the layer 2 switch.

Layer 2 Switch

An improved network technology that provides a direct data connection for network devices in a LAN

Multiport Bridge

Another name for a layer 2 switch

The **layer 2 switch** is an improved network technology that addresses the issue of providing direct data connections, minimizing data collisions, and maximizing the use of a LAN's bandwidth; in other words, that improves the efficiency of the data transfer in the network. The switch operates at layer 2 of the OSI model and therefore uses the MAC or Ethernet address for making decisions for forwarding data packets. The switch monitors data traffic on its ports and collects MAC address information in the same way the bridge does to build a table of MAC addresses for the devices connected to its ports. The switch has multiple ports similar to the hub and can switch in a data connection from any port to any other port, similar to the bridge. This is why the switch is sometimes called a **multiport bridge**. The switch minimizes traffic congestion and isolates data traffic in the LAN. Figure 5-4 provides an example of a switch being used in a LAN.

Figure 5-4 shows a switch being used in the LAN to interconnect the hosts. In this figure, the hub has been replaced with a switch. The change from a hub to a switch is relatively easy. The port connections are the same (RJ-45), and once the connections are changed and the device is powered on, the switch begins to make the direct data connections for multiple ports using layer 2 switching.

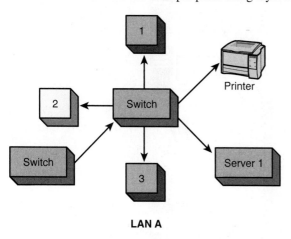

LAN A

FIGURE 5-4 A switch used to interconnect hosts in a LAN.

The LAN shown in Figure 5-5 contains 14 computers and 2 printers connected to 16 ports on the switch, configured in a star topology. If the computer connected to port 1 is printing a file on the laser printer (port 12), the switch will set up a direct connection between ports 1 and 12. The computer at port 14 could also be communicating with the computer at port 7, and the computer at port 6 could be printing a file on the color printer at port 16. The use of the switch enables simultaneous direct data connections for multiple pairs of hosts connected to the network. Each switch connection provides a link with minimal collisions and therefore maximum use of the LAN's bandwidth. A link with minimal collisions is possible because only the two computers that established the link will be communicating over the channel. Recall that in the star topology each host has a direct connection to the switch. Therefore, when the link is established between the two hosts, their link is isolated from any other data traffic. However, the exception to this is when broadcast or **multicast** messages are sent in the LAN. In the case of a broadcast message, the message is sent to all devices connected to the LAN. A multicast message is sent to a specific group of hosts on the network.

> **Multicast**
> Messages are sent to a specific group of hosts on the network

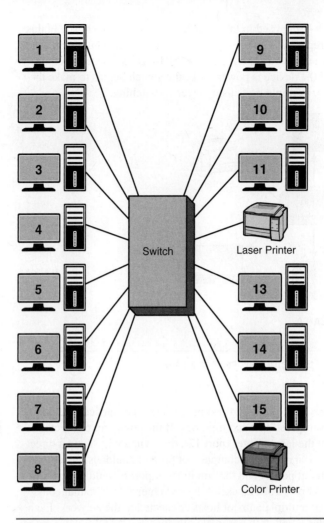

FIGURE 5-5 A switch used to interconnect the networking devices in a LAN.

Hub–Switch Comparison

An experiment was set up to test the data handling characteristics of a hub and a switch given the same input instructions. The objective of this experiment was to show that data traffic is isolated with a switch but not with a hub. For this experiment, a LAN using a hub and a LAN using a switch were assembled. The LANs are shown in Figure 5-6(a) and (b). Each LAN contains four computers connected in a star topology. The computers are marked 1–4 for reference. The IP addresses are listed for each host.

(a)   **(b)**

FIGURE 5-6   (a) The LAN experiment with a hub; (b) the LAN experiment with a switch.

The Hub Experimental Results

In this experiment, computer 1 pinged computer 3. Computer 2 was used to capture the LAN data traffic using a network protocol analyzer. What are the expected results? Remember, a hub is a multiport repeater, and all data traffic input to the hub is passed on to all hosts connected to its ports. See the Ping Command Review section that follows for a brief review of the use of the **ping** command.

Ping Command Review

The **ping** command is used to verify that a network connection exists between two computers. The command format for **ping** is:

```
ping [ip address] {for this example ping 10.10.10.3}
```

After a link is established between the two computers, a series of echo requests and echo replies are issued by the networking devices to test the time it takes for data to pass through the link. The protocol used by the **ping** command is the Internet Connection Message Protocol (ICMP).

The **ping** command is issued to an IP address; however, delivery of this command to the computer designated by the IP address requires that a MAC address be identified for final delivery. The computer issuing the **ping** might not know the MAC address of the computer holding the identified IP address (no entry in the ARP cache table); therefore, an ARP request is issued. An ARP request is broadcast to all computers connected in the LAN. The computer that holds the IP address replies with its MAC address, and a direct line of communications is then established.

The data traffic collected by computer 2 when computer 1 pinged computer 3 is provided in Figure 5-7. The first line of the captured data shows the ARP request asking who has the IP address 10.10.10.3. The second line of the captured data shows the reply from 10.10.10.3 with the MAC address of 00-B0-D0-25-BF-48. The next eight lines in the captured data are the series of four echo requests and replies associated with a ping request. Even though computer 2 was not being pinged or replying to the ARP request, the data traffic was still present on computer 2's hub port. The echo reply is from a Dell network interface card with the last six characters of the MAC address of 25-BF-48. The echo request is coming from a computer with 13-99-2E as the last six hex characters of its MAC address.

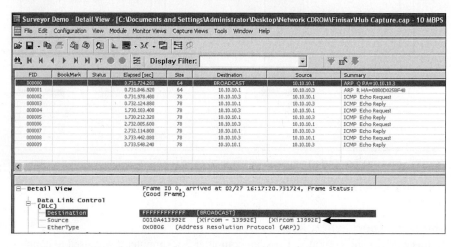

FIGURE 5-7   The captured data traffic by computer 2 for the LAN [Figure 5-6(a)] using a hub.

The Switch Experimental Results

The same experiment was repeated for the LAN shown in Figure 5-6(b), this time using a switch to interconnect the computers instead of a hub. This network consists of four computers connected in a star topology using a switch at the center of the network. The **ping** command was sent from computer 1 to computer 3, **ping 10.10.10.3**. The ARP cache for computer 1 is empty; therefore, the MAC address for computer 3 is not known by computer 1. An ARP request is issued by computer 1, and computer 3 replies. The series of echo requests and echo replies follow; however, the data traffic captured by computer 2 (Figure 5-8), shows the ARP request asking who has the IP address 10.10.10.3. This is the last of the data communications between computers 1 and 3 seen by computer 2. A direct line of communication between computers 1 and 3 is established by the switch that prevents computer 2 from seeing the data traffic from computers 1 and 3. The only data traffic seen by computer 2 in this process was the broadcast of the ARP request. This is true for any other hosts in the LAN. The results of this experiment show that the use of the switch substantially reduces data traffic in the LAN, particularly unnecessary data traffic. The experiment shows that the broadcast associated with an ARP request is seen by all computers but not the ARP replies in a LAN using a switch. This is because a direct data connection is established between the two hosts. This experiment used pings and ARPs; however, this same advantage of using a switch is true when transferring files, image downloads, file printing, and so on. The data traffic is isolated from other computers on the LAN. Remember, the switch uses MAC addresses to establish which computers are connected to its ports. The switch then extracts the destination MAC address from the Ethernet data packets to determine to which port to switch the data.

FIGURE 5-8   The data traffic captured by computer 2 for the LAN [Figure 5-6(b)] using a switch.

Managed Switches

A **managed switch** is simply a network switch that allows the network administrator to monitor, configure, and manage certain network features such as which computers are allowed to access the LAN via the switch. Access to the management features for the switch is password protected so that only the network administrators can gain entry. The following information describes some of the features of the managed interface for a Cisco Catalyst 2900 series switch established using the **Cisco Network Assistant (CNA)**. This software can be downloaded from Cisco and provides an easy way to manage the features of the Cisco switches. *(Note:* The download requires that you have set up a Cisco user account and password. The Cisco Network Assistant provides for a centralized mode for completing various network administration tasks for switches, routers, and wireless networking equipment.)

> **Managed Switch**
> Allows the network administrator to monitor, configure, and manage select network features
>
> **Cisco Network Assistant (CNA)**
> A management software tool from Cisco that simplifies switch configuration and troubleshooting

The start-up menu for a Cisco Catalyst 2960 switch obtained via the CNA is provided in Figure 5-9. The image is showing the current setup for the switch. The assigned IP address for the switch is 192.168.1.1, and a router and a switch are interconnected with the switch. The steps for setting the IP address for an interface on the switch are presented later in this section.

FIGURE 5-9   The start-up menu of a Cisco Catalyst switch using the Cisco Network Administrator software.

The current connections to the ports on the switch can be viewed by clicking the stacked switch icon at the top of the screen as shown in Figure 5-10. The image of the switch port connections shows ports 1, 2, and 3 are brighter, indicating that there are networking devices connected to the ports. The MAC addresses of the devices connected to the switch ports can be displayed by clicking the MAC address button under the Configure button as shown in Figure 5-11. Four MAC addresses are assigned to port 1, one MAC address is assigned to port 2, and one MAC address is assigned to port 3. Multiple networking devices can be connected to a port if the devices are first connected to another switch or hub and the output of the switch or hub is connected to one switch port. An example showing four devices connected through a hub to port 1 on the switch is shown in Figure 5-12. The output interface information for the MAC Addresses table shows the following information in Figure 5-11:

FastEthernet 0/1

FastEthernet 0/2

FastEthernet 0/3

Dynamic Assignment
MAC addresses are assigned to a port when a host is connected

Static Addressing
The MAC address has been manually assigned to a switch port

Secure Address
The switch port will automatically disable itself if a device with a different MAC address connects to the port

Notice that the Dynamic Address tab is highlighted. This indicates that this is a listing of the MAC addresses that have been assigned dynamically. **Dynamic assignment** means that the MAC address was assigned to a port when a host was connected. There is also a tab for Static Addresses. **Static addressing** indicates that the MAC address has been manually assigned to an interface, and the port assignment does not expire. The Secure tab shows what switch ports have been secured. A **secure address** means that a MAC address has been assigned to a port, and the port will automatically disable itself if a device with a different MAC address connects to the secured port.

Stacked Switch Icon

FIGURE 5-10 The highlighted ports showing the current connections and the location of the stacked switches icon.

The FastEthernet 0/1, FastEthernet 0/2, FastEthernet 0/3 notation indicates the [Interface Type Slot#/Interface#] on the switch, and FastEthernet indicates that this interface supports 100Mbps and 10Mbps data rate connections.

The "Aging Time" is listed to be 300 seconds. **Aging time** is the length of time a MAC address remains assigned to a port. The assignment of the MAC address will be removed if there is no data activity within this time. If the computer with the assigned MAC address initiates new data activity, the aging time counter is restarted, and the MAC address remains assigned to the port. The management window

Aging Time
The length of time a MAC address remains assigned to a port

shows a switch setting for enabling "Aging." This switch is used to turn off the aging counter so that a MAC address assignment on a port never expires.

FIGURE 5-11 The menu listing the MAC addresses currently connected to the switch.

FIGURE 5-12 An example of a hub connected to a switch port, with four computers connected to the hub.

The IP address on a switch interface can be configured using the Cisco Network Assistant software by clicking **Configure > Device Properties > IP Addresses**. This opens the IP Addresses menu shown in Figure 5-13. Click the area where the IP address should be entered. This opens a text box for entering the IP address. Enter the IP address and click **OK** to save the IP address.

FIGURE 5-13   Configuring an IP address on an interface.

Isolating the Collision Domains

Breaking the network into segments where a segment is a portion of the network where the data traffic from one part of the network is isolated from the other networking devices

The benefits of using a network switch are many in a modern computer network. These benefits include less network congestion, faster data transfers, and excellent manageability. It has been shown that a network switch can be used to replace the network hub, and the advantage is that data traffic within a LAN is isolated. The term for this is **isolating the collision domains**, which is breaking the network into segments. A segment is a portion of the network where the data traffic from one part of the network is isolated from the other networking devices. A direct benefit of isolating collision domains is that there will be an increase in the data transfer speed and throughput. This is due to the fact that the LAN bandwidth is not being shared and chances of data collisions are minimized. As a result, the LAN will exhibit faster data transfers and latency within the LAN will be significantly reduced. Reduced latency means that the data packets will arrive at the destination more quickly.

Content Addressable Memory (CAM)

A table of MAC addresses and port mapping used by the switch to identify connected networking devices

Switches learn the MAC addresses of the connected networking by extracting the MAC address information from the headers of Ethernet data packet headers of transmitted data packets. The switch will map the extracted MAC address to the port where the data packet came in. This information is stored in **Content Addressable Memory (CAM)**. CAM is a table of MAC address and port mapping used by the switch to identify connected networking devices. The extracted MAC addresses are then used by the switch to map a direct communication between two network devices connected to its ports. The MAC address and port information remain in CAM as long as the device connected to the switch port remains active. A timestamp establishes the time when the mapping of the MAC address to a switch port is established. However, switches limit the amount of time address and port information are stored in CAM. This is called *aging time*. The mapping information will be deleted from the switch's CAM if there is no activity during this set time. This technique keeps the mapping information stored in CAM up-to-date.

What happens if the destination MAC address is not stored in CAM? In this case, the packet is transmitted out all switch ports except for the port where the packet was received. This is called **flooding**.

It has been shown that switches minimize the collision domain due to the fact that a direct switch connection is made between networking devices. However, it is important to remember that switches do not reduce the broadcast domain. In a **broadcast domain**, any network broadcast sent over the network will be seen by all networking devices in the same network. Broadcasts within a LAN will be passed by switches. Refer to the discussion of Figure 5-7 and 5-8 for an example.

Two modes used in a switch to forward frames: **store-and-forward** and **cut-through**.

- **Store-and-Forward**: In this mode, the entire frame of data is received before any decision is made regarding forwarding the data packet to its destination. There is switch latency in this mode because the destination and source MAC addresses must be extracted from the packet, and the entire packet must be received before it is sent to the destination. The term **switch latency** is the length of time a data packet takes from the time it enters a switch until it exits. An advantage of the store-and-forward mode is that the switch checks the data packet for errors before it is sent on to the destination. A disadvantage is lengthy data packets will take a longer time before they exit the switch and are sent to the destination.

- **Cut-Through**: In this mode, the data packet is forwarded to the destination as soon as the destination MAC address has been read. This minimizes the switch latency; however, no error detection is provided by the switch. There are two forms of cut-through switching—Fast-Forward and Fragment Free.

    - **Fast-Forward**: This mode offers the minimum switch latency. The received data packet is sent to the destination as soon as the destination MAC address is extracted.

    - **Fragment-Free**: In this mode, fragment collisions are filtered out by the switch. Fragment-collisions are collisions that occur within the first 64 bytes of the data packet. Recall from Chapter 1, "Introduction to Computer Networks," Table 1-1 that the minimum Ethernet data packet size is 64 bytes. The collisions create packets smaller than 64 bytes, which are discarded. Latency is measured from the time the first bit is received until it is transmitted.

- **Adaptive Cut-Through**: This is a combination of the store-and-forward mode and cut-through. The cut-through mode is used until an **error threshold** (errors in the data packets) has been exceeded. The switch mode changes from cut-through to store-and-forward after the error threshold has been exceeded.

Flooding
The term used to describe what happens when a switch doesn't have the destination MAC address stored in CAM

Broadcast Domain
Any network broadcast sent over the network will be seen by all networking devices in this domain.

Store-and-Forward
The entire frame of data is received before any decision is made regarding forwarding the data packet to its destination.

Cut-Through
The data packet is forwarded to the destination as soon as the destination MAC address has been read.

Switch Latency
The length of time a data packet takes from the time it enters a switch until it exits

Error Threshold
The point where the number of errors in the data packets has reached a threshold and the switch changes from the cut-through to the store-and-forward mode

Multilayer Switches

> **Multilayer Switch (MLS)**
> Operates at layer 2 but functions at the higher layers
>
> **Wire Speed Routing**
> Data packets are processed as quickly as they arrive.

Newer switch technologies are available to help further improve the performance of computer networks. The term used to describe these switches is **multilayer switches (MLS)**. An example is a layer 3 switch. Layer 3 switches still work at layer 2 but additionally work at the network layer (layer 3) of the OSI model and use IP addressing for making decisions to route a data packet in the best direction. The major difference is that the packet switching in basic routers is handled by a programmed microprocessor. The layer 3 switch uses application-specific integrated circuits (ASICs) hardware to handle the packet switching. The advantage of using hardware to handle the packet switching is a significant reduction in processing time (software versus hardware). In fact, the processing time of layer 3 switches can be as fast as the input data rate. This is called **wire speed routing**, where the data packets are processed as fast as they are arriving. Multilayer switches can also work at the upper layers of the OSI model. An example is a layer 4 switch that processes data packets at the transport layer of the OSI model.

Section 5-3 Review

This section has covered the following **Network+** Exam objectives.

1.1 Explain the functions and applications of various network devices

This section introduced the use of the network switch. A discussion on a managed switch was presented incorporating the use of the Cisco Network Assistant. Examples of dynamic MAC address assignment and aging time were also presented.

1.8 Given a scenario, implement and configure the appropriate addressing schema

The concept of multicast messaging where messages are sent to a specific group of hosts on the network was presented in this section.

1.9 Explain the basics of routing concepts and protocols

This section presented a look at latency. A direct benefit of isolating collision domains is that there will be an increase in the data transfer speed and throughput. Reduced latency means that the data packets will arrive at the destination more quickly.

4.2 Given a scenario, analyze and interpret the output of troubleshooting tools

The use of the ping command was demonstrated in this section. This is a very important troubleshooting tool.

5-4 THE ROUTER

The router is the most powerful networking device used today to interconnect LANs. The router is a layer 3 device in the OSI model, which means the router uses the **network address** (layer 3 addressing) to make routing decisions regarding forwarding data packets. Remember from Chapter 1, section 3, that the OSI model separates network responsibilities into different layers. In the OSI model, the layer 3 or network layer responsibilities include handling of the network address. The network address is also called a *logical address,* rather than being a physical address such as the MAC address. The *physical address* is the hardware or MAC address embedded into the network interface card. The **logical address** describes the IP address location of the network and the address location of the host in the network.

> **Network Address**
> Another name for the layer 3 address
>
> **Logical Address**
> Describes the IP address location of the network and the address location of the host in the network

Essentially, the router is configured to know how to route data packets entering or exiting the LAN. This differs from the bridge and the layer 2 switch, which use the Ethernet address for making decisions regarding forwarding data packets and only know how to forward data to hosts physically connected to their ports.

Routers are used to interconnect LANs in a campus network. Routers can be used to interconnect networks that use the same protocol (for example, Ethernet), or they can be used to interconnect LANs that are using different layer 2 technologies such as an Ethernet and token ring. Routers also make it possible to interconnect to LANs around the country and the world and interconnect to many different networking protocols.

> **Router Interface**
>
> The physical connection where the router connects to the network

Routers have multiple port connections for connecting to the LANs, and by definition a router must have a minimum of three ports. The common symbol used to represent a router in a networking drawing is provided in Figure 5-14. The arrows pointing in and out indicate that data enters and exits the routers through multiple ports. The router ports are *bidirectional,* meaning that data can enter and exit the same router port. Often the router ports are called the **router interface**, the physical connection where the router connects to the network.

FIGURE 5-14   The network symbol for a router.

The Router Interface: Cisco 2800 Series

Figure 5-15 shows the rear panel view (interface side) of a Cisco 2800 series router.

FIGURE 5-15   The rear panel view of a Cisco 2800 series router.

The following describes the function of each interface:

- **USB Interface:** The USB ports are used for storage and security support.
- **FastEthernet Ports:** FE0/0: Fast Ethernet (10/100Mbps) and FE0/1: Fast Ethernet (10/100Mbps).

- **Console Input:** This input provides an RS-232 serial communications link into the router for initial router configuration. A special cable, called a *console cable*, is used to connect the console input to the serial port on a computer. The console cable can have RJ-45 plugs on each end and requires the use of an RJ-45 to DB9 adapter for connecting to the computer's COM1 or COM2 serial port. The console cable can also have an RJ-45 connector on one end and an integrated DB9 connector on the other end.

- **Auxiliary Input:** This input is used to connect a dial-in modem into the router. The auxiliary port provides an alternative way to remotely log in to the router if the network is down. This port also uses an RJ-45 connection.

- **Serial Interface:** CTRLR T1 1 and CTRLR T1 0.

  This is a serial connection, and it has a built-in CSU/DSU. This interface is used to provide a T1 connection to the communications carrier. (*Note:* The CSU/DSU function is presented in Chapter 8, "Introduction to Switch Configuration.") This type of connection (RJ-45) replaces the older cabling using V.35 cable (shown later in Figure 5-18). There are three LEDs on this interface:

  - **AL**—alarm
  - **LP**—loop
  - **CD**—Carrier Detect

- **Voice Interface Card (VIC2-4FXO):** This interface shows four phone line connections. This router can be programmed as a small Private Branch Exchange (PBX) for use in a small office. The PBX function is presented in Chapter 10, "Internet Technologies: Out to the Internet."

- **WAN Interface Card (WIC2AM):** This interface has two RJ-11 jacks and two V.90 analog internal modems. These modems can be used to handle both incoming and outgoing modem calls. This interface is listed as modem in Figure 5-15.

- **VIC-4FXS/DID:** This interface is a four-port FXS and DID voice/fax interface card. FXS is a Foreign Exchange Interface that connects directly to a standard telephone. DID is Direct Inward Dialing and is a feature that enables callers to directly call an extension on a PBX. This interface is listed as FXS/DID in Figure 5-15.

The Router Interface—Cisco 2600 Series

Figure 5-16 shows the rear panel view (interface side) of a Cisco 2600 series router.

FIGURE 5-16   The rear panel view of a Cisco 2600 series router.

The following describes the function of each interface to the network:

- **Power On/Off:** Turns on/off electrical power to the router.

- **Auxiliary Input:** Used to connect a dial-in modem into the router. The auxiliary port provides an alternative way to remotely log in to the router if the network is down. This port also uses an RJ-45 connection.

- **Console Input:** Provides an RS-232 serial communications link into the router for initial router configuration. A special cable, called a *console cable*, is used to connect the console input to the serial port on a computer. The console cable uses RJ-45 plugs on each end and requires the use of an RJ-45 to DB9 adapter for connecting to the COM1 or COM2 serial port.

- **Serial Ports:** Provides a serial data communication link into and out of the router, using V.35 serial interface cables.

- **DSU Port:** This T1 controller port connection is used to make the serial connection to Telco. This module has a built-in CSU/DSU module. There are five LEDs next to the RJ-45 jack. These LEDs are for the following:

  - **TD**—Transmit Data

  - **P**—Loop

  - **D**—Receive Data

  - **D**—Carrier Detect

  - **L**—Alarm

- **Ethernet Port:** This connection provides a 10/100Mbps Ethernet data link.

- **Analog Modem Ports:** This router has a 16-port analog network module.

> **Media Converter**
> Used to adapt a layer 1 (physical layer) technology to another layer 1 technology

A **media converter** is used to convert the 15-pin AUI port to the 8-pin RJ-45 connector. Figure 5-17 shows an example of an AUI to RJ-45 media converter. Media converters are commonly used in computer networks to adapt layer 1 or physical layer technologies from one technology to another. For example:

AUI to twisted pair (RJ-45) AUI to fiber
RJ-45 to fiber

Figure 5-18 shows a Cisco 7200 series router, which provides adaptable interfaces for connecting to many physical layer technologies such as FastEthernet, gigabit Ethernet, ATM, and FDDI.

FIGURE 5-17   A CentreCom 210TS AUI to RJ-45 media converter.

FIGURE 5-18   A Cisco 7200 series router (courtesy of Cisco Systems).

Section 5-4 Review

This section has covered the following **Network+** Exam objectives.

1.1 Explain the functions and applications of various network devices

The network router, a layer 3 device, was presented in this section. The network router is the most powerful networking device used today to interconnect LANs.

1.4 Explain the characteristics and benefits of various WAN technologies

The ATM interface for a network router was presented.

5.2 Explain the basics of network theory and concepts

This section has introduced the carrier detect/sense feature on a router. This feature was present for both Cisco 2800 and 2600 series routers.

Test Your Knowledge

1. A router uses which of the following to make routing decisions regarding forwarding data packets?

    a. Router address

    b. Network address

    c. Fast link pulse

    d. None of these answers is correct.

2. A logical address is which of the following?

    a. MAC address

    b. Router interface address

    c. Network address

    d. The ARP address

3. The physical connection where the router connects to the network is called which of the following?

    a. Console input

    b. Auxiliary input

    c. Router interface

    d. USB interface

5-5   INTERCONNECTING LANS WITH THE ROUTER

The previous section introduced the function of a router in a network. A router routes data based on the destination network address or logical address rather than the physical address used by layer 2 devices, such as the switch and the bridge. Information exchanged with bridges and layer 2 switches requires that the MAC address for the hosts be known. Routed networks such as most enterprise and campus networks use IP addressing for managing the data movement. **Enterprise network** is a term used to describe the network used by a large company. The use of the network or logical address on computers allows the information to be sent from a LAN to a destination without requiring that the computer know the MAC address of the destination computer. Remember, delivery of data packets is based on knowing the MAC address of the destination.

Enterprise Network
Term used to describe the network used by a large company

An overview of the router interface was presented in section 5-4. The router interface provides a way to access the router for configuration either locally or remotely. Interfaces are provided for making serial connections to the router and to other devices that require a serial communications link. For example, interfaces to wide area networking devices require a serial interface. RJ-45 ports are provided on the router interface for connecting the router to a LAN. Older routers can require the use of an AUI port to establish an Ethernet connection to a UTP cable. This port provides a 10Mbps data connection to Ethernet (10Mbps) networks. The RJ-45 connection is used to connect both Ethernet (10Mbps), FastEthernet (100Mbps), Gigabit Ethernet (1000Mbps), and 10 Gigabit Ethernet (10G) to a LAN. The RJ-45 connection can also support gigabit and 10G Ethernet, but high-speed data networks can also use a fiber connection.

This section introduces the information needed to design, manage, and configure campus networks. An example of a small interconnected LAN is provided in Figure 5-19. This example shows four Ethernet LANs interconnected using three routers. The LANs are configured in a star topology using switches at the center of the LAN. The LANs are labeled LAN A, LAN B, LAN C, and LAN D. The routers are labeled RouterA, RouterB, and RouterC (router naming protocols are discussed in Chapter 7, "Introduction to Router Configuration"). Connection of the routers to the LANs is provided by the router's **FastEthernet port (FA0/0, FA0/1, FA0/2, . . .)**. Look for the FA label in Figure 5-19.

FastEthernet Port (FA0/0, FA0/1, FA0/2,...)
Naming of the FastEthernet ports on the router

The interconnections for the routers and the LANs are summarized as follows:

- **Router A** connects directly to the LAN A switch via FastEthernet port FA0/0. RouterA also connects directly to RouterB via the FastEthernet port FA0/1 and connects to RouterC via FastEthernet port FA0/2.

- **Router B** connects directly to the LAN B switch via FastEthernet port FA0/0. RouterB connects to the LAN C switch via FastEthernet port FA0/1. RouterB connects directly to RouterA via FastEthernet port FA0/2 and connects to RouterC via FastEthernet port FA0/3.

- **Router C** connects directly to the LAN D switch via the FastEthernet port FA0/0. Connection to RouterB is provided via Ethernet port FA0/1. RouterC connects to RouterA via FastEthernet port FA0/2.

Router A Port Addresses (LAN A)		Router B Port Addresses (LAN B)		Router B Port Addresses (LAN C)		Router Port Addresses (LAN D)	
FastEthernet 0/0 (Gateway Address)	10.10.20.250	FastEthernet 0/0 (Gateway Address)	10.10.10.250	FastEthernet 0/1 (Gateway Address)	10.10.1.250	FastEthernet 0/0 (Gateway Address)	10.10.5.250
FastEthernet 0/1	10.10.200.1	FastEthernet 0/2	10.10.200.2	FastEthernet 0/2	10.10.200.2	FastEthernet 0/1	10.10.150.2
FastEthernet 0/2	10.10.100.1	FastEthernet 0/3	10.10.150.1	FastEthernet 0/3	10.10.150.1	FastEthernet 0/2	10.10.100.2
LAN A Computers		**LAN B Computers**		**LAN C Computers**		**LAN D Computers**	
Computer A1	10.10.20.1	Computer A1	10.10.10.1	Computer A1	10.10.1.1	Computer A1	10.10.5.1
Computer A2	10.10.20.2	Computer A2	10.10.10.2	Computer A2	10.10.1.2	Computer A2	10.10.5.2
Subnet Mask	**255.255.255.0**	**Subnet Mask**	**255.255.255.0**	**Subnet Mask**	**255.255.255.0**	**Subnet Mask**	**255.255.255.0**

FIGURE 5-19   A small interconnected LAN.

Serial Port (S0/0, S0/1, S0/2,...)
Naming of the serial ports on the router

The **serial ports (S0/0, S0/1, S0/2,...)** are not being used to interconnect the routers in this sample campus network. The serial interfaces are typically used to interconnect LANs that connect through a data communications carrier such as a telephone company (Telco).

The network configuration provided in Figure 5-19 enables data packets to be sent and received from any host on the network after the routers in the network have been properly configured. For example, computer A1 in LAN A could be sending data to computer D1 in LAN D. This requires that the IP address for computer D1 is known by the user sending the data from computer A1. The data from computer A1 will first travel to the switch where the data is passed to RouterA via the FA0/0 FastEthernet data port. RouterA will examine the network address of the data packet and use configured routing instructions stored in routing tables to decide where to forward the data. RouterA determines that an available path to RouterC is via the FA0/2 FastEthernet port connection. The data is then sent directly to RouterC. RouterC determines that the data packet should be forwarded to the FA0/0 port to reach computer D1 in LAN D. The data is then sent to D1. Alternatively, RouterA could have sent the data to RouterC through RouterB via Router A's FA0/1

FastEthernet port. Path selection for data packets is examined in Chapter 9, "Routing Protocols."

Delivery of the information over the network was made possible by the use of an IP address and **routing tables**. Routing tables keep track of the routes used for forwarding data to its destination. RouterA used its routing table to determine a network data path so computer A1's data could reach computer D1 in LAN D. RouterA determines that a path to the network where computer D1 is located can be obtained via RouterA's FA0/2 FastEthernet port to the FA0/2 FastEthernet port on RouterC. RouterC determines that computer D1 is on LAN D, which connects to RouterC's FA0/0 FastEthernet port. An ARP request is issued by RouterC to determine the MAC address of computer D1. The MAC address is then used for final delivery of the data to computer D1.

> **Routing Table**
> Keeps track of the routes to use for forwarding data to its destination

If RouterA determines that the network path to RouterC is down, RouterA can route the data packet to RouterC through RouterB. After RouterB receives the data packet from RouterA, it uses its routing tables to determine where to forward the data packet. RouterB determines that the data needs to be sent to RouterC, and it uses the FA0/3 FastEthernet port to forward the data.

Gateway Address

The term **gateway** is used to describe the address of the networking device that enables the hosts in a LAN to connect to networks and hosts outside the LAN. For example, for all hosts in LAN A, the gateway address will be 10.10.10.250. This address is configured on the host computer. Any IP packets with a destination outside the LAN will be sent to the gateway address.

> **Gateway**
> Describes the networking device that enables hosts in a LAN to connect to networks (and hosts) outside the LAN

Network Segments

The *network segment* defines the networking link between two LANs. There is a segment associated with each connection of an internetworking device (for example, router—hub, router—switch, router—router). For example, the IP address for the network segment connecting LAN A to the router is 10.10.20.0. All hosts connected to this segment must contain a 10.10.20.x because a subnet mask of 255.255.255.0 is being used. Subnet masking is fully explained in Chapter 6.

Routers use the information about the network segments to determine where to forward data packets. For example, the network segments that connect to RouterA include

    10.10.20.0
    10.10.200.0
    10.10.100.0

The computers in LAN A will have a 10.10.20.x address. All the computers in this network must contain a 10.10.20.x IP address. For example, computer A1 in LAN A will have the assigned IP address of 10.10.20.1 and a gateway address of 10.10.20.250. The computers in LAN B are located in the 10.10.10.0 network. This means that all the computers in this network must contain a 10.10.10.x IP address. The *x* part of the IP address is assigned for each host. The gateway address for the hosts in LAN B is 10.10.10.250.

Section 5-5 Review

This section has covered the following **Network+** Exam objectives.

    1.9 Explain the basics of routing concepts and protocols

The concept of routing tables was presented in this section. It is important to remember that the purpose of the routing table is to keep track of the routes used to forward data to its destination.

    4.6 Given a scenario, troubleshoot and resolve common network issues

This section introduced the gateway address, which enables the host in a LAN to connect to hosts outside the LAN.

Test Your Knowledge

1. The router's routing tables do which of the following? (Select all that apply.)

    a. Keep track of the routes to forward data to its destination

    b. Keep track of the IP addresses to forward data to its destination

    c. Keep track of the MAC addresses to forward data to its destination

    d. None of these answers is correct.

2. The term Enterprise Network is used to describe the network used by a large company. True or False?

3. A gateway address defines which of the following?

    a. The networking links between two LANs

    b. The networking device that enables hosts in a LAN to connect to networks outside the LAN

    c. The networking device that enables hosts in a LAN to connect to networks inside the LAN

    d. All of these answers are correct

5-6 CONFIGURING THE NETWORK INTERFACE—AUTO-NEGOTIATION

Most modern networking internetworking technologies (for example, hubs, switches, bridges, and routers) now incorporate the **auto-negotiation** protocol. The protocol enables the Ethernet equipment to automate many of the installation steps. This includes automatically configuring the operating speeds (for example, 10/100/1000Mbps) and the selection of full- or half-duplex operation for the data link. The auto-negotiation protocol is defined in the IEEE Ethernet standard 802.3x for FastEthernet.

The auto-negotiation protocol uses a **fast link pulse (FLP)** to carry the information between each end of a data link. Figure 5-20 shows a data link. The data rate for the fast link pulses is 10Mbps, the same as for 10BASE-T. The link pulses were designed to operate over the limited bandwidth supported by CAT3 cabling. Therefore, even if a link is negotiated, there is no guarantee that the negotiated data rate will work over the link. Other tests on the cable link must be used to certify that the cable can carry the negotiated data link configuration (refer to Chapter 2, "Physical Layer Cabling: Twisted Pair").

> **Auto-negotiation**
> Protocol used by interconnected electronic devices to negotiate a link speed

> **Fast Link Pulse (FLP)**
> Carries the configuration information between each end of a data link

FIGURE 5-20 The two ends of a data link negotiating the operating parameters.

Auto-Negotiation Steps

Each link partner shares or advertises its data link capabilities with the other link partner. The two link partners then use the advertised capabilities to establish the fastest possible data link rate for both links. In the example of the link partners shown in Figure 5-22, computer 1 advertises that its interface supports 10Mbps. The switch advertises that it supports both 10Mbps and 100Mbps. The network interfaces on each link partner are set for auto-negotiation; therefore, the 10Mbps operating mode is selected. This is the fastest data rate that can be used in this data link. The data rate is limited by the 10Mbps capabilities of the computer's network interface.

Note

Auto-negotiation is established when an Ethernet link is established. The link information is only sent one time, when the link is established. The negotiated link configuration will remain until the link is broken or the interfaces are reconfigured.

Full-Duplex/Half-Duplex

Modern network interfaces for computer networks have the capability of running the data over the links in either full- or half-duplex mode. As noted previously, *full-duplex* means that the communications device can transmit and receive at the same time. **Half-duplex** means the communications device can transmit or receive, but not at the same time.

In full-duplex operation (10/100Mbps), the media must have separate transmit and receive data paths. This is provided for in CAT6/5e/5 cable with pairs 1–2 (transmit) and pairs 3–6 (receive). Full-duplex with gigabit and 10 gigabit data rates require the use of all four wire pairs (1–2, 3–6, 4–5, 7–8). An important note is that the full-duplex mode in computer network links is only for point-to-point links. This means that there can only be two end stations on the link. The CSMA/CD protocol is turned off; therefore, there can't be another networking device competing for use of the link. An example of networking devices that can run full-duplex are computers connected to a switch. The switch can be configured to run the full-duplex mode. This also requires that each end station on the link must be configurable to run full-duplex mode.

In half-duplex operation, the link uses the CSMA/CD protocol. This means only one device talks at a time, and while the one device is talking, the other networking devices "listen" to the network traffic. Figure 5-21(a) and (b) shows examples of networks configured for full- and half-duplex mode. In full-duplex operation [Figure 5-21(a)], CSMA/CD is turned off and computers 1, 2, and the switch are transmitting and receiving at the same time. In half-duplex mode [Figure 5-21(b)], CSMA/CD is turned on, computer 1 is transmitting, and computer 2 is "listening" or receiving the data transmission.

Figure 5-22(a) and (b) provides an example of the port management features available with the Cisco switch using the Cisco Network Administrator software. The settings for the speed are shown in Figure 5-22(a). An example of setting the switch for auto, half-, and full-duplex are shown in Figure 5-22(b). The auto setting is for auto-negotiate.

Table 5-4 provides a summary of the advantages and disadvantages of the auto-negotiation protocol.

TABLE 5-4   **Summary of the Auto-negotiation Protocol**

Advantages	Disadvantages
Useful in LANs that have multiple users with multiple connection capabilities.	Not recommended for fixed data links such as the backbone in a network.
The auto-negotiation feature can maximize the data links' throughput.	A failed negotiation on a functioning link can cause a link failure.

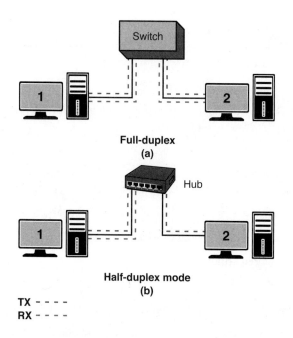

Full-duplex
(a)

Half-duplex mode
(b)

TX - - - -
RX - - - -

FIGURE 5-21 (a) Computer 1 transmits and receives at the same time; (b) computer 1 transmits; others listen.

(a)   (b)

FIGURE 5-22 An example of the port management options available with a Cisco switch: (a) 100Mbps auto-negotiation; (b) 10Mbps half-/full-duplex option.

Section 5-6 Review

This section has covered the following **Network+** Exam objectives.

5.2 Explain the basics of network theory and concepts

The changes in the CSMA/CD protocol when configuring switch ports for operation in the half- and full-duplex mode was presented.

Test Your Knowledge

1. Which of the following is a disadvantage of the auto-negotiation protocol?

   a. It is only useful in LANs that have multiple connection capabilities.

   b. A failed negotiation on a functioning link can cause a link failure.

   c. It should be used only in critical network data paths.

   d. It works at 10Mbps.

2. The fast link pulse does which of the following? (Select all that apply.)

   a. Carries the configuration information between each end of a data link

   b. Is used in auto-negotiation

   c. Uses a 100Mbps data rate

   d. Uses a 1Mbps data rate

3. Which of the following is an advantage of auto-negotiation? (Select all that apply.)

   a. Is useful in LANs that have multiple users with multiple connection capabilities

   b. Can maximize the data link throughput

   c. Simplifies the backbone configuration

   d. Simplifies the LAN configuration

   e. All of the answers are correct.

SUMMARY

This chapter has established how LANs are interconnected. The need for careful documentation was addressed in this chapter. The importance of this will become more relevant as the complexity in network topics increases from chapter to chapter. Internetworking hardware such as bridges, switches, and routers were discussed and examples of using these technologies presented.

A technique for internetworking the LANs using routers has been presented. In addition, the purpose of a router and its hardware interface has been defined. The use of switches and hubs to connect to the routers has been demonstrated. The purpose of a gateway has been explained and demonstrated. The concept of a network segment has been examined.

The concepts the student should understand from this chapter are the following:

- How bridges are used to interconnect separate LANs
- How a switch is used in a network and why the switch improves network performance
- Understand and be able to identify the various connections on a the router interface
- How a router is used to interconnect LANs
- The purpose of a gateway in a computer network
- The concept of a network segment
- The concept of auto-negotiation

QUESTIONS AND PROBLEMS

Section 5-2

1. What is a *bridge*?

2. Define a *segment*.

3. What information is stored in a bridge table?

4. What is an *association* on a bridge, and how is it used?

5. What are excessive amounts of broadcasts on a network called?

6. Which command is used on a computer to view the contents of the ARP cache?

7. An empty ARP cache indicates what?

8. Why do entries into the bridging table have a limited lifetime?

9. Which of the following are advantages of using a bridge to interconnect LANs?

   a. Works best in low traffic areas

   b. Relatively inexpensive

   c. Can be used to route data traffic

   d. Easy to install

   e. Reduces collision domains

Section 5-3

10. The network switch operates at which layer of the OSI model?

11. Another name for a switch is

    a. multiport repeater

    b. multiport bridge

    c. multiport router

    d. multiport hub

12. How does a switch provide a link with minimal collisions?

13. The link for a switch connection is isolated from other data traffic except for what type of messages?

14. Explain what data traffic is sent across a network when a computer pings another computer and a hub is used to interconnect the computers.

15. Explain what data traffic is seen by computer 3 when computer 1 pings computer 2 in a LAN. A switch is used to interconnect the computers.

16. Explain the concept of *dynamic assignment* on a switch.

17. Define *aging time* on a switch.

18. Explain how a switch learns MAC addresses, and where a switch stores the address.

19. What happens if a MAC address is not stored in CAM on a switch?

20. Which two modes are used by a switch to forward frames?

21. Which switch mode offers minimum latency?

22. What is error threshold, and which mode is it associated with?

23. Explain the difference in store-and-forward and the cut-through mode on a switch.

24. How does a layer 3 switch differ from a layer 2 switch?

25. What is meant by the term *wire-speed routing*?

Section 5-4

26. A router uses the network address on a data packet for what purpose?

27. What is the *logical address*?

28. The physical connection where a router connects to the network is called the
    a. router port
    b. network port
    c. network interface
    d. router interface

29. The connection to the router's console input is typically which of the following?
    a. RS-232
    b. RJ-45
    c. DB9
    d. RJ-11

30. AUI stands for
    a. Auxiliary Unit Input
    b. Attachment Unit Interconnect
    c. Auxiliary Unit Interface
    d. Attachment Unit Interface

31. The AUI port on a router connects to which networking protocol?

   a. 100BASE-T

   b. 10BASE-T

   c. Token Ring

   d. Ethernet

Section 5-5

32. Define enterprise network.

33. The router interface most commonly used to interconnect LANs in a campus network is

   a. serial

   b. console port

   c. Ethernet

   d. ATM

34. Serial interfaces on a router are typically used to

   a. interconnect routers

   b. interconnect hubs

   c. connect to communication carriers

   d. connect to auxiliary ports

35. The designation E0 indicates

   a. Ethernet port 0

   b. Ethernet input

   c. External port 0

   d. Exit port 0

36. Routing tables on a router keep track of

   a. port assignments

   b. MAC address assignments

   c. gateway addresses of LANs

   d. routes to use for forwarding data to its destination

37. The convention used for naming of the serial port 0 on a router is

    a. S0

    b. System 0

    c. Serial interface 0

    d. Serial AUI 0

38. Define the term *gateway*.

Section 5-6

39. What is the purpose of the fast link pulse?

40. Define *full-duplex*.

41. Define *half-duplex*.

42. Which of the following is a disadvantage of the auto-negotiation protocol?

    a. Only useful in LANs that have multiple connection capabilities.

    b. A failed negotiation on a functioning link can cause a link failure.

    c. It's recommended for use in critical network data paths.

    d. It works at 10Mbps.

CRITICAL THINKING

43. Describe how a network administrator uses the OSI model to isolate a network problem.

44. Why is auto-negotiation not recommended for use in critical network data paths?

45. What would happen if the local network devices do not have local ARP cache?

CERTIFICATION QUESTIONS

46. Which of the following best defines a *bridging table*?

    a. A list of MAC addresses and port locations for hosts connected to the bridge ports

    b. A list of IP addresses and port locations for hosts connected to the bridge ports

    c. A list of IP addresses and port locations for hosts connected to the hub ports

    d. A list of MAC addresses and port locations for hosts connected to the hub ports

47. Which of the following best defines *aging time*?

    a. The length of time a MAC address remains assigned to a port

    b. The length of time an IP address remains assigned to a port

    c. The length of time a MAC address remains assigned to a hub

    d. The length of time an IP address remains assigned to a hub

48. Dynamic assignment on a switch implies which of the following? (Select all that apply.)

    a. MAC addresses are assigned to a port when a host is connected.

    b. IP addresses are assigned to a port when a host is connected.

    c. MAC addresses are assigned to a switch when a host is connected.

    d. IP addresses are assigned to a switch when a host is connected.

49. Which of the following terms is used to describe that a MAC address has been manually assigned?

    a. Dynamic assignment

    b. ARP assignment

    c. DHCP assignment

    d. Static assignment

50. What is the purpose of the secure tab on a switch?

    a. The switchport will use port discovery to assign a MAC address to the port.

    b. The switchport will automatically disable itself if a device with a different MAC address connects to the port.

    c. The switchport will use a different MAC address than the one connected to the port.

    d. This enables the switch to select what networking devices have a selectable IP address.

51. What is the length of time an IP address is assigned to a switchport called?

    a. Delay time

    b. Enable time

    c. Aging time

    d. Access time

52. Which of the following is a table of MAC addresses and port mapping used by the switch to identify connected network devices?

    a. CAM

    b. ARP

    c. ARP-A

    d. ipconfig /all

53. Which of the following best defines store-and-forward relative to switch operation?

    a. The frame is stored in CAM and the forward to the source for confirmation.

    b. The frame is stored in CAM and the forward to the destination for confirmation.

    c. The header is received before forwarding it to the destination.

    d. The entire frame is received before a decision is made regarding forwarding to its destination.

54. In which switch mode is the data packet forwarded to the destination as soon as the MAC address has been read?

    a. Store-and-forward

    b. Adaptive fast-forward

    c. Cut-through

    d. Fast-forward

55. Which switch mode offers the minimum switch latency?

    a. Cut-through

    b. Fast-forward

    c. Store-and-forward

    d. Adaptive cut-through

TCP/IP

Chapter Outline

Objectives

- Develop an understanding of the four layers of the TCP/IP model
- Define how a TCP connection is established, maintained, and terminated
- Investigate the properties of the UDP connectionless protocol
- Define the five classes of IPv4 addresses

- Investigate the properties of basic number conversion
- Define the purpose of subnet masking
- Investigate the implementation of CIDR blocks and supernetting
- Apply subnet masking concepts to allocate space for hosts in a subnet
- Define the structure of IPv6

Key Terms

NCP
ARPAnet
well-known ports
ICANN
transport layer protocols
TCP
connection-oriented protocol
SYN, SYN ACK, ACK
UDP
Internet layer
IP (Internet Protocol)
ARP
IGMP

multicasting
multicast address
network interface layer
hex
IPv4
class A, B, C, D, and E
non-Internet routable IP addresses
RIRs
ARIN
subnet mask
classful
supernetting
CIDR

prefix length notation
CIDR block
supernets
IPv6
IPng
full IPv6 address
unicast address
multicast address
anycast address
link-local address
stateless address autoconfiguration (SLAAC)
6to4 prefix

Transmission Control Protocol/Internet Protocol (TCP/IP) is the protocol suite used for communications between hosts in most local networks and on the Internet. TCP/IP can be used to enable network communications in LANs, campus networks, and wide area networks (WANs) as long as the hosts support the protocol. TCP/IP is widely supported and is included in operating systems such as Windows 10 and 8, Mac OS, Linux, and Unix.

The Network Control Protocol (NCP) was developed by the Defense Advanced Research Projects Agency (DARPA) to provide a way to network the computers of government researchers. The DARPA-funded initiative forced the use of a standard networking protocol by all defense contractors.

6-1 INTRODUCTION

NCP
Network Control Protocol

ARPAnet
Advanced Research Projects Agency network

The Transmission Control Protocol (TCP) was first proposed in 1974 in a paper by Vint Cerf and Bob Kahn. The suite of protocols called TCP/IP was introduced in 1978. In 1983, TCP/IP replaced NCP as the standard networking protocol used by the Advanced Research Projects Agency network (ARPAnet), considered the predecessor to today's Internet.

This chapter examines the fundamentals of the TCP/IP protocol suite. The relationship of the TCP/IP model to the OSI model is presented in section 6-2. The following layers of the TCP/IP protocol are examined: the application layer, the transport layer, the Internet layer, and the network interface layer. Section 6-3 contains a discussion on the numbering systems used in TCP/IP networks, including examples of converting decimal, hexadecimal, and binary numbers. The fundamentals of IP addressing are reintroduced in section 6-4. (The concept of IP addressing was first introduced in Chapter 1, "Introduction to Computer Networks.") This section examines the 32-bit structure of IPv4 addressing, the current version used in the Internet. This section goes into detail about the role and features of IP addressing in computer networks.

The concept of subnet masking is examined in section 6-5. This section presents many examples of calculating and applying subnet masks to networks. The material presented provides the student with the knowledge base to master subnet masking–related concepts that are presented later in the text. The fundamentals of CIDR blocks and supernetting are examined in section 6-6. The chapter concludes with an overview of the new IP addressing standard, IPv6.

Table 6-1 lists and identifies, by chapter section, where each of the CompTIA Network+ objectives are presented in this chapter. At the end of each chapter section is a review with comments of the Network+ objectives presented in that section. These comments are provided to help reinforce the reader's understanding of a particular Network+ objective. The chapter review also includes "Test Your Knowledge" questions to aid in the understanding of key concepts before the reader advances to the next section of the chapter. The end of the chapter includes a complete set of question plus sample certification type questions.

TABLE 6-1   Chapter 6 CompTIA Network+ Objectives

Domain/ Objective Number	Domain/Objective Description Is Covered	Section Where Objective Is Covered
1.0	*Network Architecture*	
1.8	Given a scenario, implement and configure the appropriate addressing schema	6-2, 6-4, 6-5, 6-6, 6-7
3.0	*Network Security*	
3.2	Compare and contrast common network vulnerabilities and threats	6-2
5.0	*Industry standards, practices, and network theory*	
5.2	Explain the basics of network theory and concepts	6-2, 6-3
5.9	Compare and contrast the following ports and protocols	6-2

6-2   THE TCP/IP LAYERS

In this section we examine the four layers of the TCP/IP model: application, transport, Internet, and network interface. Each of these layers and its purpose are defined in Table 6-2. The TCP/IP protocol was established in 1978, prior to the final release of the OSI model (see Chapter 1); however, the four layers of the TCP/IP model do correlate with the seven layers of the OSI model, as shown in Figure 6-1.

TABLE 6-2 The Four Layers of the TCP/IP Model

Layer	Purpose of the Layer
Application layer	Defines the applications used to process requests and which ports and sockets are used
Transport layer	Defines the type of connection established between hosts and how acknowledgements are sent
Internet layer	Defines the protocols used for addressing and routing the data packets
Network interface layer	Defines how the host connects to the network

FIGURE 6-1 The layers of the TCP/IP model and their relationships to the OSI model.

The Application Layer

The top level of the TCP/IP stack is the *application* layer. This layer is used to process requests from hosts and to ensure a connection is made to an appropriate port. A *port* is basically an address used to direct data to the proper destination application.

There are 65,536 possible TCP/UDP ports. Ports 1–1023 are called **well-known ports** or *reserved* ports. These ports are reserved by Internet Corporation for Assigned Names and Numbers (**ICANN**). Ports 1024–49151 are called *registered* ports and are registered with ICANN. Ports 49152–65535 are called *dynamic* or *private* ports. Table 6-3 summarizes port numbers.

Well-known Ports
Ports reserved by ICANN

ICANN
Internet Corporation for Assigned Names and Numbers

TABLE 6-3   Port Number Assignments

Port Numbers	Description
1–1023	The "well-known" ports
1024–49,151	Registered ports
49,152–65,535	Private ports

Examples of well-known ports include HTTP (TCP port 80), HTTPS (TCP port 443), and SSH (TCP port 22). Applications use these port numbers when communicating with another application as illustrated in Figure 6-2. Host B is passing to Host A data that is destined for TCP port 80 (HTTP). HTTP is the HyperText Transfer Protocol, used for transferring non-secure web-based documents to a web browser such as Internet Explorer or Mozilla Firefox. Host A receives the packet and passes the application up to the port 80 application. Table 6-4 lists some popular applications and their port numbers for TCP/IP. This list includes FTP, SSH, SMTP, DNS, DHCP, HTTP, and HTTPS.

FIGURE 6-2   An example of two hosts connected for a TCP transmission.

TABLE 6-4   Common Applications and Their Port Numbers

Transport Protocol	Port Number	Application	Description
TCP	20 (data port) 21 (command/control port)	FTP	File Transfer Protocol
TCP	22	SSH	Secure Shell
TCP	23	Telnet	Virtual terminal connection
TCP	25	SMTP	Simple Mail Transfer Protocol
UDP	53	DNS	Domain name server
UDP	67, 68	(BOOTP-Server)	Dynamic Host Control Protocol
UDP	69	TFTP	Trivial File Transfer protocol
TCP and UDP	80	HTTP	Hypertext Transfer protocol
UDP	110	POP3	Post Office Protocol
NetBIOS	137–139	NetBIOS	Network Basic Input/Output System

Transport Protocol	Port Number	Application	Description
TCP	143	IMAP	Internet Message Access Protocol
UDP	161	SNMP	Simple Network Management Protocol
TCP	443	HTTPS	Secure HTTP
TCP	445	SMB	Server message block
UDP	1701	L2TP	Layer 2 Tunneling Protocol
TCP	1720	H.323/Q.931	Voice over IP
TCP/UDP	1723	PPTP	Point-to-point Tunneling Protocol
TCP/UDP	2427/2727	MGCP	Media Gateway Protocol
TCP/UDP	3389	RDP	Remote Desktop Protocol
UDP	5004/5005	RTP	Real-time Transport Protocol
TCP/UDP	5060/5061	SIP	Session Initiation Protocol

You can find a complete list of ports at http://www.iana.org/assignments/port-numbers.

The Transport Layer

The **transport layer protocols** in TCP/IP are very important in establishing a network connection, managing the delivery of data between a source and destination host, and terminating the data connection. There are two transport protocols within the TCP/IP transport layer, TCP and UDP. **TCP**, the Transport Control Protocol, is a **connection-oriented protocol**, which means it establishes the network connection, manages the data transfer, and terminates the connection. The TCP protocol establishes a set of rules or guidelines for establishing the connection. TCP verifies the delivery of the data packets through the network and includes support for error checking and recovering lost data. TCP then specifies a procedure for terminating the network connection.

A unique sequence of three data packets is exchanged at the beginning of a TCP connection between two hosts, as shown in Figure 6-3. This is a virtual connection that is made over the network. This sequence is as follows:

1. The **SYN** (Synchronizing) packet

2. The **SYN ACK** (Synchronizing Acknowledgement) packet

3. The **ACK** (Acknowledgement) packet

Transport Layer Protocols

Define the type of connection established between hosts and how acknowledgements are sent

TCP

Transport Control Protocol

Connection-Oriented Protocol

Establishes a network connection, manages the delivery of data, and terminates the connection

SYN

Synchronizing packet

SYN ACK

Synchronizing Acknowledgement packet

ACK

Acknowledgement packet

FIGURE 6-3   The three-packet initial TCP handshake.

The host initiating the connection will send a synchronizing packet (SYN) (see Figure 6-3). In this example, Host A issues a SYN packet to initiate the TCP handshake. The SYN will have a sequence number (SEQ) associated with it. In the example shown in Figure 6-3, the sequence number is x. The sequence number is used to keep track of the data packets being transferred from Host A to Host B. The length of the packet being sent by Host A is 0 (LEN 0), which indicates that the packet contains no data.

In packet 2, Host B replies with a SYN ACK packet. The ACK is an acknowledgement that Host B received the packet from Host A. A number is attached to the ACK with a value of $(x + 1)$ that should be the sum of the SEQ# from packet 1 plus the length (LEN) of packet 1. Recall that the length of packet 1 is 0 (LEN 0), but packet 1 counts as one packet; therefore, Host B replies with an acknowledgement of packet 1 sequence number plus 1 $(x + 1)$. This acknowledgement notifies Host A that the packet (packet 1) was received. Packet 2 from Host B will also have a sequence number issued by Host B. In this packet, the sequence number has a value of y. This sequence number is used to keep track of packets transferred by Host B.

In packet 3, Host A acknowledges the reception of Host B's packet. The ACK number is an increment of one higher than the SEQ# sent by Host B in packet 2 $(y + 1)$. Host A also sends an updated SEQ# that is one larger than the SEQ# Host A sent in packet 1 $(x + 1)$. Remember, Host A and Host B each have their own sequence numbers. This completes the three-packet handshake that establishes the TCP connection. This handshake appears at the beginning of all TCP data transfers.

The following is an example of a TCP packet transmission captured using a network protocol analyzer. The network setup is shown in Figure 6-4. Host A (the client) is establishing an FTP connection with Host B. The captured file is *6-a.cap* and is also provided in the Capture folder with the text's accompanying CD-ROM. Portions of the captured data packets are shown in Figure 6-5.

FIGURE 6-4   The setup for the capture of the TCP connection.

```
 ID                    Summary
000001 TCP   SP=1054 DP=21  SYN  SEQ=997462768 ACK=0 LEN=0 WS=16384    OPT
000002 TCP   SP=21 DP=1054  SYN  SEQ=3909625466 ACK=997462769 LEN=0 WS=17520
000003 TCP   SP=1054 DP=21       SEQ=997462769 ACK=3909625467 LEN=0 WS=17520
000004 FTP   R Port=1054  220 w2kserver Microsoft

000009 FTP   C Port=1054  USER administrator
000010 FTP   R Port=1054  331 Password required

000014 FTP   C Port=1054  PASS Chile
```

FIGURE 6-5   An example of the three packets exchanged in the initial TCP handshake.

Packet 1 (ID 000001) is the SYN or synchronizing packet. This packet is sent from the host computer on the network that wants to establish a TCP network connection. In this example, Host A is making a TCP connection for an FTP file transfer. The summary information for packet 1 specifies that this is a TCP packet, the source port is 1054 (SP=1054), and the destination port is 21 (DP=21). Port 1054 is an arbitrary port number that the FTP client picks or is assigned by the operating system. The destination port 21 (command/control) is the well-known FTP port (see Table 6-4). The packet has a starting sequence number, 997462768, and there is no acknowledgement (ACK=0). The length of the data packet is 0 (LEN=0). This indicates that the packet does not contain any data. The window size = 16384 (WS=16384). The *window size* indicates how many data packets can be transferred without an acknowledgement.

Packet 2 is the SYN-ACK packet from the FTP server. The sequence number SEQ=3909625466 is the start of a new sequence for the data packet transfers from Host B. The source port is 21 (SP=21) and the destination port for packet 2 is 1054 (DP=1054). ACK=997462769 is an acknowledgement by host B (the FTP server) that the first TCP transmission was received. Note that this acknowledgement shows an increment of 1 from the starting sequence number provided by host A in packet 1.

Packet 3 is an acknowledgement from the client (host A) back to the FTP server (host B) that packet 2 was received. Note that the acknowledgement is ACK=3909625467, which is an increment of 1 from the SEQ number transmitted in packet 2. This completes the initial handshake establishing the TCP connection. The next part is the data packet transfer. At this point, the two hosts can begin transferring data packets.

The last part of the TCP connection is terminating the session for each host. The first thing that happens is that a host sends a FIN (finish) packet to the other connected host. This is shown in Figure 6-6. Host B sends a FIN packet to Host A indicating the data transmission is complete. Host A responds with an ACK packet acknowledging the reception of the FIN packet. Host A then sends Host B a FIN packet indicating that the connection is being terminated. Host B replies with an ACK packet.

Figure 6-7 shows an example of terminating a TCP connection. This example was captured with a network protocol analyzer. The captured file is *6-a.cap* and is provided in the Capture folder in the companion CD-ROM.

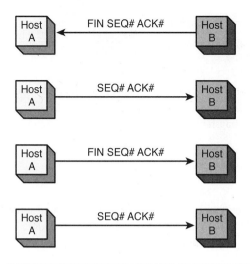

FIGURE 6-6 Terminating the TCP connection.

ID	Summary
000048 TCP	SP=21 DP=1054 FIN SEQ=3909625742 ACK=997462851 LEN=0 WS=17438
000049 TCP	SP=1054 DP=21 SEQ=997462851 ACK=3909625743 LEN=0 WS=17245
000050 TCP	SP=1054 DP=21 FIN SEQ=997462851 ACK=3909625743 LEN=0 WS=17245
000051 TCP	SP=21 DP=1054 SEQ=3909625743 ACK=997462852 LEN=0 WS=17438

FIGURE 6-7 An example of the four-packet TCP connection termination.

Packet 48 (see Figure 6-7) is a TCP packet with a source port of 21 (SP=21) and a destination port of 1054 (DP=1054). The FIN statement is shown, followed by a SEQ# and an ACK#. Remember, the SEQ and ACK numbers are used to keep track of the number of packets transmitted and an acknowledgement of the number received. The LEN of packet 48 is 0, which means the packet does not contain any data. Packet 49 is an acknowledgement from the host, at port 1054, of the FIN packet. Remember, the FIN packet was sent by the host at the source port 21. In packet 50 the host at port 1054 sends a FIN packet to the host at the destination port 21. In packet 51, the host at port 21 acknowledges the reception of the FIN packet and the four-packet sequence closes the TCP connection.

UDP, the User Datagram Protocol, is a *connectionless* protocol. This means UDP packets are transported over the network without a connection being established and without any acknowledgement that the data packets arrived at the destination. UDP is useful in applications such as videoconferencing and audio feeds, where such acknowledgements are not necessary.

> **UDP**
> User Datagram Protocol

Figure 6-8 provides an example of a UDP packet transfer. Packet 136 is the start of a UDP packet transfer of an Internet audio feed. A TCP connection to the Internet was made first, and then the feed was started. At that time, the UDP connectionless packets started. Packets 138, 139, and 140 are the same types of packets with a length of 789. No acknowledgements are sent back from the client because all the packets are coming from the Internet source. UDP does not have a procedure for terminating the data transfer; either the source stops delivery of the data packets or the client terminates the connection.

FIGURE 6-8   An example of a UDP packet transfer.

The Internet Layer

Internet Layer

Defines the protocols used for addressing and routing data packets

The TCP/IP **Internet layer** defines the protocols used for addressing and routing the data packets. Protocols that are part of the TCP/IP Internet layer include IP, ARP, ICMP, and IGMP. We examine these protocols next.

IP

IP (Internet Protocol)

Defines the addressing used to identify the source and destination addresses of data packets being delivered over an IP network

The **IP (Internet Protocol)** defines the addressing used to identify the source and destination addresses of data packets being delivered over an IP network. The IP address is a logical address that consists of a network and a host address portion. The network portion is used to direct the data to the proper network. The host address identifies the address locally assigned to the host. The network portion of the address is similar to the area code for a telephone number. The host address is similar to the local exchange number. The network and host portions of the IP address are then used to route the data packets to the destination. (IP addressing and subnet masking are examined in detail in sections 6-4 and 6-5.)

ARP

ARP

Address Resolution Protocol, used to map an IP address to its MAC address

Address Resolution Protocol (ARP) is used to resolve an IP address to a hardware address for final delivery of data packets to the destination. ARP issues a query in a network called an *ARP request*, asking which network interface has this IP address. The host assigned the IP address replies with an *ARP reply*, the protocol that contains the hardware address for the destination host. Figure 6-9 provides an example of an ARP request captured with a protocol analyzer. As shown highlighted in Figure 6-9(a), an ARP request is issued on the LAN. The source MAC address of the packet is 00-10-A4-13-99-2E. The destination address on the local area network shown is BROADCAST, which means this message is being sent to all computers in the local area network. A query (Q) is asking who has the IP address 10.10.10.1 (PA=). *PA* is an abbreviation for *protocol address*.

The highlighted area in Figure 6-9(b) shows the destination computer's ARP reply, sending its MAC address back to the source that issued the ARP request. (The *R* after the ARP indicates this is an ARP reply.) The source of the ARP reply is 00-10A4-13-6C-6E, which is replying that the MAC address for 10.10.10.1 is 00-10-A4-13-6C-6E (HA=). *HA* is an abbreviation for *hardware address*. In this case, the owner of the IP address replied to the message, but this is not always the case. Sometimes another networking device, such as a router, can provide the MAC address information. In that case, the MAC address being returned is for the next networking device in the route to the destination.

(a)

(b)

FIGURE 6-9   (a) The captured packets showing the ARP request; (b) the ARP reply.

Figure 6-10 provides a breakdown of the packet details of the ARP request. The description of the ARP request is a broadcast that is the uppercase *F*. This means that all binary data bits are set to a logical 1. The data packet with all Fs is highlighted at the bottom of the image. Can you find the source address for the ARP request? The source address of 00-10-A4-13-99-2E immediately follows the destination address. The four hexadecimal characters (0x0806) identify this as an ARP packet. The 0x indicates that the 0806 is a hexadecimal number. Section 6-3 discusses the hexadecimal numbers in more detail.

FIGURE 6-10   The details of the ARP broadcast packet.

ICMP

The Internet Control Message Protocol (ICMP) is used to control the flow of data in the network, to report errors, and to perform diagnostics. A networking device, such as a router, sends an ICMP *source-quench* packet to a host that requests a slowdown in the data transfer.

An important troubleshooting tool within the ICMP protocol is *ping,* the packet Internet groper. The **ping** command is used to verify connectivity with another host in the network. The destination host could be in a LAN, in a campus LAN, or on the Internet.

The **ping** command was introduced in Chapter 1 and used in Chapter 4 to test the data packet deliveries in a LAN using a hub or switch. The **ping** command uses a series of echo requests, and the networking device receiving the echo requests responds with a series of echo replies to test a network connection. Refer to Chapters 1 and 4 for examples.

IGMP

IGMP
Internet Group Message Protocol

Multicasting
When one host sends data to many destination hosts

Multicast Addresses
The addresses used to send a multicast data packet

IGMP is the Internet Group Message Protocol. It is used when one host needs to send data to many destination hosts. This is called **multicasting**. The addresses used to send a multicast data packet are called **multicast addresses** and are reserved addresses not assigned to hosts in a network. An example of an application that uses IGMP packets is when a router uses multicasting to share routing tables. This is explained in Chapter 7, when routing protocols are examined.

Another application of IGMP packets is when a host wants to stream data to multiple hosts. *Streaming* means the data is sent without waiting for any acknowledgement that the data packets were delivered. In fact, in the IGMP protocol, the source doesn't care whether the destination receives a packet. Streaming is an important application in the transfer of audio and video files over the Internet. Another feature of IGMP is that the data is handed off to the application layer as it arrives. This enables the appropriate application to begin processing the data for playback.

The Network Interface Layer

Network Interface Layer
Defines how the host connects to the network

The network interface layer of the TCP/IP model defines how the host connects to the network. Recall that the host can be a computer or a networking device such as a router. The type of network to which the host connects is not dictated by the TCP/IP protocol. The host could be a computer connected to an Ethernet or token-ring network or a router connected to a frame relay wide area network. TCP/IP is not dependent on a specific networking technology; therefore, TCP/IP can be adapted to run on newer networking technologies such as asynchronous transfer mode (ATM).

In the network interface layer every TCP/IP data packet must have a destination and a source MAC address in the TCP/IP header. The MAC or hardware address is found on the host's network interface card or connection and is 12 hexadecimal characters in length. For example, the network interface could have a MAC address of

00-10-A4-13-99-2E

The hardware address is used for final delivery of data packets to the next destination in a network. The first six hexadecimal numbers represent the organization that manufactured the card. This is called the organizational unit identifier (*OUI*). The last six digits are unique numbers assigned by the manufacturer of the network interface. The concept of the MAC address was fully explained in Chapter 1, and you are encouraged to refer to this material for a thorough review.

Section 6-2 Review

This section has covered the following **Network+** Exam objectives.

1.8 Given a scenario, implement and configure the appropriate addressing schema

This section introduced IGMP, the Internet Group Message Protocol. It is used when one host needs to send data to many destination hosts. This is called multicasting. The addresses used to send a multicast data packet are called multicast addresses and are reserved addresses not assigned to hosts in a network.

3.2 Compare and contrast common network vulnerabilities and threats

This section introduced common applications and port numbers, which are presented in Table 6-4. Take the time to memorize the applications and port numbers provided in this table. It is important that a network technician knows the function of all ports and understands the possible threats when a port is left open.

5.2 Explain the basics of network theory and concepts

The concepts of TCP and UDP were both presented in this section. Make sure you understand the differences between a connection-oriented protocol and a connectionless protocol.

5.9 Compare and contrast the following ports and protocols

A partial list of the possible TCP/UDP ports is provided in Table 6-4. There are 65,536 possible TCP/UDP ports. Ports 1–1023 are called well-known ports or reserved ports. These ports are reserved by Internet Corporation for Assigned Names and Numbers (ICANN). Ports 1024–49151 are called registered ports and are registered with ICANN. Ports 49152–65535 are called dynamic or private ports.

6-3 NUMBER CONVERSION

This section reviews the numbering systems used in computer networking, with a focus on converting binary, decimal, and hexadecimal numbers.

Binary-to-Decimal Conversion

Binary numbers are represented as a logical 0 or logical 1 in base 2 format. This means that each number has a place value of 2^N, where n is the place value position of the binary digit. The place values start at 2^0 with the least significant bit (LSB) position. For example, the binary number 1 0 1 1 has the place values of 2^0 for the LSB position to 2^3 for the most significant bit (MSB) position.

Place value	2^3	2^2	2^1	2^0
Binary digit	1	0	1	1
MSB→LSB	MSB			LSB

The 1 and 0 are used as a multiplier times the place value. For example, the conversion of 1 0 1 1 to decimal is as follows:

$1 \times 2^3 = 8$
$0 \times 2^2 = 0$
$1 \times 2^1 = 2$
$\underline{1 \times 2^0 = 1}$
sum = 11

Note that the place value was multiplied by the value of the binary digit.

Instead of writing 2^0, 2^1, 2^2..., it is easier to write the decimal equivalent for each place value (for example, 1, 2, 4, 8, 16, 32, 64, 128). The calculations for determining each place value are as follows:

$2^0 = 1$	$2^1 = 2$	$2^2 = 4$	$2^3 = 8$
$2^4 = 16$	$2^5 = 32$	$2^6 = 64$	$2^7 = 128$

This is shown in Table 6-5.

TABLE 6-5 **Place Values for Eight Binary Numbers (an Octet)**

Place value (decimal)	128	64	32	16	8	4	2	1
Place value	2^7	2^6	2^5	2^4	2^3	2^2	2^1	2^0
MSB—LSB	MSB							LSB

For example, the place values for the binary number 1 0 0 1 0 0 can be set up as follows:

Place value (decimal)	32	16	8	4	2	1
Place value	2^5	2^4	2^3	2^2	2^1	2^0
Binary digit	1	0	0	1	0	0
MSB→LSB	MSB					LSB

Every place value that has a binary digit of 1 is used to sum a total for determining the decimal equivalent for the binary number. In this example, the decimal equivalent is 32 + 4 = 36. After working a few examples, it becomes obvious that the base 2 place values can be written by inspection in their decimal equivalence. The rightmost place value is 1, the next place value is 2, the next is 4, and so on.

The 8-bit octet numbers used in IP addressing are converted from binary to decimal in the same manner. The following example demonstrates this.

Example 6-1

Given a 32-bit IP address number expressed in binary format, convert the number to a dotted-decimal format.

1 1 0 0 0 0 0 0	1 0 1 0 1 0 0 0	0 0 1 0 0 0 0 0	0 0 0 0 1 1 0 0
octet-4	octet-3	octet-2	octet-1

Solution:

First, assign the place value for each binary position.

	128	64	32	16	8	4	2	1
octet-1	0	0	0	0	1	1	0	0

$(1 \times 8) + (1 \times 4) = 8 + 4 = 12$

	128	64	32	16	8	4	2	1
octet-2	0	0	1	0	0	0	0	0

$(1 \times 32) = 32$

	128	64	32	16	8	4	2	1
octet-3	1	0	1	0	1	0	0	0

$(1 \times 128) + (1 \times 32) (1 \times 8) = 128 + 32 + 8 = 168$

	128	64	32	16	8	4	2	1
octet-4	1	1	0	0	0	0	0	0

$(1 \times 128) + (1 \times 64) = 128 + 64 = 192$

Therefore, the dotted decimal equivalent is 192.168.32.12.

Decimal-to-Binary Conversion

The simplest way to convert a decimal number to binary is using division, repeatedly dividing the decimal number by 2 until the quotient is 0. The division steps for converting decimal numbers to binary are as follows:

1. Divide the decimal number by 2, record the remainder of 0 or 1, and write the quotient or result of the division by 2.

2. Divide the quotient by 2 and record the remainder of 0 or 1. Write the quotient and repeat this step until the quotient is 0.

3. Write the remainder numbers (0 and 1) in reverse order to obtain the binary equivalent value.

Example 6-2

Convert the decimal number 12 to binary.

Solution:

Divide 12 by 2. This equals 6 with a remainder of 0. Divide 6 by 2. This equals 3 with a remainder of 0. Divide 3 by 2. This equals 1 with a remainder of 1. Divide 1 by 2. This equals 0 with a remainder of 1. The quotient is 0; therefore, the conversion is done. Write the remainder numbers in reverse order to generate the binary equivalent value. This yields a value of 1 1 0 0. The calculation for this is shown:

2|12
2|6   0
2|3   0
2|1   1
0   1

You can verify the answer by converting the binary number back to decimal.

8	4	2	1
1	1	0	0

$(1 \times 8) + (1 \times 4) = 12$

Example 6-3

Convert 33 to its binary equivalent.

Solution:

Use the decimal-to-binary steps listed previously.

2|33
2|16   1
2|8   0
2|4   0
2|2   0
2|1   0
0   1

The answer is 1 0 0 0 0 1.

Example 6-4

Convert the decimal number 254 to binary.

Solution

Use the decimal-to-binary steps listed previously.

```
2|254
2|127          0
2|63           1
2|31           1
2|15           1
2|7            1
2|3            1
2|1            1
0              1
```

The answer is 1 1 1 1 1 1 1 0.

Hexadecimal Numbers

Hex
Hexadecimal, base 16

Hexadecimal numbers (**hex**) are base 16 numbers. Table 6-6 provides a conversion lookup table for hexadecimal. It takes four binary numbers to represent a hexadecimal number. Notice that the letters A–F are used to represent the decimal numbers 10–15.

Converting Hexadecimal

The simplest way to convert hexadecimal numbers to binary is through the use of either a calculator or a lookup table, such as Table 6-6.

TABLE 6-6 **Hexadecimal Conversion Table**

Decimal	Hexadecimal	Binary
0	0	0 0 0 0
1	1	0 0 0 1
2	2	0 0 1 0
3	3	0 0 1 1
4	4	0 1 0 0
5	5	0 1 0 1
6	6	0 1 1 0
7	7	0 1 1 1

Decimal	Hexadecimal	Binary
8	8	1 0 0 0
9	9	1 0 0 1
10	A	1 0 1 0
11	B	1 0 1 1
12	C	1 1 0 0
13	D	1 1 0 1
14	E	1 1 1 0
15	F	1 1 1 1

Hexadecimal numbers are used in computer networks to represent the computer's 12-hex character MAC address and are used to display the packet details in a protocol analyzer, as shown in Figure 6-11. Hex numbers are also used in IPv6 addressing (discussed in section 6-7).

FIGURE 6-11   An example of the use of hex numbers in data packets.

The highlighted region in Figure 6-11 shows the destination MAC address of 01005E00000A, which is a 12-digit hexadecimal code. Notice that the EtherType number is 0x0800, defining that this is an Internet protocol packet. Also note that the numbers at the bottom of the screen are expressed in hex format. These numbers are the values in the data packets.

0x800—The 0x indicates this is a hexadecimal number.

0x800$_H$—The subscript H is sometimes used to indicate that this is a hexadecimal number. The subscript notation is not always practical to display in a text format, so this style is of limited use.

The following are examples of converting hexadecimal numbers to binary.

Example 6-5

Convert the hexadecimal number 0x48AF to binary.

Solution:

Use Table 6-6 to convert the hex numbers.

Hex:	4	8	A	F
Binary:	0 1 0 0	1 0 0 0	1 0 1 0	1 1 1 1

Example 6-6

Convert the hexadecimal number 0x0800 to binary.

Solution:

Use Table 6-6 to convert the hex numbers.

Hex:	0	8	0	0
Binary:	0 0 0 0	1 0 0 0	0 0 0 0	0 0 0 0

Converting binary numbers to hexadecimal requires that the binary numbers be separated into groups of four beginning with the LSB position. If the binary sequence doesn't have 4 bits, use leading 0s to pad the number. The binary numbers used in computer networks are always a multiple of four in length; therefore, you won't have to pad any of the numbers with leading 0s.

Example 6-7

Convert the binary number 0 1 0 0 1 1 0 0 1 0 1 0 to hexadecimal.

Solution:

Separate the binary numbers into groups of four beginning with the LSB position. Next, use the conversion lookup table (Table 6-6) to convert each 4-bit binary group to hexadecimal.

0 1 0 0	1 1 0 0	1 0 1 0
4	C	A

The answer is 0x4CA.

Section 6-3 Review

This section has covered the following **Network+** Exam objectives.

5.2 Explain the basics of network theory and concepts

The focus of this section was number conversion. An important relationship is the structure of the MAC address, which is made up of 12 hexadecimal characters. Also, the EtherType of 0x0800 was expressed in hexadecimal.

Test Your Knowledge

1. Converting 1 0 1 1 0 1 1 0 1 1 1 1 0 0 0 1 to hexadecimal yields which of the following?

    a. B6F1

    b. A6F1

    c. AAF1

    d. BAF1

    e. None of these answers is correct.

2. Converting 65 to its binary equivalent yields 1 0 0 0 0 0 1. True or False?

6-4   IPV4 ADDRESSING

IP addressing provides a standardized format for assigning a unique routable address for every host in a TCP/IP network. You might ask, "The host in a TCP/IP network already has a hardware (MAC) address, so why the need for the IP address?"

The answer is that internetworking devices need a routable network address to deliver data packets outside the LAN. The IP address is similar to a telephone number. The network portion of the IP address is similar to the telephone's area code. The host portion of the IP address is similar to the telephone's 7-bit local exchange number. This section identifies the network and host portion of an IP address and describes how IP addressing is used to identify the address for a host in a network.

The IP addressing version currently being used on the Internet and for TCP/IP data traffic is **IPv4**. There are five classes of IPv4 addresses: **class A, B, C, D, and E**. The address breakdown for each class is provided in Table 6-7. Classes A, B, and C are the primary addresses used over the Internet and for TCP/IP data traffic. Class D is used for multicasting (explained in Chapter 9, "Routing Protocols"), while the class E range is experimental and is not used on the Internet. A new IP addressing scheme called IPv6 has been developed for use on the Internet. Section 6-7 covers this address scheme in more detail.

TABLE 6-7   **IPv4 Address Classes and Address Range**

Class	IP Address Range
A	0.0.0.0–127.255.255.255
B	128.0.0.0–191.255.255.255
C	192.0.0.0–223.255.255.255
D	224.0.0.0–239.255.255.255
E	240.0.0.0 –254.255.255.255

Note

The 0.0.0.0 and 127.x.x.x addresses are special-purpose addresses. The 0.0.0.0 IP address refers to the source host on this network. The 127.x.x.x addresses are used as the Internet loopback address. A datagram sent by a higher-level protocol to an address anywhere within this block should loop back inside the host. The most common loopback address used is 127.0.0.1. The 127.x.x.x addresses should never appear on the network.

Each IP address consists of four 8-bit octets, providing a total binary data length of 32 bits. Figure 6-12 shows the 32-bit structure for the IP address. Each octet in the IP address is expressed in terms of its decimal equivalent. The decimal equivalent representation of the four octets shown in Figure 6-12 is 10.10.20.1. Table 6-8 provides the breakdown for determining each octet in decimal and binary.

FIGURE 6-12   The structure of the 32-bit IPv4 address.

TABLE 6-8   Decimal/Binary Octet Breakdown for the 10.10.20.1 IPv4 Address

Octet	Decimal	Binary
4	10	0 0 0 0 1 0 1 0
3	10	0 0 0 0 1 0 1 0
2	20	0 0 0 1 0 1 0 0
1	1	0 0 0 0 0 0 0 1

Representing the binary data in decimal form simplifies the user interface. TCP/IP uses the binary form (represented as 32 1/0 bits) for transporting the IP address, but the user interface is typically expressed in a *dotted-decimal* format. The 10.10.20.1 IP address is an example of dotted-decimal.

Each of the four octets of the IPv4 address represents either a network or a host portion of the IP address. Figure 6-13 and Table 6-9 illustrate the breakdown in each of the address classes for network and host bits. Class A has 8 bits assigned for the network address and 24 bits for the host. Class B has 16 bits for the network address and 16 bits for the host. Class C has 24 bits assigned for the network address and 8 bits for the host.

FIGURE 6-13   The octets making up the network and host portions of the IPv4 address for classes A, B, and C.

TABLE 6-9   Breakdown of the Network and Host Bits by Class

Class	Network Bits	Host Bits
A	8	24
B	16	16
C	24	8

The number of host bits in the IP address classes determines how many hosts can be created for each class of address. The equation

$2^N - 2$, where n = number of host bits

is used to calculate the number of host IP addresses that can be created for a network. For example, a class C address has 8 host bits; therefore, $2^8 - 2 = 254$ host IP addresses can be assigned to a class C network. The reason for the "– 2" value in the equation when calculating the number of host addresses is the host IP address cannot be all 1s or all 0s. The all 1s state is reserved for network broadcasts, and the all 0s state is reserved for the network address. Table 6-10 lists the total number of available host IP addresses for each class of network. (A technique called *subnetting* is introduced in this chapter in section 6-5. This section shows how host bits are borrowed and added to the network address bit to create subnets in a network.)

TABLE 6-10   Number of Host IP Addresses by Class

Class	Number of Host Bits	Number of Hosts
A	24	16,777,214
B	16	65,534
C	8	254

Private IP Addresses

Address ranges in class A, B, and C have been set aside for private use. These addresses, called *private addresses*, are not used for Internet data traffic but are intended to be used specifically on internal networks called *intranets*. Table 6-11 lists the private address ranges.

TABLE 6-11   Private IP Addresses

Class	Address Range
A	10.0.0.0–10.255.255.255
B	172.16.0.0–172.31.255.255
C	192.168.0.0–192.168.255.255

Non-Internet Routable IP Addresses

IP addresses not routed on the Internet

RIRs

Regional Internet registries, IANA-designated governing organizations responsible for IP address allocation by geographical location

The IP addresses used in this text are in the private address range. Functionally, private addresses work the same as public addresses except they are not routed on the Internet. These are called **non-internet routable IP addresses** and are blocked by Internet service providers (ISPs).

IP Address Assignment

IP address allocation is governed by the Internet Assigned Number Authority (IANA). To coordinate the global effort of IP allocation more effectively, IANA delegates the allocation to the regional Internet registries (**RIRs**), each of which is responsible for a different area. The five RIRs accounting for the different regions of the world are as follows:

- **AfriNIC**: Africa Region
- **APNIC**: Asia/Pacific Region

- **ARIN**: North America Region
- **LACNIC**: Latin America and some Caribbean Islands
- **RIPE NCC**: Europe, the Middle East, and Central Asia

In North America, IP addresses are assigned by the American Registry for Internet Numbers (**ARIN**). Their web address is http://www.arin.net. ARIN assigns IP address space to ISPs and end users, but only to those who qualify. This requires that the ISP or end user be large enough to merit a block of addresses. When blocks of addresses are allocated by ARIN to ISPs, the ISPs issue addresses to their customers. For example, a Telco could be the ISP that has a large block of IP addresses and issues an IP address to a user. A local ISP could also be assigned a block of IP addresses from ARIN, but the local ISP must have a large number of users.

ARIN also assigns end users IP addresses. Once again, the end user must qualify to receive a block of addresses from ARIN. This usually means that the end user must be large. For example, many universities and large businesses can receive a block of IP addresses from ARIN. However, most end users will get their IP addresses from an ISP (for example, Telco) or have IP addresses assigned dynamically when they connect to the ISP.

> **ARIN**
> American Registry for Internet Numbers

Section 6-4 Review

This section has covered the following **Network+** Exam objectives.

> 1.8 Given a scenario, implement and configure the appropriate addressing schema

The classes of IP addresses were presented in Table 6-7. Make sure you can identify the class for each range of addresses. This section also listed the ranges for private IP addresses in Table 6-11.

Test Your Knowledge

1. The home IP address for a network is assigned by which of these?

   a. ARIN, the association of Registered Internet Numbers

   b. ARIN, the American Registry for Internet Names

   c. ARIN, the American Registry for Internet Numbers

   d. ARNN, the American Registry for Internet Names and Numbers

2. The IP address 192.168.20.5 is an example of what? (Select all that apply.)

   a. Class C IP address

   b. Class B IP address

   c. Class A IP address

   d. A private IP address

6-5   SUBNET MASKS

The objective of this section is to demonstrate how to establish subnet masks for use in computer networks. *Subnetting* is a technique used to break down (or partition) networks into subnets. The subnets are created through the use of subnet masks. The **subnet mask** identifies which bits in the IP address are to be used to represent the network/subnet portion of an IP address.

Subnets are created by borrowing bits from the host portion of the IP address. This is shown in Figure 6-14. The network portion of the IP address and the new subnet bits are used to define the new subnet. Routers use this information to properly forward data packets to the proper subnet. The class C network shown in Figure 6-15 is partitioned into four subnets. It takes 2 bits to provide four possible subnets; therefore, 2 bits are borrowed from the host bits. This means the process of creating the 4 subnets reduces the number of bits available for host IP addresses.

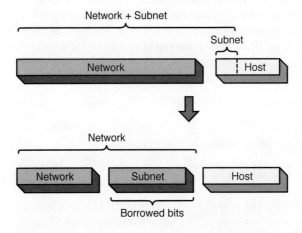

FIGURE 6-14   Borrowing bits from the host to create subnets.

FIGURE 6-15   Partitioning a network into subnets.

Assume that the network has an IP address of 192.168.12.0. The 2 bits are borrowed from the host portion of the IP address to create the 4 subnets. The class C network has 24 network bits and 8 host bits. Then 2 bits are borrowed from the host address to create the 4 subnets. The network plus subnet portion of the IP address is now 24 + 2, or 26 bits in length, and the host portion is now 6 bits. The breakdown of the 32-bit IP address is shown in Figure 6-16.

FIGURE 6-16   The breakdown of the IP address to allow for the creation of four subnets.

The equations for calculating the number of subnets created and the number of hosts/subnet are provided in Equations 6-1 and 6-2.

| # of subnets created | 2x | [Equation 6-1] |
| # of hosts/subnet | 2(y - x) | [Equation 6-2] |

where x = # of bits borrowed from the host bits

y = # host bits for the class of network

(A = 24, B = 16, C = 8)

Breaking down the 192.168.12.0 network into four subnets requires borrowing two host bits. Therefore, $x = 2$, and because this is a class C network, $y = 8$.

$x = 2$ (the number of bits used from the host)

$y = 8$ (number of bits for a class C network)

Applying these values to equation 6-2 yields

The number of subnets created = $2^x = 2^{(2)} = 4$

The number of hosts/subnet = $2^{(Y - X)} = 2^{(8 - 2)} = 64$

When creating subnets, it is important to note that each subnet will have both a network and a broadcast address. Taking this into consideration, the equations for calculating the number of hosts/subnet are modified to account for the number of usable hosts/subnet. The modified equations are as follows:

The number of usable hosts/subnet = $2^{(Y - X)} - 2$ [Equation 6-3]

The next step is to determine the subnet mask required for creating the four subnets. Recall that creating the four subnets required borrowing 2 host bits. The two most significant bit (MSB) positions, borrowed from the host and network portion of the IP address, must be included in the subnet mask selection. The purpose of the subnet mask is to specify the bit positions used to identify the network and subnet bits. Applying the subnet mask is basically a logical AND operation. Setting the subnet mask bit position to a 1 enables the bit value from the IP address to pass. Setting the subnet mask bit value to 0 disables the IP address from appearing on the output. This is shown in the truth table for a logical AND operation:

Subnet Mask Bit	IP Address Bit	Output
0	0	0
0	1	0
1	0	0
1	1	1

Notice that when the subnet mask bit is set to 0, the output is forced to 0. When the subnet mask bit is set to 1, the output follows the IP address bit.

The subnet mask consists of bit position values set to either a 1 or a 0. A bit position set to a 1 indicates that the bit position is used to identify a network or subnet bit. The subnet mask for identifying the class C network 192.168.12.0 will be 255.255.255.x. This conversion is shown next.

Binary	1 1 1 1 1 1 1 1	1 1 1 1 1 1 1 1	1 1 1 1 1 1 1 1	x x x x x x x x
Decimal	255	255	255	x

The subnet mask also identifies the subnet bits. The two MSBs were borrowed from the host bits; therefore, the last octet of the subnet mask will be

	|—Subnet—| |————Host Addresses————|							
Place Value	128	64	32	16	8	4	2	1
	1	1	x	x	x	x	x	x

where the 1 indicates this place is used for the subnet mask and the x means that the place value is left for the host address. Summing the two bit position values that have a 1 yields $128 + 64 = 192$. The 192 is placed in the last octet of the subnet mask. The complete subnet mask is 255.255.255.192.

The two subnet bits create four subnets, and each subnet has its own network address. The network addresses are used to route data packets to the correct subnet. Table 6-12 shows the four subnet addresses listed in both binary and decimal format.

(*Note:* The six host bits are all set at 0 in a subnet's network address.)

TABLE 6-12 **Binary and Decimal Equivalents for the Subnet's Network Address**

Place Value			
128	64	Host Bits	Subnet Address
0	0	0 0 0 0 0 0	0
0	1	0 0 0 0 0 0	64
1	0	0 0 0 0 0 0	128
1	1	0 0 0 0 0 0	192

Each subnet will also have its own broadcast address. The broadcast address for the subnet is used to broadcast packets to all hosts in the subnet. (*Note:* All host bits are set to 1 for a broadcast.) Table 6-13 shows the binary and decimal equivalents for the subnet's broadcast address.

TABLE 6-13 Binary and Decimal Equivalents for the Subnet's Broadcast Address

	|- Subnet -|	|——Host Bits——|					Decimal Equivalent
Place Value	128	64	32	16	8	4	2	1	
	0	0	1	1	1	1	1	1	63
	0	1	1	1	1	1	1	1	127
	1	0	1	1	1	1	1	1	191
	1	1	1	1	1	1	1	1	255
Place Value	128	64	32	16	8	4	2	1	

Given this information, the network and broadcast address can be defined for the four subnets of the 192.168.12.0 network. Table 6-14 provides these addresses for the four subnets.

TABLE 6-14 Network and Broadcast Addresses for the Four Subnets of the 192.168.12.0 Network

Subnet	Network Address	Broadcast Address
1st subnet (0)	192.168.12.0	192.168.12.63
2nd subnet (64)	192.168.12.64	192.168.12.127
3rd subnet (128)	192.168.12.128	192.168.12.191
4th subnet (192)	192.168.12.192	192.168.12.255

The same technique for subnet masking can be applied to class A, B, or C addresses. The following examples demonstrate subnet mask selection in a network.

Example 6-8

Given a network address of 10.0.0.0, divide the network into 8 subnets. Specify the subnet mask, the network and broadcast addresses, and the number of usable hosts/subnet.

Solution:

Creating 8 subnets requires borrowing 3 host bits; therefore, $x = 3$. This is a class A network, so $y = 24$.

Using Equation 6-1, the number of subnets = 23 = 8.

Using Equation 6-3, the number of usable hosts = $2^{(24-3)} - 2 = 2097150$

The 8 subnets will be:

128	64	32	Host Bits	Subnet
0	0	0	x x x x x	0
0	0	1	x x x x x	32
0	1	0	x x x x x	64
0	1	1	x x x x x	96
1	0	0	x x x x x	128
1	0	1	x x x x x	160
1	1	0	x x x x x	192
1	1	1	x x x x x	224

Therefore, the network and broadcast addresses for the 8 subnets will be

Subnet	Network Address	Broadcast Address
0 subnet (0 0 0)	10.0.0.0	10.31.255.255
32 subnet (0 0 1)	10.32.0.0	10.63.255.255
64 subnet (0 1 0)	10.64.0.0	10.95.255.255
96 subnet (0 1 1)	10.96.0.0	10.127.255.255
128 subnet (1 0 0)	10.128.0.0	10.159.255.255
160 subnet (1 0 1)	10.160.0.0	10.191.255.255
192 subnet (1 1 0)	10.192.0.0	10.223.255.255
224 subnet (1 1 1)	10.224.0.0	10.255.255.255

The subnet mask for creating the 8 subnets will be 255.224.0.0.

The 224 in Example 6-8 comes from setting the subnet mask to select the three MSB positions in the host portion of the address, as shown in Figure 6-17.

FIGURE 6-17   The network, subnet, and host bit positions for creating the eight subnets in Example 6-8.

Another way to look at selecting a subnet mask is by specifying how many usable hosts are available to be assigned in a subnet. For example, assume that 62 usable host addresses are to be available in a subnet. Assume this is for a class C network. Using Equation 6-2,

$$62 = 2^{(8-x)} - 2$$

$$64 = 2^{(8-x)}$$

Using logarithms to solve for x:

$$\log 64 = (8-x)(\log 2)$$

$$\log 64/(\log 2) = 8-x$$

$$6 = 8-x \text{ therefore, } x = 2$$

Instead of using logarithms, a table such as that shown in Table 6-15 can be used. Example 6-9 shows how the table can be used to determine the subnet mask.

TABLE 6-15   **Number of Bits Borrowed to Create a Specific Number of Usable Hosts**

	# of Host Bits Needed		
# of Usable Hosts	Class A	Class B	Class C
1022	14	6	–
510	15	7	–
254	16	8	–
126	17	9	–
62	18	10	2
30	19	11	3
14	20	12	4
6	21	13	5
2	22	14	6

Example 6-9

Determine the subnet mask required for the router-to-router link shown in Figure 6-18 if only two host addresses are required for this link.

172.16.31.1

172.16.31.2

FIGURE 6-18 Setting a subnet mask for a router-to-router link that provides two host addresses.

Solution:

Using Table 6-15 to determine the number of host bits borrowed for creating a subnet with two usable hosts, we find that 14 host bits are borrowed for this class B network. This means the first 3 octets plus the 6 MSB positions of the fourth octet will be used to create the subnet mask. The decimal equivalent for the 6 MSB bit positions is $128 + 64 + 32 + 16 + 8 + 4 = 252$.

Binary	1 1 1 1 1 1 1 1	1 1 1 1 1 1 1 1	1 1 1 1 1 1 1 1	1 1 1 1 1 1 x x
Decimal	255	255	255	252

Therefore, the subnet mask is going to be 255.255.255.252.

Computers use the subnet mask to control data flow within networks. Computers in a LAN use a subnet mask to determine whether the destination IP address is intended for a host in the same LAN or if the data packet should be sent to the gateway IP address of the LAN. The gateway IP address is typically the physical network interface on a layer 3 switch or a router.

For example, assume that the IP address of the computer in the LAN is 172.16.35.3. A subnet mask of 255.255.255.0 is being used. This means that all data packets with an IP address between 172.16.35.0 and 172.16.35.255 stay in the LAN. A data packet with a destination IP address of 172.16.34.15 is sent to the LAN gateway. The 255.255.255.0 subnet mask indicates that all bits in the first three octets must match each other to stay in this LAN.

This can be verified by "ANDing" the subnet mask with the destination address as shown:

> 172.16.35.3
> 255.255.255.0
> 172.16.35.0 is in the same LAN subnet sent to the gateway
> 172.16.34.15
> 255.255.255.0
> 176.16.34.0 not in the same subnet as the LAN

This section has demonstrated techniques for establishing subnets and subnet masks in computer networks. Examples have been presented that guide the reader through the process of borrowing bits to determine the number of available hosts in the subnet. The next section examines the concepts of expanding the subnet IP address range past the class boundaries using CIDR blocks.

Section 6-5 Review

This section has covered the following **Network+** Exam objectives.

1.8 Given a scenario, implement and configure the appropriate addressing schema

The techniques for subnetting networks was presented in this section. Make sure you understand the concept of borrowing bits to create a subnet and can identify how many host IP address are available for a given subnet. This section also showed how the subnet mask is used to determine whether the destination IP address is in the same LAN or whether the data packet is sent to the gateway address for the LAN. This is an important concept when tracking data packet travel.

Test Your Knowledge

1. The subnet mask 255.255.255.0 is applied to the IP address 10.20.35.12. Which subnet is the packet sent to?

   a. 10.20.35.32

   b. 10.20.0.0

   c. 10.0.0.0

   d. 10.20.35.192

   e. None of these answers is correct.

2. The network address for a host with an IP address of 192.168.50.146 using a subnet mask of 255.255.255.192 is which of the following?

   a. 192.168.50.128

   b. 192.168.50.191

   c. 192.168.128.0

   d. 192.168.128.192

   e. None of these answers is correct.

3. Given a network IP address of 172.16.0.0 and a subnet mask 255.255.192.0, how many subnets are in this network?

   a. 2

   b. 4

   c. 8

   d. 16

6-6 CIDR BLOCKS

Classful

The IP and subnet addresses are within the same network

Up to this point, this chapter has focused on the issues of **classful** networks. *Classful* means that the IP addresses and subnets are within the same network. The problem with classful addressing is that there is a lot of unused IP address space. For example, a class A IP network has more than 16 million possible host addresses. A Class B network has more than 65,000 host addresses, but the fact is that only a limited number of Class A and B address space has been allocated for Internet use.

Supernetting

Allows multiple networks to be specified by one subnet mask

CIDR

Classless interdomain routing

A technique called **supernetting** was proposed in 1992 to eliminate the class boundaries and to make available the unused IP address space. Supernetting allows multiple networks to be specified by one subnet mask. In other words, the class boundary could be overcome.

Supernetting required a simpler way to indicate the subnet mask. The technique developed is called classless interdomain routing (**CIDR**). CIDR (pronounced "cider") notation specifies the number of bits set to a 1 that make up the subnet mask. For example, the Class C size subnet mask 255.255.255.0 is listed in CIDR notation as /24. This indicates the 24 bits are set to a 1. A Class B size subnet is written as /16, and a Class A subnet is written as /8. CIDR can also be used to represent subnets that identify only part of the octet bits in an IP address. For example, a subnet mask of 255.255.192.0 is written in CIDR as /18. The /18 comes from the 18 bits that are set to a 1 as shown:

255	255	192	0
1 1 1 1 1 1 1 1	1 1 1 1 1 1 1 1	1 1 0 0 0 0 0 0	0 0 0 0 0 0 0 0

Prefix Length Notation

Another shorthand technique for writing the subnet mask except class boundaries are not being crossed

An alternative to the CIDR notation is the **prefix length notation**. This is another shorthand technique for writing the subnet mask. For example, the subnet mask 255.255.255.192 is written as /26. This notation shows the number of network and host bits being used to create the subnet mask. In the case of a /26 subnet mask, 24 network bits and 2 host bits are being used. Yes, this is basically the same as the CIDR except class boundaries are not being crossed and network bits are not being borrowed.

A network address and the subnet mask of 192.168.12.0 255.255.252.0 can be **written** in CIDR notation as 192.168.12.0/22. Table 6-16 provides the CIDR for the most common subnet masks.

TABLE 6-16 CIDR—Subnet Mask Conversion

CIDR	Subnet Mask	CIDR	Subnet Mask
/8	255.0.0.0	/21	255.255.248.0
/9	255.128.0.0	/22	255.255.252.0
/10	255.192.0.0	/23	255.255.254.0
/11	255.224.0.0	/24	255.255.255.0
/12	255.240.0.0	/25	255.255.255.128
/13	255.248.0.0	/26	255.255.255.192
/14	255.252.0.0	/27	255.255.255.224
/15	255.254.0.0	/28	255.255.255.240
/16	255.255.0.0	/29	255.255.255.248
/17	255.255.128.0	/30	255.255.255.252
/18	255.255.192.0	/31	255.255.255.254
/19	255.255.224.0	/32	255.255.255.255
/20	255.255.240.0		

CIDR blocks are used to break down the class barriers in IP addressing. For example, two Class C networks (192.168.78.0/24 and 192.168.79.0/24) can be grouped together as one big subnet. These two networks can be grouped together by modifying the /24 CIDR number to /23. This means that one bit has been borrowed from the network address bits to combine the two networks into one supernet. Writing these two networks in CIDR notation provides 192.168.78.0/23. This reduces the two Class C subnets to one larger network. The group of networks defined by CIDR notation is called a **CIDR block**. When you group two or more classful networks together, they are called **supernets**. This term is synonymous with CIDR blocks. The group of four IP addresses from 192.168.76.0 to 192.168.79.0 with a CIDR of /22 is a supernet. The supernet uses a CIDR subnet mask (/22) that is shorter than the number of network bits for Class C network (/24). Another example of a supernet is 172.16.0.0/12. 172.16.0.0 is a Class B address, and the CIDR subnet mask (/12) is less than the 16 bits for the network portion of a Class B address.

The problem with randomly applying CIDR blocks to Class A, B, and C addresses is that there are boundaries in each class, and these boundaries can't be crossed. If a boundary is crossed, the IP address maps to another subnet. For example, the CIDR block is expanded to include four Class C networks. This means that all four Class C networks need to be specified by the same CIDR subnet mask to avoid crossing boundaries. The new subnet mask is 255.255.252.0. The following example demonstrates what happens if a boundary is crossed.

CIDR Block
The grouping of two or more class networks together; also called supernetting

Supernets
The grouping of two or more class networks together; also called CIDR blocks

Example 6-10

Explore what happens if the boundary in IP addresses for Class C subnets is crossed. For this example, the subnets have IP addresses of

192.168.78.0/22

192.168.79.0/22

192.168.80.0/22

192.168.81.0/22

Solution:

Applying the /22 subnet mask to 192.168.78.0 and 192.168.80.0 provides the following. (*Note:* The binary values of the affected octet are shown, and applying the subnet mask means that the binary values of the IP address and the subnet mask are ANDed together.)

	Place Value	128	64	32	16	8	4	2	1
192.168.78.0 IP		0	1	0	0	1	1	1	1
255.255.252.0 SM		1	1	1	1	1	1	0	0
192.168.76.0		0	1	0	0	1	1	0	0 (76)

$$64 + 8 + 4 = 76$$

Now the same subnet mask is applied to the 192.168.80.0 subnet.

	Place Value	128	64	32	16	8	4	2	1
192.168.80.0 IP		0	1	0	1	0	0	0	0
255.255.252.0 SM		1	1	1	1	1	1	0	0
192.168.80.0		0	1	0	1	0	0	0	0 (80)

$$64 + 16 = 80$$

IP = IP Address

SM = subnet mask

Applying the /22 subnet mask places these two IP addresses in different subnets. The first IP address is placed in the "76" subnet while the second IP address is placed in the "80" subnet. The boundary line has been crossed, placing the IP addresses in different subnets when the /22 is applied.

This example shows what will happen if a boundary is crossed in IP addressing. If four Class C subnets need to be grouped into one CIDR block, IP addresses from the ranges shown could be used:

192.168.76.0–192.168.79.0 (all will be in the "76" subnet), or

192.168.80.0–192.168.83.0 (all will be in the "80" subnet)

Careful planning is required to ensure the IP addresses can all be specified by the same subnet mask. The goal of this section has been to develop an understanding of supernets, classless routing, and CIDR blocks. The reader should also understand the CIDR notation and be able to determine whether a group of IP addresses is in the same subnet.

Section 6-6 Review

This section has covered the following **Network+** Exam objectives.

> 1.8 Given a scenario, implement and configure the appropriate addressing schema

This section has presented a technique for creating "classless" CIDR blocks. It is important to understand that to create CIDR blocks, bits are borrowed from the network bits.

Test Your Knowledge

1. A network address of 192.168.6.0 and a subnet mask of 255.255.254.0 can be written in CIDR as which of the following?

    a. 192.168.6.0/23

    b. 192.168.6.0/12

    c. 192.168.6.0/15

    d. 192.168.6.0/20

2. The subnet mask for a CIDR of /22 is which of the following?

    a. 255.255.255.252

    b. 255.252.0.0

    c. 255.255.255.254

    d. 255.255.252.0

6-7 IPV6 ADDRESSING

IP version 4 (IPv4) is the current TCP/IP addressing technique being used on the Internet. Address space for IPv4 is quickly running out due to the rapid growth of the Internet and the development of new Internet-compatible technologies such as the IP addressable telephone. IP version 6 (**IPv6**) is the proposed solution for expanding the possible number of users on the Internet. IPv6 is also called **IPng,** the next generation IP.

IPv6 uses a 128-bit address technique, compared to IPv4's 32-bit address structure. IPv6 provides for a large number of IP addresses (2^{128}). IPv6 numbers are written in hexadecimal rather than dotted decimal. For example, the following is a 32-hexadecimal digit IPv6 address (*Note:* 32 hex digits × 4 bits/hex digit = 128 bits):

6789:ABCD:1234:EF98:7654:321F:EDCB:AF21

This is classified as a **full IPv6 address**. The *full* means that all 32 hexadecimal positions contain a value other than 0.

Why doesn't IPv6 use the dotted decimal format of IPv4? It would take many decimal numbers to represent the IPv6 address. Each decimal number takes at least 7 binary bits in American Standard Code for Information Interchange (ASCII) code. For example, the decimal equivalent of the first 8 hexadecimal characters in the previous full IPv6 address is

6	7	8	9	:A	B	C	D
103		.137		.171		.205	

The completed decimal equivalent number for the full IPv6 address is

103.137.171.205.18.52.239.152.118.84.50.31.237.203.175.33

The equivalent decimal number is 42 characters in length. In fact, the decimal equivalent number could be 48 decimal numbers long.

IPv6 uses seven colons (:) as separators to group the 32 hex characters into eight groups of four. Some IPv6 numbers will have a 0 within the address. In this case, IPv6 allows the number to be compressed to make it easier to write the number. For example, assume that an IPv6 number is as follows:

6789:0000:0000:EF98:7654:321F:EDCB:AF21

Consecutive 0s can be dropped and a double-colon notation can be used:

6789::EF98:7654:321F:EDCB:AF21

Recovering the compressed number in double-colon notation simply requires that all numbers left of the double notation be entered beginning with the leftmost slot of the IPv6 address. Next, start with the numbers to the right of the double colon.

Begin with the rightmost slot of the IPv6 address slots and enter the numbers from right to left until the double colon is reached. Zeros are entered into any empty slots.

6789 :0 :0 :EF98 :7654 :321F :EDCB :AF21

IPv4 numbers can be written in the new IPv6 form by writing the IPv4 number in hexadecimal and placing the number to the right of a double colon. Example 6-11 demonstrates how a dotted-decimal IP number can be converted to IPv6 hexadecimal.

Example 6-11

Convert the IPv4 address of 192.168.5.20 to an IPv6 hexadecimal address.

Solution:

First convert each dotted-decimal number to hexadecimal.

Decimal	Hex
192	C0
168	A8
5	05
20	14

(*Hint:* use a calculator or a lookup table to convert the decimal numbers to hexadecimal.) The IPv6 address will have many leading 0s; therefore, the IPv6 hex address can be written in double-colon notation as

:: C0A8:0514

IPv4 numbers can also be written in IPv6 form by writing the IPv4 number in dotted-decimal format as shown. Note that the number is preceded by 24 hexadecimal 0s.

0000: 0000: 0000: 0000: 0000: 0000:192.168.5.20

This number can be reduced as follows:

::192.168.5.20

There are three types of IPv6 addresses: **unicast, multicast,** and **anycast.** The unicast IPv6 address is used to identify a single network interface address and data packets are sent directly to the computer with the specified IPv6 address. There are several types of unicast addresses, including **link-local addresses**, global unicast addresses, and unique local addresses. Link-local addresses are designed to be used for and are limited to communications on the local link. Every IPv6 interface will have one link-local address.

Multicast IPv6 addresses are defined for a group of networking devices. Data packets sent to a multicast address are sent to the entire group of networking devices, such as a group of routers running the same routing protocol. Multicast addresses all start with the prefix FF00::/8. The next group of characters in the IPv6 multicast address (the second octet) are called the scope. The scope bits are used to identify which ISP should carry the data traffic. The anycast IPv6 address is obtained from a list of addresses but is only delivered to the nearest node.

Unicast Address
Used to identify a single network interface address, and data packets are sent directly to the computer with the specified IPv6 address

Multicast Address
Data packets sent to a multicast address are sent to the entire group of networking devices, such as a group of routers running the same routing protocol

Anycast Address
Is obtained from a list of addresses

Link-Local Address
Designed to be used for and is limited to communications on the local link

IPv6 addressing is being used in a limited number of network sites (for example, www.6bone.com and the federal government); however, the Internet is still running IPv4 and will be for some time. However, transition strategies are in place to help with the IPv4-to-IPv6 transition.

One possible transition to IPv6 is called the **6to4 Prefix**, which is essentially a technique that enables IPv6 sites to communicate over the IPv4 Internet. This requires the use of a 6to4-enabled router, which means that 6to4 tunneling has been enabled. This also requires the use of a 6to4 Relay router that forwards 6to4 data traffic to other 6to4 routers on the Internet.

Figure 6-19 illustrates the structure of the 6to4 prefix for hosts. The 32 bits of the IPv4 address fit into the first 48 bits of the IPv6 address.

6to4 Prefix

A technique that enables IPv6 hosts to communicate over the IPv4 Internet

FIGURE 6-19 The 6to4 prefix format.

Note the following in Figure 6-19:

- **FP** is the format prefix, which is made up of the higher order bits. The **001** indicates that this is a global unicast address. The current list of the IPv6 address allocation can be viewed at http://www.iana.org/assignments/ipv6-unicast-address-assignments/ipv6-unicast-address-assignments.xml.

- **TLA ID (0x2002)** is the top-level identifiers issued to local Internet registries. These IDs are administered by IANA (http://www.iana.org/). The TLA is used to identify the highest level in the routing hierarchy. The TLA ID is 13 bits long.

- **V4ADDR** is the IPv4 address of the 6to4 endpoint and is 32 bits long.

- **SLA ID** is the site-level aggregation identifier that is used by individual organizations to identify subnets within their sites. The SLA ID is 16 bits long.

- **Interface ID** is the link-level host identifier, used to indicate an interface on a specific subnet. The interface ID is equivalent to the host IP address in IPv4.

The 6to4 prefix format enables IPv6 domains to communicate with each other even if they don't have an IPv6 ISP. Additionally, IPv6 can be used within the intranet but access to the Internet is still available. The 6to4 provides unicast IPv6 connectivity between IPv6 host and via the IPv4 Internet.

Stateless address autoconfiguration (SLAAC)

Allows a server-less basic network configuration of the IPv6 computers

Stateless address autoconfiguration (SLAAC) is another important feature of IPv6. This feature allows for a server-less basic network configuration of the IPv6 computers. With IPv4, a computer generally obtains its network settings from a DHCP server. With IPv6, a computer can automatically configure its network settings without a DHCP server by sending a solicitation message to its IPv6 router. The router then sends back its advertisement message, which contains the prefix information that the computer can use to create its own IPv6 address. This feature significantly helps simplify the deployment of the IPv6 devices, especially in transient environments such as airports, train stations, stadiums, hotspots, and so on.

When will the Internet switch to IPv6? The answer is not clear, but the networking community recognizes that something must be done to address the limited availability of current IP address space. Manufacturers have already incorporated IPv6 capabilities in their routers and operating systems. What about IPv4? The bottom line is that the switch to IPv6 will not come without providing some way for IPv4 networks to still function. Additionally, techniques such as Network Address Translation (NAT; see Chapter 1, "Introduction to Computer Networks") have made it possible for intranets to use the private address space and still be able to connect to the Internet. This has significantly reduced the number of IP addresses required for each network.

Section 6-7 Review

This section has covered the following **Network+** Exam objectives.

> 1.8 Given a scenario, implement and configure the appropriate addressing schema

An overview of IPv6 addressing has been presented. Make sure you understand the structure of IPv6 addressing. Key topics include the structure of the IPv6 address, tunneling 6to4 and 4to6, and the three types of IPv6 addresses.

Test Your Knowledge

1. What is the 6to4 prefix?

   a. A technique that enables IPv4 hosts to communicate over the IPv6 Internet.

   b. A technique that enables IPv6 hosts to communicate over the IPv4 Internet.

   c. This is used to separate the IPv6 address from the hex MAC address.

   d. This is used to separate the MAC address from the IPv4 address.

2. In regards to IPv6, the SLA ID is what?

   a. It replaces the MAC address in IPv6 and is 32 bits long.

   b. This is the site-level aggregation ID and 128 bits in length and replaces the 32 bit IPv4 address.

   c. This is the site-level aggregation ID and is used by individual networks to identify the subnets within their site.

   d. It replaces the IP address in IPv6 and is 128 bits in length.

SUMMARY

This chapter has presented an overview of the fundamentals of the TCP/IP protocol suite. TCP/IP is well established and carries the data traffic over the Internet. The student should understand the following:

- The layers of TCP/IP and their relationship to the OSI layers
- The basic structure of a 32-bit IPv4 address
- How to subnet a network
- How to apply subnet masks in networks
- The purpose of CIDR blocks and supernetting
- The data structure of an IPv6 hexadecimal address
- The structure and purpose of the 6to4 protocol

QUESTIONS AND PROBLEMS

Section 6-2

1. What are the four layers of the TCP/IP model?

2. Which layer of the TCP/IP model processes requests from hosts to ensure a connection is made to the appropriate port?

3. What are well-known ports?

4. Identify the port numbers for the following applications:
    a. Telnet
    b. HTTP
    c. FTP
    d. DNS
    e. DHCP

5. Define the purpose of a *connection-oriented protocol.* Give an example.

6. Which three packets are exchanged between two hosts when establishing a TCP connection?

7. What is the purpose of a sequence number (SEQ=) in TCP data packets?

8. Explain how a host knows whether a data packet was not received.

9. Describe how a TCP connection is terminated.

10. What is a *connectionless protocol*? Give an example.

11. What is the purpose of the Internet layer in the TCP/IP protocol suite?

12. What is the purpose of an ARP request?

13. What is the purpose of an ARP reply?

14. Which important networking-troubleshooting tool is part of ICMP, and how does it test a network connection?

15. When is IGMP used?

16. The network interface layer of the TCP/IP model defines how the host connects to which network?

Section 6-3

17. Convert the following 8-bit binary number to decimal: 10010011

128	64	32	16	8	4	2	1
1	0	0	1	0	0	1	1

18. Convert the following octet to decimal: 11000000

128	64	32	16	8	4	2	1
1	1	0	0	0	0	0	0

19. Convert the following 8-bit number to decimal: 11111100

128	64	32	16	8	4	2	1
1	1	1	1	1	1	0	0

20. Convert the following binary number to decimal: 11111111

128	64	32	16	8	4	2	1
1	1	1	1	1	1	1	1

21. Convert the number 192 to its binary equivalent.

2	192	
2	96	0
2	48	0
2	24	0
2	12	0
2	6	0
2	3	0
2	1	1
	0	1

22. Convert the number 65 to its binary equivalent.

2	65	
2	32	1
2	16	0
2	8	0
2	4	0
2	2	0
2	1	0
	0	1

23. Convert the number 96 to its binary equivalent.

2	96	
2	48	0
2	24	0
2	12	0
2	6	0
2	3	0
2	1	1
0	1	1

24. What is the equivalent hexadecimal number for 13?

25. Convert 0x5AF3 to binary. Use Table 6-6.

Hex	5	A	F	3
Binary	0101	1010	1111	0011

26. Convert 1011011011110001 to hexadecimal.

Binary	1011	0110	1111	0001
Hex	B	6	f	1

Section 6-4

27. What is the IP address range for Class C addresses?

28. What is the purpose of Class D IP addresses?

29. How many bits are in an IPv4 address? How many octets?

30. The IPv4 address is typically expressed in which format for the user?

31. The IPv4 address 192.168.12.2 is an example of which format?

32. How many network bits are in each of the following classes?
    a. Class A
    b. Class B

33. How many network and host bits are in a Class C network address?

34. What is the purpose of a private IP address?

35. Can private IP addresses be routed?

36. How are private IP addresses handled on the Internet?

37. Which organization assigns IP addresses for North America?

Section 6-5

38. How many host bits are borrowed if four subnets are created?

39. What is the purpose of a subnet mask?

40. A host computer is assigned the IP address 192.168.12.8 and a subnet mask of 255.255.255.192. The host sends a packet to another host with an IP address of 192.168.12.65. Is the destination IP address in the same subnet as 192.168.12.8? Show why or why not.

41. The subnet mask 255.255.255.224 is applied to a packet with a destination IP address of 192.168.12.135. Which subnet is the packet sent to?

42. The subnet mask 255.255.255.0 is applied to a packet with the following IP addresses. Which subnet is the packet sent to?

    a. 10.20.35.12

    b. 10.20.35.3

c. 10.50.35.6

d. 192.168.12.8

43. Given an IP address of 193.10.10.0, answer the following questions if the number of subnets created is 4.

a. Determine the network address and the broadcast address for each subnet.

	Network Address	Broadcast Address
1st subnet		
2nd subnet		
3rd subnet		
4th subnet		

b. Determine the subnet mask:

c. Determine the number of usable hosts per subnet:

44. Given a network IP address of 211.123.83.0, answer the following questions if 8 subnets are to be created. The 8 subnets include the network and broadcast address.

a. Determine the network address and the broadcast address for each subnet.

	Network Address	Broadcast Address
1st subnet		
2nd subnet		
3rd subnet		
4th subnet		
5th subnet		
6th subnet		
7th subnet		
8th subnet		

b. Determine the subnet mask:

c. Determine the number of hosts per subnet 30 (32)

45. Complete the following table, given Class C subnetting.

# Mask Bits	Subnet Mask	# Subnets	# Host/Subnet
2	255.255.255.192	2	62
3			
4			
5			
6			

Section 6-6

46. Complete the following table.

Network Address	Class	Classless Interdomain Routing (CIDR)	Subnet Mask	# Subnets	# Hosts / Subnet
128.123.0.0	B	/30	255.255.255.252	16384	2
135.45.0.0		/25			
193.10.10.0		/28			
211.123.83.0		/26			
10.0.0.0		/13			
32.0.0.0		/20			
204.204.5.0		/28			
223.201.65.0		/27			
156.35.0.0		/21			
116.0.0.0		/14			
145.23.0.0		/29			
199.12.1.0		/30			
15.0.0.0		/29			

47. How is a network address of 192.168.6.0 and a subnet mask of 255.255.254.0 written in CIDR?

48. A CIDR block contains the following subnets with IP addresses of

   a. 192.168.68.0/22

   b. 192.168.69.0/22

   c. 192.168.70.0/22

   d. 192.168.71.0/22

Are there any problems with this group of subnets in the CIDR block? Show your work.

49. How many bits are in an IPv6 address?

50. IPv6 numbers are written in which format?

51. Express the following IPv6 numbers using double-colon notation:

    a. 5355:4821:0000:0000:0000:1234:5678:FEDC

    b. 0000:0000:0000:1234:5678:FEDC:BA98:7654

    c. 1234:5678:ABCD:EF12:0000:0000:1122:3344

52. Express the IPv4 IP address 192.168.12.5 in IPv6 form using dotted decimal.

53. Recover the IPv6 address from the following double-colon notation:

1234:5678::AFBC

54. Define the structure of the 6to4 prefix.

55. What is the purpose of the 6to4 relay router?

CRITICAL THINKING

56. Your boss has read about IPv6 and wants to know whether the network you oversee is ready for the transition. Prepare a response based on the networking and computer operating systems used in your facility.

57. Your company is assigned a 206.206.155.0/24 CIDR block by your ISP. Your company consists of 5 different networks.

Network A: 50 users

Network B: 26 users

Network C: 12 users

Network D: 10 users

Your job is to create four subnets and allocate enough IP addresses for the users within the network. Document how you will do this.

CERTIFICATION QUESTIONS

58. The IP address of 10.0.0.0 is a class _____ address and with a CIDR of /13 has a subnet mask of _____ with _____ subnets and _____ hosts/subnet.

    a. A, 255.248.0.0, 32, 52486

    b. A, 255.255.255.248. 2097150, 6

    c. A, 255.255.0.0, 62, 262142

    d. None of these answers is correct.

59. The IP address of 156.35.0.0 is a class _____ address and with a CIDR of /21 has a subnet mask of ____ with ____ subnets and ____ hosts/subnets.

   a. B, 255.255.255.252, 16382, 2

   b. B, 255,255,255,128, 510, 126

   c. B, 255.255.255.240, 14, 14

   d. None of these answers is correct.

60. The IP address of 192.12.1.0 is a class _____ address and with a CIDR of /30 has a subnet mask of ____ with ____ subnets and ____ hosts/subnet.

   a. C, 255.255.255.252, 64, 2

   b. C, 255.255.248.0, 30, 2046

   c. C, 255.255.255.240, 14, 14

   d. None of these answers is correct.

61. IPv4 addressing is characterized by which of the following? (select all that apply)

   a. Currently being used on the Internet

   b. Uses four classes of IP addresses

   c. Uses five classes of IP addresses

   d. Is being replaced by IPv5

   e. Is being replaced by IPv6

62. The broadcast address for a host at 192.168.20.15 using a subnet mask of 255.255.255.192 is what?

   a. 192.168.20.63

   b. 192.168.20.0

   c. 192.168.20.127

   d. 192.168.20.255

   e. None of these answers is correct.

63. Given a network IP address of 192.168.12.0 and a subnet mask of 255.255.255.252, how may usable host IP addresses are provided?

   a. 2

   b. 4

   c. 8

   d. 16

   e. 0

64. A network with an IP address of 172.16.0.0 is divided into 8 subnets. What are the network addresses for each subnet?

    a. 172.16.0.0, 172.16.32.0, 172.16.64.0, 172.16.96.0, 172.16.128.0, 172.16.160.0, 172.16.192.0, 172.16.224.0

    b. 172.16.0.0, 172.16.0.32, 172.16.0.64, 172.16.0.96, 172.16.0.128, 172.16.0.160, 172.16.0.192, 172.16.0.224

    c. 172.16.0.255, 172.16.32.255, 172.16.64.255, 172.16.96.255, 172.16.128.255, 172.16.160.255, 172.16.192.255, 172.16.224.255

    d. None of these answers is correct.

65. Well-known ports are reserved by ICANN and range from 1 to 23. True or False?

False

66. Port numbers from 1024 to 49151 are known as private ports. True or False?

False

67. The Network layer defines how data packets are routed in a network. True or False?

True

7 CHAPTER

INTRODUCTION TO ROUTER CONFIGURATION

Chapter Outline

Objectives

- Describe the purpose of a router
- Describe the purpose of a gateway
- Describe the steps (software and hardware) for connecting to a router's console port
- Describe the Cisco IOS command structure
- Define the function of the command-line interface

- Define the functional difference with the router's user and privileged EXEC modes
- Be able to enter basic router configuration modes
- Demonstrate that you can enable and disable certain router interfaces
- Describe what information is contained in the running-configuration file

Key Terms

Cisco IOS
command line interface
(CLI)
CCNA
CCNP
CCIE
broadcast domain
flat network
routed network
layer 3 network
default gateway address
next hop address
subnet, NET

RS-232
DB-9
DB-25
console cable
COM1, COM2, ...
rollover cable
hostname
user EXEC mode
user mode
?
show flash
show version
router uptime

privileged mode
enable
Router#
configure terminal (conf t)
Router(config)#
Router(config-line)#
Router(config-if)#
no shutdown (no shut)
**show ip interface brief
(sh ip int brief)**
DCE
DTE

The main objective of this chapter is to introduce the use of the **Cisco IOS** (Internetwork Operating System) software for configuring routers. Cisco IOS is the operating software used to configure all Cisco routers. It includes a **command line interface (CLI)** for inputting instructions to configure the Cisco router interface. There are many choices for routers in the market; however, Cisco routers have set the standard. Also, Cisco certifications such as the Cisco Certified Network Associate (**CCNA**); the Cisco Certified Network Professional (**CCNP**); and the professional benchmark for internetworking expertise, the Cisco Certified Internetwork Expert (**CCIE**), base their testing on the applicant's ability to configure, troubleshoot, and analyze local area networks (LANs) that incorporate Cisco routers and switches.

7-1 INTRODUCTION

An overview of router fundamentals is presented in section 7-2. Some of the router concepts and terminology presented in Chapter 4, "Wireless Networking," are reexamined, in particular the following:

- The concepts of interconnecting LANs with routers
- The concept of a network segment
- Data flow through a routed network

The procedure for configuring a router through the router's console port is presented in section 7-3. The discussion includes an overview of configuring a computer's serial communication software and selecting the proper cable and hardware for connecting the console port to a computer. Sections 7-4 and 7-5 introduce the steps for accessing and programming the router interface. The user EXEC mode is examined in section 7-4, and the privileged EXEC mode in section 7-5. These sections teach the student how to work with the Cisco IOS command structure and how to access many of the configuration layers in the Cisco IOS. Sections 7-4 and 7-5 also include networking challenges using the Net-Challenge software included with the accompanying companion CD-ROM. These challenges enable students to test their ability to access and program a router's interface. The simulator software was developed specifically for this text and emulates programming the interface of a Cisco router. The console port connection is emulated with the software, and although the simulator doesn't emulate all the router programming modes or operational features, it does emulate the functions presented in the text.

Cisco IOS

Cisco Internet Operating System, the operating software used in all Cisco routers

Command Line Interface (CLI)

The interface type used for inputting commands and configuring devices such as routers

CCNA

Cisco Certified Network Associate

CCNP

Cisco Certified Network Professional

CCIE

Cisco Certified Internetwork Expert

Table 7-1 lists and identifies, by chapter section, where each of the CompTIA Network+ objectives are presented in this chapter. At the end of each chapter section is a review with comments of the Network+ objectives presented in that section. These comments are provided to help reinforce the reader's understanding of a particular Network+ objective. The chapter review also includes "Test Your Knowledge" questions to aid in the understanding of key concepts before the reader advances to the next section of the chapter. The end of the chapter includes a complete set of question plus sample certification type questions.

TABLE 7-1 **Chapter 7 CompTIA Network+ Objectives**

Domain/ Objective Number	Domain/Objective Description Is Covered	Section Where Objective Is Covered
1.0	*Networking Architecture*	
1.1	Explain the functions and applications of various network devices	7-4
1.2	Compare and contrast the use of networking services and applications	7-5
1.5	Install and properly terminate various cable types and connectors using the appropriate tools	7-3
1.8	Given a scenario, implement and configure the appropriate addressing schema	7-2
2.0	*Network Operations*	
2.6	Given a scenario, configure a switch using the proper features	7-3
5.0	*Industry Standards, Practices, and Network Theory*	
5.1	Analyze a scenario and determine the corresponding OSI layer	7-2
5.4	Given a scenario, deploy the appropriate wired connectivity standard	7-5

7-2 ROUTER FUNDAMENTALS

This section further defines the function of a router in a network and describes how data packets travel through a layer 3 network. A layer 3 network uses IP addressing for routing data packets to the final destination. Delivery of the data packets is made possible by the use of a destination MAC address, IP address, network addresses, and routing tables. Each of these concepts is examined in this section.

LANs are not necessarily restricted in size. A LAN can have 20 computers, 200 computers, or even more. Multiple LANs also can be interconnected to essentially create 1 large LAN. For example, the first floor of a building could be set up as 1 LAN, the second floor as another LAN, and the third floor another. The 3 LANs in the building can be interconnected into essentially 1 large LAN using switches, with the switches interconnected as shown in Figure 7-1.

FIGURE 7-1 Three floors of a building interconnected using switches to form one large LAN.

Broadcast Domain
Any broadcast sent out on the network is seen by all hosts in this domain.

Is it bad to interconnect LANs this way? As long as switches are being used to interconnect the computers, the impact of the interconnected LANs has minimal impact on network performance. This is true as long as there are not too many computers in the LAN. The number of computers in the LAN is an issue because layer 2 switches do not separate **broadcast domains** by default. This means that any broadcast sent out on the network (for example, the broadcast associated with an ARP request) will be sent to all computers in the LAN. Excessive broadcasts are a problem because each computer must process the broadcast to determine whether it needs to respond; this essentially slows down the computer and the network. Virtual LANs (VLANs) are now being used to interconnect LANs. This concept is examined in Chapter 8, "Introduction to Switch Configuration."

Flat Network
A network where the LANs share the same broadcast domain

A network with multiple LANs interconnected at the layer 2 level is called a **flat network**. A flat network is where the LANs share the same broadcast domain. The use of a flat network should be avoided if possible for the simple reason that the network response time is greatly affected. Flat networks can be avoided by the use of layer 3 networks. This topic is discussed next.

Layer 3 Networks

In both the simple office-type LAN introduced in Chapter 1, "Introduction to Computer Networks," and the building LAN just discussed, the hosts are interconnected with a switch. This allows data to be exchanged within the LAN; however, data cannot be routed to other networks. Also, the broadcast domain of one LAN is not isolated from another LAN's broadcast domain. The solution for breaking up the broadcast domains and providing network routing is to incorporate routing hardware into the network design to create a **routed network**. A routed network uses layer 3 addressing for selecting routes to forward data packets, so a better name for this network is a **layer 3 network**.

In layer 3 networks, routers and layer 3 switches are used to interconnect the networks and LANs, isolating broadcast domains and enabling hosts from different LANs and networks to exchange data. Data packet delivery is achieved by handing off data to adjacent routers until the packet reaches its final destination. This typically involves passing data packets through many routers and many networks. An example of a layer 3 network is shown in Figure 7-2. This example has four LANs interconnected using three routers. The IP address for each networking device is listed. How does information get from computer A1 in LAN A to computer C1 in LAN C? The following discussion describes the travel of the data packets.

Router A Port Addresses (LAN A)		Router B Port Addresses (LAN B)		Router B Port Addresses (LAN C)		Router Port Addresses (LAN D)	
FastEthernet 0/0 (Gateway Address)	10.10.20.250	FastEthernet 0/0 (Gateway Address)	10.10.10.250	FastEthernet 0/1 (Gateway Address)	10.10.1.250	FastEthernet 0/0 (Gateway Address)	10.10.5.250
FastEthernet 0/1	10.10.200.1	FastEthernet 0/2	10.10.200.2	FastEthernet 0/2	10.10.200.2	FastEthernet 0/1	10.10.150.2
FastEthernet 0/2	10.10.100.1	FastEthernet 0/3	10.10.150.1	FastEthernet 0/3	10.10.150.1	FastEthernet 0/2	10.10.100.2
LAN A Computers		**LAN B Computers**		**LAN C Computers**		**LAN D Computers**	
Computer A1	10.10.20.1	Computer B1	10.10.10.1	Computer C1	10.10.1.1	Computer D1	10.10.5.1
Computer A2	10.10.20.2	Computer B2	10.10.10.2	Computer C2	10.10.1.2	Computer D2	10.10.5.2
Subnet Mask	*255.255.255.0*	*Subnet Mask*	*255.255.255.0*	*Subnet Mask*	*255.255.255.0*	*Subnet Mask*	*255.255.255.0*

FIGURE 7-2   An example of a layer 3 network using routers to interconnect the LANs.

Computer A1 (IP address 10.10.20.1) sends a data packet to computer C1 (IP address 10.10.1.1). First, computer A1 uses the assigned subnet mask (255.255.255.0) to determine whether the destination IP address 10.10.1.1 is in the same subnet or network as itself. Applying the subnet mask to the destination address shows the final destination of the data packet is the 10.10.1.0 network (10.10.1.0 NET). This is not the same subnet or network in which computer A1 resides (10.10.20.0 NET). Therefore, the data packet is forwarded to the **default gateway address** defined by the computer. The default gateway address is the IP address of a networking device (for example, a router) used to forward data that needs to exit the LAN. An example of setting a computer's default gateway is provided in Figure 7-3. The default gateway address for computer A1 is 10.10.20.250. This is the IP address of Router A's FastEthernet0/0 port. Figure 7-2 shows that Router A's FastEthernet FA0/0 port connects directly to the switch in LAN A.

FIGURE 7-3   The TCP/IP menu for setting the default gateway address for computer A1.

Recall that the term *gateway* describes the networking device that enables data to enter and exit a LAN and is where the host computers forward data packets that need to exit the LAN. In most networks, the gateway is typically a router or switch port address. An example of a gateway is provided in the block diagram shown in Figure 7-4. An important concept is that the IP address of the gateway must be in the same subnet as the LAN that connects to the gateway, and this same gateway enables data traffic to enter and exit the LAN. An example of using the subnet mask to determine the destination network is provided in Example 7-1.

FIGURE 7-4 Data flow to and from the gateway.

Example 7-1

Problem:

A computer host sends two data packets out on the network. Each packet has a different IP destination address. Determine whether the data packets are to be forwarded to the default gateway or should remain in the same LAN as the host. The source host IP address is 10.10.20.2, and a subnet mask of 255.255.255.0 is being used. The destination IP addresses for the data packets are 10.10.1.1 and 10.10.20.3.

Solution:

First, determine the network or subnet where the source host resides. This can be determined by "ANDing" the subnet mask with the source host IP address as shown. Subnet masks and subnets were presented in Chapter 6, "TCP/IP," section 6-5, and should be reviewed if this concept is difficult to follow. Remember, subnet masking is a binary AND operation. The decimal numbers are the equivalent of the 8-bit binary number. For example:

255	1 1 1 1 1 1 1 1
20	0 0 0 1 0 1 0 0
10	0 0 0 0 1 0 1 0
2	0 0 0 0 0 0 1 0

Source IP address	10. 10. 20. 2
Subnet mask	<u>255.255. 255. 0</u>
Subnet	10. 10. 20. 0

Therefore, the source host is in the 10.10.20.0 subnet (10.10.20.0 NET).

a. Determine the destination network for a data packet given the following information:

Destination IP address   10. 10. 1. 1

Subnet mask   <u>255.255.255. 0</u>

Subnet   10. 10. 1. 0

Answer: The destination subnet address for Part a is 10.10.1.0. This is not in the same subnet as the 10.10.20.2 host (10.10.20.0 NET). Therefore, the data packet is forwarded to the default gateway.

b. Determine the destination network for a data packet given the following information:

Destination IP address   10. 10. 20. 3

Subnet mask   <u>255.255.255. 0</u>

Subnet   10. 10. 20. 0

Answer: The destination subnet address for Part b is 10.10.20.0, which is the same subnet as the host. Therefore, the data packet remains in the 10.10.20.0 subnet.

Next Hop Address

The IP address of the next networking device that can be used to forward the data packet to its destination

The IP address of the data packet sent from the source computer to the gateway is examined by the router, and a next hop address is selected. The gateway examines the destination IP address of all data packets arriving at its interface. The router uses a routing table to determine a network data path and the next hop address. As noted previously, a *routing table* is a list of the possible networks that can be used to route the data packets. Alternative data paths are usually provided so that a new route can be selected and data delivery maintained even if a network route is down. The **next hop address** is the IP address of the next networking device that can be used to forward the data packet to its destination.

For example, assume that a data packet is to be delivered from a host in LAN A to a destination address in LAN C (see Figure 7-2). The data packet is forwarded to the LAN A gateway, which is the FastEthernet 0/0 (FA0/0) port on Router A. The router examines the data packet and determines that the data can be sent to the host in LAN C via Router A's FastEthernet 0/2 (FA0/2) interface over the 10.10.100.0 NET to Router C, then to Router B, and finally to LAN C. The routing table also shows that there is a route to LAN C via Router A's FastEthernet 0/1 (FA0/1) interface over the 10.10.200.0 NET. The next hop off Router A's FastEthernet 0/1 (FA0/1) interface is the FA0/2 FastEthernet interface on Router B. Which is the better route?

In terms of hops, data from LAN A will have to travel over two hops (Router C and Router B) to reach LAN C. The route to LAN C via Router B requires only one hop; therefore, Router A will select the 10.10. 200.0 NET to route the data to LAN C because it has fewer router hops. The IP address of the FastEthernet 0/2 (FA0/2) port on Router B is called the next hop address. In each case, the next hop address is the IP address of the next networking device. For example, if the data travels to LAN C via Router B, the next hop address off Router A is the IP address of the FastEthernet 0/2 (FA0/2) port on Router B (10.10.200.2).

The MAC addresses are used to define the hardware address of the next hop in the network. When the next hop is defined, its MAC address is determined and the data packet is relayed.

When the routes are fully configured, data packets can be exchanged between any LANs in the interconnected routed network. For example, data can be exchanged between any of the hosts in any of the LANs shown in Figure 7-2. Computer A2 in LAN A can exchange data with computer D1 in LAN D, and computer C1 in LAN C can exchange data with computer B2 in LAN B. This differs from the simple office LAN that has restricted data packet delivery: The data packets can be exchanged only within the LAN. Using IP addressing and routers enables the data to be delivered outside the LAN. Recall that a *segment* in a network defines the physical link between two internetworking devices (for example, router-hub, router-switch, or router-router). For example, in an interconnected network, a segment is the name of the link between a router and another router. Another example is the segment that connects a router to a LAN via a hub or a switch. Each network segment has its own network address. For the small campus network shown in Figure 7-2, the network IP address for the segment connecting LAN A to the router is 10.10.20.0. All hosts connected to this segment must contain a 10.10.20.#. For example, Computer A1 is assigned the IP address 10.10.20.1.

The segment is sometimes called the **subnet** or **NET**. These terms are associated with a network segment address, such as 10.10.20.0. In this case, the network is called the 10.10.20.0 NET. All hosts in the 10.10.20.0 NET will have a 10.10.20.# IP address. The network addresses are used when configuring the routers and defining which networks are connected to the router. For example, the networks attached to Router A in Figure 7-2 are listed in Table 7-2.

> **Subnet, NET**
> Other terms for the segment

The physical layer interface on the router provides a way to connect the router to other networking devices on the network. For example, the FastEthernet ports on the router are used to connect to other FastEthernet ports on other routers. Gigabit and 10 gigabit Ethernet ports are also available on routers to connect to other high-speed Ethernet ports. (The sample network shown in Figure 7-2 includes only FastEthernet ports.) Routers also contain serial interfaces that are used to interconnect the router and the network to other serial communication devices. For example, connection to wide area networks (WANs) requires the use of a serial interface to connect to a communications carrier such as Sprint, MCI, AT&T, and so on. The data speeds for the serial communication ports on routers can vary from slow (56Kbps) up to high-speed DS3 data rates (47+Mbps), OC3 (155Mbps), OC12 (622Mbps), or even OC192 (9953Mbps).

The following is a summary of the discussion on layer 3 networks. The components of a layer 3 network are shown in Figure 7-5. The source host computer has an installed network interface card (NIC) and an assigned IP address and subnet mask.

TABLE 7-2 The Networks (Subnets) Attached to Router A in Figure 7-2

Router Port	Subnet
FA0/0	10.10.20.0
FA0/1	10.10.200.0
FA0/2	10.10.100.0

FIGURE 7-5 The components of a layer 3 network.

The subnet mask is used to determine whether the data is to stay in the LAN or is to be forwarded to the default gateway provided by the router. The router uses its subnet mask to determine the destination network address. The destination network address is checked with the router's routing table to select the best route to the destination. The data is then forwarded to the next router, which is the next hop address. The next router examines the data packet, determines the destination network address, checks its routing table, and then forwards the data to the next hop. If the destination network is directly connected to the router, it issues an ARP request to determine the MAC address of the destination host. Final delivery is then accomplished by forwarding the data using the destination host computer's MAC address. Routing of the data through the networks is at layer 3, and the final delivery of data in the network is at layer 2.

Section 7-2 Review

This section has covered the following **Network+** Exam objectives.

1.8 Given a scenario, implement and configure the appropriate address schema

The concept that a switch does not separate broadcast domains was reviewed in this section. The term next hop *address, which is the IP address of the next networking device in the route of a data packet, was introduced.*

5.1 Analyze a scenario and determine the corresponding OSI layer

This section provided a review of layer 3 networks and the steps for creating a routed network.

Test Your Knowledge

1. The purpose of a gateway is to allow data to enter and exit a LAN. True or False?

2. What is a broadcast domain?

    a. A network where the LANs share broadcasts.

    b. Where networks forward data packets that need to leave the domain.

    c. Any broadcast sent out on the network is seen by all hosts in this domain.

    d. Another name for a routed network.

3. What is a next hop address?

    a. It is also called the default gateway address.

    b. The IP address of the next networking device that can be used to forward the data packet to its destination.

    c. The IP address of the next networking device that can be used to forward the data packet to its source.

    d. It does not have a purpose in routed networks.

7-3   THE CONSOLE PORT CONNECTION

The router's console port is used as the initial interface for configuring the router. It is a slow-speed serial communications link (9600 bps) and is the only way to communicate with the router until the router interfaces have been configured. Specifically, the console connection is an **RS-232** serial communications port that uses an RJ-45 jack to connect to its interface. The RS-232 protocol running on the console port is the same communications protocol format used on a computer's (COM1, COM2) port; however, the connector for the serial communications port on the computer is either a **DB-9**–or **DB-25**–type connector. (*Note:* DB25 connectors are seldom used.) Figure 7-6(a) and (b) shows drawings of the DB-9 and DB-25 connector ends. The DB-9 connection uses 9 pins, and the DB-25 connection uses 25 pins.

> **RS-232**
> Serial communications port
>
> **DB-9**
> 9-pin connector
>
> **DB-25**
> 25-pin connector

(a)

(b)

FIGURE 7-6   (a) DB-9 connector; (b) DB-25 connector (courtesy of StarTech.com).

Console Cable

A cable that connects a router's console port to a computer's serial port

The connection from the router to the serial port on the computer requires a cable run from the computer's serial port to the RJ-45 console jack input on the router. This can be accomplished using a cable with the DB-9 and RJ-45 plug ends, as shown in Figure 7-7(a), or using an RJ-45 rollover cable and a DB-9 to RJ-45 adapter, as shown in Figure 7-7(b). The serial connection is being replaced by the USB connection. In this case, the option is to use a USB to 9-pin RS-232 adapter, as shown in Figure 7-7(c). A cable that connects the router's console port to the computer's serial port is called a **console cable**.

FIGURE 7-7   (a) A console cable with an integrated DB-9 connector; (b) a console cable using an RJ-45 rollover cable and a DB-9 to an RJ-45 adapter; (c) a USB to RS-232 adapter (courtesy of StarTech.com).

COM1, COM2...

The computer's serial communication ports

Rollover Cable

A cable with the signals reversed at each end

Connect the DB-9 end of the console cable to any of the available serial ports (**COM1, COM2...**) on the computer. The router's console input uses an RJ-45 jack, and the console cable must have an RJ-45 plug. The cable used to connect the RJ-45 plug to the computer is called a **rollover cable**, which is a flat cable that reverses signals on each cable end; for example, pins 1–8, 2–7, 3–6, and so on. Table 7-3 shows the signal assignments and pin number for each end of the rollover cable. Note that the pin numbers for the cables are swapped at each end.

TABLE 7-3 Signal and Pin Assignments for the Console Rollover Cable

Signal	Function	RJ-45 End A	RJ-45 End B
RTS	Ready-to-Send	1	8
DTR	Data Terminal Ready	2	7
TXD	Transmit Data	3	6
GND	Ground	4	5
GND	Ground	5	4
RXD	Receive Data	6	3
DSR	Data Send Ready	7	2
CTS	Clear-to-Send	8	1

A serial communications software package such as HyperTerminal or PuTTY can be used to establish the communications link to the router's console input. Table 7-4 outlines the settings for the serial interface on a Cisco router's console port.

TABLE 7-4 Settings for Connecting to the Router Console Port

Bits per second	9600
Data bits	8
Parity	None
Stop bits	1
Flow control	none

The next step is to set up the console connection from a computer to the router. This requires that one RJ-45 end of a rollover cable be connected to the console port in the back of the router. The other end of the cable connects to one of the 9-pin serial communication ports (COM ports) of the computer. Note which serial port you connect to. You will have to specify the serial port (for example, COM1, COM2, and so on) when configuring the HyperTerminal or PuTTY serial communications software.

Configuring the HyperTerminal Software (Windows)

The HyperTerminal software is available on Windows XP but must be purchased separately for Windows 10. PuTTY is free software. After HyperTerminal is installed, click **Start > Programs > Accessories > Communications** and click **HyperTerminal** to start the HyperTerminal software on your computer. Click **Start > Programs > Hyperterminal** on Windows 10. The **Connection Description** menu shown in Figure 7-8 will appear. Enter a name for your connection, such as **Cisco-Router**, and select an icon to be associated with the connection. Click **OK** when done.

FIGURE 7-8   The HyperTerminal Connection Description menu.

The next menu displayed is shown in Figure 7-9. This is the **Connect To** menu, which lets you specify how you are making the serial connection to the router. This example shows that the connection is configured to use the computer's COM2 serial port. Change the **Connect using** parameter to match the connection (COM1, COM2...) you have made on your computer. Click **OK** when done.

FIGURE 7-9   The HyperTerminal Connect To menu.

The next menu is the **Properties** menu for your serial connection. This menu is labeled **COM2 Properties** because the Connect Using COM2 parameter was specified in the previous menu. Recall that the settings for connecting to the router's serial console port were provided in Table 7-4. The COM2 properties will have to be set to match these settings. Figure 7-10 shows the **COM2 Properties** menu for Hyperterminal with the settings entered. Also shown is the PuTTY Configuration window, Click **OK** for Hyperterminal and **Open** for PuTTY when done After doing this, the **CiscoRouter >** screen will be displayed. Press **Enter** to start the terminal communications. You should see the image shown in Figure 7-11 when a connection has been established. If the text does not display **Press RETURN to get started**, press **Enter** to see whether the router resets itself. Another possible screen you might see might have only the **Router>** prompt. Press **Enter**, and if the

Router> prompt remains, you are connected. If this doesn't correct the displayed text, the router might need to be restarted.

(a)   (b)

FIGURE 7-10   The Properties menu for configuring the serial port connection for (a) HyperTerminal and (b) PuTTY.

FIGURE 7-11   The Cisco router console port—HyperTerminal screen.

Configuring the Z-Term Serial Communications Software (Mac)

The following are the steps for establishing a console port via the USB serial connection on the Mac computer. This requires the following:

- A serial communication software such as ZTerm. ZTerm is a shareware program for the Mac that can be downloaded from the Internet.
- A USB to a 9-pin RS-232 male serial adapter, such as the USB to 9-pin adapter cable shown previously in Figure 7-7(c). (*Note:* The USB serial adapter can require that an additional driver be installed.)

Install the serial communications software and the driver. Start the serial communications software. Click **Setting > Modem Preferences** as shown in Figure 7-12. This opens the window shown in Figure 7-13. You will need to change the serial port so that it is set to **PL2303-000** and then click **OK** when the change to usbserial0 has been made. Next, click **Settings > Connection** to open the menu shown in Figure 7-14. The following settings need to be set for the serial console connection. Click **OK** when done.

Data Rate: 9600

Data Bits: 8

Parity: N

Stop Bits: 1

Hardware Handshake

FIGURE 7-12   The Mac OS X menu for configuring the settings for the serial interface.

FIGURE 7-13   The Mac OS X menu for setting the serial port to PL2303-000.

FIGURE 7-14   The Mac OS X window listing the serial communication link settings.

Section 7-3 Review

This section has covered the following **Network+** Exam objectives.

1.5 Install and properly terminate various cable types and connectors using the appropriate tools.

This section provided a review of the RS-232 DB9 connector and the steps for configuring the serial port so that a console port connection can be established.

Test Your Knowledge

1. The connection to a router's console port input is typically which of the following? (Select two.)

    a. RS-232

    b. USB

    c. DB-9

    d. DB-25

    e. None of these answers is correct.

2. What is the cable used to connect the RJ-45 plug to a computer called?

    a. RS-232

    b. USB

    c. Rollover

    d. Patch cable

7-4 THE ROUTER'S USER EXEC MODE (ROUTER>)

This section introduces the use of the Cisco Internetwork Operating System (Cisco IOS) used for configuring Cisco routers. Cisco IOS, the standard interface software available on all Cisco routers, is regularly updated, thus providing improved configuration, management, and monitoring capabilities.

The Cisco IOS structure is fairly easy to navigate after you learn a few basic commands. Cisco IOS uses a command line interface (CLI) for inputting commands when configuring Cisco routers. This section explains some simple concepts, such as how to access the Help menu, using the **show** commands, and configuration options. The text comes with the Net-Challenge Companion CD-ROM that includes a router simulator specifically developed for this text. The simulator enables you to practice accessing various router modes and gain practice configuring a router for use in a network. The networking challenges presented in the text are available with the Companion CD-ROM for testing your knowledge.

The User EXEC Mode

The first text you see on the terminal screen after a console connection is made to the router is **Router con0 is now available**. This text confirms that you have connected to the router's console port.

```
Router con0 is now available Press RETURN to get started! Router>
```

You are prompted to **Press Return to get started.** Press **Return** (the **Enter** key on the keyboard) to connect to the router. The prompt **Router>** indicates that you have connected to a router with the hostname Router, and the **>** symbol indicates that you have entered the user EXEC mode on the router. The user EXEC mode, also called the user mode, is the unsecured first level of entry passed through when accessing the router's interface. It does not allow the user any access to the router's configuration options. However, some of the router parameters, such as the version of the Cisco IOS software running on the machine, memory, flash, and the available commands, can be viewed.

Hostname
The name assigned to a networking device

User EXEC Mode
Used by a user to check to router status

User Mode
Same as the user EXEC mode

One caveat to keep in mind when connecting serially to the router is that the router's logging messages will be displayed on the console terminal. These messages are useful when troubleshooting but could be annoying when they show up in the middle of entering commands for the configuration. Recommended practice dictates that you *not* enable the debug mode and configure the router at the same time due to the sheer number of logging messages.

You can view the commands that are recognized at the user level by entering a **?** after the **Router>** prompt. The **?** is the universal help command in Cisco IOS that allows you to view the available commands from any prompt. The following shows an example of using the **?** command to display the available commands from the **Router>** prompt:

```
Router>?
Exec commands:
access-enable    Create a temporary Access-List entry
clear            Reset functions
connect          Open a terminal connection disable Turn off
                 privileged commands
disconnect       Disconnect an existing network connection
enable           Turn on privileged commands
exit             Exit from the EXEC
help             Description of the interactive help system lock
                 Lock the terminal
login            Log in as a particular user logout Exit from the
                 EXEC
mrinfo           Request neighbor and version information from a
                 multicast router
mstat            Show statistics after multiple multicast
                 traceroutes
mtrace           Trace reverse
multicast        path from destination to source
name-connection  Name an existing network connection
pad              Open a X.29 PAD connection ping Send echo messages
ppp              Start IETF Point-to-Point Protocol (PPP)
resume           Resume an active network connection
rlogin           Open an rlogin connection
set              Set system parameter (not config) show
Show             running system information
slip             Start Serial-line IP (SLIP)
systat           Display information about terminal lines
telnet           Open a telnet connection
terminal         Set terminal line parameters
traceroute       Trace route to destination
tunnel           Open a tunnel connection
where            List active connections
x28              Become an X.28 PAD
x3               Set X.3 parameters on PAD
```

It's obvious from the **Router>** help listing that the command options are quite extensive, and it takes some time to master them all. The objective of this chapter is to introduce the fundamental commands required for navigating the Cisco IOS

?

The help command that can be used at any prompt in the command line interface for the Cisco IOS software and configuring the router's interface. In particular, this section concentrates on the commands and procedures for configuring the router's FastEthernet and serial ports.

Another way to display commands or features is to place a **?** after the command. The **?** can be used after any command from any prompt in the command line interface in the Cisco IOS Software. Placing the **?** after the **show** command at the **Router>** prompt lists the available options in the user mode for the **show** command, as demonstrated here:

```
Router>show ?
backup              Backup status
clock               Display the system clock
dialer              Dialer parameters and statistics
flash               display information about flash: file system
history             Display the session command history
hosts               IP domain-name, lookup style, nameservers, and
                    host table location  Display the system location
modemcap            Show Modem Capabilities database
ppp                 PPP parameters and statistics
rmon                rmon statistics
rtr                 Response Time Reporter (RTR)
sessions            Information about Telnet connections
snmp                snmp statistics
tacacs              Shows tacacs + server statistics
terminal            Display terminal configuration parameters
traffic-shape       Traffic rate shaping configuration
users               Display information about terminal lines
version             System hardware and software status
```

show flash
Lists the details of the router's flash memory

Two key options for **show** in the user (**Router>**) mode are **show flash** and **show version**. The **show flash** command lists the details of the router's flash memory, while **show version** lists the version of the Cisco IOS Software running on the router. Examples of each are provided in the output samples that follow.

The **show flash** command displays the flash memory available and the amount of flash memory used. This command is typically used to verify whether sufficient memory is available to load a new version of the Cisco IOS Software. In this example, IOS is already installed, the file length is 6788464, and the name of the file is *c2800-d-1.120-4*.

```
Router>show flash
System flash directory: File Length Name/status
1 6788464 c2800-d-1.120-4
[6788528 bytes used, 1600080 available, 8388608 total]
8192K bytes of processor board System flash (Read ONLY)
```

show version
Lists the version of the Cisco IOS software running on the router

Router Uptime
The amount of time the router has been running

The following listing for **show version** indicates that the router is operating version 12.4. Notice that the *show version* command also lists the amount of time that the router has been running. This is listed as the **Router uptime**. In this example the router has been running 41 minutes, and it indicates that the system was restarted by power-on. This is a good place to check when troubleshooting intermittent problems with a router. Recurring statements that the router was restarted by power-on could indicate that the router has an intermittent power supply problem or that the power to the router is intermittent. Another possibility is that someone is resetting the router. This is not common because access to the router is typically password protected.

```
Router>show version
Cisco Internetwork Operating System Software
    IOS (tm) 2800 Software (C2800-D-L), Version 12.4, RELEASE SOFTWARE
(fc1) Copyright  1986-2006 by Cisco Systems, Inc.
Compiled Wed 14-Apr-06 21:21 by prod_rel_team
Image text-base: 0x03037C88, data-base: 0x00001000

ROM: System Bootstrap, Version 12.04(10c), SOFTWARE
    BOOTFLASH: 3000 Bootstrap Software (IGS-BOOT-R), Version 12.2(10c),
RELEASE SOFTWARE (fc1)

Router uptime is 41 minutes
System restarted by power-on
System image file is "flash:c2800-d-1.120-4"

    cisco 2800 (68030) processor (revision N) with 2048K/2048K bytes of
memory. Processor board ID 14733315, with hardware revision 00000000

Bridging software.
X.25 software, Version 3.0.0.
1 FastEthernet/IEEE 802.3 interface(s)
2 Serial network interface(s)
32K bytes of non-volatile configuration memory
8192K bytes of processor board System flash (Read ONLY)

Configuration register is 0x42
```

Router Configuration Challenge: The User EXEC Mode

Use the Net-Challenge software included with the companion CD-ROM to complete this exercise. Place the disk in your computer's CD-ROM drive. The Net-Challenge software is located in the *Net-Challenge* folder on the CD-ROM. Open the folder and click the *Net-ChallengeV4.exe* file. The program will open on your desktop with the screen shown in Figure 7-15. The Net-Challenge software is based on a three-router campus network setting. The software allows the user to configure each of the three routers and to configure the network interface for computers in the LANs attached to each router. Connection to each router is provided by clicking one of the three router buttons shown in Figure 7-15. Clicking a router button connects the selected router to a console session, thus enabling the simulated console terminal access to all three routers. The routers are marked with their default hostnames of Router A, Router B, and Router C. This challenge tests your ability to use router commands in the user EXEC mode. Click the *Net-ChallengeV4.exe* file to start the software. Then click the **Select Challenge** button to open a list of challenges available with the software. Select the **Chapter 7 - User EXEC Mode** challenge. Selecting a challenge will open a check box window, as shown in Figure 7-16. The tasks in each challenge will be checked as completed, as appropriate.

FIGURE 7-15 The Net-Challenge screen.

FIGURE 7-16 The check box for the User EXEC Net-Challenge software.

1. Make sure you are connected to Router A by clicking the appropriate selection button.

2. Demonstrate that you can enter the router's user EXEC mode. The router screen will display **Router>** when you are in the user EXEC mode.

3. Use the **?** command for help to see the available command options in the Net-Challenge simulation software. You should see that the **enable**, **exit**, and **show** commands are available from the **Router>** prompt. The Net-Challenge software displays only the available commands and options within the software. The text provides examples of what the full command and help options look like.

4. Enter **exit** from the **Router>** prompt (**Router>exit**). Where does this place you? You should be back at the **Press RETURN** screen, as shown in Figure 7-15.

5. Reenter the user EXEC mode by pressing **Enter**.

6. Enter the command **show** after the **Router>** prompt (**Router>show**).

   This step generates an "error unknown command" message. Include a **?** after the **show** command to see which options are available for **show**. The text displayed on the terminal screen should look like Figure 7-17.

FIGURE 7-17   The display for Step 6 using the **show** command.

7. Enterthe command **show flash** at the **Router>** prompt on the command line interface. Describe the information displayed.

8. Enter the command **show version** at the **Router>** prompt on the command line interface. Describe the information displayed.

9. Enter the command **show history** at the **Router>** prompt on the command line interface. Describe the information displayed.

Section 7-4 Review

This section has covered the following **Network+** Exam objectives.

1.1 Explain the functions and applications of various network devices

This section introduced the Cisco Internetworking Operating System (IOS). The steps for establishing the router's console connection and operating in the user EXEC mode were explained.

Test Your Knowledge

1. Which command can be used to see the uptime for a router?

   a. **show uptime**

   b. **sh uptime**

   c. **show time**

   d. **show version**

2. The prompt for a router's user EXEC mode is **router/>**. True or False?

3. The command to view the details of the routers flash memory is which of these?

   a. **show mem**

   b. **show details**

   c. **show history**

   d. **show flash**

4. What is the help command in Cisco IOS?

   a. **?**

   b. **-help**

   c. **-h**

   d. **- help**

7-5 THE ROUTER'S PRIVILEGED EXEC MODE (ROUTER#)

Configuring a router interface requires you to enter **privileged mode** on the router. The privileged EXEC mode allows full access for configuring the router interfaces and configuring a routing protocol. This section focuses on general configuration steps for the router and configuring the router's interfaces, FastEthernet, and serial ports. Configuring routing protocols is examined in Chapter 9, "Routing Protocols."

You enter the privileged mode using the command **enable** at the **Router>** prompt as shown. The # sign after the router name indicates you are in the privileged EXEC mode (**Router#**).

```
Router> enable
Password:
Router#
```

Entry into the router's privileged mode is typically password protected. The exception to this is when a router has not been configured and a password has not been assigned to it. In this case, pressing Enter on the keyboard from the **Router>** prompt places you in the router's privileged mode (**Router#**). The two different steps for entering the router's privileged mode are shown in Figure 7-18: (a) no password protection and (b) password required.

(a)

(b)

FIGURE 7-18   The steps for entering the router's privileged EXEC mode: (a) no password; (b) password required.

Use caution when you have entered the privileged mode in a router. It is easy to make mistakes, and incorrectly entered router configurations will adversely affect your network. This text comes with the Net-Challenge router simulator on the companion CD-ROM to help you gain experience with router configuration. In fact, most of the router configuration commands presented in the text can be implemented in the router simulator on the companion CD-ROM. Many options are available for configuring the router and the router's interfaces from the **Router#** prompt. This section presents the key options needed to configure the router.

> **Privileged Mode**
> Allows the router ports and routing features to be configured
>
> **enable**
> The command used to enter the router's privileged mode
>
> **Router#**
> The pound sign indicates that the user is in the router's privileged EXEC mode.

Hostname

> **configure terminal (conf t)**
>
> The command to enter the router's terminal configuration mode

The next commands examined require that the router's terminal configuration mode be entered. To do this, enter the command **configure terminal** (abbreviated **conf t**) at the **RouterA#** prompt to enter the router's configuration mode.

```
Router#conf t
Enter configuration commands, one per line. End with CNTL/Z.
RouterA(config)#
```

or

```
Router#configure terminal
Enter configuration commands, one per line. End with CNTL/Z.
Router(config)#
```

Note the change in the prompt to **Router(config)#**. This indicates that the router is in terminal configuration mode.

The first router configuration option examined enables the user to assign a hostname to the router. The generic name or the name of an unconfigured Cisco router is *router*, and the **hostname** command enables the user to change the name to specifically identify the router. For example, valid hostname structures include RouterA, Router-A, or Router_A, while Router A is not valid. Valid router hostnames may not have any spaces. The word *router* does not have to be used in the hostname. The hostname can reflect the manner in which the router is being used. A router can serve as the network gateway for the LANs in a building; for example, for a building named Goddard the router could be called *Goddard_gate*. This tells the network administrator the location and purpose of the router.

In the privileged mode (**Router#**), enter the command **hostname** [*router-name*] **<enter>**. This sets the hostname for the router to *router-name*. The following example demonstrates how the router's hostname is changed to **RouterA**. Notice the change with the router's name from the first to the second line after the **hostname** command is entered.

```
Router(config)# hostname RouterA
RouterA#(config)
```

Enable Secret

Password protection for the privileged (enable) mode is configured by setting **enable secret**. The steps are as follows:

1. Enter the router's configure terminal mode by entering **configure terminal** or **conf t** at the **Router#** prompt.

2. Enter the command–**enable secret** [*your-password*] **<enter>**.

The following is an example of the commands to enable password protection for privileged mode:

```
Router# conf t
Router(config)#
Router(config)# enable secret my-secret
```

This example sets the password for entering the router's privileged EXEC mode to **my-secret**. The password for entering the router's privileged mode must now be entered to gain access to the mode.

Setting the Line Console Passwords

The router has three line connections through which a user can gain access to the router. The line connections available on a router can be displayed using the **line ?** command at the **Router(config)#** prompt. The available line connections are as follows:

- **aux**: Auxiliary line
- **console**: Primary terminal line (console port)
- **vty**: Virtual terminal (for a telnet connection)

Router(config)#
The prompt for the router's terminal configuration mode

The *console* (primary terminal line) is the console port, *vty* is the virtual terminal used for Telnet connections, and *aux* is used to establish an external modem connection. The following steps demonstrate how to configure password protection for the console port and the virtual terminal.

The console port configuration is as follows:

1. Enter the command **line console 0 <enter>**.
2. Enter the command **login**, and then press **Enter**,
3. Type the command **password [my-secret2]**, where **my-secret2** is the console port password.

The following is an example of using these commands to configure a console port:

```
Router(config)# line console 0
Router(config-line)# login
Router(config-line)# password [my-secret2]
```

Note the change in the router prompt to **Router(config-line)#**, indicating you are in the router's line configuration mode.

Password protection for the virtual terminal (line vty) is set from the router's configuration mode. The virtual terminal is the method for entering the router via a Telnet connection:

Router(config-line)#
The prompt indicating you are in the router's line configuration mode

1. Enter the command **line vty 0 4**. This places the router in the line configuration mode (config-line). The **0 4** represents the number of vty lines to which the following configuration parameters will be applied. The five virtual terminal connections are identified as 0, 1, 2, 3, and 4.
2. Enter the command **password [*my-secret3*]**. The entry **my-secret3** is the password for the virtual terminal connection.
3. Enter **login**, and press **Enter**.

The following is an example of using these commands for enabling password protection for a virtual terminal:

```
Router(config)# line vty 0 4
Router(config-line)# password [my-secret3]
Router(config-line)# login
```

Fast Ethernet Interface Configuration

Routers can have Ethernet (10Mbps), Fast Ethernet (100Mbps), gigabit Ethernet (1000Mbps), and ten gigabit (10GB) interfaces. These routers can have multiple interfaces supporting 10/100/1000Mbps and 10Gbps connections, and the steps for configuring each interface are basically the same. Each interface is assigned a number. For example, a router could have three FastEthernet interfaces identified as

> FastEthernet 0/0
> FastEthernet 0/1
> FastEthernet 0/2

The notation 0/0 is indicating the [interface-card-slot/port]

The following steps describe how to configure a router's FastEthernet 0/0 port (FastEthernet 0/0, also listed as fa0/0 and FA0/0).

<table>
<tr><td>

Router(config-if)#

Indicates that you are in the router's interface configuration mode

</td><td>

1. In the router's configuration mode [**Router(config)#**], enter **interface fa0/0** and press **Enter**. This changes the router's prompt to **Router(config-if)#**, indicating you are in the router's interface configuration mode. The router keeps track of the interface you are configuring. The abbreviated command **int fa0/0** is used to access the FastEthernet0/0 interface. The router prompt will still show **Router(config-if)#**.

2. Enter the assigned IP address for the FastEthernet 0/0 port—for example, **ip address 10.10.20.250 255.255.255.0**—and press **Enter**.

</td></tr>
<tr><td>

no shutdown (no shut)

Enables a router's interface

</td><td>

3. Enable the router interface using the **no shutdown (no shut)** command.

</td></tr>
</table>

The following is an example of using these commands to configure a Fast-Ethernet interface:

```
Router(config)# int fa0/0
Router(config-if)# ip address 10.10.20.250 255.255.255.0
Router(config-if)#no shut
2w0d: %LINEPROTO-5-UPDOWN: Line protocol on Interface FastEthernet0/0,
   changed state to up
```

<table>
<tr><td>

show ip interface brief (sh ip int brief)

The command used to verify the status of the router's interfaces
Router# **sh ip int brief**

</td><td>

Notice that the router prompts you that the line protocol on interface FastEthernet 0/0 changed state to up. Repeat the previous steps for each of the FastEthernet interfaces. The command **show ip interface brief (sh ip int brief)** entered at the enable prompt (**Router#**) can be used to verify the status of the router interfaces. The following is an example:

</td></tr>
</table>

Interface	IP-Address	OK?	Method	Status	Protocol
FastEthernet0	10.10.20.250	YES	manual	up	up
FastEthernet1	10.10.200.1	YES	manual	up	up
FastEthernet2	10.10.100.1	YES	manual	up	up

Serial Interface Configuration

The router's serial ports are used to interface to other serial communication devices. The serial communications link is often used in campus networks to connect to WANs or the Internet. Configuring the serial port requires that the following questions be answered:

- What is the IP address of the interface?
- What is the subnet mask for the interface?
- Which interfaces are responsible for providing clocking?

In the router's serial communication links, there will be a **DCE** and a **DTE** end. The serial cables on older routers are called *V.35* cables. Examples are shown in Figure 7-19. DCE stands for Data Communication Equipment; DTE stands for Data Terminal Equipment. The DTE interface on the V.35 cable is designed for connecting the router to a CSU/DSU and outside digital communication services. In regards to clocking, the serial interface defined to be the DCE is responsible for providing clocking. This section shows how to check to see whether your serial connection is DCE or DTE. Modern routers have a built-in CSU/DSU and use an RJ-45 cable to establish the WAN or Internet connection.

(a)   (b)

FIGURE 7-19   The (a) DCE and (b) DTE ends of V.35 serial cable (courtesy of StarTech.com).

1. From the router's config prompt, enter the command **int s0/0** to access the Serial0/0 interface. The router's prompt changes to **Router(config-if)#** to indicate that the interface configuration has been entered. Notice that this is the same prompt as when configuring the FastEthernet interfaces.

2. Configure the IP address and subnet mask for the serial interface by entering the command **ip address 10.10.50.30 255.255.255.0**.

These steps are shown as follows:

```
Router(config)# int s0/0
Router(config-if)# ip address 10.10.50.30 255.255.255.0
```

If this is a serial DCE connection, you must set the clock rate. The serial connection can have either a DCE or DTE end. Routers use RJ-45 and V.35 connections to connect to the serial interface. In the case of V.35 cables, the DCE end of the serial connection is defined to be the female end of the V.35 cable. The DTE end of the cable is defined to be the male end of the V.35 cable. The female and male ends of V.35 cables are shown in Figure 7-19(a) and (b). There are three ways to check the cable to see whether the connection is DCE or DTE:

1. The command **show controllers serial** *[interface number]* can be used to determine whether your serial interface is a DCE or DTE interface. An abbreviated listing of the displayed results for the **show controllers serial 0/0** command is shown. The Serial0/0 interface is a V.35 DCE cable. This command should be used when you have an RJ-45 connection.

2. The V.35 cables are typically labeled to indicate whether they are a DTE or DCE cable.

3. Inspect the end of the V.35 cable to determine whether it is male (DTE) or female (DCE).

The customer is usually the DTE end, and the clock rate will be set by the communications carrier. The exception to this is when the customer is setting up a back-to-back serial connection within his own network. In this case, the customer sets the clock rate. The following is an example of using the **show controllers** command for a DCE interface:

```
Router# sh controllers serial 0/0
HD unit 0,    idb    0xCF958, driver structure at 0xD4DC8
buffer size 1524 HD unit 0, V.35 DCE cable
cpb    0x21, eda    0x4940, cda    0x4800
.
.

```

The next example shows the results of the **show controllers serial** *[interface number]* for a DTE interface. This example shows that the Serial0/1 interface is being checked.

```
RouterA#sh controllers serial 0/1
HD unit 1, idb    0xD9050, driver structure at 0xDE4C0
buffer size 1524 HD unit 1, V.35 DTE cable
cpb 0x22, eda    0x30A0, cda    0x30B4
.
.

```

The clocking for the serial interface is set using the **clock rate** command followed by a data rate. The clock rate for the serial interface on the router can be set from 1200bps to 4Mbps. The following is the command for setting the clock rate to 56000:

```
Router(config-if)# clockrate 56000
```

Next, the serial interface must be enabled using the **no shut** command. The router prompts the console port that interface Serial 0/0 changed state to up. These steps are repeated for all the serial interfaces.

```
Router(config-if)# no shut
2w0d: %LINK-3-UPDOWN: Interface Serial0/0, changed state to up
2w0d: %LINEPROTO-5-UPDOWN: Line protocol on Interface Serial0/0,
   changed state to up
```

The status of the serial interfaces can be checked using the **sh ip int brief** command as demonstrated here:

```
Router# sh ip int brief
Interface       IP-Address     OK?    Method     Status     Protocol
FastEthernet0   10.10.20.250   YES    manual     up         up
FastEthernet1   10.10.200.1    YES    manual     up         up
FastEthernet2   10.10.100.1    YES    manual     up         up
Serial0         10.10.128.1    YES    manual     up         up
Serial1         10.10.64.1     YES    manual     up         up
```

Router Configuration Challenge: The Privileged EXEC Mode

Use the Net-Challenge software included with the companion CD-ROM to complete this exercise. Place the CD-ROM in your computer's drive. The software is located in the *NetChallenge* folder on the CD-ROM. Open the folder and click the *Net-ChallengeV4.exe* file. The program will open on your desktop with the screen shown previously in Figure 7-15. The Net-Challenge software is based on a three-router campus network setting. The topology for the network can be viewed by clicking the **View Topology** button. The network topology used in the software is shown in Figure 7-20. The software allows the user to configure each of the three routers and to configure the network interface for computers in the LANs attached to each router. Clicking one of the router symbols in the topology will enable you to view the IP address for the router required for the configuration.

FIGURE 7-20 The network topology for Net-Challenge. The arrows indicate where to click to display the router IP address configurations.

Connection to each router is provided by clicking one of the three router buttons shown previously in Figure 7-17. An arrow is pointing to the buttons used to establish a console connection. Clicking a button connects the selected router to a terminal console session, enabling the simulated console terminal access to all three routers. The routers are marked with their default hostnames of Router A, Router B, and Router C. This challenge tests your ability to use router commands in the privileged EXEC mode, also called the enable mode. Click the *Net-ChallengeV4. exe* file to start the software. Next, click the **Select Challenge** button to open a list of challenges available with the software. Select the **Chapter 7 - Privileged EXEC Mode** challenge to open a check box screen. Each challenge will be checked when the task has been successfully completed:

1. Make sure you are connected to Router A by clicking the appropriate selection button.

2. Demonstrate that you can enter the router's privileged EXEC mode. The router screen should display **Router#**. The password is **Chile**.

3. Place the router in the terminal configuration mode [**Router(config)#**].

4. Use the **hostname** command to change the router hostname to RouterA.

5. Set the **enable secret** for the router to **Chile**.

6. Set the vty password to ConCarne.

7. Configure the three FastEthernet interfaces on RouterA as follows:

```
FastEthernet0/0    (fa0/0)    10.10.20.250    255.255.255.0
FastEthernet0/1    (fa0/1)    10.10.200.1     255.255.255.0
FastEthernet0/2    (fa0/2)    10.10.100.1     255.255.255.0
```

8. Enable each of the router FastEthernet interfaces using the **no shut** command.

9. Use the **sh ip interface brief** (**sh ip int brief**) command to verify that the interfaces have been configured and are functioning. For this challenge, the interfaces on Router B and Router C have already been configured.

10. Configure the serial interfaces on the router. Serial interface 0/0 is the DCE. The clock rate should be set to 56000. (use clock rate 56000) The IP addresses and subnet masks are as follows:

```
Serial 0/0    10.10.128.1    255.255.255.0
Serial 0/1    10.10.64.1     255.255.255.0
```

11. Use the **sh ip int brief** command to verify that the serial interfaces are properly configured. For this challenge, the interfaces on Router B and Router C have already been configured.

12. Use the **ping** command to verify that you have a network connection for the following interfaces:

```
RouterA FA0/1 (10.10.200.1) to RouterB FA0/2 (10.10.200.2)
RouterA FA0/2 (10.10.100.1) to RouterC FA0/2 (10.10.100.2)
```

Section 7-5 Review

This section has covered the following **Network+** Exam objectives.

1.1 Explain the functions and applications of various network devices

The steps for operating in the privileged EXEC mode and configuring the router were explained in this section.

5.4 Given a scenario, deploy the appropriate wired connectivity standard

The steps for configuring the Ethernet and serial interfaces were introduced in this section.

Test Your Knowledge

1. The router interface most commonly used to interconnect LANs to a campus network is which of these?

   a. Serial

   b. Parallel

   c. Console port

   d. Ethernet

   e. None of these answers is correct.

2. Serial interfaces on a router are typically used to

   a. Connect to console ports

   b. Connect to communication carriers

   c. Connect to auxiliary ports

   d. Interconnect routers

3. The prompt for a router's terminal configuration mode is **router(config-term)#**. True or False?

SUMMARY

This chapter presented an overview of routers, a technique for establishing a console port connection, and the basic steps for configuring the router's interface. The student should understand the difference in the router's user and privileged EXEC modes. A list of the router prompts encountered in this chapter appears in Table 7-5.

TABLE 7-5   Router Prompts and Their Definitions

Prompt	Definition
Router>	User EXEC mode
Router#	Privileged EXEC
mode Router(config)#	Configuration mode
Router(config-if)#	Interface configuration mode
Router(config-line)#	Line terminal configuration mode

The student should understand and be able to demonstrate the steps for configuring the Ethernet and serial interfaces. These concepts are used repeatedly in the next chapters. A new router troubleshooting command (**sh ip int brief**) was added to the list of networking troubleshooting steps.

QUESTIONS AND PROBLEMS

Section 7-1

1. What is the command line interface used for on a Cisco router?

2. Define Cisco IOS.

Section 7-2

3. Define a broadcast domain.

4. What is a flat network?

5. What is a layer 3 network?

6. Define the purpose of a gateway.

7. Where is the default gateway address assigned on Windows?

8. A computer with a host IP address of 10.10.5.1 sends a data packet with a destination IP address of 10.10.5.2. A subnet mask of 255.255.255.0 is being used. Determine whether the packet stays in the LAN or is sent to the gateway. Show your work.

9. Repeat problem 8 if the destination IP address for the data packet is 10.5.10.2. The subnet mask is still the same. Show your work.

10. Repeat problem 8 if the subnet mask is changed to 255.0.0.0. Show your work.

11. Repeat problem 8 if the subnet mask is changed to 255.255.0.0. Show your work.

12. The IP address for computer C2 is 10.10.1.2. The IP address for computer B1 is 10.10.10.1. A subnet mask of 255.255.0.0 is being used. Are the computers in the same network? Show your work.

13. Determine the router hop count from Router A to Router D in the network shown in Figure 7-21 for the route with the fewest hops.

FIGURE 7-21 Network topology for problem 13.

14. List all of the possible routes from Router B to Router D in the network shown in problem 13.

15. What subnets are attached to Router B in Figure 7-21?

16. List the subnets attached to Router C in Figure 7-21.

17. What is the next hop address for FastEthernet port 1, Router A in Figure 7-21?

18. What is the next hop address for the FastEthernet port 2, Router C in Figure 7-21?

Section 7-3

19. What is a rollover cable?

20. What values are used when configuring HyperTerminal for connecting to a Cisco router's console port?

Section 7-4

21. What command is used to find out the version of the IOS running on a Cisco router? Show the prompt and the command.

22. What is the help command in Cisco IOS?

23. What command can be used to see the uptime for a router?

24. What command is used to verify that there is sufficient memory available to load a new version of the Cisco IOS software?

25. What is the router prompt for the user EXEC mode?

26. If you enter **exit** from the **Router>** prompt, where does it place you?

Section 7-5

27. What is the router prompt for the privileged EXEC mode?

28. What command is used to enter the router's privileged mode?

29. What command is used to configure a router's hostname to *Tech-router*?

30. What command is used to enter the router's terminal configuration mode?

31. What is the router prompt for the terminal configuration mode?

32. What is the command for setting password protection for the privileged mode? The password is **Tech**.

33. What does the command **line vty 0 4** mean?

34. Describe the steps to configure and enable a FastEthernet0/1 router interface with the IP address 10.10.20.250 and a subnet mask of 255.255.0.0.

35. What is the best command to view the router interface status and protocol?

36. Is clocking of a router's serial interface set by the DCE or the DTE?

37. What are the three ways to see if your router's serial port is a DCE or DTE end?

38. What command is used to set the data speed on a router's serial port to 56 Kbps?

39. What is the router prompt for the interface configuration mode?

CRITICAL THINKING

40. What does the command line **vty 0 1** mean?

41. How can you check to see if the FastEthernet interface on a router is connected to the FastEthernet interface on another networking device?

42. You suspect that a router's LAN gateway is down. Describe how you would troubleshoot the problem.

43. Can the following configurations be accomplished on a router A? Please explain your answer.

    a.
    ```
    interface Fastethernet 0
    ip address 10.1.0.5 255.255.255.252

    interface Fastether 1
    ip address 10.1.0.5 255.255.255.252
    ```

    b.
    ```
    interface Fastethernet 0
    ip address 10.1.0.5 255.255.255.252

    interface Fastether 1
    ip address 10.1.0.6 255.255.255.252
    ```

    c.
    ```
    interface Fastethernet 0
    ip address 10.1.0.4 255.255.255.252

    interface Fastether 1
    ip address 10.1.0.5 255.255.255.252
    ```

    d.
    ```
    interface Fastethernet 0
    ip address 10.1.0.5 255.255.255.252

    interface Fastether 1
    ip address 10.1.0.9 255.255.255.252
    ```

CERTIFICATION QUESTIONS

44. What is the best command to use to view the router's interface status and protocol status?

    a. sh int brief

    b. show interface brief

    c. show ip interface brief

    d. show status

45. The designation of fa0/0 indicates

    a. the FastEthernet interface 0/0.

    b. external port 0/0.

    c. exit port 0/0

    d. Fast Ethernet input port 0/0.

    e. Fast Ethernet output port 0/0.

46. The IP address of the networking device used for the default gateway must (select all that apply)

    a. be in the same subnet as the LAN.

    b. use a subnet mask of 255.255.255.0.

    c. use a CIDR block of /22.

    d. None of these answers is correct.

47. What is the command for setting password protection for the privileged mode. The password is tech.

    a. enable tech

    b. enable secret tech

    c. enabling secret tech

    d. enabling tech

48. Clocking for the serial port on a router is at the DTE end. True or False?

49. The three ways to see if your router's serial port is a DTE or the DCE are:

    1. Inspect the ends of the V.35 cable, DCE-male.

    2. Check the label on the V.35 cable.

    3. Use the **show serial** (*interface name*) command.

    True or False?

50. The sequence of commands and prompts used to change the hostname of a router to **Network** is:

```
router> enable
router# enable
router# conf t
router# hostname Network
Network#
```

True or False?

51. The router prompt for the interface configuration mode on a Cisco router is **router (config-if)#**. True or False?

52. The settings for the console serial communication port on a Cisco router are:

Bits per seconds 9600

Data bits 8

Parity none

Stop bits 1

Flow control none

True or False?

53. The command **sh ip int brief** is executed from what prompt?

    a. Router(config)

    b. Router(config-if)#

    c. Router#

    d. Router(config)#

INTRODUCTION TO SWITCH CONFIGURATION

Chapter Outline

Objectives

- Be able to identify and describe the three types of VLANs
- Discuss two ways for establishing VLAN membership
- Understand how to use the commands to configure a network switch
- Be able to explain the steps for configuring a static VLAN
- Explain the purpose of the Spanning-Tree Protocol
- Discuss the purpose of the five Spanning-Tree Protocol states
- Understand how to use SNMP tools for network management
- Discuss the advantages of using Power over Ethernet

Key Terms

VLAN (virtual LAN)
port-based VLAN
tag-based VLAN
protocol-based VLAN
static VLAN
dynamic VLAN
configure terminal (conf t)
switch#
Switch(config)#
Switch(config-line)#
Spanning-Tree Protocol

Bridge Protocol Data Unit (BPDU)
Configuration BPDU
Topology Change Notification (TCN)
Topology Change Notification Acknowledgement (TCA)
SNMP (SNMPv1)
Management Information Base (MIB)
SNMPv2

SNMPv3
Power over Ether (PoE)
PD
PSE
endpoint PSE
midspan (mid-point) PSE
Resistive Power Discovery
PoE Plus

The objective of this chapter is to examine the computer networking issues that arise when configuring a network switch. The previous chapter introduced the Cisco IOS and the steps for connecting to and configuring a network router. In this chapter, the commands for configuring a network switch are presented. An introduction to virtual local area networks (VLANs) is presented in section 8-2. The section begins with an overview of the three types of VLANs followed by a discussion on the two ways for establishing VLAN membership. The basics of configuring a Cisco switch are presented in section 8-3. This section provides an introduction to the commands needed for configuring the VLAN and also demonstrates how to configure a static VLAN. Section 8-4 examines the Spanning-Tree Protocol (STP), a link management protocol that prevents looping and also controls data flow over possible redundant data paths. The next section (8-5) addresses network management. An overview of configuring a Cisco router for SNMP operation is first presented. This section also includes an example of using SNMP management software to collect router information and data statistics. Section 8-6 provides an overview of Power over Ethernet (PoE) and the benefits of implementing this technology in a network.

8-1 INTRODUCTION

Table 8-1 lists and identifies, by chapter section, where each of the CompTIA Network+ objectives are presented in this chapter. At the end of each chapter section is a review with comments of the Network+ objectives presented in that section. These comments are provided to help reinforce the reader's understanding of a particular Network+ objective. The chapter review also includes "Test Your Knowledge" questions to aid in the understanding of key concepts before the reader advances to the next section of the chapter. The end of the chapter includes a complete set of question plus sample certification type questions.

TABLE 8-1   Chapter 8 CompTIA Network+ Objectives

Domain/Objective Number	Domain/Objective Description	Section Where Objective Is Covered
2.0	*Network Operations*	
2.1	Given a scenario, use the appropriate monitoring tools	8-5
2.4	Explain the importance of implementing network segmentation	8-2, 8-5
2.6	Given a scenario, configure a switch using the proper features	8-2, 8-3, 8-4, 8-6
3.0	*Network Security*	
3.2	Compare and contrast common network vulnerabilities and threats	8-5
3.3	Given a scenario, implement network-hardening techniques	8-5
4.0	*Troubleshooting*	
4.2	Given a scenario, analyze and interpret the output of troubleshooting tools	8-4
4.7	Given a scenario, troubleshoot and resolve common security issues	8-3

8-2   INTRODUCTION TO VLANS

This section provides an overview to VLANs, an important networking concept in modern computer networks. A discussion on port-based, tagged-based, and protocol-based VLANs is presented. This section also examines static and dynamic VLANs.

Virtual LAN

A switch can be configured with **VLANs (virtual LANs)** where a group of host computers and servers are configured as if they are in the same LAN even if they reside across routers in separate LANs. The advantage of using VLANs is that the network administrator can group computers and servers in the same VLAN based on the organizational group (for example, Sales, Engineering, and so on), the geographical location (for example, first floor, second floor, and so on), or the network purpose (for example, office network, Voice over IP phone network, utility network, and so on). This can be done even if they are not on the same physical segment or even in the same building.

There are three types of VLANs: **port-based**, **tag-based**, and **protocol-based**. The port-based VLAN is one where the host computers connected to specific ports on a switch are assigned to a specific VLAN. For example, assume the computers connected to switch ports 2, 3, and 4 are assigned to the Sales VLAN 2 while the computers connected to switch ports 6, 7, and 8 are assigned to the Engineering VLAN 3, as shown in Figure 8-1. The switch will be configured as a port-based VLAN so that the groups of ports [2, 3, 4] are assigned to the sales VLAN while ports [6, 7, 8] belong to the Engineering VLAN. The devices assigned to the same VLAN will share broadcasts for that LAN; however, computers that are connected to ports not assigned to the VLAN will not share the broadcasts. For example, the computers in VLAN 2 (Sales) share the same broadcast domain and computers in VLAN 3 (Engineering) share a different broadcast domain.

FIGURE 8-1   An example of the grouping for port-based VLANs.

In tag-based VLANs, a tag is added to the Ethernet frames. This tag contains the VLAN ID that is used to identify that a frame belongs to a specific VLAN. The addition of the VLAN ID is based on the 802.1Q specification. An advantage of an 802.1Q VLAN is it helps to contain broadcast and multicast data traffic that helps to minimize data congestion and improve throughput. This specification also provides guidelines for a switch port to belong to more than one VLAN. Additionally, the tag-based VLANs can help provide better security by logically isolating and grouping users.

In protocol-based VLANs, the data traffic is connected to specific ports based on the type of protocol being used. The packet is dropped when it enters the switch if the protocol doesn't match any of the VLANs. For example, an IP network could be set up for the Engineering VLAN on ports 6, 7, and 8 and a network for the Sales VLAN on ports 2, 3, and 4. The advantage of this is that the data traffic for the two networks is separated.

The two approaches for assigning VLAN membership are as follows:

- **Static VLAN**: Basically a port-based VLAN. The assignments are created when ports are assigned to a specific VLAN.
- **Dynamic VLAN**: Ports are assigned to a VLAN based on either the computer's MAC address or the username of the client logged on to the computer. This means that the system has been previously configured with the VLAN assignments for the computer or the username. The advantage of this is that the username and/or the computer can move to a different location but VLAN membership will be retained.

> **Static VLAN**
> Basically a port-based VLAN
>
> **Dynamic VLAN**
> Ports are assigned to a VLAN based on either the computer's MAC address or the username of the client logged on to the computer

Section 8-2 Review

This section has covered the following **Network+** Exam objectives.

2.4 Explain the importance of implementing network segmentation

The technique of using VLANs to help provide better security by logically isolating and grouping users was presented in this section.

2.6 Given a scenario, configure a switch using proper features

This section introduces port-based, tag-based, and protocol-based VLANs. Also discussed is the VLAN ID, which is based on the 802.1Q specification. In a tag-based VLAN, a tag containing the VLAN ID is added to the Ethernet frame.

Test Your Knowledge

1. What are the three types of VLANs?

    a. Port-based

    b. Tag-based

    c. Pd-based

    d. Protocol-based

    e. Label-based

    f. Routing-based

2. A static VLAN is basically which of the following?

    a. Seldom used

    b. A MAC VLAN

    c. Port-based VLAN

    d. None of these answers is correct.

8-3 INTRODUCTION TO SWITCH CONFIGURATION

This section examines the basics of configuring a Cisco switch. The commands for switch configuration are similar to that of a router. Configuring a switch requires that a console connection is first established and the privileged mode is entered on the switch. The procedure for establishing a console connection to a switch is the same as the router. Refer to section 7-3 for the steps for establishing a console connection. The privileged EXEC mode (also called the enable mode) allows full access for configuring the switch ports and establishing a VLAN. This section focuses on general configuration steps for the switch, examining MAC address information and IP address configuration of the VLANs.

The privileged mode is entered using the command **enable** at the Switch> prompt as shown. The # sign after the switch name indicates you are in the privileged EXEC mode (Switch#):

```
Switch> enable
Password:
Switch#
```

Entry into the switch's privileged mode is typically password-protected. The exception to this is when a switch has not been configured and a password has not been assigned to it. In this case, pressing **Enter** on the keyboard from the Switch> prompt promotes the user to the privilege mode (Switch#) without requesting a password.

Use caution after you have entered the privileged mode in a switch. It is easy to make mistakes, and incorrectly entered switch configurations will adversely affect your network. This text comes with the Net-Challenge switch simulator on the companion CD-ROM to help you gain experience with switch configuration. In fact, most of the switch configuration commands presented in this section can be implemented in the switch simulator on the companion CD-ROM.

Hostname

The next commands examined require that the switch's terminal configuration mode be entered. To do this, enter the command **configure terminal** (abbreviated **conf t**) at the switch# prompt to enter the switch's configuration mode:

```
switch#conf t
Enter configuration commands, one per line. End with CNTL/Z.
switch(config)#
```

or

```
switch#configure terminal
Enter configuration commands, one per line. End with CNTL/Z.
switch(config)#
```

> **configure terminal (conf t)**
> Command to enter the switch's terminal configuration mode

Note the change in the prompt to switch(config)#. This indicates that the switch is in terminal configuration mode.

The first switch configuration option examined enables the user to assign a hostname to the switch. The generic name or the name of an unconfigured Cisco switch is **switch**, and the **hostname** command enables the user to change the name to specifically identify the switch. For example, valid hostname structures include switchA, switch-A, or switch_A, while switch A is not valid. Valid switch hostnames may not have any spaces. The word *switch* does not have to be used in the hostname.

In the privileged mode (switch#), enter the command **hostname** [*switch-name*] **<enter>**. This sets the hostname for the switch to *switch-name*. The following example demonstrates how the switch's hostname is changed to *SwitchA*. Notice the change with the switch's name from the first to the second line after the **hostname** command is entered:

```
switch(config)# hostname SwitchA
SwitchA#
```

Enable Secret

Password protection for the privileged (enable) mode is configured by setting the enable secret. The steps are as follows: Enter the switch's configure terminal mode by entering **configure terminal** or **conf t** at the **Switch#** prompt. Enter the command **enable secret** [*your-password*] **<enter>** as demonstrated here:

```
SwitchA# conf t
SwitchA(config)#
SwitchA(config)# enable secret my-secret
```

This example sets the password for entering the switch's privileged EXEC mode to **my-secret**. The password for entering the switch's privileged mode must now be entered to gain access to the mode.

Setting the Line Console Passwords

The switch has two line connections through which a user can gain access to the switch. The line connections available on a switch can be displayed using the **line ?** command at the **Switch(config)#** prompt. The available line connections typically are as follows:

- **console**: Primary terminal line (console port)
- **vty**: Virtual terminal (for a telnet connection)

The *console* (primary terminal line) is the console port, and *vty* is the virtual terminal used for Telnet connections. The following steps demonstrate how to configure password protection for the console port and the virtual terminal.

Switch#
The prompt for the switch's privileged EXEC mode

Switch(config)#
The prompt for the switch's terminal configuration mode

Configuring the console port consists of the following steps:

1. Enter the command **line console 0 <enter>**.

2. Enter the command **login** *and* press **Enter.**

3. Input the command **password [my-secret2]**, where **my-secret2** is the console port password.

An example of using these commands follows:

```
SwitchA(config)# line console 0
SwitchA(config-line)# login
SwitchA(config-line)# password my-secret2
```

Switch(config-line)#
The prompt indicating you are in the switch's line configuration mode

Note the change in the switch prompt to **Switch(config-line)#**, indicating you are in the switch's line configuration mode.

Password protection for the virtual terminal (line vty) is set from the switch's configuration mode. The virtual terminal is the method for entering the switch via a Telnet connection:

1. Enter the command **line vty 0 15**. This places the switch in the line configuration mode (config-line). The **0 15** indicates that 16 virtual terminal connections can be simultaneously made. The 16 virtual terminal connections are identified as 0, 1, 2, 3, 4, and so on.

2. Enter **login**, press **Enter**, followed by entering the command **password [my-secret3]**. The **entry my-secret3** is the password for the virtual terminal connection:

   ```
   SwitchA(config)# line vty 0 4
   SwitchA(config-line)# password my-secret3
   SwitchA(config-line)# login
   ```

3. Layer 3 access to the switch is set by using the following command sequence:

   ```
   SwitchA(config)# interface VLAN 1
   SwitchA(config-if)# ip address 172.16.32.2 255.255.255.0
   SwitchA(config-if)# no shutdown
   ```

Note that the IP address is being set for VLAN 1. The interface for the switch is also enabled at this same point using the **no shutdown** command as shown.

Configuring an IP address on a router's interface enables a layer 3 routed network. In addition, the interface IP address becomes a gateway address of that network as shown in Chapter 7, "Introduction to Router Configuration." However, it is not the same as on layer 2 switches. When configuring an IP address on a VLAN interface such as this, it merely assigns an IP address to a switch. So, a switch can communicate with other network devices on the same VLAN and vice versa. This is an important addition to the switch for management purposes because it enables the networking staff to connect remotely and configure the switch. The IP VLAN interface does not perform any routing functions when running as a layer 2 switch. As a matter of fact, the IP VLAN interface is not required for a switch to start forwarding packets and perform its other layer 2 functions.

The configuration settings entered on the VLAN 1 interface can be viewed by entering the following command:

```
SwitchA#show interface VLAN 1
```

For the interface VLAN to be up, at least one switch port in the VLAN must be up or have a physical link. The status of a switch port can be verified by entering the following command:

```
SwitchA#show interface Fastethenet0/1
```

To see the status of all the switch ports including their speed, duplex, and VLAN, use the following command:

```
SwitchA#show interface status
```

Port	Name	Status	Vlan	Duplex	Speed Type
Fa0/1	connected	1	a-full	a-100	10/100BaseTX
Fa0/2	connected	1	a-full	a-100	10/100BaseTX
Fa0/3	connected	1	a-full	a-100	10/100BaseTX
Fa0/4	connected	1	a-full	a-100	10/100BaseTX
Fa0/5	connected	1	a-full	a-100	10/100BaseTX
Fa0/6	connected	1	a-full	a-100	10/100BaseTX

You can view the running configuration for the switch using the **show running-config** command as shown. To display the startup configuration, use the **show startup-config** command. To copy the running-configuration file to NVRAM, use the **copy running-config startup-config** command.

These examples show that there is a lot of similarity between switch and router configuration at the command line interface. However, the major differences are apparent when configuring a VLAN. The next section demonstrates the steps for configuring a static VLAN.

Static VLAN Configuration

This section demonstrates the steps for configuring a static VLAN. In this example, the ports for VLAN 2 (Sales) and VLAN 3 (Engineering) will be defined. This requires that VLAN memberships be defined for the required ports. The steps and the commands are demonstrated.

The first step for configuring the VLAN is to establish a terminal connection to the switch using the Cisco console cable. The console connection is used to perform the initial configurations needed to use the Cisco Network Assistant software:

1. Connect the Console cable to your workstation and switch.

2. Open the HyperTerminal software on your workstation.

3. Make a HyperTerminal connection to the switch. (These are the same steps as connecting to a router.)

    Now that you have made a HyperTerminal connection to the switch, the switch's initial prompt should appear as **Switch>**.

4. At the initial prompt, type **enable** or **en**. After this is done, the prompt should change to Switch#. This allows you to enter the privileged mode of the switch.

5. Next, type **configure terminal** or **conf t**. After this is done, the prompt should change to Switch(config)#. Doing this places you in the global configuration mode of the switch.

6. Now type **interface Vlan1** or **int Vlan1**. The prompt should now change to Switch(config-if)#. You are now able to make changes to Vlan1's interface.

7. Next, enter **ip address 192.168.1.1 255.255.255.0**. This command changes the switch's IP address to 192.168.1.1.

8. Type **no shut**. This is needed for Vlan1 to stay up and active.

You have now set the IP address of the switch to 192.168.1.1. Notice that the subnet mask is set to 255.255.255.0, which places the switch in the 192.168.1.0 network. The IP address is set for Vlan1 because this is the default administrative VLAN for the switch, and it can never be removed. The workstation should be connected to port 1 on the switch, and the computers' IP addresses should be configured for 192.168.1.2. This places the computer in the same network as that defined for the VLAN1 interface. At this point, use the **ping** command to verify network connectivity from the computer to the switch.

The next step is to use the **show vlan** command to verify which ports have been defined for the switch. By default, all ports are assigned to VLAN 1, as demonstrated in the following example:

```
Switch# show vlan
VLAN   Name        Status                    Ports
_ _ _ _ _ _ _ _ _ _ _ _ _ _ _ _ _ _ _ _ _ _ _ _ _ _ _ _     _

1      default     active                    Fa0/1, Fa0/2, Fa0/3, Fa0/4
                                             Fa0/5, Fa0/6, Fa0/7, Fa0/8
                                             Fa0/9, Fa0/10
```

This shows that all the FastEthernet interfaces are currently assigned to VLAN 1. In the next step, two additional VLANs will be created for both Sales and Engineering.

The following is an example of configuring a VLAN. This requires that the configuration mode on the switch be entered. In this case, the Sales and Engineering VLANs are being created.

```
SwitchA#configure terminal
Enter configuration commands, one per line.  End with CNTL/Z.
SWitchA(config)#vlan 2
SWitchA (config-vlan)#name Sales

Switch(config)#vlan 3
Switch(config-vlan)#name Engineering
```

The next step is used to verify that the new VLANs have been created:

```
Switch(config-vlan)#     exit
Switch(config)#     exit
Switch#     show     vlan

VLAN  Name            Status      Ports
- -   - - - - - - -  - - -  - - - - - - - - - - - -
1     default         active      Fa0/1,   Fa0/2,   Fa0/3,   Fa0/4
                                  Fa0/5,   Fa0/6,   Fa0/7,   Fa0/8
                                  Fa0/9,   Fa0/10
2     Sales           active
3     Engineering     active
```

In the next steps, ports will be assigned to the newly created VLANs. This requires that the configuration mode be entered and each FastEthernet interface (port) must be assigned to the proper VLAN. An example is presented for FastEthernet interface 0/2 being assigned to VLAN 2.

```
Switch#conf t
Enter configuration commands, one per line. End with CNTL/Z.
Switch(config)#int fa 0/2
Switch(config-if)#switchport mode access
Switch(config-if)#switchport access vlan 2
Switch(config-if)#end
```

The next step is used to verify that FastEthernet 0/2 has been assigned to the Sales VLAN (VLAN2). This can be verified using the **show vlan brief** command as shown. This command displays only the interfaces assigned to each VLAN.

```
Switch# show vlan

VLAN      Name         Status      Ports
- -     - - - - - - - - - - - - - - - - - - - - - - -
1         default      active      Fa0/1, Fa0/3, Fa0/4, Fa0/5
                                   Fa0/6, Fa0/7, Fa0/8, Fa0/9
                                   Fa0/10
2         Sales        active      Fa0/2
```

The next steps are to assign ports 3 and 4 to the Sales VLAN (VLAN 2) and ports 6, 7, and 8 to Engineering (VLAN 3). After this is completed, the port assignments can be verified using the **show vlan** command as shown.

```
Switch#show vlan

VLAN    Name         Status        Ports
- -    - - - - - - - -      - - - - - - - - - - - - -
1       default      active        Fa0/1, Fa0/5, Fa0/9, Fa0/10

2       Sales        active        Fa0/2, Fa0/3, Fa0/4

3       Engineering  active        Fa0/6, Fa0/7, Fa0/8
```

You can look specifically at the assignments for only one of the VLANs by entering the command **show vlan name** *<vlan-name>*, where *vlan-name* is the name assigned to the VLAN. Please note that the name is case-sensitive. You can also use the number of the VLAN instead of using the command **sh vlan id** *<vlan#>*. Examples of both are presented:

```
Switch#sh vlan name Engineering

VLAN    Name              Status          Ports
- -     - - - - - - - -   - - - - - - -   - - - - - - - - - - - - - -
3       Engineering       active          Fa0/6, Fa0/7, Fa0/8

Switch#show vlan id 3

VLAN    Name              Status          Ports
- -     - - - - - - - -   - - - - - - -   - - - - - - - - - - - - - -
3       Engineering       active          Fa0/6, Fa0/7, Fa0/8
```

The overall configuration of the switch can be viewed using the **show running-config (sh run)** command as shown. Only a part of the configuration is displayed:

```
Switch#sh run        -    -
Building configuration...

Current configuration : 1411 bytes
!
version 12.1
no service pad
service timestamps debug uptime
service timestamps log uptime
no service password-encryption
!
hostname Switch
!
ip subnet-zero
!
spanning-tree mode pvst
no spanning-tree optimize bpdu transmission
spanning-tree extend system-id
!
interface FastEthernet0/1
!-
 interface FastEthernet0/2
 switchport access vlan 2
 switchport mode access
    .    .
    .    .
    .    .
    .    .

interface FastEthernet0/5
!
```

```
interface FastEthernet0/6
 switchport access vlan 3
 switchport mode access
!
interface FastEthernet0/9
!
interface FastEthernet0/10
!
!
interface Vlan1
 ip address 192.168.1.1 255.255.255.0
 no ip route-cache
!
ip http server
!
line con 0
line vty 0 15
 login
end
```

The running-configuration for the switch shows that the FastEthernet interfaces have been assigned to the proper VLANs. Additionally, this shows that an IP address has been assigned to the default VLAN1.

This portion of the text has demonstrated the steps for creating a static VLAN. Both Sales and Engineering VLANs were created, and specific ports on the switch were assigned to the respective VLANs. Unassigned ports remained as part of the default VLAN 1.

Networking Challenge—Switch Configuration

Use the simulator software included with the text's companion CD-ROM to demonstrate that you can perform basic switch and static VLAN configuration. Place the CD-ROM in your computer's drive. Open the *Net-Challenge* folder, and click **Net-ChallengeV4.exe**. After the software is running, click the **Select Challenge** button. This opens a Select Challenge drop-down menu. Select the **Chapter 8 - Switch Configuration** challenge to open a check box that can be used to verify that you have completed all the tasks. Do the following:

1. Enter the privileged EXEC mode on the switch (password: **Chile**).

2. Enter the switch's configuration mode, **Router(config)**.

3. Set the hostname of the switch to switch-A.

4. Configure the IP address for VLAN 1 interface with the following:

   - IP address: 10.10.20.250
   - Subnet mask: 255.255.255.0

5. Enable the VLAN 1 interface.

6. Use the command to display the current VLAN settings for the switch.

7. Create a VLAN 2 named Sales.

8. Verify that a new Sales VLAN has been created.

9. Issue the command to enter the fa0/2 interface configuration mode.

10. Enter the sequence of commands that are used to assign interface fa0/2 to the Sales VLAN.

11. Enter the command that enables you to display the interface assigned to each VLAN.

12. Enter the command that enables you to view specifically the assignments for the Sales VLAN.

13. Issue the command that allows you to view the switch's running-configuration.

Section 8-3 Review

This section has covered the following **Network+** Exam objectives.

2.6 Given a scenario, configure a switch using the proper features

The basics of configuring a Cisco switch are presented in this section. You should have noticed the similarity and distinct differences between router and switch IOS commands. Spend time working through the Net-Challenge exercises. These exercises will help you remember the commands needed for configuring a switch, creating VLANs, and configuring the default gateway.

4.7 Given a scenario, troubleshoot and resolve common security issues

This section presented the steps to enable password protection for the privileged (enable) mode for a switch. This is configured by setting the enable secret.

Test Your Knowledge

1. Which of the following is used to look specifically at the assignments for the Administrator VLAN?

   a. Switch(config)#**sh vlan name Administrator**

   b. Switch(vlan)#**sh vlan name Administrator**

   c. Switch#**sh vlan name Administrator**

   d. Switch#**sh vlan Administrator**

2. Which of the following command sequences is used to set password protection for the console port?

a. SwitchA(config)# **line console 0**

   SwitchA(config-line)# **login**

   SwitchA(config-line)# **password my-secret2**

b. SwitchA# **line console 0**

   SwitchA(config-line)# **login**

   SwitchA(config-line)# **password my-secret2**

c. SwitchA# **line console 0**

   SwitchA# **login**

   SwitchA#**password my-secret2**

d. SwitchA(config)# **line console 0**

   SwitchA(config)# **login**

   SwitchA(config)# **password my-secret2**

8-4 SPANNING-TREE PROTOCOL

This section examines the **Spanning-Tree Protocol (STP)**. STP is a link management protocol that prevents looping and controls data flow over possible redundant data paths. Looping is bad for Ethernet networks because duplicate packets can be sent over redundant paths. The switches should only send the packets over one path. The Spanning-Tree Protocol is used to ensure only one data path is selected. The Spanning-Tree Protocol also forces one of the redundant data paths into a stand-by mode by placing the path in a blocked state.

Switches that are participating in the Spanning-Tree Protocol exchange information with other switches in the form of **bridge protocol data units (BPDUs)**. Switches use the BPDUs for the following:

- Election of a root switch for the spanning-tree network topology.

- Removing redundant data paths.

- The shortest distance to a root switch is calculated.

- A port from each switch is selected as the best path to the root switch.

- Ports that are part of the Spanning-Tree Protocol are selected.

Switches assume they are the root switch until the BPDUs are exchanged and a root switch is elected. The root switch elected is the switch with the lowest MAC address. Part of the BPDU packet is shown. In this case a switch with the MAC

Spanning-Tree Protocol
A link management protocol that prevents looping and controls data flow over possible redundant data paths

Bridge Protocol Data Unit (BPDU)
Used by switches to share information with other switches that are participating in the Spanning-Tree Protocol

address 0030194A6940 is issuing that data packet as start of the bidding process to see which switch will be elected as the "root" switch.

BPDU Config BID=0030194A6940 PID=0x801B

The "Config" indicates this is a **Configuration BPDU** and is used by the switches to elect the "root" switch. Two other types of packets that can come from the switch are the **Topology Change Notification (TCN)**, which is used to indicate that there has been a change in the switch network topology, and the **Topology Change Notification Acknowledgement (TCA)**, which is an acknowledgement from another switch that the TCN has been received.

Figure 8-2 illustrates an example of the contents of a BPDU. This is showing that the Root ID—MAC address is 0030194A6940. The BPDUs are exchanged at regular intervals and are used to keep the switches notified of any changes in the network topology. The default notification interval is 2 seconds and is called the "Hello Time," as shown in Figure 8-2.

```
   IEEE 802.1D - Bridge
 Management Protocol
   (IEEE 802.1D)
     Protocol ID            0x0000   (Bridge PDU)
   Bridge Protocol Data
 Unit   (BPDU)
     Version                0
     Type                   0x00   (Configuration)
   Flags                    0x00
     >                      0... ....   Not Topology Change Acknowledgment
     >                      .... ...0   Not Topology Change
     >                      .000 000.   Not Used (MBZ)
     Root ID - Settable     32768
     Priority
     Root ID - MAC Address  0030194A6940   [No Vendor Name. - 4A6940]   [0030194A6940]
     Root Path Cost         0
     Bridge ID - Settable   32768
     Priority
     Bridge ID - MAC Address 0030194A6940   [No Vendor Name. - 4A6940]   [0030194A6940]
     Port Identifier        0x801B
     Message Age            0.000000 secs
     Max Age                20.000000 secs
     Hello Time             2.000000 secs
     Forward Delay          15.000000 secs
```

FIGURE 8-2   An example of a BPDU packet information.

The switch will not begin to forward data packets when a networking device is connected to a port. Instead, during this delay, the switch will first begin to process the BPDUs to determine the topology of the switch network. This is called the forward delay, which is listed in Figure 8-2. This is showing that the forward delay is 15 seconds, which is the default value set by the root switch. During the delay period, the switch is going through the listening and learning states.

The five Spanning-Tree Protocol states are as follows:

- **Blocking State:** In this state, the switch is not sending data out of the ports. However, the switch is receiving and monitoring the BPDUs. This state is used to prevent any possible switching loops.

- **Listening State:** BPDUs are being processed.

- **Learning State:** The switch is learning source MAC addresses from the received data packets and will add the addresses to the MAC address table.

- **Forwarding State:** The switch is now sending and receiving data packets. The BPDUs are still to be monitored for any possible change in the switch network.

Configuration BPDU
Used by switches to elect the "root" switch

Topology Change Notification (TCN)
Used to indicate that there has been a change in the switch

Topology Change Notification Acknowledgement (TCA)
An acknowledgement from another switch that the TCN has been received

- **Disabled:** This is a setting available for the network administrator to manually disable the port. This is not part of the Spanning-Tree Protocol but rather a function available on the switch.

The Spanning-Tree Protocol has been a standard feature in all layer 2 switches for many years. Many improvements have been made based upon original STP. Rapid Spanning-Tree Protocol (RSTP) is an improvement over STP because it reduces the convergence time to less than 10 seconds. RSTP proactively monitors switch ports for status change and allows a port to safely transition to the forwarding state. RSTP is also backward compatible with STP switches. Multiple Spanning Tree Protocol (MSTP) is another improvement. MSTP is VLAN aware, thus allowing each VLAN to have its own MST instance, or MSTI. This enables load balancing of network traffic across redundant links so that all the links in a network can be used by at least one MSTI. There are also other improved proprietary spanning tree protocols. For example, Cisco developed Per-VLAN Spanning Tree (PVST) and PVST+, and Juniper developed VLAN Spanning Tree Protocol (VSTP).

Section 8-4 Review

This section has covered the following **Network+** Exam objectives.

2.6 Given a scenario, configure a switch using the proper features

The Spanning-Tree Protocol (STP) is introduced in this section. Make sure you know the five STP states.

4.2 Given a scenario, analyze and interpret the output of troubleshooting tools

Switches assume they are the root switch until the BPDUs are exchanged and a root switch is elected. The root switch elected is the switch with the lowest MAC address. This concept was presented in this section.

Test Your Knowledge

1. Which of the following are the five Spanning-Tree Protocol states?

    a. Blocking

    b. Listening

    c. Selecting

    d. Learning

    e. Forwarding

    f. Disabled

    g. Passing

    h. Cut-through

2. Spanning-Tree Protocol is which of the following? (Select all that apply.)

   a. Link-management protocol

   b. Replaces RIP as the routing protocol for switches

   c. Used to minimize hops

   d. Used to prevent loops

8-5   NETWORK MANAGEMENT

A network of moderate size has a tremendous number of data packets entering and leaving. The number of routers, switches, hubs, servers, and host computers can become staggering. Proper network management requires that all network resources be managed. This requires that proper management tools be in place.

A fundamental network management tool is **SNMP (SNMPv1)**, the Simple Network Management Protocol. SNMPv1, developed in 1988, is widely supported in most modern network hardware. SNMP is a connectionless protocol using the User Datagram Protocol (UDP) for the transmission of data to and from UDP port 161.

SNMP uses a **management information base (MIB)**, which is a collection of standard objects that are used to obtain configuration parameters and performance data on a networking device such as a router. For example, the MIB (ifDescr) returns a description of the router's interfaces as demonstrated in Figure 8-3. An SNMP software tool was used to collect the interface description information. The IP address of the router is 10.10.10.1, and a **get request ifDescr** was sent to port 161, the UDP port for SNMP. The descriptions of the interfaces were returned as shown.

SNMP (SNMPv1)
Simple Network Management Protocol

Management Information Base (MIB)
A collection of standard objects that are used to obtain configuration parameters and performance data on a networking device

FIGURE 8-3   An example of using an SNMP software management tool to obtain descriptions of a router's interfaces using the MIB (ifDescr).

Obtaining the SNMP data requires that SNMP be configured on the router. The following discussion demonstrates how to configure SNMP on a Cisco router.

Configuring SNMP

The first step for configuring SNMP on a Cisco router is to enter the router's configuration mode using the **conf t** command:

```
RouterB#conf t
Enter configuration commands, one per line. End with CNTL/Z.
```

From the router's (config)# prompt, enter the command **snmp community** [*community string*] [*permissions*]. The community string can be any word. The permissions field is used to establish whether the user can read only (**ro**), write only (**wo**), or both (**rw**). The options for configuring SNMP on the router are shown here:

```
RouterB(config)#snmp community ?
WORD SNMP community string
```

The router was connected to the computer running the SNMP management software, as shown in Figure 8-4. The router's configuration mode was entered, and the **snmp community public ro** command was issued. The word **public** is used as the community string. The community string is the password used by the SNMP software to access SNMP (port 161) on the router. The **ro** sets the permission to read only:

```
RouterB(config)#snmp community public ro
```

FIGURE 8-4   The setup for connecting the SNMP management software tool to the router.

In the next example, the community string password is set to **makesecret**, and the permission is set to read write (rw). Once again, the router's (config)# mode is entered and the command **snmp community makesecret rw** is entered:

```
RouterB(config)#snmp community makesecret rw
```

The configuration for SNMP can be verified using the **show run** command from the router's privileged mode prompt. A portion of the configuration file that lists the SNMP configuration for the router is shown here:

```
RouterB#sh run
 .

 .

snmp-server community makesecret RW
 .

 .
```

Figure 8-4 shows the setup of the configured router and the computer running the SNMP management software. The SNMP management software issues the MIB to the router at port 161, and the router returns the response. Figure 8-5 shows another example of using SNMP to obtain interface information about a router. The SNMP manager was configured with the host IP address of 10.10.10.1, a set value (port #) of 161 and the 10 character community string of **makesecret** shown as * * * * * * * * * *. The MIB (ifspeed) was sent to the router and a status for each of the interfaces was provided. The data displayed shows the speed settings for the router's interfaces.

FIGURE 8-5   Using an SNMP software management tool to obtain interface speed settings.

Another important application of SNMP is for obtaining traffic data statistics. An example of this is shown in Figure 8-6. The SNMP management program issued the MIB (ifOutOctets), which returns the number of octets of data that have left the router. (The router has a counter that keeps track.) The first result shows ifOutOctets 7002270. The next result display shows that the ifOutOctets returns a value of 7002361.

The SNMP management program collecting the statistics keeps track of the time interval between measurements and the number of octets that have passed. This information can be used to calculate the average traffic flow by hour, day, week, or month, depending on the information needed. An example of collecting traffic route statistics is provided in section 6 of Chapter 10, "Internet Technologies: Out to the Internet." A final note about the router's counter: The counter does not reset unless the router is rebooted.

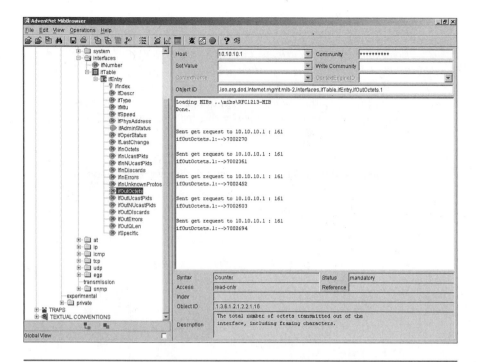

FIGURE 8-6 An example of using SNMP to collect data traffic statistics.

Two other versions of SNMP have been developed for network management. These versions are **SNMPv2** and **SNMPv3**. SNMPv2 was developed in 1993; however, this version was not directly compatible with SNMPv1. SNMPv2 attempted to address security issues, but this led to the development of many variants and SNMPv2 was never fully accepted by the networking industry. One of the variants called SNMPv2c (Community-based SNMP version 2) was adopted more widely than the others. SNMPv3 was developed in 1998 and achieved the important goal of maintaining compatibility with SNMPv1 and adding security to SNMP. The security features of SNMPv3 include confidentiality, integrity, and authentication. *Confidentiality* means the packets are encrypted to prevent snooping; *integrity* ensures the data being transferred has not been tampered with; and *authentication* means the data is from a known source.

> **SNMPv2**
> Simple Network Management Protocol version 2
>
> **SNMPv3**
> Simple Network Management Protocol version 3

Section 8-5 Review

This section has covered the following **Network+** Exam objectives.

2.1 Given a scenario, use the appropriate monitoring tools

The Simple Network Management Protocol is presented in this section. An important concept is that SNMP uses network port 161 for the transmission of data. Also, make sure you have an understanding of MIBs.

2.4 Explain the importance of implementing network segmentation

This section examined the security features of SNMPv3. SNMPv3 was developed in 1998 and achieved the important goal of maintaining compatibility with SNMPv1 and adding security to SNMP. The security features of SNMPv3 include confidentiality, integrity, and authentication. Confidentiality means the packets are encrypted to prevent snooping; integrity ensures the data being transferred has not been tampered with; and authentication means the data is from a known source.

3.2 Compare and contrast common network vulnerabilities and threats

This section presented a look at SNMPv1 and SNMPv2. The security issues and vulnerabilities were examined.

3.3 Given a scenario, implement network-hardening techniques

This section introduced SNMPv3. SNMPv3 was developed in 1998 and achieved the important goal of maintaining compatibility with SNMPv1 and adding security to SNMP. The security features of SNMPv3 include confidentiality, integrity, and authentication.

Test Your Knowledge

1. Which of the following is the *best* example of a fundamental network management tool?

   a. SNMP

   b. **ping**

   c. **trace route**

   d. Documentation

2. Which of the following best characterizes a MIB? (Select all that apply.)

   a. The Management Internet Base is a collection of standard objects that are used to obtain certain configuration parameters and performance data on a networking device.

   b. The Management Information Base is a collection of standard objects that are used to obtain performance data on a networking device.

   c. The Management Information Base is a collection of standard multicast addresses that are used to obtain certain configuration parameters.

   d. The Management Information Base is a collection of standard objects that are used to obtain certain configuration parameters.

8-6 POWER OVER ETHERNET

One of the challenges the network administrator faces as the campus network grows is making sure that electrical power is available for the networking devices (for example, switches, wireless access points, and IP phones). It is not always practical or affordable to run electrical power every place a networking device is needed. This challenge is met with **Power over Ethernet (PoE)**. The Power over Ethernet standard (IEEE 802.3af) was approved in 2003 for networks running 10BASE-T, 100BASE-T, and 1000BASE-T technologies. This provided a standardized technology that could be used to supply power over existing CAT5 or better network cabling (CAT5 or better) to the networking devices.

The benefits of PoE include the following:

- It is not necessary to run external power to all networking devices.
- You can run power and data over one cable.
- Monitoring of power management can be done via SNMP.
- Networking devices can be moved easily.

The power provided by PoE as defined by IEEE 802.3af is as follows:

- 15.4 watts per port to Ethernet devices
- 48 volt system

Two pieces of networking hardware are defined in PoE. These are the **Powered Device (PD)** and the **Power Sourcing Equipment (PSE)**. The three main functions provided by the PSE are as follows:

- Capability of detecting a PD
- Supplying power to the PD
- Power supply monitoring

The two types of power sourcing equipment (PSE) are the **endpoint PSE** and the **midspan (mid-point) PSE**. These types of network switches are usually referred to as *PoE switches*. Besides being a PSE, they still provide typical switching functions. They are not meant to be the replacement for the layer 2 switches because they are more expensive. These switches are used extensively in the Voice over IP

> **Power over Ethernet (PoE)**
> Technology developed to supply power over the network cabling (CAT5 or better)

> **PD**
> Powered Device
>
> **PSE**
> Power Sourcing Equipment

> **Endpoint PSE**
> Example is the source port on an Ethernet switch that connects to the PD
>
> **Midspan (Mid-point) PSE**
> Used to provide power to a PD when a powered Ethernet port is not available

(VoIP) environment to power up the IP phones. One useful command to check the power status of the switch ports is **show power inline**, as demonstrated here:

```
SwitchA#sh power inline
```

Module	Available (Watts)	Used (Watts)	Remaining (Watts)
1	740.0	0.0	740.0

Interface	Admin	Oper	Power (Watts)	Device	Class	Max
Gi1/0/1	auto	off	0.0	n/a	n/a	30.0
Gi1/0/2	auto	off	0.0	n/a	n/a	30.0
Gi1/0/3	auto	off	0.0	n/a	n/a	30.0
Gi1/0/4	auto	off	0.0	n/a	n/a	30.0
Gi1/0/5	auto	off	0.0	n/a	n/a	30.0
Gi1/0/6	auto	off	0.0	n/a	n/a	30.0

An example of an endpoint PSE is the source port on an Ethernet switch that connects, via a cable, to a PD. The power to the PD can be delivered in two ways, over the active data pairs (for example, 1–2, 3–6) or via pairs 4–5, 7–8, as demonstrated in Figure 8-7 (a and b). Both types of power delivery can be used for 10BASE-T, 100 BASE-T, and 1000 BASE-T. The most common way of power delivery is over pairs 1–2/3–6, as shown in Figure 8-7(a).

A midspan or mid-point PSE is used to provide power to a PD when a powered Ethernet port is not available. This setup requires the use of a power injector and typically uses pairs 4–5/7–8, and this does not support 1000 BASE-T connections.

FIGURE 8-7   The two ways to deliver power to the PD: (a) pairs 1–2/3–6 and (b) 4–5/7–8.

The PD is the actual device receiving power such as wireless access points and an IP phone. Here are four classes of PD devices:

- Class 0 (.44 to 12.95 watts)
- Class 1 (.44 to 3.84 watts)
- Class 2 (3.84 to 6.49 watts)
- Class 3 (6.49 to 12.95 watts)

PD devices are "discovered" by the PSE by sending discovery signals on active and inactive Ethernet ports. The discovery process (called **Resistive Power Discovery**) is basically looking for devices that support PoE. Valid PDs will have a 25kΩ resistor connected between the transmit and receive pairs. Before full power is delivered to the PD, two low-voltage "discovery" signals are sent out to verify that a compatible PoE device is attached. The second of the two signals is a slightly higher voltage than the first, but neither is large enough to damage an incompatible device. If the PSE detects a compatible PD, then the full 48 volts is applied to all ports that have compatible PDs connected.

A new version of Power over Ethernet, called **PoE Plus**, based on the IEEE 802.3at standard is now available. PoE Plus provides the following features:

- Supports both 802.3af (PoE) and 802.3at (PoE Plus) PDs
- Support for midspan PSEs for 10000 BASE-T
- Supports a minimum of 30 watts of power for the PD
- Support for 10GBASE-T
- Will operate with CAT5 and higher cabling

There are a limited number of problems with PoE as long as the devices support IEEE 802.3af. In cases where a vendor proprietary PoE equipment is being used, the PSEs and PDs must be compatible. Also, the network administrator must be aware of how many PDs are connected to the PSE and that the total power requirements for the PDs does not exceed the PSEs limit. For example, a network could have 10 access points and 25 IP phones all requiring a PoE connection. The total number of devices requiring power can exceed the power output for a PSE and possibly damaging the device.

> **Resistive Power Discovery**
> Looking for devices that support PoE and have a 25kΩ resistor connected between the transmit and receive pairs

> **PoE Plus**
> A new version of PoE based on IEEE 802.3at

Section 8-6 Review

This section has covered the following **Network+** Exam objectives.

2.6 Given a scenario, configure a switch using the proper features

Providing electrical power for a growing network is addressed in this section's discussion on Power over Ethernet (PoE) and PoE+. Make sure you know and understand the process of how power is delivered using UTP cables. Also, make sure you understand and can explain the Resistive Power Discovery.

Test Your Knowledge

1. Which of the following is an advantage of running Power over Ethernet? (Select all that apply.)

   a. It is not necessary to run external power to all networking devices.

   b. PoE allows an improvement in data throughput.

   c. PoE works with all networking devices regardless of the manufacturer.

   d. You can run power and data over one cable.

2. How are PD devices discovered, and which device discovers them?

    a. Resistor Power Discovery/ESE

    b. PoE Discovery/PSE

    c. Resistive Power Discovery/PSE

    d. PoE Discovery/ESE

SUMMARY

The fundamentals of VLANs and switch configuration have been presented in this chapter. You have also been introduced to the Spanning-Tree Protocol and the process of selecting the root bridge. You were also introduced to the SNMP network management tool and associated MIBs. Lastly, the operation of Power over Ethernet was presented. Make sure you understand the following concepts presented in this chapter:

- Understand and be able to describe the three types of VLANs.
- Understand the basics of switch configuration and static VLAN configuration.
- Be able to explain the Spanning-Tree Protocol.
- Explain how SNMP management tools can be used to monitor the data traffic and performance within a campus network.
- Discuss the operation of Power over Ethernet.

QUESTIONS AND PROBLEMS

Section 8-2

1. What is a VLAN?

2. List the three types of VLANs.

3. When a port is not assigned to any VLAN, is it still a member of a VLAN?

4. What is an advantage of using VLANs?

5. What is a port-based VLAN?

6. What is a tag-based VLAN?

7. What is a protocol-based VLAN?

8. What is a VLAN ID?

9. What are the two approaches for assigning VLAN membership? Explain the function of each.

Section 8-3

10. What is the purpose of the enable secret for a switch?

11. What commands are used to assign the IP address 192.168.20.5 to VLAN1?

12. Which switch command is used to display the interfaces assigned to a VLAN?

13. What is the purpose of the VLAN database?

14. List the commands used to create VLAN5, and name this the VLAN Marketing group.

15. List the commands used to assign FA0/5 to the Marketing-group VLAN (VLAN5). Show the switch prompts.

16. Which command is used to display the port assignments for the Software-Development VLAN? List both the prompt and the command.

17. List the steps to configure the IP address for the default interface VLAN1. The IP address should be set to 10.10.20.1 with a subnet mask of 255.255.255.0.

Section 8-4

18. What is the purpose of the Spanning-Tree Protocol?

19. What is a BPDU, and what is its purpose?

20. Discuss how a root switch is elected.

21. What are the five STP protocol states?

22. A BPDU data packet shows that the "Hello Time" is 2.0 secs. What information does this provide?

23. A BPDU data packet lists the "Forward Delay" as 15 seconds. What information does this provide?

Section 8-5

24. Which port number does SNMP use and which transport protocol?

25. The SNMP MIB get request **ifDescr** returns what information from a router?

26. What is the purpose of the MIB?

27. Write the Cisco router command for configuring SNMP on a Cisco router. Assume a community string of networking and set the permissions to read-only.

28. The command `show run` is entered on a Cisco router. Describe what the output "SNMP-server test RO" means.

29. Which SNMP MIBs were most likely issued to the router discussed in section 8-5?

Use Figure 8-8 to answer questions 30–34.

FIGURE 8-8   For problems 30–34.

30. Which MIB was issued?

31. What information was returned?

32. Which port number was used?

33. Which protocol is being used? How do you know?

34. Who is the manufacturer of this networking device?

Section 8-6

35. What are the two types of devices defined by PoE?

36. What should you check if you are installing a Power over Ethernet connection using computer equipment from two different manufacturers?

37. Cite four benefits of Power over Ethernet.

38. What is resistive power discovery, and how does it work?

39. Which wire pairs are used in PoE?

40. How much power can a class 0 PD PoE device source?

41. What are the benefits of PoE Plus?

CRITICAL THINKING

42. Your supervisor asks you if a layer 2 switch could be used in the core of the campus network. Prepare a response to your supervisor. Be sure to justify your recommendation.

43. A 1Gbps data link is to be set up between building A and building B in a campus network. Does it matter if the link is fiber or microwave or some other media? Explain your answer.

44. You've just configured a IP VLAN interface on a switch and the interface is not up. How do you troubleshoot the issue?

CERTIFICATION QUESTIONS

45. You have been asked as the network administration to create a VLAN called **Administrator.** The command used on a Cisco switch for creating an **Administrator** VLAN 2 is which of the following?

a.

```
SwitchA#vlan
Switch#vlan 2 name Administrator
```

b.

```
SwitchA#vlan
Switch(data)#vlan 2 name Administrator
```

c.

```
SwitchA(config)#vlan 2
Switch(config-vlan)#name Administrator
```

d.

```
SwitchA#vlan database
Switch(vlan)#vlan name Administrator
```

46. You are configuring a switch so that a specific port on the switch is assigned to **vlan3**. The steps for assigning the FastEthernet port 0/4 to VLAN 3 on a Cisco switch are which of the following?

a.

```
Switch(config)#int fa 0/4
Switch(config-if)#switchport mode access
Switch(config-if)#switchport access vlan 3
```

b.

```
Switch(config)#int fa 0/4
Switch(config-if)#switchport mode access
Switch(config-if)#switchport access 3
```

c.

```
Switch(config)#int fa 0/4
Switch(config)#switchport mode access
Switch(config-if)#switchport access vlan 3
```

d.

```
Switch(config)#int fa 0/4
Switch(config-if)#switchport mode access 3
Switch(config-if)#switchport access vlan
```

47. You are cabling a UTP connection to a switch that will also be used for supplying power via Power over Ethernet. The power to the PoE devices is provided using which of the following pairs? (Select all that apply.)

    a. 1-3 / 4-6

    b. 1-6 / 5-8

    c. 1-2 / 3-6

    d. 4-5 / 7-8

48. The source port of an Ethernet switch that connects to a PD is an example of which of the following?

    a. A mid-point PSE

    b. An endpoint PSE

    c. A start PSE

    d. None of these answers is correct.

49. You are the network administrator and are configuring an SNMP connection. You need to be able to set permissions for both read and write. What is the command for setting the community string to **Chile** with a permission of read and write on a Cisco router?

    a. **snmp community Chile rw**

    b. **snmp makesecret Chile rw**

    c. **Chile rw makesecret**

    d. **snmp Chile Read/Write**

50. Switches use bridge protocol data units for which of the following? (Select all that apply.)

    a. Ports that are part of the STP are selected.

    b. The longest distance to a root switch is calculated.

    c. Election of a root switch for the spanning-tree network topology.

    d. Removing redundant data paths.

51. What is the purpose of a VLAN?

    a. A VLAN is a group of host computers and servers that are configured as if they are not in the same LAN even if they reside across routers in separate LANs.

    b. A VLAN is a group of host computers and servers that are configured as if they are in the same LAN even if they reside in the same LAN.

    c. A VLAN is a group of host computers and servers that are configured as if they are in the same LAN even if they reside across routers in separate LANs.

    d. A VLAN is comprised of a single host computer and servers that are configured as if they are in the same LAN even if they reside across routers in separate LANs.

52. Your supervisor asks you to create a port-based VLAN to support the development group. Specifically, you are being asked to do which of the following? (Select all that apply.)

    a. Use the 802.1Q protocol for VLAN assignment.

    b. Assign specific ports on a switch to a specific VLAN.

    c. Specify which protocols control port assignment.

    d. Specify which ports will share broadcasts.

53. The network administrator is configuring a VLAN named "Development." Which of the following are the correct steps for creating the VLAN?

    a. `SwitchAvlan database`

        `Switch(vlan)#vlan 2 name Development`

        `VLAN 2 modified:`

          `Name: Sales`

    b. `SwitchA(config)#vlan`

        `Switch(config-vlan)#name Development`

    c. `SwitchA#vlan`

        `Switch(int-vlan)#vlan 2 name Development`

        `VLAN 2 modified:`

          `Name: Sales`

    d. `SwitchA#vlan`

        `Switch(config-vlan)#vlan 2 name Development`

        `VLAN 2 modified:`

          `Name: Sales`

54. The network administrator sees that the following data packet has been sent: BPDU Config BID=0030194A6940 PID=0x801B. What is the purpose of this data packet?

    a. This BPDU indicates the peripheral interface device (PID=0x801B) requesting a data packet.

    b. This BPDU indicates the peripheral interface device (PID=0x801B) requesting to send a data packet.

    c. The "Config" indicates this is a configuration **BPDU** and is used by the switches to elect the "root" switch.

    d. The "Config" indicates this is a static BPDU and is configured by the user that connects to the root bridge.

9
CHAPTER

ROUTING PROTOCOLS

Chapter Outline

Objectives

- Describe the difference between static and dynamic routing protocols
- Describe the difference in distance vector and link state protocols
- Be able to configure a basic setup for static routing protocol
- Understand the relative amount of traffic generated by each protocol
- Understand the basics for OSPF, IS-IS, and the EIGRP routing protocols
- Be able to configure a basic setup for the RIP and RIP v2 routing protocols
- Be able to configure a basic setup for the OSPF and EIGRP routing protocols

Key Terms

static route
netstat -r
route print
loopback
ip route
variable length subnet masking
show ip route (sh ip route)
routing table code S
routing table code C
gateway of last resort
show ip route static (sh ip route static)
show running-config (sh run)
show startup-config (sh start)
copy run start
write memory (wr m)
dynamic routing protocols

administrative distance
path determination
metric
convergence
load balancing
hop count
reliability
bandwidth
delay
cost
load
ticks
distance vector protocols
RIP
routing loop
advertise
class network address
classful addressing
contiguous network

show ip protocol
link state protocol
OSPF
IETF
link state advertisement (LSA)
"Hello" packets
areas
backbone
variable length submasks (VLSM)
route flapping
IS-IS
NET
router ospf [number]
network number
wildcard bits
Area 0
EIGRP

This chapter introduces the basic concepts of routing protocols. Routing protocols provide a standardized format for route management, including route selection, sharing route status with neighbor routers, and calculating alternative routes if the best path route is down. The focus of this chapter is on the use of routing protocols in a campus network environment.

Static routing protocols are presented in section 9-2. This section includes examples of how to configure static routes and view the routes in a routing table. The material includes a discussion of when and where static protocols are used and also when and why it is not advantageous to use a static routing protocol. An overview of the concept of dynamic protocols is presented in section 9-3. Dynamic protocols are divided into two areas: distance vector and link state. Distance vector protocols are introduced in section 9-4. The steps for configuring the distance vector protocols RIP and RIPv2 are presented in section 9-5. A discussion on link state protocols is presented in section 9-6. The steps for configuring OSPF, the Open Shortest Path First routing protocol, are presented in section 9-7. An overview of hybrid protocols is presented in section 9-8, which concludes with an introduction to configuring the EIGRP hybrid routing protocol.

9-1   INTRODUCTION

The static, RIPv2, OSPF, and EIGRP routing protocols introduced in this chapter contain a networking challenge that is included with the Net-Challenge companion CD-ROM. These challenges enable you to test your ability to configure static, RIPv2, OSPF, and EIGRP routing on a virtual router.

Table 9-1 lists and identifies, by chapter section, where each of the CompTIA Network+ objectives are presented in this chapter. At the end of each chapter section is a review with comments of the Network+ objectives presented in that section. These comments are provided to help reinforce the reader's understanding of a particular Network+ objective. The chapter review also includes "Test Your Knowledge" questions to aid in the understanding of key concepts before the reader advances to the next section of the chapter. The end of the chapter includes a complete set of question plus sample certification type questions.

TABLE 9-1   Chapter 9 CompTIA Network+ Objectives

Domain/Objective Number	Domain/Objective Description	Section Where Objective Is Covered
1.0	**Networking Concepts**	
1.3	Install and configure the following services/applications	9-8
1.9	Explain the basics of routing concepts and protocols	9-2, 9-3, 9-4, 9-5, 9-6, 9-7, 9-8
1.10	Identify the basic elements of unified communication technologies	9-6, 9-7
2.4	Explain the importance of implementing network segmentation	9-3

9-2   STATIC ROUTING

The objective of this section is to demonstrate how data packets are routed in a network using a static routing protocol. The techniques for configuring static routes so that data packets can be forwarded are presented. A **static route** is a list of IP addresses to which data traffic can be forwarded and has been manually entered into either a router's or computer's routing table. A static route is specified in a PC computer in terms of the computer's default gateway, and routers sometimes use a static route when specifying where the network data traffic is to be forwarded. Examples of specifying the static route(s) for a computer are first examined.

> **Static Route**
> A data traffic route that has been manually entered into either a router's or a computer's routing table

The most common static route used in a host computer is the default gateway. The *default gateway* specifies where the data traffic is to be sent when the destination address for the data is not in the same LAN or is unknown. If you don't have a route specified for a subnet in your network, the default route is used. For example, if your PC is on the 10.10.0.0 network and it wants to send data to 100.100.20.1, the data is sent to the default gateway as specified by the TCP/IP setup on your PC. An example of setting the host computer's default gateway is shown in Figure 9-1 for both (a) Windows and (b) Mac OS X. In this example, the default gateway IP address is 10.10.20.250 with a subnet mask of 255.255.255.0 for the computer in LAN A with the IP address of 10.10.20.1.

FIGURE 9-1   Setting the default gateway address or default static route on the host computer (PC and Mac OS X).

netstat -r

The command used to obtain the routing table for a host PC computer

route print

Produces same displayed result as **netstat -r**

Loopback

The data is routed directly back to the source

The routing tables for the host PC computer can be obtained by entering the command **netstat -r** at the PC's command prompt and from the Mac OS X terminal screen. An example is shown in Figure 9-2(a). The command **route print** can also be used to view the active routes from the host PC, as shown in Figure 9-2(b).

The default route is specified in the routing table by a 0.0.0.0 network address entry with a subnet mask of 0.0.0.0. The gateway address of 10.10.20.250 is the IP address of the FastEthernet port of the router connected to the LAN. The IP address of 10.10.20.1 for the interface is the IP address for the host computer's network interface card (NIC). The network destination of 10.10.20.0 is returned to the computer's NIC at IP address 10.10.20.1. The gateway for the network destination of 10.10.20.1 is 127.0.0.1, which is a **loopback** to the host computer. A loopback means the data is routed directly back to the source. In this case, the source is the computer's NIC. The loopback can be used to check whether the network interface is working; if it is, pinging IP address 127.0.0.1 will generate a reply.

What about setting static routes for a router in a small campus network? First, let's examine how data packets travel from one LAN to another in the three-router campus network shown in Figure 9-3. Specifically, how is information sent from a host computer in LAN A (10.10.20.0 subnet) to a host computer in LAN B (10.10.10.0 subnet)? The data packets must travel from LAN A to the RouterA gateway (FA0/0 interface), from RouterA to RouterB via the 10.10.200.0 subnet, and then to LAN B via the RouterB gateway (FA0/0 interface). This requires that a physical communications link be established between the routers and a routing protocol defined for Routers A and B before data packets can be exchanged. The physical connection will typically be CAT6/5e UTP or a fiber connection.

```
C:\netstat -r

Route Table
----------------------------------------------------------------------------
Interface List
0x1 .......................... MS TCP Loopback interface
0x2 ...00 b0 d0 25 bf 48 ...... 3Com 3C920 Integrated Fast Ethernet Controller
3C905C-TX Compatible) — Packet Scheduler Miniport
----------------------------------------------------------------------------
----------------------------------------------------------------------------
Active Routes:
Network Destination         Netmask          Gateway        Interface     Metric
          0.0.0.0           0.0.0.0      10.10.20.250      10.10.20.1        20
       10.10.20.0     255.255.255.0       10.10.20.1      10.10.20.1        20
       10.10.20.1   255.255.255.255        127.0.0.1       127.0.0.1        20
   10.255.255.255   255.255.255.255       10.10.20.1      10.10.20.1        20
        127.0.0.0         255.0.0.0        127.0.0.1       127.0.0.1         1
        224.0.0.0         240.0.0.0       10.10.20.1      10.10.20.1        20
  255.255.255.255   255.255.255.255       10.10.20.1      10.10.20.1         1
Default Gateway:           10.10.20.250
----------------------------------------------------------------------------
Persistent Routes:
  None
                                    (a)
```

```
C:\route print
----------------------------------------------------------------------------
Interface List
0x1 .......................... MS TCP Loopback interface
0x2 ...00 b0 d0 25 bf 48 ...... 3Com 3C920 Integrated Fast Ethernet Controller
3C905C-TX Compatible) — Packet Scheduler Miniport
----------------------------------------------------------------------------
----------------------------------------------------------------------------
Active Routes:
Network Destination         Netmask          Gateway        Interface     Metric
          0.0.0.0           0.0.0.0      10.10.20.250      10.10.20.1        20
       10.10.20.0     255.255.255.0       10.10.20.1      10.10.20.1        20
       10.10.20.1   255.255.255.255        127.0.0.1       127.0.0.1        20
   10.255.255.255   255.255.255.255       10.10.20.1      10.10.20.1        20
        127.0.0.0         255.0.0.0        127.0.0.1       127.0.0.1         1
        224.0.0.0         240.0.0.0       10.10.20.1      10.10.20.1        20
  255.255.255.255   255.255.255.255       10.10.20.1      10.10.20.1         1
Default Gateway:           10.10.20.250
----------------------------------------------------------------------------
Persistent Routes:
  None
                                    (b)
```

FIGURE 9-2   (a) A host computer's static route listing obtained using the netstat
-r command; (b) a host computer's static route listing obtained using the route print
command.

A simplified network can be used to demonstrate what is required to develop static
routes in a multiple-router network. For this example, two routers from the campus
network are used. The two routers, RouterA and RouterB, connect to LANs A and
B as shown in Figure 9-4. This simplified network will be used to describe how
data packets travel from LAN A > RouterA > RouterB > LAN B and what is required to define the static routes.

FIGURE 9-3 A three-router campus network.

Router A Port Addresses (LAN A):

FastEthernet 0/0 (Gateway Address)	10.10.20.250
FastEthernet 0/1	10.10.200.1
FastEthernet 0/2	10.10.100.1

LAN A Computers

Computer A1	10.10.20.1
Computer A2	10.10.20.2
Subnet Mask	**255.255.255.0**

Router B Port Addresses (LAN B):

FastEthernet 0/0 (Gateway Address)	10.10.10.250
FastEthernet 0/2	10.10.200.2
FastEthernet 0/3	10.10.150.1

LAN B Computers

Computer B1	10.10.10.1
Computer B2	10.10.10.2
Subnet Mask	**255.255.255.0**

Router B Port Addresses (LAN C):

FastEthernet 0/1 (Gateway Address)	10.10.1.250
FastEthernet 0/2	10.10.200.2
FastEthernet 0/3	10.10.150.1

LAN C Computers

Computer C1	10.10.1.1
Computer C2	10.10.1.2
Subnet Mask	**255.255.255.0**

Router Port Addresses (LAN D):

FastEthernet 0/0 (Gateway Address)	10.10.5.250
FastEthernet 0/1	10.10.150.2
FastEthernet 0/2	10.10.100.2

LAN D Computers

Computer D1	10.10.5.1
Computer D2	10.10.5.2
Subnet Mask	**255.255.255.0**

FIGURE 9-4 A simplified two-router network.

The data packets pass through three subnets (indicated by *NET*) when traveling from LAN A to LAN B. The IP subnets for each network are as follows:

10.10.20.0 NET	LAN A
10.10.200.0 NET	RouterA connection to RouterB
10.10.10.0 NET	LAN B

In this network, there are only two routers, with RouterA directly connected to RouterB. This means that the only route between the routers is via the 10.10.200.0 NET, which is the connection between Routers A and B. The static route information is entered from the router's configure terminal prompt **(config)#** using the **ip route** command. The command structure for **ip route** is

```
Router(config)#ip route <destination> <subnet mask> <next hop>
```

where the *destination* is the network's destination IP address (NET), the *subnet mask* is what has been defined for the subnets, and the *next hop* is the IP address of the next router's interface in the link. The command for routing the data to the 10.10.10.0 subnet is as follows:

```
RouterA(config)#ip route 10.10.10.0 255.255.255.0 10.10.200.2
```

The following configuration information is entered into RouterA:

Destination Subnet IP Address	Subnet Mask	Next Hop IP Address
10.10.10.0	255.255.255.0	10.10.200.2

The next hop IP address is the IP address of the Ethernet2 port on RouterB. Now the router knows how to deliver data packets from host computers in the 10.10.20.0 NET (LAN A) to destination computers in the 10.10.10.0 NET (LAN B). (*Note:* Each static route can use a different subnet mask. This is called **variable length subnet masking**. For example, one static route could have a subnet mask of 255.255.255.0 and another could have a subnet mask of 255.255.255.252.)

The routing address entry into the routing table can be verified by entering the command **show ip route (sh ip route)** from the router's **(config)#** prompt. An example of this is shown:

```
show ip route (sh ip route)
RouterA#show ip route
Codes: C connected, S static, I IGRP, R RIP, M mobile, B BGP
D EIGRP, EX EIGRP external, O OSPF, IA OSPF inter area
N1 OSPF NSSA external type 1, N2 OSPF NSSA external type 2
E1 OSPF external type 1, E2 OSPF external type 2, E EGP
i IS-IS, L1 IS-IS level-1, L2 IS-IS level-2, * candidate default
U per-user static route, o ODR T traffic engineered route
Gateway of last resort is not set
10.0.0.0/24 is subnetted, 2 subnets
S 10.10.10.0 [1/0] via 10.10.200.2
C 10.10.200.0 is directly connected, FastEthernet1
```

The static route configured on Router A only dictates how the 10.10.10.0 network should be routed from Router A's perspective and that is in outgoing direction or egress only. This does not influence how the returned traffic will come back to Router A. Routing is a bidirectional traffic type; therefore, when a route is configured at one end, the reverse has to be configured at the other end.

ip route
The router configuration command for manually setting the next hop IP address

Variable Length Subnet Masking
Routes can be configured using different subnet masks

show ip route (sh ip route)
The command that displays the routes and the routing address entry into the routing table

What about data traffic flow from the 10.10.10.0 NET (LAN B) to the 10.10.20.0 NET (LAN A)? Once again, the data packets pass through three subnets (indicated by NET) when traveling from LAN B to LAN A. The IP addresses for each subnet are as follows:

10.10.10.0 NET	LAN B
10.10.200.0 NET	RouterB connection to RouterA
10.10.20.0 NET	LAN A

In this scenario, LAN B connects directly to RouterB and the only route to LAN A from RouterB is via the 10.10.200.0 NET, which is the connection between Routers B and A. The destination network IP address is 10.10.20.0. The command input to RouterB for routing the data to the 10.10.20.0 subnet is as follows:

```
RouterB(config)#ip route 10.10.20.0 255.255.255.0 10.10.200.1
```

The following information is entered into the router:

Destination Subnet IP Address	Subnet Mask	Next Hop IP Address
10.10.20.0	255.255.255.0	10.10.200.1

The next hop IP address is the IP address of the FastEthernet0/1 port on RouterA. Now a static route has been configured on RouterB to route data packets from host computers in the 10.10.10.0 NET (LAN B) to destination computers in the 10.10.20.0 NET (LAN A). The entries into RouterB's routing table can be confirmed by using the command **sh ip route** at the **Router#** prompt, as shown:

```
RouterB#sh ip route
Codes: C connected, S static, I IGRP, R RIP, M mobile, B BGP
D EIGRP, EX EIGRP external, O OSPF, IA OSPF inter area
N1 OSPF NSSA external type 1, N2 OSPF NSSA external type 2
E1 OSPF external type 1, E2 OSPF external type 2, E EGP
i IS-IS, L1 IS-IS level-1, L2 IS-IS level-2, * candidate default
U per-user static route, o ODR T traffic engineered route
Gateway of last resort is not set
10.0.0.0/24 is subnetted, 2 subnets
S 10.10.20.0 [1/0] via 10.10.200.1
C 10.10.200.0 is directly connected, FastEthernet0/2
```

routing table code S
The router code for a static route

routing table code C
The router code for specifying a directly connected network

The **sh ip route** command lists a table of codes first, followed by the routes. This listing shows a static route (S) 10.10.20.0 via 10.10.200.1, which indicates that a static route to the destination 10.10.20.0 subnet can be reached via the next hop of 10.10.200.1. The C indicates that the 10.10.200.0 network is directly connected to the FastEthernet02 port.

This simplified network has only one route; therefore, the entries for the static routes using the **ip route** command are limited but were required for each router. Static routes are sometimes used when configuring the routers for routing in a small network. Static routing is not the best choice, as you will learn, but it can be suitable if the network is small (for example, the two-router network). It can be suitable for situations in which there is only one route to the destination, such as a wide area network or Internet feed. This concept is examined in Chapter 10, "Internet Technologies: Out to the Internet."

What about using static routes in the three-router campus network shown in Figure 9-3? A computer in LAN A (10.10.20.0 NET) sends data to a computer in LAN B (10.10.10.0 NET). This is the same requirement specified in the two-router network example. Once again, a static route must be entered into RouterA's routing table telling the router how to forward data to the 10.10.10.0 NET. However, in this example there are two possible choices for a data packet to travel to the 10.10.10.0 NET from RouterA. The IP addresses for the two possible next hops are 10.10.200.2 and 10.10.100.2. The following are the router commands:

```
RouterA(config)#ip route 10.10.10.0 255.255.255.0 10.10.200.2
RouterA(config)#ip route 10.10.10.0 255.255.255.0 10.10.100.2
```

What about sending information from LAN A to LAN C or to LAN D? This requires four additional **ip route** entries into the router's routing table, as shown:

```
RouterA(config)#ip route 10.10.1.0 255.255.255.0 10.10.200.2
RouterA(config)#ip route 10.10.1.0 255.255.255.0 10.10.100.2
RouterA(config)#ip route 10.10.5.0 255.255.255.0 10.10.200.2
RouterA(config)#ip route 10.10.5.0 255.255.255.0 10.10.100.2
```

But wait, we aren't done. We must enter return static routes for all the LANs back to LAN A and then enter the static routes for the other three LANs. For troubleshooting purposes, we want to be able to ping all the Ethernet interfaces on the subnets, so we need to add static IP routes to each subnet (NET). For example, defining a route to the 10.10.150.0 NET, the following are the static IP route entries:

```
RouterA(config)#ip route 10.10.150.0 255.255.255.0 10.10.200.2
RouterA(config)#ip route 10.10.150.0 255.255.255.0 10.10.100.2
```

This means that many static route entries must be made for the routes in this network to be completely defined. This requires a lot of time, and if routes change in the network, new static entries must be made and old static routes must be deleted. The problem with using a static routing protocol in your network is the amount of maintenance required by the network administrator just to keep the route selections up-to-date in a large network. Assume that the network connection uses five router hops. The entries for the static routes on each router are numerous, and if the routes change, the routing tables in all routers must be manually updated to account for the data path changes.

When static routes are used, the network administrator in essence becomes the routing protocol. In other words, the network administrator is making all the decisions regarding data traffic routing. This requires the administrator to know all network data routes, set up the routes to each subnet, and be constantly aware of any route changes. This is in contrast to dynamic routing protocols that communicate routing information between the routers to determine the best route to use to forward the data packets. The concept of a dynamic routing protocol is introduced in section 9-3.

Gateway of Last Resort

One of the most important applications for using a static route is for configuring the **gateway of last resort** on a router. The gateway of last resort is the IP address of the router in your network where data packets with unknown routes should be forwarded. The purpose of this is to configure a route for data packets that do not have a destination route configured in the routing table. In this case, a default route can be configured that instructs the router to forward the data packet(s) with an unknown route to another router. The command for doing this is

```
ip route 0.0.0.0            0.0.0.0            <next hop address>
```

If this static route has not been configured, the router will display the following message when the **show ip route** command is entered:

```
Gateway of last resort is not set
```

This means the router does not know how to route a data packet with a destination IP address that differs from the routes stored in the routing table. This will result in the router dropping the packet to the destination IP address. Without the gateway of last resort, a router will drop any data packets with destination networks that are not in its routing table.

Configuring Static Routes

The following discussion describes how to configure static routes on a Cisco router. The topology being used is the three-router campus network shown in Figure 9-3. This demonstration is for configuring the static routes for RouterA only.

The first step is to connect to the router via a console or virtual terminal connection. Next, enter the privileged EXEC mode as shown:

```
Router con0 is now available Press RETURN to get started!
RouterA>en
RouterA#
```

Next, enter the configure terminal mode on the router [**RouterA(config)#**] using the **configure terminal (conf t)** command. Before configuring the static routes, make sure the interfaces are configured. The FastEthernet0/1 interface is configured with the assigned IP address of 10.10.200.1 and a subnet mask of 255.255.255.0, and the FastEthernet0/2 interface is assigned the 10.10.100.1 IP address and a subnet mask of 255.255.255.0. The **no shut** command is used to enable the FastEthernet ports.

```
RouterA#conf t
Enter configuration commands, one per line. End with CNTL/Z.
RouterA(config)#int fa0/1
RouterA(config-if)#ip address 10.10.200.1 255.255.255.0
RouterA(config-if)#no shut
00:19:07: %LINK-3-UPDOWN: Interface FastEthernet0/1, changed state to
up
RouterA(config)#int fa0/2
RouterA(config-if)#ip address 10.10.100.1 255.255.255.0
RouterA(config-if)#no shut
00:21:05: %LINK-3-UPDOWN: Interface FastEthernet0/2, changed state to
up
```

Notice that the FastEthernet0/1 and FastEthernet0/2 interfaces change state to **up** after the **no shut** command is issued. It is good to verify the interface status using the **show ip interface brief (sh ip int brief)** command as shown.

```
RouterA#sh ip int brief
00:22:18: %SYS-5-CONFIG_I: Configured from console
Interface          IP-Address    OK?   Method Status        Protocol
FastEthernet0/1    10.10.200.1   YES   manual up            down
FastEthernet0/2    10.10.100.1   YES   manual up            down
```

The status for both FastEthernet ports show that they are **up**; however, the line protocol **down** tells us that no physical connection is established between the routers. This problem with the "protocol down" is fixed by reestablishing the physical connection between the routers.

The static routes are entered using the **ip route** command after the interfaces are configured. You don't have to enter all routes at once, but all routes must be properly entered for the network to work. Only the routes to the 10.10.10.0 NET have been listed to shorten the example.

```
RouterA(config)#ip route 10.10.10.0 255.255.255.0 10.10.200.2
RouterA(config)#ip route 10.10.10.0 255.255.255.0 10.10.100.2
```

There are two places to verify whether the static routes are properly configured. First, verify that the routes are in the routing table using either the **show ip route** or the **show ip route static (sh ip route static)** command. Adding the word **static** after **show ip route** limits the routes displayed to only **static**. An important note is that the routes are displayed using the **show ip route** command only if the line protocol is **up**.

> **show ip route static (sh ip route static)**
> Limits the routes displayed to only static

```
RouterA#sh ip route
Codes: C connected, S static, I IGRP, R RIP, M mobile, B BGP
D EIGRP, EX EIGRP external, O OSPF, IA OSPF inter area
N1 OSPF NSSA external type 1, N2 OSPF NSSA external type 2
E1 OSPF external type 1, E2 OSPF external type 2, E EGP
i IS-IS, L1 IS-IS level-1, L2 IS-IS level-2, * candidate default
U per-user static route, o ODR T traffic engineered route
Gateway of last resort is not set
10.0.0.0/24 is subnetted, 2 subnets
S   10.10.10.0 [1/0] via 10.10.200.2
S   10.10.10.0 [1/0] via 10.10.100.2
C   10.10.200.0 is directly connected, FastEthernet0/1
C   10.10.100.0 is directly connected, FastEthernet0/2
```

The command for showing only the static routes is

```
RouterA#sh ip route static
```

The other place to check the routing configuration is by examining the router's running-configuration file using the command **show running-config (sh run)** as shown. The command displays the current configuration of the router, but it does not show what is currently saved in the router's nonvolatile memory (NVRAM). The command **show startup-config (sh start)** displays the router's configuration saved in NVRAM.

> **show running-config (sh run)**
> The command that displays the router's running-configuration
>
> **show startup-config (sh start)**
> The command that displays the router's startup-configuration

```
RouterA#sh run
Using 519 out of 32762 bytes
!
version 12.0
service timestamps debug uptime service timestamps log uptime no
service password-encryption
!
hostname Router
!
!
ip subnet-zero
!
interface FastEthernet0/1
ip address 10.10.200.1 255.255.255.0
no ip directed-broadcast no keepalive
!
interface FastEthernet0/2
ip address 10.10.100.1 255.255.255.0
no ip directed-broadcast no keepalive
!
ip classless
ip route 10.10.10.0 255.255.255.0 10.10.200.2
ip route 10.10.10.0 255.255.255.0 10.10.100.2
!
line con 0
transport input none line aux 0
line vty 0 4
!
end
```

copy run start
The command for copying the running-configuration to the startup-configuration

write memory (wr m)
The command that saves your configuration changes to memory. This is the same as issuing the **copy run start** command, which is the most common command for saving your configuration.

It is important that you save your configuration changes to the router as you go. Save changes to the router configuration using the **copy running-configuration startup-configuration** command (**copy run start**) or **write memory (wr m)** as shown:

```
RouterA#copy run start
RouterA#wr m
```

Table 9-2 in the section that follows shows a summary of the commands used when configuring the static routes.

Networking Challenge: Chapter 9—Static Routes

TABLE 9-2 Summary of Commands Used to Configure the Static Routing Protocol

Command	Use
ip route	Used to specify the destination IP address, the subnet mask, and the next hop IP address
show ip route	Displays the IP routes listed in the routing table
show ip route static	Displays only the static IP routes listed in the routing table
show running-configuration	Displays the router's running-configuration
show startup-configuration	Displays the router's saved configuration in NVRAM
write memory	Copies the current router changes to memory (NVRAM)
copy run start	Copies the current router changes to memory (NVRAM)

Use the Network Challenge software included with the text's companion CD-ROM to demonstrate that you can configure static routes for a router. Place the CD-ROM in your computer's drive. Open the Net-Challenge folder and double-click the *Net-ChallengeV4 .exe* file. Select the **Static Routes** challenge. Use the software to demonstrate that you can complete the following tasks.

This challenge requires you to configure the static routes for RouterA. Do the following:

1. Click the RouterA select button and press Return to get started.

2. Configure the IP address, subnet mask and the default gateway address for computerA1 in LAN A (10.10.20.250). To do so, click the computer A1 icon in LAN topology to bring up the **TCP/IP Properties** menu. Click **OK** on the menu, and press Enter to see the check.

3. Enter the privileged EXEC mode using the password "Chile".

4. Configure the IP addresses for the FastEthernet0/0 and FastEthernet0/1 ports. Note: Click the RouterA symbol in the topology to display the IP addresses and subnet mask for the router.

5. Use the **no shut** command to enable both FastEthernet ports.

6. Use the **show ip int brief** command to view the current interface status.

7. Use the **ip route** command to configure two routes to the 10.10.10.0 subnet (NET). Note: Click the RouterB and RouterC symbols in the network topology to display the IP addresses for the router interfaces. (Use a 255.255.255.0 subnet mask.)

8. Use the **show ip route** command to view whether the routes are entered into the router's routing table.

9. Use the **show run** command to verify whether the static routes are listed in the router's running-configuration.

Section 9-2 Review

This section has covered the following **Network+** Exam objectives.

1.9 Explain the basics of routing concepts and protocols

The use of the next-hop address is demonstrated using the **ip route** *command for configuring a static route. Make sure you fully understand the concept of the destination network and the next-hop address. Also, use the Net-Challenge static route challenge to test your ability in configuring a static route.*

Test Your Knowledge

1. The default gateway specifies which of the following? (Select one.)

    a. Where the data is to be sent when the source address for the data is not in the same subnet or is unknown

    b. Where the data is to be sent when the destination address for the data is in the same subnet or is unknown

    c. Where the data is to be sent when the destination address for the data is not in the same subnet or is unknown

    d. Where the data is to be routed when both the source and the destination addresses for the data is not in the same subnet or is unknown

    e. None of these answers is correct.

2. Which of the following is the generic command for configuring a static route? (select one)

    a. `router(config) ip route <destination> <subnet mask> <next hop          ip address>`

    b. `router(config-static)# ip route <destination> <subnet mask> <next hop ip address>`

    c. `router(config)# router static router(config)# ip route <destination> <subnet mask> <next hop          ip address>`

    d. `router(config)# ip route <destination ip address> <subnet mask>          <next hop ip address>`

    e. `router(config)# ip route <next hop ip address> <subnet mask>          <destination ip address>`

9-3 DYNAMIC ROUTING PROTOCOLS

The concept of configuring a network using a static routing protocol was presented in section 9-2. It became obvious that the time required for entering and maintaining the static routes can be a problem. Therefore, a static routing protocol is of limited use for campus wide network routing but is essential when configuring the default route (gateway of last resort) on routers. However, static routes are used in situations such as configuring small networks with few routes.

This section introduces an improvement over static routing through the use of **dynamic routing protocols**. Dynamic routing protocols enable the router's routing tables to be dynamically updated to account for loss or changes in routes or changes in data traffic. The routers update their routing tables using information obtained from adjacent routers. Table 9-3 defines the features of dynamic routing protocols. The routing protocol is responsible for managing the exchange of routing information between the routers, and the choice of protocol defines how the routing information is exchanged and used.

> **Dynamic Routing Protocols**
> The routing table is dynamically updated to account for loss or changes in routes or changes in data traffic

The primary features of dynamic routing protocols are as follows:

- What information is exchanged between routers
- When updated routing information is exchanged
- Steps for reacting to changes in the network
- Criteria for establishing the best route selection

Four key issues are associated with dynamic routing protocols:

- **Path determination:** A procedure in the protocol that is used to determine the best route.
- **Metric:** A numeric measure assigned to routes for ranking the routes best to worst; the smaller the number, the better.
- **Convergence:** This happens when a router obtains a clear view of the routes in a network. The time it takes for the router to obtain a clear view is called the convergence time.
- **Load balancing:** A procedure in the protocol that enables routers to use any of the multiple data paths available from multiple routers to reach the destination.

Examples of route metrics are as follows:

- **Hop count:** The number of routers the data packet must pass through to reach the destination network.
- **Reliability:** A measure of the reliability of the link, typically in terms of the amount of errors.

- **Bandwidth:** Having to do with the data capacity of the networking link. A Fast-Ethernet 100Mbps link has greater data capacity than a 10Mbps Ethernet link.
- **Delay:** The time it takes for a data packet to travel from source to destination.
- **Cost:** A value assigned by the routing protocol or the network administrator to the link or the interface. Typically, the value is based on the referenced bandwidth.
- **Load:** Having to do with the network activity on a link or router.
- **Ticks:** The measured delay time in terms of clock ticks, where each tick is approximately 55 milliseconds (1/18 second).

There are two types of internal dynamic routing protocols: distance vector and link state. These protocols are briefly introduced in sections 9-4 and 9-5. Another concept related to metrics is **administrative distance.** Administrative distance is a feature used by routing protocols to select the best path when more than one path is available. For example, let's assume there are two network routes. One is an OSPF route, and the other is EIGRP. The OSPF route has an administrative distance of 110, whereas EIGRP has an administrative distance of 90. The EIGRP route will be selected as the preferred route. Table 9-3 provides a short list of administrative distances for common routing protocols.

TABLE 9-3   **A List of Administrative Distances for Common Routing Protocols**

Routing Protocol	Default Distance Values
connected	0
Static	1
EIGRP	90
OSPF	110
RIP	120

Section 9-3 Review

This section has covered the following **Network+** Exam objectives.

1.9 Explain the basics of routing concepts and protocols

Various routing metrics are introduced in this section, including hop counts, bandwidth, cost, latency, and administrative distance. Understanding these metrics is important when planning routing for a network.

Test Your Knowledge

1. What is a metric?

   a. A numeric measure assigned to routes for ranking the routes best to worst; the larger the number, the better.

   b. A numeric measure assigned to routes for ranking the routes best to worst; the smaller the number, the better.

   c. A numeric measure assigned to routes for ranking the routes best to worst; number equal to 100 indicate the best route.

   d. A numeric measure assigned to routes for ranking the routes best to worst; the number indicates the ticks.

2. What is a hop count?

   a. A value typically assigned by the network administrator that takes into account bandwidth and expense.

   b. The number of routers the data packet must pass through to reach the destination network.

   c. Having to do with the data capacity of the networking link; a Fast-Ethernet 100Mbps link has greater data capacity than a 10Mbps Ethernet link.

   d. The measured delay time in terms of clock ticks, where each tick is approximately 55 milliseconds (1/18 second).

9-4 DISTANCE VECTOR PROTOCOLS

A **distance vector protocol** is a routing algorithm that periodically sends the entire routing table to its neighboring or adjacent router. When the neighboring router receives the table, it assigns a distance vector number to each route. The distance vector number is typically specified by some metric such as hop count.

In a distance vector protocol, the router first determines its neighbors or adjacent routers. All the connected routes will have a distance or hop count of 0 as illustrated in Figure 9-5. Routers use the hop count metric to determine the best route to forward a data packet. Figure 9-6 provides an example of determining the hop count to a destination subnet.

> **Distance Vector Protocol**
> A routing algorithm that periodically sends the entire routing table to its neighboring or adjacent router

10.10.10.0   10.10.20.0

B

A   C

neighbor   neighbor
router   router
(hop count = 0)   (hop count = 0)

FIGURE 9-5 An example of router neighbors (hop count = 0).

RouterA

10.10.200.0 NET   10.10.50.0 NET

10.10.150.0 NET
RouterB   RouterC

	Hop Count	
From:	To:	Hop Count
Router A	10.10.200.0	0
Router A	10.10.150.0	1
Router A	010.10.50.0	2

FIGURE 9-6 An example of determining the router hops.

The hop count from RouterA to the 10.10.200.0, 10.10.150.0, and 10.10.50.0 subnets are as follows:

From	To	Hop Count
RouterA	10.10.200.0	0
RouterA	10.10.150.0	1
RouterA	10.10.50.0	2

In a distance vector protocol, each router determines its neighbors, builds its list of neighboring routers, and sends its routing table to its neighbors. The neighboring routers update their routing table based on the received information. When complete, each router's routing table provides a list of known routes within the network.

Routing Information Protocol (**RIP**) is a dynamic routing protocol, meaning the routers periodically exchange routes. RIP is classified as a distance vector protocol using router hop count as the metric. RIP permits a maximum of 15 hops to prevent **routing loops**. Routing loops occur when a router forwards packets back to the router that sent them, as graphically shown in Figure 9-7. RIP and other distance vector routing protocols send the entire routing table to neighbor routers at regular time intervals. Sometimes the routing tables can be quite large and the transfer can consume network bandwidth. This is of great concern in networks with limited bandwidth because the periodic exchange can lead to slowdowns in data traffic. The default time interval for RIP for exchanging routing tables is 30 seconds. This results in slow route convergence, and if multiple routers are sharing RIP routes, there will be even longer convergence time.

FIGURE 9-7 An example of data packet travel in a routing loop. Note that the packets never leave the routes between the two routers.

RIP is a relatively simple routing protocol to configure. However, RIP is good only for very small networks that have a limited staff size to manage the network and is not suited for networks that need fast convergence. RIP is a standard protocol, not a proprietary protocol—meaning the use of the protocol is not limited to certain equipment manufacturers. Section 9-7 examines the procedures for configuring a router to use the RIP and RIP V2 dynamic routing protocol.

Section 9-4 Review

This section has covered the following **Network+** Exam objectives.

1.9 Explain the basics of routing concepts and protocols

This section introduced the concept of the distance vector protocol.

Test Your Knowledge

1. RIP is classified as which of the following?

   a. Distance vector protocol

   b. Dynamic routing protocol

   c. Link state protocol

   d. Both a and c

   e. Both a and b

   f. Both b and c

2. When does a routing loop occur?

    a. Routing loops occur if the cost of a route is too low.

    b. Routing loops occur if the cost of a route is too high.

    c. Routing loops occur when a router forwards packets back to the router that sent them.

    d. Routing loops occur only when static routing is used.

9-5 CONFIGURING RIP AND RIPV2

Advertise
The sharing of route information

Class Network Address
The network portion of the IP address based on the class of the network

Classful Addressing
The network portion of a particular network address

The RIP routing protocol is enabled on the router by entering the command **router rip** at the **Router(config)#** prompt in the privileged EXEC mode. Next, **network** statements are required to declare which networks will be advertised by the RIP routing protocol. To **advertise** the network means the routing table containing the network is shared with its neighbors. The **network** command requires the use of a **class network address** (class A, class B, class C) after the **network** command. This is called **classful addressing**. A class network address or classful address is the network portion of the address for the particular class of the network. For example, LAN A in our campus network is on the 10.10.20.0 NET, as shown in Figure 9-8. This is a class A network, and the network portion of the address is 10.0.0.0. The structure of the network command is **network** *[network address]*, where the *network address* is the network where RIP is to be advertised; therefore, the command in RIP will be **network 10.0.0.0**.

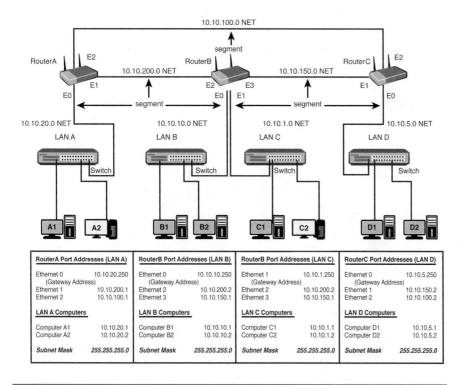

FIGURE 9-8 LAN A in the campus network.

The following discussion explains how to initialize RIP and how to set the networks attached to the router. After these commands are entered, any interfaces that are part of the 10.0.0.0 network will run the RIP routing protocol. Note that subnets or subnet masks are not specified in the RIP network command because the class network address is used and all IP addresses in the network (for example, 10.0.0.0) are enabled to use RIP.

```
Router(config)#router rip
Router(config-router)#network 10.0.0.0
```

RIP can be used only in **contiguous networks**, meaning the networks and routes must have the same class network address. This means the router addresses for the network connecting the routers must be the same class as the LAN connected to the router. This is shown in Figure 9-9(a) and (b). LAN A and B have a 10.#.#.# address (also called a *10 network* address). The network address connecting the two routers must also be a "10" network address. The IP address for the network connecting the two routers in Figure 9-9(a) is 10.10.200.0. This is a "10" network address. The network shown in Figure 9-9(b) uses the IP address of 192.168.10.0 for the network connecting the two routers. An address of 192.168.10.0 is in the 192.168.10.0 network. This is not part of the 10.0.0.0 network; therefore, the 192.168.10.0 address is not suitable for use in RIP.

> **contiguous network**
> means the networks and routes must have the same class network address

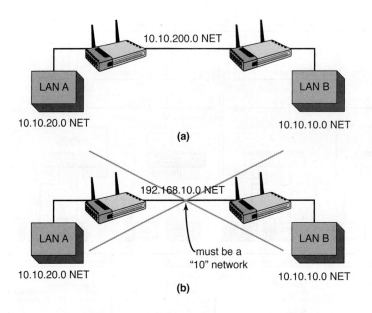

FIGURE 9-9   An example of (a) a contiguous network and (b) a discontiguous network.

Configuring Routes with RIP

The first step in configuring the router for RIP is to set up the interfaces. This includes assigning an IP address and a subnet mask to the interface using the command **ip address** *A.B.C.D. subnet-mask*. Next, the interface is enabled using the **no shut** command. The following are the steps for configuring the FastEthernet0/0 and FastEthernet 0/1 interfaces on RouterA in the campus network shown previously in Figure 9-9:

```
Router con0 is now available
Press RETURN to get started.
RouterA>en
Password:
RouterA#conf t
Enter configuration commands, one per line. End with CNTL/Z.
RouterA(config)#int fa0/0
RouterA(config-if)#ip address 10.10.20.250 255.255.255.0
RouterA(config-if)#no shut
00:59:03: %LINEPROTO-5-UPDOWN: Line protocol on Interface
FastEthernet1, changed state to up Router(config)#int fa0/1
RouterA(config-if)#ip address 10.10.200.1 255.255.255.0
RouterA(config-if)#no shut
00:59:03: %LINEPROTO-5-UPDOWN: Line protocol on Interface
FastEthernet1, changed state to up
```

Next, enter the router's configuration mode [**RouterA(config)#**] and input the command **router rip** to use RIP as the routing protocol. The next step is to specify the network that uses RIP for routing. These two steps are shown next:

```
RouterA(config)#router rip
RouterA(config-router)#network 10.0.0.0
```

The command **router rip** enables the RIP routing protocol, and the command
network 10.0.0.0 instructs the router to use RIP on the "10" network. Remember,
RIP requires the use of a class network address (for example, 10.0.0.0). Notice that
the **router rip** command places the router in the **(config-router)** mode, as shown in
the prompt. This indicates that the router is in the state for specifying the networks
using RIP.

It's a good idea to periodically check that the router interfaces are properly configured. The command **show ip interface brief (sh ip int brief)** is used to check the
interfaces. This is an important troubleshooting command when looking for reasons
the router is not working. Use this command to check whether the IP address has
been assigned to the interface and to check the status and protocol settings. In this
case, the FastEthernet0/1 port has been assigned the IP address 10.10.200.1, the
status is *up*, and the protocol is *up*. The FastEthernet 0/2 port for RouterA have not
been configured, as shown; the status is administratively down; and the protocol is
down:

```
RouterA#sh ip int brief
Interface       IP-Address      OK?  Method  Status                  Protocol
FastEthernet 0/0 10.10.20.250   YES  manual  up                      up
FastEthernet 0/1 10.10.200.1    YES  manual  up                      up
FastEthernet 0/2 unassigned     YES  unset   administratively  down down
```

The command **show ip protocol (show ip protocol)** is used to display the routing
protocols running on the router, as shown. This command will display protocol
information only after the routing protocol has been enabled and the network addresses are specified. Notice that there are no values specified for the FastEther-
net0/0 and FastEthernet0/2 ports. Neither of these interfaces has been configured.
The **show ip protocol** command also shows that router updates are being sent every
30 seconds and indicates that the next update is due in 5 seconds.

> **show ip protocol (sh ip protocol)**
> Displays the routing protocol running on the router

```
RouterA#sh ip protocol
Routing Protocol is "rip"
Sending updates every 30 seconds, next due in 5 seconds
Invalid after 180 seconds, hold down 180, flushed after 240
Outgoing update filter list for all interfaces is Incoming update fil-
ter list for all interfaces is Redistributing: rip
Default version control: send version 1, receive any version
Interface                                Send Recv Key-chain
FastEthernet0/0            1             1       2
FastEthernet0/1           1              1       2
FastEthernet0/2           0              0       0
Routing for Networks:
10.0.0.0
Routing Information Sources:
Gateway Distance Last Update
10.10.200.2 120 00:00:14
Distance: (default is 120)
```

The routes configured for the router can be displayed using the **show ip route (sh ip route)** command as shown. In this example, the FastEthernet0/0, FastEthernet 0/0 and FastEthernet0/1 ports for RouterA have been configured and are displayed as connected networks:

```
RouterA#sh ip route
Codes: C—connected, S—static, I—IGRP, R—RIP, M—mobile, B—BGP D—EIGRP,
EX—EIGRP external, O—OSPF, IA—OSPF inter area
N1—OSPF NSSA external type 1, N2—OSPF NSSA external type 2
E1—OSPF external type 1, E2—OSPF external type 2, E—EGP
I—IS-IS, L1—IS-IS level-1, L2—IS-IS level-2, * candidate default
U—per-user static route, o—ODR T—traffic engineered route
Gateway of last resort is not set
10.0.0.0/24 is subnetted, 1 subnets
C 10.10.20.0 is directly connected, FastEthernet0/0
C 10.10.200.0 is directly connected, FastEthernet0/1
```

This table shows the connected networks, but RIP (R) is not enabled for any networks. Why? At this point, RIP has been enabled only on RouterA in the campus network. RouterB and RouterC also need to have RIP enabled. Use the commands **router rip** and **network** to enable RIP on RouterB. RIP was next configured on RouterB and the updated routing table for RouterA is provided:

```
Router#sh ip route
Codes: C—connected, S—static, I—IGRP, R—RIP, M—mobile, B—BGP D—EIGRP,
  EX—EIGRP external, O—OSPF, IA—OSPF inter area
N1—OSPF NSSA external type 1, N2—OSPF NSSA external type 2
E1—OSPF external type 1, E2—OSPF external type 2, E—EGP
I—IS-IS, L1—IS-IS level-1, L2—IS-IS level-2, * candidate default
U—per-user static route, o—ODR T—traffic engineered route
Gateway of last resort is not set
10.0.0.0/24 is subnetted, 5 subnets
R 10.10.1.0 [120/1] via 10.10.200.2, 00:00:05, FastEthernet0/1
R 10.10.10.0 [120/1] via 10.10.200.2, 00:00:05, FastEthernet0/1
C 10.10.20.0 is directly connected, FastEthernet0/0
C 10.10.200.0 is directly connected, FastEthernet0/1
```

Now, the networks (10.10.10.0 and 10.10.1.0) from LAN B and LAN C, respectively, are shown in this table. RouterA learns these network routes via its FastEthernet0/1 from the IP address 10.10.200.2, which is the FastEthernet0/2 interface of RouterB.

Verify the settings in the running-configuration file by using the **sh run** command. Recall that this is the abbreviated command for **show running-configuration**. The configuration list should show that the interfaces have been assigned an IP address and that RIP has been configured. Table 9-4 provides some commented output from the **sh run** command.

TABLE 9-4   sh run Command Output

CLI	Comments
RouterA#sh run	! 1. sh run command
Building configuration	! 2. assembling the data file
!	! 3. ! is used for spaces or comments
Current configuration:	
version 12.0	! 6. displays the Cisco IOS version
service timestamps debug uptime	
service timestamps log uptime	
no service password-encryption	! 9. the enable (line 14) and vty (line 42) passwords appear as plaintext
!	
hostname RouterA	! 11. the name of the router
!	
enable secret 5 $1$6EWO$kWlakDz89zac.koh/pyG4.	! 13. the encrypted enable secret
enable password Salsa	! 14. the enable password
!	
ip subnet-zero	! 16. enables subnet zero routing
!	
interface FastEthernet0/0 ip address 10.10.20.0 255.255.255.0 no ip directed-broadcast	! 18. FastEthernet0/0 settings
!	
interface FastEthernet0/1 ip address 10.10.200.1 255.255.255.0 no ip directed-broadcast no mop enabled	! 22. FastEthernet0/1 settings
!	
interface FastEthernet0/2 ip address 10.10.100.1 255.255.255.0 no ip directed-broadcast no mop enabled	! 27. FastEthernet0/2 settings
!	
router rip	! 33. enable RIP
network 10.0.0.0	! 34. specify a network class address
!	
ip classless	

CLI	Comments
!	
line con 0	
transport input none	
line aux 0	
line vty 0 4	! 41. virtual terminal settings for telnet
password ConCarne	! 42. telnet password
!	login
end	

Lines 18, 22, and 27 list the assigned IP addresses for the interface. Lines 33 and 34 show that RIP has been configured for the router. The **sh run** command displays the router's running configuration. The **copy run start** command must be entered to save to NVRAM the changes made to the router's configuration.

RIP is among the oldest protocols; it was introduced in 1988. It has a number of limitations that makes it inefficient in handling a lot of newer IP features. Some of its limitations are as follows:

- **RIP is a classful routing only protocol**: It therefore does not support VLSM and CIDR. This prevents it from being the routing protocol of choice when having to deal with different sized subnets in a network.

- **RIP does not support router authentication**: As a result, this can be exploited as vulnerability.

- **RIP has a hop count limit of 15**: Means a destination that is 15 hops away is considered to be unreachable.

- **RIP uses hop count as a metric**: RIP determines the best route by counting the number of hops to reach the destination. A lower hop count wins over the higher hop count. This is a disadvantage when dealing with different bandwidth between hops. RIP does not take into consideration whether the higher hop count route might have higher bandwidth. Therefore, the lower bandwidth route could be taken.

The following example demonstrates one of RIP's limitations. In this example, the subnet mask of the LAN C network will be changed to 255.255.255.128. To accomplish this task, the FastEthernet 0/1 interface for the RouterB needs to be reconfigured as follow:

```
RouterB# conf t
Enter configuration commands, one per line. End with CNTL/Z.
RouterB(config)#int fa0/1
RouterB(config-if)#ip address 10.10.1.250 255.255.255.128
```

Because RIP does not support VLSM, what will happen to the newly reconfigured subnet? The answer is that the network 10.10.1.0 will not be advertised by RIP. The route for network 10.10.1.0 is not displayed in the routing table of the RouterA as shown with the command **sh ip route**.

```
RouterA#sh ip route
Codes: C—connected, S—static, I—IGRP, R—RIP, M—mobile, B—BGP D—EIGRP,
EX—EIGRP external, O—OSPF, IA—OSPF inter area
N1—OSPF NSSA external type 1, N2—OSPF NSSA external type 2
E1—OSPF external type 1, E2—OSPF external type 2, E—EGP
I—IS-IS, L1—IS-IS level-1, L2—IS-IS level-2, * candidate default
U—per-user static route, o—ODR T—traffic engineered route
Gateway of last resort is not set
10.0.0.0/24 is subnetted, 5 subnets
R 10.10.10.0 [120/1] via 10.10.200.2, 00:00:05, FastEthernet0/1
C 10.10.20.0 is directly connected, FastEthernet0/0
C 10.10.200.0 is directly connected, FastEthernet0/1
```

To address some of RIP's limitations, the second version of RIP was developed as RIP version 2 (RIPv2) in 1993. The original version of RIP is then called RIP version 1 (RIPv1). RIPv2 is not quite a redesign RIPv1; it could be thought more of an enhanced version of RIP version 1. RIPv2 works basically just like RIPv1. It introduced new features such as support for VLSM and CIDR, router authentication, next hop specification, route tag, and the use of multicasting. However, it still cannot resolve the hop count and metric decision limitations of RIPv1.

Configuring Routes with RIP Version 2

The steps needed to configure RIPv2 are almost exactly the same as configuring RIPv1. The only difference is the version must be specified in the **router rip** configuration. Let's take the RIP configuration that was done earlier in this segment and then enter the router's configuration mode [**Router(config)#**] and input the command **router rip** to use the RIP routing protocol. The next step is to configure RIPv2 to be used with the command **version 2.** Without specifying the version, RIPv1 will be used by default. These two steps are shown next:

```
RouterA(config)#router rip
RouterA(config-router)#version 2
```

To verify that RIPv2 is the routing protocol, use the **sh ip protocol** command. Notice the line **Default version control**—it is confirmed that RIP version 2 is being sent as well as being received by the RouterA. The rest of the information shown is similar to the protocol result of RIP version 1.

```
RouterA#sh ip protocol
Routing Protocol is "rip"
Sending updates every 30 seconds, next due in 17 seconds
Invalid after 180 seconds, hold down 180, flushed after 240
Outgoing update filter list for all interfaces is not set
Incoming update filter list for all interfaces is not set
Redistributing: rip
Default version control: send version 2, receive version 2
  Interface                      Send Recv Triggered RIP Key-chain
  FastEthernet0/0                 2      2
```

```
FastEthernet0/1                                    2          2
FastEthernet0/2                                    2          2
Automatic network summarization is in effect
Maximum path: 4
Routing for Networks:
10.0.0.0
Routing Information Sources:
Gateway                              Distance            Last Update
10.10.200.2                             120                00:00:20
Distance: (default is 120)
```

Now, let's reexamine the previous demonstration of RIPv1 limitation where the VLSM was being used, where the subnet mask for the network 10.10.1.0 was changed to 255.255.255.128. This resulted in the network no longer showing up in the routing table. The same command **version 2** needs to be applied under **router rip** on RouterB. With RIP version 2 enabled, the command **sh ip route** is reissued at the RouterA. This time, the routing table shows the LAN C network 10.10.1.128/25 is being displayed, even though it has a different sized subnet than the others.

```
RouterA#sh ip route
Codes: C—connected, S—static, I—IGRP, R—RIP, M—mobile, B—BGP D—EIGRP,
  EX—EIGRP external, O—OSPF, IA—OSPF inter area
N1—OSPF NSSA external type 1, N2—OSPF NSSA external type 2
E1—OSPF external type 1, E2—OSPF external type 2, E—EGP
I—IS-IS, L1—IS-IS level-1, L2—IS-IS level-2, * candidate default
U—per-user static route, o—ODR T—traffic engineered route
Gateway of last resort is not set
10.0.0.0/24 is subnetted, 5 subnets
R 10.10.10.0 [120/1] via 10.10.200.2, 00:00:05, FastEthernet0/1
C 10.10.20.0 is directly connected, FastEthernet0/0
R 10.10.1.128/25 [120/1] via 10.10.200.2, 00:00:15, FastEthernet0/1
C 10.10.200.0 is directly connected, FastEthernet0/1
```

Networking Challenge—RIP V2

Use the router simulator software included with the text's companion CD-ROM to demonstrate that you can configure RIP for RouterA in the campus LAN. (*Note:* The campus LAN is shown in Figure 9-8 and is displayed on the computer screen after the software is started and you click on "View Topology".) Place the CD-ROM in your computer's drive. Open the *Net-Challenge* folder, and click **Net-ChallengeV4.exe.** When the software is running, click the **Select Challenge** button to open a **Select Challenge** drop-down menu. Select **Chapter 9 - RIP V2**. This opens a checkbox that can be used to verify that you have completed all the tasks:

1. Enter the privileged EXEC mode on the router (password "Chile").

2. Enter the router configuration mode, **Router(config)**.

3. Configure the FastEthernet0/0 interface with the following:
   - IP address 10.10.20.250
   - Subnet mask 255.255.255.0

4. Enable the FA0/0 interface.

5. Configure the FastEthernet0/1 interface with the following:
   - IP address 10.10.200.1
   - Subnet mask 255.255.255.0

6. Enable the FA0/1 interface.

7. Configure the FastEthernet0/2 interface with the following:
   - IP address 10.10.100.1
   - Subnet mask 255.255.255.0

8. Enable the FA0/2 interface.

9. Enable RIPv2.

   a. Specify that RIP version 2 is to be used.

   b. Use the **network** command to specify the class network address to be used by RIP (10.0.0.0).

   c. Use the **sh ip int brief** command to check the interface status.

   d. Use the **sh ip protocol** command to see whether RIP is running. (Note: This requires that steps 9 and 10 are complete; otherwise, the response will be "no protocol.")

   e. Use the **show ip route** command to verify whether the three FastEthernet ports are connected to the router.

   f. Display the contents of the **running-configuration** file. Verify that RIP is enabled and the proper network address is specified.

   g. Copy the router's running-configuration to the startup configuration.

   h. Display the contents of the startup configuration.

Section 9-5 Review

This section has covered the following **Network+** Exam objectives.

   1.3 Install and configure the following networking services/applications

This section introduced the dynamic routing protocol RIP.

   1.9 Explain the basics of routing concepts and protocols

The steps for configuring RIP routing were introduced. Use the Net-Challenge exercise to verify your understanding of using the commands to configure RIP and RIPv2 routing.

9-6 LINK STATE PROTOCOLS

Link State Protocol

Establishes a relationship with a neighboring router and uses route advertisements to build routing tables

Link state protocols establish a relationship with a neighboring router. The routers exchange link state advertisements to update neighbors regarding route status. The link state advertisements are sent only if there is a change or loss in the network routes and the link state protocols converge to route selection quickly. This is a distinct advantage over distance vector protocols that exchange updated routing tables at fixed time intervals and are slow to converge. In fact, link state routing protocols are replacing distance vector protocols. Link state protocols are also called *shortest-path first protocols,* based on the algorithm developed by E. W. Dijkstra. Link state protocols use "Hello" packets to verify that communication is still established with neighbor routers.

The key issues of link state protocols are summarized as follows:

- Finds neighbors/adjacencies
- Uses route advertisements to build routing table
- Sends "Hello" packets
- Sends updates when routing changes

OSPF

Open Shortest Path First routing protocol

Open Shortest Path First (**OSPF**) is a dynamic routing protocol, classified as a link state protocol. It was developed by the Interior Gateway Protocol (IGP) working group for the Internet Engineering Task Force (**IETF**) specifically for use in TCP/IP networks. OSPF is an open, not proprietary, protocol and is supported by many vendors. The main advantages of OSPF are rapid convergence and the consumption of very little bandwidth. When a network is completely *converged*, all the routers in the network agree on the best routes. After the initial flooding of routes in the form of **link state advertisements (LSAs)**, OSPF sends route updates only when there is a change in the network. Every time LSAs are sent, each router must recalculate the routing table.

This is a distinct advantage over RIP. Recall that RIP exchanges the entire routing table at fixed time intervals. RIP updates every 30 seconds. Also, in RIP, the routing table update is propagated through the network at regular timer intervals, and therefore the convergence to final routes is slow. In OSPF, an LSA is sent as soon as the loss of a route has been detected. The loss is immediately reported to neighbor routers, and new routes are calculated much faster than with RIP.

OSPF sends small **"Hello" packets** at regular time intervals to adjacent routers to verify that the link between two routers is active and the routers are communicating. If a router fails to respond to a "Hello," it is assumed that the link or possibly the router is down.

OSPF uses the concept of **areas** to partition a large network into smaller networks. The advantage of this is that the routers have to calculate routes only for their area. If a route goes down in a given area, only the routers in that area have to calculate new routes. Any number between 0 and 4294967295 (2^{32}—1) can be used; however, area 0 is reserved for the root area, which is the **backbone** for the network. The backbone is the primary path for data traffic to and from destinations and sources in the campus network. All areas must connect to area 0, and area 0 cannot be split. The area numbers can also be expressed in IP notation—for example, area 0 could be 0.0.0.0—or you can specify an area as 192.168.25.0 or in subnet notation. Hence the need for the large upper area number. (2^{32}—1) = 255.255.255.255 when converted to a decimal number.

OSPF allows the use of **variable length subnet masks (VLSMs)**, which enable different size subnets in the network to better meet the needs of the network and more efficiently use the network's limited IP address space. For example, point-to-point inter-router links don't need a large block of addresses assigned to them. An example of an inter-router link is shown in Figure 9-10.

FA0/0   FA0/1
10.10.250.1/30   10.10.250.2/30

255.255.255.252 Subnet Mask
10.10.250.0 Network Address
10.10.250.3 Broadcast Address
10.10.250.0 Subnet

FIGURE 9-10 An inter-router link subnetted to provide for two host IP address, a network address, and a broadcast address.

IETF
Internet Engineering Task Force

Link State Advertisement (LSA)
The exchange of updated link state information when routes change

"Hello" Packets
Used in the OSPF protocol to verify that the links are still communicating

Areas
The partition of a large OSPF network into smaller OSPF networks

Backbone
The primary path for data traffic to and from destinations and sources in the campus network

Variable Length Subnet Masks (VLSM)
Allows the use of subnet masks to better fit the needs of the network, thereby minimizing the waste of IP addresses when interconnecting subnets

A subnet of size 4 is sufficient for the inter-router link that includes the IP addresses for the router interfaces, the network address, and the broadcast address. A subnet mask of 255.255.255.252 meets this requirement of a subnet size 4 and is permissible in OSPF. This subnet mask provides for the addressing of the two host addresses (the router interfaces on each end) and the network and broadcast addresses, which provides the total subnet size of 4. (Refer to Chapter 6, "TCP/IP," to review subnet masking if needed.) This is an important advantage of OSPF because using variable-length subnet masks minimizes the waste of IP addresses when interconnecting subnets. Table 9-5 summarizes the advantages and disadvantages of OSPF.

TABLE 9-5 **Summary of Advantages and Disadvantages of OSPF**

Advantages	Disadvantages
Not proprietary—available for use by all vendors.	Can be very complicated to implement.
Link state changes are immediately reported, which enables rapid convergence.	Is process intensive due to routing table calculations.
Consumes very little network bandwidth.	Intermittent routes that are going up and down will create excessive LSA updates—this is called **route flapping**.
Uses variable length subnet masking (VLSM).	
Uses areas to partition the network into smaller networks, minimizing the number of route calculations.	

Route Flapping
Intermittent routes going up and down creating excessive LSA updates

IS-IS
Intermediate System to Intermediate System

Another link state protocol is Intermediate System to Intermediate System (**IS-IS**). This link state protocol was developed by the Digital Equipment Corporation for its DECnet phase V. Later, it was adopted by International Organization for Standardization (ISO) around the same time that the IETF was developing OSPF. The term *intermediate system* refers to a router. Even though IS-IS is not as well known as its counterpart OSPF, it is still being used largely in many service provider core networks.

There are many similarities between IS-IS and OSPF. They both use the link state protocol with the Dijkstra algorithm. They both are classless protocols, which enable the support of variable length subnet mask. They both use Hello packets to form and maintain adjacencies and both use the area concept. However, there is a difference in the way in which the areas are defined. In IS-IS, there are two hierarchical topology areas: level 1 (Intra-area) and level 2 (Inter-area). A router can either be a level 1 (L1) router, a level 2 (L2) router, or both (L1/L2) router. L1 routers are analogous to OSPF non-backbone routers, L2 routers are analogous to OSPF backbone routers, and L1/L2 routers are analogous to OSPF area border routers (ABR). Unlike OSPF ABRs, L1/L2 routers do not advertise routes from L2 routers to L1 routers. The packets from different areas can only be routed through the L1/L2 routers. Essentially, L1/L2 routers are default gateways to L1 routers. Another big difference is that the IS-IS backbone area can be segmented. Unlike the backbone area in OSPF, all routers in area 0 must be connected; the IS-IS L2 routers do not need to be connected directly together.

IS-IS was originally designed as part of the Open System Interconnection (OSI) network layer service called Connectionless Network Service (CLNS). This means that IS-IS is designed to work on the same network layer just like IP; therefore, it does not require IP protocol for it to function. Later, it was adapted to work with IP. Hence, it is sometimes referred to as *integrated* IS-IS. In IS-IS, every router uses the Network Entity Title (**NET**) to define its process. The NET address is unique to each router; it is comprised of the following components in hexadecimal format:

> **NET**
> In ISIS, this is the Network Entity Title

- The Area ID in IS-IS is analogous to OSPF area number, and it is used by L2 routers.
- The System ID is analogous to the OSPF router ID, and it is used by L1 routers.
- The Network Service Access Point Selector (NSEL) identifies the network service type.

The NET address can look intimidating due to its long hexadecimal format, but it is not as bad as it seems. The way to work with a NET address is to start from right and work left. For example, in a NET address of 49.0001.0014.a909.5201.00, the last 1 byte from the right is NSEL, which is always set to 00 on a router. The next 6 bytes separated into 3 groups of 2 bytes are the system ID, which is 0014. a909.5201 in this example. This is always unique and is typically represented as the MAC address of the router. The rest to the left of the System ID is the Area ID, which is 49.0001. The Area ID has a variable length, but its first number must be at least 1 byte long.

Section 9-6 Review

This section has covered the following **Network+** Exam objectives.

> 1.9 Explain the basics of routing concepts and protocols

The basics of the link state protocols, OSPF, and IS-IS were introduced. Remember the purpose of link state advertisements and how this technique speeds up route selection. Also, make sure you understand the purpose of the "Hello" packets.

Test Your Knowledge

1. Which of the following are key issues of link state protocols? (Select all that apply.)

   a. Finds neighbors/adjacencies

   b. Sends "Hello" packets

   c. Sends updates when routing changes

   d. Can be used to minimize route flapping

2. What is the purpose of a "Hello" packet?

    a. It is used to partition a large network into smaller networks.

    b. It verifies that the link between two routers is active and the routers are communicating.

    c. This enables variable-length subnet masking.

    d. It is assigned to a protocol or route to declare its reliability.

9-7 CONFIGURING THE OPEN SHORTEST PATH FIRST (OSPF) ROUTING PROTOCOL

This section describes a procedure for configuring OSPF on a router. The first example is for configuring the three routers in the campus LAN shown in Figure 9-11. The routers will be configured to run OSPF on each of the router's three Ethernet interfaces. The example begins with configuring RouterA. RouterA must first be placed in the router's configuration mode (**Router(config)#**), as shown here:

```
RouterA#conf t
Enter configuration commands, one per line. End with CNTL/Z.
RouterA(config)#
```

The next step is to enter the information about the IP address for each of the Ethernet interfaces. The IP addresses for RouterA are as follows:

- FastEthernet0/0: 10.10.20.250
- FastEthernet0/1: 10.10.200.1
- FastEthernet0/2: 10.10.100.1

A subnet mask of 255.255.255.0 is assigned to each of the FastEthernet interfaces. After the FastEthernet interfaces are configured, verify the configuration settings using the **sh ip int brief** command, as shown. Make sure the status for the FastEthernet interfaces are *up*. This indicates that the interfaces are turned on and an Ethernet networking device is connected. The protocol will show *down* until the Ethernet cable is connected and the connecting interface is enabled. In this case, the connecting interfaces to FA0/1 and FA0/2 are not enabled and therefore show a status of *down*.

```
RouterA#sh ip int brief
Interface       IP-Address     OK?  Method  Status  Protocol
FastEthernet0/0 10.10.20.250   YES  manual  up      up
FastEthernet0/1 10.10.200.1    YES  manual  up      down
FastEthernet0/2 10.10.100.1    YES  manual  up      down
```

10.10.100.0 Net

segment

FA0/2 Router A   Router B   Router C FA0/2

10.10.200.0 Net   10.10.150.0 Net

FA0/1   FA0/2   FA0/3   FA0/1

FA0/0   FA0/0 FA0/1   FA0/0

segment   segment

10.10.20.0 Net   10.10.10.0 Net   10.10.1.0 Net   10.10.5.0 Net

LAN A   LAN B   LAN C   LAN D

Switch   Switch   Switch   Switch

A1   A2   B1   B2   C1   C1   D1   D2

LAN A Server   LAN C Server

Router A Port Addresses (LAN A)		Router B Port Addresses (LAN B)		Router B Port Addresses (LAN C)		Router Port Addresses (LAN D)	
FastEthernet 0/0 (Gateway Address)	10.10.20.250	FastEthernet 0/0 (Gateway Address)	10.10.10.250	FastEthernet 0/1 (Gateway Address)	10.10.1.250	FastEthernet 0/0 (Gateway Address)	10.10.5.250
FastEthernet 0/1	10.10.200.1	FastEthernet 0/2	10.10.200.2	FastEthernet 0/2	10.10.200.2	FastEthernet 0/1	10.10.150.2
FastEthernet 0/2	10.10.100.1	FastEthernet 0/3	10.10.150.1	FastEthernet 0/3	10.10.150.1	FastEthernet 0/2	10.10.100.2
LAN A Computers		**LAN B Computers**		**LAN C Computers**		**LAN D Computers**	
Computer A1	10.10.20.1	Computer B1	10.10.10.1	Computer C1	10.10.1.1	Computer D1	10.10.5.1
Computer A2	10.10.20.2	Computer B2	10.10.10.2	Computer C2	10.10.1.2	Computer D2	10.10.5.2
Subnet Mask	*255.255.255.0*	*Subnet Mask*	*255.255.255.0*	*Subnet Mask*	*255.255.255.0*	*Subnet Mask*	*255.255.255.0*

FIGURE 9-11   The three-router campus LAN.

Next, the command **router ospf** *<process id>* is used to enable OSPF routing. In this case, the command **router ospf 100** is entered. The 100 is the *process ID num-ber*. This number must be the same on each router for OSPF to exchange routes. The process ID number is selected by the network administrator and is not used for routing outside the network. It is customary to use the same process ID throughout the network for ease of management, but it is not required. Entering the **router ospf 100** command places the router in the **RouterA(config-router)#** prompt:

> **router ospf [*number*]**
> The command used to enable OSPF routing

```
RouterA(config)#router ospf 100
RouterA(config-router)#
```

The next step is to define the network running OSPF by entering the **network** com-mand followed by the IP address of the interface, the OSPF wildcard bits, and then an area number. The following text shows each step and lists the results of entering a question mark as the command is entered. When you are entering the command **network ?**, the router prompts you to enter the IP address of the interface.

```
RouterA(config-router)#network ?
A.B.C.D Network number
```

A.B.C.D is the IP address, or **network number**, for the Ethernet interface. Next, entering **network 10.10.20.250 ?** prompts you to enter the OSPF wildcard bits in the form of A.B.C.D. The **wildcard bits**, also called the *inverse mask bits,* are used to match the network IP addresses (A.B.C.D format) to interface IPs. If there is a match, the subnet on the interface is advertised out OSPF, and OSPF packets are sent out the interface. A 0 wildcard bit is used to indicate a "must" match. A 255 is a "don't care," hence the name *inverse mask.*

The last entry when defining an OSPF route is for the area. Remember, areas are used to partition a large network into smaller networks. **Area 0** is the root area and is the backbone for the network. All other areas must connect to area 0. Area 0 cannot be split. Other area numbers are specified by the network administrator.

Assume that the router command **network 10.10.20.250 0.0.0.0 area 0** is entered. The wildcard bits indicate that any interface with an address of 10.10.20.250 must run OSPF on the interface and will be assigned to area 0 (the network backbone). Assume that the router command **network 10.10.20.250 0.255.255.255 area 0** is entered. The wildcard bits indicate that any interface with an IP address of 10.x.x.x must run OSPF on the interface and will be assigned to area 0.

```
RouterA(config-router)#network 10.10.20.250 ? A.B.C.D OSPF wildcard
bits
RouterA(config-router)#network 10.10.20.250 0.0.0.0 ?
area Set the OSPF area ID
RouterA(config-router)#network 10.10.20.250 0.0.0.0 area 0
```

The following text details the three OSPF network entries needed to configure OSPF routing for RouterA:

```
RouterA(config-router)#network 10.10.20.250 0.0.0.0 area 0
RouterA(config-router)#network 10.10.200.1 0.0.0.0 area 0
RouterA(config-router)#network 10.10.100.1 0.0.0.0 area 0
```

Note that the RouterA interface to LAN A (10.10.20.250 NET) is listed when configuring OSPF. This is used in OSPF to advertise the LAN to the other routers. Also note that the network has been assigned to area 0 (the backbone). The command **sh ip int brief** is used to check the status of the interfaces. The text protocol *down* indicates that the cable to the interface is either unplugged or the interface is shut down.

```
RouterA#show int brief
Interface        IP-Address      OK?    Method     Status    Protocol
FastEthernet0/0  10.10.20.250    YES    NVRAM      up        up
FastEthernet0/1  10.10.200.1     YES    manual     up        down
FastEthernet0/2  10.10.100.1     YES    manual     up        down
```

This problem with the "protocol down" is fixed by reestablishing the physical connection between the routers.

The next step is to configure RouterB. First, configure the four FastEthernet interfaces on RouterB. Next, the OSPF routing protocol for RouterB is set. In this example, one command-line instruction is used to configure RouterB to run OSPF on all four of its interfaces. This is done with a subnet mask or wildcard in OSPF.

First, enter RouterB's configuration mode using the **configure terminal** command. The command **router ospf 100** is entered. Note that the same process ID number of 100 is being used. The next step is to enter **network 10.0.0.0 0.255.255.255 area 0**. This command tells the router that any address that starts with "10" belongs to area 0 on RouterB.

```
RouterB#configure terminal
Enter configuration commands, one per line. End with CNTL/Z.
RouterB(config)#router ospf 100
RouterB(config-router)#network 10.0.0.0 0.255.255.255 area 0
```

Verify that the interfaces are properly configured using the **sh ip int brief** command, as shown:

```
RouterB#sh ip int brief
Interface        IP-Address     OK?  Method  Status  Protocol
FastEthernet0/0  10.10.10.250   YES  manual  up      up
FastEthernet0/1  10.10.1.250    YES  manual  up      up
FastEthernet0/2  10.10.200.2    YES  manual  up      up
FastEthernet0/3  10.10.150.1    YES  manual  up      down
```

The FastEthernet0/3 interface shows the protocol is *down* because the connecting interface is shut down on RouterC.

The next step is to configure RouterC. The OSPF routing protocol for RouterC is set using the command **router OSPF 100** followed by **network 10.0.0.0 0.255.255.255 area 0**, as shown:

```
RouterC(config)#router ospf 100
RouterC(config-router)#network 10.0.0.0 0.255.255.255 area 0
```

The interfaces on RouterC are checked using the **sh ip int brief** command, as shown:

```
RouterC#sh ip int brief
Interface        IP-Address     OK?  Method  Status  Protocol
FastEthernet0/0  10.10.5.250    YES  manual  up      up
FastEthernet0/1  10.10.150.2    YES  manual  up      up
FastEthernet0/2  10.10.100.2    YES  manual  up      up
```

Notice that protocol shows *up* for all interfaces. This is because all interfaces are connected and the interfaces are enabled.

The following is a partial listing of the running-configuration file on RouterA that shows the router OSPF network configuration. Similar information will appear on RouterB and RouterC.

```
.
.
router ospf 100
 network 10.10.200.1 0.0.0.0 area 0 network 10.10.20.250 0.0.0.0 area 0
 network 10.10.100.1 0.0.0.0 area 0
.
.
```

The routing table for RouterA can be checked using the command **show ip route**, as shown next. The routing table indicates there are seven subnets in the campus network shown in Figure 9-12. The instances of "O" indicate the subnets running OSPF, and "C" indicates the subnets directly connected to the router.

```
RouterA#show ip route
Codes: C connected, S static, I IGRP, R RIP, M mobile, B BGP D EIGRP,
EX EIGRP external, O OSPF, IA OSPF inter area
N1 OSPF NSSA external type 1, N2 OSPF NSSA external type 2
E1 OSPF external type 1, E2 OSPF external type 2, E EGP
i IS-IS, L1 IS-IS level-1, L2 IS-IS level-2, * candidate default
U per-user static route, o ODR T traffic engineered route
Gateway of last resort is not set
10.0.0.0/24 is subnetted, 7 subnets
O 10.10.5.0 [110/74] via 10.10.100.2, 00:03:28, FastEthernet0/2
O 10.10.10.0 [110/74] via 10.10.200.2, 00:03:28, FastEthernet0/1
O 10.10.1.0 [110/74] via 10.10.200.2, 00:03:28, FastEthernet0/1
C 10.10.20.0 is directly connected, FastEthernet0/0
C 10.10.100.0 is directly connected, FastEthernet0/2
O 10.10.150.0 [110/128] via 10.10.200.2, 00:03:28, FastEthernet0/1
[110/128] via 10.10.100.2, 00:03:28, FastEthernet0/2
C 10.10.200.0 is directly connected, FastEthernet0/1
```

A command used to display only the OSPF routes is **show ip route ospf**. The following are the results for this command from RouterA:

```
RouterA#show ip route ospf
10.0.0.0/24 is subnetted, 6 subnets
O 10.10.5.0 [110/74] via 10.10.100.2, 00:10:03, FastEthernet0/2
O 10.10.10.0 [110/74] via 10.10.200.2, 00:10:03, FastEthernet0/1
O 10.10.150.0 [110/128] via 10.10.200.2, 00:10:03, FastEthernet0/1
[110/128] via 10.10.100.2, 00:10:03, FastEthernet0/2
```

Another command used for displaying protocol information for the router is **sh ip protocol**. The following are the results from entering this command for RouterA:

```
RouterA#show ip protocol
Routing Protocol is "ospf 100" Sending updates every 0 seconds
Invalid after 0 seconds, hold down 0, flushed after 0
Outgoing update filter list for all interfaces is Incoming update
  filter list for all interfaces is Redistributing: ospf 100
Routing for Networks:
10.10.20.250/32
10.10.100.1/32
10.10.200.1/32
Routing Information Sources:
Gateway Distance Last Update
10.10.100.1 110 00:06:01
10.10.200.2 110 00:06:01
Distance: (default is 110)
```

Networking Challenge: OSPF

Use the Net-Challenge simulator software included with the text's companion CD-ROM to demonstrate that you can configure OSPF for RouterB in the campus LAN (the campus LAN is shown in Figure 9-11 and is displayed on the computer screen when the software is started). Place the Net-Challenge CD-ROM in your computer's drive. Open the **Net-Challenge** folder and click **Net-ChallengeV4.exe.** When the software is running, click the **Select Router Challenge** button to open a **Select Router Challenge** drop-down menu. Select **Chapter 9 OSPF**. This opens a checkbox that can be used to verify that you have completed all the tasks.

1. Enter the privileged EXEC mode on the router.

2. Enter the router's terminal configuration mode, **Router(config)**.

3. Set the hostname to *RouterA*.

4. Configure the FastEthernet0/0 interface with the following:

    - IP address: 10.10.20.250
    - Subnet mask: 255.255.255.0

5. Enable the FA0/0 interface.

6. Configure the FastEthernet0/1 interface with the following:

    - IP address: 10.10.200.1
    - Subnet mask: 255.255.255.0

7. Enable the FA0/1 interface.

8. Configure the FastEthernet0/2 interface with the following:

    - IP address: 10.10.100.1
    - Subnet mask: 255.255.255.0

9. Enable the FA0/2 interface.

10. Enable OSPF with a network number of 100.

11. Use a single command-line instruction to configure RouterA to run OSPF on all three of the FastEthernet interfaces (use area 100).

12. Use the **sh ip int brief** command to check the interface status.

13. Use the **sh ip protocol** command to see whether OSPF is running on RouterA.

14. Use the **sh ip route** command to verify that the three FastEthernet ports are connected to RouterA.

15. Use the **sh run** command to view the running-configuration file on RouterA. Verify that OSPF is enabled and the proper network address is specified.

Section 9-7 Review

This section has covered the following **Network+** Exam objectives.

> 1.9 Explain the basics of routing concepts and protocols

The technique for configuring OSPF routing was introduced.

9-8 HYBRID PROTOCOLS: CONFIGURING THE ENHANCED INTERIOR GATEWAY ROUTING PROTOCOL (EIGRP)

This section introduces the Enhanced Interior Gateway Routing Protocol (**EIGRP**), which is an enhanced version of the Interior Gateway Routing Protocol (IGRP). EIGRP is a Cisco proprietary protocol and is often called a *hybrid routing protocol* that incorporates the best of the distance vector and link-state algorithms.

EIGRP

Enhanced Interior Gateway Routing Protocol

EIGRP allows the use of variable-length subnet masks, which is beneficial when you're trying to conserve the uses of IP addresses. EIGRP also uses "Hello" packets to verify that a link from one router to another is still active. The routing table updates are exchanged when there is a change in the network. In other words, the routers don't exchange unnecessary information unless a route changes. This helps conserve the limited bandwidth of the network data link. When route information is exchanged, EIGRP quickly converges to the new route selection.

The four components of EIGRP are as follows:

- **Neighbor Discovery Recovery:** Used to learn about other routers on directly attached networks. This is also used to discover whether neighbor routers are unreachable. This discovery is accomplished by periodically sending "Hello" packets. The "Hello" packets are used to verify that a neighbor router is functioning.

- **Reliable Transport Protocol:** Used to guarantee delivery of EIGRP packets to neighbor routers. Both unicast and multicast packet transmission are supported.

- **DUAL Finite State Machine:** Used to track all routes advertised by its neighbors and is used for route computation to obtain loop-free routing.

- **Protocol Dependent Modules:** Responsible for handling network layer, protocol-specific requirements. For example, the IP-EIGRP module is responsible for extracting information from the EIGRP packets and passing this information to DUAL. DUAL uses this information to make routing decisions, and IP-EIGRP then redistributes the learned routes.

Configuring Routes with EIGRP

This section describes a procedure for configuring EIGRP on a router. The first example is for configuring RouterA in the campus LAN shown in Figure 9-12.

FIGURE 9-12   The three-router campus LAN.

The three routers in the campus LAN will be configured to run EIGRP. The first step is to configure the interfaces on each of the three routers. The IP addresses and the subnet masks for the router interfaces are as follows:

```
RouterA
FA0/0     10.10.20.250     255.255.255.0
FA0/1     10.10.200.1      255.255.255.0
```

```
FA0/2      10.10.100.1      255.255.255.0
RouterB
FA0/0      10.10.10.250     255.255.255.0
FA0/1      10.10.1.250      255.255.255.0
FA0/2      10.10.200.2      255.255.255.0
FA0/3      10.10.150.1      255.255.255.0
RouterC
FA0/0      10.10.5.250      255.255.255.0
FA0/1      10.10.150.2      255.255.255.0
FA0/2      10.10.100.2      255.255.255.0
```

After the router interfaces are configured, the EIGRP routing protocol for RouterA will be configured. Use the **configure terminal** command to enter the router's configuration mode. Next enter the command **router eigrp** *[AS number]*. The AS number is the same as that for the IGRP routing protocol: Any AS number can be used. The router uses the AS numbers to determine which routers share routing tables. Only routers with the same AS number will share routing updates. The command **router eigrp 150** is entered as shown. The prompt changes to (**config-router**) and the next command entered sets the network to run EIGRP. In this example, the command **network 10.0.0.0** is entered. This instructs the router to run EIGRP on any of the router's interfaces that have an IP address that begins with 10. A different network command will be used on RouterB to show how the command can be used to specify a limited IP address range.

```
RouterA(config)#router eigrp 150
RouterA(config-router)#network 10.0.0.0
```

Now the 10.x.x.x interfaces on RouterA are configured to run EIGRP. The command **show ip protocol** is entered to verify that the EIGRP routing protocol is enabled on RouterA.

```
RouterA# show ip protocol
Routing Protocol is "eigrp 150"
Outgoing update filter list for all interfaces is Incoming update fil-
ter list for all interfaces is Default networks flagged in outgoing
updates Default networks accepted from incoming updates EIGRP metric
weight K1 1, K2 0, K3 1, K4 0, K5 0
EIGRP maximum hopcount 100
EIGRP maximum metric variance 1
Redistributing: eigrp 150
Automatic network summarization is in effect
Routing for Networks:
10.0.0.0
Routing Information Sources:
Gateway Distance Last Update
10.10.200.2 90 00:00:09
Distance: internal 90 external 170
```

The top line states that the routing protocol is "eigrp 150" and indicates that it has been nine seconds since the last update to the routing table. In EIGRP, updates to the routing table are made when there are changes in the network.

Another useful command is **show ip route**. The following are the results of entering the command. In this case, the router does not show any EIGRP routes to the subnets in the network because EIGRP has not been configured on RouterB or RouterC.

```
RouterA#show ip route
Codes: C connected, S static, I IGRP, R RIP, M mobile, B BGP D EIGRP,
EX EIGRP external, O OSPF, IA OSPF inter area
N1 OSPF NSSA external type 1, N2 OSPF NSSA external type 2
E1 OSPF external type 1, E2 OSPF external type 2, E EGP
i IS-IS, L1 IS-IS level-1, L2 IS-IS level-2, * candidate default
U per-user static route, o ODR T traffic engineered route
Gateway of last resort is not set
10.0.0.0/24 is subnetted, 3 subnets
C 10.10.20.0 is directly connected, FastEthernet0/0
C 10.10.200.0 is directly connected, FastEthernet0/1
C 10.10.100.0 is directly connected, FastEthernet0/2
```

The command **show ip int brief** is entered and the status and protocols for the Ethernet interfaces are *up*. These will show *up* as long as there is a network connection to the interfaces.

```
RouterA#show ip int brief
Interface       IP-Address     OK?  Method  Status  Protocol
FastEthernet0/0 10.10.20.250   YES  NVRAM   up      up
FastEthernet0/1 10.10.200.1    YES  manual  up      up
FastEthernet0/2 10.10.100.1    YES  manual  up      up
```

The **show run** command is used to view the contents of the router's running-configuration file. The following is the part of the configuration file that shows the entries for EIGRP. Notice that these entries are the same as the commands entered earlier when configuring EIGRP.

```
!
router eigrp 150
 network 10.0.0.0
!
```

The next step is to configure RouterB. The configuration mode **(config)#** for RouterB is entered and the command **router eigrp 150** is entered. Remember, 150 is the AS number, which is the same number used when configuring RouterA. The next command is used to set the network that is running EIGRP. In this case, the command **network 10.10.0.0** is entered. This means that on RouterB, all interfaces with a 10.10.x.x address will run the EIGRP protocol. In this case, all interfaces on RouterB have a 10.10.x.x address and will run EIGRP.

```
RouterB#configure terminal
Enter configuration commands, one per line. End with CNTL/Z.
RouterB(config)#router eigrp 150
RouterB(config-router)#network 10.10.0.0
```

The command **show ip protocol** is used to verify that EIGRP is running on RouterB. The text shows that eigrp 150 is running on RouterB and it has been 27 seconds since the last update to the routing table.

```
RouterB#sh ip protocol
Routing Protocol is "eigrp 150"
Outgoing update filter list for all interfaces is Incoming update fil-
ter list for all interfaces is Default networks flagged in outgoing
updates Default networks accepted from incoming updates EIGRP metric
weight K1 1, K2 0, K3 1, K4 0, K5 0
EIGRP maximum hopcount 100
EIGRP maximum metric variance 1
Redistributing: eigrp 150
Automatic network summarization is in effect
Routing for Networks:
10.0.0.0
Routing Information Sources:
Gateway Distance Last Update
10.10.200.1 90 00:00:27
Distance: internal 90 external 170
```

The **show ip route** command for RouterB shows that six routes are on RouterB and there are EIGRP routes to the 10.10.20.0 and 10.10.100.0 subnets. The code for the EIGRP routes is "D." Remember, the "C" code is for the subnets directly connected to the router.

```
RouterB#show ip route
Codes: C connected, S static, I IGRP, R RIP, M mobile, B BGP D EIGRP,
EX EIGRP external, O OSPF, IA OSPF inter area
N1 OSPF NSSA external type 1, N2 OSPF NSSA external type 2
E1 OSPF external type 1, E2 OSPF external type 2, E EGP
i IS-IS, L1 IS-IS level-1, L2 IS-IS level-2, * candidate default
U per-user static route, o ODR T traffic engineered route
Gateway of last resort is not set
10.0.0.0/24 is subnetted, 6 subnets
C 10.10.10.0 is directly connected, FastEthernet0/0
C 10.10.1.0 is directly connected, FastEthernet0/1
D 10.10.20.0 [90/2195456] via 10.10.200.1, 00:00:09, FastEthernet0/2
D 10.10.100.0 [90/2681856] via 10.10.200.1, 00:00:09, FastEthernet0/2
C 10.10.150.0 is directly connected, FastEthernet0/3
C 10.10.200.0 is directly connected, FastEthernet0/2
```

A check of the IP routes on RouterA also shows that RouterA and RouterB are exchanging routes with each other. RouterA now shows six subnets. Once again, the "D" indicates the EIGRP routes and the "C" indicates the directly connected subnets.

```
RouterA#show ip route
Codes: C connected, S static, I IGRP, R RIP, M mobile, B BGP D EIGRP,
EX EIGRP external, O OSPF, IA OSPF inter area
N1 OSPF NSSA external type 1, N2 OSPF NSSA external type 2
E1 OSPF external type 1, E2 OSPF external type 2, E EGP
```

```
i IS-IS, L1 IS-IS level-1, L2 IS-IS level-2, * candidate default
U per-user static route, o ODR T traffic engineered route
Gateway of last resort is not set
10.0.0.0/24 is subnetted, 6 subnets
D 10.10.10.0 [90/2195456] via 10.10.200.2, 00:00:50, FastEthernet0/1
D 10.10.1.0 [90/2195456] via 10.10.200.2, 00:00:50, FastEthernet0/1
C 10.10.20.0 is directly connected, FastEthernet0/0
C 10.10.100.0 is directly connected, FastEthernet0/2
D 10.10.150.0 [90/2681856] via 10.10.200.2, 00:00:50, FastEthernet0/1
C 10.10.200.0 is directly connected, FastEthernet0/1
```

The last step is to configure EIGRP for RouterC using the **router eigrp 150** command. The command **network 10.10.0.0** is used to instruct the router to assign EIGRP to all interfaces that are under the 10.10.0.0 network. In this case, all interfaces on RouterC have a 10.10.x.x address and therefore will run EIGRP.

```
RouterC(config)#router eigrp 150
RouterC(config-router)#network 10.10.0.0
```

The **sh ip route** command is used to display the IP routes for RouterC. RouterC shows seven subnets. In fact, there are seven subnets in the campus LAN shown in Figure 7-13. This completes the setup for running EIGRP on the campus LAN.

```
RouterC#show ip route
Codes: C connected, S static, I IGRP, R RIP, M mobile, B BGP D EIGRP,
EX EIGRP external, O OSPF, IA OSPF inter area
E1 OSPF external type 1, E2 OSPF external type 2, E EGP
i IS-IS, L1 IS-IS level-1, L2 IS-IS level-2, * candidate default
Gateway of last resort is not set
10.0.0.0 255.255.255.0 is subnetted, 7 subnets
C 10.10.5.0 is directly connected, FastEthernet0/0
D 10.10.10.0 [90/2195456] via 10.10.150.1, 00:00:01, FastEthernet0/1
D 10.10.1.0 [90/2195456] via 10.10.150.1, 00:00:01, FastEthernet0/1
D 10.10.20.0 [90/2195456] via 10.10.100.1, 00:00:01, FastEthernet0/2
C 10.10.100.0 is directly connected, FastEthernet0/2
C 10.10.150.0 is directly connected, FastEthernet0/1
D 10.10.200.0 [90/2681856] via 10.10.150.1, 00:00:01, FastEthernet0/1
         [90/2681856] via 10.10.100.1, 00:00:01, FastEthernet0/2
```

Networking Challenge—EIGRP

Use the router simulator software included with the text's companion CD-ROM to demonstrate that you can configure EIGRP for RouterA in the campus LAN (the campus LAN is shown in Figure 9-12 and is displayed on the computer screen when the software is started). EIGRP has already been configured for RouterB and RouterC. Place the CD-ROM in your computer's drive. Open the **Net-Challenge** folder and click **Net-ChallengeV4.exe**. When the software is running, click the **Select Router Challenge** button to open the **Select Router Challenge** drop-down menu. Select **Chapter 9 EIGRP**. This opens a checkbox that can be used to verify that you have completed all the tasks.

1. Enter the privileged EXEC mode on the router.

2. Enter the router configuration mode, **Router(config)**.

3. Set the hostname to *RouterA*.

4. Configure the FastEthernet0/0 interface with the following:
   - IP address: 10.10.20.250
   - Subnet mask: 255.255.255.0

5. Enable the FA0/0 interface.

6. Configure the FastEthernet0/1 interface with the following:
   - IP address: 10.10.200.1
   - Subnet mask: 255.255.255.0

7. Enable the FA0/1 interface.

8. Configure the FastEthernet0/2 interface with the following:
   - IP address: 10.10.100.1
   - Subnet mask: 255.255.255.0

9. Enable the FA0/2 interface.

10. Enable EIGRP with an AS number of 200.

11. Enter the network command that enables EIGRP on the router.

12. Use the **show ip int brief** command to check the interface status.

13. Use the **show ip protocol** command to see whether EIGRP is running on RouterA.

14. Use the **show ip route** command to verify that the three FastEthernet ports are connected to RouterA.

15. Use the **show run** command to view the running-configuration file on RouterA. Verify that EIGRP is enabled and the proper network address is specified.

Section 9-8 Review

This section has covered the following **Network+** Exam objectives.

1.9 Explain the basics of routing concepts and protocols

The hybrid routing protocol, EIGRP, is introduced. This protocol incorporates the best of distance vector and link state algorithms.

1.10 Identify the basic elements of unified communication technologies

This section introduced the Reliable Transport Protocol, which is used to guarantee delivery of EIGRP packets to neighbor routers. Both unicast and multicast packet transmission are supported. Recall that with unicast, this is the transmission of a data packet to a single recipient.

Test Your Knowledge

1. EIGRP is classified as which of the following?

   a. Link state protocol

   b. Distance vector protocol

   c. Hybrid routing protocol

   d. All of these answers are correct

2. Route information with EIGRP routes:

   a. Is exchanged every 90 seconds

   b. Is exchanged every 300 seconds

   c. Is exchanged when there is a change in the network

   d. Is exchanged only when IP addresses are reconfigured

SUMMARY

This chapter presented examples of configuring static and dynamic routing protocols. No matter what type of routing protocol is chosen, you must remember that routing is a bidirectional communication. When configuring a network route on a router, the reverse has to be configured at the corresponding router. At the most basic level, all the routers involved in routing must use the same routing protocol for them to communicate and exchange routing information. The network challenge exercises provided the opportunity for the student to test her configuration skill prior to actually configuring a real router. The student should be able to configure and verify operation of the following protocols: static, RIP, RIP V2, OSPF, and EIGRP. Additionally, this chapter introduced the IS-IS routing protocol.

QUESTIONS AND PROBLEMS

Section 9-2

1. What is a routing table?

2. What is the most common static route used in a host computer?

3. Which command is used to view a PC computer's routing table?

4. What is meant by a 0.0.0.0 network address entry with a subnet mask of 0.0.0.0 in a PC's routing table?

5. What is the 127.0.0.1 IP address, and what is it used for?

6. What is the router command to configure a static route from LAN A to LAN B for the network shown in Figure 9-13?

FIGURE 9-13   The network for Problem 9-6.

7. What is the difference in a router's running configuration and startup configuration?

8. What is the router command used to view the routes entered into the router's routing table?

9. What is the router command used to configure a static route for a router?

10. List two static routes to route data from LAN A to LAN C. The network is shown in Figure 9-14. Assume a subnet mask of 255.255.255.0.

FIGURE 9-14 The network for Problems 9-10 through 9-13.

11. List two static routes to route data from LAN B to LAN C in Figure 9-14. Assume a subnet mask of 255.255.255.0.

12. Which of the following are suitable subnet masks for use in configuring static routes for the network shown in Figure 9-14?

    a. 255.255.0.0

    b. 255.0.0.0

    c. 255.255.255.224

    d. All these answers are correct.

    e. None of these answers is correct.

13. A static route is configured to route data from LAN A to LAN B on Router1 in Figure 9-14. Which of the following are appropriate static routes to achieve this goal?

    a. **ip route 10.10.16.0 255.255.255.255 10.20.100.2**

    b. **ip route 10.10.16.0 255.255.255.0 10.20.100.2**

    c. **ip route 10.10.16.0 255.255.255.255 10.10.10.2**

    d. **ip route 10.10.16.0 255.255.0.0 10.10.10.2**

Section 9-3

14. What is the difference between a *static* and a *dynamic* routing protocol?

15. What are the four key issues in dynamic routing protocols?

16. Define hop count.

17. Which of the following is *not* a metric used in dynamic routing protocols?

    a. Hop count

    b. Cost

    c. Runs

    d. Ticks

18. Determine the hop count for Router2 to subnet B in Figure 9-15.

A, B, C, E, F, G, H, I are segments.

FIGURE 9-15   The network for Problems 9-18 through 9-20.

19. In Figure 9-15, what is the hop count from Router5 to subnet G?

20. In Figure 9-15, what is the hop count from Router3 to subnet A?

21. Link state protocols issue what to update neighbor routers regarding route status?

   a. Hop status

   b. Link state advertisements

   c. "Hello" packets

   d. Adjacencies

22. Which of the following is a key issue of link state protocols?

   a. Send updates every 90 seconds.

   b. Send update when routing changes.

   c. Use link lights to establish adjacencies.

   d. Use a hop count metric to determine the best route to a destination.

Section 9-4

23. Define *routing loops*.

24. Which of the following is an example of a classful address?

    a. 10.10.0.0

    b. 192.168.0.0

    c. 10.1.0.0

    d. 10.0.0.0

25. All connected routes off a router have a distance or hop count of what value?

26. In a distance vector protocol, the neighboring routers update their routing table based on what received information?

    a. The cost of each route

    b. Its list of neighboring routers

    c. The hop count off each router

    d. All of these answers are correct

27. RIP permits a maximum of 15 hops to prevent what?

    a. Routing metrics

    b. Router table exchanges

    c. Bandwidth issues

    d. Routing loops

Section 9-5

28. What is the router command to enable the RIP routing protocol on a router?

    a. **config router RIP**

    b. **router rip**

    c. **rip 10.0.0.0**

    d. **network 10.0.0.0**

29. What does it mean to *advertise* a network?

30. Write the commands to enable RIP on an interface with an IP address of 192.168.10.0.

31. The command **show ip protocol** is used on a router to do which of the following?

    a. Display the routing protocol that can run on the router.

    b. Display the IP address of the routers running an IP protocol.

    c. Display the routing protocols running on the router.

    d. None of these answers is correct.

32. The command **show ip interface brief** is used on a router to do which of the following?

    a. Check the current configuration of the interfaces.

    b. Check the assigned IP addresses for the interface.

    c. Check the status of the interfaces.

    d. All these answers are correct.

    e. None of these answers is correct.

33. The command **show ip route** is used on a router to do which of the following?

    a. Set a static route.

    b. Configure a static route.

    c. Display the configured routes on a router.

    d. Display how often routing updates are sent.

    e. Both c and d.

    f. Both b and d.

34. What is the command used to display the router's current running configuration?

    a. **show run**

    b. **show routing**

    c. **show interface**

    d. **show controller**

35. The network shown in Figure 9-16 is an example of which of the following?

    a. Contiguous network

    b. Discontiguous network

10.10.20.0 NET   10.10.100.0 NET

192.168.10.0 NET

FIGURE 9-16   The network for Problem 9-35.

36. OSPF is what? (Select all that apply.)

    a. Open Shortest Path First routing protocol

    b. An open protocol

    c. Developed specifically for TCP/IP networks

    d. Developed specifically for IPX networks

    e. A distance vector protocol

    f. A dynamic routing protocol

    g. A link state protocol

    h. A high consumer of bandwidth

37. In OSPF, route updates are sent in the form of which of the following?

    a. Link state advertisements

    b. Exchanging routing tables every 30 seconds

    c. Exchanging routing tables every 90 seconds

    d. IETF packets

38. The OSPF routing protocol uses which of the following to verify that a link between two routers is active and the routers are communicating?

    a. LSAs

    b. "Hello" packets

    c. ARP messages

    d. Ping

39. Which of the following best defines how areas are used in the OSPF protocol?

    a. Areas are not used.

    b. Used to partition a large network into small networks.

    c. Used to combine small networks into one large network.

    d. An inefficient use of bandwidth.

40. Which of the following best characterizes variable-length subnet masks?

    a. Minimize wasted IP address space when interconnecting subnets

    b. Are not recommended in modern computer networks

    c. Reduce the number of bits required in a subnet mask from 32 to 24

    d. Are the same as classful addressing

41. Which is *not* an advantage of OSPF?

    a. Very easy to implement.

    b. Uses VLSM.

    c. Link state changes are immediately reported.

    d. Not a proprietary protocol.

42. Define *router flapping*.

Section 9-7

43. Areas in the OSPF protocol are

    a. not used

    b. used to partition a large network into small networks

    c. used to combine small networks into one large network

    d. an inefficient use of bandwidth

44. Variable length subnet masks

    a. minimize wasted IP address space when interconnecting subnets

    b. are not recommended in modern computer networks

    c. reduce the number of bits required in a subnet mask from 32 to 24

    d. are the same as classful addressing

45. The command structure for enabling OSPF routing on a router is

    a. **router ospf**

    b. **router ospf** *[area]*

    c. **routing protocol ospf**

    d. **router ospf** *[process ID]*

46. Another name for wildcard bits is

    a. OSPF pass-through bits

    b. Area 0 selection bits

    c. inverse mask bits

    d. route selection bits

47. Area 0 is

    a. used to hide data packets

    b. the root or backbone for the network

    c. the inverse mask bits

    d. the route selection bits

48. Which of the following is *not* a correct statement for configuring a route to run over OSPF? Assume that the OSPF protocol has been enabled.

    a. **network 10.10.20.1 1.1.1.1 area 0**

    b. **network 10.10.20.1 1.0.0.0 area 0**

    c. **network 10.0.0.0 1.0.0.0**

    d. **network 10.10.100.1 0.0.0.0 area 0**

49. The command **show ip route ospf**

    a. is not valid in OSPF

    b. displays only the IP routes

    c. displays only the OSPF routes

    d. enables OSPF routing

50. The **sh ip route** command is entered on RouterB in the campus LAN shown in Figure 9-17. The LAN has been fully configured to run the OSPF protocol.

Router A Port Addresses (LAN A)		Router B Port Addresses (LAN B)		Router B Port Addresses (LAN C)		Router Port Addresses (LAN D)	
FastEthernet 0/0 (Gateway Address)	10.10.20.250	FastEthernet 0/0 (Gateway Address)	10.10.10.250	FastEthernet 0/1 (Gateway Address)	10.10.1.250	FastEthernet 0/0 (Gateway Address)	10.10.5.250
FastEthernet 0/1	10.10.200.1	FastEthernet 0/2	10.10.200.2	FastEthernet 0/2	10.10.200.2	FastEthernet 0/1	10.10.150.2
FastEthernet 0/2	10.10.100.1	FastEthernet 0/3	10.10.150.1	FastEthernet 0/3	10.10.150.1	FastEthernet 0/2	10.10.100.2
LAN A Computers		**LAN B Computers**		**LAN C Computers**		**LAN D Computers**	
Computer A1	10.10.20.1	Computer B1	10.10.10.1	Computer C1	10.10.1.1	Computer D1	10.10.5.1
Computer A2	10.10.20.2	Computer B2	10.10.10.2	Computer C2	10.10.1.2	Computer D2	10.10.5.2
Subnet Mask	**255.255.255.0**	**Subnet Mask**	**255.255.255.0**	**Subnet Mask**	**255.255.255.0**	**Subnet Mask**	**255.255.255.0**

FIGURE 9-17 Network topology for questions 50 and 51.

    a. How many OSPF subnets are running on the network?

    b. Identify the connected C and OSPF O subnets.

51. The **sh ip route** command is entered on RouterC in the campus LAN shown in
    Figure 9-17. The LAN has been fully configured to run the OSPF protocol.

    a. How many OSPF subnets are running on the network?

    b. Identify the connected C and OSPF O subnets.

Section 9-8

52. *EIGRP* stands for which of the following?

    a. Enhanced Interior Routing Protocol

    b. Enhanced Interior Gateway Routing Protocol

    c. Enhanced Internet Gateway Routing Protocol

    d. None of these answers is correct.

53. Why is it beneficial to use variable-length subnetting?

54. This is used to verify that a link from one router to another is active.

55. What are the four components of EIGRP?

56. When are routing tables exchanged with EIGRP?

57. The command for enabling EIGRP on a router is

    a. **router igrp** *[as number]*

    b. **router eigrp**

    c. **router eigrp** *[as number]*

    d. **router eigrp enable**

58. The command **network 10.10.0.0** is entered on a router after EIGRP has been enabled. Define what this means.

59. What router command can be used to verify EIGRP is running on the router?

    a. **show run**

    b. **show ip int brief**

    c. **show history**

    d. **show ip protocol**

60. What router command will show how many subnets are configured?

    a. **show run**

    b. **show ip int brief**

    c. **show list**

    d. **show ip route**

61. What router command will show whether the router is exchanging routes?

   a. **show run**

   b. **show ip int brief**

   c. **show list**

   d. **show ip route**

62. The **sh ip route** command is entered on RouterA in the campus LAN shown in Figure 9-18. The LAN has been fully configured to run the EIGRP protocol.

FIGURE 9-18 Network topology for questions 62 and 63.

   a. How many EIGRP subnets are running on the network?

   b. Identify the connected C and EIGRP D subnets.

63. The **sh ip route** command is entered on RouterB in the campus LAN shown in Figure 9-18. The LAN has been fully configured to run the EIGRP protocol.

    a. How many EIGRP subnets are running on the network?

    b. Identify the connected C and EIGRP D subnets.

CRITICAL THINKING

64. You are configuring a router connection to a remote network. Which protocol would you select if there is only one network route to the remote network? Explain why you selected the protocol.

65. You are configuring the routing protocols for a small network. Which routing protocol would you select, and why?

CERTIFICATION QUESTIONS

66. Which subnets are connected to Router 4 in Figure 9-15?

    a. A, G, D

    b. F, G, H, I

    c. H, I, B

    d. G, G, H

67. Which router command will display how many subnets are configured?

    a. **show run**

    b. **show ip int brief**

    c. **show list**

    d. **show ip route**

68. The command **show ip protocol** is used to do which of the following?

    a. Display the routing protocols that can run on the router

    b. Display the IP address of the routers running an IP protocol

    c. Display the routing protocols running on the router

    d. None of these answers is correct.

69. The command **show ip route** is used on a router to do what? (Select all that apply.)

    a. Set a static route

    b. Configure a static route

    c. Display the configured routes on a router

    d. Display how often routing updates are sent

70. Which router command will display the configured routes on a router?

    a. **show run**

    b. **show ip int brief**

    c. **show list**

    d. **show ip route**

71. The command used to display the router's current running configuration is what?

    a. **show run**

    b. **show routing**

    c. **show interface**

    d. **show controller**

    e. **sh config**

72. What is the router command for displaying the startup configuration?

    a. **show run**

    b. **show flash**

    c. **show history**

    d. **show start**

73. What is the router command to enable the RIP routing protocol on a router?

    a. **config router RIP**

    b. **router rip**

    c. **router rip** [*area*]

    d. **router rip** [*as number*]

74. RIP is classified as a what? (Select all that apply.)

    a. Distance vector protocol

    b. Dynamic routing protocol

    c. Link state protocol

    d. Multivendor protocol

75. All subnets connected to Router3 in the network shown in Figure 9-14 are:

    10.10.10.0

    10.50.10.0

    10.10.200.0

    True or False?

76. Router flapping is when intermediate routers are going up and down creating excessive LSA updates. True or False?

77. A computer with an IP address of 10.10.5.1 sends a data packet with a destination IP address of 10.10.5.20 using a subnet mask of 255.255.255.0. The packet stays in the LAN. True or False?

78. A computer with an IP address of 10.10.5.1 sends a data packet with a destination IP address of 10.5.10.10 and a subnet mask of 255.0.0.0 is being used. The packet stays in the LAN. True or False?

79. A router has three network routes to a destination. The routing protocols used for each path are OSPF, EIGRP, and RIP. Based on administrative distance, specify the routing protocol with the smallest default distance value.

10
CHAPTER

INTERNET TECHNOLOGIES: OUT TO THE INTERNET

Chapter Outline

Objectives

- Describe line connection, data channels, and point of presence
- Describe the function of the CSU/DSU
- Discuss the HDLC and PPP encapsulation protocols
- Describe modern remote access technologies including DSL and cable modems
- Describe the purpose of the remote access server
- Describe Metro Ethernet and Carrier Ethernet and related services types
- Describe the purpose of DHCP and DNS network services
- Discuss internet routing with BGP
- Describe Internet data traffic

Key Terms

wide area network (WAN)
HSSI
OC
DS-0 to DS-3, T1 to T3
DS
telco
telco cloud
multiplexed
point of presence (POP)
line of demarcation
CSU/DSU
HDLC
PPP
V.44/V.34
V.92/V.90
asymmetric operation
cable modem
DOCSIS
ranging
xDSL
DSL

ADSL (asymmetric DSL)
discrete multitone (DMT)
RAS
client
peer
peer-to-peer network
client/server network
Metro Ethernet
Carrier Ethernet
Metro Ethernet Forum (MEF)
User-network interface (UNI)
Ethernet Service Definition
Ethernet Virtual Channel (EVC)
E-Line Service Type (E-Line)
E-LAN Service Type (E-LAN)
E-Tree Service Type (E-Tree)
CIR (Committed Information Rate)
CBS (Committed Burst Size)

EIR (Excess Information Rate)
EBS (Excess Burst Size)
BOOTP
DHCP
Lease Time
APIPA
Unicast
MT Discover
MT Offer
MT Request
MT ACK
SOHO
DNS
Forward Domain Name Service
Reverse Domain Name Service
TLD
Country Domain
Root Servers

NS Record	TXT record	Peering
ICANA	SPF	iBGP
ICANN	SRV record	eBGP
domain registrar	Stubby Areas	NOC
Reverse DNS	Totally Stubby Areas	outbound data traffic
PTR record	BGP	inbound data traffic
CNAME record	Multi-homed	IPX
NS record	AS	
MX record	ASN	

This chapter examines the concepts and technologies for establishing **wide area network (WAN)** connections. WANs use the telecommunication network to interconnect sites that are geographically distributed throughout a region, the country, or even the world. Connections can include extensions of the campus LAN to remote members of the network. For example, the corporate office for a company could be located in one part of a state and the engineering, manufacturing, and sales sites could be at different locations in the state. Figure 10-1 shows an example of a WAN. The WAN in this example shows connections for the Internet, a Frame Relay network, a virtual private network (VPN), and remote client access through a remote access server.

10-1   INTRODUCTION

FIGURE 10-1   An example of a wide area network.

An introduction to setting up a connection to the communications carrier (Telco), the important concept of the point of presence, and the line of demarcation are examined in section 10-2. The section concludes with a look at the Channel Service Unit/Data Service Unit (CSU/DSU) and serial line protocols. Section 10-3 examines establishing a point-to-point dial-in connection using a phone modem, cable modem, digital subscriber line (DSL) service, and other technologies.

Section 10-4 examines the technique of using Ethernet as a WAN connection. This is called Metro Ethernet or Carrier Ethernet. Section 10-5 provides a look at both DHCP and DNS network services. An overview of the issues of WAN routing are presented in section 10-6. Next, the BGP protocol that is used for routing Internet data traffic is examined. The chapter concludes with an example of using a network protocol analyzer to examine Internet data traffic entering and exiting a campus LAN.

Table 10-1 lists and identifies, by chapter section, where each of the CompTIA Network+ objectives are presented in this chapter. At the end of each chapter section is a review with comments of the Network+ objectives presented in that section. These comments are provided to help reinforce the reader's understanding of a particular Network+ objective. The chapter review also includes "Test Your Knowledge" questions to aid in the understanding of key concepts before the reader advances to the next section of the chapter. The end of the chapter includes a complete set of question plus sample certification type questions.

TABLE 10-1   Chapter 10 CompTIA Network+ Objectives

Domain/ Objective Number	Domain/Objective Description	Section Where Objective Is Covered
1.0	**Network Architecture**	
1.1	Explain the function and applications of various network devices	10-3
1.2	Compare and contrast the use of networking services and applications	10-5
1.3	Install and configure the following networking services/applications	10-5
1.4	Explain the characteristics and benefits of various WAN technologies	10-1, 10-2, 10-3, 10-4
1.6	Differentiate between common network topologies	10-3
1.7	Differentiate between network infrastructure implementations	10-1
1.8	Given a scenario, implement and configure the appropriate addressing schema	10-5
1.9	Explain the basics of routing concepts and protocols	10-6

Domain/ Objective Number	Domain/Objective Description	Section Where Objective Is Covered
1.10	Identify the basic elements of unified communication technologies	10-5
2.0	*Network Operations*	
2.2	Given a scenario, analyze metrics and reports from monitoring and tracking	10-7
2.3	Given a scenario, use appropriate resources to support configuration management	10-7
2.4	Explain the importance of implementing network segmentation	10-3, 10-5
2.6	Given a scenario, configure a switch using the proper features	10-4
3.0	*Network Security*	
3.2	Compare and contrast common network vulnerabilities and threats	10-5
3.3	Given a scenario, implement network-hardening techniques	10-6
5.0	Industry standards, practices, and network theory	
5.2	Explain the basics of network theory and concepts	10-2, 10-3
5.4	Given a scenario, deploy the appropriate wired connectivity standard	10-3

10-2   THE LINE CONNECTION

This section introduces the basic knowledge needed for configuring the high-speed serial data transmission interfaces used to connect LANs and to connect the campus network to the outside world. The term *high-speed* is relative. For large networks, a high-speed connection could be a DS-3 (44.7+Mbps) or a connection to a high-speed serial interface (**HSSI**) that supports data rates from 300Kbps to 52Mbps. For small networks, the high-speed serial connection out of the network could be a T1 (1.544Mbps). The T1 data rate is fast relative to the connection speed provided by a dial-up phone modem, so some users would call this a "high-speed" connection. Topics in this section include an introduction to the data standards currently being used in data communications and the data formats being used. These data standards include T1 to T3, DS-1 to DS-3, E1, E-3, and the **OC** (optical carrier) data rates of OC-1 to OC-192.

Data Channels

The most common communications data rates for end users are **DS-0 to DS-3** and **T1 to T3**. The T1/DS-1 and T3/DS-3 designations are actually the same data rates and the terms are used interchangeably. The Bell system *T* carriers were established in the 1960s primarily for transporting digitized telephone conversations. In the early 1980s, the digital signal (**DS**) subscriber lines became available. The data rates for the T/DS carriers are listed in Table 10-2. The DS0 designation is for the base rate of the digital signal lines, basically the data rate of a digitized telephone call.

TABLE 10-2 **Data Rates for the T and DS Carriers**

Designation	Data Rate
DS-0	64Kbps (56Kbps)
T1 (DS-1)	1.544Mbp
T2 (DS-2)	6.312Mbps
T3 (DS-3)	44.736Mbps
T4 (DS-4)	274.176Mbps

The T1 line is capable of carrying 24 DS-0 transmissions or 24 voice channels. Each DS-0 line uses 64Kbps (56Kbps) of data, but the data rate of 56Kbps in parentheses after 64Kbps indicates the rate actually available to the user in some cases. In other words, the DS-0 line does not guarantee that the full 64Kbps line is available. This depends on the connection provided by the communications carrier (**telco**—the local telephone company) and the equipment used to make the connection. When a 56Kbps connection is used, the other part of the data is for the overhead (synchronization and framing) required for the digital transmission.

The data lines are leased from a communications carrier for carrying any type of data, including voice, data, and video. It is important to note that when you lease a T1 (DS-1) line from the communications carrier to provide a data connection from point A to point B, the communications carrier does not provide you with your own point-to-point private physical connection. The communications carrier provides you with sufficient data bandwidth and a switched connection in its system to carry your data traffic to the destination. Most likely, your data will be multiplexed with hundreds of other T1/DS-1 data channels. An example of this is shown in Figure 10-2. Networks A and B each have established and configured a T1 data connection to the **telco cloud**. The telco cloud is the switched network the telecommunications carrier uses to get the data to its destination. The data from network A enters the telco cloud and is routed to the destination, network B. The term *cloud* is often used to describe the interconnection of networks via the Internet.

Telco Cloud

The telecommunications carrier's switched network used to transport data to its destination; also used to describe the interconnected networks on the Internet

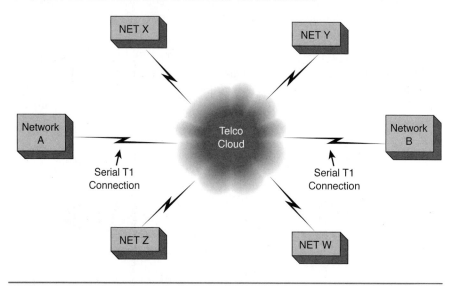

FIGURE 10-2   Transporting data over a T1/DS-1 line to the destination.

Note that networks W, X, Y, and Z also interconnect to the telco cloud. These networks can also be exchanging data packets, possibly over the same lines carrying data to and from networks A and B. In other words, the data from each network is being **multiplexed** together to reach the destination.

Multiplexed

Combining data packets for transport

Two other designations for data rates are E1 and E3. These designations are used throughout the world where the T-carrier designation is not used. For example, these designations are primarily used in Europe. The data rates for E1 and E3 are listed in Table 10-3.

TABLE 10-3   **E1 and E3 Data Transmission Rates**

Designation	Data Rate
E1	2.048Mbps
E3	34.368Mbps

Point of Presence

Point of Presence (POP)

The point where the customer connects the network data traffic to the communications carrier

Line of Demarcation

The point where ownership of the communications equipment changes from the communications carrier to the user

CSU/DSU

The channel service unit/data service unit

The place where the communications carrier brings in service to a facility is called the **point of presence (POP)**. This is where users connect their networks to the communications carrier. The link to the communications carrier can be copper, fiber, digital microwave, or digital satellite. Another term related to this is the **line of demarcation**, which is the point where ownership of the communications equipment changes from the communications carrier to the customer.

The communications carrier will require that the data connection be made through a channel service unit/data service unit (**CSU/DSU**). The CSU/DSU provides the hardware data interface to the carrier. This includes adding the framing information for maintaining the data flow, storing performance data, and providing line management. Figure 10-3 illustrates an example of inserting the CSU/DSU in the connection to the telco cloud.

FIGURE 10-3   The placement of the CSU/DSU in the connection to the telco cloud.

The CSU/DSU also has three alarm modes for advising the user of problems on the link: red, yellow, and blue. Table 10-4 defines the conditions for each alarm.

TABLE 10-4   **CSU/DSU Alarms**

Red alarm	A local equipment alarm that indicates that the incoming signal has been corrupted
Yellow alarm	Indicates that a failure in the link has been detected
Blue alarm	Indicates a total loss of incoming signal

HDLC

High-level data link control, a synchronous proprietary protocol

PPP

Point-to-Point Protocol

Two serial line protocols commonly used in wide area networking are high-level data link control (**HDLC**) and Point-to-Point Protocol (**PPP**). Both of these protocols are used by routers to carry data over a serial line connection, typically over direct connections such as with T1. PPP is used for serial interface connections such as that provided by modems. PPP is a full duplex protocol and is a subset of the HDLC data encapsulation. Figure 10-4 shows examples of direct connections using HDLC and PPP.

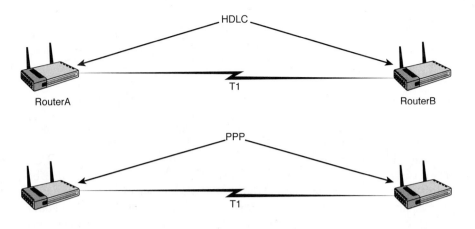

FIGURE 10-4 An example of a direct connection.

The routers at each end must be configured with the proper data encapsulation. *Data encapsulation* means the data is properly packaged for transport over a serial communications line. The type of encapsulation depends on the hardware being used to make the connection. The command for setting the data encapsulation is **encapsulation (encap)**. The options for the data encapsulation on the router can be viewed by entering **encap ?** at the router's **(config-if)#** prompt. The following shows an example of using the **encap ?** command:

```
Router(config-if)#encap ?
atm-dxi ATM-DXI encapsulation frame-relay Frame Relay networks hdlc
Serial HDLC synchronous lapb LAPB (X.25 Level 2)
ppp Point-to-Point protocol
smds Switched Megabit Data Service (SMDS)
x2 X.25
```

The serial interface can be configured to run HDLC from the **(config-if)#** prompt.

(Note: The **(config-if)#** prompt is the prompt for the interface currently being configured and is the same for all interfaces. Examples for setting the data encapsulation to HDLC and PPP on the Serial0 interface are shown.)

```
Router# conf t
Router(config)# int s0
Router(config-if)#encap hdlc
Router# conf t
Router(config)# int s0
Router(config-if)#encap ppp
```

The data encapsulation can be verified by using the **sh int s0** command. The seventh line in this example shows that the encapsulation is HDLC:

```
Router#sh int s0
Serial0 is up, line protocol is up
Hardware is HD64570
Description: ISP Connection
```

```
Internet address is 192.168.1.2/24
MTU 1500 bytes, BW 1544 Kbit, DLY 20000 usec, rely 255/255, load 1/255
Encapsulation HDLC, loopback not set, keepalive set (10 sec)
  .
  .
  .
```

The type of network being configured and the equipment being used to make the direct connection determine the selection of the format for data encapsulation. For example, Cisco routers automatically configure the serial interfaces to run HDLC but the Cisco routers support many data encapsulation formats. The HDLC data encapsulation formats are implemented differently by some vendors, and sometimes some equipment is not interoperable with other equipment even though they both have specified the HDLC encapsulation. In that case, another encapsulation format such as PPP can be used to make the direct connection.

Section 10-2 Review

This section has covered the following **Network+** Exam objectives.

1.4 Explain the characteristics and benefits of various WAN technologies

The concepts of the various data transmission rates, from DS0 to OC192, were presented. It is very important for the network administrator to know about all available network connection speeds.

5-2 Explain the basics of network theory and concepts

This chapter introduced the concept of encapsulation and its various configuration options.

Test Your Knowledge

1. What is the data rate of a DS-3 line?

   a. 44,735Mbps

   b. 44.736Mbps

   c. 44.735Mbps

   d. 1.544Mbps

2. This indicates a total loss of the incoming signal on a CSU/DSU.

   a. Red alarm

   b. Blue alarm

   c. Yellow alarm

   d. All of these answers are correct.

10-3 REMOTE ACCESS

This section addresses the technologies used to facilitate dial-in access to a network. This includes an overview of analog, digital, and hybrid techniques used for establishing a remote network connection via the telephone connection.

The limitations of a modem connection are first examined, followed by an overview of the V.92/V.90 standard (hybrid connection). Next, high-speed access is examined using high-speed cable modems and high-speed remote digital access using DSL. This section concludes with the last piece needed for remote access—the remote access server.

Analog Modem Technologies

The voice frequency (analog) channels of the public switched telephone network (PSTN) are used extensively for the transmission of digital data. Transporting data over analog channels requires that the data be converted to an analog form that can be sent over the bandwidth-limited line voice-grade channels. In voice-grade telephone lines, the bandwidth is limited by transformers, carrier systems, and line loading. Each of these factors contributes to attenuation of all signals below 300Hz and above 3400Hz. While the bandwidth from 300Hz to 3400Hz is suitable for voice transmission, it is not appropriate for digital data transmission because the digital pulse contains *harmonics* (higher frequencies) well outside this range. To transmit data via a phone requires the conversion of a signal to fit totally within the 300Hz–3400Hz range. This conversion is provided by a modem.

There are currently two major modem standards for providing high-speed modem connections to an analog telephone line. These standards are **V.44/V.34**, which is totally analog and supports data rates up to 33.6Kbps, and **V.92/V.90**, which is a combination of digital and analog and supports data rates up to 56Kbps. The V.92/V.90 modem connection requires a V.92- or V.90-compatible modem and an Internet service provider (ISP) that has a digital line service back to the phone company. The data transfer with V.92/V.90 is called **asymmetric operation** because the data rate connection to the service provider is typically at V.34 speeds, whereas the data rate connection from the service provider is at the V.92/V.90 speed (56Kbps). The difference in the data rates in asymmetric operation is due to the noise introduced by the analog-to-digital conversion.

The modem link from your computer to the PSTN (your telephone connection) is typically analog. This analog signal is converted to digital at the phone company's central office. If the Internet service provider (ISP) has a digital connection to the phone company, an analog-to-digital conversion is not required. However, the signal from the ISP through the phone company is converted back to analog for reception by your modem. The digital-to-analog process does not typically introduce enough noise to affect the data rate. Figure 10-5 shows the digital–analog path for V.92/V.90.

V.44/V.34

The standard for all analog modem connections with a maximum data rate of up to 34Kbps; V.44 provides improved data compression, smaller file sizes that provide faster file transfers, and improved web browsing

V.92/V.90

The standard for a combination analog and digital modem connection with a maximum data rate of 56Kbps; V.92 provides a quick connect feature that cuts down on negotiation and handshake time compared to V.90

Asymmetric Operation

Describes the modem operation when the data transfer rates to and from the service provider differ

FIGURE 10-5 The digital–analog data path for V.92/V.90.

Cable Modems

Cable Modem

A modem that can use the high bandwidth of a cable television system to deliver high-speed data to and from the service provider

DOCSIS

Data Over Cable Service Interface Specification

Ranging

A technique used by cable modems to determine the time it takes for data to travel to the cable head end

Cable modems provide an alternative way to access a service provider. This is also identified by the term **DOCSIS**, which stands for Data Over Cable Service Interface Specification. DOCSIS is an international standard that enables high-speed data transfers over the cable system. Cable modems capitalize on their high-bandwidth network to deliver high-speed, two-way data. Data rates range from 128Kbps to 100Mbps upstream (computer to the cable head end) and 10Mbps to 150Mbps downstream (cable head end back to the computer). The cable modem connections can also be one-way when the television service implemented on the cable system precludes two-way communications. In this case, the subscriber connects to the service provider via the traditional telephone and receives the return data via the cable modem. The data service does not impair the delivery of the cable television programming. Currently, cable systems are using the Ethernet protocol to transfer the data over the network. Many subscribers use the same upstream connection. This leads to a potential collision problem, so a technique called **ranging** is used. With ranging, each cable modem determines the amount of time needed for its data to travel to the cable head end. This technique minimizes the collision rate, keeping it to less than 25 percent.

xDSL Modems

xDSL

A generic representation of the various DSL technologies that are available

DSL

Digital subscriber line

The **xDSL** modem is another high-speed Internet access technology. **DSL** stands for *digital subscriber line*, and the *x* generically represents the various types of DSL technologies currently available. The DSL technology uses existing copper telephone lines to carry data. Copper telephone lines can carry high-speed data over limited distances, and the DSL technologies use this capability to provide a high data rate connection. However, the actual data rate depends on the quality of the copper cable, the wire gauge, the amount of crosstalk, the presence of load coils, the bridge taps, and the distance of the phone service's central office.

DSL is the base technology in xDSL services. It is somewhat related to the ISDN service; however, the DSL technologies provide a significant increase in bandwidth and DSL is a point-to-point technology. ISDN is a switch technology and can experience traffic congestion at the phone service's central office. Table 10-5 provides the available xDSL services and their data rates.

TABLE 10-5   xDSL Services and Data Rates

Technology	Data Rate	Distance Limitation
ADSL	1.5Mbps–8Mbps downstream; up to 1.544Mbps upstream	18,000 ft.
IDSL	Up to 144Kbps full duplex	18,000 ft.
HDSL	1.544Mbps full duplex	12,000 ft. to 15,000 ft.
SDSL	1.544Mbps full duplex	10,000 ft.
VDSL	13Mbps–52Mbps downstream; 1.5Mbps–16Mbps upstream	1,000 ft. to 4,500 ft.
VDSL2	Up to 100Mbps full duplex	12,000 ft.

DSL services use filtering techniques to enable the transport of data and voice traffic on the same cable. Figure 10-6 shows an example of the ADSL frequency spectrum. Note that the voice channel, the upstream data connection (from the home computer), and the downstream data connection (from the service provider) each occupy its own portion of the frequency spectrum. **ADSL (asymmetric DSL)** is based on the assumption that the user needs more bandwidth to receive transmissions (downstream link) than for transmission (upstream link). ADSL can provide data rates up to 1.544Mbps upstream and 1.5Mbps–8Mbps downstream.

ADSL (Asymmetric DSL)
A service providing up to 1.544Mbps from the user to the service provider and up to 8Mbps back to the user from the service provider

FIGURE 10-6   The ADSL frequency spectrum. (Source: Modern Electronic+ Communication 9/e, by G. M. Miller & J. S. Beasley, 2008, p. 502. Copyright ©2008 Pearson Education, Inc. Reprinted by permission of Pearson Education, Inc., Upper Saddle River, NJ.)

The bandwidth of a copper telephone line is limited to 300Hz–3400Hz. The xDSL services use special signal-processing techniques for recovering received data and a unique modulation technique for inserting the data on the line. For ADSL, a multicarrier technique called **discrete multitone (DMT)** modulation is used to carry the data over the copper lines. It is well understood that the performance of copper lines can vary from site to site. DMT uses a technique to optimize the performance of each site's copper telephone lines. The DMT modem can use up to

Discrete Multitone (DMT)
A multicarrier technique used to transport digital data over copper telephone lines

256 subchannel frequencies to carry the data over copper lines. A test is initiated at startup to determine which of the 256 subchannel frequencies should be used to carry the digital data. The system then selects the best subchannels and splits the data over those available for transmission.

ADSL is receiving the most attention because its data modulation technique, DMT, is already an industry standard. Figure 10-7 provides an example of an xDSL network. The ADSL system requires an ADSL modem, which must be compatible with the service provider. Additionally, a Plain Old Telephone Service (POTS) splitter is required to separate the voice and data connection. The filter is placed inline with the phone connection to remove any of the high-frequency upstream data noise that gets into the voice frequency spectrum (refer to Figure 10-6). A filter is required for all telephone connections to eliminate noise interference any time a computer is in use on the connection.

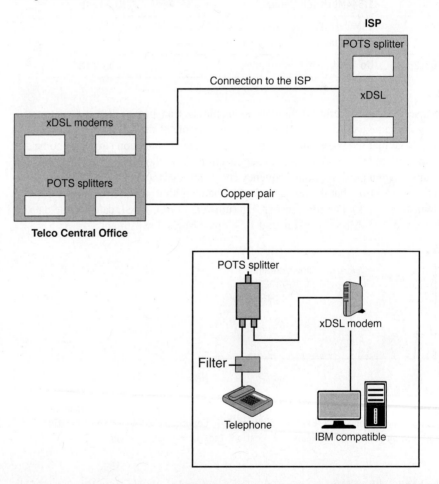

FIGURE 10-7 An xDSL connection to an ISP. (Source: Modern Electronic Communication 9/e, by G. M. Miller & J. S. Beasley, 2008, p. 503. Copyright ©2008 Pearson Education, Inc. Reprinted by permission of Pearson Education, Inc., Upper Saddle River, NJ.)

The Remote Access Server

The remote access server (**RAS**) is the last piece needed for completing a dial-up connection to the network. The RAS provides a way for the outside user to gain access to a network. The connection to a RAS can be provided through a telephone line provided by the PSTN; in other words, the basic telephone service or the dial-up connection could also be via cable modem, or DSL technology.

The protocol typically used for connecting to a RAS is PPP, introduced in section 10-2. PPP helps establish the dial-up connection, manages data exchanges between the user and the RAS, and manages the data packets for delivery over TCP/IP.

The server connects to the PSTN through a modem (analog, cable, DSL) to the telephone connection. The outside client also connects his PC to the PSTN through a modem as illustrated in Figure 10-8.

FIGURE 10-8   A RAS connection.

When the connection to the network is made, a client/server or a peer-to-peer network is created. The following information defines the advantages and disadvantages of the two network types. A **client** is a computer connected to the network that uses services from the server. A **peer** is a computer that uses and provides resources to the network. In a **peer-to-peer network**, all computers connected in the network use and provide similar services. The client computer can also function as a server for the network. The small office LAN introduced in Chapter 1, "Introduction to Computer Networks," and shown in Figure 10-9 is an example of a peer-to-peer network.

In a **client/server network,** the server handles multiple requests from multiple clients for multiple services. An example of a client/server network is provided in Figure 10-10.

> **RAS**
> Remote access server

> **Client**
> Computer connected to the network that accesses services from the server
>
> **Peer**
> Computer that uses and provides resources to the network
>
> **Peer-to-Peer Network**
> All computers in the network provide similar services, including server functions.
>
> **Client/Server Network**
> The server handles multiple requests from multiple clients for multiple services.

FIGURE 10-9   An example of a peer-to-peer network.

FIGURE 10-10   An example of a client/server network.

It isn't practical to say which network choice, peer-to-peer or client/server, is best for all applications. Both types are used, and it is up to the users and the administrator for the LAN to make the choice. There are definite advantages and disadvantages for each, as outlined in Tables 10-6 and 10-7.

TABLE 10-6 Advantages and Disadvantages of a Peer-to-Peer Network

Advantages	Disadvantages
Easy to set up the network.	Resource sharing can affect the performance of the computers.
No centralized network administration.	Poor security.
Low cost.	Users must administer their own computer.
Users control the resource sharing.	No central file server.
	No centralized administration of the computer's resources.

TABLE 10-7 Advantages and Disadvantages of a Client/Server Network

Advantages	Disadvantages
Centralized file storage	Client/server software and licenses can be expensive.
Centralized network security	Server hardware can be expensive.
Easy sharing of the network resources	Requires a network administrator.
	Network bandwidth/resource requirements.

Section 10-3 Review

This section has covered the following **Network+** Exam objectives.

1.1 Explain the function and applications of various network devices

This section examined three remote access technologies: DSL, cable modems, and dial-up. It is important that the network administrator has a good understanding of each technology.

1.4 Explain the characteristics and benefits of various WAN technologies

This section introduced the various DSL technologies: DSL/ADSL. The purpose of the analog modem was also examined.

1.6 Differentiate between common network topologies

This section examined the advantages and disadvantages of both the client/server and peer-to-peer networks.

2.4 Explain the importance of implementing network segmentation

The purpose of the RAS was introduced. Make sure you understand the role of the RAS and how this provides a way for outside users to gain access to a network.

5.2 Explain the basics of network theory and concepts

This section presented modulation techniques used in various modem technologies.

5.4 Given a scenario, deploy the appropriate wired connectivity standard

This section introduced cable modems and the DOCSIS (Data Over Cable Service Interface Specification).

Test Your Knowledge

1. Discrete multitone is a single-carrier technique used for transporting digital data over copper telephone lines. A test is initiated at start-up to determine which of 256 subchannel frequencies should be used to carry the digital data. True or False?

2. The data transfer for V.92/90 is called asymmetric operation because the data rate connection to the ISP is at V.24 speeds, whereas the data rate connection from the ISP is at V.92/90 speeds. True or False?

10-4   METRO ETHERNET/CARRIER ETHERNET

The number of Internet users is growing at a staggering rate. One key factor that brings people to the Internet is its application. The systems have evolved so much from the day of standalone applications running on computers to the day of real-time and collaborative applications that connect via the Internet. Many applications on the Internet are available for people to download and add to their computer systems. Coupled with the wealth of applications is the ever-increasing need for more bandwidth. It is no longer sufficient for some of these applications to run on a lower bandwidth modem connection. In a business environment, even the T1 speed (1.544Mbps) is not adequate to accommodate the number of concurrent users and the increased data demands of an application. As discussed in the previous sections, there have been many developments in both the commercial side and the residential side (for example, fiber to the business [FTB]) to bring more bandwidth to the consumers.

What every network infrastructure has in common is the Ethernet infrastructure. The design might be different, the equipment might be from different vendors, the backbone speed might not be the same; however, nonetheless everyone is running the same Ethernet-based infrastructure. The IT world has been investing a lot of time and money to improve the Ethernet speed. Ethernet has come a long way from the old 10Base5 technology running over coaxial cable to the high-speed 10 Gigabit fiber-optic networks. Ethernet is a standard network protocol used to connect virtually all networking devices. So, wouldn't it be logical to extend the Ethernet infrastructure beyond one's internal network infrastructure? Why not use Ethernet as a WAN connection? Hence, the idea of **Metro Ethernet** was born originally to connect subscribers and businesses in the metropolitan area networks (MANs). Later, it evolved into **Carrier Ethernet** that covers much more than just a metropolitan area.

Metro Ethernet and Carrier Ethernet specifications are defined by a nonprofit organization called the **Metro Ethernet Forum (MEF)**. Within the context of the MEF specifications, Metro Ethernet and Carrier Ethernet can be used interchangeably. The term *Carrier Ethernet* will be used for the rest of this chapter. Ethernet service is provided by the Carrier Ethernet provider and is delivered at the **user-network interface (UNI)** where the customer equipment (CE) attaches to the network. A UNI is defined by the MEF as the demarcation point between the customer equipment and the service provider. Sometimes, it is referred to as a *subscriber site*. Generally, the UNI is an Ethernet physical interface operating at 10Mbps, 100Mbps, 1Gbps, or 10Gbps.

The MEF develops the **Ethernet Service Definition** framework, which defines the Ethernet service types. These services are based on the types of the **Ethernet Virtual Connection (EVC)**. An EVC is defined by MEF as "an association of two or more UNIs" that essentially creates a logical path that connects two or more subscriber sites. Because the UNI is a physical connection and the EVC is a logical connection, a UNI might contain more than one EVC as depicted in Figure 10-11.

FIGURE 10-11   The UNI and EVC relationship.

Similar to WAN technologies, Frame Relay, or ATM Permanent Virtual Circuit (PVC), an EVC creates a protection and data privacy for the subscriber sites on the same EVC and prevents data transfer between subscriber sites that are not part of the same EVC. From the EVC types, the MEF derived the following three Ethernet service types:

- **Ethernet Line Service (E-Line)**—Point-to-Point Ethernet service based on a point-to-point EVC

- **Ethernet LAN Service (E-LAN)**—Multipoint-to-Multipoint service based on a Multipoint-to-Multipoint EVC

- **Ethernet Tree Service (E-Tree)**—Point-to-Multipoint service based on a Routed-Multipoint EVC

Metro Ethernet

An extension of the Ethernet infrastructure beyond one's internal network infrastructure

Carrier Ethernet

Another name for Metro Ethernet

Metro Ethernet Forum (MEF)

A nonprofit organization that defines Metro/Carrier Ethernet specifications

User-network Interface (UNI)

The demarcation point between the customer equipment and the service provider

Ethernet Service Definition

Defines the Ethernet service types

Ethernet Virtual Connection (EVC)

An association of two or more UNIs

Ethernet Service Types

E-Line Service Type (E-Line)

Provides a point-to-point Ethernet Virtual Connection between two UNIs

E-Line service type provides a point-to-point Ethernet Virtual Connection between two UNIs or subscriber sites as shown in Figure 10-12. It is analogous to a dedicated leased line or a Frame Relay PVC. This type of Carrier Ethernet service is the most popular one of all due to its simplicity. The Internet service is usually provided using the E-Line service type.

FIGURE 10-12   E-Line service.

E-LAN Service Type (E-LAN)

Provides connectivity to two or more subscriber sites using the same EVC

E-Tree Service Type (E-Tree)

Provides more of a hub-and-spoke environment or a root-and-leaf environment

The **E-LAN service type** can provide connectivity to two or more subscriber sites using the same EVC as shown in Figure 10-13. This type of service is more advantageous when adding new subscriber sites as they can be added to the same multipoint EVC without disturbing the existing subscriber sites on same EVC. A transparent LAN service is one of a well-known service offered by E-LAN service type. From the subscriber's standpoint, it appears as everyone is on the same LAN.

E-Tree service type provides more of a hub-and-spoke environment, or in this case a root-and-leaf environment. The E-Tree provides traffic separation between subscriber sites. Traffic from any leaf can only be sent to and received from a root. Traffic can never be forwarded directly to other leaves in the EVC. This service type is geared toward ISPs that want to provide multicast type service such as video on demand. Figure 10-14 illustrates the E-Tree service type.

FIGURE 10-13   E-LAN service.

FIGURE 10-14 E-Tree service.

Service Attributes

Many service attributes define the capabilities of the previously mentioned Ethernet service types. These attributes are under constant revision by the MEF. This section details some attributes that are more pertinent to typical IT users.

The bandwidth profile service attribute is a commonly used attribute. As a matter of fact, the first thing a subscriber must do is to choose the bandwidth when ordering the Carrier Ethernet Service. It is either applied at the UNI or to an EVC to limit the rate at which the Ethernet frames can transverse the applied point. Even though the UNI might be delivered as a 1Gbps physical connection, the subscriber might choose to subscribe to only 500Mbps worth of bandwidth. This is when traffic rate limiting is needed. The Bandwidth profile service attribute uses the following parameters to rate limit the traffic:

- **CIR (Committed Information Rate)** is same parameter used in Frame Relay. It is used to guarantee the bandwidth the network must deliver. This is an average rate measured in bits per second.

- **CBS (Committed Burst Size)** is the traffic size that is allowed to burst; it is not discarded or shaped by the profile. The CBS is measured in KB.

- **EIR (Excess Information Rate)** is an average rate parameter in bps used to allow traffic greater than the Committed Information Rate to transverse and may deliver it when the network is not congested.

- **EBS (Excess Burst Size)** is the burstable size allowed when the traffic is in the EIR mode.

Another useful service attribute is VLAN Tag Preservations. In a typical campus infrastructure, VLANs are used to separate physical segments into many logical segments. These VLANs reside locally. When connecting multiple campuses across the WAN, the VLANs cannot be extended; the separation has to be done at the higher OSI layer. It is typically carried out as different routed networks. With Carrier Ethernet Network, LAN extension is no longer an issue. The VLAN Tag Preservations service attribute can be used to carry out the mission. With this attribute, all Ethernet frames received from a subscriber will transverse untouched across the EVC. Therefore, when an 802.1Q VLAN Tag is provisioned and applied at the customer equipment (CE), its Customer Edge VLAN ID (CE-VLAN ID) will be preserved.

Section 10-4 Review

This section has covered the following **Network+** Exam objectives.

1.4 Explain the characteristics and benefits of various WAN technologies

A comparison of the attributes assigned to carrier Ethernet to Frame Relay and ATM were presented. Make sure you have an understanding of CIR, CBS, EIR, and EBS and how each of these relates to bandwidth.

2.6 Given a scenario, configure a switch using the proper features

This section introduced the 802.1 Q VLAN tag and its role with the Carrier Ethernet Network. The addition of this tag enables the Ethernet LAN to be extended.

Test Your Knowledge

1. How does Carrier Ethernet differ from Metro Ethernet?

    a. They are exactly the same.

    b. Carrier Ethernet covers much more than just a metropolitan area.

    c. Metro Ether covers much more than just a metropolitan area.

    d. All of these answers are correct.

2. Which service type can provide connectivity to two or more subscriber sites using the same EVC?

    a. E-Tree service type

    b. E-Line service type

    c. E-LAN service type

    d. All of these answers are correct.

10-5 NETWORK SERVICES—DHCP AND DNS

An IP address is one of the most basic pieces of information needed for a computer to communicate on the network. As discussed in Chapter 1 an IP address can be configured either manually or it can be assigned dynamically. In the manual process, a network administrator assigns an IP address to a user computer. Then, either the administrator or the user has to configure the computer's network settings with the assigned IP address along with other network parameters, such as the subnet mask, default gateway, domain name, and domain name servers. This could be a tedious process especially when it involves multiple machines.

This process can be automated to some extent using a program called **BOOTP** for IP assignment. BOOTP stands for *Bootstrap Protocol*, and it enables computers to discover their own IP addresses. When a client requests an IP address, it is assigned to the Ethernet address (MAC address) based on the BOOTP record. In this case, the IP and MAC addresses have a one-to-one relationship.

> **BOOTP**
> Bootstrap Protocol

Dynamic Host Configuration Protocol (**DHCP**) simplifies the steps for IP assignment even further. DHCP's function is to assign a pool of IP addresses to requesting clients. DHCP is a superset of BOOTP and runs on the same port number. In this process, DHCP requests an IP address from the DHCP server. The DHCP server retrieves an available IP address from a pool dedicated to the subnet of the requesting client. The IP address is passed to the client, and the server specifies a length of time that the client can hold the address. This is called the **lease time**. This feature keeps an unused computer from unnecessarily tying up an IP address.

> **DHCP**
> Dynamic Host Configuration Protocol
>
> **Lease Time**
> The amount of time that a client can hold an IP address

In a situation where a DHCP server isn't available, the Windows operating system can automatically self-configure its IP address and subnet mask. This is called Automatic Private IP Addressing (**APIPA**). APIPA uses a class B IP address space of 169.254.0.0/16, which ranges from 169.254.0.0 to 169.254.255.255.

> **APIPA**
> Automatic Private IP Addressing

When a computer is configured to obtain an IP address automatically or to use the DHCP option, the process of requesting an IP address with DHCP is as follows:

1. The client boots up and sends out a DHCP request. This is a broadcast, meaning that the message is sent to all computers in the LAN.

   A DHCP server listening on the LAN will take the packet, retrieve an available IP address from the address pool, and send the address to the client. The server sends the IP address, and the server will send the lease time and other necessary network parameters, such as subnet mask, default gateway, domain name server, and so on.

2. The client applies the IP address and its network settings to the computer; then it is ready to make network connections.

Figure 10-15 provides an example of this process.

FIGURE 10-15 An example of a DHCP server and client in the same LAN.

<table>
<tr><td>

Unicast

The packet has a fixed destination.

</td></tr>
</table>

What if a DHCP server is on the other side of the router (for example, not in the same LAN)? Remember, routers don't pass broadcast addresses, so the DHCP broadcast is not forwarded. This situation requires that a DHCP relay be used, as shown in Figure 10-14. The DHCP relay sits on the same LAN as the client. It listens for DHCP requests and then takes the broadcast packet and issues a **unicast** packet to the network DHCP server. *Unicast* means that the packet is issued a fixed destination and therefore is no longer a broadcast packet. The DHCP relay puts its LAN address in the DHCP field so the DHCP server knows the subnet the request is coming from and can properly assign an IP address. The DHCP server retrieves an available IP address for the subnet and sends the address to the DHCP relay, which forwards it to the client.

FIGURE 10-16 An example requiring the use of a DHCP relay.

Cisco routers have a DHCP relay built in to their operating systems. The router command to enable the DHCP relay is

```
Router(config-if)# ip helper [ip address of the DHCP server]
```

Notice that this command is issued from the interface that connects to the LAN. In fact, the IP address for the interface is typically the gateway address for the LAN.

DHCP is a UDP protocol and uses port number 68 for the BOOTP-client and port 67 for the BOOTP-server. (BOOTP and DHCP use the same port numbers.) The BOOTP-client is the user requesting the DHCP service. The BOOTP-server is the DHCP server. The following discussion describes how these services are used in a DHCP request. The DHCP proxy on the router listens for the packets that are going to DHCP or BOOTP port numbers.

The DHCP Data Packets

The following is a discussion on the TCP packets transferred during a DHCP request. The network setup is the same as shown in Figure 10-16. The data traffic shown in this example will contain only the data packets seen by the client computer. A protocol analyzer was used to capture the data packets. Figure 10-17 provides a portion of the captured data packets. Packet 10 is a DHCP request with a message type discover (**MT Discover**). This is also called the DHCP Discover packet. The destination for the packet is a broadcast. The message source has a MAC address of Dell 09B956, and the IP address is 0.0.0.0. The IP address is shown in the middle panel, and the *0.0.0.0* indicates that an IP address has not been assigned to the computer. The source and destination ports are shown in the third panel in Figure 10-15. The source port is 68, which is for the Bootstrap Protocol Client (the computer requesting the IP address). The destination port is 67, the Bootstrap Protocol Server (the DHCP server).

> **MT Discover**
> Message type discover, a DHCP Discover packet

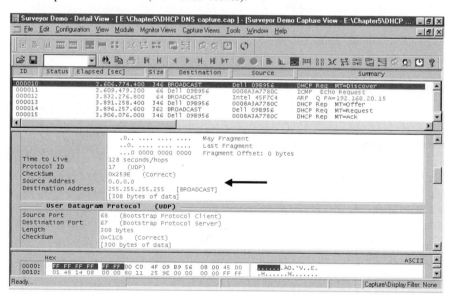

FIGURE 10-17 The captured DHCP packets.

Packet 13 is a reply from the DHCP server, an offer of the IP address to the client. This is called the DHCP Offer packet (**MT Offer**). This packet contains the domain name, the domain name server, the default gateway, and other network information the client may need to connect to the network. Packet 14 has a message type of **MT Request**. This packet is sent from the client back to the server that has been selected to provide the DHCP service. (Note: It is possible for a campus LAN to have more than one DHCP server answering the DHCP request.) The packet is sent through the DHCP relay to the DHCP server. This means that the client is accepting the IP address offer. Packet 15 is a message type of ACK (**MT ACK**). The DHCP server is acknowledging the client's acceptance of the IP address from the DHCP server. The client computer now has an IP address assigned to it.

DHCP Deployment

In a small office/home office (**SOHO**) environment, the network is typically small and only one router is needed. In this kind of network, a router performs simple routing functions, acts as a gateway to the outside world, and manages IP assignment via DHCP. Most of network routers are capable of running DHCP service, so it makes sense and is more cost-effective to deploy DHCP service at the router.

In a larger and more complex environment where there are multiple networks and multiple routers, deploying DHCP service at the routers is not as simple. Having to manage a different DHCP service for each network on multiple routers can be tedious, time-consuming, and inefficient. This is where centralized DHCP service fares better. This setup offers a centralized management, which scales better and is easier to support. A typical setup is to run a DHCP service program on a centralized server. With centralized DHCP service, the IP address assignment is typically tracked by the network administrator or the network operations center (NOC). The tracking information can include more than the IP and MAC addresses—the user information can also be included. The information can be kept in a central log file or in the database so that the administrator can troubleshoot network problems. For example, a machine could be causing network problems possibly due to hacked or corrupted software. The NOC needs to be able to track down the network problem(s). The NOC database will have the MAC address, the IP address, and the name of the person who uses the computer.

In a large environment, DCHP pools are usually planned and pre-allocated. IP addresses are assigned by NOC based on where the subnet for the computer is located. The subnet could be in a building, a floor of the building, a department, and so on. The subnets are created by the network administrators based on the expected number of users (hosts) in a subnet (refer to Chapter 6, "TCP/IP"). For example, the 192.168.12.0 network shown in Figure 10-18 has been partitioned into four subnets. The network addresses for each of the subnets are provided in Table 10-6. Any computer in subnet B is assigned one of the 62 IP addresses from the range 192.168.12.65–192.168.12.126. Remember that the first IP address in the subnet is reserved for the network address and the last is reserved for the broadcast address.

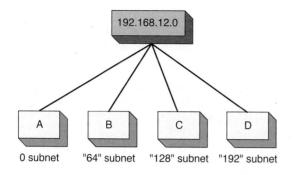

FIGURE 10-18 IP assignment of computers in a network's subnet.

TABLE 10-6 Subnet Addresses for the Subnets Shown in Figure 10-18

Subnet	Network Address	Broadcast Address
A	192.168.12.0	192.168.12.63
B	192.168.12.64	192.168.12.127
C	192.168.12.128	192.168.12.191
D	192.168.12.192	192.168.12.255

Network Services: DNS

This section examines the DNS services typically available in a campus network. **DNS** is the domain name service. DNS translates a human readable name to an IP address or an IP address to a domain name. The translation of a name to an IP address is called **forward domain name service**, and translation of an IP address to a domain name is called **reverse domain name service**.

The domain name service is a tree hierarchy. It starts with the top-level domains and then extends to subdomains. Examples of top-level domains (**TLD**) are as follows: .com, .net, .org, .edu, .mil, .gov, .us, .ca, .info, .biz, and .tv.

Country domains are usually defined by two letters, such as .us (United States) and .ca (Canada). The primary domain server for that domain has to exist in the same country; for example, the .us primary domain server is located in the United States. Figure 10-19 shows the top-level domains and their relationship to the subdomains and root servers.

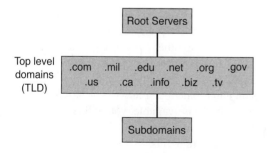

FIGURE 10-19 The domain name service tree hierarchy.

DNS
Domain name service

Forward Domain Name Service
Translation of a name to an IP address

Reverse Domain Name Service
Translation of an IP address to a name

TLD
Top-level domain

Country Domain
Usually two letters, such as United States (.us) or Canada (.ca), that define the location of the domain server for that country

The **root servers** use well-known IP addresses that have been programmed into DNS servers. When the DNS is installed on a server, the root server's IP addresses are automatically configured in the DNS. The campus DNS will query the root servers to try to find name servers of known domains.

For example, if network-A wants to know the IP address for the www server at network-B.edu, DNS queries one of the root servers and returns the IP address for the .edu domain. Then the network-A DNS queries the .edu domain for the IP address of the network-B DNS. The network-A DNS then queries the network-B DNS to obtain the IP address for www.network-B.edu. There are many steps for obtaining the IP address via DNS. However, the DNS server keeps a cache of recent queries so this multiple-step process of obtaining an IP address does not have to be repeated unnecessarily. The *www* entry, called the *A record,* is the name for an IP address. The A record is used by a DNS server at the parent company for network-B to convert the name www.network-B.edu to an IP address.

The top-level domain for network-B.edu is .edu, and the subdomain is network-B.edu. At the top-level of the .edu domain, and all domains, are the root servers, as shown in Figure 10-19. The .edu domain has an **NS record**, basically a record that points to a name server. They will have an NS record for network-A that points to the IP address of the network-A domain name server and the secondary DNS server's IP address and its DNS names.

The root servers have information only about the next level in the tree. Root servers know only about the top-level domains (for example, .com, .gov, .mil, and so on). They will not know anything about www.network-B.edu. They only know the .edu domain server's IP address.

Internet Domain Name

People generally connect to Internet services via Internet hostnames, not by the IP addresses. The Internet hostname is a subset of the Internet domain name that people can identify with—for example, www.example.com is a web server for the domain example.com. Internet domain name is the identity of the organization. The first step to obtain an Internet domain name is to find a domain name registrar.

The **Internet Assigned Numbers Authority (IANA)** was set up to be in charge of Internet registration authorities. Today, they are working under the direct support from the **Internet Corporation of Assigned Names and Numbers (ICANN)**; however, these organizations do not directly register domain names for the general public. ICANN delegates the top-level domain (TLD) registry to other companies or organizations. A couple of the most notable TLD registrars are Verisign, which is a company authorized to operate the TLD for .com and .net, and Educause, which is an organization operating the TLD for the .edu domain. The company, such as Verisign, delegates the responsibilities further to other **domain registrars** such as networksolutions.com, godaddy.com, tucows.com, and so on. An Internet domain can be purchased from any of these registrars. When you get on the registrar's website you will be able to input a domain name. The registrar will check whether the domain name is available. If the domain name is available, you will be prompted to complete the application for the domain name and enter the DNS servers that are to be used to host the domain. The DNS servers will be assigned an IP address and names. When the network's DNS servers are placed online, the root servers will point to the network's DNS servers. These DNS servers then become the authoritative DNS servers for the domain.

Administering the Local DNS Server—A Campus Network Example

The primary records are the A records of a campus network. These contain the hostname and IP addresses for the computers. For example, network-B.edu has an assigned IP address of 172.16.12.1:

1. When a host pings www.network-B.edu, the host computer first checks its DNS cache; assuming the DNS cache is empty, the host then sends a DNS request to the campus DNS server. Typically the host will know the IP addresses of the primary and secondary DNS server through either static input or dynamic assignment.

2. The request is sent to the primary DNS server requesting the IP address for www.network-B.edu. The primary DNS server is the authority for network-B.edu and knows the IP address of the hosts in the network.

3. The primary DNS server returns the IP address of www.network-B.edu, and then the ICMP process associated with a ping is started.

One might ask, "How does a PC in the campus network become part of the campus domain?" Specifically, how is an A record entered into the campus domain? Recall that the A record provides a host to IP address translation. Adding the PC to the campus domain is done either manually or dynamically.

The Steps for Manually Adding a Client to the Campus Network

The steps for manually updating the DNS A records are graphically shown in Figure 10-20 and are listed as follows:

1. A client PC updates the A record when an IP address is requested for a computer.

2. The user obtains the PC name and the PC's MAC address.

3. This information is sent to the network administrator or the NOC.

4. The NOC issues an IP address to the client, updates the NOC database of clients on the network, and enters a new A record into the primary DNS. The entry is made only on the primary DNS.

5. The entry will be later replicated on the secondary DNS.

FIGURE 10-20 Manually updating the A record.

The Steps for Dynamically Adding a Client to the Campus Network

A new A record can be entered dynamically when the client computer obtains an IP address through DHCP registration. This is graphically depicted in Figure 10-21. The DHCP server will issue an IP address to the client and at the same time send an updated A record to the network's primary DNS. The client name and the IP and MAC addresses are stored in the DHCP database.

Why obtain the MAC address when entering the information into DNS? This record is used to keep track of all the machines operating on the network. The MAC address is a unique identifier for each machine. The MAC address is also used by BOOTP, which is a predecessor to DHCP. This is where a MAC address is specifically assigned to one IP address in the network.

Reverse DNS
Returns a hostname for an IP address

Reverse DNS returns a hostname for an IP address. This is used for security purposes to verify that your domain is allowed to connect to a service. For example, pc-salsa1-1 (10.10.20.1) connects to an FTP server that allows only machines in the salsa domain to make the connection. When the connection is made, the FTP server knows only the IP address of the machine making the connection (10.10.20.1). The server will use the IP address to request the name assigned to that IP. A connection is made to the salsa domain server, and the salsa DNS server returns pc-salsa1-1 as the machine assigned to 10.10.20.1. The FTP server recognizes this is a salsa domain machine and authorizes the connection.

FIGURE 10-21 Dynamic updating of the A record using DHCP.

PTR Record (Pointer Record)
The reverse of an A record

The **PTR record** or **Pointer record** is the reverse of an A record. It is a mapping of an IP address to a hostname and is sometime referred to as a reverse record. The following example uses the **nslookp** command to find the PTR record (or the reverse record) of the IP address given as the result of www.example.com.

```
C:\nslookup -query=PTR 192.0.43.10
  Server:   192.168.1.1
  Address:  192.168.1.1#53

    Non-authoritative answer:
    10.43.0.192.in-addr.arpa      name = 43-10.any.icann.org.
```

Interestingly, the answer is not the exact reverse hostname that one would expect. One would think that the name result would be the reciprocal to the previous exercise, which is www.example.com. In this case, the name listed is 43-10.any.icann.org instead. This is quite common on the Internet. This has to do with how the Internet domain name is registered and how the IP address is acquired. As you have learned, the Internet domain name can come from different sources. An Internet domain name is generally purchased from a domain registrar, and the IP address has to be allocated from ARIN (in North America) or from an ISP. This results in one entity being in charge of the forward DNS zone and another entity being in charge of the reverse DNS zone. The information is not usually synchronized, hence the preceding result.

The **CNAME record** or **Canonical Name record** is generally called an alias. It allows another name to be defined and points to the real name. The CNAME record is mapped to an A record. Similar to an A record query, it is not necessary to specify the option for a CNAME record when using **dig** or **nslookup**. Both commands will yield a canonical name or an alias of a hostname, if it exists. The following example reveals that www.iana.org is actually the name of an A record of ianawww. vip.icann.org.

> **CNAME Record (Canonical Name Record)**
> Generally called an alias of a hostname

```
C:\nslookup  www.iana.org
  Server:   192.168.1.1
  Address:  192.168.1.1#53

Non-authoritative answer:
www.iana.org    canonical name = ianawww.vip.icann.org.
Name:     ianawww.vip.icann.org
Address: 192.0.32.8
```

CNAME is very useful in applications such as virtual web hosting. Being able to create multiple names and mapping these names to one canonical name, which in turn associates to one IP address, allows multiple websites to be served by one server. The effect is seamless to general users. As a matter of fact, this is how most of the virtual service and cloud service providers are able to provide their services. For example, what if the website www.example.com moved to a cloud service provider by creating a CNAME record and then mapped the website to a specific cloud service provider's server? To general users, the website is still www.example.com, but the destination where the service is hosted is now different.

The **NS record** or **Name Server record** is another mandatory RR for a zone. This specifies the name of the authoritative name server of the domain. The record must map to a valid A record, not an IP address or a CNAME. The NS records are associated with the domain, not a particular host. Therefore, one will need to look up the name server information based on the domain. The following example demonstrates the use of the **nslookup** command to look up the NS records of the domain example.com.

> **NS Record (Name Server)**
> Specifies the name of the authoritative name server of the domain

```
C:\nslookup  -query=NS example.com
  Server:   192.168.1.1
  Address:  192.168.1.1#53

    Non-authoritative answer:
    example.com    nameserver = a.iana-servers.net.
    example.com    nameserver = b.iana-servers.net.
```

In this case, the authoritative name servers are a.iana-servers.net and b.iana-servers. net.

The MX record or **Mail Exchange record** specifies the email-handling server of the domain. This is the server where all the incoming emails to the domain will go. The MX record must also map to a valid A record, not an IP address or a CNAME. The MX record is a crucial piece of information in today's Internet. Without correct MX records, emails to the domain will stop flowing. The following example demonstrates the use of the **nslookup** command to search the MX records information of the domain network-b.edu. The command is issued per entire domain, just like the NS information.

```
C:\nslookup  -query=MX network-b.edu
 Server:  192.168.1.1
 Address:  192.168.1.1#53


   Non-authoritative answer:
network-b.edu    mail exchanger = 20 mx02.cloud.example.com.
network-b.edu    mail exchanger = 30 mx03.cloud.example.com.
network-b.edu    mail exchanger = 10 mx01.cloud.example.com.
```

The MX records yields three email servers for the domain network-b.edu. Each server has a different preference number. The lowest preference number signifies the most preferred server. Email service is another popular service offered by many cloud service providers. Many entities do not have resources to manage the amount of emails going to and coming from their domain. Similar to how CNAME records are used to map to the cloud server, the MX records can be used in similar fashion. To move the email service of the domain to the cloud service, the MX will need to be changed to the cloud service provider's email servers. As shown in the preceding example, the domain network-b.edu is using cloud.example.com as their email cloud service.

The TXT record or **Text record** is used to hold arbitrary text information of the domain. Besides storing arbitrary information or comments for the domain, this record is being used increasingly more to validate the authenticity of the domain. One of its popular applications is to authenticate the email sender domain. **SPF** or **Sender Policy Framework** can be entered into a TXT record. This piece of information can be used as a validation of the legitimate sources of email from a domain. Another application is for the cloud service providers to validate the authenticity of the domain ownership. Many cloud service providers will ask for the proof of the domain ownership by providing the domain owner with a token value that needs to be added to the TXT record. The following example shows the TXT record with the specific token value (t=) for a cloud service.

```
C:\nslookup  -query=TXT network-b.edu
 Server:  192.168.1.1
 Address:  192.168.1.1#53


   Non-authoritative answer:
alumni.nmsu.edu    text = "v=msv1 t=3b6735dd2923c44e99c313ac4adb65"
```

The **SRV record** or **Service record** is used to identify a host (or hosts) that offers a specific type of service. This is sometime called a service location record. The uniqueness of this type of record is its syntax. The SRV record has a syntax of _service._protocol.name (for example _ldap._tcp.network-b.edu or _http._tcp. example.com). Not only does the SRV record provide typical host information, it also provides the TCP or UDP port of the service. The SRV record is used all the time with Microsoft Windows, especially in the Active Directory environment. The following example shows the SRV record of _ldap._tcp.network-b.edu. This service record allows a client to locate a server that is running the LDAP service for the domain network-b.edu.

```
C:\nslookup  -query=SRV _ldap._tcp.network-b.edu
 Server:   192.168.1.1
 Address:   192.168.1.1#53

Non-authoritative answer:
_ldap._tcp.network-b.edu     service = 0 100 389 dc2.network-b.edu.
_ldap._tcp.network-b.edu     service = 0 100 389 dc1.network-b.edu.
```

The output yields two servers that can provide the service. Both of them have a priority of 0, which is the highest, and a weight value of 100. Both of them provide the LDAP service on TCP port 389.

The DNS record for IPv6 is called the **AAAA** (quad-A) **record**. It is very important that IPv6 addresses be added to the name server. This makes it possible for the DNS server to be reachable for IPv6. This means that today your DNS server will need to have both A and AAAA (quad-A) records.

Section 10-5 Review

This section has covered the following **Network+** Exam objectives.

1.3 Install and configure the following networking services/applications

The role of the DNS server was presented in this section. Make sure you understand the role of the root servers. A good review is the domain name service hierarchy service shown in Figure 10-19. This section also presented an overview of DHCP. Important concepts to remember are BOOTP and the DHCP relay. Also, make sure you review the discussion on the TCP packets transferred during a DHCP request.

1.8 Given a scenario, implement and configure the appropriate addressing schema

The concept of APIPA (Automatic Private IP Addressing) was presented in this section.

10-6 INTERNET ROUTING—BGP

This section examines the routing issues for WAN and Internet routing. WAN connections typically link remote sites and branch offices to the main network. These links usually have slower connection speeds than LAN connections and usually incorporate smaller and less-powerful routers. It is critical that the network administrator be aware of these limited resources when choosing a routing protocol for a link to a WAN.

The easiest routing protocol for WAN links is the *static route*. At the main site you need a static route for each subnet at the remote end, as shown in Figure 10-22. At the remote site you also need a default static route. Each remote site router has a static route, attached to the network's WAN router, that goes back to the main network. No routing updates are passed across the link, and the routing table is very small and takes up very little memory in the router. This works well for single connections to the remote sites, as shown in Figure 10-22. For multiple connections you should use a dynamic routing protocol such as OSPF or EIGRP.

When choosing the routing protocol, you must be cautious about the amount of routing updates traversing the link. Remember that distance vector protocols send the entire routing table at set intervals. RIP typically sends routing table updates every 30 seconds. This is an issue when large routing tables are exchanged. In some cases, the exchange of the routing table traffic could consume more than an acceptable amount of data bandwidth. OSPF and EIGRP are more desirable protocols because they send updates only when routing changes occur.

The size of the router at the remote site will also play a part in the routing protocols you implement. The amount of memory in the remote routers is usually smaller than in the LAN routers. Therefore, the size of the routing table that can be passed to the remote site might need to be smaller than the routing table at the LAN site. Access lists (see Chapter 12, "Network Security") can be used to filter out routes passed to the remote sites. Route filters or access lists are implemented in most modern routers, including Cisco routers. Some routing protocols, such as OSPF, have built-in functions to filter out routes. These are called **stubby areas** and **totally stubby areas**. Stubby areas give only inter-area routes and do not accept routes from the external network—that is, routes from the Internet. Totally stubby areas use only a default route to reach destinations external to the autonomous system (AS). For a more detailed discussion of route filters and OSPF routing, you should seek out a routing reference book.

> **Stubby Areas**
> Do not accept routes from the Internet
>
> **Totally Stubby Areas**
> Use only a default route to reach destinations external to the autonomous system

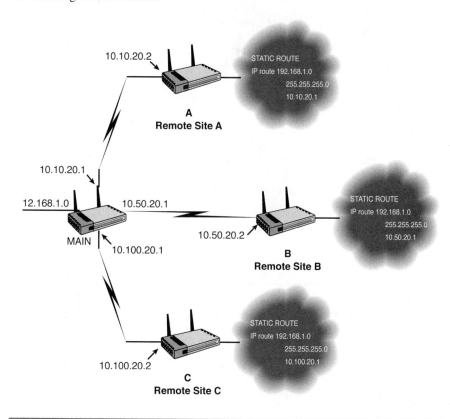

FIGURE 10-22 An example of configuring the static routes for the remote ends on a WAN.

Configuring an Internet connection is similar to configuring a WAN connection. The Internet connection can use the same type of link. For example, the link to the Internet could be made using a T1 connection or a high-speed link such as a DS-3 (44.7Mbps), OC-3 (155Mbps), or Carrier Ethernet (100Mbps and above). WAN connections typically connect sites that belong to the same organization, such as a branch office of a business. Internet connections are usually between an ISP and its customers. Typically, the ISP and its customers do not use routing protocols such as OSPF for the Internet connection because these protocols do not scale well to this type of implementation. Instead, the two main routing protocol options that are available for making the Internet connection to the ISP are static routes and **BGP**.

Static routes are implemented in the same fashion as in the WAN routing section. The procedure for configuring static routes was presented in Chapter 9. Static routes are used only when the customer has a single Internet connection. If the customer is **multihomed**, meaning the customer has more than one Internet connection, BGP is used. The most current version of BGP is version 4. An example of a single and multihomed customer is provided in Figure 10-23.

(a)

(b)

FIGURE 10-23   An example of (a) a single Internet connection and (b) a customer that is multihomed.

BGP is considered to be an external routing protocol. This protocol is designed for routing between separate organizational networks. The BGP term for these networks is *autonomous systems* (**AS**). An AS is assigned an AS number (**ASN**) by the same organization that assigns North American IP addresses—ARIN. The ASN has a different use than the ASN used in such IGP protocols as EIGRP and IGRP. The ASN in BGP is used to distinguish separate networks and prevent routing loops.

Each router participating in BGP must manually make a **peering** with its BGP neighbor. Peering is an agreement made for the exchange of data traffic between large and small ISPs or, as in this case, between a router and its neighbor router. The agreement on peering is how different networks are joined to form the Internet. The network administrator configuring the Internet connection must know the remote IP address and ASN to make this peering. An AS path is created when a network is connected. This is demonstrated in the next subsection. (Note: If BGP routers in the same AS peer with each other—that is, have the same ASN—this is called internal BGP [**iBGP**], whereas the BGP between separate ASs is called external BGP [**eBGP**]. The protocols are collectively referred to as BGP.)

ASNs have a set of numbers reserved for private use. These numbers are 64512–65535 and cannot be passed into the Internet.

> **Peering**
> How an agreement is made for the exchange of data traffic between large and small ISPs or between a router and its neighbor router
>
> **iBGP**
> Internal Border Gateway Protocol
>
> **eBGP**
> External Border Gateway Protocol

Section 10-6 Review

This section has covered the following **Network+** Exam objectives.

1.9 Explain the basics of routing concepts and protocols

This section examined the steps for configuring routing over the Internet. This requires the use of BGP and static routes. Make sure you understand peering and the purpose of the ASN.

Test Your Knowledge

1. A multihomed customer has which of the following?

    a. A single Internet connection

    b. More than one Internet connection

    c. Static routes

    d. None of these answers is correct.

2. BGP is considered to be which of the following?

    a. An external routing protocol

    b. An internal routing protocol

    c. Used for routing between the same network

    d. Outdated

10-7   ANALYZING INTERNET DATA TRAFFIC

NOC
Network operations center

Outbound Data Traffic
Data traffic leaving the network

Inbound Data Traffic
Data traffic entering the network

A campus **NOC** receives many emails and calls about suspected problems with the network. Many times network problems are due to operational errors by the users and possible hacker attacks. Occasionally, network equipment failure can be causing the problem. The bottom line is that the network administrator must have some expected performance measure (baseline) of the network. The administrator will want to know the expected normal usage of the network, which type(s) of normal data traffic is expected, what is typical of outbound and inbound Internet data traffic, and who are the "big" data users on the network. **Outbound data traffic** is data leaving the network, and **inbound data traffic** is data entering the network. This section provides an overview of the Internet data traffic patterns a NOC might monitor. These patterns are only examples of data traffic activity for a network. Data traffic patterns will vary significantly for each network, and each network will have its own typical data traffic. Also, data traffic will change during the day. The data traffic images shown in this section were captured using a network protocol analyzer such as Wireshark.

The first capture, shown in Figure 10-24, is a composite view of the data traffic activity for an Internet connection to and from a campus network. The image has four screens showing various data traffic information. This screen setup might be typical of the screen display at a network monitoring center. This does not imply that someone watches the screen continually, but the screen is looked at when a possible data traffic problem is mentioned.

FIGURE 10-24   A composite view of network data traffic activity.

Utilization/Errors Strip Chart

One of the areas NOC monitors is the typical percentage utilization of the network bandwidth. Figure 10-25 is a utilization/errors chart of an Internet feed to and from a campus network. The Utilization/Errors Strip chart shows that the network is running about 60%–65% utilization and no errors are reported. This is a 45Mbps network; therefore, the utilization is about 30Mbps. Is this a good percentage of utilization? You can't answer this from the picture, but you *can* answer it if you know the expected utilization of your network. In this example, the network operations center expects an average of about 60% utilization of their Internet feed. The graph shows that the utilization is within this range, so a quick glance at the screen indicates that the utilization is typical. This demonstrates why you need to learn and know the expected utilization of your network. The utilization chart shows stable behavior during the brief time it was monitored. There are peaks and valleys in the network utilization, but this is to be expected. Downloading large files from the Internet will temporarily increase the network utilization.

FIGURE 10-25   A Utilization/Errors strip chart for an Internet feed.

Network Layer Matrix

The top 10 network layer conversations on the campus Internet feed are shown in Figure 10-26. The chart is obtained by starting the protocol analyzer, starting a capture, and clicking **Capture View > Monitor Views > Network Layer Matrix**. The network layer is layer 3 in the OSI model, and this is the layer where IP addressing is defined. The monitoring software is reporting 1024 IP conversations and 8 IPX conversations. **IPX** is Novell's Internetworking Packet Exchange networking protocol. The top conversation is between the machines at IP addresses 192.168.15.25 and 10.10.20.2. The 10.10.20.2 machine is on the home 10.0.0.0 network. This one conversation is consuming more than 1.5% of the network's Internet bandwidth. This chart provides the network administrator with a quick look at which host computer is tying up the network resources. It is not possible to make a reasonable guess whether this is a normal network layer graph for your network by looking at only this one picture. This requires that the network administrator develop knowledge of expected behavior over a long term.

> **IPX**
> Novell's Internetworking Packet Exchange networking protocol

FIGURE 10-26   The Network Layer Matrix graph.

Notice that the machine with the IP address of 10.10.20.2 is listed three times in the top 10 conversations. The 10.10.20.2 machine is a web server on the 10.0.0.0 network, and it is expected that this machine will experience a fair amount of data activity.

Network Layer Host Table

The network layer host table (see Figure 10-27) provides a look at the top 10 network stations. The information is plotted by the IP address of the host (computer). Notice that the IP addresses for 7 of the network stations are outside the 10.0.0.0 network. Remember, the 10.0.0.0 IP address is the network address for the home network of the campus LAN discussed in this text. This indicates that the network consumes more data traffic than it exports to the Internet.

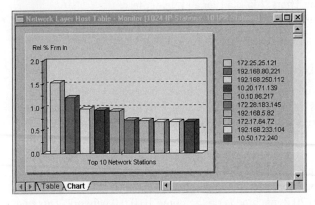

FIGURE 10-27   The Network Layer Host table.

Frame Size Distribution

Figure 10-28 shows the frame size distribution of packets in bytes being delivered to and from the campus network's Internet connection. The average frame size is

1132, which is listed at the top of the chart. The frame sizes for Ethernet packets are limited to 1500. The frame size distribution for this network has a somewhat *J* shape. The *J* in this case is skewed by the large percentage of frame size in the 1024–1518 frame size range. A *J* shape is expected because many small data frames are expected for negotiating the transfer of data over the network (frame size 65–127) and then many large frames for exchanging the data (frame size 1024–1518). There is a small peak with the 65–127 frame size, the few 128–255 and 256–511 frame size packets, and the frame sizes then begin to increase at 512–1023 and then the larger increase in the 1024–1518 region. The graph shows few data packets in the >1518 region.

FIGURE 10-28   The Frame Size Distribution graph.

Section 10-7 Review

This section has covered the following **Network+** Exam objectives.

2.2 Given a scenario, analyze metrics and reports from monitoring and tracking

The use of a network protocol analyzer was demonstrated in this section. This is a powerful tool that provides the network administrator with the capability to fully understand data traffic and resource utilization.

2.3 Given a scenario, use appropriate resources to support configuration management

An example was presented in this section that showed how the network administrator can develop baseline measurements using a protocol analyzer. Also presented was a section that examined the network data traffic and the need for additional bandwidth. The analysis techniques show how a protocol analyzer enables the network administrator to determine whether there is justification to add more bandwidth.

Test Your Knowledge

1. The frame size distribution for a network has a somewhat of a *J* shape. This is indicating which of the following? (Select all that apply.)

   a. The *J* shape is expected because many small data frames are expected for negotiating the transfer of data over the network (frame size 65–127).

   b. The frame sizes for Ethernet packets are limited to 1500.

   c. There are few large frames for exchanging the data (frame size 1024–1518).

   d. There are many large frames for exchanging the data (frame size 1024–1518).

2. What is expected utilization for an Ethernet network?

   a. The utilization is based on the CSMA/CD throughput, which is defined by telco.

   b. You *can* answer it if you know the expected utilization of your network, which is usually 10Gbps.

   c. The expected utilization is defined by the data traffic in each network. There is not a specific answer.

   d. This will vary based on the cost of using the network and the expected number of remote access clients.

SUMMARY

This chapter presented the fundamentals of wide area networking. The student should understand and appreciate the role that the PSTN—telco plays in wide area networking. Many associated issues and technologies have been presented. This chapter has only introduced a fraction of the technologies and issues needed to be understood by an Internet expert such as a Cisco Certified Internet Expert (CCIE). However, the chapter has tried to address the fundamental or base knowledge needed for a networking administrator to start working in this field.

The student should understand the following:

- The basics of a line connection to the telco
- The technologies used for establishing a remote connection to a network
- The concepts of Metro Ethernet and Carrier Ethernet and extending the Ethernet network out into the metropolitan network
- The function of DHCP and DNS network services
- The fundamental concept of wide area networking
- The issues for Internet routing
- The issue of analyzing Internet data traffic

QUESTIONS AND PROBLEMS

Section 10-2

1. What is the data rate of a DS-3 line?

2. What is the data rate of a T1 line?

3. Define the *telco cloud.*

4. Define fractional T1.

5. Define point of presence.

6. Explain the difference between line of demarcation and point of presence.

7. A CSU/DSU has a blue alarm. What does this indicate?

8. Which command do you enter to view the options for data encapsulation on a Cisco router (show the router prompt)?

Section 10-3

9. What is the bandwidth of a voice channel in the public switched telephone network?

10. Why is the data transfer for V.92/V.90 called *asymmetric* operation?

11. What are the data speeds for V.44/V.34 and V.92/V.90?

12. Cable modems use a technique called *ranging*. Define this term.

13. What are the data rates for basic access service ISDN and the ISDN primary access channel?

14. What is *ADSL* and what are its data rates?

15. Define *discrete multitone*.

16. What is the purpose of a remote access server?

17. Define *PPP* and state its purpose.

18. This international standard enables high-speed data transfers over the cable system.

    a. DCC

    b. DOCSIS

    c. SYSDOC

    d. SYSLOG

19. Which of the following is an advantage of a peer-to-peer network? (Select two.)

    a. Poor security

    b. No centralized network administration

    c. Easy to set up network

    d. Users must administer their own network

    e. Resource sharing

20. Which is a disadvantage of a client/server network? (Select three.)

    a. Client/server software and licenses can be expensive.

    b. Requires a network administrator.

    c. Network bandwidth/resource requirements.

    d. Easy sharing of network resources.

Section 10-4

21. What is Metro Ethernet?

22. How does Carrier Ethernet differ from Metro Ethernet?

23. What is an Extended Virtual Connection?

24. Which type of Carrier Ethernet service is the most popular due to its simplicity.

25. What is a Committed Information Rate?

Section 10-5

26. In regard to campus DHCP service, the IP address assignment is based on what?

27. How are BOOTP and DHCP related?

28. Define *lease time*.

29. What networking function is required if the DHCP server is not on the same LAN? Why is this networking function required?

30. What command enables a DHCP relay on a Cisco router?

31. Why is packet 14 in the captured DHCP packets shown in Figure 10-17 (from earlier in the chapter) a broadcast?

32. What are the port numbers for the DHCP protocol?

33. What command is used to release a current IP address on a computer?

34. What command is used to initiate the DHCP process?

35. What happens if a DHCP server is not available?

    a. The client will issue a global broadcast to search for available DHCP server.

    b. The host computer will issue a unicast packets to the 169.254.1.1 address and then obtain an IP address.

    c. A DHCP client will use a self-assigned IP address known as Automatic Private IP addressing (APIPA).

    d. The **ipconfig/redo** command is automatically issued to establish connectivity.

36. What is the command on the router to enable the DHCP relay function?

37. What information is contained in the MT offer (DHCP Offer) packet? (Select three.)

    a. Default gateway

    b. Leased time

    c. Internet address

    d. IP address of the domain name server

    e. Host name

38. What is a gratuitous ARP broadcast?

39. What information does NOC typically associate with an IP address?

40. What is the PTR record? (select two)

    a. Identifies the MAC address

    b. Is only used for IPv6

    c. The reverse of an "A" record

    d. Mapping of an IP address to a hostname

41. Which is true for the CNAME record?

    a. Generally called an alias

    b. Maps the MAC address on the Internet

    c. The reverse of the "A" record

    d. Also called the canonical record

42. Which record specifies the email-handling server on the domain?

    a. PTR record

    b. MX record

    c. TXT record

    d. SRV record

43. Which record is used to identify a host or hosts that offer a specific type of service?

    a. MX record

    b. SRV record

    c. PTR record

    d. TXT record

Section 10-6

44. What is the purpose of a wide area network connection?

45. What is the easiest routing protocol to use for WAN links? What if there are multiple connections to the remote sites?

46. Define the following:

    a. Stubby areas

    b. Totally stubby areas

47. A multihomed customer has which of the following?

    a. A single Internet connection

    b. More than one Internet connection

    c. Static routes

    d. None of these answers is correct.

48. BGP is considered to be which of the following?

    a. An external routing protocol

    b. Used for routing between the same networks

    c. Used for routing between switches and routers on the same networks

    d. Outdated

Section 10-7

49. Define the following:

    a. Outbound data traffic

    b. Inbound data traffic

50. What is an expected percentage utilization for a network?

51. The protocol analyzer shows that the average frame size of data packets being delivered to and from the campus network's Internet connection is 1203. Is this a reasonable average? Justify your answer.

CERTIFICATION QUESTIONS

52. The network administrator notices that the hourly plot of a router's data traffic varies from hour to hour. What does this information tell the network administrator?

    a. This is most likely normal operation.

    b. The network administrator needs to compare this hourly plot with expected hourly plots of the router's data traffic.

    c. The network administrator should run diagnostics on the router.

    d. The router needs to be rebooted.

53. The difference between line of demarcation and point of presence is:

    Line of Demarcation: Defines the connection point to the communication carrier.

    Point of Presence: The point where ownership of the communication equipment changes

    True or False?

54. The network administrator is examining the data capture for an Internet feed. The network layer host table in the network analyzer provides a look at which of the following?

    a. The top ten network stations

    b. The top five network stations

    c. The layer 4 conversations

    d. The layer 2 conversations

    e. 44.736 bps

55. If a client and the DHCP server are not on the same LAN, a DHCP relay is used. This is important because the computer can't access the DHCP server without consent of the DHCP server. True or False?

56. The BOOTP protocol is characterized best by which of the following?

    a. It enables computers to broadcast their own IP address.

    b. It enables computers to discover their own MAC address.

    c. It enables computers to discover their own IP address.

    d. It is outdated and no longer used.

57. In DHCP data packets, a DHCP discover packet is

    a. Message = Discover

    b. MT = Discover

    c. Discover = Type

    d. Type = Discover

58. Data traffic plots are not necessary for which of the following?

    a. Hourly plots

    b. Daily plots

    c. Weekly plots

    d. Monthly plots

    e. None of these answers is correct.

59. What is the command to enable the DHCP relay on a Cisco router?

    a. Router(config-if)# **ip helper** [*ip address of the DHCP server*]

    b. Router(config)# **ip helper** [*ip address of the DHCP server*]

    c. Router# **ip helper** [*ip address of the DHCP server*]

    d. Router(config-dhcp)# **ip helper** [*ip address of the DHCP server*]

60. What are the ports for the BOOTP-server and BOOTP client?

    a. BOOTP-server 68, BOOTP-client 67

    b. BOOTP-server 21, BOOTP-client 22

    c. BOOTP-server 67, BOOTP-client 68

    d. None of these answers is correct.

61. A DHCP server isn't available. What process allows a Windows system to automatically configure its IP address and subnet mask?

    a. IP helper

    b. Reverse DHCP lookup

    c. APIPA (Automatic Private IP Addressing)

    d. None of the above

62. The network technician notices that the network is working fine for IPv4. However, IPv6 traffic is not able to reach the DNS server. Which of the following is most likely the problem?

    a. The A record is missing.

    b. The AAAA record is not updated.

    c. The DHCP server is down.

    d. The system requires rebooting.

TROUBLESHOOTING

Chapter Outline

Objectives

- Describe the purpose of a network protocol analyzer
- Describe the to analyze captured data packets
- Describe the contents of an FTP data transfer
- Describe the data traffic patterns a NOC (network operation center) might monitor
- Discuss the commands used to troubleshoot a router interface
- Describe the purpose of an optical time domain reflectometer
- Describe the steps for troubleshooting wireless networks

Key Terms

Address Resolution Protocol (ARP)

arp reply

arp request

FTP

SFTP

keepalive packet

administratively down

Visual Fault Locator (VFL)

OTDR

event

This chapter examines the various tools and troubleshooting techniques needed by the network administrator. An introduction to capturing and analyzing network data traffic is examined in sections 11-2, 11-3, and 11-4. In section 11-2, the steps for installing the Wireshark protocol analyzer are presented. In this section the student will gain an introductory understanding of how to capture network data traffic and analyze the results. Section 11-3 explores the data packet contents of a File Transfer Protocol (FTP) data transfer. In this section, the reader will gain a deeper understanding of how data packets are transferred using the FTP. Section 11-4 provides an overview of the data traffic patterns a network operation center (NOC) might monitor. Included in this section are examples of data traffic activity for a network.

11-1   INTRODUCTION

Section 11-5 examines one of the most commonly used router commands for troubleshooting and isolating problems **show ip interface brief (sh ip int brief)**. This command enables the network administrator to verify the IP address for each interface and determine its status and protocol state. This command is useful when looking for problems that might be related to the router configuration and router interfaces operation. Section 11-6 examines the basic concepts of troubleshooting the network switch. The use of the **show ip interface brief** and the **show interface status** commands are demonstrated. The switch is an OSI layer 2 device and the command **show mac address-table** is demonstrated for displaying the switch's MAC address table. The chapter concludes with a look at one of the tools used to troubleshoot fiber-optic cable—the optical time domain reflectometer (OTDR). The OTDR sends a light pulse down the fiber and measures the reflected light. This provides a way to verify the quality of each fiber span and obtain some measure of performance.

Table 11-1 lists and identifies, by chapter section, where each of the CompTIA Network+ objectives are presented in this chapter. At the end of each chapter section is a review with comments of the Network+ objectives presented in that section. These comments are provided to help reinforce the reader's understanding of a particular Network+ objective. The chapter review also includes "Test Your

Knowledge" questions to aid in the understanding of key concepts before the reader advances to the next section of the chapter. The end of the chapter includes a complete set of question plus sample certification type questions.

TABLE 11-1 **Chapter 11 CompTIA Network+ Objectives**

Domain/Objective Number	Domain/Objective Description	Section Where Objective Is Covered
1.0	*Network Architecture*	
1.5	Install and properly terminate various cable types and connectors using the appropriate tools	11-7
2.0	*Network Operations*	
2.1	Given a scenario, use appropriate monitoring tools	11-2, 11-4
2.6	Given a scenario, configure a switch using the proper features	11-6
3.0	*Network Security*	
3.2	Compare and contrast network vulnerabilities and threats	11-2, 11-3, 11-4, 11-5
3.3	Given a scenario, implement network-hardening techniques	11-5
4.0	*Troubleshooting*	
4.1	Given a scenario, implement the following network troubleshooting methodology	11-5, 11-6
4.2	Given a scenario, analyze and interpret the output of troubleshooting tools	11-2, 11-3, 11-4, 11-6
4.3	Given a scenario, troubleshoot and resolve common wireless issues	11-8
4.6	Given a scenario, troubleshoot and resolve common network issues	11-8

11-2 ANALYZING COMPUTER NETWORKS

The objective of this section is to introduce the techniques for using a protocol analyzer to examine how networking packets are exchanged in a TCP/IP network. The TCP/IP protocol was previously examined in Chapter 6, "TCP/IP." By using a protocol analyzer, such as Wireshark, you will actually be able to develop a better understanding of the protocols being used and how the data packets are being transferred.

The Wireshark software includes many advanced features for packet capture and analysis. The capabilities of this software will help you gain a thorough understanding of packet transfers and networking protocols. In this chapter, you will gain an introductory understanding of the capabilities and techniques for using a sophisticated software protocol analyzer. The protocol analyzer has the capability to capture and decode data packets and allows the user to inspect the packet contents. This enables the user to investigate how information is being transferred in the network. Additionally, the information provided by the protocol analyzer enables the user to detect, identify, and correct network problems. In this section, you are guided through the steps of using the Wireshark Network Analyzer.

The following steps guide you through installing and using the Wireshark software. To download the latest version of the software, visit www.Wireshark.org. At the Wireshark.org home page, select **Download Wireshark**; once completed, select your corresponding operating system. Click **Run** when the dialog box appears to initiate the download process. At the prompt of the setup wizard, select **Next** and agree to the license agreement. Choose the components you would like to install and click **Next** to continue. At the next screen, select your program shortcuts and click **Next** to continue. Use the default directory paths specified in the setup menu. To complete the setup, click **Install** to start the installation process. After installation, you are ready to begin using the software.

In our first exercise, the Wireshark software is used to examine the packets transferred in the process of pinging a computer. This exercise is based on the ping exercise presented in section 1-7, "Testing and Troubleshooting a LAN," from Chapter 1, "Introduction to Computer Networks," and uses the IP and MAC addresses specified in Table 11-2.

Using Wireshark to Inspect Data Packets

The following are steps to guide you through the use of the Wireshark Network Protocol Analyzer. This first exercise demonstrates how to use the protocol analyzer to inspect captured packets.

1. In Windows, Click **Start > Programs > Wireshark** to start the analyzer program. The procedure for starting the Wireshark Network Analyzer is the same for a MAC OS X operating in the dual-boot mode with XP.

2. Once Wireshark is open, click **File > Open**, select your CD-ROM drive, and select the Wireshark file folder. Double-click the **Ch11-6.cap** file to open the file.

Once you have opened the Ch11-6.cap capture in Wireshark, you should see the captured packets displayed on the detail view screen, as shown in Fig. 11-1. In this example, the information on the screen shows the transfer of packets that occurs when one computer pings another. In this case, computer 1 pinged computer 2. The MAC and IP addresses are listed for your reference in Table 11-2.

TABLE 11-2   **The MAC and Assigned IP Addresses for Computer 1 and Computer 2**

Name (Hostname)	MAC Address	IP Address
Computer 1	00-10-A4-13-99-2E	10.10.10.1
Computer 2	00-10-A4-13-6C-6E	10.10.10.2

In this example, a **ping** command is issued from computer 1 to computer 2. The structure of the command issued by computer 1 at the command prompt is as follows:

```
ping 10.10.10.2
```

Shown in packet number 1 in Figure 11-1, computer 1 issues an Address Resolution Protocol **(ARP)** request on the LAN. ARP is a protocol used to map an IP address to its MAC address. The source of the packet is 00-10-A4-13-99-2E (computer 1). The destination address on the local area network (LAN) shown is BROADCAST, which means this message is being sent to all computers on the network. A query (Q) being asked is who has the IP address 1 0.10.10.2 (PA). In Figure 11-1, the wording to the right of ARP says, "Who has 10.10.10.2?"

> **Address Resolution Protocol (ARP)**
> Used to map an IP address to its MAC address

The highlighted area (Number 2) in Figure 11-2 shows computer 2 replying with its MAC address back to computer 1. This is called an **ARP reply**, which is a protocol where the MAC address is returned. The source of the ARP reply is from 00-10-A4-13-6C-6E (computer 2), which is replying that the MAC address for 10.10.10.2 is 00-10-A4-13-6C-6E (HA). In this case, the owner of the IP address replied to the message.

> **ARP Reply**
> A network protocol where the MAC address is returned

FIGURE 11-1   The captured packets showing the ping from computer 1 to computer 2.

FIGURE 11-2 Computer 2 replying with its MAC address back to computer 1.

<table>
<tr><td>**Echo Request**

Part of the ICMP protocol that requests a reply from a computer</td></tr>
</table>

Figure 11-3 shows computer 1 sending an **echo request** directly to computer 2. An echo request is the part of the ICMP protocol that requests a reply from a computer. Notice in the echo request that the destination address is 00-10-A4-13-6C-6E (computer 2's MAC address) and the source is 00-10-A4-13-99-2E (computer 1's MAC address). Recall that computer 1 now knows the MAC address for IP address 10.10.10.2 so the **ping** request can be sent directly. In this step, computer 1 uses the ICMP **ping** command to verify network connectivity. The highlighted area in Figure 11-4 (Number 4) shows computer 2's echo reply. This series of echo requests and replies repeats three more times for a total of four cycles.

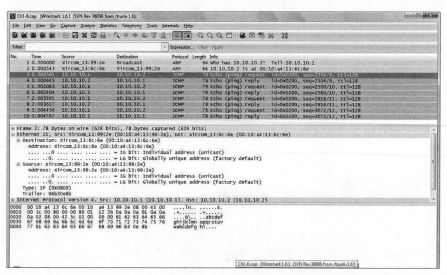

FIGURE 11-3 Computer 1 is sending an echo request to computer 2.

FIGURE 11-4 The echo reply from computer 2.

Using Wireshark to Capture Packets

The first exercise with the Wireshark software demonstrated how to use the protocol analyzer to inspect captured packets. In most cases, the user will want to capture data packets from her own network. The following steps describe how to use the software to capture packets.

1. In Windows, click **Start > Programs > Wireshark >** and select **Wireshark** to start the program.

2. To capture packets on an operating network, you first need to select the interfaces in which you would like to obtain the capture (see Figure 11-5). You can do this by going to **Capture > Interfaces**. After selecting your interfaces, click **Start** to start capturing as shown in Figure 11-6. You can also get to the interface list by clicking on **Interface List** from the Wireshark home screen.

3. To examine the packets, stop the simulation by clicking **Capture > Stop.** Remember, there must be some activity on your network for packets to be transferred. You might see little traffic activity if your network is in the lab and there is limited network activity. You can always use the **ping** command to generate some network data activity if needed.

To open a saved capture file, click **File > Open** or click **Open** from the Wireshark home screen.

To change capture options, click **Capture > Options** to change the options to your preferred settings.

FIGURE 11-5   Initializing Wireshark to capture data packets from your network.

FIGURE 11-6   Starting the capture.

Section 11-2 Review

This section has covered the following **Network+** Exam objectives.

> 2.1 Given a scenario, use the appropriate monitoring tools

This section introduced the use of the Wireshark Network Protocol analyzer. The steps for capturing and displaying data packets were examined.

> 4.2 Given a scenario, analyze and interpret the output of troubleshooting tools

This section has demonstrated how to use the Wireshark protocol analyzer to analyze captured data packets.

11-3 ANALYZING COMPUTER NETWORKS—FTP DATA PACKETS

This section explores the data packet contents of an FTP data transfer. FTP is the File Transfer Protocol defined in the TCP/IP model. The captured file is available on the companion CD-ROM in the *Capture* folder. The filename is *11-D.cap*. This file contains several TCP transactions. This discussion will identify the packet IP for reference.

Figure 11-7 provides the setup for this data capture. The MAC addresses for the client and server are provided as a reference. The beginning of the FTP is shown in packet 5 in Figure 11-8(a). The packet shows that a connection is being made from a Windows server to port 1054 on a client computer. In packet 8, the client is responding with a username of *administrator*. In packet 9, the server is telling the client that a password is required. The client responds with the password *Chile* in packet 11.

FIGURE 11-7   The computer setup for the FTP packet transfer.

Notice that the password is in plaintext (not encrypted). This is why most FTP applications use Secure FTP (**SFTP**). With SFTP, all messages between the server and the client are encrypted.

In packet 14, the server acknowledges that the user *administrator* is connected to the server. In packet 18, the client is notifying the server that an ASCII data transfer is requested. This is indicated in the Type A statement. In packet 19, the server acknowledges that an ASCII transfer is requested (*Type set to A*). Packet 24 [Figure 11-8(b)] is a request from the client to start the data packet transfer from the server. The text *STOR text.txt* signifies this. In packet 25, the server indicates that it is

SFTP
Secure File Transfer Protocol

opening the ASCII mode for the transfer. When the FTP connection is established, the port numbers change to handle the data transfer as shown in packet 31, SP = 20 DP = 1055. Packets 38, 40, and 41 are the closing of the FTP transfer. The FTP data packets examined are part of a TCP connection. This required that a TCP connection was both established and closed. In fact, the TCP initial handshake and the connection closing for this FTP session were presented in section 6-2.

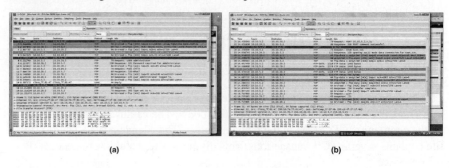

(a)   (b)

FIGURE 11-8 (a) The beginning of the FTP data packet transfer and the request for an ASCII data transfer by the client. (b) The FTP data packet transfer and the closing of the FTP transfer.

Section 11-3 Review

This section has covered the following **Network+** Exam objectives.

> 3.2 Compare and contrast network vulnerabilities and threats

This section examined the security issues of transferring data packets using FTP. A secured FTP transfer is provided with SFTP.

> 4.2 Given a scenario, analyze and interpret the output of troubleshooting tools

This section examined the packets exchanged during an FTP file transfer using the Wireshark network protocol analyzer. You should be able to follow the transfer from the opening the connection to data transfer and then the closing of the connection.

Test Your Knowledge

1. Which TCP port number does FTP use?

    a. 20

    b. 25

    c. 20, 21

    d. 80, 443

2. Which packets are exchanged when an FTP transfer is being established from the client to the server?

    a. SYN + ACK

    b. ACK

    c. SYN + (SYN+ACK) + ACK

    d. ASK + SYN

11-4 ANALYZING CAMPUS NETWORK DATA TRAFFIC

Section 8-5 in Chapter 8, "Introduction to Switch Configuration," introduced the SNMP protocol for use in network management. An example was presented that shows how to obtain the number of octets leaving a router. This type of information can be used in a campus network to monitor the flow of data for many points in the network. Statistics can be obtained for hourly, daily, weekly, and monthly data traffic. This section discusses plots of network router utilization obtained via the router's SNMP port.

Figure 11-9 is a plot of a router's hourly data traffic. The plot shows the average number of bits coming into the router and the average number of bits out. The network administrator should become familiar with the typical hourly data traffic pattern for his network. Notice the decrease in data traffic in the early morning and the dramatic increase in data traffic around 12:00. The traffic clearly shows some type of disturbance around 12:00. The plot is showing that the bit rate significantly increases for a few minutes. This is not necessarily a problem, but it is something that a network administrator should watch.

FIGURE 11-9 The hourly plot of a router's data traffic.

In this case, the network administrator looked at the daily log of network activity for the same router. This plot is shown in Figure 11-10. The cycle of the data traffic from morning to night is as expected, heavy data traffic about noon and very low data traffic in the mornings. An interesting note is that the noon data traffic spikes on the first Wednesday and then repeats the following Wednesday. Whatever is causing the change in traffic appears to happen on Wednesdays. If this sudden change in data traffic turned out to be something of concern, a protocol analyzer could be set up to capture the data traffic on Wednesdays around noon so that the traffic pattern could be explained.

FIGURE 11-10 The daily plot of a router's data traffic.

Sometimes the graph of the network traffic over a longer period of time is needed. Figure 11-11 shows the data traffic through the router over a six-week period. The traffic shows some consistency except for a change from week 11 to week 12. Most likely this can be explained by examining the network trouble reports and maintenance logs to see if this router was briefly out of service.

FIGURE 11-11 The weekly plot of a router's data traffic.

Justifying the expansion of a network's capability (for example, higher data rate or better core or distribution service) requires showing the manager data traffic statistics. Figure 11-12 is a plot of the router's monthly data traffic. The summer shows a significant decrease in data traffic. The plot also shows that the network was down once in the June–July period and again in January. The manager wants to know whether there is justification to increase the data rate of the router to 1 gigabit (1GB). (The router's current data rate is 100Mbps.) Is there justification to upgrade the router to 1GB? Probably not, at least not immediately. The maximum measured average data rate is about 16Mbps. The router's 100Mbps data rate does not seem to be causing any traffic congestion problems.

FIGURE 11-12   The monthly plot of a router's data traffic.

SNMP can be used to collect much more information other than utilization usage in bits per second (bps) for capacity planning. Most Network Operations Centers would also collect SNMP information, such as packets per second, errors per second, unicast per second, multicast per second, broadcast per second, and so on. All this information can be graphed for better visualization and help illustrate the overall health of the network through time.

This section has shown how keeping logs of data traffic can be used to spot potential network problems and to help plan for possible future expansion of the network.

Section 11-4 Review

This section has covered the following **Network+** Exam objectives.

2.1 Given a scenario, use appropriate monitoring tools

This section examined the flow of data in a network. The use of SNMP and the importance of keeping logs of network performance were presented.

3.2 Compare and contrast vulnerabilities and threats

This section examined network data traffic and presented examples with data spikes that could be an indication of unauthorized file transfers taking place.

4.2 Given a scenario, analyze and interpret the output of troubleshooting tools

This section has shown how keeping logs of data traffic can be used to spot potential network problems and to help plan for possible future expansion of the network.

11-5 TROUBLESHOOTING THE ROUTER INTERFACE

This section examines one of the most commonly used router commands for troubleshooting and isolating problems that might be related to the router configuration and router interfaces: **show ip interface brief (sh ip int brief)**. Typically, the network administrator will be able to SSH into the router to establish a secure virtual terminal connection. The virtual terminal enables the administrator to connect to the router without physically plugging in to it. The onscreen appearance of the virtual terminal connection will appear the same as the console port connection. Remember, the virtual interface is password protected and only authorized users can access the router through this interface.

The first step is to check the status of the interfaces and verify that the interfaces are attached to another networking device using the **sh ip int brief** command. The command provides a quick look at information about the interfaces, such as the following:

Interface	The type of interface:
	Ethernet: 10Mbps
	Fast Ethernet: 100Mbps
	Gigabit Ethernet: 1000Mbps
	Serial: From 2500bps to 4Mbps and higher for high-speed serial interfaces
IP-Address	The IP address assigned to the interface
OK?	Indicates whether the interface is functioning
Method	"How the interface was brought up" (for example, manual, tftp)
Status	{current router status "up", "down", or "administratively down"}
	Line Protocol displayed results differ for FastEthernet and the Serial interfaces. For FastEthernet, status "up" indicates that the FastEthernet interface has been administratively brought up.
Protocol	The protocol "up" indicates that you are seeing the **Keepalive packet**. Keepalive indicates that the FastEthernet interface is connected to another networking device such as a hub, switch, or router. A protocol status of "down" indicates that the Ethernet port is not physically connected to another network device. This is not the same as the link integrity pulse that activates the link light. The link integrity pulse does not send a small Ethernet packet; Keepalive sends such a packet.

> **Keepalive Packet**
> Indicates that the Ethernet interface is connected to another networking device such as a hub, switch, or router

The following demonstrates how **sh ip int brief** can be used to check the status of the interfaces for different conditions such as status down, status up/protocol down, and status/protocol down. This includes examples of how to interpret the results displayed by the **sh ip int brief** command. This is of particular importance when troubleshooting a possible cable or link failure. When a FastEthernet interface cable is not attached or the link is broken, the protocol shows "down." If a serial interface cable is not attached or the link is broken, the status and the protocol both show "down."

The following are text outputs from a Cisco router that demonstrate how the router status and protocol settings change based on the interface configuration and setup. The first text displays that the three Ethernet interfaces and two serial interfaces are properly configured. The status "up" means that the interface has been administratively turned on by the network administrator.

```
RouterA#sh ip int brief
Interface       IP-Address     OK?  Method   Status   Protocol
FastEthernet0/0 10.10.20.250   YES  manual   up       up
FastEthernet0/1 10.10.200.1    YES  manual   up       up
FastEthernet0/2 10.10.100.1    YES  manual   up       up
Serial0/0       10.10.128.1    YES  manual   up       up
Serial0/1       10.10.64.1     YES  manual   up       up
```

The next example demonstrates that the router provides a prompt if the link between the router's FastEthernet0/0 interface and another networking device is lost. Within a few seconds of losing the link, the prompt shown appears:

```
2w0d: %LINEPROTO-5-UPDOWN: Line protocol on Interface
FastEthernet0/0, changed state to down
```

The **sh ip int brief** command shows that the protocol for FastEthernet0/0 is "down" and the status is still "up," meaning the interface is still enabled but the router is not communicating with another networking device such as a hub, switch, or router. Therefore, the protocol "down" condition for the FastEthernet interface, as viewed by the **sh ip int brief** command, indicates that there is a loss of communications between the router and a connected networking device. You might have to physically check the router's FastEthernet interface for a link light. In this example, a link light check on the router showed that there was not a link and, in fact, the RJ-45 plug connected to the router had come loose.

```
RouterA#sh ip int brief
Interface        IP-Address      OK?   Method   Status   Protocol
FastEthernet0/0  10.10.20.250    YES   manual   up       down
FastEthernet0/1  10.10.200.1     YES   manual   up       up
FastEthernet0/2  10.10.100.1     YES   manual   up       up
Serial0/0        10.10.128.1     YES   manual   up       up
Serial0/1        10.10.64.1      YES   manual   up       up
```

Reconnecting the RF-45 cable reestablishes the link for the FastEthernet0/0 interface and the networking device. The router provides a prompt that the FastEthernet0/0 line protocol has changed state to "up." The **sh ip int brief** command now shows that all interface status is "up" and protocol is "up."

```
2w0d: %LINEPROTO-5-UPDOWN: Line protocol on Interface FastEthernet0/0,
changed state to up
RouterA#sh ip int brief
Interface        IP-Address      OK?   Method   Status   Protocol
FastEthernet0/0  10.10.20.250    YES   manual   up       up
FastEthernet0/1  10.10.200.1     YES   manual   up       up
FastEthernet0/2  10.10.100.1     YES   manual   up       up
Serial0/0        10.10.128.1     YES   manual   up       up
Serial0/1        10.10.64.1      YES   manual   up       up
```

The router's serial ports behave differently from the FastEthernet interfaces, as shown with the following examples. The previous router text display using the **sh ip int brief** command shows that the Serial0/0 interface status is "up" and the protocol is "up." If the serial link is lost or disconnected, the interface goes down and a prompt is sent to the console screen, as shown. The prompt advises the administrator that the Serial0/0 interface has changed state to "down" and the line protocol for Serial0/0 is also "down." The **sh ip int brief** command now shows that the status and line protocol for Serial0/0 are "down."

```
2w0d: %LINK-3-UPDOWN: Interface Serial0/0, changed state to down
2w0d: %LINEPROTO-5-UPDOWN: Line protocol on Interface Serial0/0,
changed state to down
```

```
RouterA#sh ip int brief
Interface         IP-Address      OK?   Method   Status    Protocol
FastEthernet0/0   10.10.20.250    YES   manual   up        up
FastEthernet0/1   10.10.200.1     YES   manual   up        up
FastEthernet0/2   10.10.100.1     YES   manual   up        up
Serial0/0         10.10.128.1     YES   manual   down      down
Serial1/1         10.10.64.1      YES   manual   up        up
```

Reestablishing the serial connection will change the status back to "up" and the
protocol back to "up" as shown. Note that the prompt includes a statement that
communication to 10.10.128.1 has been resumed. This is the IP address of the serial interface attached to the router's Serial0 interface.

```
2w0d: %LINK-3-UPDOWN: Interface Serial0, changed state to up
2w0d: %LINEPROTO-5-UPDOWN: Line protocol on Interface Serial0, changed
state to up
[Resuming connection 1 to 10.10.128.1 ... ]
RouterA#sh ip int brief
Interface         IP-Address      OK?   Method   Status    Protocol
FastEthernet0/0   10.10.20.250    YES   manual   up        up
FastEthernet0/1   10.10.200.1     YES   manual   up        up
FastEthernet0/2   10.10.100.1     YES   manual   up        up
Serial0/0         10.10.128.1     YES   manual   up        up
Serial10/1        10.10.64.1      YES   manual   up        up
```

This screen shows that the Serial0 interface is "administratively down." The term
administratively down indicates that the router interface has been shut off by the
administrator. Note the difference with the terms *down* and *administratively down*.
Reissuing the command **no shut** for the Serial0/0 interface should correct the
problem.

> **Administratively Down**
>
> Indicates that the router interface has been shut off by the administrator

```
RouterA#sh ip int brief
Interface         IP-Address     OK?  Method  Status                   Protocol
FastEthernet0/0   10.10.20.250   YES  manual  up                       up
FastEthernet0/1   10.10.200.1    YES  manual  up                       up
FastEthernet0/2   10.10.100.1    YES  manual  up                       up
Serial0/0         10.10.128.1    YES  manual  administratively down    up
Serial0/1         10.10.64.1     YES  manual  up                       up
```

The command **show ip int brief** gives a summary view of the interface's status. If
you would like to examine an interface more in detail, using the command **show
interface** would be more suitable. This command gives detailed information of all
interfaces belonging to the router. The following output is part of the result from
the command **show int**. Not only does the command show the status of the interface FastEthernet0/0, but it displays statistical information regarding the interface,
such as input and output rate in bits per second and packets per second, broadcast

packets, as well as error packets. Here, it shows the interface received two input errors, both CRC-type errors. This command is very useful when troubleshooting something beyond basic connectivity issues such as speed, performance, and throughput.

```
RouterA #sh int
FastEthernet0/0 is up, line protocol is up
  Hardware is MV96340 Ethernet, address is 40f4.ecb9.1010 (bia
40f4.ecb9.1010)
  Internet address is 10.10.20.250/24
  MTU 1500 bytes, BW 100000 Kbit/sec, DLY 100 usec,
     reliability 255/255, txload 7/255, rxload 6/255
  Encapsulation ARPA, loopback not set
  Keepalive set (10 sec)
  Full-duplex, 100Mb/s, 100BaseTX/FX
  ARP type: ARPA, ARP Timeout 04:00:00
  Last input 00:00:00, output 00:00:00, output hang never
  Last clearing of "show interface" counters never
  Input queue: 0/75/0/0 (size/max/drops/flushes); Total output drops: 0
  Queueing strategy: fifo
  Output queue: 0/40 (size/max)
  5 minute input rate 2623000 bits/sec, 556 packets/sec
  5 minute output rate 2892000 bits/sec, 485 packets/sec
     48430288 packets input, 206222517 bytes
     Received 633291 broadcasts, 0 runts, 0 giants, 0 throttles
     2 input errors, 2 CRC, 0 frame, 0 overrun, 0 ignored
     0 watchdog
     0 input packets with dribble condition detected
     43353888 packets output, 2673132365 bytes, 0 underruns
     0 output errors, 0 collisions, 0 interface resets
     0 unknown protocol drops
     0 babbles, 0 late collision, 0 deferred
     0 lost carrier, 0 no carrier
     0 output buffer failures, 0 output buffers swapped out
```

It is a best practice to always verify the router configuration. At the end, the status of the interface is a reflection of how the router is programmed. When making changes to the router configuration, the changes are made to the running configuration. The command **show running-config** (**sh run**) can be used to display the most current configuration of the router. The running configuration is stored in random access memory (RAM), which loses its content when the router is powered off. The router configuration can be saved by issuing the command **copy running-config startup-config** (**copy run start**). This will save the router configuration to the startup configuration, which is stored in non-volatile random access memory (NVRAM). This type of memory does not lose its content after the power down.

This section has presented the **show ip int brief** command and shown how it can be used to troubleshoot and isolate router interface problems. The status differs for the Ethernet and serial interfaces. This is an important concept and something you will encounter when working with routers.

11-6   TROUBLESHOOTING THE SWITCH INTERFACE

This section examines how to troubleshoot another type of network equipment, the switch. The troubleshooting concepts from the previous section still apply to the switch troubleshooting. Similar to troubleshooting a router, you should verify the switch configuration to ensure that it is correct and verify the switch interfaces to make sure they are up and operating in the right mode. Many commands from the router can also be used for the switch. On Cisco routers and switches, commands such as **show running-config** are universal. This command is used to display the currently running configuration of the network device.

In previous section, the command **show ip int brief** was introduced to check the status of the interfaces on a router; the same command can also be used on a switch. The output of the command will show the status of the physical interfaces as well as the VLAN interfaces, if any are configured. Here, it shows that the VLAN1 is configured and is up and operational.

```
SwitchA#sh ip int brief
Interface          IP-Address     OK?    Method   Status   Protocol
Vlan1              10.123.124.2   YES    NVRAM    up       up
FastEthernet0/1    unassigned     YES    unset    up       up
FastEthernet0/2    unassigned     YES    unset    up       up
FastEthernet0/3    unassigned     YES    unset    up       up
FastEthernet0/4    unassigned     YES    unset    up       up
FastEthernet0/5    unassigned     YES    unset    down     down
```

You might find that the command **show ip int brief** does not offer enough layer 2 or layer 1 information. Another useful command for displaying the status of the switch interfaces is **show interface status** (**sh int status**). This command provides the following switch port information:

Port	The type of interface:
	Ethernet: 10Mbps
	Fast Ethernet: 100Mbps
	Gigabit Ethernet: 1000Mbps
Name	The description of the interface, if it is configured.
Status	**"connect"** indicates the interface is physically connected to another network device.
	"notconnect" indicates the switch port has no physical link to an active network device.
Vlan	This displays the VLAN ID, which indicates the VLAN port membership.
Duplex	This indicates the duplexing mode of the connection. The duplex can be a-full (auto-negotiation full-duplex), a-half (auto-negotiation half-duplex), full (manual full-duplex), or half (manual half-duplex).
Speed	This indicates the speed at which the connection is negotiated or configured. The speed can be a-1000 (auto-negotiation 1Gbps), a-100 (auto-negotiation 100Mbps), a-10 (auto-negotiation 10Mbps), 1000 (manual 1Gbps), 100 (manual 100Mbps), or 10 (manual 10Mbps).
Type	This indicates the physical connection type of the interface, whether it is a 100Mbps copper (100BaseTX), 1Gbps copper (1000BaseTX), 100Mbps fiber (100BaseFX), 1Gbp multimode fiber (1000BaseSX), or 1Gbps single-mode fiber (1000BaseLX).

The following example shows the outputs from a Cisco switch. It shows the status of the gigabit interfaces from 0/1 to 0/6, where only gigabit interfaces 0/1–0/4 have connections. All the ports are configured to be auto-negotiated. All the active ports are connected at 1Gbps full-duplex. The physical connection on the gigabit interface 0/1 is 1000BaseLX, which indicates that a single-mode fiber-type connection and that the rest of the active ports are using multimode fiber-type connectors (1000BaseSX). The gigabit interfaces 0/1 and 0/4 are configured to be members of VLAN 1, while gigabit interfaces 0/2 and 0/3 are members of VLAN2. Because gigabit interfaces 0/5 and 0/6 are not used, their statuses are shown as "notconnect" and their types are "unknown." It shows that these two ports are configured to be auto-negotiated and are configured to be members of VLAN 1.

```
SwitchA#sh interfaces status
Port    Name        Status       Vlan    Duplex  Speed   Type
Gi0/1   main feed   connected    1       a-full  a-1000  1000BaseLX
Gi0/2   BuildingA   connected    2       a-full  a-1000  1000BaseSX
Gi0/3   BuildingB   connected    2       a-full  a-1000  1000BaseSX
Gi0/4   BuildingC   connected    1       a-full  a-1000  1000BaseSX
Gi0/5               notconnect   1       auto    auto    unknown
Gi0/6               notconnect   1       auto    auto    unknown
```

The duplex and speed are good information when you're troubleshooting performance issues. When the reported duplex or speed does not match what the NIC is using, this will result in performance degradation due to collisions and packet drops. Most NICs are typically left to auto-negotiate their speed and duplex. If auto-negotiation is configured at the switch interface and at the device NIC, then it will be no problem because auto-negotiation will do its job to find the proper speed and duplex. Issues arise when one end is configured to use auto-negotiation and the other end is not, or when both ends are configured for manual duplex and speed and their settings do not match. It is a good fundamental troubleshooting practice to make sure the duplex and speed of the connection are matched at both ends.

When a network device is connected to an available port and the physical link is successful, messages are displayed on the switch console. An example of the messages displayed is provided for the gigabit interface 0/5 indicating the interface has successfully linked with an active network device.

```
2w0d: %LINK-3-UPDOWN: Interface GigabitEthernet 0/5, changed state to
up
2w0d: %LINEPROTO-5-UPDOWN: Line protocol on Interface GigabitEthernet
0/5, changed state to up
```

Unlike a router, a switch is an OSI layer 2 device that operates by storing and forwarding the MAC addresses. Also, a switch generally services more directly connected network devices than a router does. More populated switch ports mean more network clients, which makes troubleshooting more difficult. So, it is very important to know how to isolate network devices. Being able to tell to which switch port a particular network device is connected comes in handy. On Cisco switches, the switch command **show mac-address-table** or the command **show mac address-table** on the newer switches can be used to display the MAC address table of the switch as shown here:

```
SwitchA#sh mac address-table
                        Mac Address Table
- - - - - - - - - - - - - - - - - - - - - - -

    Vlan            Mac Address        Type            Ports
- -         - - - - - - - - -        - - -
    All             0100.0ccc.cccc     STATIC          CPU
    All             0100.0ccc.cccd     STATIC          CPU
    All             0180.c200.0000     STATIC          CPU
```

```
All                    0180.c200.0001          STATIC          CPU
All                    0180.c200.0002          STATIC          CPU
All                    0180.c200.0003          STATIC          CPU
All                    0180.c200.0004          STATIC          CPU
All                    0180.c200.0005          STATIC          CPU
All                    0180.c200.0006          STATIC          CPU
All                    0180.c200.0007          STATIC          CPU
All                    0180.c200.0008          STATIC          CPU
All                    0180.c200.0009          STATIC          CPU
All                    0180.c200.000a          STATIC          CPU
All                    0180.c200.000b          STATIC          CPU
All                    0180.c200.000c          STATIC          CPU
All                    0180.c200.000d          STATIC          CPU
All                    0180.c200.000e          STATIC          CPU
All                    0180.c200.000f          STATIC          CPU
All                    0180.c200.0010          STATIC          CPU
All                    ffff.ffff.ffff          STATIC          CPU
1                      0003.ba53.164d          DYNAMIC         Gi1/0/9
1                      0006.5bf7.6e9a          DYNAMIC         Gi1/0/8
1                      000c.0c01.4711          DYNAMIC         Gi1/0/11
1                      000f.1f64.978b          DYNAMIC         Gi1/0/13
1                      000f.1f64.979f          DYNAMIC         Gi1/0/14
1                      0013.210b.20c8          DYNAMIC         Gi1/0/10
1                      0013.211d.6475          DYNAMIC         Gi1/0/5
1                      0016.3e09.39e7          DYNAMIC         Gi1/0/7
1                      0016.3e32.3198          DYNAMIC         Gi1/0/7
1                      0017.0850.17f0          DYNAMIC         Gi1/0/6
1                      001e.c9b5.1dd2          DYNAMIC         Gi1/0/3
1                      001e.c9b5.1e4f          DYNAMIC         Gi1/0/4
1                      0050.8bc2.5471          DYNAMIC         Gi1/0/12
1                      0060.2e00:529b          DYNAMIC         Gi1/0/1
1                      02d0.6819.1854          DYNAMIC         Gi1/0/2
Total Mac Addresses for this criterion: 35
```

A network administrator can use this command to map a network device by its MAC address to a switch port. The connected device's MAC address is a dynamic type because it is not stationary or specific to a switch port. When a device moves from one switch port to another, the switch relearns the MAC address's new location. The switch deletes its old MAC entry and updates its database with the new MAC entry mapping. The static MAC addresses shown previously are those assigned to the switch interfaces. These MAC addresses do not change.

A common task for the network technician is to verify the uptime for a switch. This will help identify potential problems with switches that might be intermittently resetting. The command for viewing the switch uptime is

```
switch#show version
```

The reason to check the uptime is to see if a switch has been rebooting. Rebooting problems can be due to power fluctuations or a switch problem. In either case, the network technician will need to know how to identify this problem and propose a solution. The following is sample output from the **show version** command, which shows that SwitchA has been up for 5 weeks, 8 hours, and 24 minutes.

```
ROM: Bootstrap program is Alpha board boot loader
BOOTLDR: C2960S Boot Loader (C2960S-HBOOT-M) Version 12.2(55r)SE,
RELEASE SOFTWARE (fc1)

SwitchA uptime is 1 year, 5 weeks, 8 hours, 24 minutes
System returned to ROM by power-on
System restarted at 06:11:00 MDT Sat Jul 12 2014
System image file is "flash:/c2960s-universalk9-mz.122-55.SE7/c2960s-
universalk9-mz.122-55.SE7.bin"
```

Section 11-6 Review

This section has covered the following **Network+** Exam objectives.

2.6 Given a scenario, configure a switch using the proper features

*This section examined the use of the **show ip interface brief** and **show interface status** commands and how to interpret the results for a switch. Additionally, the **show mac address-table** command and how this command can be used to display the MAC address table of the switch were discussed.*

4.1 Given a scenario, implement the following network troubleshooting methodology

This section introduced an example of the messages displayed when the interface has successfully linked with an active network device. This is a very useful troubleshooting tool.

4.2 Given a scenario, analyze and interpret the output of troubleshooting tools

An example was presented using the switch command **show mac-address-table**, or the command **show mac address-table** on the newer switches, to display the MAC address table of the switch. This is a very useful troubleshooting tool used by the network administrator to map a network device by its MAC address to a switch port.

Test Your Knowledge

1. Unlike a router, a switch is an OSI layer 2 device and operates by storing and forwarding the MAC addresses. True or False?

2. On a switch, static MAC addresses are best characterized by which of the following?

   a. They are dynamic and change as the device changes interface ports.

   b. They are assigned to a specific interface and do not change.

   c. They are not stationary for a switch port.

   d. All of these answers are correct.

11-7   TROUBLESHOOTING FIBER OPTICS—THE OTDR

Several techniques are used to measure and troubleshoot fiber links. A common technique is to use an optical power meter to determine power loss. Another tool used is a **visual fault locator (VFL)**, which shines light down the fiber to help locate broken glass. Figure 11-13(a) and (b) are traces obtained from an optical time-domain reflectometer (**OTDR**) for two different sets of multimode fibers. In field terms, this is called *shooting* the fiber. The OTDR sends a light pulse down the fiber and measures the reflected light. The OTDR enables the installer or maintenance crew to verify the quality of each fiber span and obtain some measure of performance. The X axis on the traces indicates the distance, whereas the Y axis indicates the measured optical power value in decibel (dB). Both OTDR traces are for 850-nm multimode fiber.

In regard to Figure 11-13(a), point A is a "dead" zone or a point too close to the OTDR for a measurement to be made. The measured value begins at about 25 dB and decreases in value as the distance traveled increases. An **event**, or a disturbance in the light propagating down the fiber, occurs at point B. This is an example of what a poor-quality splice looks like (in regard to reflection as well as insertion loss). Most likely, this is a mechanical splice. The same type of event occurs at points C and D. These are also most likely mechanical splices. Points F and G are most likely the jumpers and patch-panel connections at the fiber end. The steep drop at point H is actually the end of the fiber. Point I is typical noise that occurs at the end of an unterminated fiber. Notice at point G that the overall value of the trace has dropped to about 17 dB. There has been about 8 dB of optical power loss in the cable in a 1.7km run.

An OTDR trace for another multimode fiber is shown in Figure 11-13(b); the hump at point A is basically a dead zone. The OTDR cannot typically return accurate measurement values in this region. This is common for most OTDRs, and the dead zone will vary for each OTDR. The useful trace information begins at point B with a measured value of 20 dB. Point C shows a different type of event. This type of event is typical of coiled fiber or fiber that has been tightly bound, possibly with a tie-wrap, or that has had some other disturbance affecting the integrity of the fiber. Points D and F are actually the end of the fiber. At point D the trace level is about 19 dB for a loss of about 1 dB over the 150m run. Point G is just the noise that occurs at the end of a terminated fiber.

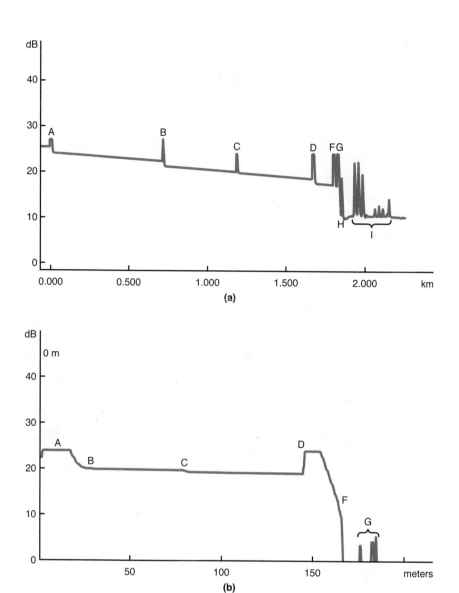

FIGURE 11-13 An OTDR trace of an 850-nm fiber. (From Modern Electronic Communication 9/e, by J. S. Beasley & G. M. Miller, 2008, p. 814. Copyright © 2008 Pearson Education, Inc. Reprinted by permission of Pearson Education, Inc., Upper Saddle River, NJ.)

11-8   TROUBLESHOOTING WIRELESS NETWORKS

This section examines some common techniques for troubleshooting wireless networks. Wireless networks have greatly simplified the steps for connecting to a network, but they do occasionally fail. The following are some scenarios that the user might encounter and outlines steps for troubleshooting and resolving the wireless issues:

- **Hardware issues:** Your primary hardware device in wireless networks is the access point. In some cases, you might have multiple access points. A simple first step is to ping the IP address for the access point. The purpose of the ping is to verify you have network connectivity. You should expect a reply to the ping, but if you don't get a reply, verify the IP address and repeat the ping. If it still doesn't work, there is a good chance that there is a problem with the access point. Try unplugging the access point and plugging it back in. This will reset the access point. Try the ping again, but if it still doesn't work, the access point might have a problem.

- **Signal strength problem**: The purpose of measuring the signal strength is to verify that you have "good" signal level at the receive location. Typically, the signal strength of the wireless connection can be adjusted at the access point to expand or reduce the area of coverage. Things change, and a loss in signal strength might not be a problem with the access point. It is possible that something could have been moved and is physically blocking the signal.

- **Frequency interference problem**: There might also be an electrical device such as a microwave oven that's causing interference. Microwave ovens operate at the frequency 2.4GHz, which is the same band as 802.11b/g/n devices. It is always good to have a baseline measurement of the signal strength expected at each location for situations such as this.

- **Load issues**: Wireless users share the same frequency channel to communicate to same access point. If too many users are connecting at the same time to the same access point, they will start experiencing slowness and packet drops will occur. For the optimum load capacity, one should consult the documentation of the access point manufacturer.

- **DHCP issues**: Your access points typically assign a 192.168.0.x address to the client. You can verify the IP address assigned by entering the command **ipconfig** from the command prompt (see section 1-4 in Chapter 1).

- **SSID issues**: Once the SSID (Service Set Identifier) has been configured for a computer, it normally does not require reconfiguration. However, in your travels, you might have reconfigured the SSID to connect to a different network. The simple fix is the reset your SSID when you return to your home network.

- **Securing Wi-Fi issues**: Most wireless systems support multiple network security protocols (for example, different versions of WPA/WEP). Make sure the client and access point are running the same security mode. Any time you are connecting your wireless device to a public hot spot, there is a chance that someone using a packet sniffer can see your data traffic. You can avoid possible problems by enabling WPA to secure your data traffic.

- **Wireless printer issues**: If you are experiencing problems with a wireless printer that was recently working, your first step is to restart the printer, your computer, and your wireless router. If this doesn't fix the problem, then print the network configuration off the printer. Check the IP address for the printer and verify it is assigned an IP address in your network. You can check the IP address of your computer by issuing the command **ipconfig** from the command prompt (see section 1-4 in Chapter 1).

- **Wireless router issues**: Make sure your client and wireless router support the same type of Wi-Fi version. For example, if your client computer's Wi-Fi card only supports 802.11b, your wireless router must also support 802.11b or must be configured to run in a mixed mode, where multiple protocols are being supported. Also, in the case where multiple clients are connecting to the wireless router, it is important to understand that when an association is made between the client and the wireless router, the client with the lowest 802.11 system will set the clock speed. For example, let's assume that a client running 802.11b and another running 802.11g connect to the same wireless router. The data transfer for 802.11b is 11bps and 802.11g is 54Mbps. The wireless router will select the 802.11b's lower clock rate for all associations. This can be of some concern to clients who have the capability to connect at a higher data transfer rate.

- **Extending the wireless range**: The following are some general tips for extending your wireless range: Make sure your antenna is placed high and is not obstructed by any metal. It is important to remember that radio waves will reflect off metal surfaces. Also, surfaces such as concrete and brick will attenuate the signal. In some cases you might have to use a high-gain antenna (see Chapter 4, "Wireless Networking") to help boost your receive signal strength.

- **Selecting wireless channels**: The default channel for 802.11b and 802.11g routers is channel 6. If you have interference problems, you can change the channel to 1 or 11. The RF spectrums on these channels do not overlap (refer to Figure 4-4 in Chapter 4). This will most likely solve your problem. 802.11b and 802.11g wireless routers have 11 possible channels, and selection of an alternate channel is managed via the wireless router's setting.

- **Wireless compatibility**: Not all wireless clients are created equal, as wireless clients depend on their hardware and software. They have to be kept up to date. Also, in order to have reliable and good throughput wireless connectivity, both the wireless access point and the wireless clients must be compatible and use the same standard. 802.11n is a standard that can offer connectivity in either 2.4GHz or 5GHz, or both. This means a wireless client can be 802.11n compatible just by operating in one frequency, not both. Therefore, an 802.11n wireless client with only 2.4GHz radio will never achieve the high speed of 300Mbps offered by 5GHz.

- **Cable issues**: Even though you are focusing on troubleshooting wireless issues, sometimes the problem could be due to a simple physical cable connection. The cable could be loose, has become disconnected, or is bad. It is always good to have a spare cable just in case. Remember, you can always verify you have a connection by checking for the presence of a link light!

- **Switch uptime**: A common task for the network technician is to verify the uptime for a switch. This will help identify potential problems with switches that might be intermittently resetting. The command for viewing the switch uptime is **switch#show version**. The reason to check the uptime is to see if a switch has been rebooting. Rebooting problems can be due to power fluctuations or a switch problem. In either case, the network technician will need to know how to identify this problem and propose a solution.

Section 11-8 Review

This section has covered the following **Network+** Exam objectives.

4.3 Given a scenario, troubleshoot and resolve common wireless issues

This section presented examples of several scenarios involving troubleshooting common wireless issues.

4.6 Given a scenario, troubleshoot and resolve common network issues

This section presented examples of several scenarios involving common network-troubleshooting issues.

Test Your Knowledge

1. Which of the following is a step the network technician could use to trouble-shoot switch uptime?

    a. View the switch uptime using the command **switch#show version**.

    b. View the switch uptime using the command **switch>show version**.

    c. View the switch uptime using the command **switch#show uptime**.

    d. View the switch uptime using the command **switch-show uptime**.

2. What issue could happen if one wireless client is running 802.11b and another is running 802.11g, and both connect to the wireless router at the same time?

    a. There are no issues.

    b. The wireless router will select 802.11g for setting the data transfer rate.

    c. The wireless router will select 802.11b for setting the data transfer rate.

    d. The access point will temporarily shut down until one client goes offline.

SUMMARY

This chapter presented an introduction to a network protocol analyzer. The student should have developed an understanding of the steps for capturing data packets as well as analyzing the captured data. The steps for troubleshooting the router and switch interfaces have also been presented. The chapter introduced analysis of data traffic a NOC might monitor. The various commands were also presented as was a look at using an OTDR to troubleshoot fiber-optic cable. The chapter concluded with a look at troubleshooting wireless networks.

QUESTIONS AND PROBLEMS

Section 11-2

1. Expand the acronym *ARP.*

2. What is the purpose of an ARP request?

3. Expand the acronym *ICMP.*

4. What is an *echo request*?

5. What is the purpose of a protocol analyzer?

   Included on the companion CD-ROM in the Wireshark capture file folder is a network packet capture file called *Packet11a.cap.* Open this file using Wireshark. The following five questions refer to this file.

7. Which IP addresses correspond to each MAC address?

8. Which packet IDs correspond to ARP requests?

9. Which packet IDs correspond to ARP replies?

10. Which computers are pinging which computers?

11. In terms of computer security, a switch offers better security than a hub. Why is this?

Section 11-3

12. What are the server port numbers for an FTP transfer?

13. How does a client notify a server that an ASCII data transfer is requested?

    The following questions use the *chapter 11-hw.cap* file included on the companion CD-ROM in the Wireshark capture file folder.

14. What routing protocols are used in this network?

15. In the FTP exchange, what operating system is the server running?

16. What is the destination address for the FTP server?

17. What is the source address for the FTP transfer?

18. What is the username sent to the FTP server?

19. What is the password sent to the FTP server?

20. What is the name of the file sent over FTP?

21. What are the contents of the file?

22. From Packet ID# 8, what is the FTP server requesting from the host?

Section 11-4

22. What is an expected percentage utilization for a network?

23. If you suspect you have a physical OSI layer 1 issue with one of the router interfaces, which SNMP information is a good indication?

24. The protocol analyzer shows that the average frame size of data packets being delivered to and from the campus network's Internet connection is 1203. Is this a reasonable average? Justify your answer.

Section 11-5

25. What is the purpose of the Keepalive packet?

26. The **sh ip int brief** command has indicated that the protocol for a FastEthernet interface is "down." What does this mean?

27. What is the difference in a serial interface with a status of *down* and a status of *administratively down*?

28. To look at collision errors, what command should be used?

Section 11-6

29. How does the **show ip interface brief** command differ for a switch as compared to a router?

30. What does the following information indicate if the **show interfaces status** command is entered on a switch?

```
Gi0/2          notconnect   1          auto   auto unknown
```

31. The **show interface status** command is entered on a switch. What does it mean if the switch interface's status shows "connect"?

32. Which command is used to display the MAC address of a switch port?

33. If the command **show ip int brief** shows the interface status of "administratively down" and the protocol status of "down," what will be the status of the port reported by the command **show int status**?

Section 11-7

34. Examine the OTDR trace provided in Figure 11-14. Explain the trace behavior of points A, B, C, D, and E.

FIGURE 11-14   Figure for Problem 36. (From Modern Electronic Communication 9/e, by J.S. Beasley & G. M. Miller, 2008, p. 833. Copyright © 2008 Pearson Education, Inc. Reprinted by permission of Pearson Education, Inc., Upper Saddle River, NJ.)

Section 11-8

35. What step can the network technician take to verify connectivity with an access point?

   a. Verify the SSID.

   b. Ping the IP address for the access point.

   c. Ping the access point's MAC address.

   d. Call the network administrator.

36. Can a metal cabinet affect the receive signal strength? Yes or no?

37. You are attempting to connect to a wireless printer, but the printer is not responding. Which of the following are viable solutions to resolve the problem?

   a. Change the IP address of the printer to 127.0.0.1.

   b. Restart the printer.

   c. Verify that the IP address for the printer is correct.

   d. Change the SSID to "public."

38. Which of the following are appropriate steps to extend the wireless range?

   a. Make sure the antenna is in a high place that is unobstructed.

   b. Select an omnidirectional antenna for both receive and transmit.

   c. Select a high-gain antenna.

   d. The range cannot be altered. This is a limit of the technology.

39. Which of the following have non-overlapping RF spectrums in 802.11b/g?

   a. Channel 1

   b. Channel 3

   c. Channel 6

   d. Channel 9

   e. Channel 11

40. What are some reasons the network technician would have for monitoring switch uptime?

   a. Problems with network connectivity

   b. Problems with the switch resetting

   c. Checking to see if the switch is rebooting

   d. Checking to see if permissions are still valid

41. The command to verify the IP address of a PC computer is which of the following?

    a. **ifconfig**

    b. **ip config**

    c. **ipconfig**

    d. **if config**

CERTIFICATION QUESTIONS

42. A segment is used to do what? (Select all that apply.)

    a. Break up broadcast domains

    b. Isolate data traffic

    c. Connect the hub to the router

    d. Separate the MAC address

43. ARP stands for Address Resolution Protocol. True or False?

44. What is the difference in a serial interface with a status of down and a status of administratively down?

    Status of down: Interface is shut down.

    Administratively down: Link is lost, probably disconnected.

    True or False?

45. The status of protocol up indicates which of the following? (Select all that apply.)

    a. Keepalive packets are being exchanged.

    b. The Ethernet interface is connected to another networking device.

    c. The routing protocol has been configured.

    d. The router is ready to be configured.

46. When you're viewing the interface status, the Method field indicates which of the following?

    a. The interface was brought up manually.

    b. The interface was brought up using tftp.

    c. How the interface was brought up.

    d. The interface is exchanging Keepalive packets.

    e. None of these answers is correct.

Included on the companion CD-ROM in the Wireshark folder is the packet capture file called *Packet11a.cap.* Open this file with the Wireshark program. The following five questions refer to this file.

47. What is the frame length of packet #4?

    a. 78 bytes

    b. 32 bytes

    c. 64 bytes

    d. 128 bytes

48. What is the data length of packet #2?

    a. 78 bytes

    b. 32 bytes

    c. 64 bytes

    d. 128 bytes

49. What is an OUI for Dell Computers?

    a. 27:1f:6b

    b. d0:b0:00

    c. 00.10:7b

    d. 00:b0:d0

50. What is the destination for packet #10?

    a. 10.10.20.1

    b. 10.10.10.2

    c. 10.10.10.1

    d. 10.10.1.3

12

CHAPTER

NETWORK SECURITY

Chapter Outline

Objectives

- Examine how an attacker gains control of a network
- Understand how denial of service attacks are initiated
- Examine the security software and hardware used to protect the network
- Understand the VPN technologies
- Understand wireless security issues

Key Terms

social engineering
password cracking
dictionary attack
brute force attack
packet sniffing
IPsec
buffer overflow
netstat -a -b
nmap
penetration testing
virus
worm
malware
denial of service (DoS)
directed broadcast
spoof
NAQC
firewall
access lists (ACLs)
permit ip any any

demilitarized zones (DMZ)
packet filtering
proxy server
stateful firewall
IP tunnel
GRE
SHA
PPP
PAP
CHAP
EAP
MD5
RADIUS
PPTP
L2F
L2TP
AH
ESP
SHA-1

DES, 3DES
AES
IKE
ISAKMP
Diffie-Hellman
jamming
SSID
beacon
open authentication
shared key authentication
WEP
WPA
TKIP
AES
CCMP
LEAP
EAP
RADIUS

The objective of this chapter is to provide an overview of network security. An enterprise network is vulnerable to many types of network attacks. While network attacks can't be prevented, there are some steps you can take to minimize the impact an attack has on the network.

The first type of attack examined in this chapter is intrusion, where an attacker gains access to a remote network system. There are many ways by which an attacker can gain access to the network. These include social engineering, password cracking, packet sniffing, vulnerable software, and viruses. These issues are examined in section 12-2. Denial of service is an attack with a goal of preventing services to a machine or network. This can be accomplished by flooding the network with lots of data packets or through hacking vulnerable software. For example, a certain software package might reboot if a certain sequence of data packets is sent to the host computer. This is a common problem because many software packages have this vulnerability. Denial of service (DoS) and distributed denial of service (DDoS) attacks are examined in section 12-3.

12-1 INTRODUCTION

Techniques for using security software and hardware such as firewalls to protect a network are examined in section 12-4. This section discusses the role of stateful firewalls in protecting a network. The last section (12-5) explains VPN technologies as well as instructions on configuring the VPN clients.

Table 12-1 lists and identifies, by chapter section, where each of the CompTIA Network+ objectives are presented in this chapter. At the end of each chapter section is a review with comments of the Network+ objectives presented in that section. These comments are provided to help reinforce the reader's understanding of a particular Network+ objective. The chapter review also includes "Test Your Knowledge" questions to aid in the understanding of key concepts before the reader advances to the next section of the chapter. The end of the chapter includes a complete set of question plus sample certification type questions.

TABLE 12-1   Chapter 12 CompTIA Network+ Objectives

Domain/ Objective Number	Domain/Objective Description	Section Where Objective Is Covered
1.0	***Networking Architecture***	
1.2	Compare and contrast the use of networking devices and applications	12-2, 12-5
1.12	Given a set of requirements, implement a basic network	12-4, 12-5, 12-6
2.0	***Network Operations***	
2.1	Given a scenario, use the appropriate monitoring tools	12-2,
2.4	Explain the importance of implementing segmentation	12-4
2.5	Given a scenario, install and apply patches and updates	12-2
3.0	***Network Security***	
3.1	Compare and contrast risk-related concepts	12-2
3.2	Compare and contrast common network vulnerabilities and threats	12-2, 12-3, 12-4, 12-5
3.3	Given a scenario, implement network-hardening techniques	12-4, 12-5
3.5	Given a scenario, install and configure an edge firewall	12-4
3.6	Explain the purpose of various network access control models	12-4
3.7	Summarize basic forensic concepts	12-4
4.0	***Troubleshooting***	
4.2	Given a scenario, analyze and interpret the output of troubleshooting tools	12-2, 12-5
4.7	Given a scenario, troubleshoot and resolve common security threats	12-2, 12-3, 12-4, 12-5, 12-6
5.0	***Industry standards, practices, and network theory***	
5.5	Given a scenario, implement the appropriate policies or procedures	12-4, 12-6

12-2   INTRUSION (HOW AN ATTACKER GAINS CONTROL OF A NETWORK)

Hackers use many techniques to gain control of a network, as shown in Figure 12-1. The network administrator needs to be aware of the various ways an intruder can gain network access or even control. The information presented in this chapter is an example of what the hacker already knows and what the network administrator needs to know to protect the network.

FIGURE 12-1   The ways an attacker can gain access to a remote network.

Social Engineering

The first issue of intrusion is **social engineering**. This is a way for an intruder to gain enough information from people to gain access to the network. As an example, an attacker calls a user on a network and claims he is from the computer support division of the network. The attacker tells the user that there is a problem with the user's account and then asks for the user's name and password, as illustrated in Figure 12-2. Often a user will blindly provide the information, not realizing that the person calling is not associated with the network and is in fact an attacker. This gives the attacker an account (username and password) to attack the network from. This is just one example of social engineering. Some attackers search through discarded trash to gain access to user passwords. This problem is not completely solvable because as the number of users increases, so do the possible ways to attack the network. The solution is educating users about not sharing information on how they access the network and to always require identification from support staff.

FIGURE 12-2   An example of social engineering.

Password Cracking

If the attacker has access to the user's network but can't get the password from the user, the attacker can use **password cracking**. This can be done via brute force or via checking for "weak" passwords. Most networks require their users to use strong passwords.

In password cracking, the attacker can try to guess the user's password. One method is the dictionary attack. The **dictionary attack** (see Figure 12-3) uses known passwords and many variations (upper- and lowercase and combinations) to try to log in to your account. This is why many network systems prompt you not to use a dictionary word as a password. A **brute-force attack** means the attacker uses every possible combination of characters for the password. (Note: Some attackers will use a combination of brute-force and dictionary attacks.)

Password Cracking
The attacker tries to guess the user's password

Dictionary Attack
Uses known passwords and many variations (upper- and lowercase and combinations) to try to log in to your account

Brute Force Attack
Attacker uses every possible combination of characters for the password

FIGURE 12-3   The dictionary attack.

Here are some guidelines that will help prevent password cracking:

- Don't use passwords that are dictionary words.
- Don't use your username as your password.
- Don't use your username spelled backward as your password.

- Limit the number of login attempts.
- Make your password strong, which means it is sufficiently long (eight or more characters) and is an alphanumeric combination (for example, A b 1 & G 2 5 h).
- Change passwords often.

Packet Sniffing

Another way attackers can obtain a password is by sniffing the network's data packets. **Packet sniffing** assumes that the attacker can see the network data packets. The attacker will have to insert a device on the network that allows her to see the data packets (see Figure 12-4). The attacker then watches the data packets until a telnet or FTP data packet passes (or one from many of the other applications that have unencrypted logins). Many of these applications pass the username and password over the network in plain text. *Plain text* means that the information is in a human readable form. If the attacker captures all data packets from a user's computer, then the chances are good that the attacker can obtain the user's login name and password on one of the network's computers. The way to prevent this is by encrypting the user's name and password. An encrypted alternative to telnet is secure shell (SSH). The packets that pass across this SSH connection are encrypted. Secure socket layer (SSL) is an encryption used by web servers. For example, the packet transmission is encrypted when a credit card number is entered. There is also a secure version of FTP called Secure FTP (STFP).

In these examples, the security is implemented at the application layer. Security can also be implemented at layer 3 using IP security (**IPsec**). In IPsec each packet is encrypted prior to transmission across the network link. IPsec is also a method used to encrypt VPN tunnels (see section 12-5).

Attacker

Computer 1

Hub

The attacker sees the data packets being exchanged between computers 1 and 2.

Computer 2

FIGURE 12-4 An example of packet sniffing.

Vulnerable Software

In the process of writing large amounts of code, errors happen that can open access to the code and to a network. The basic attack that capitalizes on these errors is the **buffer overflow**. The buffer overflow occurs when a program attempts to put more data into a buffer than it was configured to hold and the overflow writes past the end of the buffer and over adjacent memory locations. The program stack contains data plus instructions that it will run. Assume, for example, that a program includes a variable size of 128 bytes. It is possible that the programmer didn't include instructions to check the maximum size of the variable to make sure it is smaller than 128 bytes. An attacker will look through pages and pages of source code searching for a vulnerability that allows her to issue a buffer overflow. The attacker finds the variable and sends data to the application assigned to that variable. For example, a web application could have a vulnerability with long URLs assigned to a variable within it. If the attacker makes the URL long enough, then the buffer overflow could allow her code to be placed in the stack. When the program counter gets to the inserted code, the inserted code is run and the attacker then has remote access to the machine, as illustrated in Figure 12-5.

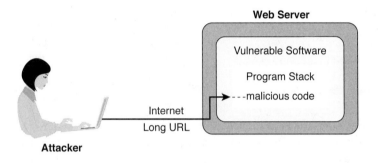

FIGURE 12-5   An example of a buffer overflow attack.

Sometimes buffer overflows don't allow instructions to be run, but rather the application crashes. This is used in denial of service attacks, examined in section 12-3. A common code that gets run in buffer overflow attacks is setting up a *backdoor* to gain entry into the computer. What the attacker is doing is creating an application on a port and then connecting to the port. The attacker can also use this to place viruses in the computer. For example, say the attacker finds a vulnerability in the source code for an operating system, such as the SSL code on a web server. The attacker downloads malicious code onto the server and then connects to the machine and instructs the code to begin attacking other machines.

Steps for Preventing Vulnerable Software Attacks

It is important to do the following to prevent vulnerable software attacks:

- Keep software patches and service packs for the operating system current, update software regularly.
- Turn off all services and ports that are not needed on a machine. For example, if your machine does not use web service, turn off this service. Leaving these services on is like leaving the windows and doors open

to your house. You are just inviting an attacker to come in. If you aren't using a service, shut the access. The command **netstat -a** can be used to display the ports currently open on the Windows operating system. This command shows who is connected to your machine and the port numbers. An example is provided here:

```
c: netstat -a
Active Connections
Proto Local              Address      Foreign Address       State
TCP           pcsalsa2   :1087        PC-SALSA2:0           LISTENING
TCP           pcsalsa2   :1088        PC-SALSA2:0           LISTENING
TCP           pcsalsa2   :1089        PC-SALSA2:0           LISTENING
TCP           pcsalsa2   :1090        PC-SALSA2:0           LISTENING
TCP           pcsalsa2   :135         PC-SALSA2:0           LISTENING
TCP           pcsalsa2   :1025        PC-SALSA2:0           LISTENING
TCP           pcsalsa2   :1087        salsa.chile.Edu:80   ESTABLISHED
TCP           pcsalsa2   :1088        salsa.chile.Edu:80   ESTABLISHED
TCP           pcsalsa2   :1089        salsa.chile.Edu:80   CLOSE_WAIT
TCP           pcsalsa2   :1090        salsa.chile.Edu:80   CLOSE_WAIT
TCP           pcsalsa2   :137         PC-SALSA2:0           LISTENING
TCP           pcsalsa2   :138         PC-SALSA2:0           LISTENING
TCP           pcsalsa2   :nbsession   PC-SALSA2:0           LISTENING
UDP           pcsalsa2   :nbname      *:                   *
UDP           pcsalsa2   :nbdatagram  *:                   *
```

Another useful command is **netstat -b**, which shows the executable involved in creating the connection or listening port. An example is provided next; it shows that Internet Explorer was used to establish the connection.

```
c: netstat - b
Active Connections

Proto    Local Address    Foreign Address        State          PID
TCP      pc-salsa:1152    salsa.chile.edu:http   ESTABLISHED    876
[iexplore.exe]
```

The ports that are listening are just waiting for a connection. For example, ports 135 and 137 (shown in the **netstat –a** example) are the NETBIOS and file sharing ports for Microsoft. Every port that is established shows listening, and that port can accept a connection. For example, if your application is vulnerable and is listening, then the machine is vulnerable to an attack. It is good idea to check which applications are running on your machine. And again, it is a good idea to turn off ports that are not needed. The steps for turning off ports depend on the application. For example, if port 80 (HTTP) is running, go to the Windows services and turn off the web application.

An excellent security tool that runs on Linux is **nmap**. The application can be installed using the command **yum install nmap**, if it's not already installed. This is a port scanner that is used by the network administrator to scan a local computer or other computers internal to the network to determine what network ports and services are being made available to users. For example, the command **nmap**

netstat -a
(**a**) Command used to display the ports currently open on a Windows operating system and (**b**) used to display the executable involved in creating the connection or listening port

nmap
A Linux port scanner

localhost can be entered to scan the Linux machine named *localhost*. Figure 12-6 shows the results of the scan. The scan shows that ftp, telnet, smtp (email server), sunrpc (network file server), and X11 (the GUI for Linux) are all available. Notice that each service has a port number assigned to it. (The concept of *port numbers* was presented in Chapter 5, "Interconnecting the LANs.") For example, FTP is on port 21 and is running TCP. Telnet is running on port 23 and is also running TCP. The network administrator may decide that the ftp or the non-secure telnet service is a security threat and that it needs to be disabled. Note that this command can also be used to scan machines outside your network by simply substituting an IP address for the machine name. For example, **nmap 192.168.12.5** can be used to scan the machine at IP address 192.168.12.5. (Note: You should only use the nmap port scanning utility on your own machines!)

FIGURE 12-6 An example using the **nmap** command to scan a local computer to determine what network ports and services are being made available to users.

There are many important issues that the network/system administrator faces, but security should be the top concern. When you first go out to install a new service or are maintaining existing systems, the most important issue is the system security and preventing outside threats. You want to fully understand the implications of installing the software and how the installation can possibly affect the overall network. The following is a list of some of the questions that should be asked:

- Who will be the users of the software, and what applications are they going to be running?
- Will they need special permissions?
- Will the software being installed require a firewall?
- Does the software introduce any security threats?

Another test that needs to be implemented to protect the network is **penetration testing**. A penetration test is a way to evaluate the security of the user's network. This is accomplished by trying to exploit vulnerabilities in the network. This includes identifying any potential problems with the operating systems, services, and

> **Penetration Testing**
> A way to evaluate the security of the user's network

applications as well as verifying user adherence to policies. The penetration test will also validate any protection mechanisms currently in place.

Viruses and Worms

A **virus** is a piece of malicious computer code that when run on your machine can damage your hardware, software, or other files. Computer viruses typically are attached to executable files and can be spread when the infected program is run. The computer virus is spread by sharing infected files or sending emails with the attached files that are infected with the virus.

> **Virus**
>
> A piece of malicious computer code that, when opened, can damage your hardware, software, or other files

Problems caused by viruses include the following:

- Annoyance
- Clogging up the mail server
- Denial of service
- Data loss
- Open holes for others to access your machine

Viruses used to be a problem passed along by exchanging computer disks. Today, most viruses are exchanged via attachments to email, as shown in Figure 12-7. For example, a user receives an email that says "Look at this!" trying to coax him into opening the attachment. By opening the attachment, the user could possibly infect his computer with a virus.

FIGURE 12-7   An example of how computer viruses are spread.

> **Worm**
>
> A type of virus that attacks computers, typically proliferates by itself, and can deny service to networks

A computer **worm** is a type of computer virus that attacks computers, typically proliferating by itself (self-replicating); it can deny service to networks. Computer worms do not need to be attached to an executable file to be distributed but can use the network to send copies of themselves to other computers. A common objective of a worm is to establish a backdoor in the infected computer, which enables an attacker access to someone's computer.

The following are steps to take to prevent viruses:

- Open only attachments that come from known sources. Even this can be a problem because email addresses can be spoofed or the message can come from a known person whose computer has been infected.
- Require that the emails you receive be digitally signed so you can verify the sender.
- Always run antivirus software on the client machines. The antivirus software is not 100% effective but will catch most viruses.

- Include email server filters to block specific types of emails or attachments.
- Keep the antivirus software up to date.
- Keep the operating system and applications software current.
- Use personal firewalls when possible

Nowadays, **malware** is the term used to encompass all malicious programs intended to harm, disrupt, deny, or gain unauthorized access to a computing system. Malware is short for *malicious software*. Viruses and worms are considered a type infectious malware.

> **Malware**
> Malicious programs

It is important to understand that an intruder can gain network access or even control of your network. And remember, the information presented in this chapter is an example of what the hacker already knows and what the network administrator needs to know to protect the network.

Section 12-2 Review

*This section has covered the following **Network+** Exam objectives:*

1.2 Compare and contrast the use of networking devices and applications

This section examined various security measures, including IPsec, and steps to prevent viruses and password cracking.

2.1 Given a scenario, use appropriate monitoring tools.

This section introduced an excellent security monitoring tool called nmap. This is a port scanner that is used by the network administrator to scan a local computer or other computers internal to a network to determine what network ports and services are being made available to users.

2.5 Given a scenario, install and apply patches and updates

The basics of worms, viruses, and packet sniffing were examined in this section. These threats underscore the importance of using antivirus software and making sure your software is up-to-date.

3.1 Compare and contrast risk-related concepts

This section introduced the concept of the buffer overflow. The attack resulting from this attack occurs when a program attempts to put more data into a buffer than it was configured to hold and the overflow writes past the end of the buffer and over adjacent memory locations.

3.2 Compare and contrast common network vulnerabilities and threats

This sections introduced the concepts of brute force attacks, social engineering, and the issue of insider threats.

4.2 Given a scenario, analyze and interpret the output of troubleshooting tools

The command **netstat -a** *was introduced in this section. This command can be used to display the ports currently open on the Windows operating system. This command shows who is connected to your machine and the port numbers*

4.7 Given a scenario, troubleshoot and resolve common security threats.

This section introduced the concept of packet sniffing. This is another way attackers can obtain a password. Packet sniffing assumes that the attacker can see the network data packets. The attacker will have to insert a device on the network that allows her to see the data packets

Test Your Knowledge

1. Which of the following best defines *social engineering*?

    a. It's a way for the host to obtain enough information to prevent intrusion.

    b. It's intrusion prevention from information passed along via email.

    c. It's a way for an intruder to obtain enough information to gain access to the network.

    d. It's a technique for breaking passwords.

2. An attacker tries to guess the user's password using which of the following techniques?

    a. Password sniffing

    b. Password cracking

    c. Password sampling

    d. Password interrogation

12-3   DENIAL OF SERVICE

Denial of Service (DoS)
A service is being denied to a computer, network, or server

Denial of service (DoS) means that a service is being denied to a computer, network, or network server. Denial of service attacks can be on individual machines, on the network that connects the machines, or on all machines simultaneously.

A denial of service attack can be initiated by exploiting software vulnerabilities. For example, a software vulnerability can permit a buffer overflow, causing the machine to crash. This affects all applications, even secure applications.

The vulnerable software denial of service attack attacks the system by making it reboot repeatedly. DoS attacks can also occur on routers via the software options available for connecting to a router. For example, SNMP management software is marketed by many companies and is supported by many computer platforms. Many of the SNMP packages use a similar core code that could contain the same vulnerability.

Another denial of service attack is a SYN attack. This refers to the TCP SYN (synchronizing) packet (introduced in Chapter 6, "TCP/IP"). An attacker sends many TCP SYN packets to a host, opening up many TCP sessions. The host machine has limited memory set aside for open connections. If all the TCP connections are opened by the SYN attack, other users are kept from accessing services from the computer because the connection buffer is full. Most current operating systems take countermeasures against the SYN attack.

Denial of service attacks can affect the network bandwidth and the end points on the network. The classic example is the Smurf attack (Figure 12-8), which required few resources from the attacker. The attacker sent a small packet and got many packets in return. The attacker would pick a victim and an intermediate site. Figure 12-8 shows an attacker site, an intermediate site, and a victim site. The intermediate site has subnets of 10.10.1.0 and 10.10.2.0. The victim is at 10.10.1.0. The attackers send a packet to 10.10.1.255, which is a broadcast address for the 10.10.1.0 subnet. The attacker then spoofs the source address information, making it look as if the packet came from the victim's network. All the machines on the 10.10.1.0 subnet send a reply to the source address. Remember, the attacker has spoofed the source address so the replies are sent to the victim's network. If this attack were increased to all the subnets in the 10.0.0.0 network, an enormous amount of data packets are sent to the victim's network. This enables the attacker to generate a lot of data traffic on the victim's network without requiring the attacker to have many resources.

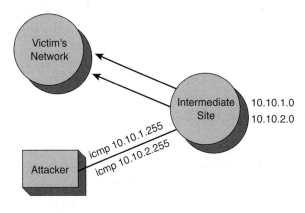

FIGURE 12-8   An example of a Smurf attack.

This type of attack is not new, and you can take certain steps to stop a network from becoming an intermediate site. Cisco routers have an interface command that blocks broadcast packets to that subnet. This prevents a network from becoming an intermediate site for a network attack such as this. Make sure this command or a similar command is a default or has been enabled on the router's interface:

```
no ip directed-broadcast
```

But aren't layer 3 devices supposed to stop broadcasts? This is true for general broadcasts (all 32 bits set to 1s or "F F F F F F F F" or 255.255.255.255). Routers will always stop these broadcasts. The type of broadcast used in this attack is a **directed broadcast**, which is passed through the router. The **no ip directed-broadcast** command enables only the router to reply.

> **Directed Broadcast**
> The broadcast is sent to a specific subnet.

To prevent your network from becoming a host for an attacker, use access lists to allow only specific sources from the network to enter the router's interfaces. For example, network B connects to a router. Only packets sourced from network B are allowed to pass through the router. The downside of this is that it does become a maintenance problem: Keeping track of the access lists can be a challenge for the network administrator and processing access lists on the router is processor intensive and can slow the throughput of the packets. However, this does help eliminate spoofed packets. **Spoof** means the attacker doesn't use his IP address but will insert an IP address from the victim's network or another network as the source IP. There is a lot of software on the Internet that enables someone to spoof an IP address.

> **Spoof**
> Inserting a different IP address in place of an IP packet's source address to make it appear that the packet came from another network

To prevent yourself from becoming a victim, well…there isn't a way unless you aren't connected to any network or to any other users.

Distributed Denial of Service Attacks

The number of packets that can be generated by a single packet as in the Smurf attack can be limited on a router; however, attackers now use worms to distribute an attack. In a distributed denial of service (DDoS) attack, the attacker will do a port scan and look for an open port or a software application that is vulnerable to an attack. The machine is *hacked* (attacked) and distributes the malicious software. The attacker will repeat this for many victim machines. After the software is on the victim machines, the attacker can issue a command or an instruction that starts the attack on a specific site. The attack comes from a potentially massive amount of machines the worm has infected.

To stop DDoS attacks, you must stop intrusions to the network, as discussed in section 12-2. The bottom line is *PREVENT INTRUSIONS*.

Section 12-3 Review

This section has covered the following **Network+** Exam objectives:

3.2 Compare and contrast common network vulnerabilities and threats

The concepts of buffer overflow and denial of service attacks were introduced in this section. Additionally, this section discussed how access lists can be used to allow only specific sources from the network to enter the router's interfaces.

4.7 Given a scenario, troubleshoot and resolve common security threats.

This section introduced the various types of denial of service attacks. The student should recognize that preventing denial of service attacks requires that the attacker be prevented from gaining access to the network.

12-4 SECURITY SOFTWARE AND HARDWARE

A healthy network starts from within, and the most basic component in the network is an individual computer. An individual computer should have protection similar to its big network. Remember, the fundamental goal of DDoS is to take control of vulnerable machines and launch the attack. This can be prevented. Even though it is not cost effective to guard each computer with dedicated hardware, there is a plethora of security software that can help.

Antivirus Software

The first line of defense against the viruses, worms, and general malware is antivirus software. Recommended practice dictates that every computer should have an antivirus program installed. Even though antivirus software cannot provide 100% protection, it will protect against most of the viruses out there. Antivirus software uses so-called *signatures* or *definitions* to match against the viruses and worms. Each virus or worm has its own trait, and this trait is defined in a signature or a definition. When a new virus or worm is found, a new signature or a new definition has to be created. Most of the commercial antivirus companies will have the new signature/definition ready and available for their customers to download within hours of its spread. So, this is why it is important to keep the antivirus software up-to-date. Most of the antivirus software is launched at the startup of the operating system, and it will try to update its signatures or definitions at that time. When a virus is found on the computer, the virus program is usually quarantined or removed. Network Access Quarantine Control (**NAQC**) is a Resource Kit tool in Windows Server

> **NAQC**
> Network Access
> Quarantine Control

2003 and 2008 that allows administrators to prevent remote client computers from connecting to their network with machines that aren't secure. Some of the popular antivirus software available include McAfee, Norton, Trend Micro, Sophos, AVG, and so on.

Personal Firewall

Another form of software protection readily available for a computer is a personal firewall. Most of the operating systems (Windows, Mac OS, and Linux) today are equipped with a personal firewall. Some of them might not be enabled by default. The personal firewall software is typically based on basic packet filtering inspections where the firewall accepts or denies incoming network traffic based on information contained in the packets' TCP or IP headers. Some personal firewalls provide more granular control to allow specific hosts or subnets. Some of the personal firewalls also offer an application-based firewall, where trusted programs can be defined. The network traffic originated from or destined to the trusted programs is allowed by the firewall.

In the Windows operating system world, firewall protection was introduced as part of the Windows XP service pack 2. It has evolved from a simple firewall in Windows XP to have more granular control in Windows 10. The Windows 10 firewall allows for both packet filtering and application-based firewall. It also gives the firewall software both inbound and outbound control. In the Linux world, iptables has been a de facto firewall program for a long time. iptables is a network packet filtering firewall program. The recent Mac OS X is deploying PF (Packet Filter) as its OS firewall. PF is a BSD-based stateful packet filter firewall. The following examples demonstrate how to configure firewall settings for Windows 7, XP, Mac OS X, and Linux.

Windows 10

The following steps illustrate how to configure the firewall to restrict Ping traffic on Windows 10. These instructions also apply to Windows 7 and 8, with only minor variations.

1. Click **Start** and select **Control Panel > Connect To**; then select **System and Security**.

   The Windows Firewall is shown in Figure 12-9, and it presents 2 options: **Check firewall status** and **Allow a program through Windows Firewall**.

2. Select **Check firewall status** to display the status window shown in Figure 12-10. This screen indicates that the firewall is on for the public network connection named "Network," and the firewall is blocking all connections to the programs that are not on the list of allowed programs.

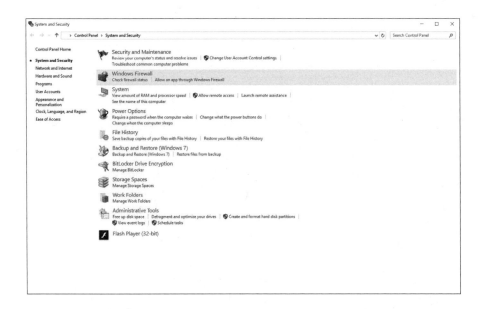

FIGURE 12-9   Windows 10: Firewall.

FIGURE 12-10   Windows 10: Firewall status.

3. Select **Allow a program or feature through Windows Firewall** to display the Allowed Programs to communicate through Windows Firewall window, as shown in Figure 12-11. This screen shows the programs that are allowed through the firewall, depending on which network location profile the computer is using. Every time a Windows 10 computer is making a new network connection for the first time, Windows 10 prompts the user to identify whether this network connection is for home/work (private) or a public location. It then adjusts the firewall and security settings accordingly.

FIGURE 12-11   Windows 10: Allowed programs.

4. Windows 10 also offers advanced firewall settings. Use the Advanced settings option to control both the inbound and outbound traffic to the computer. The Advanced settings firewall option can be found on the left column of the firewall status window shown in Figure 12-10. Figure 12-12 shows the Windows Firewall with Advanced Security.

FIGURE 12-12   Windows 7: Advanced settings.

The following example examines an inbound "File and Printer Sharing" (Echo Request – ICMPv4-in) rule by Windows 10. This rule is known as "Ping Request" on Windows 7 and Windows 8. This is a simple rule to control the Ping traffic to the computer. Open the Advanced security windows; you'll see that with Inbound Rules selected, the middle pane shows all the firewall inbound rules. There are a lot of roles, but not all of them are enabled. The enabled rules are indicated by the value **Yes** in the column **Enabled**. Right next to the **Enabled** column is the **Action** column. This column displays the action of **Allow** as to allow the connection or **Block** as to deny the connection.

5. When you double-click the rule **File and Printer Sharing (Echo Request – ICMPv4-in)** in the middle pane, the properties window is displayed, as shown in Figure 12-13. On the General tab of this window, this rule is currently set to **Disabled** and the action is set to **Allow the connection**. By selecting the **Enabled** box and changing the action to **Block the connection**, you will change the conditions of the rule to be active and to block all incoming echo request or Ping request traffic.

FIGURE 12-13   Windows 7: Ping request properties.

6. Select the Protocols and Ports tab to see the window shown in Figure 12-14. This illustrates how the firewall program matches the Ping Request by defining its protocol as an ICMPv4 protocol. The **Customize** button will bring up the Customize ICMP Settings window, which shows the Echo Request ICMP type is selected.

FIGURE 12-14   Windows 10: Ping request protocol.

Mac OS X

To start the Mac OS X firewall configuration, use the following steps:

1. Go to **System Preferences** and select **Security & Privacy**.

2. In the Security & Privacy window, select **Firewall**. The firewall window displays the status of the firewall and lets you turn off the firewall as shown in Figure 12-15.

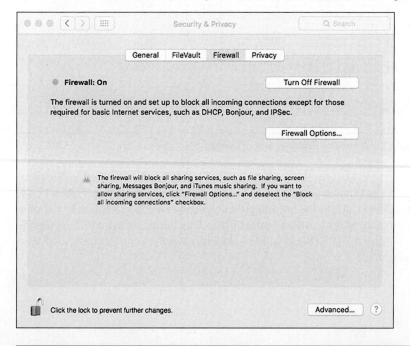

FIGURE 12-15   Mac OS X: Firewall.

3. Click **Firewall Options** button to open another window for more advanced settings, as shown in Figure 12-16. The firewall options are

- **Block all incoming connections**: This option blocks all incoming connections except a limited list of necessary services, such as DHCP and DNS.

- **Automatically allow signed software to receive incoming connections**: Because newer Mac OS X version runs application-based firewall, this option adds all the so-called digitally signed applications certified by Apple to the trusted list. The connections to and from these applications are trusted. The window above the option allows for manual entry of your own trusted software.

- **Enable stealth mode**: This option basically stops the computer from responding to an ICMP Ping request packet. Hence, this makes it difficult for attackers to identify the computer.

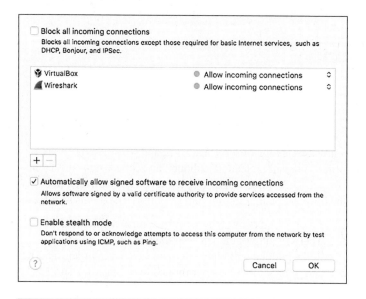

FIGURE 12-16   Mac OS X: Advanced settings.

Linux

To start the Linux firewall (iptables) configuration, use the following steps:

1. The command to view/add/modify/delete the Linux firewall configuration is **iptables**. For example, to view the firewall configuration, simply issue the command **iptables–list** as root or **sudo iptables–list**. The user must be connected as root or must open **System Preferences** and select **Security**.

2. The output of the command **iptables–list** is shown in Figure 12-17. It shows a list of chains: **INPUT, FORWARD, OUTPUT**, and **RH-Firewall-1-INPUT**. A chain can consist of firewall rules or another chain. Obviously, the only chain in this example that contains firewall rules is the RH-Firewall-1-INPUT. This chain allows incoming HTTP, HTTPS, SSH, SMTP, domain (DNS), and IMAP traffic and will reject any incoming traffic that does not match the allowed list.

FIGURE 12-17   Linux: iptables.

Firewall

Firewalls are used in computer networks for protection against the "network elements" (for example, intrusions, denial of service attacks, and so on). **Access lists (ACLs)** are the basic form of firewall protection, although an access list is not stateful and is not by itself a firewall. Access lists can be configured on a router, on a true dedicated firewall, or on the host computer. Firewalls are examined first in this section.

The access lists consist of permit and deny statements to control traffic in and out of the network interface. There is an implicit denial at the end of an access list in Cisco routers, and this statement alone will block all data packets. In order to allow other data packets that do not match the ACL's permit and deny statements to enter and exit the LAN, the command **access-list permit ip any any** must be added to the last line of an access list to explicitly allow all other data packets. If the intention is to deny other data packets that do match the permit statements, then the explicit permit statement is not needed. An example is shown here. This instruction is for access-list 100, and it instructs the router to permit IP packets from any source to any destination:

```
RouterB(config)# access-list 100 permit ip any any
```

Firewalls allow traffic from inside the network to exit but don't allow general traffic from the outside to enter the network. The firewall monitors the data traffic and recognizes where packets are coming from. The firewall will allow packets from the outside to enter the network if they match a request from within the network. Firewalls are based on three technologies:

- Packet filtering
- Proxy server
- Stateful packet filtering

Firewall

Used in computer networks for protecting the network

Access Lists (ACLs)

A basic form of firewall protection

permit ip any any

The instruction added to the last line of an access list to allow all other data packets to enter and exit the router

A general rule of thumb is to place the firewall close to the machines you want to protect (for example, the network servers). Do not assume that the clients on the network will never attack your system. Clients can and will get viruses on their machines. Create **demilitarized zones** (**DMZs**) for the outside servers, which mean that they are moved to a place on the network so that they are isolated. If the machines are compromised, the intruder will have limited access to the inside of the network.

In **packet filtering**, a limit is placed on the packets that can enter the network. Packet filtering can also limit information moving from one segment to another. ACLs are used to enable the firewall to accept or deny data packets. The disadvantages of packet filtering are

- Packets can still enter the network by fragmenting the data packets.
- It is difficult to implement complex ACLs.
- Not all network services can be filtered.

A **proxy server** is used by clients to communicate with secure systems using a proxy. The client gets access to the network via the proxy server. This step is used to authenticate the user, establish the session, and set policies. The client must connect to the proxy server to connect to resources outside the network. The disadvantages of the proxy server are

- The proxy server can run very slowly.
- Adding services can be difficult.
- There can be a potential problem with network failure if the proxy server fails or is corrupted.

In a **stateful firewall** the inbound and outbound data packets are compared to determine if a connection should be allowed. This includes tracking the source and destination port numbers and sequence numbers as well as the source and destination IP addresses. This technique is used to protect the inside of the network from the outside world but still allow traffic to go from the inside to the outside and back. The firewall needs to be stateful to accomplish this.

But what if the campus network has a web server? How are outside users allowed access? This requires that holes must be opened in the network that allow data packets to pass through. The three most common traffic types that require holes to be opened are web servers, DNS, and email. The firewall must be modified so that anybody can connect to the web server via port 80. But what if a vulnerability is discovered on port 80 for the server's operating system? When you open ports, the network administrator must continually upgrade the software so that vulnerabilities are removed. The web server also might need to have its own firewall. Most firewalls can perform deep packet inspection. This can catch some of protocol vulnerabilities.

A firewall is usually placed inline between a trusted (internal) network and an untrusted (external) network. Its primary function is to protect its trusted network. Figure 12-18 illustrates an example of how a perimeter firewall is often deployed. A perimeter firewall is physically placed between the public Internet and its internal networks. All incoming traffic is considered untrusted and is inspected by the firewall according to its rules. Sometimes, a firewall might be connected to a campus

Demilitarized Zones (DMZs)
Used to isolate the servers

Packet Filtering
A limit is placed on the information that can enter the network

Proxy Server
Clients go through a proxy to communicate with secure systems

Stateful Firewall
Keeps track of the data packet flow

router. A router might be needed to aggregate multiple networks or to handle more complicated network routing. At the firewall, NAT or PAT is typically configured to handle the translation between the private IP addresses to the public IP addresses.

FIGURE 12-18 Perimeter firewall deployment.

A big problem with firewalls is that users assume a firewall catches all possible problems. This is a wrong assumption. The user might be slow to update the patches and fixes to the software. For example, an attacker sends an email message with an attachment to a user. The user opens the attachment and unknowingly loads a Trojan horse on his computer that scans all the machines on the LAN, checking for any possible open ports and compromising the entire LAN. A firewall is not the end-to-end solution.

Other Security Appliances

There are more security appliances in the market today that help protect the network. Most of these appliances work in conjunction with the firewall or as a supplement. An intrusion prevention system (IPS) monitors and analyzes the network traffic. In real time, it identifies misuse and anomaly on the network. The IPS detects a misuse intrusion by matching the network packets with its IPS signatures for known attacks or activities that are classified as bad. The network anomaly can be detected by building up a profile of the system being monitored and detecting significant deviations from this profile. The IPS has the capability to stop or prevent malicious attacks that it detects by interacting with the firewall.

Another appliance that is widely deployed is a web filter appliance. Lots of places have very strict policies on how their users can use the network. Web traffic is usually one of the first to be monitored and filtered, and a web filter appliance is designed to do just that. In the K-12 school environment, web filtering is critical. K-12 school districts are required by law to implement filtering to block adult, illegal, or offensive content from minors. The law is known as the Children's Internet Protection Act (CIPA). A web filter appliance has a database containing inappropriate websites. A web filter appliance monitors the web traffic both via HTTP and HTTPS and matches it against the database. If an inappropriate website is detected, it is either discarded or the user is redirected to a security web page for further action. The web filter appliance gets its database updated perpetually. Also, there is always an option for a network administrator to manually mark a website as appropriate.

Another aspect associated with the security appliances is to make sure the IT staff is continually updated on technology and receive proper training. Additionally, make sure the critical systems are on a UPS system and incorporating regular back-ups. Also, validate that the security appliances incorporate redundancy and are not subject to a single point of failure.

A final comment related to security has to do with computer forensics. Computers are subject to attacks from the "bad guys," and in some cases a crime may have been committed. In this case, the network technician and network administrators must know the proper steps to take to preserve the evidence. The following are some basic guidelines for the first responders:

- No action should change data held on a computer or storage media that may be subsequently relied upon in court.

- In circumstances where a person finds it necessary to access original data held on a computer or storage media, that person must be competent to do so and be able to give evidence explaining the relevance and the implications of their actions.

- An audit trail or other record of all processes applied to computer-based electronic evidence should be created and preserved. An independent third party should be able to examine those processes and achieve the same result.

- The person in charge of the investigation has the overall responsibility for ensuring that the law and these principles are adhered to.

There are six stages of a forensics examination. These stages are as follows:

1. **Readiness**: This includes appropriate training, regular testing, and verification of software and equipment, familiarity with legislation, and ensuring that the onsite acquisition (data extraction) kit is complete and in working order.

2. **Evaluation**: The evaluation process includes receiving instructions, clarifying the instructions, completing risk analysis, and allocating resources.

3. **Collection**: This step involves collecting evidence and interviewing relevant personnel as well as the IT administration responsible for the affected system.

4. **Analysis**: This step involves the use of the appropriate tools needed to provide thorough and repeatable analysis of the compromised system.

5. **Presentation**: In this step the examiner will provide a structured report on the findings of the examination. This will also include addressing key points and any additional information relevant to the investigation.

6. **Review**: At this point the examiner should review what went wrong, what was done properly, and what can be learned and improved on based on this incident.

This is only a brief overview of computer forensics and the concept of preserving evidence. The bottom line is that the network technician should make sure a qualified forensics specialist is involved if a crime has been committed.

Section 12-4 Review

This section has covered the following **Network+** Exam objectives:

1-12 Given a set of requirements, implement a basic network

This section examined the basics of firewall protection. Firewall rules were examined as well as port security and stateful inspection of data packets.

2-4 Explain the importance of implementing segmentation

This section addressed the concept of NAT or PAT. These are typically configured to handle the translation between the private IP addresses to the public IP addresses.

3.2 Compare and contrast common network vulnerabilities and threats

Examples are presented in this section that demonstrate how to configure firewall settings for Windows 7, XP, Mac OS X, and Linux to help mitigate network threats.

3.3 Given a scenario, implement network hardening techniques

This section introduced the basics of firewall protection. A general rule of thumb is to place the firewall close to the machines you want to protect (for example, the network servers). Do not assume that the clients on the network will never attack your system.

3.5 Given a scenario, install and configure an edge firewall

This section introduced the concept of the demilitarized zones (DMZs) for the outside servers, which mean that they are moved to a place on the network so that they are isolated. If the machines are compromised, the intruder will have limited access to the inside of the network. The firewalls are to be placed close to the machines you want to protect.

3.6 Explain the purpose of various network access control models

When a virus is found on the computer, the virus program is usually quarantined or removed. Network Access Quarantine Control (NAQC) is a Resource Kit tool in Windows Server 2003 and 2008 that allows administrators to prevent remote client computers from connecting to their network with machines that aren't secure.

3.7 Summarize basic forensic concepts

Computers are subject to attacks from the "bad guys," and in some cases a crime may have been committed. In this case, the network technician and network administrators must know the proper steps to take to preserve the evidence. This section presented some basic guidelines for the first responders.

4.7 Given a scenario, implement and resolve common security threats

This section examines techniques to address common security threats such as malware, open/closed ports, and malicious users.

Test Your Knowledge

1. A stateful firewall does which of the following? (Select the best answer.)

   a. Keeps track of the data packet flow

   b. Keeps track of the data collisions

   c. Enables the access list

   d. Prevents unnecessary pings

2. An advantage of a firewall is that it catches all possible problems. True or False?

12-5 INTRODUCTION TO VIRTUAL PRIVATE NETWORK

When a network is protected behind the firewall, it is sometimes referred to as a *private* network. Only computers on the same private network are considered to be trusted. Public access to this kind of network could be very limited. Access to a private network requires special permission to be granted on the firewall. Imagine a sales company that has its sales workforce throughout the country. The salespeople need to access the company's servers and databases at its headquarters, which is protected behind a firewall. It would be a network administrator's nightmare to grant individual access through the company's firewall. This idea does not allow for flexibility and mobility. A virtual private network (**VPN**) offers a solution to this problem. As the name implies, VPN is a concept of extending a private or a trusted network over public infrastructure like the Internet. A VPN accomplishes this by establishing a secure connection between the remote end and the private network, therefore enabling the remote clients to become part of the trusted network.

> **VPN**
> Virtual private network

A secure VPN connection between two endpoints is known as an **IP tunnel**. A tunnel is created by an encapsulation technique, which encapsulates the data inside a known protocol (IP) that is agreed upon by the two end points. A tunnel creates a virtual circuit-like between the two endpoints and makes the connection appear like

> **IP Tunnel**
> An IP packet encapsulated in another IP packet

a dedicated connection even though it spans over the Internet infrastructure. Two types of VPNs are commonly used today:

- **Remote access VPN**: A remote access VPN is used to facilitate network access for users in remote office networks or for remote users that travel a lot and need access to the network. The client usually initiates this type of VPN connection.
- **Site-to-site VPN**: A site-to-site VPN is used to create a virtual link from one site to the other. It essentially replaces the traditional WAN-type connection used in connecting typical sites. This type of VPN requires network hardware like a router or a firewall to create and maintain the connection.

VPN Tunneling Protocols

GRE
Generic Routing Encapsulation

This section provides a quick overview of the protocols used in the creation of these VPN tunnels. One of the original tunneling protocols is the Generic Routing Encapsulation (**GRE**). GRE was developed by Cisco in 1994 and is still being used today. GRE is commonly used as a site-to-site VPN solution because of its simplicity and versatility. It is the only tunneling protocol that can encapsulate up to 20 types of protocols. In the past when protocols such as AppleTalk, Novell IPX, and NetBEUI roamed the network, GRE was the tunneling protocol of choice to carry these protocols to other remote sites.

PPP
Point-to-Point Protocol

PAP
Password Authentication Protocol

CHAP
Challenge Handshake Authentication Protocol

MD5
Message Digest 5

SHA
The secure hash algorithm

The tunneling protocols commonly used in remote access VPNs are mentioned throughout the rest of this section. To better understand remote access VPN, you should at least understand the importance of **PPP**. In the days when modems and dial-ups were kings, PPP was the key to the remote access solution; it was the de facto protocol of the dial-up networking. In those days, people would make a dial-up connection to their ISP and establish a PPP session to the Internet. Even though authentication is optional for PPP, most implementations of PPP provide user authentication using protocols such as Password Authentication Protocol (**PAP**) or Challenge Handshake Authentication Protocol (**CHAP**). PAP is a simple, clear-text (unencrypted) authentication method, which is superseded by CHAP, an encrypted authentication method that uses the **MD5** hashing algorithm. Related to MD5 is **SHA**, which is the secure hash algorithms required by law for use in certain government applications. This includes cryptographic algorithms and protocols that are used for the protection of sensitive, unclassified information. SHA comes in many types: SHA-0, -1, -2, and -3.

EAP
Extensible Authentication Protocol

RADIUS
Remote Authentication Dial-In User Service

Later, Extensible Authentication Protocol (**EAP**) was introduced as another PPP authentication method. During the PPP authentication phase, the ISP dial-up server collects the user authentication data and validates it against an authentication server like a **RADIUS** server. RADIUS stands for Remote Authentication Dial-In User Service. RADIUS is an IETF standard protocol that is widely used for authenticating remote users and authorizing user access. The RADIUS server supports many methods of user authentication including PAP, CHAP, and EAP. Even though PPP dial-up is not as prevalent today, the concepts of central authentication still lend themselves to many technologies and applications.

PPTP
Point-to-Point Tunneling Protocol

Point-to-Point Tunneling Protocol (**PPTP**) was developed jointly by Microsoft, 3Com, and Alcatel-Lucent in 1996. It has never been ratified as a standard. Microsoft was a big advocate of PPTP and made PPTP available as part of Microsoft

Windows Dial-up Networking. A PPTP server was included in Microsoft NT 4.0 server, and PPTP was widely used as a remote access solution. PPTP was designed to work in conjunction with a standard PPP. A PPTP client software would establish a PPP connection to an ISP, and once the connection is established, it would then make the PPTP tunnel over the Internet to the PPTP server. The PPTP tunnel uses a modified GRE tunnel to carry its encapsulated packet for IP transmission. The diagram of typical PPTP connection and other tunneling protocols is represented in Figure 12-19. PPTP does not have any authentication mechanism, so it relies heavily on the underlying PPP authentication.

FIGURE 12-19   Tunneling diagram of PPTP and L2TP.

Layer 2 Forwarding Protocol (**L2F**) was developed by Cisco around the same time as PPTP. L2F was not used widely in the consumer market due to its requirement of L2F hardware. Unlike PPTP where the VPN client software is installed and initiated from the client, L2F does not require any VPN client software. A L2F connection is intended to be done by L2F hardware. This hardware is designed to be at the ISP. A client would make a typical PPP connection to the ISP. The ISP will then initiate the L2F tunnel connection on UDP port 1701 to the L2F server at the corporate headquarters. This requires coordination between the ISP and the corporate network. L2F relies on the PPP authentication to be passed on to the corporate authentication server.

| L2F |
| Layer 2 Forwarding |

Layer 2 Tunneling Protocol (**L2TP**) was developed by the Internet Engineering Task Force (IETF) in 1999. L2TP was created with the intention of merging two incompatibles proprietary tunneling protocols, PPTP and L2F. L2TP is considered to be an enhancement of the two previous protocols. L2TP does not require a specific hardware. It can be initiated directly from the client. L2TP Tunnel encapsulation is done on UDP port 1701. L2TP allows for tunnel authentication, so it does not have to rely heavily on the underlying PPP. If L2TP is used over an IP network where PPP is not used, the tunnel can be created with its own authentication mechanism.

| L2TP |
| Layer 2 Tunneling Protocol |

All of the previously mentioned tunneling protocols are lacking one important security feature—encryption. An encryption can guarantee data confidentiality in the tunnel. IPsec offers encryption features that the others lack. IPsec was designed for the purpose of providing a secure end-to-end connection. The VPN can take advantage of IPsec to provide network layer encryption as well as authentication techniques. IPsec are versatile in that it can be implemented easily as a remote access VPN or as a site-to-site VPN. For IPv6, IPsec becomes an even more integral part as it is embedded within the IPv6 packets. There are two primary security protocols

AH
Authentication Header

ESP
Encapsulating Security Protocol

SHA-1
Secure Hash Algorithm

DES, 3DES
Data Encryption Standard, Triple Data Encryption Standard

AES
Advanced Encryption Standard

IKE
Internet Key Exchange

ISAKMP
Internet Security Association and Key Management Protocol

Diffie-Hellman
Key generation algorithm

used by IPsec. They are Authentication Header (**AH**) and Encapsulating Security Payload (**ESP**). AH guarantees the authenticity of the IP packets. It uses a one-way hash algorithm such as Message Digest 5 (MD5) or Secure Hash Algorithm 1 (**SHA-1**) to ensure the data integrity of the IP packets. ESP provides confidentiality to the data messages (payloads) by ways of encryption. It uses symmetrical encryption algorithms like Data Encryption Standard (**DES**), Triple Data Encryption Standard (**3DES**), and Advanced Encryption Standard (**AES**).

Before an IPsec tunnel can be established, quite a few security parameters have to be negotiated and agreed upon by both ends. IPsec uses the Internet Key Exchange (**IKE**) protocol to manage such process. IKE is a hybrid protocol that encompasses several key management protocols, most notably Internet Security Association and Key Management Protocol (**ISAKMP**). Many times, the term IKE and ISAKMP are often mentioned alongside each other. There are two negotiation phases that the two network nodes must perform before the IPsec tunnel is complete. The IKE Phase 1 is a phase where both network nodes authenticate each other and set up an IKE SA (Security Association). In phase 1, the **Diffie-Hellman** key exchange algorithm is used to generate a shared session secret key to encrypt the key exchange communications. This phase is essentially to set up a secure channel to protect further negotiations in phase 2. IKE Phase 2 uses the secure channel established in phase 1 to negotiate the unidirectional IPsec SAs—inbound and outbound—to set up the IPsec tunnel. This is where the parameters for AH and ESP would be negotiated.

Configuring a Remote Access VPN Server

Configuring a Windows 2010 and 20008 VPN server is fairly simple and only requires the routing and remote access server configuration be started by clicking **Start > Programs > Administrative Tools > Routing and Remote Access**. Right-click the server name and select **Configure and Enable Routing and Remote Access**. Follow the installation steps and choose the manually configured server option. Select **Virtual Private Network (VPN) Server** from the Common Configurations menu. The last step in this process is to set the pool of IP addresses to be used by the VPN server. To do this, right-click the server name and select **Properties**; then click the **IP** tab and select **Static Address Pool > Add > Set range of IP addresses and input the desired IP address range**. The Windows 2003 server will issue a default IP address in the 169.x.x.x range if this step is not completed and your client computers will be assigned an IP address that is not valid for your network.

Configuring a Remote Client's VPN Connection

The following examples demonstrate how to configure a VPN remote client running Windows Vista, XP, or Mac OS X. These examples assume that the client has permission to connect to the VPN server on your home network.

Windows 10/8/7/Vista—VPN Client

To start the Windows 10/8/7/Vista VPN client configuration, complete the following steps:

1. Click **Start** and select **Control Panel > Connect To**; then select **Set-up a connection or network**.

2. Select **Connect to a workplace** and click **Next**.

3. You may get a prompt that asks, "Do you want to use a connection that you already have?" If so, select **No, create new connection**, click **Next**, and select **Use my Internet Connection (VPN)**.

4. You will be asked to input the Internet address or the name of the VPN server.

   - In the Destination Name field, enter the name for the VPN connection (for example, **salsa-vpn**).

   - In the User Name field, enter the username for your VPN account. This is the account name set up on the VPN server.

   - In the Domain field, enter the name of your domain.

5. Click the **Create** and **Close** buttons to complete the setup.

6. When the setup is complete, you can establish a VPN connection by clicking **Start > Connect To** and then right-clicking the VPN connection you just created and selecting **Properties**.

7. Click the **Networking** tab. This gives you the option of selecting the type of VPN security. Select the type that matches the requirements for your VPN connection.

Windows XP—VPN Client

The following example demonstrates how to configure a VPN remote client running Windows XP. This example assumes that the client has permission to connect to the VPN server on your home network.

1. Click **Start > Control Panel > Network connections > Network Connections**. This opens the Network Connection window.

2. Select **Create a New Connection**. The New Connection Wizard window opens; choose **Next**.

3. Select **Connect to the Network at My Workplace** and click **Next**.

4. Select **Virtual Private Network Connection** and click **Next**. You will be asked for a company name; click **Next**.

5. The next screen asks you to type a Host Name or IP Address; after entering it, click **Next** and then click **Finish**.

6. You will be asked to input a connection name for the VPN connection. This example uses the name **VPN-Remote**. Click **Next**. This opens the Public Network Connection menu.

7. You will be asked how you are to connect to the public network. Select either **Do not dial** or **Automatically dial** based on your need. Click **Next**.

   The next menu is for specifying the IP address of the VPN server on the home network.

8. Click **Next** and you should be notified that installation is complete. Click **Finish**.

The setup for the VPN connection is now complete for the Windows XP remote client. To start a VPN connection, click **Start > Control Panel > Network and Internet connections > Network Connections**. Select the VPN-Remote connection just created by double-clicking the icon. You will see a prompt that states that to connect to VPN-Remote you must first connect to your Internet or dial-in connection. Click **Yes**. You will be asked to input the username and password for the dial-in connection. Click the **Dial** button. After the network connection is established, a new window labeled **Connect VPN-Remote** appears. Enter the username and password for the VPN connection and click **Connect**.

Mac OS X—VPN Client

The following example demonstrates how to configure a VPN remote client running Mac OS X. This example assumes that the client has permission to connect to the VPN server on your home network.

1. Click the **Apple icon > System Preferences > Network** and then click the plus sign to create a new service.

2. A new window will appear. Select **VPN** as the new interface.

3. Select the appropriate VPN type depending on the server configuration. The VPN type options are L2TP over IPSec, PPTP, Cisco IPSec or IKEv2.

4. Leave the service name as default or select a new name, then click **Create** to create a new VPN service.

5. Next, select **Apply** to save the configuration.

After completing the VPN setup, VPN connections can be established by selecting the VPN service under the **System Preferences > Network** window and click **Connect** button. You can also establish the VPN connection by clicking the VPN icon at the top of your Mac OS X main screen.

The VPN connection to the home network VPN server should now be made. Remember, the remote client must have a user account and password on the Window 2008/2003 VPN server. In this example, the user's account name is *jtest*. The IP address of 192.168.20.31 is assigned to the VPN remote client by the VPN server when a connection is made. The available IP addresses were specified when the VPN server was configured. Running a **tracert** (**traceroute**) from the VPN server (192.168.20.2) to the client on the VPN network (192.168.20.31) shows a single hop. The VPN remote client appears to be on the same home network. The **traceroute** is shown in Figure 12-20.

```
Select C:\WINNT\System32\cmd.exe                                    _ □ X
Pinging 192.168.20.31 with 32 bytes of data:

Reply from 192.168.20.31: bytes=32 time=203ms TTL=128
Reply from 192.168.20.31: bytes=32 time=203ms TTL=128
Reply from 192.168.20.31: bytes=32 time=188ms TTL=128
Reply from 192.168.20.31: bytes=32 time=188ms TTL=128

Ping statistics for 192.168.20.31:
    Packets: Sent = 4, Received = 4, Lost = 0 (0% loss),
Approximate round trip times in milli-seconds:
    Minimum = 188ms, Maximum =  203ms, Average =  195ms

C:\>tracert 192.168.20.31

Tracing route to PINDLESKIN [192.168.20.31]
over a maximum of 30 hops:

  1    172 ms    157 ms    171 ms  PINDLESKIN [192.168.20.31]

Trace complete.

C:\>
```

FIGURE 12-20   The traceroute from the VPN server to the VPN remote client.

Cisco VPN Client

This section examines setting up an end-to-end encrypted VPN connection using the Cisco VPN Client software. These connections can be used for both onsite and mobile (remote) users. The Cisco VPN Client uses IPsec with the option of two encryption modes: tunnel and transport. The tunnel mode encrypts the header and the data (payload) for each packet. The transport mode only encrypts the data (payload). IPsec can be used to encrypt data between various networking devices such as PC to server, PC to router, and router to router.

The first step for setting up the Cisco VPN Client is to install the software on the server that is to be used to establish the VPN connections. The Cisco VPN Client software must be licensed for each server installation. After the software is installed on the server, the clients connect to the server and download the Cisco VPN Client software. The individual requesting the software must have network access to the software. This usually requires that the user must have an authorized username and password. The next step is to install the client software. After the software is installed, start the Cisco VPN Client software by clicking **Start > Programs > Cisco VPN Client**.

The first window displayed after starting the VPN client is shown in Figure 12-21. This window indicates that the current status is Disconnected. Click in the **Connection Entries** tab. This will list the configured connections for establishing the VPN connection. Note: The Cisco VPN Client software will automatically set up the connections available for the client. The available connections for the client are configured when the server software is installed. An example is shown in Figure 12-22. Select the desired link by double-clicking **Connection Entry**. The next window displayed will be the initial handshake screen as shown in Figure 12-23.

> **IPsec**
> Used to encrypt data between various networking devices

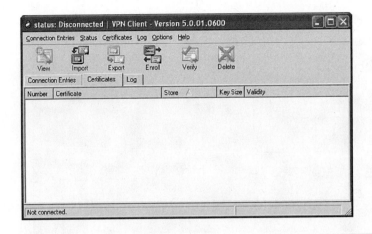

FIGURE 12-21 The first window, the VPN Client window, is displayed after starting the VPN client software. This window is showing that the current status is Disconnected.

The next window (Figure 12-24) shows that you have connected to the Virtual Private Network. It says Welcome to Chile-VPN—the Chile-Virtual Private Network.

FIGURE 12-22 The listing of the available connections for establishing the VPN link.

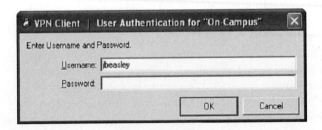

FIGURE 12-23 The initial handshake screen for the VPN client.

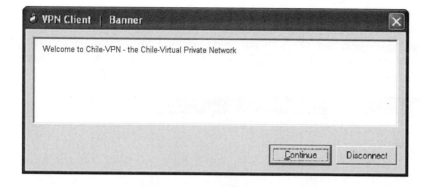

FIGURE 12-24   The welcome menu for Chile-VPN—the Chile Virtual Private Network.

After the VPN connection has been established, you can click the VPN Client icon that should be displayed in the bottom-right of your computer screen. Select the connection (for example, Chile-VPN). The properties for Chile-VPN will be displayed as shown in Figure 12-25(a). This window shows that Group Authentication has been selected. Additionally, the group name and password are entered. In this case, all authorized users are using the same group name and password. This username and password enables the user to access the VPN, but the user will have to enter an authorized username and password to actually establish a VPN connection. The certification authentication is used to verify whether the client is authorized to establish the VPN. The client must have this in their computer (installed or downloaded). This is the first step before the VPN tunnel is set up. Figure 12-25(b) shows additional properties for the VPN connection. This window indicates that IPsec over UDP has been selected.

(a)   (b)

FIGURE 12-25   The Properties window for the VPN client.

The next window, shown in Figure 12-26, lists the statistics for the VPN session. The IP addresses for both the VPN server and client are listed. This screen indicates that a 168-bit 3-DES encryption is being used and the authentication type is

HMAC-MD5. 3-DES is called Triple DES, and it uses the same procedure as DES except the encryption procedure is repeated three times, hence the name. HMAC-MD5 (the keyed-Hash Message Authentication Code) is a type of message authentication code (MAC) that is being used with the MD5 cryptographic function. This window also shows that UDP port 10000 is being used.

FIGURE 12-26   The Statistics window for the VPN client.

This section has demonstrated the setup and configuration of two types of VPN connections. The next was setting up a VPN link from a VPN client to a VPN server. The client configuration was demonstrated for Windows Vista/XP and Mac OS X. The last configuration was using the Cisco VPN Client software. This requires setting up the software on both a server and client computer. Each type of VPN connection has its use, and the network administrator must be familiar with Windows 7, Vista, and XP.

Section 12-5 Review

This section has covered the following **Network+** Exam objectives:

1.2 Compare and contrast the use of networking devices and applications

This section introduced the use of the GRE and PTP./PPTP tunneling protocols.

1.12 Given a set of requirements, implement a basic network

This section examined the use of a virtual circuit that spans over the Internet infrastructure. This virtual circuit is a VPN connection.

3.2 Compare and contrast common network vulnerabilities and threats

This section introduce PAP, a simple, clear-text (unencrypted) authentication method, which is superseded by CHAP, an encrypted authentication method that uses the MD5 hashing algorithm.

3.3 Given a scenario, implement network hardening techniques

This section examined setting up an end-to-end encrypted VPN connection. This is an important feature when trying to maintain a secure connection for a remote user.

4.2 Given a scenario, analyze and interpret the output of troubleshooting tools.

*In this section an example was presented on running a **tracert** (**traceroute**) from the VPN server to the client on the VPN network that shows a single hop.*

4.7 Given a scenario, troubleshoot and resolve common security threats

This section looked at the following authentication methods: PAP, CHAP, EAP, and the RADIUS server.

Test Your Knowledge

1. What is the purpose of an IP tunnel?

   a. An IP tunnel creates a physical circuit between the two endpoints and makes the connection appear like a dedicated connection even though it spans over the network infrastructure.

   b. An IP tunnel creates a virtual circuit between the two endpoints and makes the connection appear like a dedicated connection even though it spans over the Internet infrastructure.

   c. An IP tunnel creates a physical circuit between the two endpoints and makes the connection appear like a dedicated connection even though it spans over the internal network infrastructure.

   d. An IP tunnel creates a physical circuit between the two endpoints and makes the connection appear like a dedicated connection even though it spans over the internal Internet infrastructure.

2. What must happen before an IPsec tunnel can be established?

   a. Security parameters have to be negotiated and publicly agreed upon by both ends.

   b. IKE Phase 1 is a phase where both network nodes authenticate each other and set up an IKE SA. IKE Phase 2 uses the plain-text channel established in phase 1 to negotiate the unidirectional IPsec SAs, inbound and outbound, to set up the IPsec tunnel.

   c. IKE Phase 1 is a phase where one network node authenticates the other and sets up an IKE SA. IKE Phase 2 uses the open channel established in phase 1 to negotiate the unidirectional IPsec SAs, inbound and outbound, to set up the IPsec tunnel.

   d. Security parameters have to be negotiated and agreed upon by both ends.

12-6   WIRELESS SECURITY

This section provides an overview of securing 802.11 wireless LANs. The network administrator must be aware of the security issues when configuring a wireless LAN. The fact is, RF (radio frequencies) will pass through the walls, ceilings, and floors of a building even with low signal power. Therefore, the assumption should never be made that the wireless data is confined to only the user's area. The network administrator must assume that the wireless data can be received by an unintended user. In other words, the use of an unsecured wireless LAN is opening a potential threat to network security. The additional issue is that the radio frequencies (RF) used in wireless communications are an open medium. This means that anybody with the right type of equipment can create problems. One particular problem is called **jamming**. In this case, the wireless network is overwhelmed with wireless traffic, thereby jamming the network and preventing authorized users to access the network.

To address threats to WLAN security, the network administrator must ensure that the WLAN is protected by firewalls and intrusion detection, and most importantly the network administrator must make sure that the wireless security features are *turned on!* This might seem to be a bold statement, but surprisingly enough, many WLANs are placed on a network without the available wireless security features being turned on. Many times the user in the WLAN assumes that no one would break into their computer because nothing important exists on the system. This may be true, but to an attacker, the user has one very important item: access to the wired network through an unsecured client.

WLANs use an **SSID** (service set identifier) to authenticate users, but the problem is that the SSID is broadcast in radio link beacons about 10 times per second. In WLAN equipment, the **beacons** are transmitted so that a wireless user can identify an access point to connect to. The SSID can be turned off, so it isn't transmitted with a beacon, but it is still possible for the SSID to be obtained by packet sniffing. As noted previously, packet sniffing is a technique used to scan through unencrypted data packets to extract information. In this case, an attacker uses packet sniffing to extract the SSID from data packets. Disabling SSID broadcasting will make it so that most client devices (such as Windows devices and Mac devices) won't notice that the wireless LAN is present. This at least keeps "casual snoopers" off the network. Enterprise-grade access points implement multiple SSIDs, with each configured SSID having its own VLAN and wireless configuration. This allows the deployment of a common wireless LAN infrastructure that supports multiple levels of security, which is important for some venues such as airports and hospitals (where there are both public and private users).

IEEE 802.11 supports two ways to authenticate clients: open and sharekey. **Open authentication** basically is a null authentication that can enable any client to authenticate to an AP as long as the client knows the correct SSID. In **shared key authentication**, both the client and the access point share a key called a pre-shared key (PSK). The client sends a shared key authentication request, and then a packet of text called a challenge text is sent by the access point to the client with the instruction to encrypt the text and return it to the access point. This requires that wired equivalent privacy (**WEP**) be turned on. WEP is used to encrypt and decrypt wireless data packets. The exchange and the return of the encrypted text verifies that the client has the proper WEP key and is authorized to be a member of the wireless network. It is important to note that shared key authentication is extremely vulnerable. As a result, it's standard practice to avoid the use of shared key authentication. An example of the setting for WEP encryption is provided in Figure 12-27 (a and b). In Figure 12-27(a), the user has the WEP options of disabled (No Privacy), 64-bit WEP (Privacy), and 128-bit WEP (More Privacy). Figure 12-27(b) shows the wireless security settings in Windows Vista. There are clearly more options, and these newer wireless security settings are discussed next.

Open Authentication
Basically a null authentication that can enable any client to authenticate to an AP

Shared key Authentication
Both the client and the access point share a key called a pre-shared key (PSK).

WEP
Wired equivalent privacy

FIGURE 12-27 An example of setting WEP encryption on a wireless client.

It is well-known that WEP is a weak wireless security system. It doesn't use a strong enough encryption to secure a wireless network. The RC4 algorithm is used for encryption in WEP. A couple of the weaknesses of WEP include that the challenge text in WEP is sent in clear text. Additionally, the WEP initialization vector is only 24 bits in size and is always static. WEP also does not use a key management, and its pre-shared key never changes. Because of these factors, it is not too difficult to obtain the pre-shared key. There is published information about WEP vulnerabilities, but even with this, WEP does provide some basic security and is certainly better than operating the network with no security.

WPA

Wi-Fi Protected Access

TKIP

Temporal Key Integrity
Protocol

AES

Advance Encryption
Standard

CCMP

Counter Mode with Cipher
Block Chaining Message
Authentication Code
Protocol

LEAP

A wireless security
system used by Cisco

EAP

Extensible Authentication
Protocol

RADIUS

Remote Authentication
Dial-In User Service

An improvement with wireless security is provided with WPA and WPA2. **WPA** stands for Wi-Fi Protected Access, and it supports the user authentication provided by 802.1x and replaces WEP as the primary way for securing wireless transfers. WPA still uses RC4 as the encryption algorithm, but it provides a key management mechanism via **TKIP** (Temporal Key Integrity Protocol). TKIP basically generates a sequence of WEP keys based on a master pre-shared key and rekeys periodically every 10,000 packets. TKIP also uses an integrity check value to ensure that the packet is not tampered with. If so, WPA will stop using the current key and will rekey. WPA2 is an improved version of WPA. It uses **AES** (Advance Encryption Standard) as its encryption algorithm and **CCMP** (Counter Mode with Cipher Block Chaining Message Authentication Code Protocol) as its key management.

The encryption algorithm and key management alone cannot truly secure the wireless connection. The 802.1x standard enhances wireless security by incorporating authentication of the user. Cisco Systems uses an 802.1x authentication system called **LEAP**. In Cisco LEAP, the user must enter a password to access the network. This means that if the wireless client is being used by an unauthorized user, the password requirement will keep the unauthorized user out of the network.

WPA is considered to be a higher level of security for wireless systems. In the 802.1x system, a user requests access to the wireless network via an access point. The next step is for the user to be authenticated. At this point, the user can only send EAP messages. **EAP** is the Extensible Authentication Protocol and is used in both WPA and WPA2 by the client computer and the access point. The access point sends an EAP message requesting the user's identity. The user (client computer) returns the identity information that is sent by the access point to an authentication server. The server will then accept or reject the user's request to join the network. If the client is authorized, the access point will change the user's (client's) state to authorized. A Remote Authentication Dial-In User Service (**RADIUS**) is sometimes used to provide authentication. This type of authentication helps prevent unauthorized users from connecting to the network. Additionally, this authentication helps to keep authorized users from connecting to rogue or unauthorized access points.

Another way to further protect data transmitted over a WLAN is to establish a VPN connection. In this way, the data is protected from an attacker. The following are basic guidelines for wireless security:

- Make sure the wireless security features are turned on.
- Use firewalls and intrusion detection on your WLAN.
- Improve authentication of the WLAN by incorporating 802.1x features.
- Consider using third-party end-to-end encryption software to protect the data that might be intercepted by an unauthorized user.
- Whenever possible, use encrypted services such as SSH and Secure FTP.

**Acceptable Use Policy
(AUP)**

Defines the constraints and
practices the user must
agree to in order to have
access to the network.

The bottom line is that the choice of the level of security will be based on multiple factors within the network. For example, what is the cost benefit ratio of increased security? How will incorporating or not incorporating increased wireless security affect users? The network administrator and the overall management will have to make the final decision regarding wireless security before it is installed and the network becomes operational. Networks will typically have an **acceptable use policy (AUP)** that defines the constraints and practices the user must agree to in order to have wireless access to the network. Without this use of an AUP, the network could be in great peril. This type of policy has become an integral part of securing networks.

Section 12-6 Review

This section has covered the following **Network+** Exam objectives:

1.12 Given a set of requirements, implement a basic network

This section introduced procedures for securing the wireless LAN. The network administrator must be aware of the security issues when configuring a wireless LAN.

4.7 Given a scenario, troubleshoot and resolve common security threats

This section introduced the concept of jamming. In this case, the wireless network is overwhelmed with wireless traffic, thereby jamming the network and preventing authorized users to access the network.

5.5 Given a scenario, implement the appropriate policies and procedures

This section introduce the AUP—Acceptable Use Policy. Networks will typically have a policy that defines the constraints and practices the user must agree to in order to have wireless access to the network.

Test Your Knowledge

1. Disabling SSID broadcasting will make it so that most client devices (such as Windows devices and Mac devices) won't notice that the wireless LAN is present. True or False?

2. What are the two ways IEEE 802.11 supports authenticating clients?

SUMMARY

This chapter has presented a short overview of network security. The role of the network administrator is not only to design, assemble, and maintain a good network, but also to protect the network and its users from both external and internal threats. This chapter has introduced some of the concepts critical to network security. The reader should understand the following concepts:

- The various ways an attacker can gain control of a network
- How denial of service attacks are initiated and how they can be prevented
- How the security software like antivirus and personal firewall work and why they are important for protecting a computer
- How the security appliances such as firewall, IPS, and web filter work and why they are important for protecting a network the VPN technologies work and how to set up simple VPN clients

QUESTIONS AND PROBLEMS

Section 12-2

1. List six ways an attacker gains access to a network.

2. Describe a way social engineering can be used by an attacker to gain control of a network.

3. Describe how social engineering attacks can be avoided.

4. What is a dictionary attack?

5. Can password cracking be prevented? How?

6. How does the use of a networking switch minimize problems with packet sniffing in a LAN?

7. Describe the concept of *software vulnerabilities.*

8. What is a buffer overflow?

9. List two ways to prevent vulnerable software attacks.

10. What are simple ways to minimize or prevent viruses?

Section 12-3

11. What is a denial of service attack?

12. Describe a SYN attack.

13. Cisco routers use what command to block broadcasts to a subnet?

14. Define a directed broadcast.

15. What is the best way to keep from contributing to DDoS attacks?

Section 12-4

16. What is the purpose of a firewall?

17. Why is a stateful firewall important?

18. What is the first line against viruses and worms?

    a. A personal firewall

    b. The Mac OS X operating system

    c. Antivirus software

    d. The Linux operating system

19. The personal firewall software is typically based on which of the following?

    a. Using only trusted sites

    b. Configuring non-stateful firewall protection

    c. The 802.11x protocol

    d. Basic packet filtering inspections

20. Access lists are which of the following? (Select all that apply.)

    a. A basic form of firewall protection

    b. Basically a firewall

    c. An improvement over firewall protection

    d. A replacement for proxy servers

21. Which of the following best defines packet filtering?

    a. It implies that data rates are smoothed out.

    b. A limit is placed on the packets that can enter the network.

    c. It should be avoided when ACLs are used.

    d. A limit is not placed on the packets that can exit the network.

Section 12-5

22. What is the goal of a VPN tunnel?

23. Explain the expected difference when running a traceroute from the home network to the remote user using the IP address for the remote user's router interface, and then running a traceroute from the home network to the remote user's VPN tunnel address.

24. List five steps for troubleshooting the VPN tunnel link.

25. Identify two tunneling protocols that can be used to configure a remote user's PC.

26. What does encryption guarantee?

27. What are the two primary security protocols used by IPsec?

28. What is IKE?

Section 12-6

29. What is the most important thing to do when using a wireless network?

30. What is the purpose of wireless beacons?

31. What information can be obtained from a wireless beacon?

32. What is the purpose of WEP?

33. List five guidelines for wireless security.

34 Describe the steps used by WPA2 to authenticate a user.

35. What is a RADIUS server?

CRITICAL THINKING

36. Your network is experiencing an excessive amount of pings to your network server. The pings are from outside the network. Someone suggests that you set an access list to block ICMP packets coming into the network. How would you respond?

37. Your supervisor informs you that a user on the network has requested a VPN connection. Prepare a response to the supervisor discussing what is needed to provide the connection.

CERTIFICATION QUESTIONS

38. In regard to firewalls, packet filtering accomplishes which of the following?

    a. Not all network services can be filtered.

    b. A limit is placed on the amount of information that can enter a network.

    c. Simplifies creating access-lists.

    d. All of these answers are correct.

39. Which of the following best defines what intrusion detection is? (Select all that apply.)

    a. The monitoring of data packets passing through the network to catch potential attacks.

    b. The monitoring of data packets passing through the network to catch ongoing attacks.

    c. The monitoring of data packets with invalid IP addresses that pass through the network.

    d. None of these answers is correct.

40. Which of the following best defines what signatures are?

    a. IP addresses of known hackers.

    b. The email address of known attackers.

    c. Indicators of known attacks.

    d. None of these answers is correct.

41. What are indicators of repeated attempts to make connections to certain machines called?

    a. Operation errors

    b. Pinging

    c. Tracing

    d. Probing

42. Eavesdropping on network data traffic can be minimized by using which of the following? (Select all that apply.)

    a. Hubs

    b. Switches

    c. Ports

    d. Gigbit networks

43. It is important to block ICMP packets coming into a network to prevent intrusion. True or False?

44. What is the name for a broadcast sent to a specific subnet?

    a. Multicast

    b. Broadcast

    c. Directed broadcast

    d. Sweep

45. The command used to display the ports currently open on a Windows operating system is **netstat –r**. True or False?

46. Which of the following is the command used to display currently open ports on a Windows operating system?

    a. **netstat -a**

    b. **netstat -r**

    c. **netstat -o**

    d. **netstat - a**

47. What is a piece of malicious computer code that, when opened, starts a program that attacks a computer called?

    a. An overflow

    b. A virus

    c. A worm

    d. Denial of service

13
CHAPTER

CLOUD COMPUTING AND VIRTUALIZATION

Chapter Outline

Objectives

- Describe the concept and benefit of virtualization
- Discuss the concept of the "cloud"
- Explain the purpose of a Hypervisor

- Develop an appreciation of the benefit of outsourcing services to the cloud
- Understand the steps to set up virtualization on a PC

Key Terms

core
cache
host machine
guest machine
virtualization
VM (virtual machine)
VMM

Hypervisor
Type-1 Hypervisor
Type-2 Hypervisor
vMotion, XenMotion, Live Migration
cloud
outsource

cloud service/cloud computing
SLA
Infrastructure as a Service
Platform as a Service
Software as a Service

This chapter examines virtualization technology and its applications. Also, it explores the cloud computing services that are offered.

13-1 INTRODUCTION

Table 13-1 lists and identifies, by chapter section, where each of the CompTIA Network+ objectives is presented in this chapter. At the end of each chapter section is a review with comments of the Network+ objectives presented in that section. These comments are provided to help reinforce the reader's understanding of a particular Network+ objective. The chapter review also includes "Test Your Knowledge" questions to aid in the understanding of key concepts before the reader advances to the next section of the chapter. The end of the chapter includes a complete set of questions plus sample certification-type questions.

TABLE 13-1   Chapter 13 CompTIA Network+ Objectives

Domain/Objective Number	Domain/Objective Description	Section Where Objective Is Covered
1.0	*Networking Architecture*	
1.11	Compare and contrast technologies that support cloud and virtualization	13-2, 13-3

13-2 VIRTUALIZATION

In the past, having multiple CPUs in one computer was not a norm. Only high-end server-class machines would have the architecture that could take advantage of multi-CPU processing. Also, it was expensive to run a server with multiple CPUs, lots of RAM, and a big hard drive. This has changed due to the latest development of microprocessor technology, computer architecture, and more affordable prices.

The development of microprocessor technology has seen incredible growth. A single CPU architecture has evolved to a single CPU with multiple **cores**. The core is an independent actual processing unit, which is responsible for reading and executing program instructions. So, instead of having multiple physical CPUs, a single integrated circuit can contain two or more processors and their associated local **caches**. A cache is block of memory set aside for temporary storage of information. Similar to having a multiple-CPU architecture, a multicore CPU can execute more than one independent instruction at the same time, thus allowing for true multitasking. The multicore processor is not limited to only the server platform. In the mid-2000s, desktops, laptops, and workstations started to ship with dual-core processors. Today, computers are shipped with multicore CPUs. Buying a quad-core processor computer is not something extraordinary, as the CPU prices have become more affordable.

Also, the market started to see a shift from 32-bit CPUs to 64-bit CPUs around the same time. In the past, 64-bit CPUs were used more in supercomputers and high-end servers, which have a 64-bit hardware architecture and 64-bit operating system. This allows for supercomputers and servers to compute twice as many data bits in the same clock cycle. Another big advantage of the 64-bit architecture is the maximum supported RAM. Whereas 32-bit architecture can only support up to 4GB of RAM, 64-bit architecture can support more. This is very significant for servers because they can run more programs and support more users at the same time. Overall, the 64-bit architecture provides faster and higher performance than the 32-bit architecture.

The operating systems also have evolved to take full advantage of the 64-bit architecture. More and more 64-bit operating systems are becoming available. Even personal operating systems such as Microsoft Windows now are shipped with both 32-bit and 64-bit versions. Currently, we see that most operating systems are standardized on CPU platforms such as Intel and AMD and on 32-bit and 64-bit hardware architectures. Microsoft Windows, Linux, and even Mac operating systems can all run on the Intel 64-bit platform. This is an extraordinary convergence considering where they were in the past.

With all these developments in technology, it paves the way for virtualization. **Virtualization** is a technology concept of creating a virtual computer that can contain (but is not limited to) a virtual CPU, virtual operating system, virtual storage, or virtual network card. This virtual computer—or virtual machine or **guest machine**—can live inside a physical machine or **host machine** or virtual host. The virtual host machine can spawn as many guest machines as its physical hardware or platform can allow. A key idea behind virtualization is that the CPU and memory often are underutilized; they are not always tasked with processes to execute. It is extremely common to see the CPU in an idle state, where it is not being used by any program. This is more common in personal computers than in servers, but the time computers spend in idle state is more than the active one.

Because the CPU is idle, in most circumstances the rest of the hardware, such as the RAM, disk I/O, and NIC, will stay idle as well. Therefore, virtualization takes advantage of this concept via virtualization software to carve out enough CPU processing time, enough RAM, and enough disk space to create a virtual machine within a host machine. This way, the available computing resources of the physical host machine are used more efficiently. The number of active guest machines will

Core
The core is an independent actual processing unit, which is responsible for reading and executing program instructions.

Caches
The block of memory set aside for temporary storage of information

Host Machine
Another name for the physical machine

Guest Machine
Another name for the virtual computer

Virtualization
A technology concept of creating a virtual computer

depend on how powerful the host machine is. Please note that when a guest machine is shut down, it only requires storage space, but not other computing resources.

The software used to provide virtualization is referred to as a **Hypervisor**. This provides a Virtual Machine Monitor (**VMM**) used for managing and controlling the underlying physical hardware with the associated virtual hardware.

There are two types of Hypervisors.

- **Type-1 Hypervisor**: This type of Hypervisor is loaded directly on the hardware to abstract the hardware to the virtualization layer and is commonly used on servers. It is sometimes called a bare-metal Hypervisor. Some well-known type-1 Hypervisors are VMware's vSphere/ESXi, Microsoft's Hyper-V, Linux's KVM, Red Hat Enterprise Virtualization, and Citrix's Xenserver.

- **Type-2 Hypervisor**: This type of Hypervisor is loaded on an operating system and abstracts the virtualization layer through its host operating system and is commonly used on personal computers. It is sometimes called a hosted Hypervisor. Some of the well-known type-2 Hypervisors are VMware Workstation, Oracle's VirtualBox, VMware Fusion for Mac, and Parallels for Mac.

It used to be when an organization needed a server, a dedicated server with the right CPU, the right amount of RAM, and the right number of hard drives would be identified and purchased. The specifications would also depend on the functions or services that the server would perform. For example, a database server would need to have more memory than a file server, whereas the file server would need to have more storage space.

Virtualization, however, has brought a more cost-effective way to provide server management and maintenance. Instead of the organization buying different servers for different services, only one server has to be purchased. For example, an organization can purchase a server with two 18-core processors, 24 units of 32GB RAM, and four 6TB hard drives, which will yield computing resources of 36 processors, 768GB of RAM, and 24TB of storage space. Thus, there are enough computing resources to provision many powerful virtual servers serving different functions. When a virtual server needs more resources in the future, more CPU and RAM can be assigned to it and more disk space can be provisioned for it. This is all done via the virtualization software, which makes it more convenient than having to open up the physical unit to upgrade CPU, RAM, and hard drives.

An additional benefit of virtualization is that it reduces the physical footprint of servers. The number of physical servers will be less; hence, reduced space used in the data center, which helps reduce the power consumption and heat dissipation.

Virtualization's skeptics would argue about a single point of failure. Having multiple and critical virtual machines running on one physical server presents a great risk. It is like putting all your eggs in one basket, which every good IT person was taught not to do. Virtualization software vendors responded by introducing a feature that can move a live virtual machine from one physical server to another. In case a physical host server fails, all the virtual machines can be moved to a designated host server. Many vendors have implemented this concept but have called it

---

Hypervisor
Used for managing and controlling the underlying physical hardware with the associated virtual hardware

VM
Virtual machine

VMM
Virtual Machine Monitor

Type-1 Hypervisor
This type of Hypervisor is loaded directly on the hardware to abstract the hardware to the virtualization layer and is commonly used on servers.

Type-2 Hypervisor
This type of Hypervisor is loaded on an operating system and abstracts the virtualization layer through its host operating system and is commonly used on personal computers.

different names. VMware calls it **vMotion**, Citrix calls it **XenMotion**, and Microsoft calls it **Live Migration**.

The personal computing world also has gained some benefits from virtualization. It used to be when you wanted to run two or more operating systems simultaneously, you would need to own multiple computers to do that.

Today, it is more affordable to buy personal desktops or laptops with 64-bit multicore CPUs, 4GB of RAM or more, and more than 500GB of disk space. With type-1 Hypervisor installed, you can run virtual machines of Windows 7, Windows 8, and even Linux at the same time on the same physical computer. Better yet, Mac users can enjoy running virtual machines of Windows and Linux on Apple Mac hardware. Sadly, the same cannot be said about running a virtual copy of Mac OS on the other hardware platforms.

One has to keep in mind that not everything is designed or is allowed to be virtualized. Our prime example is Mac OS. No Hypervisor at this moment is capable of virtualizing Mac OS. This is not a technical issue, because Mac OS can run on an Intel CPU just like other operating systems. Apple has strict licensing restrictions that prohibit running Mac OS on non Apple-labeled hardware. Virtualization may also not be possible due to software restriction such as software that requires an attached piece of physical hardware called a dongle or hardware key. Without this piece of hardware, the software program cannot work properly. Many have also suggested that certain systems that require extreme I/O performance such as backup servers or high-performance computing such as supercomputers should not be virtualized.

> **vMotion, XenMotion, Live Migration**
> Different vendor options for moving a virtual machine to another host server in the event of a physical server failure

Setting Up Virtualization on Windows 8/10

Microsoft does provide a virtualization program as part of their Windows operating systems. In the personal computing realm, Windows 7 has Windows Virtual PC, and Windows 8 and Windows 10 have a client Hyper-V, which uses the same virtualization technology as a Windows server. Client Hyper-V lacks some features that are available in Server Hyper-V. These features, including Live Migration, Fibre channel, Network Virtualization, and Hyper-V replica, are more suitable on server hardware. Client Hyper-V allows users to run more than one 32-bit or 64-bit operating system at the same time on the same computer by running them inside a virtual machine. The Hyper-V feature is not enabled by default. The following steps illustrate how to configure a client Hyper-V on a Windows 8 or Windows 10 computer.

> **Hyper-V**
> A virtualization program that's part of the Windows operating systems

1. Go to Windows Control Panel, select **Programs** and then select **Programs and Features**. Under the Programs and Features, select **Turn Windows Features on or off**. A window will be presented with many Windows features. Search for Hyper-V and then select **Hyper-V**. The computer will need to be restarted in order to enable Hyper-V on Windows 8. This is shown in Figure 13-1.

2. When Hyper-V is enabled, virtualization can be controlled via Hyper-V Manager. Select **Hyper-V Manager** from the programs menu or in Administrative Tools. This is shown in Figure 13-2.

FIGURE 13-1 Restarting the computer to enable Hyper-V.

FIGURE 13-2 Selecting Hyper-V Manager.

3. Before creating any virtual machine, it is recommended that you create a virtual switch first so that the network environment is prepared. Select **Virtual Switch Manager** for the Actions pane. This is shown in Figure 13-3.

FIGURE 13-3 Creating the virtual switch in Hyper-V.

4. Select the type of virtual switch and then select **Create Virtual Switch**.

    - **External** allows the VM (virtual machine) to access all resources available to the physical network, including the host machine and the Internet.

    - **Internal** allows the VM to communicate with the host machine only, but not the Internet.

    - **Private** is the option when multiple VMs are running at the same time, and it allows them to communicate to each other.

5. Specify the name of the switch and click **OK**, as shown in Figure 13-4.

6. Back to the Hyper-V Manager screen, select **New** and then **Virtual Machine** from the Actions pane to create a virtual machine. This is shown in Figure 13-5.

FIGURE 13-4 Specifying the name of the virtual switch.

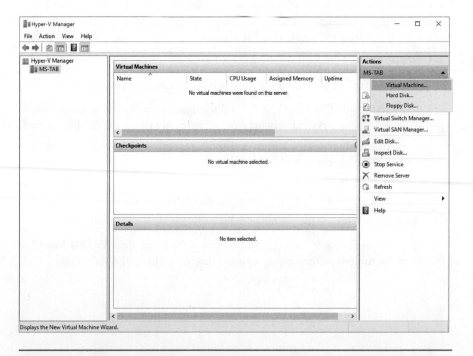

FIGURE 13-5 Creating the virtual machine.

7. Specify the name of the VM. Specify the new installation location or leave it at the default location, as shown in Figure 13-6.

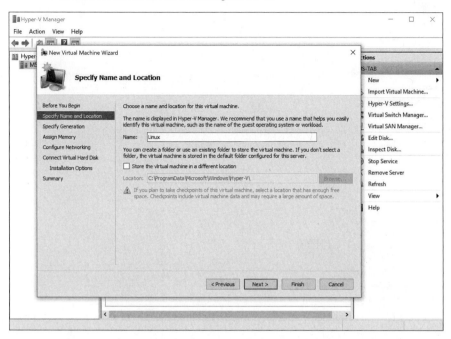

FIGURE 13-6 Specifying the name of the virtual machine.

8. Specify the generation of the virtual machine. The screen is shown in Figure 13-7.

   Generation 1 is backward compatible with an older version of Hyper-V and supports both 32-bit and 64-bit virtual machines, whereas Generation 2 only works with a 64-bit virtual machine.

9. On the Assign Memory screen, specify a desired memory size for the VM, as shown in Figure 13-8.

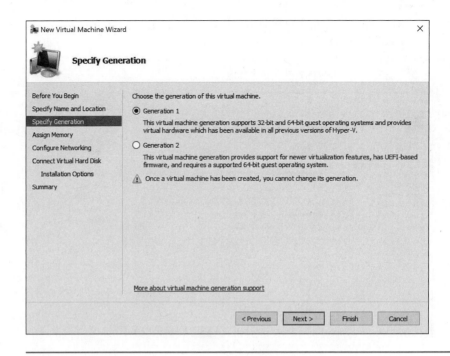

FIGURE 13-7 Specify the generation of the virtual machine.

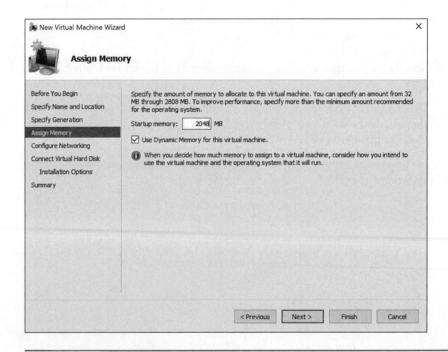

FIGURE 13-8 Specifying the desired memory size for the VM.

10. On the Configure Networking screen, select the connection name of the virtual switch that was previously created in Step 5. This is shown in Figure 13-9.

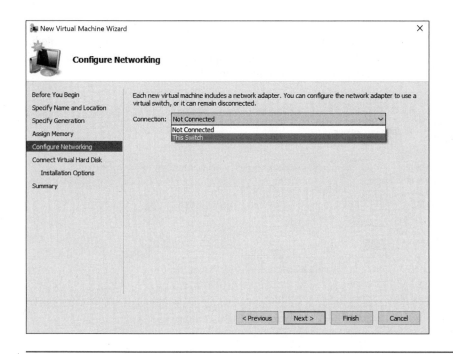

FIGURE 13-9   Select the connection name of the virtual switch.

11. The Connect Virtual Hard Disk screen (shown in Figure 13-10) gives the option
     of specifying a virtual hard disk name, location, and size. Make the necessary
     adjustments and click **Next**.

FIGURE 13-10   Specify a virtual hard disk name, location, and size.

12. The Installation Options screen presents different options for how the VM's operating system can be installed. The OS can be installed from physical media such as a CD/DVD, a virtual bootable floppy disk, an image file such as .iso, or a network server. This is shown in Figure 13-11.

FIGURE 13-11 The screen showing the different options for how the VM's operating system can be installed.

13. Before selecting **Finish** to create the VM, you can view the summary of the machine.

14. Back in the Hyper-V Manager, the Virtual Machines pane should show the new VM in the Off state (see Figure 13-12). To start the VM, select **start** under the VM name from the Actions pane or right-click on the VM. This will start or power up the VM. You can connect to the VM directly like a console by selecting **Connect** from the Actions pane or right-clicking on the newly created VM and selecting **Connect**.

15. The Virtual Machine Connection will show up, and the usual installation of the operating system can proceed. When you're done, the full-fledged running VM with operating system is ready for use. Figure 13-13 shows the final screen.

FIGURE 13-12 The screen for starting the VM.

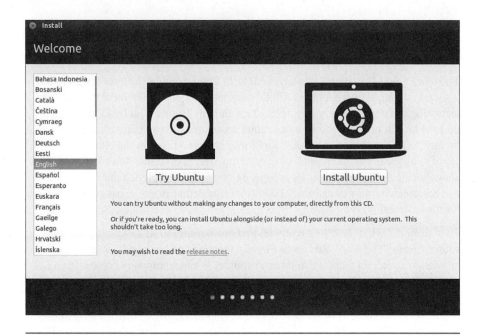

FIGURE 13-13 The final VM screen showing the machine is up.

13-3 CLOUD COMPUTING

Cloud
Another name for the Internet.

The word "cloud" is such a nontechnical term that when it represents a technology, it sounds so vague and nebulous. Cloud computing is one of the most talked-about technologies in the recent years. It has been thrown around a lot by IT people and users alike. Cloud has become a new noun, as in "people can connect to the cloud" or "my stuff is stored on the cloud" or "I migrate everything to the cloud." The cloud is magically in the middle of everything. Yet, people still don't know what and where the cloud really is. Its famous existence has developed many punch lines and has created many questions. The bottom line is that **cloud** is just another name for the Internet/intranet.

Outsource
To obtain goods or services from an outside source in place of an internal source

To understand what the cloud really is, perhaps we should first explore what outsource means. The word **outsource** literally means to obtain goods or services from an outside source in place of an internal source. When a company outsources a service, this means that someone outside of the company has been hired to perform that work or service. In the computing world, if you outsource your IBM mainframe administration to Company A, then Company A will be responsible for having someone either remotely or locally manage your own IBM mainframe system, which is housed on your premises.

Similar to the outsourcing concept, a cloud service is referred to an outsourced service; however, the service is not hosted on the local premises and is not running on the on-premises hardware. With a cloud computing service, not only is a cloud company responsible for providing users with a service, the service can be hosted on the cloud company's hardware and software, which can be anywhere on the Internet.

Cloud service or **cloud computing** is an outsourced and hosted computing environment that delivers IT services to users via a network. It adds the hosting element to the outsourcing. This hosting element typically contains features such as self-service, automation, and application catalogs. This means end users can manage the service directly, or the administrators of the organization that uses the cloud can provision services for their users. As a matter of fact, the two services that have been around for some time and have been provided in the cloud fashion are email hosting and web hosting.

> **Cloud Service or Cloud Computing**
> An outsourced and hosted computing environment that delivers IT services to users via a network

These hosting services have been quite popular because typical users do not want to run their own email servers or web servers. It is much more economical and more convenient for them to subscribe to these services. Especially with email, this service is offered for free to the public; Google offers gmail.com email accounts, Microsoft offers hotmail.com and outlook.com email accounts, Yahoo! offers yahoo.com email accounts, and Apple offers me.com and icloud.com email accounts. Any user can simply create an email account on the company website, and as long as the email username is not already taken, the user can have it. Even though web-hosting services are typically not offered for free, they have found popularity among small businesses and personal websites. For a small monthly fee, one can run a website with a design chosen from available templates. These websites may offer their users some add-ons such as a database, shopping cart, and picture gallery.

Today, these cloud-based services are being offered to enterprise-level organizations for a subscription price. Let's take an email service for example; instead of maintaining its own email system, a company can off-load its entire email operations to a cloud service provider. Running an enterprise email service is more than just bringing up a couple of email servers and then off it goes. Many details have to be thought through, from the design to the implementation, and let's not forget about the procurement.

The email administrators and the server administrators will need to work together to procure the servers. The size and the number of the servers will all depend on the number of users and their mailbox sizes. In addition, the potential growth of the system must be considered. Because email is such a critical mission to every organization, the email system must be designed with high availability and with high performance and throughput. Typically, that means multiple servers spread throughout multiple data centers. Then, the underlying infrastructure, such as the network and storage, has to be considered so that it can provide the availability the email system would need. After the system is implemented, then comes the support and the maintenance; someone has to maintain the system, and the software and operating system have to be patched and updated.

Cloud email service providers can assume all the roles and responsibilities mentioned earlier for an organization. They make use of virtualization technology to create a virtual email system for the size of your organization. Your email system can live anywhere among many data centers that are dispersed throughout a continent (or many continents) for big providers. They are responsible for maintaining your email system, from updating to applying patches. If the system needs more memory or is running out of disk space, the cloud service provider can perform those upgrades for you. All of these tasks are part of the service level agreement (**SLA**) that your organization has with the cloud service provider.

One important technical point must be mentioned. Email will not magically flow to the cloud without being directed that way. The DNS resource record called **MX** (Mail Exchange) points to the incoming email servers of the organization. This MX record must be changed to the cloud email servers' so that all email can be directed to the cloud servers. Manipulating DNS records is a technique often used to direct traffic to the cloud. An organization's website can be hosted in the cloud just by changing the DNS A record to the IP address of the cloud server or creating a DNS **CNAME** (Canonical Name) record pointing to the cloud server hostname.

Many organizations have responded to cloud computing in positive way. Many of their services have been migrated to the cloud, surprisingly with many of them being critical services such as web, email, and ERP (Enterprise Resource Planning). The cloud market is doing well and has captured many business's attention due to its many advantages. From an economic standpoint, cloud computing is the most cost-effective solution. It helps reduce capital costs, technology infrastructure costs, and personnel costs.

This has struck a chord with new businesses and small companies, as they do not have to commit excess financial resources for server hardware, software, storage, network equipment, and data centers. What's more, they don't have to hire many knowledgeable workers to manage and maintain the systems. From an operational standpoint, cloud computing helps improve efficiency in system management and maintenance, expand availability, create disaster recovery, and increase accessibility. This relieves the company's IT department from the duties of maintaining the systems and keeping them up to date; instead, they can use their time for other IT initiatives. With virtualization and dispersed data centers, the systems will be up and available to users who, as long as they have Internet access, are guaranteed to have access to them.

Cloud computing can be broken down to three major categories:

- Infrastructure as a Service (IaaS)
- Platform as a Service (PaaS)
- Software as a Service (SaaS)

Infrastructure as a Service (IaaS)

Infrastructure as a Service focuses on the facilities and infrastructure within the data center and the virtualization and abstraction layer that exists on top of the physical facilities and infrastructure. It allows for more effective sharing of the underlying physical resources. IaaS encompasses the computing power of servers, storage, network elements, power, and cooling. Instead of running servers in the company's data center, IaaS allows an organization to create virtualized servers in the cloud or to virtualize their servers and move their server systems and data center infrastructure to the cloud. This category of cloud computing is the fundamental and underlying layer of other cloud categories. Some examples of IaaS are Amazon Web Services (AWS), Microsoft Azure, and Google Compute Engine.

Platform as a Service (PaaS)

Platform as a Service focuses on application development on any desired platform utilizing cloud computing. It incorporates platform elements such as operating systems, databases, programming language, and middleware installed on top of the abstracted infrastructure. It allows developers to design, test, and implement their software on the same platform that their clients will use in a quick, simple, and cost-effective manner. This category of cloud computing service is popular among software developers for web applications and mobile applications as it allows them to frequently change or upgrade any platform elements and helps them collaborate on projects. Some examples of PaaS are Google App Engine, Heroku, and Salesforce1.

> **Platform as a Service (PaaS)**
> Focuses on application development on any desired platform utilizing cloud computing

Software as a Service (SaaS)

Software as a Service focuses on the application component and delivery. It provides the applications that run on top of the platform and the abstracted infrastructure, and the applications are delivered via the Internet. Most SaaS applications can be run directly from a web browser, but some may require plug-ins to be installed. Because SaaS eliminates the need to install and run applications on individual computers, it is easy for organizations to streamline their product delivery, maintenance, and support. This category of cloud computing is the most widely used. Email and collaboration tools are among the popular SaaS applications. Some examples of SaaS are Microsoft Office 365, Google Apps, Cisco WebEx, Citrix GoToMeeting.

> **Software as a Service SaaS**
> Focuses on the application component and delivery

Section 13-3 Review

This section has covered the following **Network+** Exam objectives.

> 1.11 Compare and contrast technologies that support cloud and virtualization

This section examined the concept of the cloud. It also examined the benefit of outsourcing services.

Test Your Knowledge

1. What is the cloud?

2. What is a cloud service?

SUMMARY

This chapter introduced the basic concepts of cloud computing and virtualization. It also introduced the concept of cloud services and setting up your own virtual environment.

- Define the "cloud" and "cloud services."
- Discuss the evolution of computing devices.
- Discuss the concept of "virtualization."
- Define the purpose of a Hypervisor and the two types.
- Understand the process of setting up virtualization on a Windows computer.
- Define "cloud computing."
- Understand the purpose of a service level agreement.
- Discuss the three major categories of cloud computing.

QUESTIONS AND PROBLEMS

Section 13-2

1. What is the core relative to a computer?

2. What is a cache relative to a computer?

3. Why is 64-bit architecture an improvement in computer processing? List three reasons.

4. What is virtualization?

5. What is the purpose of the Hypervisor?

6. What is a Type-1 Hypervisor?

7. What is Type-2 Hypervisor?

8. How has virtualization helped companies?

9. How has virtualization helped the personal computing world?

10. What limitation is there for the Mac OS environment and virtualization?

Section 13-3

11. What is cloud computing?

12. What does it mean to outsource services?

13. What is required to make email flow properly to the cloud?

14. What is an SLA?

15. With virtualization and dispersed data centers, the systems will be up and available to users as long as they have what?

    a. Server access

    b. Software access

    c. Internet access

    d. Mac OS installed

16. Define Infrastructure as a Service (IaaS). (Select one.)

    a. It focuses on the software external to the data center that exists on top of the software infrastructure.

    b. It focuses on the facilities and infrastructure within the data center and the virtualization and abstraction layer that exist on top of the physical facilities and infrastructure.

    c. It focuses on the hardware external to the data center that exists under of the software infrastructure.

    d. It focuses on the facilities external to the data center that exist on top of the software infrastructure.

17. Define Platform as a Service (PaaS).

    a. It focuses on the facilities and infrastructure within the data center and the virtualization and abstraction layer that exist on top of the physical facilities and infrastructure.

    b. It focuses on application development on any desired platform utilizing cloud computing.

    c. It focuses on the application component and delivery of the desired platform.

    d. It focuses on the software external to the data center that exists on top of the software platform.

18. Define Software as a Service (SaaS).

    a. It focuses on the application component and delivery.

    b. It focuses on the software external to the data center that exists on top of the software infrastructure.

    c. It focuses on the virtual network component and delivery.

    d. It focuses on the application development and storage.

CERTIFICATION QUESTIONS

19. The network technician is experiencing an error when trying to install Mac OS X in the virtual environment. What did the network technician forget?

    a. The incorrect name of the VM was specified; it should be Apple 2.

    a. An incorrect virtual switch was configured.

    a. You can't use Mac OS X in a virtual environment.

    a. You can't virtualize Mac OS X without a Hyper-V key.

20. A virtual machine was created with 8GB of RAM and 100GB of hard drive space. Which of the following operating systems can maximize all its hardware abstraction potentials?

    a. Linux Red Hat 7 64-bit

    a. Windows 10 64-bit

    a. Windows 7 32-bit

    a. Windows XP

21. A physical host machine has four quad-core CPUs, 16GB of RAM, 1TB of hard drive space, and two 1Gbps NICs. If we need to create four Windows 2008 servers, what will be the first bottleneck we should upgrade?

    a. CPU

    a. RAM

    a. Hard drive

    a. NIC

22. Which of the following are Type-1 Hypervisors?

    a. VMware ESXi

    a. VMware Workstation

    a. Parallels

    a. VirtualBox

    a. Hyper-V

23. In what situations would one likely run a Type-2 Hypervisor?

    a. When running on a Windows 2008 server

    a. When running on Mac hardware

    a. When running on a server with 48 CPUs, 768 GB of RAM, and 24TB of storage space

    a. When running on a laptop

14

CHAPTER

CODES AND STANDARDS

Chapter Outline

Objectives

- Define relevant safety standards and codes related to the IT business
- Define the requirement for an organization to have an emergency action plan
- Provide an overview of fire extinguishing systems used to protect critical data-processing equipment

- Examine regulations that can pertain to an IT organization
- Define the business and policies an organization might have to comply with or utilize in the daily management of the data center

Key Terms

OSH Act	HVAC	PCI DSS
OSHA	biometric systems	MSDS
NFPA	FERPA	MOU
CFR	FISMA	SLA
EAP	GLBA	MSA
FPP	HIPAA	SOW

14-1 INTRODUCTION

Table 14-1 lists and identifies, by chapter section, where each of the CompTIA Network+ objectives is presented in this chapter. At the end of each chapter section is a review with comments of the Network+ objectives presented in that section. These comments are provided to help reinforce the reader's understanding of a particular Network+ objective. The chapter review also includes "Test Your Knowledge" questions to aid in the understanding of key concepts before the reader advances to the next section of the chapter. The end of the chapter includes a complete set of questions plus sample certification-type questions.

TABLE 14-1   Chapter 14 CompTIA Network+ Objectives

Domain/Objective Number	Domain/Objective Description	Section Where Objective Is Covered
2.0	***Network Operations***	
2.1	Given a scenario, use the appropriate monitoring tools	14-2, 14-3
2.3	Given a scenario, use the appropriate resources to support configuration management	14-3
3.4	Compare and contrast physical security controls	14-2
5.5	Given a scenario, implement the appropriate policies or procedures	14-4
5.6	Summarize safety practices	14-2
5.8	Explain the basics of change management procedures	14-4

14-2 SAFETY STANDARDS AND CODES

Safety should always be the number-one priority in every operation and for every workplace, even though it does not appear that way in many workplaces. Therefore, the United State government passed the Occupational Safety and Health Act (**OSH Act**) in 1970 and created the Occupational Safety and Health Administration (**OSHA**) to oversee and enforce the safety standards at the workplace. OSHA's mission is to ensure safe and healthful workplaces by setting and enforcing standards, and by providing training, outreach, education, and assistance. Every employer must comply with all applicable OSHA standards.

> **OSH Act**
> Occupational Safety and Health Act
>
> **OSHA**
> Occupational Safety and Health Administration

The National Fire Protection Association (**NFPA**) is an organization that works closely with OSHA to create standards and codes to help create safe environments and to prevent accidents. OSHA has requested NFPA to develop many standards that would assist employers and employees in complying with the safety regulations. Compliance with OSHA codes and regulations is mandatory. However, compliance with NFPA is not mandatory, but it is the way for employers to demonstrate and ensure compliance with OSHA requirements. To put it simply, OSHA tells us what to do and NFPA tells us how to do it. Therefore, many OSHA standards have references to NFPA codes.

> **NFPA**
> National Fire Protection Association

Under the OSH Act, OSHA regulations are in Code of Federal Regulations (**CFR**) title 29 part 1910, which can be represented as 29 CFR 1910. Some of the applicable and well-known OSHA's safety standards are detailed in the following sections.

> **CFR**
> Code of Federal Regulations

Design and Construction Requirements for Exit Routes (29 CFR 1910.36)

An exit route is a continuous and unobstructed path of travel from any location within a workplace to a place of safety. This standard specifies the basic location requirements for the proper design and construction of exit routes.

- Each exit route must be a permanent part of the workplace.

- Each exit must be separated from other parts of the workplace, and the separation materials must be fire resistant.

- An opening into an exit must be protected by a self-closing fire door that remains closed and must be limited to only allow exit access.

- The number of exit routes must be adequate for all employees to be able to evacuate safely during an emergency.

- Each exit discharge must lead directly outside or to a street, walkway, refuge area, public way, or an open space, which must be large enough to accommodate the building occupants.

- Each exit door must be unlocked from the inside so employees can open the exit door at all times.

- A side-hinged exit door must be used, so that the door can swing out in the direction of exit travel.

- An exit route must be at least 7 feet, 6 inches high and at least 28 inches wide at all points.

- An outdoor exit route is permitted with the same height and width requirement as the indoor exit route.

Maintenance, Safeguards, and Operational Features for Exit Routes (29 CFR 1910.37)

This standard specifies requirements for employers to properly maintain their exit routes in order to prepare the workplace for a successful emergency evacuation and minimize further danger to employees.

- Each exit route must be free of explosive or highly flammable furnishings and other decorations.
- Exit routes must be arranged so employees will not have to travel toward a high-hazard area.
- Each exit route must not be obstructed by any materials or equipment. It must not go through locked doors or dead-end corridors.
- Safeguards designed to protect employee, such as sprinkler systems, alarm systems, exit lighting, and fire doors, must be working properly.
- There must be adequate lighting for each exit route.
- Each exit must be clearly visible and marked by a sign reading "Exit."
- Each exit door must be free of decorations or signs that obscure the visibility of the exit door.
- If the direction to the exit is not apparent, signs must be posted to show the direction to the exit.
- Each exit sign must be illuminated and the word "Exit" must be in plainly legible letters.
- Fire-retardant paints or solutions must be maintained often enough to renew their properties.
- During construction, repairs, or alterations, exit routes must be maintained and available at all times.
- Employers must install and maintain an operable alarm system to alert employees of fire and other emergencies.

Emergency Action Plans (29 CFR 1910.38)

EAP
Emergency action plan

An employer must have an emergency action plan (**EAP**). An emergency action plan facilitates and organizes employer and employee actions during workplace emergencies. If there are more than 10 employees, the plan must be in writing and it must be kept in the workplace and available for employee review. An emergency action plan must include the following, at a minimum:

- Procedures for reporting fires and other emergencies
- Procedures for emergency evacuation, including the type of evacuation and exit route assignments
- Procedures for employees who stay behind to continue critical plant operations
- Procedures to account for all employees after evacuation
- Procedures for employees performing rescue or medical duties
- Names or job titles of the persons who can be contacted for further information or explanation of duties under the plan

In addition, employers should have an alarm system to alert employees. Employers must designate and train enough people to assist in the safe and orderly emergency evacuation of employees. Employers must review the emergency action plan with each employee when the plan is initially developed, or when an employee is initially hired to the job, or when actions or responsibilities under the plan change, or when the plan changes.

Fire Prevention Plans (29 CFR 1910.39)

Similar to having an emergency action plan, an employer is required to have a fire prevention plan (FPP). As a matter of fact, both the emergency action plan and fire prevention plan typically come hand in hand. Many organizations combine the two plans into one document. The written fire prevention plan must be available to the employees and kept at the workplace. For employers with 10 or fewer employees, the plan may be communicated orally. The purpose of the fire prevention plan is to prevent a fire from occurring or spreading in a workplace. A fire prevention plan must include the following, at a minimum:

> **FPP**
> Fire prevention plan

- A list of all major fire hazards, proper handling and storage procedures for hazardous materials, potential ignition sources and their control, and the type of fire protection equipment necessary to control each major hazard

- Procedures to control accumulations of flammable and combustible waste materials

- Procedures for regular maintenance of safeguards installed and heat-producing equipment to prevent the accidental ignition of combustible materials

- Name or job title of employees responsible for maintaining equipment to prevent or control sources of ignition or fires

- Name or job title of employees responsible for the control of fuel source hazards

In addition, employers must inform employees of any fire hazards they may be exposed to and must review with each employee the fire prevention plan necessary for self-protection.

Portable Fire Extinguishers (29 CFR 1910.157)

When used properly, fire extinguishers can save lives and property by putting out small fires or controlling a fire until additional help arrives. This standard specifies the placement, use, maintenance, and testing of portable fire extinguishers provided for the use of employees. Employers may exempt themselves from most of the portable fire extinguisher requirements if they develop a written emergency action plan that is complete and in compliance with 29 CFR 1910.38.

- Employers must mount, locate, and identify portable fire extinguishers for easy employee access.

- Portable fire extinguishers cannot have carbon tetrachloride or chlorobromomethane extinguishing agents.

- Employers must remove portable fire extinguishers that use soldered or riveted shell self-generating soda acid, self-generating foam, and gas cartridge water from service.

- Employers must provide, select, and distribute portable extinguishers based on the class of anticipated workplace fires because fire extinguishers are classified by their ability to handle specific classes and sizes of fires.

- Employers are responsible for the inspection, maintenance, and testing of all portable fire extinguishers in the workplace.

- Employers must ensure that portable fire extinguishers are fully charged, operable, and kept in their designated place at all times.

- Employers must provide equivalent protection when extinguishers are removed for maintenance or recharging.

- Portable fire extinguishers must be subjected to annual maintenance checks. The maintenance date must be recorded, and the record must be retained for one year after the last entry or for the extinguisher's shell life.

- Employers must have trained persons with suitable testing equipment and facilities conduct hydrostatic testing on portable fire extinguishers.

- Employers must remove portable fire extinguishers that fail hydrostatic pressure testing.

In addition to these requirements, employers must provide training upon initial assignment and at least annually for employees who use fire extinguishers. The training program must familiarize employees with the general principles of fire extinguisher use, fire hazards, and the use of appropriate equipment.

Fixed Extinguishing Systems (29 CFR 1910.160)

Fixed fire extinguishing/suppression systems are commonly used to protect areas containing valuable or critical equipment such as data-processing rooms, telecommunication switches, and process control rooms. Their main function is to quickly extinguish a developing fire before extensive damage occurs by filling the protected area with a gas or chemical extinguishing agent. The purpose of this standard is to ensure the safety of employees and prevent possible injury, death, or adverse health consequences caused by the extinguishing agent.

- If the system becomes inoperable, employers must notify employees and take the necessary temporary precautions to ensure their safety until the system is restored to operating order. Any defects or impairments must be properly corrected by trained personnel.

- A distinctive alarm or signaling system must be capable of being perceived above ambient noise or light levels when the extinguishing system is discharging.

- Effective safeguards must be provided to warn employees against entry into discharge areas where the atmosphere remains hazardous to employee safety or health.

- Hazard warning or caution signs must be posted at the entrance to, and inside of, areas protected by fixed extinguishing systems that use agents in concentrations known to be hazardous to employee safety and health.

- Fixed extinguishing systems must be inspected annually by a knowledgeable person to ensure that the system is maintained in good operating condition.

- The weight and pressure of refillable containers must be checked at least semi-annually.

- Factory-charged nonrefillable containers, which have no means of pressure indication, must be weighed at least semi-annually. If a container shows a loss in net weight or more than 5 percent, it must be replaced.

- Inspection and maintenance dates must be recorded, and the record of the last semi-annual check must be maintained until the container is checked again or for the life of the container, whichever is less.

- Employers must ensure the designated employees who inspect, maintain, operate, or repair fixed extinguishing systems are regularly trained, and their training must be reviewed annually.

- Chlorobromomethane or carbon tetrachloride may not be used as an extinguishing agent where employees may be exposed.

- Fixed extinguishing systems installed in the presence of corrosive atmospheres must be constructed of noncorrosive material or otherwise protected against corrosion.

- Automatic detection equipment must be approved, installed, and maintained in accordance with the fire detection system.

- All systems designed for and installed in areas with climatic extremes must operate effectively at the expected extreme temperatures.

- At least one manual station must be provided for discharge activation of each fixed extinguishing system.

- Manual operating devices must be identified as to the hazard against which they will provide protection.

- Employers must provide and ensure the use of the personal protective equipment needed for immediate rescue of employees trapped in hazardous atmospheres created by an agent discharge.

Fire Detection Systems (29 CFR 1910.164)

Automatic fire detection systems, when combined with other elements of an emergency response and evacuation plan, can significantly reduce property damage, personal injuries, and loss of life from fire in the workplace. Automatic fire detection systems do this by using electronic sensors to detect the smoke, heat, or flames from a fire and providing an early warning. Their main function is to quickly identify a developing fire and alert building occupants and emergency response personnel before extensive damage occurs.

- Employers must restore all fire detection systems and components to normal operating condition as promptly as possible after each test or alarm.

- Employers must maintain all systems in an operable condition.

- Employers are responsible for servicing, testing, and adjusting fire detectors and fire detection systems as often as needed to maintain proper reliability and operating condition. The work must be performed by a trained person.

- Fire detectors must be cleaned at regular periodic intervals.

- Employers must ensure that fire detection equipment be protected from mechanical or physical impact, weather, and corrosion.

- Employers must ensure that fire detectors are supported independently of their attachment to wires or tubing.

- Fire detection systems installed for the purpose of actuating fire extinguishment or suppression systems must operate in time to control or extinguish a fire.

- Fire detection systems installed for the purpose of employee alarm or evacuation systems must provide a warning in time for emergency action and safe escape of employees.

- Employers cannot delay alarms or devices initiated by fire detector actuation for more than 30 seconds unless it is necessary for the immediate safety of employees, which then must be addressed in the emergency action plan.

- Employers must ensure that the number, spacing, and location of fire detectors is based upon design data obtained from field experience, or tests, engineering surveys, the manufacturer's recommendations, or a recognized testing laboratory listing.

Employee Alarm Systems (29 CFR 1910.165)

The purpose of the employee alarm systems standard is to reduce the severity of workplace accidents and injuries by ensuring that alarm systems operate properly and procedures are in place to alert employees to workplace emergencies.

- An employee alarm must be perceived above ambient noise or light levels by all employees. It must be distinctive and recognizable as a signal to evacuate the work area.

- Employers must explain to each employee the preferred means of reporting emergencies. If telephones serve as a means of reporting emergencies, emergency telephone numbers must be posted near telephones, or employee notice boards, and other conspicuous locations.

- Employers must establish procedures for sounding emergency alarms in the workplace. For employers with 10 or fewer employees, direct voice communication is an acceptable procedure.

- All devices, components, combinations of devices, or systems constructed and installed must be approved by OSHA.

- All employee alarm systems must be restored to normal operating condition as promptly as possible after each test or alarm.

- Employers must ensure that all employee alarm systems are maintained in operating condition.

- Employers must test the reliability and adequacy of both supervised and unsupervised employee alarm systems. Supervised alarm systems can monitor the condition of their detectors and circuitry, whereas non-supervised alarm systems cannot. Unsupervised employee alarm systems must be tested every two months. Supervised employee alarm systems installed after January 1, 1981, must be tested at least annually and working properly in supervised mode.

- Employers must maintain or replace power supplies to the systems as often as is necessary to ensure a fully operational condition.

- Employers must ensure that employee alarms are serviced, maintained, and tested by properly trained persons.

- Employers must ensure that manually operated actuation devices for use in conjunction with employee alarms are unobstructed and readily accessible.

Hazard Communication (29 CFR 1910.1200)

The purpose of this standard is to ensure that the hazards of all chemicals are classified and the information concerning the classified hazards is communicated to employers and employees. It requires that the chemical manufacturer, distributor, or importer provide safety data sheets (SDS), formerly known as material safety data sheets (MSDS), for each hazardous chemical they produce or import. Employers must have an SDS in the workplace for each hazardous chemical they use. The SDS includes information such as product identifier or manufacturer, physical and chemical properties, chemical hazards, chemical ingredients and composition, first-aid measures, fire-fighting measures, accidental release measures, handling and storage, personal protection, chemical stability and hazardous reactions, and toxicological information.

> **SDS**
> Safety data sheets
>
> **MSDS**
> Material safety data sheets

The network technician needs to be aware of this particularly because network closets are sometimes used incorrectly to temporarily store chemicals. The safety data sheets provide the workers and emergency personnel with procedures for handling the chemicals in a safe manner.

HVAC Systems

Another building issue for networks is the HVAC (heating, ventilation, and air conditioning) system. HVAC systems are critical for computing and data centers. The system must be properly planned and maintained to ensure that the operating environment is properly maintained. The physical hardware used in a computer center will have recommendations for temperature and humidity. Additionally, the maintenance personnel for HVAC systems will have access to protected areas, and these people must have proper clearance and safeguards must be in place to allow non-IT staff to have access to these areas.

> **HVAC**
> Heating, ventilation, and air conditioning

Door Access

In computer networks and enterprise data centers, door access should be controlled through the use of proximity readers or key fobs. Other options for access control include biometrics, such as hand scanners and retinal scanners. Biometric systems measure and analyze specific characteristics of the human body for the purpose of authentication. This includes DNA, fingerprints, voice and facial patterns, eye retinas, and hand measurements.

> **Biometric Systems**
> Measure and analyze specific characteristics of the human body for the purpose of authentication

Door access control could also be managed using keypads and cipher locks. This ensures that only authorized personnel will have entry access. In some cases, a security guard could be in position to help control physical access to these areas. Video monitoring in computer spaces is a necessity to prevent theft and to provide a video record of personnel who access the systems. It is important to remember that internal threats are always a major concern.

Section 14-2 Review

This section has covered the following **Network+** Exam objectives:

> 2.1 Given a scenario, use the appropriate monitoring tools

This section provided an overview of the HVAC system and concern for the operating environment.

> 3.4 Compare and contrast physical security controls

This section provided an overview of the very important process of controlling and monitoring access to your data center.

> 5.6 Summarize safety practices

This section provided an overview of emergency procedures and their importance in data centers.

Test Your Knowledge

1. What scenario is the only exception to the rule of having a written emergency action plan (EAP)?

2. True or False? According to OSHA, portable fire extinguishers can be operated by anyone.

14-3 INDUSTRY REGULATORY COMPLIANCE

There are numerous rules and regulations nationally as well as internationally. Regulations that pertain to one organization may not pertain to another. An organization must know what regulations it must comply with in order to operate. Organizations from the same industry will most likely have to adhere to the same regulations. Industry regulatory compliance is an adherence to laws, regulations, guidelines, and specifications relevant to the industry's business. The following are some prevalent regulatory compliance laws and regulations from different industries.

FERPA

FERPA stands for Family Educational Rights and Privacy Act, which is a federal law that requires all educational institutions to protect the privacy of student education records. FERPA imposes confidentiality requirements around student educational records, prohibiting institutions from disclosing such information such as grades or financial aid without the student's written permission. The law applies equally to both electronic and hardcopy records.

Education records, as defined by FERPA, are "records that are directly related to a student and that are maintained by an educational agency or institution or a party acting for or on behalf of the agency or institution. These records include but are not limited to grades, transcripts, class lists, student course schedules, health records (at the K–12 level), student financial information (at the postsecondary level), and student discipline files. The information may be recorded in any way, including, but not limited to, handwriting, print, computer media, videotape, audiotape, film, microfilm, microfiche, and e-mail."

> **FERPA**
> Family Educational Rights and Privacy Act, a federal law that requires all educational institutions to protect the privacy of student education records

FISMA

FISMA stands for Federal Information Security Management Act, which is a federal law that was developed to protect government information, operations, and assets against security threats. Every agency is responsible for ensuring information security in the federal government and is subject to FISMA audit. The National Institute of Standards and Technology (NIST) has developed Federal Information Processing Standards (FIPS) that will help agencies to become FISMA compliant. FIPS 199: Information Systems Security Categorization of Federal Information and Information Systems and FIPS 200: Minimum Information Security Requirements are approved standards by the Secretary of Commerce and required standards by FISMA.

> **FISMA**
> Federal Information Security Management Act, a federal law that was developed to protect government information

GLBA

GLBA stands for Gramm-Leach-Bliley Act, which is a federal law that requires all financial institutions to protect customer financial information data, to safeguard the financial information from security threats, and to deny any unwarranted access to financial data. Financial institutions are defined to be institutions that engage in financial institution activities, which include services such as loans, financial or investment advice, and insurance. By this definition of that term under the GLBA regulations has brought a wide range of entities, including colleges and universities, under the jurisdiction of the GLBA.

> **GLBA**
> Gramm-Leach-Bliley Act, a federal law that requires all financial institutions to protect customer financial information data

HIPAA

HIPAA stands for Health Insurance Portability and Accountability Act, which is a federal law that requires all health-related agencies to protect the personal identifiable information (PII) of patients. This law specifies the administrative processes, IT standards, and policies and procedures to protect patient information gathered in the healthcare process as well as mandates the standardization of electronic transactions, code sets, and identifiers.

> **HIPAA**
> Health Insurance Portability and Accountability Act, a federal law that requires all health-related agencies to protect the personal identifiable information (PII) of patients

PCI DSS

PCI DSS, which stands for Payment Card Industry Data Security Standard, is not a federal law, but it is a standard set by the Payment Card Industry (Visa, MasterCard, Discover, and American Express) that holds banks and merchants accountable for any credit card breach. The compliance requires all merchants to process, store, and transmit credit card information in a secure environment. IT specifies the administrative processes, IT standards, policies, and procedures to protect the privacy and confidentiality of the credit card transaction.

In order for an organization to conform to these stringent and complex regulations, it takes a great deal of collaboration from many units within the organization. Information technology plays a very important role in fulfilling these mandates because the data that these regulations are trying to protect is stored in some database or server, processed by some software application, and transmitted on some network. Therefore, safeguarding the data requires IT involvement.

These regulations have a common theme of protecting the confidentiality, the integrity, and the availability of the information that impacts consumers. In accordance with NIST's Framework for Improving Critical Infrastructure Cybersecurity, an IT organization can use this guidance to help facilitate the compliance goal. The following are components of this framework:

- The data, personnel, devices, systems, and facilities that enable the organization to achieve business purposes are identified and managed consistent with their relative importance to business objectives and the organization's risk strategy.

- The organization's mission, objectives, stakeholders, and activities are understood and prioritized; this information is used to inform cybersecurity roles, responsibilities, and risk management decisions.

- The policies, procedures, and processes to manage and monitor the organization's regulatory, legal, risk, environmental, and operational requirements are understood and inform the management of cybersecurity risk.

- The organization understands the cybersecurity risk to organizational operations (including mission, functions, image, or reputation), organizational assets, and individuals.

- The organization's priorities, constraints, risk tolerances, and assumptions are established and used to support operational risk decisions.

- Access to assets and associated facilities is limited to authorized users, processes, or devices, and to authorized activities and transactions.

- The organization's personnel and partners are provided cybersecurity awareness education and are adequately trained to perform their information security-related duties and responsibilities consistent with related policies, procedures, and agreements.

- Information and records (data) are managed consistent with the organization's risk strategy to protect the confidentiality, integrity, and availability of information.

- Security policies (that address purpose, scope, roles, responsibilities, management commitment, and coordination among organizational entities), processes, and procedures are maintained and used to manage the protection of information systems and assets.

- Maintenance and repairs of industrial control and information system components are performed consistent with policies and procedures.

- Technical security solutions are managed to ensure the security and resilience of systems and assets, consistent with related policies, procedures, and agreements.

- Anomalous activity is detected in a timely manner, and the potential impact of events is understood.

- The information system and assets are monitored at discrete intervals to identify cybersecurity events and verify the effectiveness of protective measures.

- Detection processes and procedures are maintained and tested to ensure timely and adequate awareness of anomalous events.

- Response processes and procedures are executed and maintained, to ensure timely response to detected cybersecurity events.

- Response activities are coordinated with internal and external stakeholders, as appropriate, to include external support from law enforcement agencies.

- Analysis is conducted to ensure adequate response and support recovery activities.

- Activities are performed to prevent expansion of an event, mitigate its effects, and eradicate the incident.

- Organizational response activities are improved by incorporating lessons learned from current and previous detection/response activities.

- Recovery processes and procedures are executed and maintained to ensure timely restoration of systems or assets affected by cybersecurity events.

- Recovery planning and processes are improved by incorporating lessons learned into future activities.

- Restoration activities are coordinated with internal and external parties, such as coordinating centers, Internet service providers, owners of attacking systems, victims, other CSIRTs (Computer Security Incidence Response Team), and vendors.

Section 14-3 Review

This section has covered the following **Network+** Exam objectives:

> 2.1 Given a scenario, use the appropriate monitoring tools

This section provided a discussion on the policies, procedures, and processes to manage and monitor the organization's regulatory, legal, risk, environmental, and operational requirements. This was presented in terms of a cybersecurity risk.

> 2.3 Given a scenario, use appropriate resources to support configuration management

This section provided an overview of internal operation procedures/policies/ standards.

1. Why is FERPA and HIPAA important to the IT staff?

2. Name a compliance standard that is not a federal regulation?

3. You are working for a loan company. Your loan officers often dispose of the client paperwork by throwing them away in a trash can. What is the compliance regulation your company may be violating?

14-4   BUSINESS POLICIES AND PROCEDURES

Regulations and compliance are mandatory rules that are set by government or authorized entities. Organizations will have to certify that they have complied with all the rules as well as have a way to show that their compliance can be validated through a process such as an audit. This helps set many guidelines and practical standards for their day-to-day operations. There are also rules that can be set between entities without being regulated by government. Similar to regulations and compliance, these rules define how business should be done, what services can be exchanged, what the service expectations are, what the rules of engagement are, and so on. These rules, once agreed upon by all parties, are legal in the court of law. It can hold a party accountable and responsible for their actions. In the IT world, two or more parties can enter into a formal agreement that articulates the terms and conditions of a service called a service agreement. The agreement specifies many criteria, which include but are not limited to the nature, description, and scope of the service as well as how the service will be governed, implemented, operated, tested, reported, and financed. Many types of service agreements are used in business. The following are the more prevalent service agreements used as standard business documents in the IT world.

Memorandum of Understanding

> **MOU**
> Memorandum of understanding

Memorandum of understanding, or **MOU**, is a formal agreement between two or more parties to establish official service partnerships. It outlines the terms and details of each party's requirements and responsibilities. This document is sometimes called a letter of intent (LOI) because it can be followed with a legal binding contract.

MOUs are much less formal than contracts, but are far more formal than a gentlemen's handshake. Many IT organizations use MOUs to create guidelines with one another as they contribute their efforts and resources toward important projects or for sharing or exchanging of IT services without having to enter into a detailed and complex process of contracts.

Service Level Agreement

A service level agreement, or **SLA**, is a formal agreement typically from a service provider to its client or end user. This agreement defines the level of service expected from the service provider. Unlike MOUs, SLAs do not contain details regarding how a service will be provided or delivered, nor do they provide operational guidelines. SLAs simply define what service the end user should expect to receive as well as the levels of service the service provider will guarantee. In case of failure to provide the guaranteed level of service, SLAs define the responsibilities of the service provider to restore the guaranteed level of service.

> **SLA**
> Service level agreement

Internet service is a prime example of service with an SLA. SLAs for Internet service are varied depending on many factors, such as Internet service provider (ISP), type of Internet technology, class of Internet service, and so on. For example, the SLA for business Internet service will be far more stringent and detailed than the SLA for residential Internet service. Most SLAs for business Internet service will include the guaranteed speed, the guaranteed Internet service availability or uptime, the expected response time for repair or service restoration, and the service provider's penalty for not meeting the guaranteed service level.

Many organizations use SLAs as a way to benchmark their performance. SLAs are very common and popular among cloud service providers. They are used to assure their customers of the quality of the service they will receive.

Master Service Agreement

A master service agreement (**MSA**) is an overarching document that lays the framework for multiple service level agreements, hence the term *master*. An MSA is typically used when entering into a long negotiation of services, where multiple contracts or agreements might be needed. It is set up as the initial agreement to include most but not all the terms and conditions between two or more parties. These terms, such as service definitions, payment terms, warranties, limitations on liability, and termination, are likely not to change. Its purpose is to speed up and simplify the process for future subsequent agreements. Future subsequent agreements only need to contain the differences from the MSA, thus reducing the time and involvement from all parties.

> **MSA**
> Master service agreement

Statement of Work

Statement of work (**SOW**) is a document often used in conjunction with an MSA. Whereas an MSA defines general terms of service, an SOW has all the specifics of the service. SOWs define in detail the deliverables, schedules, and timelines, roles and responsibilities, and price agreed by all parties. Under one MSA, there may be multiple SOWs.

> **SOW**
> Statement of work

SOWs are common in the information technology field when an organization has to engage third-party companies to implement or deploy new IT services. SOWs are used to define what the service provider is committing to deliver as well as to outline the steps and procedures of work to be done.

Acceptable Use Policy

In the workplace, many policies are established to give guidelines to employees. A simple and short policy, such as a dress code policy, is very common in business places. There could be a long and complex policy for the whole organization, such as an Employee Policy Manual or Employee Handbook. Policies should be reviewed often to keep the contents up to date, especially when there have been any recent issues in a relevant section of the policy. Another common policy found in all organizations with IT services is an acceptable use policy, or AUP. This policy outlines the acceptable use of computer equipment, network, Internet, and other IT-related services. The policy defines rules and constraints that users must accept before accessing IT services. By accepting this policy, users are held accountable to their actions while using the organization's IT services. Typically, AUPs contain a segment referencing the organization's policies and standards as well as adhering to local and federal laws.

Section 14-4 Review

This section has covered the following **Network+** Exam objectives:

5.5 Given a scenario, implement the appropriate policies or procedures

This section provided an overview of standard business documents.

5.8 Explain the basics of change management procedures

Many types of service agreements are used in business. This section provided an overview of the more prevalent service agreements used as standard business documents in the IT world.

Test Your Knowledge

1. Your company has suffered an Internet outage for two straight days and you want to take a legal action against the Internet service provider. What is the document you must review before pursuing with legal action?

2. List five types of service agreements.

SUMMARY

The following is a summary of the key topics presented in this chapter:

- An introduction to safety standards and codes
- The role of OSHA
- A look at the various CFRs—code of federal regulations
- An overview of fire protection systems and exit routes
- An overview of HVAC systems
- A look at door access control
- A discussion of business policies and procedures and the more prevalent service agreements used as standard business documents in the IT world

QUESTIONS AND PROBLEMS

Section 14-2

1. What is OSHA's mission?

2. Every employer must comply with all applicable OSHA standards. True or False?

3. What is the purpose of NFPA?

4. Compliance with NFPA is mandatory. True or False?

5. Provide a definition of an exit route as defined by 29CFR1910.36?

6. What is the purpose of 29CFR1910.37?

7. What is the purpose of an emergency action plan?

8. The organization's written FPP must be available to the employees and kept at the workplace. True or False?

9. What is FERPA?

10. How does FERPA define education records?

11. What is FISMA?

12. What is GLBA?

13. What is HIPAA?

14. What is the purpose of PCI DSS?

15. How is the IT part of an organization involved with the regulations defined by FERPA, FISMA, GLBA, HIPAA, and PCI DSS?

16. Which of the following are components of the NIST's Framework for Improving Critical Infrastructure Cybersecurity? (Select all that apply.)

    a. The organization understands the cybersecurity risk to organizational operations (including mission, functions, image, or reputation), organizational assets, and individuals.

    b. Information and records (data) are managed consistent with the organization's risk strategy to protect the confidentiality, integrity, and availability of information.

    c. Security policies (that address purpose, scope, roles, responsibilities, management commitment, and coordination among organizational entities), processes, and procedures are maintained and used to manage protection of information systems and assets.

    d. The information system and assets are monitored at discrete intervals to identify cybersecurity events and verify the effectiveness of protective measures.

    e. Recovery processes and procedures are executed and maintained to ensure timely restoration of systems or assets affected by cybersecurity events.

17. Which of the following is (are) not part of the NIST Framework for Improving Critical Infrastructure Cybersecurity?

    a. Technical security solutions are managed to ensure the security and resilience of systems and assets, consistent with related policies, procedures, and agreements.

    b. Anomalous activity is detected within a one-month period and the potential impact of events is understood.

    c. Detection processes and procedures are maintained and tested to ensure timely and adequate awareness of anomalous events.

    d. Response processes and procedures are executed and maintained, to ensure timely response to detected cybersecurity events.

    e. Activities are performed to prevent expansion of an event, mitigate its effects, and eradicate the incident.

Section 14-4

18. What is the purpose of a service agreement relative to the IT world?

19. What is an MOU and what is its purpose?

20. Why do organizations use MOUs?

21. What is a service level agreement?

22. How does the SLA differ from the MOU?

23. Which of the following is a prime example of service with an SLA related to IT work?

    a. Rental space

    b. Food service

    c. Internet service

    d. All of the above

24. This type of agreement is used when entering into a long negotiation of services when multiple contracts or agreements might be needed.

    a. Service level agreement

    b. MSDS sheets

    c. Statement of work

    d. Master service agreement

25. This is used to define deliverables, schedules and time lines, and roles and responsibilities.

    a. Statement of work

    b. Memorandum of understanding

    c. Business plan

    d. PCI DSS

26. There can be multiple SOWs under one MSA. True or False?

CERTIFICATION QUESTIONS

27. Which of these documents should be reviewed in preparation for the OSHA inspection?

    a. MSDS

    b. MOU

    c. SLA

    d. EAP

28. Related to IT, the acceptable use policy outlines which of the following?

    a. Network

    b. Break time

    c. Annual leave

    d. Internet

    e. Use of computer equipment

29. The network technician is setting up access for the HVAC to do maintenance in the server room. What safeguards need to be in place? (Select all that apply.)

    a. Guard on duty.

    b. Make sure all servers are fully password protected.

    c. Make sure all monitors are turned off.

    d. Make sure the water lines are turned off.

30. Door access to an organization's server room is being scheduled. Which of the following are best practices for door access control? (Select all that apply.)

    a. Require a proximity reader.

    b. Require multiple keys.

    c. Use biometrics.

    d. Require key fobs.

    e. All of the above.

31. This is a formal agreement between two or more parties to establish official service partnerships.

32. Which of the following is a critical component in avoiding accidents by identifying potential hazards?

    a. Fire extinguisher

    b. Exit route

    c. SDS

    d. SLA

    e. None of the above

33. What policy informs users of proper system usage?

A

APPENDIX

NETWORK + EXAM SUPPLEMENT

1.0 NETWORK ARCHITECTURE

1.1 Explain the functions and applications of various network devices

HIDS—Host-based intrusion detection system. This is an intrusion detection system that monitors the computer system for changes such as system file modifications, changes to the registry, file changes, and system logs. HIDS software packages are configured to prevent malicious activity on the host system, and if an unauthorized change or activity is detected, an alert is issued. Based on policy settings, the central server could be notified or the activity could be blocked.

IDS/IPS—Intrusion detection system/intrusion prevention system. Intrusion detection systems are designed to monitor both inbound and outbound data traffic and report any suspicious activity that could indicate an attack. The IDS system identifies misuse or potential attacks by matching the data packets against known signatures that have been classified as bad. IDS solutions are available in terms of shareware and open source programs, to more expensive vendor software solutions. In some cases, an IDS solution might be in the form of both a software package and a hardware appliance installed at various places within your network.

An intrusion prevention system (IPS) monitors and analyzes the network traffic. In real time, it identifies misuse and any anomaly on the network. The IPS detects a misuse intrusion by matching the network packets with its IPS signatures for known attacks or activities classified as bad. The network anomaly can be detected by building up a profile of the system being monitored and detecting significant deviations from this profile. The IPS has the capability to stop or prevent malicious attacks that it detects by interacting with the firewall.

Content filter (also known as information filtering)—Many organizations have strict policies on how their users can use the network. Web traffic is usually one of the first things to be monitored and filtered, and a content filter appliance is designed to do just that. In the K-12 school environment, web filtering is critical. K-12 school districts are required by law to implement filtering to block adult, illegal, or offensive content from minors. The law is known as the Children's Internet Protection Act (CIPA). A content filter appliance has a database containing inappropriate websites. A web filter appliance monitors the web traffic both via HTTP and HTTPS and matches it against the database. If an inappropriate website is detected, either it is discarded or the user is redirected to a security web page for further action. The web filter appliance gets its database updated continually. Also, there is always an option for a network administrator to manually mark a website as inappropriate.

Packet shaper—This is a device that sits between the campus network and the outside network. The device is set up so that all data traffic, incoming and outgoing, passes through it. The packet shaper box is configured with a set of "rules" used to prioritize data traffic. This is important when it comes to better managing your network's data bandwidth. The *packet shaper* can be used to set rules to limit download traffic off the Internet. It can also be used to make sure that applications such as VoIP are given a higher priority so that the operation and quality of service are not affected.

VPN concentrator—The purpose of the VPN concentrator is to manage a secure VPN connection. The VPN concentrator is essentially an advanced router enabled to handle multiple connections (tunnels) into a network. A tunnel is created by an encapsulation technique, which encapsulates the data inside a known protocol (IP) agreed upon by the two endpoints. A tunnel creates a virtual *circuit* between the two endpoints and makes the connection appear like a dedicated connection even though it spans the Internet infrastructure. Two types of VPNs commonly used today are

- **Remote access VPN (Host-to-site)**: A remote access VPN is used to facilitate network access for users in remote office networks or for remote users who travel a lot and need access to the network. The client usually initiates this type of VPN connection.

- **Site-to-site VPN**: A site-to-site VPN is used to create a virtual link from one site to the other. It essentially replaces the traditional WAN-type connection used in connecting typical sites. This type of VPN requires network hardware like a router or a firewall to create and maintain the connection.

You might also see mentioned a *host-to-host VPN,* which deals with a single connection between two machines. The machines could be using VPN software or hardware for establishing the VPN connection.

In regards to tunneling, one of the original tunneling protocols is Generic Routing Encapsulation (*GRE*). GRE was developed by Cisco in 1994 and is still being used today. GRE is commonly used as a site-to-site VPN solution because of its simplicity and versatility. It is the only tunneling protocol that can encapsulate up to 20 types of protocols. Other protocols include the Point-to-Point Tunneling Protocol (*PPTP*) developed jointly by Microsoft, 3Com, and Alcatel-Lucent in 1996. Layer 2 Forwarding Protocol (*L2F*) was developed by Cisco around the same time as PPTP. L2F does not require any VPN client software. An L2F connection is intended to be done by L2F hardware. Layer 2 Tunneling Protocol (*L2TP*) was developed by the Internet Engineering Task Force (IETF) in 1999. L2TP was created with the intention of merging two incompatible proprietary tunneling protocols, PPTP and L2F. L2TP is considered to be an enhancement of the two previous protocols. L2TP does not require a specific hardware.

1.2 Compare and contrast the use of networking services and applications

Network Controllers—The purpose of this device is to authenticate users and network devices using Kerberos in domain environments. Kerberos is a network authentication protocol for client/server applications. In non-domain environments, certificates are required for authentication. Associated with the Network Controller is the API (Application Programming Interface). The API is defined in southbound and northbound applications. Southbound applications allow a controller to define switches while the northbound applications gather information used to monitor and configure the network.

1.3 Install and configure the following networking services/ applications

Reservations—This is used to ensure that a DHCP client always receives the same IP address when it reconnects.

Scopes—This is a grouping of IP addresses that use the DHCP (Dynamic Host Control Protocol) service for a group of computers located on a subnet.

SNAT—This stands for Source Network Address Translation, which enables private network data traffic to go out to the Internet. SNAT enables multiple VMs so they can reach the public network through a single gateway public IP address.

DNAT—This stands for Destination Network Address Translation. DNAT allows any host on the "outside" of the network to get to a single host on the "inside" of the network.

Reverse proxy—A *proxy server* is used by clients to communicate with secure systems using a proxy. The client gets access to the network via the proxy server. This step is used to authenticate the user, establish the session, and set policies. The client must connect to the proxy server to connect to resources outside the network. In reverse proxy, the client computer is outside the network trying to gain access to the server inside the network. The client computer issues the request for website information, which is sent to the proxy. The proxy obtains information from the website and sends it to the client. Its function is to provide control for traffic flow from the server to the client.

Dynamic DNS—This is a method where name server and Domain Name Server are automatically updated.

1.4 Explain the characteristics and benefits of various WAN technologies

CWDM—This stands for coarse wavelength division multiplexing. This is a technique for combining multiple signals on laser beams for transmission. The signals are at different wavelengths but have less total wavelengths compared to dense wavelength division multiplexing (DWDM).

MPLS—This is Multiprotocol Label Switching, which is a data-carrying service for telecommunication networks that route data from one network node to the next based on labels for short path rather than long network addresses.

1.5 Install and properly terminate various cable types and connectors using appropriate tools

UTP coupler—This is a small device used to connect two UTP cables. It is also called an inline coupler. UTP couplers can be used to couple CAT5 and RJ-11 phone lines but can introduce signal degradation.

BNC connectors—BNC stands for Bayonet Neill-Concelman, which is a quick connector for coaxial cable. This was a common connector used with ThinNet Ethernet cabling.

Fiber coupler—These couplers come in a variety of styles that support single-mode and multimode fibers. These devices allow a single fiber to be split into two outputs, and multiple input fibers can be combined into one output fiber.

APC versus UPC—APC stands for angled physical contact and UPC stands for ultra physical contact. The difference between the two types of connectors is the fiber endface. APC has a polished endface at an 8-degree angle. UPC endfaces are polished with no angle. APC and UPC connectors are easily identified by their color. APC adapters are green, and UPC adapters are blue.

Fiber to coaxial—This device is used to convert an optical signal carried over fiber to an electrical signal carried over coaxial cable. A typical application for this is coupling cabling that carries digital optical signals to a digital coaxial cable.

PVC versus Plenum—PVC cable is a common plastic cable insulation or jacket that consists of polyvinyl chloride chemical compounds that emit toxic smoke when burned. Plenum rated cable has special coating that emits less toxic smoke when burned.

1.6 Differentiate between common network topologies

Hybrid—This is simply a combination of two or more network topologies. For example, a STAR and a BUS topology combination.

1.7 Differentiate between network infrastructure implementations

NFC—This stands for near field communication. NFC is a set of communication protocols used to enable two electronic devices to communicate. A typical NFC device is a smartphone, and NFC smartphones can establish communication if they are within 4 cm of each other. Applications of NFC include reading electronic tags or even making payments.

SCADA/ICS—SCADA stands for supervisory control and data acquisition. ICS stands for industrial control systems. Applications for SCADA systems include electrical power systems, railroads, and pipelines. ICS systems are computer-based systems associated with the monitoring and control of industrial processes. The difference between SCADA and ICS systems is SCADA systems are large systems or systems that extend over many miles or multiple sites. Industrial control systems are designed to operate and monitor the critical industrial infrastructure.

ICS server—Industrial control systems servers are designed to withstand the harsh environment of industry. The physical cabinet housing the server has a heavier enclosure, improved electronics, and a high-watt power supply. The operating systems for ICS servers are typically more robust to better protect the system from cyber threats. Typical components that can be included in a control system configuration are

- Distributed Control Systems (DCS)
- Programmable Logic Controllers (PLC)
- (SCADA) systems
- Control server
- Master Terminal Unit (MTU)
- Remote Terminal Unit (RTU)
- Intelligent Electronic Devices (IED)
- Data Historian
- Input/Output (IO) server

DCS/closed circuit—Distributed Control System (DCS) is a system that has multiple subsystem controllers geographically dispersed throughout the network. In modern DCS systems, the local controllers connect to the ICS server. A human interacts with the controllers through what is called a human machine interface (HMI). DCS systems have been the primary solution for automation in a process environment; however, many PLC (Programmable Logic Controller) vendors are advocating that PLCs or PACs (Programmable Automation Controllers) are an improved solution.

Remote Terminal Unit (RTU)—This is a control unit designed to support SCADA remote stations.

Programmable logic controller (PLC)—A PLC is used for control of machinery in manufacturing and related industries. PLCs handle both analog and digital inputs, are designed for the harsh environment of a manufacturing floor, and have excellent noise immunity. A PLC is designed to provide responses to inputs in real time. Remote PLCs are also called *field devices*.

Medianets—This is an intelligent network that has been optimized for high traffic video applications. The system has the capability of identifying whether the destination is a smartphone or a desktop computer and can adjust bandwidth based on the target. Medianets also have the capability to deliver surveillance video over the same IP network carrying the company's data traffic. Cisco's Medianet technologies enable the video applications to better interact with the overall system thereby improving the Quality of Service (QoS) for the deployment.

VTC—This stands for video teleconferencing. Medianets improve the QoS for video teleconferencing by integrating complex equipment to distribute the video teleconference. Some older systems use ISDN (Integrated Services Digital Network); however, IP/SIP based VTC is now the norm. SIP is the Session Initiation Protocol used for the signals and control of multimedia sessions such as a video teleconference and Internet telephony.

1.8 Given a scenario, implement and configure the appropriate addressing schema

Autoconfiguration—This is an IPv6 feature. With IPv6, a computer can automatically configure its network settings without a DHCP server by sending a solicitation message to its IPv6 router. The router then sends back its advertisement message, which contains the prefix information that the computer can use to create its own IPv6 address. This feature significantly helps simplify the deployment of the IPv6 devices, especially in the transient environments such as airports, train stations, stadiums, hotspots, and so on.

To complete the autoconfiguration IPv6 address, the subnet prefix of *FE80::/64* is then prepended to the interface identifier resulting in a 128-bit link-local address. To ensure that there is no duplicate address on the same link, the machine sends a Neighbor Solicitation message out on the link. The purpose of this solicitation is to discover the link-layer address of another IPv6 node or to confirm a previously determined link-layer address. If there is no response to the message, it assumes that the address is unique and therefore assigns the link-local address to its interface. The process of detecting another machine with the same IPv6 address is called Duplicate Address Detection (DAD).

EUI 64—This stands for Extended Universal Identifier-64, and this option allows the router to choose its own host identifier (rightmost 64 bits) from the EUI-64 (Extended Universal Identifier-64) of the interface. The following example uses the IPv6 address of 2001:DB88:FEED:BEEF::1 on the router interface. This has a 64-bit network prefix of 2001:DB88:FEED:BEEF. The interface identifier of the link-local address is derived by transforming the 48 bits of the EUI-48 MAC address to 64 bits for EUI-64. This EUI-48 to EUI-64 transform algorithm is also used to derive the interface identifier for the global unicast address.

The following example demonstrates how to convert an EUI-48 MAC address of 000C291CF2F7 to a modified EUI-64 format.

1. Expand the 48-bit MAC address to a 64-bit format by inserting "FFFE" in the middle of the 48 bits.

   000C29 **FFFE** 1CF2F7

2. Change the 7th bit starting with the leftmost bit of the address from 0 to 1. This 7th bit is referred to as the U/L bit or universal/local bit. 000C29 is 0000 0000 0000 1100 0010 1001 in binary format. When its 7th bit is changed to 1, it becomes 0000 0010 0000 1100 0010 1001, which is 020C29 in hexadecimal number.

3. The result is a modified EUI-64 address format of 020C29FFFE1CF2F7.

Toredo, miredo—Toredo is a tunneling protocol that provides IPv6 connectivity for IPv6 capable devices that are on an IPv4 platform. Toredo is a temporary measure for clients that don't have IPv6 capability and is expected to be removed as IPv6 networks mature. Miredo works behind NAT (Network Address Translation) devices. It also doesn't require that tunnel endpoints or accounts be defined.

DHCP6—This is the Dynamic Host Control Protocol for DHCP6. An IPv6 client can request an IPv6 address, and it can request a DHCPv6 prefix.

1.9 Explain the basics of routing concepts and protocols

Routing redistribution—Routing redistribution is another important practice that a network engineer may have to face when working in a big network environment. Routing redistribution is the technique of injecting routes from one routing protocol to another routing protocol. Routes are only exchanged automatically with routers running the same routing protocol. Each routing protocol speaks its own language; they do not automatically communicate with each other. Each routing protocol has its own metric or cost. Static routes use administrative distance, OSPF uses cost, IS-IS uses metric, and EIGRP uses composite metric. Therefore, routes from different routing protocols cannot be exchanged automatically. This process has to be configured manually.

There are several reasons why routing redistribution is necessary. One common reason is to redistribute static routes. These routes are not learned but are configured manually. They must be redistributed into a dynamic routing protocol so that they can be advertised. Another reason is when two or more dynamic routing protocols are used on the network. This scenario happens often when connecting one network to another either for peering purposes or for business acquisition. When connecting to another network of different routing protocols, rather than converting to a single routing protocol, it is much easier to accept the new routing protocol and to distribute the new routes into the existing routing protocol. This saves time and money. Another reason for routing redistribution is that certain routing protocols may not be supported by certain network devices. A prime example of this is the EIGRP, which is a Cisco proprietary protocol and is not supported by any other network vendors. If a non-Cisco router were to connect to an existing EIGRP-running Cisco router, the Cisco router will need to redistribute routes learned from another routing protocol into EIGRP.

Route aggregation—This is a technique used to minimize the number of routing tables required in an IP network.

High availability—This refers to information technology systems that are in continuous operation for a long time and downtime must be minimal. Typical high availability systems include hospitals and data centers. These systems are intended to be in operation 100% of the time. There are three principles in engineering high availability systems:

1. Eliminate single points of failure by adding high redundancy.

2. Provide reliable crossovers to avoid a single point of failure.

3. The systems must be able to detect failures. A reliable/redundant system might make it so that failures are not seen, but the failures must be noted in the maintenance log.

VRRP—This is the Virtual Router Redundancy Protocol that provides automatic assignment of routers to hosts participating in the network. The objective is to increase reliability and availability of routes. For participating hosts, the default gateway is assigned to a virtual router instead of a physical router. Each VRRP is limited to a single subnet. VRRP also functions with IPv6, IPv4, MPLS, and Token Ring. The virtual IP address for VRRP can be assigned manually or via DHCP (Dynamic Host Configuration Protocol). The most common application for VRRP is to have one router dedicated to forwarding data packets from hosts in a LAN.

Virtual IP—This is a virtual IP address also called a VIPA. When using a VIPA, there isn't an actual or physical network device. The virtual IP address is shared among multiple servers and domains. Data packets still travel over existing network paths but are no longer dependent on a single network interface card (NIC). A reason to implement a virtual IP address is to improve redundancy and provide failover capabilities for the machine.

HSRP—This is the Hot Standby Router Protocol. This protocol enables a framework of routers so that a default gateway always is available, hence the status of "Hot Standby." HSRP does not advertise routes and is not a routing protocol. However, if a router goes down, the backup router takes over as the primary router and still provides a default gateway.

SPB—This is stands for shortest path bridging. It is based on the IEEE 802.1aq standard for enabling multipath routing. It is a replacement for the IEEE 802.1D, IEEE 802.1w, and IEEE 802.1s spanning tree protocols. While the intent of the older spanning tree protocol was to block a layer 2 loop, SPB lets all paths be active with equal costs, thereby providing a larger layer 2 topology.

1.10 Identify the basic elements of unified communication technologies

VoIP—Voice over IP (VoIP), or IP telephony, is the transport of phone conversations over packet networks. Many companies and individuals are taking advantage of the development of new technologies that support the convergence of voice and data over their existing packet networks. The network administrator can also see an additional benefit with the cost savings using a converged voice/data network. This has created a new role for the network administrator, that of a telecommunications manager. The network administrator must not only be aware of the issues of data transport within and external to the network, but also the issues of incorporating voice data traffic into the network.

QoS—An important issue in the delivery of real-time data over a network (for example, voice over IP) is quality of service (QoS). The following are QoS issues for a VoIP network:

- Jitter
- Network latency and packet loss
- Queuing

Jitter—Digitized voice data requires a fixed time interval between data packets for the signal to be properly converted back to an audible analog signal. However, there is a delay problem with transported voice data over a packet network. Variability in data packet arrival introduces jitter in the signal, which produces a poorly reconstructed signal at the receiver. For example, assume that a 1000 Hz tone is sent over a VoIP network. The tone is digitized at regular time intervals, assembled into frames and packets, and sent out as an RTP packet. Random delays in the packets' travel to the destination result in their arriving at irregular time intervals. The reproduced 1000 Hz analog tone will contain jitter because the arrival time for each data packet varies.

Buffering the data packets long enough for the next data packet to arrive can minimize the effects of jitter. A *buffer* is temporary storage for holding data packets until it is time for them to be sent. The buffer enables the data packets to be output at regular time intervals, thereby removing most of the jitter problem. Buffering works as long as the arrival time of the next packet is not too long. If the arrival time is too late, the data packet might have to be considered "lost" because the real-time data packets can't wait too long for the buffered packet without affecting the quality of the reconstructed signal. Another issue is that the buffering stage introduces delay, and having to wait additional time only introduces more delay.

Network latency—It takes time for a data packet to travel from the source to the destination. This is called network latency, and it becomes an important issue in VoIP data traffic. Telephones (both traditional and IP) feed a portion of the user's voice into the earpiece. If the round-trip delay of the voice data is too lengthy (> 50 ms), the user begins to hear an annoying echo in the earpiece.

Delay issues can be minimized by making sure the network routers and switches are optimized for VoIP data traffic. The VoIP network can be configured so that high-priority data packets (for example, voice packets) are transported first over the IP network. Nonsensitive data packets are given a low-priority status and are transmitted only after the high-priority packets are sent.

Another source of packet delay is network congestion. This can have a negative effect on any type of data traffic but is disruptive to VoIP telephony. The network administrator must make sure that congestion problems are avoided or at least minimized and could have the option of configuring the routers to optimize routes for IP telephony.

Queuing—This is another technique the network administrator can use to improve the quality of service of data traffic by controlling the transfer of data packets. The administrator must identify the data traffic that must be given priority for transport. The queuing decision is made when the data packet arrives, is first queued, and is placed in a buffer. There are many types of queuing arrangements, with the most basic being FIFO (first in, first out). In this case, the data packets are placed in the queue on arrival and transmitted when the channel is available.

A technique called *weighted fair queuing (WFQ)* is available on many routers and is used to determine what data traffic gets priority for transmission. This technique applies only if the buffer is full, and a decision must be made as to which data packet goes first. WFQ can be modified to provide a class-based weighted fair queuing (CBWFQ). This improvement enables the network administrator to define the amount of data traffic allocated to a class of data traffic (for example, VoIP).

Other queuing techniques are PQ and CQ. Priority queuing (PQ) is used to make sure the important data traffic gets handled first. Custom queuing (CQ) reserves a portion of the channel bandwidth for selected data traffic (for example, VoIP traffic). This is a decision made by the network administrator based on experience with the network. The problem with CQ is it doesn't make allowances for other traffic management when the channel is full; therefore, queuing techniques such as WFQ or WRED can't be used to manage the data flow.

DSCP—This is the Differentiated Services Code Point. A field is placed in the IP data packet that is used to enable services. It is a combination of the IP Precedence and Type of Service fields.

COS—This stands for Class of Service. With COS, flow control for data throughput can be better managed.

UC servers—The UC stands for unified communication. This refers to the integration of various real-time technologies such as IP telephony, instant messaging, audio and video conferencing. Essentially, UC enables a message that is sent using one technology to be received using a different technology.

UC devices—This refers to unified communication devices.

UC gateways—This refers to gateways used by unified communication technologies.

1.11 Compare and contrast technologies that support cloud and virtualization

Virtual firewall—This is a network device running in a virtual environment. This device provides the same functionality as a physical firewall.

Software-defined networking—This enables network administrators' manageability of the network, enabling network control to be programmable.

Storage area network (SAN)—This network is used to provide access to storage devices for multiple servers. The SAN is robust and is built to handle any type of failure. Additionally, the SAN must be able to grow as the network grows. The main benefit of SANs is that storage is treated as a pool of resources. These storage resources are centrally managed and made available as needed.

ISCSI—This stands for Internet Small Computer System Interface. This feature allows SCSI commands to be sent over the LAN or Internet.

Jumbo frame—These are simply Ethernet frames that contain more than 1500 bytes of data. A jumbo frame can carry up to 9216 bytes and is supported by most Gigabit switches. Not all Fast Ethernet switches support jumbo frames. The advantage with jumbo frames is the reduced overhead; however, jumbo frames can have a negative impact on network performance, in particular latency, in low bandwidth networks.

Network attached storage (NAS)—This is a type of storage for nodes on the local area network. This device has its own Ethernet connection and IP address. NAS also provides the ability to share its files with multiple clients on the network.

Cloud concepts—The word "cloud" is such a nontechnical term that when it represents a technology, it sounds so vague and nebulous. Cloud computing is one of the most talked about technologies in recent years, discussed by IT people and users alike. Cloud has become a new noun, as in "people can connect to the cloud," or "my stuff is stored on the cloud," or "I migrate everything to the cloud." The cloud is magically in the middle of everything. Yet, people still don't know what and where the cloud really is. Its famous existence has developed many punch lines of its own and created many questions. The bottom line is that the *cloud* is just another name for the Internet.

Cloud infrastructure—There are different types of cloud infrastructures used by IaaS, PaaS, and SaaS. These infrastructures offer different levels of security, resource restrictions, and management. Most notable cloud models are

- **Public cloud**—This cloud infrastructure is owned and operated by the cloud service company but made available for use by the general public.

- **Private cloud**—This cloud infrastructure is operated by the organization and is made available only to members of the organization.

- **Community cloud**—This cloud infrastructure offers two or more organizations exclusive access to the infrastructure and computing resources. These organizations may have shared common policies that allow them to operate in a distributed mode.

- **Hybrid cloud**—This cloud infrastructure offers a combination of at least one private cloud and one public cloud.

1.12 Given a set of requirements, implement a basic network

Environment limitations—Access to the network and in particular the Internet can be limited for users. For example, download times and saturated networks can have a negative impact on the computer's Internet access and frustrate users. This limitation on the networking environment is constantly being addressed by network engineers.

Compatibility requirements—One significant improvement in today's networks is the interoperability of most network devices. Setting up and physically connecting any device to an Ethernet connection is virtually the same for all operating systems (OS) and computers. Yes, the underlying OS differs, but they all function pretty much the same and provide similar features and TCP/IP support. Access to the Internet is also similar for each OS and computer system regardless of whether you are operating at a home or at a business. The difference is typically a home supports a few computer systems and maybe one or two Internet connections. The business might have numerous computers and a high bandwidth Internet connection.

2.0 NETWORK OPERATIONS

2.1 Given a scenario, use appropriate monitoring tools

TRAP—SNMP TRAP is one of the SNMP protocol data unit (PDU) types. It is used to enable an agent to notify the SNMP network management station (NMS) of significant events. Instead of an NMS polling information and getting a response from an SNMP agent, the agent sends an unsolicited SNMP message to the NMS as triggered by specified events.

Walk—In the situation where an OID (object identifier) is not returned, snmpwalk searches SNMPv2-SMI::mig-2.

SYSLOG—It is a standard protocol used to collect log messages sent from devices to a server running a SYSLOG service or daemon. The server is typically known as a SYSLOG server. SYSLOG servers run on UDP port 514 or TCP port 601.

SIEM—Security Information and Event Management is an IT security system that can provide a holistic view and real-time analysis of an organization's IT security. A SIEM system combines the Security Event Management (SEM) and the Security Information Management (SIM) by gathering security alerts and information generated by the network or security hardware, servers, and applications.

2.2 Given a scenario, analyze metrics and reports from monitoring and tracking performance tools

Log management—This is a way to collect log files from different devices and to store the log data over time, so that information can be extracted, analyzed, and reviewed. Log files can be gathered from many different sources in many different ways, and they can have different formats. The standard is to use SYSLOG so the log files from devices such as routers, switches, web servers, database servers, and so on can be generated with a consistent format, and they all can be sent to the same aggregation point like SYSLOG server.

Graphing—Graphing is a standard representation used by many monitoring tools to show the performance, behaviors and trends of interested targets over time. These tools convert the raw data collected from log files, SNMP messages, or proprietary system information into useful and readable reports by illustrating them in graphical formats. For the computing hardware, one might be interested in tracking the CPU utilization, memory usage, I/O rate, and storage or disk consumption. For the network devices, one might be interested in tracking the network device CPU, network device memory, interface or link status, network utilization, network packets, network errors, and network discards.

Utilization storage—They key point is you want as much memory as you can afford and you also want fast devices. Solid state memory (storage) is the best choice.

Network device CPU—The issue with the CPU is an overtaxed CPU is slow. This can be because too many processes are running or you don't have sufficient memory to handle the workload.

Network device memory—You want to install as much memory as your system can handle, and you want to use fast devices.

Link status—The easiest way to verify link status is by using the **ping** command. You can verify the link lights when possible.

Discards—Data packets have what is called a "Time-to-Live," which is the number of routers the data packet can pass through before it is discarded.

SMS—Short message service can send text messages of alerts and notifications. This is a feature that typically is integrated into most monitoring tools.

2.3 Given a scenario, use appropriate resources to support configuration management

NAC—Network Access Control is sometimes known as Network Admission Control. It is a security mechanism that can be implemented on a network to register, authenticate, authorize, and enforce security policies on all endpoint devices before they are allowed to access the network. NAC is gaining popularity as a method to manage BYOD (Bring Your Own Device) and keep track of these devices. It can be deployed in many forms from hardware appliance, virtual appliance, client agent, or clientless agent. It can be used to manage the on-boarding and off-boarding of mobile devices.

To manage network devices and resources properly, an organization must have a good policy for change management for network device configuration and standard procedures for network maintenance. To prepare for disaster recovery, an organization must have a backup plan, which entails backing up network equipment configurations and archiving them for recovery. One of the most fundamental elements of network operations is documentation. Documentation can consist of network drawings and diagrams, asset management, and even vendor documentation. Having network diagrams helps engineers visualize and understand how things are connected. Asset management gives engineers details of their network equipment from model numbers to software version and their locations.

2.4 Explain the importance of implementing network segmentation

SCADA systems/Industrial control systems—Industrial Control Systems (ICS) are command and control networks designed to support industrial processes in critical infrastructures such as power plants, transportation systems, utility facilities, refineries, and factories. The largest subgroup of ICS is Supervisory Control and Data Acquisition (SCADA) systems. Since critical infrastructures are controlled and monitored by ICS/SCADA over the network, they need to be secured and protected against vulnerabilities, exploitations, and malicious attacks. An ICS/SCADA system must be on its own network; it must be segmented off from other networks and must be placed behind the network firewall with strict access.

Legacy systems—Legacy systems can be categorized as "end-of-life" or "end-of-support." This means that they are no longer supported by their vendors and manufacturers. One of the biggest security risks for a legacy system is there will not be a firmware, hardware, or software update. This makes a legacy system more vulnerable and susceptible to security hacks and exploitations. If it is on a network, a hacker can exploit it via its known vulnerabilities. Legacy systems should be decommissioned as soon as possible. If needed services are running on these systems, an organization must plan to transition these services to another system. If legacy systems must be on the network, it is best to segment the legacy systems off to a protected network and restrict access to these systems.

Honeypot—Honeypot is a computing environment specifically set up to gather information regarding network attacks and intrusions and to study the vulnerabilities of a system. A honeypot typically consists of decoy servers or systems including a real network that connects to the Internet. The honeypot environment is designed to be more vulnerable, which allows for easier access and intrusion than the real protected environment. It is also designed to be on a separate network with constant monitoring and logging to gain more insights of how attackers can break into or penetrate into the systems.

Testing lab—Testing lab is another good environment to have for an IT organization. It is a best practice for an IT organization to have both a production environment and a testing environment, where the testing environment is almost a clone of the real production environment. For a smaller IT shop, a testing lab can be set up to mimic the hardware environment in a much smaller scale. However, it serves the same purpose of testing the software and hardware installations, upgrades, and patches before doing it on the production environment. For mission critical services, it is imperative to do all the necessary testing in the testing environment or lab, so the detrimental issues can be discovered and worked out and to lessen the negative impact on users.

2.5 Given a scenario, install and apply patches and updates

Driver updates—These updates are required for the operating system or the software to operate the hardware component. Also, when there are changes to the OS or the software, the driver may need to be reinstalled or updated.

Major versus minor updates—Typically, minor updates are subsets of a major update. Major updates are strongly recommended by the vendors, while minor updates are done as needed.

2.6 Given a scenario, configure a switch using proper features

Interface configuration—VLAN interface configuration is different from a router interface configuration. With a router interface configuration, a subnet is created, and it is local to that router interface. With VLAN interface configuration, a subnet is created, and it is local to that VLAN. Since more than one switch port can be assigned to a specific VLAN, this means the same subnet can span different physical ports or user locations. This allows for greater flexibility to have many locations sharing the same subnet.

VTP—VTP or VLAN Trunking Protocol is Cisco's proprietary protocol used to manage and propagate the VLAN definitions to all the VTP capable switches. This is to reduce the administrative overhead in maintaining the VLANs in all the switches on the network. With VTP, a new VLAN can be defined on a VTP server, and then the VLAN information gets propagated to every switch on the network.

Port bonding (LACP)—Link Aggregation Control Protocol (LACP), sometimes called port bonding, is part of an IEEE specification (802.3ad) that allows for multiple physical ports on an Ethernet switch to be bundled as one single logical channel. LACP is a standard protocol supported by most network switches, while PAgP (Port Aggregation Protocol) is a Cisco proprietary protocol that performs a similar function to create an EtherChannel.

Port mirroring (local versus remote)—Port mirroring is a capability offered by many network switches. Port mirroring, as implied by the name, makes a copy of the network traffic from a specified port or ports and sends the traffic to a specified destination. When a copy of the traffic is sent to another port on the switch, it is local port mirroring. When the destination is on another switch, it is remote port mirroring. For remote mirroring, the copy of traffic is sent over a dedicated VLAN created for this purpose. Port mirroring is essential for monitoring and logging the network traffic without having to install a device in-line with the traffic and disrupt the network traffic flow.

In-band/Out-of-band management—The management of the remote network devices can be done in two ways. One is in-band management, and another is out-of-band management. In-band management refers to when the management traffic is using the same network channel as the regular network traffic on the managed network device. Out-of-band management refers to when the management traffic is using a different or dedicated network channel than the regular network traffic on the managed network device.

AAA—AAA stands for authentication, authorization, and accounting. It is a common access control used by RADIUS and Kerberos.

2.7 Install and configure wireless LAN infrastructure and implement the appropriate technologies in support of wireless capable devices

Device density—The device density is the number of connecting wireless clients. Every wireless access point has a maximum device density that it can handle at one time. This is crucial in wireless AP deployment planning. More WAPs are always needed in a more populated area to handle more wireless devices.

Wireless controllers—Wireless controllers are used more in an enterprise wireless environment when managing hundreds of APs or more. In a traditional standalone wireless environment, each AP is managed individually. With an enterprise wireless controller environment, an AP communicates with its controller when booting up to download its necessary firmware and software, to register and authenticate itself, to receive its network information settings, and to receive its wireless LAN (WLAN) configuration. The wireless controller becomes the brain and manager of the whole operations. When wireless changes need to be made, it can be done at the controller, which pushes the changes out to all of the APs.

VLAN pooling—VLAN pooling is a solution offered by many wireless manufacturers to deal with the large number of connecting wireless devices, and every device is required to have an IP address. Multiple VLANs of different subnets can be grouped together with VLAN pooling to accommodate the large number of IP addresses needed. Every device shares the same WLAN, but may have an IP address of a different subnet.

LWAPP—Lightweight Access Point Protocol (LWAPP) is a Cisco Proprietary Protocol that has been superseded by the standard called CAPWAP (Configuration and Provisioning of Wireless AP). LWAPP is the underlying wireless control protocol for Cisco APs to communicate with their wireless controllers.

Goodput—Goodput refers to the actual wireless data throughput as measured by an application on the end device. It is a way to represent the actual transmission rate of a wireless connection, which is not the maximum theoretical transmission rate.

High throughput—A wireless adapter with high throughput or high successful data delivery rate can be referred to as 802.11a-ht or 802.11g-ht depending on the protocol 802.11a or 802.11g protocol used by the adapter.

Ad hoc—Ad hoc wireless connection is a peer-to-peer connection between wireless devices. This connection does not require a wireless access point, as wireless devices communicate directly with each other.

Cell phone—Another way to connect a wireless device to the Internet is via a cell phone. A cell phone can be set up as a hotspot that a wireless device can connect to and use the data plan to connect to the Internet.

3.0 NETWORK SECURITY

3.1 Compare and contrast risk related concepts

Business continuity—The IT group is responsible for servicing all organizations within a business. The IT group needs to have a plan because everyone uses computers and the network. Software and hardware decisions need to have input from all organizations so that there is good continuity among all groups requiring IT support.

3.2 Compare and contrast common vulnerabilities and threats

Botnet—A group of infected or compromised computers on the Internet that are being used to launch coordinated denial of service attacks against another system on the network. A botnet computer is controlled via an Internet Relay Chat (IRC) channel by a server called a command and control server.

Coordinated attack—A type of distributed denial of service attack that is deliberate toward a specific target and is orchestrated by a controller source like the command and control server in a botnet. In recent news, the Anonymous group is synonymous with the coordinated attacks as they planned many attacks to bring down websites deliberately to send their political message.

Friendly/unintentional DOS—This type of denial of service is not a malicious attack. It is typically caused by heavy legitimate traffic to a server or a website that inadvertently overwhelms the server resources or the network connection. So, the server or the network cannot handle the massive volume of traffic.

Permanent DOS—Permanent DOS or PDOS is a malicious type of attack that aims to sabotage the hardware and render it useless. A PDOS attack can damage a hardware system to the point that it requires replacement or reinstallation of hardware.

Reflective/amplified—A recent reflective attack used DNS servers configured as open resolvers on the Internet. These open resolvers answer any DNS queries from anyone. A small DNS query asking for all information about the DNS zone is sent to an open resolver; then in turn the open resolver replies with the huge DNS zone information. The message has increased or amplified, hence the name DNS amplification attack. When a botnet sends these small DNS query messages to a list of open DNS resolvers with the source IP being the victim, the amplified messages are then sent or reflected back to the victim overwhelming the resources on the victim.

NTP—Similar to DNS amplification attacks, this is another reflective attack using public Network Time Protocol (NTP) servers. This time a botnet sends an old NTP remote command called monlist requesting a list of the last 600 hosts connected to the server and spoofs the source IP to be the victim. Again, this DDOS is used to overwhelm the victim and bring down the system.

Packet/protocol abuse—Hackers can compromise a system or gain valuable information from a system by taking advantage of inherent weaknesses in network packet and network protocols. Ping of Death, SYN attack, and DNS reflective attack are just a few examples of packet/protocol abuse.

Man-in-the-middle—Man-in-the-middle is an attack where an attacker seamlessly places itself in the middle of the conversation of others. Therefore, the attacker becomes the recipient of all information sent by victim computers.

ARP cache poisoning—This is a technique used in man-in-the-middle attacks. On the same network segment, network devices communicate using MAC addresses. These MAC addresses are stored in the ARP cache, which contains IP address to MAC address mappings. If an attacker can change the MAC addresses in the victim's ARP cache or *"poison the ARP cache,"* then the conversations get redirected to the attacker.

Evil twin—Evil twin can be categorized as a man-in-the-middle attack in which a rogue wireless access point poses as a legitimate one by broadcasting a legitimate SSID and eavesdropping on the wireless network. Typical users only recognize the SSID and do not know behind the scene which APs are broadcasting this wireless network. Attackers can collect information from wireless users connecting through this wireless access point.

War chalking—War driving is a process in which attackers search for locations with an open wireless network or a weak wireless network, so that they can gain more access to collect information or data of connecting users. War chalking is the next step after war driving, which leaves marks or symbols on the premise, outside the premise, or even online to notify other hackers about the wireless vulnerabilities of the location.

Bluejacking/Bluesnarfing—Both Bluejacking and Bluesnarfing are attacks on Bluetooth devices. Bluejacking is considered more annoying than harmful as it sends unsolicited messages to other Bluetooth devices in the vicinity, while Bluesnarfing is truly an attack to gain unauthorized access of another Bluetooth device over the Bluetooth connection with the intention to obtain information stored on the Bluetooth device.

WPA/WEP/WPS attacks—To crack encrypted systems requires the "bad guy" to collect a lot of information. For example, a lot of information is transmitted with an ARP request in a wireless system. The "bad guy" can use this information to extract the WEP key from this data. It is not simple, but it can be done.

Session hijacking—Session hijacking is the exploitation of a valid computer session to gain unauthorized access to information or services on a computer. It is more synonymous with the exploitation of the web session control by stealing a session cookie and using it to establish a session with remote servers that still think the session is valid.

VLAN hopping—VLAN hopping is an attack to gain information or resources only available in specific VLANs. There are two types of VLAN hopping attacks. A switch spoofing attack works by taking advantage of an incorrectly configured trunk port whereby the attacker tricks a switch into thinking that another switch is forming a trunk port and therefore gaining access to all the VLANs allowed on the trunk port. Another type of VLAN hopping attack is the double-tagging attack whereby the attacker embeds a second 802.1Q tag inside the frame. This second tag allows the frame to be forwarded to a VLAN that the original 802.1Q did not intend.

Compromised system—Compromised system is generally referred to as a computer, a group of computers, or a part of the network that has been adversely impacted by an untrusted source.

Zero-day attacks—A zero-day attack refers to the exploitation of vulnerability in software that is unknown to the developer. Since the developer is not aware of it, there is no patch to fix it.

Unencrypted channels—Any network transmission done by using a protocol that does not encrypt the data is said to be an unencrypted channel. Some of the protocols that cannot encrypt data are TELNET, FTP, HTTP, TFTP, TEMPEST, and SNMP v1 and v2.

TEMPEST/RF emanation—TEMPEST is a standard for computer systems certification commenced by the US government in the late 1950s. TEMPEST standard specifies the amount of Electromagnetic Interference (EMI) and Radio Frequency Interference (RFI) or RF emanation emitted by a device. The purpose of TEMPEST is to shield the wireless RF signal within the area and not divulge intelligence about system information.

3.3 Given a scenario, implement network hardening techniques

Anti-malware network-based—This type of anti-malware is installed on a device connected to the network that is capable of monitoring all traffic in and out of the network. Intrusion Detection System (IDS), Intrusion Prevention System (IPS), and Application or a Next-Generation Firewall can be equipped with anti-malware capability.

Cloud/server-based antimalware—This type of antimalware has a lightweight agent installed on a device. The agent then communicates with and sends its information to a server or a cloud server for signature definition detection and analysis. So the heavy lifting is done by the server or the cloud server instead of by the software on the device.

Switch Port Security—This security option is prominent in Cisco switches where it can be configured to enable many switch port security features.

DHCP snooping—This security feature detects any rogue DHCP server and stops DHCP packets from untrusted ports from propagating.

Personal WPA/WPA2—Wi-Fi Protected Access (WPA) and its successor WPA2 are wireless security standards developed by the Wi-Fi Alliance. Both personal WPA and WPA2, also known as WPA-PSK (Personal Shared Key), use a passphrase consisting of 8 to 63 ASCII characters. The big difference is WPA uses Temporal Key Integrity Protocol (TKIP), which is based on RC4 stream cipher. WPA2 uses Counter Mode Cipher Block Chaining Message Authentication code protocol (CCMP), which is based on the Advanced Encryption Standard (AES) and is significantly stronger than RC4-based TKIP.

TLS/TTLS—Transport Layer Security (TLS) is the successor to the Secure Sockets Layer (SSL), and it is designed to ensure privacy between the communicating parties. TLS ensures that no third party may eavesdrop or tamper with any messages between a server and a client. TLS requires both the client and the server to use certificates to verify their identities to each other.

Tunneled Transport Layer Security (TTLS) is similar to TLS in that it also ensures the privacy, but it does not require that each party be issued a certificate. Instead, only the authentication server is issued a certificate. The client authentication is performed by password, but the password credentials are transported in a securely encrypted tunnel established based upon the server certificate.

Kerboros—Kerboros is the authentication protocol for Windows Active Directory. When users log on, a special token or ticket containing information linking it to the users is issued by the Kerboros authentication server. Kerboros uses this ticket to validate user access to a resource or a service.

Multifactor/two-factor authentication—When two different authentication factors are used, that is called two-factor authentication. An example of a two-factor authentication would be password (what you know) and smartcard token (what you have). When two or more factors of authentication are used, it is a multifactor authentication. An example would be password, smartcard token, and biometrics (what you are).

Authentication/Single sign-on—Single sign-on (SSO) is a process that permits the users to access different systems after one successful authentication. For an enterprise environment, this makes it convenient for users not having to enter the same credentials to access different systems such as file server, email, and ERP.

MSCHAP—This was created by Microsoft for authenticating remote Windows-based systems. **CHAP** and **MSCHAP** both use a challenge response mechanism to authenticate connections without requiring sending any passwords.

3.4 Compare and contrast physical security controls

Mantraps—A mantrap is an interlocking door controller in a small room, where one door of a mantrap cannot be unlocked or opened until the other door has been closed or locked. Mantraps are used in high security areas where only authorized personnel are allowed.

3.5 Given a scenario, install and configure a basic firewall

UTM—Unified Threat Management (UTM) is an all-in-one solution that integrates a wide range of security features into one appliance. A UTM appliance may have a combination of firewall, network IDS/IPS, VPN, gateway antivirus, gateway antispam, load balancing, and content filtering. This type of appliance is popular in small to medium businesses where the network is too big and complicated. It helps reduce administrative time and cost overhead.

Virtual wires versus routed—With a virtual wire, the firewall takes the data packets coming into one port and sends these to another port. Data packets from the outside are sent inside. In a way, this is just a transparent bridge between the two ports.

Application aware/context aware—This type of firewall is sometimes known as a next generation firewall because of its capability to operate beyond the typical layer 4 of the OSI model. This type of firewall can perform deep packet inspection to analyze each packet. It can incorporate application and context information with other network information to make security decisions.

3.6 Explain the purpose of various network access control models

Posture assessment—Posture assessment is the evaluation of system security based on the applications and settings that a particular system is using. A posture assessment is typically performed on a device before it is permitted to access the network. If a device is found not to have all necessary security settings or software, it can be placed in a quarantine network until it can pass the assessment.

Guest network—A guest network is a special segmented network provided to visitors to access the Internet and certain unrestricted networks. However, visitors are not allowed to access the secure corporate network or corporate resources. Sometimes, certain restriction controls such as bandwidth, time, and network protocols are implemented.

Persistent versus nonpersistent agents—A persistent agent is already installed on the system and is waiting to be used as needed. This agent can be detecting incidents or just waiting to be called on. A nonpersistent agent is typically installed and used as needed.

Edge versus access control—Edge control is applied at the boundary of the network, where firewalls or routers are used to protect the network. This control can restrict access in and out of the network. Access control has an advantage over edge control in that it can be more granular as the control is applied at the resource itself.

4.0 TROUBLESHOOTING

4.1 Given a scenario, implement the following network troubleshooting methodology

Divide and conquer—Using this troubleshooting approach, an OSI layer is selected and tested for its functionality. If this layer is good, the technician tests the next layer, which could be higher or lower. Selecting the layer you start with in the troubleshooting process varies depending on the technician's experience. An experienced technician has a better understanding where to start.

4.2 Given a scenario, analyze and interpret the output of troubleshooting tools

tracert/tracert -6/traceroute6/traceroute -6—These are all commands used to trace the routes that data packets take in an IP network. The commands with a (6) after the command indicate they are for tracing routes in an IPv6 network.

nbstat—This is a diagnostic tool for checking NetBIOS over TCP/IP. The following are some basic functions:

- **nbstat –a <name>**—This checks the NetBIOS adapter status on the computer <name>.
- **nbstat –a <IP address>**—This checks the NetBIOS adapter status on the computer with the specified IP address.
- **nbstat –c /**—This displays the contents of the NetBIOS name cache.
- **nbstat—n /**—This lists the names that are locally registered by NetBIOS applications.
- **nbstat—r -/**—This command lists the count of NetBIOS names.
- **nbstat—R /**—This command purges the name cache.
- **nbstat –RR /**—This command releases packets to the WINS and starts a refresh.
- **nbstat—S /**—This command lists the current NetBIOS sessions.

Multimeter—This is a device used to measure voltage, current, and resistance. A basic function related to cabling is conducting a continuity check, which is used to verify two ends are connected.

Light meter—The function of a light meter is to shine light down a fiber. This assumes that the fiber is not connected to anything at either end.

Toner probe—The function of a toner probe is to inject a tone on a cable. The technician can then use a speaker/sensor to verify that a tone is present at the other cable end. This is also useful when having to locate a cable end. The cable being searched for will have the tone.

Speed test sites—These are used so a speed test can be run to measure a computer's upload and download speeds.

Looking glass sites—These sites are used to obtain routing information related to the network's backbone and efficiency.

4.3 Given a scenario, troubleshoot and resolve common wireless issues

Signal-to-noise ratio—This is a measure of the signal level relative to the noise level. The value is usually expressed in dB, and a high dB value is desirable.

Window film—Sometimes the covering on windows interferes with the propagation of wireless signals. The technician must be aware of this possible problem.

Mismatched channels—Wireless access points and the client computer must use the same frequencies to communicate. The most common frequencies are channels 1, 6, and 11 since these are nonoverlapping channels.

Device saturation—Wireless networks use a shared media, and as the number of wireless units trying to access the network increases, data throughput declines. Remember, wireless networks use the CSMA/CA Carrier Sense Multiple Access/ Collision Avoidance.

Bandwidth saturation—A communication channel has a limited bandwidth. In other words, the channel can carry only so much data. As the user demand increases, the capacity is limited and only so much information can be carried. This is similar to the concept that a garden hose can carry only so much water. If more water capacity is required, you have to get a bigger pipe.

Untested updates—In this case, the updates have not been fully tested for your network. Potential compatibility issues have not been identified. Network administrators normally wait so that problems can be isolated and fixed or wait for a software update that fixes known problems.

Open networks—This is a wireless network that is not using encryption or is using the factory default SSID. In either case, security is now a big threat since the "bad guys" have access to your network.

Incompatibilities—Compatibility issues are important in wireless networks. You need to know the operating frequency for each standard. The current wireless standards are listed here:

- **802.11a (Wireless-A):** This standard can provide data transfer rates up to 54Mbps and an operating range up to 75 feet. It operates at 5 GHz. (Modulation OFDM)

- **802.11b (Wireless-B):** This standard can provide data transfer rates up to 11Mbps with ranges of 100–150 feet. It operates at 2.4 GHz. (Modulation DSSS)

- **802.11g (Wireless-G):** This standard can provide data transfer rates up to 54Mbps up to 150 feet. It operates at 2.4 GHz. (Modulation DSSS or OFDM)

- **802.11n (Wireless-N):** This high-speed wireless connectivity promises data transfer rates over 200+ Mbps. It operates at 2.4 GHz and 5 GHz. (Modulation DSSS or OFDM)

- **802.11i:** This standard for WLANs provides improved data encryption for networks that use the 802.11a, 802.11b, and 802.11g standards.

- **802.11r:** This standard is designed to speed hand-offs between access points or cells in a WLAN. This standard is a critical addition to 802.11 WLANs if voice traffic is to become widely deployed.

- **802.11ac:** This is the next generation of high-speed wireless connectivity. This technology promises data rates up to 1 Gbps. It operates over the 5 GHz band.

Wrong encryption—There are several encryption types for wireless networks. When setting up a wireless router, you find multiple options for encryption. There are options for WEP (not very secure), WPA, and WPA2. *WPA* stands for Wi-Fi Protected Access, and it supports the user authentication provided by 802.1x and replaces WEP as the primary way for securing wireless transfers. WPA2 is an improved version of WPA. The 802.1x standard enhances wireless security by incorporating authentication of the user. It is important that your networking devices use the same encryption. *(WEP, WPA, and WPA2 are discussed in Chapter 4 section 5.)*

Bounce—This refers to the fact that wireless networks use signal radio waves to communicate. Radio waves bounce off metal surfaces. As a result, the radio signals experience signal loss. Wireless LANs have a maximum distance the signal can be transmitted. This is a critical issue inside buildings when user mobility is required. Many obstacles can reflect and attenuate the signal, causing reception to suffer. Also, the signal level for mobile users is hampered by the increased distance from the access point. Distance is also a critical issue in outdoor point-to-multipoint wireless networks. *(Additional information is provided in Chapter 4 section 3.)*

AP configurations—One of the biggest misconceptions about a wireless network is that it does not require a wired connection. This is not quite correct. The connection to a wired LAN is provided by a wireless access point, which provides a bridge between the wireless LAN and the wired network. A physical cable connection (typically CAT6/5e) ties the access point to the wired network's switch or hub (typically Ethernet). It is also necessary that the SSID, type of encryption, and the channel be specified. *(Additional information on all aspects related to configuring the access point is provided in Chapter 4 sections 2-3 and 5)*

LWAPP—This is the Lightweight Access Protocol. This protocol can be used to simplify the control of multiple wireless access points at the same time. With Cisco's LWAPP, the controller is also used as the gateway from the WLAN to the LAN. The system provides for the assignment of a primary, secondary, and even a tertiary controller for the wireless network.

Thin versus thick—A "thick" network is also called an "intelligent" network. Its purpose is to handle authentication, encryption, and management of the wireless devices connected to it. A "thin" network is referring to "dependent" access points. They are called dependent because they can't operate as a stand-alone device.

4.4 Given a scenario, troubleshoot and resolve common copper cable issues

Cable placement—Cable placement is an important consideration, especially when running cable in high EMF environments or next to electrical mains. Electrical noise can be induced in unshielded cable and can affect data reception. You should not suspend cabling from ceiling tiles for safety and fire regulations. The cable bends should be limited to less than four times the diameter of the cable.

Bad SFP/GBIC (cable mismatch)—There can be compatibility issues using the SFP (Small Form Factor Pluggable), and this is replacing the GBIC. Make sure you have the correct connector.

4.5 Given a scenario, troubleshoot and resolve common fiber cable issues

There is always a chance that your fiber link has gone down or the fiber has been cut. Use the appropriate troubleshooting techniques to fix this.

4.6 Given a scenario, troubleshoot and resolve common network issues

Incorrect IP configuration/default gateway—The most common static route used in a host computer is the default gateway. The *default gateway* specifies where the data traffic is to be sent when the destination address for the data is not in the same LAN or is unknown. If you don't have a route specified for a subnet in your network, the default route is used. For example, if your PC is on the 10.10.0.0 network and it wants to send data to 100.100.20.1, the data is sent to the default gateway as specified by the TCP/IP setup on your PC. If you input an incorrect IP address for the default gateway, your data packets will be discarded.

Duplicate IP address—It is possible that a network could have a duplicate IP address. This typically happens when the ID addresses are configured manually. Most systems detect that a duplicate IP address has been assigned and issue an error message. If two devices are configured with the same IP address, there will be a lot of communication problems, but most likely an error message will be issued first and prevent the IP address assignment.

End-to-end connectivity—This can be verified using the **ping** command. After you have the networking devices physically connected, use the **ping** command to verify that the networking devices are communicating. **ping** uses *Internet Control Message Protocol (ICMP)* echo requests and replies to test that a device on the network is reachable. The ICMP protocol verifies that messages are being delivered. The **ping** command is available in the command window of Windows to verify the networking devices are communicating. The command structure for the **ping** command is as follows:

```
Usage ping[-t][-a][-n count)[-1 size][-f -i TTL][-v TOS] [-r count][-s
  count]
[[-j host-list]:[-k host-list][-w timeout] destination-list
Options
-t Ping the specified host until stopped
To see statistics and continue, type Control-Break
To stop, type Control-C
```

Incorrect VLAN assignment—If you suspect a misconfigured VLAN, simply use the command **show vlan brief** to check what VLAN a switch port has been assigned to. If you spot an error, then reconfigure the settings to correct the problem.

Misconfigured DHCP—Dynamic Host Configuration Protocol (DHCP) simplifies the steps for IP assignment even further. DHCP's function is to assign a pool of IP addresses to requesting clients. A possible error could be that the MAC address assigned to an IP address is misconfigured and the DHCP server doesn't know what computer to assign the IP address to since the MAC-IP addresses relationship is not known. This results in an error, and a valid IP address is not assigned from the DHCP pool of addresses.

Misconfigured DNS—*DNS* is the domain name service. DNS translates a human readable name to an IP address or an IP address to a domain name. The translation of a name to an IP address is called *forward domain name service*, and translation of an IP address to a domain name is called *reverse domain name service*. It is possible that a misconfigured DNA will prevent access to the Internet. When troubleshooting this type of problem, first check to see what the primary and secondary IP addresses for your DNS are. Verify the IP addresses are correct. The *NS record* or *Name Server record* is another place to check. This specifies the name of the authoritative name server of the domain. The record must map to a valid A record, not an IP address or a CNAME. The NS records are associated with the domain, not a particular host. Therefore, one needs to look up the name server information based on the domain. The following example demonstrates the use of the **nslookup** command to look up the NS records of the domain example.com:

```
C:\nslookup -query=NS example.com
Server:  192.168.1.1
Address:  192.168.1.1#53
Non-authoritative answer:
example.com    nameserver = a.iana-servers.net.
example.com    nameserver = b.iana-servers.net.
```

Cable placement—Cable placement is an important consideration especially when running cable in high EMF environments or next to electrical mains. Electrical noise can be induced in unshielded cable and can affect data reception. You should not suspend cabling from ceiling tiles for safety and fire regulations. The cable bends should be limited to less than four times the diameter of the cable.

Interface errors—Connecting to the Internet is possible via multiple interfaces on the computer. For example, the Internet interface could be an Internet connection to your Internet Service Provider (ISP). This typically involves a cable or DSL modem connection. The most common types of errors experienced are loss of connectivity. The problem could be as simple as a loose cable, or it could be that the system is down due to bad weather conditions or loss of power at the ISP. A good troubleshooting step is to verify that your wireless router is still functioning before passing on the blame to the ISP. You can also try rebooting your modem and/or computer to see whether this corrects the problem.

Simultaneous wired/wireless connections—Sometimes a wireless bridge might have a full-duplex wired connection on one side, but the radio side is not full-duplex. It is possible that data packets continue to be delivered on the cable connected side resulting in the buffer filling up. This is because the ACK packet is not being returned quickly. As a result, the same packet gets retransmitted.

Discovering neighboring devices/nodes—During the power-up process for a wireless router, it starts searching for any wireless signals and indicates whether the channels are unlocked or locked. Locked channels require a secure login.

Power failure/power anomalies—Temporary loss of power is not uncommon with any network. Data loss can be minimized by utilizing a UPS (Uninterruptable Power Supply). These devices can be used to keep the local system functioning until the main power is restored.

MTU/MTU black hole—MTU stands for Maximum Transmission Unit. For Ethernet networks, the MTU is 1518 bytes. An MTU black hole is a result of a misconfigured router resulting in data packets not being properly delivered. In this case the router is called an MTU black hole router.

Missing IP routes—Missing IP routes are due to misconfiguration of the router. When a routing protocol is configured, the network routes are entered for the desired destination networks. A misconfigured route results in nondelivery of the data packet. The network routes can be checked by issuing the **show ip route** command from the router's privilege EXEC mode.

NIC teaming misconfiguration—An NIC is a network interface card. Sometimes more than one NIC is installed on a computer. The purpose is to provide load balancing and fault tolerance (traffic failover). The idea of traffic failover is to keep the computer connected even if there is a failure of the NIC.

Active-active versus active-passive—This addresses the concept of providing high availability (H/A) networks. The term active/passive addresses failover and load balancing. The term active/active supports redundancy for either databases or sessions. An advantage of active/passive configuration using load balancers is providing uninterrupted service. In the active/active mode, the servers working in tandem keep requests stored in cache and as a result improve access time because the server that handled the previous request will be able to respond to the request.

4.7 Given a scenario, troubleshoot and resolve common security issues

TACACS—This stands for the Terminal Access Controller Access Control System and is an older protocol used for user authentication.

Ping of death—This is a type of denial of service attack intended to crash the victim's system or to inject malicious code onto the system. The attack is a malformed ping packet that is too large for the victim to handle and therefore causes a buffer overflow.

Firmware/OSs—It is best practice to keep the firmware of the network equipment such as routers and switches up to date. Also, patches, especially security patches, must be applied to operating systems and software applications regularly.

Misconfigured firewall—The purpose of a firewall is to prevent unauthorized access to your network. Firewall protection is available in both the Windows and MAC operating environments. If a firewall is misconfigured, meaning the rules are not configured properly, errors can occur and worse yet, the "bad guys" can gain access to your network and data. If you still suspect problems with your firewall, you should check the firewall's logging and look for errors. You might also check the security policies that have been set on the firewall.

Misconfigured ACLs/applications—Access lists (ACLs) are the basic form of firewall protection, although an access list is not stateful and is not by itself a firewall. Access lists can be configured on a router, on a true dedicated firewall, or on the host computer. The access lists consist of permit and deny statements to control traffic in and out of the network interface. There is an implicit denial at the end of an access list in Cisco routers, and this statement alone blocks all data packets. To allow other data packets that do not match the ACL's permit and deny statements to enter and exit the LAN, the command **access-list permit ip any any** must be added to the last line of an access list to explicitly allow all other data packets. If the intention is to deny other data packets that do match the permit statements, the explicit permit statement is not needed. The issue with misconfigured access lists is you may have opened a hole in the network allowing unauthorized user access. It is important that you test your own network and conduct penetration testing. A penetration test is a way to evaluate the security of the user's network. This is accomplished by trying to exploit vulnerabilities in the network. This includes identifying any potential problems with the operating systems, services, and applications as well as verifying user adherence to policies. The penetration test also validates any protection mechanisms currently in place.

Unreachable default gateway—When something like this happens, the problem could be a router has failed or the connection is down. A troubleshooting command to use is **tracert <*host*>** so that the router hops are listed and you can tell whether the gateway is reached. Make sure you either enter the default gateway's IP address or use an IP address not in the router's routing table so the data packets are sent to the default gateway.

Banner grabbing/OUI—Banner grabbing refers to error messages generated when a bad request is issued to a device in the network. The information contained in the error message might be enough for the "bad guy" to gain access to the network. It is also possible that the error message can contain its MAC address. The MAC address is 6 bytes, or 48 bits, in length. The address is displayed in 12 hexadecimal digits. The first six digits are used to indicate the vendor of the network interface, also called the **organizationally unique identifier (OUI)**, and the last six numbers form a unique value for each NIC assigned by the vendor. The OUI information lets the intruder know what kind of equipment is being used. At least for the network interface card, this provides the intruder with one piece of the puzzle about your network.

4.8 Given a scenario, troubleshoot and resolve common WAN issues

Loss of Internet connectivity—The connection to the Internet does go down on occasion. To verify that the Internet is down, try connecting to a different Internet site. If you still can't connect, then try a different computer. You need to eliminate any unknowns and the problem could possibly be with your computer, so try it and if the Internet connection is still down, you might try a different computer with a different Internet Service Provider.

Interface errors—It is important to verify that the interface to the WAN is properly configured. Next, ping the ISP's IP address. If this fails you can issue the **ping 127.0.0.1** command. This is the loopback address for your NIC. A reply back lets you know that your NIC is working. If the WAN connection is properly configured and the NIC is functioning, the problem could be with your ISP or telco (telephone company).

Split horizon—This is a technique used to prevent routing loops caused by a routing path being specified to send data packets back to the router that sent them. In split horizon, the packets are sent in a forward direction. The split horizon feature is integrated into distance vector routing protocols.

Interference—Interference problems with your WAN connection are not common, but any problems should be reported to your ISP or telco (telephone company). Interference problems can adversely affect your data throughput.

Smart jack/NIU—A smart jack is a network interface device that provides additional capabilities such as diagnostics. An NIU (Network Interface Unit) defines the demarcation point between telco and the customer's equipment (Customer Premise Equipment—CPE).

Copper line drivers/repeaters—This is primarily an issue with telco (telephone company). Land-based telephone systems use many miles of copper wire to get from the customer's site to the phone company's central office. The phone company provides line drivers and repeaters so that an acceptable signal can be received after traveling many miles.

Throttling—This is a technique used by communication carriers to regulate and manage network data traffic. The purpose of this is to minimize congestion on the network. This is also a technique used to prevent server crashes. Throttling limits upload and download capabilities.

Fair Access Policy/utilization limits—A Fair Access Policy or FAP is a company's policy used to set a network usage guideline for its users. This policy is intended for all users to receive an equitable share of network bandwidth. Also, this policy can be used to set the priority of the traffic based on the types of traffic. As a result, utilization limits can be set for users and different types of traffic.

5.0 INDUSTRY STANDARDS, PRACTICES, AND NETWORK THEORY

5.2 Explain the basics of network theory and concepts

De-multiplexing—Multiplexing is a communications system in which more than one signal is within a single channel. The process of de-multiplexing simply reverses the process and separates the multiplexed channel back into the individual channels.

Encapsulation/de-encapsulation—*Encapsulation* is a process where information is attached to the data packets in the *headers*. *De-encapsulation* is the process used when a data packet is received and the header is extracted.

Octal—This refers to the base-8 numbering system. The digits run from 0-1-2-3-4-5-6-7. It can also refer to the grouping of four numbers such as the four octets associated with an IPv4 address, 192.168.20.5, where each decimal number is represented by 8 binary numbers.

Speed—Speed is the rate in which data can be transmitted in a time interval. It currently is measured in bits per second (bps). In the old days, data transmission was modulated and transmitted over analog medium. Speed was measured as baud rate, which is a modulation rate.

Sampling size—The sampling size of digitized signals determines the dynamic range of the sampled systems. A general rule of thumb is that you get 6db/bit when sampling. Audio systems for CDs use 16-bit sampling and use an oversampling technique to provide 96db of dynamic range.

5.4 Given a scenario, deploy the appropriate wired connectivity standard

100BaseFX—This is a multimode fiber technology. It uses a 1300nm wavelength and is good for transmission lengths of 2km.

10Base2—This is a legacy coax cable network called ThinNet. The cable is terminated with BNC connectors, and the cable type is RG-58A/U.

10GBaseSR—This is a10-Gigabit Ethernet physical layer *standard* for use with multimode fibers for a short range of 300 meters to 400 meters.

10GBaseER—This is a10-Gigabit Ethernet physical layer *standard* for use with single mode fibers for extended range or reach up to 40 km.

10GBaseSW—This is a10-Gigabit Ethernet physical layer *standard* for WAN connection, which is designed for longer distance type connections like SONET by adding extra encapsulation support. The maximum distance for this standard is up to 80 km.

IEEE 1905-1-2013—This is an IEEE standard that integrates wired technologies with wireless connectivity. This standard includes the IEEE 1901 Standard for Broadcast over Power Lines.

Ethernet over HDMI—This standard provides for Ether connectivity via HDMI. The benefit is another cable is not required for an Ethernet connection. This enables multiple network devices to share a connection. Additionally this provides the potential for simplifying home theatre systems' connectivity.

Ethernet over power line—Simply put, this is a system that uses the electrical wiring in your home or business to transmit a modulated carrier signal containing Ethernet data. The technology requires an adapter connected to the home's Ethernet connection, and another adapter is connected anywhere in the house where an Ethernet connection is needed. These adapters can support data rates up to 80 Mbps.

Wiring standards—The wiring standards for modern computer networks are defined by the EIA/TIA 568-C standard. This standard defines specifications for 4-pair 100-ohm category 5e twisted-pair cabling. Defined within this standard are the CAT5e, CAT6, CAT7, and the RJ-45 (8P8C) twisted pair cable terminations.

5.5 Given a scenario, implement the appropriate policies or procedures

Consent to monitoring—Organizations are required to have a consent to monitoring policy in place. The intent is to protect the individual from unlawful observation. Most facilities also have guidelines in place about the use of cameras, particularly IP cameras. Your facility should have a checklist and training related to monitoring. All installations of cameras and their locations should be monitored, and installation should be coordinated with your organization's administration. The networking group should be involved with this so access to IP cameras is restricted.

MLA—MLA is a master license agreement that defines the owner rights, terms, and conditions of the intellectual property.

5.6 Summarize safety practices

Electrical safety—Some computers connect to the electrical outlet. You should always use caution when working with any electrical system. Best practice is to always disconnect electrical power prior to working inside any electrical device including computers. Always use caution when working with power supplies because the filter capacitors can hold a charge.

Grounding—All electrical devices should have a ground for safety. This includes the electrical devices used in computer networks, including devices mounted in the racks and the rack itself. Never remove the ground pin from an electrical device. That ground connection is there for a very good reason, to protect you.

ESD—ESD stands for electrostatic discharge. ESD can damage integrated circuits, so the technician should always use a grounding strap connected to his wrist to prevent any unwanted static discharge. The grounding strap is typically connected to the electrical ground.

Static—Any type of static discharge is undesirable around electronic systems. A static discharge can damage integrated circuits, so the technician should always use a grounding strap connected to her wrist to prevent any unwanted static discharge. The grounding strap typically connects to the electrical ground. The power should be disconnected and a grounding strap should be placed on the technician's wrist prior to opening any electronic equipment.

Installation safety—Installation safety rules are outlined in Federal Regulation 29 CFR PART 1926—SAFETY AND HEALTH REGULATIONS FOR CONSTRUCTION. Cabling installers are required to follow OSHA rules and general construction safety guidelines. It is critical that the technician be careful when climbing ladders installing racks.

Lifting equipment—Always use due caution when lifting heavy boxes. It is recommend that when lifting, you should bend at the knees and get someone to help you.

Rack installation—Racks are used in a multitude of places in network systems. The racks could be installed in closets or there could be many racks in a data center. You can also expect to have server rack frames with air blowing over the devices for cooling. Racks must be securely installed and grounded. Rack types vary for sites, but the most common are 19-inch rack frames. There also two-post racks used for smaller telecommunication equipment. Four-post racks are typically used for servers.

Placement—In a data center, you can expect the equipment to have locks on the racks for security reasons. These racks are placed in a well monitored area. You also have "hot" and "cold" aisles. The hot air from the equipment in the hot aisles is blown out of the racks and recirculates to the ceiling ducts. The cold aisles are where the air is being pulled through the equipment using its fans.

Tool safety—Tool safety is always of concern especially when power tools are involved. The technician must make sure all power tools are properly grounded. It is also important that you understand the purpose or intent of any tool you are working with. There is always a risk if you are trying to use the wrong tool for a job. Don't take shortcuts.

Building layout—Always seek advice from an expert when planning the building layout for a networking or data center. There are many issues concerning safety, power distribution/requirements, grounding, shielding, heating and cooling considerations, fire suppressant systems, security, door access control, security cameras, and video monitoring. You also want to make sure you have room for growth. An expert can help you with planning this.

Fail-open/fail-close—When systems fail, there are two ways of responding. The two ways are fail-open and fail-closed. If a systems fails-open, this means everything is left the same as it was before the failure. Fail-closed implies that the system closes down when the problem occurs. The proper response depends on the system you are working with.

5.7 Given a scenario, install and configure equipment in the appropriate location using best practices

Cable management—If you are in a large office and campus network, cable management becomes an issue. The ANSI/TIA/EIA Administrative Standard for Telecommunications Infrastructure of Commercial Buildings describes how to manage your cable installation. This standard describes how your cable structure should be managed. Some of the topics outlined in the standard include drawings, reports, work orders, labeling, grounding, fire stopping, backbone cabling, cross connects, intra- and interbuilding cabling, building records, horizontal cabling, and types of cable.

Power management—Power for a campus network or a large data center has specific needs that must be addressed. For example, how do you address the failure of a power supply? The good news is it is practical to have redundant power supplies so that the system can switch to a new power supply if there is a failure. It is also possible that the electrical power could be coming from two different sources or two separate feeds from the electric company. How do you manage the loss of one power source? The threat of the loss of power is something you need to plan for because if it can happen, it will.

Power converters—The basic power converter is the power supply that converts the AC voltage from the electric company to a DC voltage used by the networking devices. Power supplies fail, so you need to have a plan in place to replace power supplies for your various networking devices. Other examples of power converters are solar panels (convert photons to electricity) and backup generators, which convert mechanical energy to electrical energy.

Circuits—This is referring to the electrical circuits that power your clients' networking equipment or the equipment in your data center. There are many issues concerning power distribution/requirements, grounding, and shielding. Consulting with an expert is a good step.

Inverters—An inverter or a power inverter is a device that converts DC (direct current) into AC (alternating current). This enables generation of AC power for your appliances when your only power source is a DC voltage source, such as a battery.

Power redundancy—Simply put, this means that you are operating with backup power supplies and/or a backup generator. The system is typically designed to automatically switch over to the backup system if power is lost.

Device placement—Device placement in a networking facility or a data center can be important. You don't want to have your staff bumping into each other or continually having to walk long distances to fix problems. Your objective is to thoughtfully place your equipment so that access is easy, and normal operations are not impeded.

Cable trays—The purpose of cable trays is to provide a place to hold cable runs to keep the cables secured away from other items such as pipes, steam, water, people, and so on. Cable trays are found in ceilings, tunnels, and inside walls.

Rack systems—The purpose of your rack systems is to mount your equipment. While mounting the equipment make sure you have equipment properly consolidated and you have allowed sufficient access to the back side of the equipment for the technician to troubleshoot problems and make repairs/changes. You also want to make sure that cable pathways in the racks are well defined and you have provided room for growth.

Server rail racks—This provides an easy way to replace servers by simply pulling them out from the racks and installing the replacement device.

Two-post racks—Two-post racks are often used for smaller telecommunication equipment. These systems just provide two rack posts for rack mounting the equipment. There are also less expensive than racks that have doors and are fully enclosed.

Four-post racks—Four-post racks are typically used for servers and larger electronic systems. They can have open sides or do have the options for enclosures and doors.

Free-standing racks—These are just racks of different sizes and shapes that are free-standing and used for many different situations.

Labeling—Labeling is important for all aspects of your computer network and data center. To begin with, all racks should be labeled identifying the purpose of the equipment installed in the rack. For example, maybe the rack houses the telecommunication equipment that connects to your WAN connection. Another example is to label names for your server that identify the purpose and possibly the name of the server machine. Another important label is for cabling. Both cable ends or wall plates should be labeled with some identifying marks that correspond to your building drawings. This makes it possible for the technician to easily identify the cable and its path.

Port labeling—When labeling your equipment and cabling, develop a standardized format that contains all the information you will need at a later time. Remember, your facility will eventually have a lot of equipment and cables, and being able to easily identify these will be of great benefit to the technical staff. Also make sure the labels correspond to your drawings.

System labeling—These labels are important so that the technical staff are referencing the same system. A large facility will eventually have many systems doing similar tasks, and being able to identify the correct system will simplify your work.

Circuit labeling—In this case, we are referring to labeling your electrical power circuits. This is important for documenting breakers that trip and identifying why this happened. It could be that you have too many devices on the circuit. You also want to have circuits labeled so you know exactly what systems are being affected if the breaker has to be shut off.

Naming conventions—You will probably want to develop a naming strategy for your networking equipment. For example, maybe your computers are named according to the building and room number and then machine number. For example brown-rm35-275. This makes it easy for the technician to easily identify the location of the machine.

Patch panel labeling—You need to label all patch panels so you can easily identify the source and destination when connecting a jumper cable. The normal convention is that sources (outputs) are on top, and destination (inputs) are on the bottom.

Rack monitoring—Critical systems need to be monitored for possible tampering or just to have visual confirmation why something is being changed. You might be monitoring who entered certain locked cabinets. A quick review of the trouble reports should quickly explain who and why someone was in the rack.

Rack security—The racks could house equipment that processes secure data or could be connected to a secure connection, and monitoring the rack would be mandatory. Racks can also provide protection against unauthorized access and prevent unauthorized changes to the network.

Intermediate distribution frame—An intermediate distribution frame or IDF connects back to the main distribution frame (MDF). This wiring closet typically exists when an MDF cannot support the distance of the cable run.

Air flow—In data centers, server racks must be positioned in such a way to take advantage of air flow. Racks are positioned with alternating cold aisles and hot aisles, where equipment fans can draw cold air from a cold aisle and vent its hot air to a hot aisle.

5.8 Explain the basics of change management procedures

Configuration procedures—What operating system are you going to install on the many computers you manage? What problems do you foresee if you upgrade the OS? What about people's preferences? How will this configuration change affect your company? The bottom line is you need to have a procedure in place to manage changes to your system and your equipment so your questions and concerns can be addressed. It is important that your changes be well documented.

Rollback process—You just made changes to your network, but it doesn't work properly. In your configuration process, you want to have a plan for a rollback to the previous version or hardware. Good documentation is still a must, and notifying all affected personnel is extremely important.

Potential impact—Anytime you make changes, particularly technical changes, it is going impact your staff and your system. What if you are planning to make the move to cloud-based services? How is this going to impact your staff and your overall operation? Don't make changes without putting a lot of thought into it. The objective is to plan your transitions carefully to avoid major disturbances with your budget, your technical operations, and your staff.

Notification—It is of paramount importance that you make sure all users of your system are notified of any planned downtimes for scheduled maintenance and upgrades. It is also equally important to notify your users, staff, and help desk of any plans to discontinue support for software or hardware or your plan to upgrade to a newer software or hardware technology.

Approval process—Make sure you have an approval process in place to monitor changes. You always want to have a record that the change was approved. This can be online or a paper trail, but it is important to keep a record. The approval process should outline the steps for approval and who should approve each step in the process. The approval process can also outline what steps are to be taken if the request is withdrawn or rejected.

Authorized downtime—It is important that planned downtime be authorized. You need to have an approval process in place to track this. It is also important to know what downtime is actually costing you and your organization. You also want to know whether a recovery time is associated with the planned downtime. Downtime is unavoidable, but the objective is to keep this to a minimum. It is also important to know how much downtime your organization can afford. Some highly critical systems can't afford any downtime.

Notification of change—If a change is planned for your organization, make sure your support staff, the help desk personnel, and your customers are aware of this change. It is also a good idea to let everyone know what the possible impact of the change might be.

5.9 Compare and contrast the following ports and protocols

2427/2727 MGCP—This is the Media Gateway Protocol. The Media Gateway Control Protocol (MGCP) is a protocol used within a distributed Voice over IP system. This is also called H.248, and its purpose is to handle signal and session management that is used in real-time multimedia conferences. It essentially provides a way to convert data from a packet-switched network to a circuit-switched network.

PROBLEMS

Section 1.0—Network Architecture (supplement)

1. What is the purpose of HIDS?

   a. This system identifies misuse or potential attacks by matching the data packets against known signatures that have been classified as bad.

   b. A device that sits between the campus network and the outside network. The device is set up so that all data traffic, incoming and outgoing, passes through it.

   c. This is an intrusion detection system that monitors the computer system for changes, such as system file modifications, changes to the registry, file changes, and system logs.

   d. All of the above.

2. What is the purpose of a content filter?

   a. This is a web filter appliance that monitors the web traffic via both HTTP and HTTPS and matches it against the database. If an inappropriate website is detected, it is either discarded or the user is redirected to a security web page for further action.

   b. This device is used to stop or prevent malicious attacks that it detects by interacting with the firewall.

   c. This device identifies misuse and any anomaly on the network by matching the network packets with its IPS signatures for known attacks or activities that are classified as bad.

   d. This device is configured to prevent malicious activity on the host system, and if an unauthorized change or activity is detected, an alert is issued.

3. What is the purpose of SNAT?

   a. This is used to ensure that a DHCP client always receives the same IP address when it reconnects.

   b. This device enables private network data traffic to go out to the Internet, so it can reach the public network through a single gateway public IP address.

   c. This allows any host on the "outside" of the network to get to a single host on the "inside" of the network.

   d. None of the above.

4. What is the purpose of scopes ?

   a. This step is used to authenticate the user, establish the session, and set policies.

   b. This allows any host on the "outside" of the network to get to a single host on the "inside" of the network.

   c. The purpose of this is to authenticate users and network devices in domain environments.

   d. This is a grouping of IP addresses that use the DHCP (Dynamic Host Control Protocol) service for a group of computers located on a subnet.

5. Define MPLS.

   a. This is a technique for combining multiple signals on laser beams for transmission.

   b. This device is used to connect two UTP cables.

   c. This is a data-carrying service for telecommunication networks that route data from one network node to the next based on labels for short path rather than long network addresses.

   d. These devices allow a single fiber to be split into two outputs, and multiple input fibers can be combined into one output fiber.

6. What is near field communications?

   a. NFC systems are computer-based systems associated with the monitoring and control of industrial processes.

   b. NFC is a set of communication protocols used to enable two electronic devices to communicate.

   c. NFC systems are designed to withstand the harsh environment of industry.

   d. NFC systems are designed to operate and monitor the critical industrial infrastructure.

7. What is an ICS server?

   a. ICS systems are computer-based systems associated with the monitoring and control of industrial processes.

   b. This is a data-carrying service for telecommunication networks that route data from one network node to the next based on labels for short path rather than long network addresses.

   c. Industrial control systems servers are designed to withstand the harsh environment of industry.

   d. None of the above.

8. What is a medianet?

    a. This is an intelligent network that has been optimized for high traffic video applications.

    b. This is a system that has multiple subsystem controllers geographically dispersed throughout the network.

    c. This is a control unit designed to support SCADA remote stations.

    d. This device is used for control of machinery in manufacturing and related industries.

9. What is the purpose of autoconfiguration?

    a. This option allows the router to choose its own host identifier (rightmost 64 bits) from the EUI-64 (Extended Universal Identifier-64) of the interface.

    b. This is an IPv6 feature. With IPv6, a computer can automatically configure its network settings without a DHCP server by sending a solicitation message to its IPv6 router.

    c. This is a data-carrying service for telecommunication networks that route data from one network node to the next based on labels for short path rather than long network addresses.

    d. None of the above.

10. What is EUI 64?

    a. This is a tunneling protocol that provides IPv6 connectivity for IPv6 capable devices that are on an IPv4 platform.

    b. This is a data-carrying service for telecommunication networks that route data from one network node to the next based on labels for short path rather than long network addresses.

    c. This is an intelligent network that has been optimized for high traffic video applications.

    d. This option allows the router to choose its own host identifier (rightmost 64 bits) from the EUI-64 (Extended Universal Identifier-64) of the interface.

11. What is route redistribution?

    a. This is a preferred method for router IP packets.

    b. Routing redistribution is the technique of injecting routes from one routing protocol to another routing protocol.

    c. This is the replacement for RIP.

    d. This is a low overhead solution to routing.

12. What is HSRP?

   a. This is the Hot Standby Router Protocol. This protocol enables a framework of routers so that a default gateway is always available, hence the status of "Hot Standby."

   b. This is the High Source Routing Protocol, and this protocol enables a framework of routers so that a default gateway is always available.

   c. This is the Hot Standby Router Protocol, and it provides automatic assignment of routers to hosts participating in the network.

   d. All of the above.

13. Select three QoS issues for VoIP networks. (Select three of the following.)

   a. Route selection

   b. Jitter

   c. Shortest path bridging

   d. Network latency and packet loss

   e. Queuing

   f. Unified communications

14. What is a virtual firewall?

   a. This device is built to handle any type of failure.

   b. This network device is used to provide access to multiple servers.

   c. This network device provides access to the network and in particular the Internet.

   d. This is a network device running in a virtual environment. This device provides the same functionality as a physical firewall.

15. Which of the following is true about the cloud?

   a. The cloud is just another name for the Internet.

   b. Setting up and physically connecting to the cloud is virtually the same for all operating systems (OS) and computers.

   c. Access to the cloud can be limited for users.

   d. The advantage of the cloud is the reduced overhead.

Section 2—Network Operations (supplement)

16. What is the name for an operation used to enable an agent to notify the SNMP network management station (NMS) of significant events?

   a. SIEM

   b. MIB

   c. Walk

   d. TRAP

17. What is SYSLOG? (Select two.)

    a. IT security system that can provide a holistic view and real-time analysis of an organization's IT security.

    b. It is a standard protocol used to collect log messages sent from devices to a server running a SYSLOG service or daemon.

    c. Servers run on UDP port 514 or TCP port 601.

    d. None of the above.

18. What is NAC?

    a. This is an IT security system that can provide a holistic view and real-time analysis of an organization's IT security.

    b. It is a security mechanism that can be implemented on a network to register, authenticate, authorize, and enforce security policies on all endpoint devices before they are allowed to access the network.

    c. This is a network device running in a virtual environment.

    d. All of the above.

19. Which of the following applies to "legacy systems?" (Select the best answer.)

    a. Legacy systems can be categorized as "end-of-life" or "end-of-support."

    b. Legacy systems should be decommissioned as soon as possible.

    c. A legacy system is more vulnerable and susceptible to security hacks and exploitations.

    d. One of the biggest security risks for a legacy system is there will not be a firmware, hardware, or software update.

    e. All of the above.

20. This is a computing environment specifically set up to gather information regarding network attacks and intrusions and to study the vulnerabilities of a system.

    a. Honeypot

    b. SCADA

    c. NAC

    d. Scope

21. Define VTP.

    a. VTP or VLAN Tunneling Protocol is Cisco's proprietary protocol used to manage and propagate the VLAN definitions of all the VTP-capable switches.

    b. VTP or VLAN Tunneling Protocol is Cisco's proprietary protocol used to manage and store the VLAN definitions of all the VTP-capable switches.

    c. VTP or VLAN Trunking Protocol is Cisco's proprietary protocol used to manage and propagate the VLAN definitions of all the VTP-capable switches.

    d. This means the same subnet can span different physical ports or user locations. This allows for greater flexibility to have many locations sharing the same subnet.

22. This allows for multiple physical ports on an Ethernet switch to be bundled as one single logical channel.

    a. Port mirroring

    b. Port enabling

    c. Port sharing

    d. Port bonding

23. What is VLAN pooling?

    a. This is a technique where a MAC address is shared with multiple computers in the same VLAN.

    b. VLAN pooling is a solution offered by many wireless manufacturers to deal with the large number of connecting wireless devices, and every device is required to have an IP address.

    c. VLAN pooling is a solution offered by many wireless manufacturers to deal with connecting wireless devices, and every device is required to have a MAC address.

    d. This is a technique where an IP address is shared with multiple computers in the same VLAN.

24. Define Goodput. (Select two.)

    a. Goodput refers to the actual wireless data throughput as measured by an application on the end device.

    b. Goodput is the underlying wireless control protocol for Cisco APs to communicate with wireless controllers.

    c. Goodput is a way to represent the actual transmission rate of a wireless connection, which is not the maximum theoretical transmission rate.

    d. Goodput is the underlying wireless control protocol for Cisco APs to communicate with Ethernet controllers.

25. Define device density.

    a. This defines the number of Ethernet clients.

    b. This is defined by Thick clients.

    c. This means the same subnet can span different physical ports or user locations.

    d. This is the number of connecting wireless clients.

Section 3—Network Security (supplement)

26. What is a botnet?

    a. This is an IT group responsible for servicing all organizations within a business. Also call a BizNet.

    b. This is an attack where an attacker can seamlessly place itself in the middle of the conversation of others.

    c. This is a group of infected or compromised computers on the Internet that is being used to launch coordinated denial of service attacks against another system on the network.

    d. This is a technique used in man-in-the-middle attacks.

27. What is a type of distributed denial of service attack that is deliberately toward a specific target and is orchestrated by a controller source like the command and control server in a botnet?

    a. Evil twin

    b. Coordinated attack

    c. Reflective attack

    d. War chalking

28. What is Bluejacking? (Select two.)

    a. These are attacks on Bluetooth devices.

    b. This is an attack to gain unauthorized access of another Bluetooth device over the Bluetooth connection with the intention to obtain information stored on the Bluetooth device.

    c. This is a process in which attackers search Bluetooth devices for an open wireless network connection, so that they can gain more access to collect information or data of connecting users.

    d. This is the exploitation of a valid Bluetooth device with the intent to gain unauthorized access.

29. Define session hijacking.

    a. This is an attack to gain information or resources that are only available in specific VLANs.

    b. This is generally referred to as a computer, a group of computers, or a part of the network that has been adversely impacted by an untrusted source.

    c. This is an exploitation of vulnerability in software that is unknown to the developer.

    d. This is the exploitation of a valid computer session to gain unauthorized access to information or services on a computer.

30. What is TEMPEST? (Select the correct answer.)

   a. This is a standard for computer systems certification commenced by the US government in the late 1950s.

   b. This refers to the exploitation of vulnerability in government software that is unknown to the developer.

   c. This specifies the amount of Electromagnetic Interference (EMI) and Radio Frequency Interference (RFI) or RF emanation emitted by a device.

   d. The purpose of TEMPEST is to shield the wireless RF signal within the area and not divulge intelligence about system information.

31. What is TLS? (Select two.)

   a. This is used by the **ping** command to verify packet delivery.

   b. This is an authentication protocol for Windows Active Directory.

   c. This is the successor to the Secure Sockets Layer (SSL), and it is designed to ensure the privacy between the communicating parties.

   d. TLS ensures that no third party may eavesdrop or tamper with any messages between a server and a client.

32. What is Unified Threat Management (UTM)?

   a. This is generally referred to as a computer, a group of computers, or a part of the network that has been unified.

   b. This is the authentication protocol for Windows Active Directory.

   c. This is an all-in-one solution that integrates a wide range of security features into one appliance.

   d. None of the above.

33. This is a special segmented network provided to visitors to access the Internet and certain unrestricted networks. (Select one.)

   a. Persistent agent

   b. Guest network

   c. Posture

   d. Virtual segment

34. What is single sign-on? (Select the best answer.)

   a. Single sign-on (SSO) is a process that permits users to access different systems after one successful authentication.

   b. Single sign-on (SSO) is a process that permits guests to access different systems.

   c. This is used to control or minimize internal access by limiting the number of times you can connect to a system.

   d. All of the above.

Section 4—Troubleshooting (supplement)

35. What is meant by divide and conquer?

    a. This is a basic troubleshooting approach for UTP cable.

    b. Using this troubleshooting approach, an OSI layer is selected and tested for its functionality. If this layer is good, then the technician tests the next layer, which could be higher or lower.

    c. A basic function related to cabling that is used to verify two ends are connected.

    d. All of the above.

36. What is a looking glass site?

    a. A site used to run connectivity tests.

    b. A site used to obtain routing information related to the network's backbone and efficiency.

    c. A network site that has a fragile connection.

    d. A site used so a speed test can be run to measure a computer's upload and download speeds.

37. What are the most common frequency channels used in wireless communication?

    a. 1,6,11

    b. 2,7,9

    c. 1,2,3

    d. 1, 5, 10

38. What is the operating frequency for 802.11a?

    a. 5 GHz

    b. 2.4 GHz

    c. 2.4 GHz and 5 GHz

39. What is the operating frequency for 802.11b?

    a. 5 GHz

    b. 2.4 GHz

    c. 2.4 GHz and 5 GHz

40. What is the operating frequency for 802.11n?

    a. 5 GHz

    b. 2.4 GHz

    c. 2.4 GHz and 5 GHz

41. What is the operating frequency for 802.11ac?

    a. 5 GHz

    b. 2.4 GHz

    c. 2.4 GHz and 5 GHz

42. What is LWAPP?

    a. The system provides for the assignment of a primary, secondary, and even a tertiary controller for the wireless network.

    b. This protocol can be used to simplify the control of multiple wireless access points at the same time.

    c. This is the Lightweight Access Protocol.

    d. All of the above.

43. Which of the following is true for MTU? (Select two.)

    a. MTU stands for Maximum Transmission Unit. For Ethernet networks, the MTU is 1518 bytes.

    b. This stands for Multimedia Transcriber Unit. It is assigned to data packets to avoid black holes.

    c. A misconfigured MTU results in nondelivery of the data packet.

    d. An MTU black hole is a result of a misconfigured router resulting in data packets not being properly delivered.

44. Which of the following are issues with a misconfigured firewall?

    a. A bad request is issued to the network.

    b. Timing on stateful connection is affected.

    c. Penetration testing will be useless.

    d. Errors can occur and worse yet, the "bad guys" can gain access to your network and data.

45. What is banner grabbing and why is this important? (Choose two.)

    a. Refers to error messages generated when a bad request is issued to a device in the network.

    b. This is used to verify that a penetration test was successful.

    c. This is used to verify the integrity of the MAC address.

    d. The information contained in the error message might be enough for the "bad guy" to gain access to the network.

46. Which of the following is a technique used to prevent routing loops caused by a routing path being specified to send data packets back to the router that sent them?

a. Loop grabbing

b. TTL

c. Throttling

d. Split horizon

Section 5—Industry standards, practice, and network theory (supplement)

47. What is Ethernet over HDMI?

a. This made RJ-45 connectors compatible with HDMI.

b. This made 8P8C connectors compatible with HDMI.

c. This is intended to speed up HDMI network connections.

d. This standard provides for Ether connectivity via HDMI.

48. This is a system that uses your electrical wiring in your home or business to transmit a modulated carrier signal containing Ethernet data.

a. Ethernet over 120

b. Ethernet over AC

c. Ethernet over power line

d. Ethernet over zip line

49. What is the name for the wiring standards for modern computer networks?

a. IEEE 802.1

b. IEEE 802.11

c. EIA/TIA 568-C

d. EIA/TIA 395-B

50. What is the purpose of a consent to monitoring policy? (Select the best answer.)

a. The intent is to protect the individual from excessive oversight.

b. To ensure the IT group adheres to copyright laws.

c. To maintain oversight of computer installations.

d. The intent is to protect the individual from unlawful observation.

51. This is the power supply that converts the AC voltage from the electric company to a DC voltage used by the networking devices. (Select two.)

a. Power inverter

b. Inverter

c. Induction system

d. Sweeping system

52. Why is labeling important? (Select the best answer.)

    a. All racks should be labeled identifying the purpose of the equipment installed in the rack.

    b. Label names for your server that identify the purpose and possibly the name of the server machine.

    c. Cable ends or wall plates should be labeled with some identifying marks that correspond to your building drawings.

    d. All of the above.

53. What is the rollback process?

    a. A plan to decrease data storage

    b. A plan to make room for upgrades

    c. A plan for a rollback to the previous version or hardware

    d. None of the above

54. What is the purpose of the Media Gateway Protocol and the port numbers?

    a. MGCP is a protocol used within a distributed Voice over IP system. It uses ports 2427/2727.

    b. MGCP is a protocol used within data storage for multimedia applications. It uses ports 2001/2002.

    c. MGCP is a protocol used for distributed Internet connections. It uses ports 1298/1398.

    d. MGCP is a protocol used within a distributed Voice over IP system. It uses ports 2427/2428.

GLOSSARY

? The help command that can be used at any prompt in the command line interface for the Cisco IOS software

"Hello" Packets Used in the OSPF protocol to verify that the links are still communicating

10GBASE-T 10GB over twisted-pair copper

3G/4G 3G (third generation) was developed to provide broadband network wireless services. The standard defining 3G wireless is called international mobile communications, or IMT 2000. 4G (fourth generation) is the successor to 3G technology and provides download speeds of 100Mbps.

6to4 Prefix A technique that enables IPv6 hosts to communicate over the IPv4 Internet

AAAA (Quad-A) Record The DNS record for IPv6

Absorption Light interaction with the atomic structure of the fiber material; also involves the conversion of optical power to heat

Acceptable Use Policy (AUP) Defines the constraints and practices the user must agree to in order to have access to the network.

Access Lists (ACLs) A basic form of firewall protection

Access Point A transceiver used to interconnect a wireless and a wired LAN

ACK Acknowledgement packet

Ad Hoc Another term used to describe an independent network

Address Resolution Protocol (ARP) Used to map an IP address to its MAC address

Administratively Down Indicates that the router interface has been shut off by the administrator

ADSL (Asymmetric DSL) A service providing up to 1.544Mbps from the user to the service provider and up to 8Mbps back to the user from the service provider

Advertise The sharing of route information

AES Advance Encryption Standard

AES Advanced Encryption Standard

Aging Time The length of time a MAC address remains assigned to a port

AH Authentication Header

Alien Crosstalk (AXT) Unwanted signal coupling from one permanent link to another

Anycast Address Is obtained from a list of addresses

APIPA Automatic Private IP Addressing

Application Layer Interacts with application programs that incorporate a communication component such as your Internet browser and email

Area 0 In OSPF, this is the root area and is the backbone for the network.

Areas The partition of a large OSPF network into smaller OSPF networks

ARIN American Registry for Internet Numbers

ARP Cache Temporary storage of MAC addresses recently contacted

ARP Reply A network protocol where the MAC address is returned

ARP Table Another name for the ARP cache

ARP Address Resolution Protocol

ARP Address Resolution Protocol, used to map an IP address to its MAC address

ARPAnet Advanced Research Projects Agency network

AS Autonomous systems

ASN Autonomous systems number

Association Indicates that the destination address is for a networking device connected to one of the ports on the bridge

Asymmetric Operation Describes the modem operation when the data transfer rates to and from the service provider differ

Attenuation (Insertion Loss) The amount of loss in the signal strength as it propagates down a wire or fiber strand

Auto-negotiation Protocol used by interconnected electronic devices to negotiate a link speed

Backbone Main fiber distribution. The primary path for data traffic to and from destinations and sources in the campus network

Backscatter Refers to the reflection of the radio waves striking the RFID tag and reflecting back to the transmitter source

Balanced Mode Neither wire in the wire pairs connects to ground

Basic Service Set (BSS) Term used to describe an independent network

Beacon Used to identify a wireless link and to verify the integrity of a wireless link

Beamforming A technique used to direct transmission of the radio signal to a specific device

BGP Border Gateway Protocol

Biometric Systems Measure and analyze specific characteristics of the human body for the purpose of authentication

BOOTP Bootstrap Protocol

Bottlenecking Another term for network congestion

Bridge Protocol Data Unit (BPDU) Used by switches to share information with other switches that are participating in the Spanning-Tree Protocol

Bridge A networking device that uses the MAC address to forward data and interconnect two LANs

Bridging Table List of MAC addresses and port locations for hosts connected to the bridge ports

Broadcast Domain Any broadcast sent out on the network is seen by all hosts in this domain.

Broadcast Domain Any network broadcast sent over the network will be seen by all networking devices in this domain.

Broadcast Storm Excessive amounts of broadcasts

Broadcast Transmission of data by a hub to all devices connected to its ports

Broadcast Transmission of the data to all connected devices

Brute Force Attack Attacker uses every possible combination of characters for the password

Buffer Overflow Happens when a program tries to put more data into a buffer than it was configured to hold netstat -a -b   (a) Command used to display the ports currently open on a Windows operating system and (b) used to display the executable involved in creating the connection or listening port

Building Entrance The point where the external cabling and wireless services interconnect with the internal building cabling

Bus Topology The computers share the media (co-axial cable) for data transmission

BWA Broadband wireless access

Cable Modem A modem that can use the high bandwidth of a cable television system to deliver high-speed data to and from the service provider

Caches The block of memory set aside for temporary storage of information

Campus Network A collection of two or more interconnected LANs in a limited geographic area

Campus Network Interconnected LANs within a limited geographic area

Carrier Ethernet Another name for Metro Ethernet

CAT6 (category 6) Twisted-pair cables capable of carrying up to 1000Mbps (1 gigabit) of data up to a length of 100 meters

CAT7/7a and CAT6a UTP cable standards that support 10GB date rates for a length of 100 meters

CCIE Cisco Certified Internetwork Expert

CCMP Counter Mode with Cipher Block Chaining Message Authentication Code Protocol

CCNA Cisco Certified Network Associate

CCNP Cisco Certified Network Professional

CDMA (Code Division Multiple Access) This is a communications system in which spread-spectrum techniques are used to multiplex more than one signal within a single channel. In this case, each device uses a different binary sequence to modulate the carrier, spreading the spectrum of the waveform (spread-spectrum). The signals are separated at the receiver by using a "correlator" that accepts only the signal from the selected binary sequence.

CFR Code of Federal Regulations

CHAP Challenge Handshake Authentication Protocol

CIDR Block The grouping of two or more class networks together; also called supernetting

CIDR Classless interdomain routing

Cisco IOS Cisco Internet Operating System, the operating software used in all Cisco routers

Cisco Network Assistant (CNA) A management software tool from Cisco that simplifies switch configuration and troubleshooting

Cladding Material surrounding the core, which must have a lower index of refraction to keep the light in the core

Class A, B, C, D, and E The five classes of IPv4

Class Network Address The network portion of the IP address based on the class of the network

Classful Addressing The network portion of a particular network address

Classful The IP and subnet addresses are within the same network

Client/Server Network The server handles multiple requests from multiple clients for multiple services.

Client Computer connected to the network that accesses services from the server

Cloud Service or Cloud Computing An outsourced and hosted computing environment that delivers IT services to users via a network

Cloud Another name for the Internet.

CNAME Record (Canonical Name Record) Generally called an alias of a hostname

CNAME Used to specify that a domain name is an alias for another domain

Color Map The specification of which wire color connects to which pin on the connector

COM1, COM2... The computer's serial communication ports

Command Line Interface (CLI) The interface type used for inputting commands and configuring devices such as routers

Configuration BPDU Used by switches to elect the "root" switch

configure terminal (conf t) Command to enter the switch's terminal configuration mode

configure terminal (conf t) The command to enter the router's terminal configuration mode

Connection-Oriented Protocol Establishes a network connection, manages the delivery of data, and terminates the connection

Console Cable A cable that connects a router's console port to a computer's serial port

Content Addressable Memory (CAM) A table of MAC addresses and port mapping used by the switch to identify connected networking devices

contiguous network Means the networks and routes must have the same class network address

copy run start The command for copying the running-configuration to the startup-configuration

Core The core is an independent actual processing unit, which is responsible for reading and executing program instructions.

Country Domain Usually two letters, such as United States (.us) or Canada (.ca), that define the location of the domain server for that country

Cross-connect A space where you are going to take one or multiple cables and connect them to one or more cables or equipment

Crossover Cable Transmit and receiver wire pairs are crossed

Crossover Transmit and receive signal pairs are crossed to properly align the transmit signal on one device with the receive signal on the other device

Crosstalk Signal coupling in a cable

CSMA/CA Carrier sense multiple access/collision avoidance

CSMA/CD The Ethernet LAN media-access method, carrier sense multiple access with collision detection

CSU/DSU The channel service unit/data service unit

Cut-Through The data packet is forwarded to the destination as soon as the destination MAC address has been read.

Data Link Layer Handles error recovery, flow control (synchronization), and sequencing

DB-25 25-pin connector

DB-9 9-pin connector

DCE Data Communications Equipment (the serial interface responsible for clocking)

Default Gateway Address The IP address of the networking device used to forward data that needs to leave the LAN

Demilitarized Zones (DMZs) Used to isolate the servers

Denial of Service (DoS) A service is being denied to a computer, network, or server

Dense Wavelength Division Multiplex (DWDM) Incorporates the propagation of several wavelengths in the 1550-nm range for a single fiber

DES, 3DES Data Encryption Standard, Triple Data Encryption Standard

Deterministic Access to the network is provided at fixed time intervals

DHCP Dynamic Host Configuration Protocol

Dictionary Attack Uses known passwords and many variations (upper- and lowercase and combinations) to try to log in to your account

Diffie-Hellman Key generation algorithm

Directed Broadcast The broadcast is sent to a specific subnet.

Discrete Multitone (DMT) A multicarrier technique used to transport digital data over copper telephone lines

Dispersion Compensating Fiber Acts like an equalizer, canceling dispersion effects and yielding close to zero dispersion in the 1550-nm region

Dispersion Broadening of a light pulse as it propagates through a fiber strand

Distance Vector Protocol A routing algorithm that periodically sends the entire routing table to its neighboring or adjacent router

Distributed Feedback (DFB) Laser A more stable laser suitable for use in DWDM systems

DL Diode laser

DNS Domain name service

DOCSIS Data Over Cable Service Interface Specification

Domain Registrar An organization that is authorized to register Internet domain names

DS Digital signal

DS-0 to DS-3; T1 to T3 Common telecommunication data rates

DSL Digital subscriber line

DSSS Direct sequence spread spectrum

DTE Data Terminal Equipment (the serial interface designed for connecting to a CSU/DSU to outside digital communication services)

Dynamic Assignment MAC addresses are assigned to a port when a host is connected

Dynamic Routing Protocols The routing table is dynamically updated to account for loss or changes in routes or changes in data traffic

Dynamic VLAN Ports are assigned to a VLAN based on either the computer's MAC address or the username of the client logged on to the computer

EAP Emergency action plan

EAP Extensible Authentication Protocol

eBGP External Border Gateway Protocol

Echo Request Part of the ICMP protocol that requests a reply from a computer

Edge EDGE (Enhanced Data GSM Evolution) provides download speeds of 384Kbps.

EIA/TIA 568-B The standard that defines the six subsystems of a structured cabling system

EIA Electronic Industries Alliance

EIGRP Enhanced Interior Gateway Routing Protocol

E-LAN Service Type (E-LAN) Provides connectivity to two or more subscriber sites using the same EVC

E-Line Service Type (E-Line)   Provides a point-to-point Ethernet Virtual Connection between two UNIs

ELTCTL   Equal Level Transverse Conversion Transfer Loss

EMI   Electromagnetic interference

enable   The command used to enter the router's privileged mode

Endpoint PSE   Example is the source port on an Ethernet switch that connects to the PD

Enterprise Network   Term used to describe the network used by a large company

Entrance Facilities (EF)   A room set aside for complex electronic equipment

Equipment Room (ER)/Backbone Cabling   Cabling that interconnects telecommunication closets in the same building and between buildings

Error Threshold   The point where the number of errors in the data packets has reached a threshold and the switch changes from the cut-through to the store-and-forward mode

ESP   Encapsulating Security Protocol

Ethernet Service Definition   Defines the Ethernet service types

Ethernet Virtual Connection (EVC)   An association of two or more UNIs

E-Tree Service Type (E-Tree)   Provides more of a hub-and-spoke environment or a root-and-leaf environment

Event   A disturbance in the light propagating down a fiber span that results in a disturbance on the OTDR trace

Extended Service Set (ESS)   The use of multiple access points to extend user mobility

F/UTP   Foil over twisted-pair cabling

FastEthernet Port (FA0/0, FA0/1, FA0/2,...)   Naming of the FastEthernet ports on the router

FastEthernet   An Ethernet system operating at 100Mbps

FERPA   Family Educational Rights and Privacy Act, a federal law that requires all educational institutions to protect the privacy of student education records

FHSS   Frequency hopping spread spectrum

Fiber Bragg Grating   A short strand of modified fiber that changes the index of refraction and minimizes intersymbol interference

Fiber Cross-connect   Optical patch panel used to interconnect fiber cables

Fiber, Light Pipe, Glass   Terms used to describe a fiber-optic strand

Firewall Protection   Used to prevent unauthorized access to your network

Firewall   Used in computer networks for protecting the network

FISMA   Federal Information Security Management Act, a federal law that was developed to protect government information

Flat Network   A network where the LANs share the same broadcast domain

Flooding   The term used to describe what happens when a switch doesn't have the destination MAC address stored in CAM

Forward Domain Name Service   Translation of a name to an IP address

FPP   Fire prevention plan

Frame   Provides grouping of the information for transmission

FTTB   Fiber to the business

FTTC   Fiber to the curb

FTTD   Fiber to the desktop

FTTH   Fiber to the home

Full Channel   Consists of all the link elements from the wall plate to the hub or switch

Full Duplex   Computer system can transmit and receive at the same time

Full IPv6 Address   All 32 hexadecimal positions contain a value other than 0.

Fusion Splicing A long-term method where two fibers are fused or welded together

Gateway of Last Resort The IP address of the router in your network where data packets with unknown routes should be **forwarded**

Gateway Describes the networking device that enables hosts in a LAN to connect to networks (and hosts) outside the LAN

GBIC Gigabit interface converter

Gigabit Ethernet 1000Mbps Ethernet

GLBA Gramm-Leach-Bliley Act, a federal law that requires all financial institutions to protect customer financial information data

Graded-index Fiber The index of refraction is gradually varied with a parabolic profile

GRE Generic Routing Encapsulation

Guest Machine Another name for the virtual computer

Half-Duplex The communications device can transmit or receive but not at the same time

Hand-off When the user's computer establishes an association with another access point

HDLC High-level data link control, a synchronous proprietary protocol

Hex Hexadecimal, base 16

HIPAA Health Insurance Portability and Accountability Act, a federal law that requires all health-related agencies to protect the personal identifiable information (PII) of patients

Hopping Sequence The order of frequency changes

Horizontal Cabling Cabling that extends out from the telecommunications closet into the LAN work area

Horizontal Cross-connect (HC) The connection between the building distributors and the horizontal cabling to the work area or workstation outlet—another term used for the HC is the floor distributors (FD)

Host Address Same as host number

Host Machine Another name for the physical machine

Host Number The portion of the IP address that defines the location of the networking device connected to the network; also called the host address

Hostname The name assigned to a networking device

Hotspots A limited geographic area that provides wireless access for the public

HSPA+ HSPA+ (Evolved High-Speed Packet Access) has been developed to provide network speeds comparable to LTE networks. Theoretical speeds for download are said to be 168Mbps and uplink 22Mbps.

HSSI High-speed serial interface

Hub Broadcasts the data it receives to all devices connected to its ports

HVAC Heating, ventilation, and air conditioning

Hybrid Echo Cancellation Circuit Removes the transmitted signal from the receive signal

Hyper-V A virtualization program that's part of the Windows operating systems

Hypervisor Used for managing and controlling the underlying physical hardware with the associated virtual hardware

IANA The agency that assigns IP addresses to computer networks

IANA The Internet Assigned Numbers Authority

iBGP Internal Border Gateway Protocol

IC Interconnect fibers branch exchange—item D shows the jumpers connecting the main fiber cross-connect (item B) to the active equipment (item C)

ICANN The Internet Corporation of Assigned Names and Numbers

ICMP Internet Control Message Protocol

IDC Intermediate distribution closet

IEEE 802.3an-2006 10GBASE-T The standard for 10Gbps

IEEE Institute of Electrical and Electronics Engineers, one of the major standards-setting bodies for technological development

IETF   Internet Engineering Task Force

IGMP   Internet Group Message Protocol

IKE   Internet Key Exchange

Inbound Data Traffic   Data traffic entering the network

Index-matching Gel   A jellylike substance that has an index of refraction much closer to glass than to air

Infrared Light   Light extending from 680 nm up to the wavelengths of the microwaves

Infrastructure as a Service (IaaS)   Focuses on the facilities and infrastructure within the data center and the virtualization and abstraction layer that exists on top of the physical facilities and infrastructure

Intermediate Cross-connect (IC)   Also called the building distributor (BD), this is the building's connection point to the campus backbone. The IC links the MC to the horizontal cross-connect (HC).

Internet Layer   Defines the protocols used for addressing and routing data packets

Intranet   An internal network that provides file and resource sharing but is not accessed from the Internet

IP (Internet Protocol)   Defines the addressing used to identify the source and destination addresses of data packets being delivered over an IP network

IP Internetwork   A network that uses IP addressing for identifying devices connected to the network

ip route   The router configuration command for manually setting the next hop IP address

IP Tunnel   An IP packet encapsulated in another IP packet

ipconfig /all   Enables the MAC address information to be displayed from the command prompt

ipconfig   Command used to display the computer's address

IPng   The next generation IP

IPsec   IP security

IPsec   Used to encrypt data between various networking devices

IPv4   The IP version currently being used on the Internet

IPv6   IP version 6

IPX   Novell's Internetworking Packet Exchange networking protocol

ISAKMP   Internet Security Association and Key Management Protocol

IS-IS   Intermediate System to Intermediate System

ISM   Industrial, scientific, and medical

Isolating the Collision Domains   Breaking the network into segments where a segment is a portion of the network where the data traffic from one part of the network is isolated from the other networking devices

Isolator   An inline passive device that allows optical power to flow only in one direction

ISP   Internet service provider

Jamming   The wireless network is overwhelmed with wireless traffic, thereby jamming the network.

Keepalive Packet   Indicates that the Ethernet interface is connected to another networking device such as a hub, switch, or router

L2F   Layer 2 Forwarding

L2TP   Layer 2 Tunneling Protocol

Last Mile   The last part of the connection from the telecommunications provider to the customer

Layer 2 Switch   An improved network technology that provides a direct data connection for network devices in a LAN

Layer 3 Network   Another name for a routed network

LCL   Longitudinal Conversion Loss

LEAP   A wireless security system used by Cisco

Lease Time   The amount of time that a client can hold an IP address

LED   Light-emitting diode

Line of Demarcation   The point where ownership of the communications equipment changes from the communications carrier to the user

Link Integrity Test   Protocol used to verify that a communication link between two Ethernet devices has been established

Link Light   Indicates that the transmit and receive pairs are properly aligned

Link Pulses   Sent by each of the connected devices via the twisted-pair cables when data is not being transmitted to indicate that the link is still up

Link State Advertisement (LSA)   The exchange of updated link state information when routes change

Link State Protocol   Establishes a relationship with a neighboring router and uses route advertisements to build routing tables

Link   Point from one cable termination to another

Link-Local Address   Designed to be used for and is limited to communications on the local link

Local Area Network (LAN)   Network of users that share computer resources in a limited area

Logical Address   Describes the IP address location of the network and the address location of the host in the network

Logical Fiber Map   Shows how the fiber is interconnected and data is distributed throughout a campus

Long Haul   The transmission of data over hundreds or thousands of miles

Loopback   The data is routed directly back to the source

LTE/4G   LTE, or Long Tem Evolution, is a 4G Wireless communications standard. It has been designed to provide up to 10 times 3G network speeds.

MAC Address   A unique 6-byte address assigned by the vendor of the network interface card

Macrobending   Loss due to light breaking up and escaping into the cladding

Main Cross-connect (MC)   Usually connects two or more buildings and is typically the central telecommunications connection point for a campus or building. It is also called the main distribution frame (MDF) or main equipment room. The MC connects to Telco, an ISP, and so on. Another term for the MC is the campus distributor (CD).

Malware   Malicious programs

Managed Switch   Allows the network administrator to monitor, configure, and manage select network features

Management Information Base (MIB)   A collection of standard objects that are used to obtain configuration parameters and performance data on a networking device

Mbps   Megabits per second

MD5   Message Digest 5

Mechanical Splices   Two fibers joined together with an air gap, thereby requiring an index-matching gel to provide a good splice

Media Converter   Used to adapt a layer 1 (physical layer) technology to another layer 1 technology

Mesh Topology   All networking devices are directly connected to each other

Metro Ethernet Forum (MEF)   A nonprofit organization that defines Metro/Carrier Ethernet specifications

Metro Ethernet   An extension of the Ethernet infrastructure beyond one's internal network infrastructure

Microbending   Loss caused by very small mechanical deflections and stress on the fiber

Midspan (Mid-point) PSE   Used to provide power to a PD when a powered Ethernet port is not available

MIMO   A space-division multiplexing technique where the data stream is split into multiple parts called spatial streams

mm   Multimode

Mode Field Diameter   The actual guided optical power distribution, which is typically a micron or so larger than the core diameter; single-mode fiber specifications typically list the mode field diameter

MOU   Memorandum of understanding

MSA   Master service agreement

MSDS   Material safety data sheets

MT ACK   Message type acknowledgement, a DHCP ACK packet

MT Discover   Message type discover, a DHCP Discover packet

MT Offer   Message type offer, a DHCP offer packet

MT Request   Message type request, a DHCP request packet

Multicast Address   Data packets sent to a multicast address are sent to the entire group of networking devices, such as a group of routers running the same routing protocol

Multicast   Messages are sent to a specific group of hosts on the network

Multicasting   When one host sends data to many destination hosts

Multihomed   This means the customer has more than one Internet connection

Multilayer Switch (MLS)   Operates at layer 2 but functions at the higher layers

Multilevel Encoding   Technique used to reduce in the required bandwidth required to transport the data

Multimode Fiber   A fiber that supports many optical waveguide modes

Multiplexed   Combining data packets for transport

Multiport Bridge   Another name for a layer 2 switch

Multiport Repeater   Another name for a hub

Multiuser MIMO (MUMIMO)   Use of MIMO technology with eight spatial streams

MX (Mail Exchange) Record   Specifies the email handling server of the domain

MX Record   Mail Exchange

NAQC   Network Access Quarantine Control

NCP   Network Control Protocol

Near-end Crosstalk (NEXT)   A measure of the level of crosstalk or signal coupling within the cable, with a high NEXT (dB) value being desirable

NET   In ISIS, this is the Network Entity Title

netstat -r   The command used to obtain the routing table for a host PC computer

Network Address Translation (NAT)   Translates the private IP address to a public address for routing over the Internet

Network Address   Another name for the layer 3 address

Network Congestion   A slowdown on network data traffic movement

Network Interface Card (NIC)   The electronic hardware used to interface the computer to the network

Network Interface Layer   Defines how the host connects to the network

Network Layer   Accepts outgoing messages and combines messages or segments into packets, adding a header that includes routing information

Network Number   The portion of the IP address that defines which network the IP packet is originating from or being delivered to. Also another name for the IP subnet

Network Slowdown   Degraded network performance

Next Hop Address   The IP address of the next networking device that can be used to forward the data packet to its destination

NFPA   National Fire Protection Association

NLOS   Non-line-of-sight

nmap   A Linux port scanner

no shutdown (no shut)   Enables a router's interface

NOC   Network operations center

NS Record (Name Server)   Specifies the name of the authoritative name server of the domain

NS Record   A record that points to a name server

Numerical Aperture   A measure of a fiber's ability to accept light

Numerics   A numerical representation

OC   Optical carrier

OFDM   Orthogonal frequency division multiplexing

Optical Ethernet   Ethernet data running over a fiber link

Optical Spectrum   Light frequencies from the infrared on up

OSH Act   Occupational Safety and Health Act

OSHA Occupational Safety and Health Administration

OSI Model The seven layers describing network functions

OSI Open system interconnect

OSPF Open Shortest Path First routing protocol

OTDR Sends a light pulse down the fiber and measures the reflected light, which provides a measure of performance for the fiber

Outbound Data Traffic Data traffic leaving the network

Outsource To obtain goods or services from an outside source in place of an internal source

Overloading Where NAT translates the home network's private IP addresses to a single public IP address

Packet Filtering A limit is placed on the information that can enter the network

Packet Sniffing A technique in which the contents of data packets are watched

Paging Procedure Used to establish and synchronize a connection between two Bluetooth devices

Pairing When a Bluetooth device is set up to connect to another Bluetooth device

PAP Password Authentication Protocol

Passkey Used in Bluetooth Security to limit outsider access to the pairing

Password Cracking The attacker tries to guess the user's password

PCI DSS Payment Card Industry Data Security Standard

PD Powered Device

Peer Computer that uses and provides resources to the network

Peering How an agreement is made for the exchange of data traffic between large and small ISPs or between a router and its neighbor router

Peer-to-Peer Network All computers in the network provide similar services, including server functions.

Penetration Testing A way to evaluate the security of the user's network

permit ip any any The instruction added to the last line of an access list to allow all other data packets to enter and exit the router

Physical Fiber Map Shows the routing of the fiber but also shows detail about the terrain, underground conduit, and entries into buildings

Physical Layer Describes the media that interconnects networking devices

Physical Layer Provides the electrical and mechanical connection to the network

Piconet An ad hoc network of up to eight Bluetooth devices

Ping Command used to test that a device on the network is reachable

Platform as a Service (PaaS) Focuses on application development on any desired platform utilizing cloud computing

PoE Plus A new version of PoE based on IEEE 802.3at

Point of Presence (POP) The point where the customer connects the network data traffic to the communications carrier

Port Address Translation (PAT) A port number is tracked with the client computer's private address when translating to a public address

Port-based VLAN Host computers connected to specific ports on a switch are assigned to a specific VLAN

Ports The interface for the networking devices

Ports The physical input/output interfaces to the networking hardware

Power over Ethernet (PoE) Technology developed to supply power over the network cabling (CAT5 or better)

PPP Point-to-Point Protocol

PPTP Point-to-Point Tunneling Protocol

Prefix Length Notation   Another shorthand technique for writing the subnet mask except class boundaries are not being crossed

Presentation Layer   Accepts and structures the messages for the application

Private Addresses   IP addresses set aside for use in private intranets

Privileged Mode   Allows the router ports and routing features to be configured

Protocol   Set of rules established for users to exchange information

Protocol-Based VLAN   Connection to ports is based on the protocol being used

Proxy Server   Clients go through a proxy to communicate with secure systems

PSAACRF   Power-Sum Alien Attenuation Cross-talk Ratio Far-End

PSANEXT   Power-Sum Alien Near-End Crosstalk

PSE   Power Sourcing Equipment

Pseudorandom   The number sequence appears random but actually repeats

PTR Record (Pointer Record)   The reverse of an A record

Pulse Dispersion   Stretching of received pulse width because of multiple paths taken by the light

Radio Frequency Identification (RFID)   A technique that uses radio waves to track and identify people, animals, objects, and shipments

RADIUS   Remote Authentication Dial-In User Service

Range Extender   Device that relays the wireless signals from an access point or wireless router into areas with a weak signal or no signal at all

Ranging   A technique used by cable modems to determine the time it takes for data to travel to the cable head end

RAS   Remote access server

Received Signal Level (RSL)   The input signal level to an optical receiver

Refractive Index   Ratio of the speed of light in free space to its speed in a given material

Resistive Power Discovery   Looking for devices that support PoE and have a 25kΩ resistor connected between the transmit and receive pairs

Reverse Domain Name Service   Translation of an IP address to a name

RIP   Routing Information Protocol

RJ-45   The 8-pin modular connector used with CAT6/5e/5 cable

Roaming   The term used to describe a user's' ability to maintain network connectivity as he moves through the workplace

Rollover Cable   A cable with the signals reversed at each end

Root Servers   A group of servers that exist using well-known IP addresses that have been programmed into DNS servers

Route Flapping   Intermittent routes going up and down creating excessive LSA updates

route print   Produces same displayed result as netstat -r

Routed Network   Uses layer 3 addressing for selecting routes to forward data packets

Router Interface   The physical connection where the router connects to the network

router ospf [*number*]   The command used to enable OSPF routing

Router Uptime   The amount of time the router has been running

Router#   The pound sign indicates that the user is in the router's privileged EXEC mode.

Router(config)#   The prompt for the router's terminal configuration mode

Router(config-if)#   Indicates that you are in the router's interface configuration mode

Router(config-line)#   The prompt indicating you are in the router's line configuration mode

Routing Loop   Data is forwarded back to the router that sent the data packets

routing table code C   The router code for specifying a directly connected network

routing table code S   The router code for a static route

Routing Table   Keeps track of the routes to use for forwarding data to its destination

RS-232   Serial communications port

RX   Abbreviation for receive

Scattering   Caused by refractive index fluctuations; accounts for 96 percent of attenuation loss

SDS   Safety data sheets

Secure Address   The switch port will automatically disable itself if a device with a different MAC address connects to the port

Serial Port (S0/0, S0/1, S0/2,...)   Naming of the serial ports on the router

Session Layer   Provides the control functions necessary to establish, manage, and terminate the connections

SFP   Small Form Pluggable

SFTP   Secure File Transfer Protocol

SHA   The secure hash algorithm

SHA-1   Secure Hash Algorithm

Shared key Authentication   Both the client and the access point share a key called a pre-shared key (PSK).

show flash   Lists the details of the router's flash memory

show ip interface brief (sh ip int brief)   The command used to verify the status of the router's interfaces

show ip protocol (sh ip protocol)   Displays the routing protocol running on the router

show ip route (sh ip route)   The command that displays the routes and the routing address entry into the routing table

show ip route static (sh ip route static)   Limits the routes displayed to only static

show running-config (sh run)   The command that displays the router's running-configuration

show startup-config (sh start)   The command that displays the router's startup-configuration

show version   Lists the version of the Cisco IOS software running on the router

Single-mode Fiber   Fiber cables with core diameters of about 7–10 μm; light follows a single path

Site Survey   Performed to determine the best location(s) for placing the access point(s) to provide maximum RF coverage for the wireless clients

SLA   Service level agreement

Slotted Aloha   A wireless network communications protocol technique similar to the Ethernet protocol

sm   Single mode

SNMP (SNMPv1)   Simple Network Management Protocol

SNMPv2   Simple Network Management Protocol version 2

SNMPv3   Simple Network Management Protocol version 3

Social Engineering   A way for an intruder to obtain enough information from people to gain access to the network

Software as a Service SaaS   Focuses on the application component and delivery

SOHO   Small office or home office network

SONET/SDH   Synchronous optical network; protocol standard for optical transmission in long-haul communication/synchronous digital hierarchy

SOW   Statement of work

Spanning-Tree Protocol   A link management protocol that prevents looping and controls data flow over possible redundant data paths

SPF   Sender Policy Framework

Spoof   Inserting a different IP address in place of an IP packet's source address to make it appear that the packet came from another network

SRV (Service) Record   Used to identify a host (or hosts) that offers a specific type of service

SSID   Service set identifier

Star Topology   The most common networking topology in today's LANs where all networking devices connect to a central switch or hub

Stateful Firewall   Keeps track of the data packet flow

Stateful Packet Inspection (SPI)   Type of firewall that inspects incoming data packets to make sure they correspond to an outgoing request

Stateless address autoconfiguration (SLAAC)   Allows a server-less basic network configuration of the IPv6 computers

Static Addressing   The MAC address has been manually assigned to a switch port

Static Route   A data traffic route that has been manually entered into either a router's or a computer's routing table

Static VLAN   Basically a port-based VLAN

Store-and-Forward   The entire frame of data is received before any decision is made regarding forwarding the data packet to its destination.

STP   Shielded twisted pair

Straight-through Cable   The wire pairs in the cable connect to the same pin numbers on each end

Straight-through   Transmit and receive signal pairs are aligned end-to-end

STS   Synchronous transport signals

Stubby Areas   Do not accept routes from the Internet

Subnet Mask   Identifies the network/subnet portion of an IP address

Subnet, NET   Other terms for the segment

Supernets   The grouping of two or more class networks together; also called CIDR blocks

Switch Latency   The length of time a data packet takes from the time it enters a switch until it exits

Switch#   The prompt for the switch's privileged EXEC mode

Switch(config)#   The prompt for the switch's terminal configuration mode

Switch(config-line)#   The prompt indicating you are in the switch's line configuration mode

Switch   Forwards a frame it receives directly out the port associated with its destination address

SYN ACK   Synchronizing Acknowledgement packet

SYN   Synchronizing packet

T568A   Wire color guidelines specified under the EIA/TIA568B standard

T568B   Wire color guidelines specified under the EIA/TIA568B standard

Tagged-based VLAN   Used VLAN ID based on 802.1Q

TCL   Transverse Conversion Loss

TCO   Telecommunications outlet

TCP/IP   Transmission Control Protocol/Internet Protocol, the protocol suite used for internetworks such as the Internet

TCP   Transport Control Protocol

TCTL   Transverse Conversion Transfer Loss

Telco Cloud   The telecommunications carrier's switched network used to transport data to its destination; also used to describe the interconnected networks on the Internet

Telco   The local telephone company

Telecommunications Closet   The location of the cabling termination points that includes the mechanical terminations and the distribution frames

TIA   Telecommunications Industry Association

TKIP   Temporal Key Integrity Protocol

TLD   Top-level domain

Token Passing   A technique where an electrical token circulates around a network—control of the token enables the user to gain access to the network

Token Ring Hub   A hub that manages the passing of the token in a Token Ring network

Token Ring Topology   A network topology configured in a logical ring that complements the token passing protocol

Topology Change Notification (TCN)   Used to indicate that there has been a change in the switch

Topology Change Notification Acknowledgement (TCA)   An acknowledgement from another switch that the TCN has been received

Topology   Architecture of a network

Totally Stubby Areas   Use only a default route to reach destinations external to the autonomous system

TR   Another name for the telecommunications closet

Transceiver   A transmit/receive unit

Translation Bridge   Used to interconnect two LANs that are operating two different networking protocols

Transparent Bridge   Interconnects two LANs running the same type of protocol

Transport Layer Protocols   Define the type of connection established between hosts and how acknowledgements are sent

Transport Layer   Is concerned with message integrity between source and destination

Tunable Laser   Laser in which the fundamental wavelength can be shifted a few nanometers, ideal for traffic routing in DWDM systems

TX   Abbreviation for transmit

TXT Record   Used to hold arbitrary text information of the domain

Type-1 Hypervisor   This type of Hypervisor is loaded directly on the hardware to abstract the hardware to the virtualization layer and is commonly used on servers.

Type-2 Hypervisor   This type of Hypervisor is loaded on an operating system and abstracts the virtualization layer through its host operating system and is commonly used on personal computers.

UDP   User Datagram Protocol

Unicast Address   Used to identify a single network interface address, and data packets are sent directly to the computer with the specified IPv6 address

Unicast   The packet has a fixed destination.

U-NII   Unlicensed National Information Infrastructure

Uplink Port   Allows the connection of a switch to another r switch without having to use a crossover cable

User EXEC Mode   Used by a user to check to router status

User Mode   Same as the user EXEC mode

User-network Interface (UNI)   The demarcation point between the customer equipment and the service provider

V.44/V.34   The standard for all analog modem connections with a maximum data rate of up to 34Kbps; V.44 provides improved data compression, smaller file sizes that provide faster file transfers, and improved web browsing

V.92/V.90   The standard for a combination analog and digital modem connection with a maximum data rate of 56Kbps; V.92 provides a quick connect feature that cuts down on negotiation and handshake time compared to V.90

Variable Length Subnet Masking   Routes can be configured using different subnet masks

Variable Length Subnet Masks (VLSM)   Allows the use of subnet masks to better fit the needs of the network, thereby minimizing the waste of IP addresses when interconnecting subnets

Vertical Cavity Surface Emitting Lasers (VCSELs)   Lasers with the simplicity of LEDs and the performance of lasers

Virtual Private Network (VPN)   Establishes a secure network connection and is a way to protect your LAN's data from being observed by outsiders

Virtualization   A technology concept of creating a virtual computer

Virus   A piece of malicious computer code that, when opened, can damage your hardware, software, or other files

Visual Fault Locator (VFL) Device that shines light down the fiber to help locate broken glass

VLAN (Virtual LAN) A group of host computers and servers that are configured as if they are in the same LAN even if they reside across routers in separate LANs

VM Virtual machine

VMM Virtual Machine Monitor

vMotion, XenMotion, Live Migration Different vendor options for moving a virtual machine to another host server in the event of a physical server failure

VPN Virtual private network

War Driving Using wireless equipment to detect wireless management packets

Well-known Ports Ports reserved by ICANN

WEP Wired equivalent privacy

Wide Area Network (WAN) Uses the telecommunication network to interconnect sites that are geographically distributed throughout a region, the country, or the world

Wi-Fi Wi-Fi Alliance—an organization that tests and certifies wireless equipment for compliance with the 802.11x standards

WildCard Bits Used to match network IP addresses to interface IPs

WiMAX A broadband wireless system based on the IEEE 802.16e standard

Wire Speed Routing Data packets are processed as quickly as they arrive.

Wired Network Uses cables and connectors to establish the network connection

Wireless Network Uses radio signals to establish the network connection

Wire-map A graphical or text description of the wire connections from pin to pin

WLAN Wireless local area network

Work Area The location of the computers and printers, patch cables, jacks, computer adapter cables, and fiber jumpers

Workstation or Work Area Outlet (WO) Also called the TO (telecommunications outlet), it's used to connect devices to the cable plant. The cable type typically used is CAT3, CAT5, CAT5e, CAT6, CAT6A, and various coaxial cables. Devices typically connected to these outlets are PCs, printers, servers, phones, televisions, and wireless access points.

Worm A type of virus that attacks computers, typically proliferates by itself, and can deny service to networks

WPA Wi-Fi Protected Access

WPA Wi-Fi Protected Access

write memory (wr m) The command that saves your configuration changes to memory. This is the same as issuing the copy run start command, which is the most common command for saving your configuration.

xDSL A generic representation of the various DSL technologies that are available

XENPAK, XPAK, X2, XFP, SFP+ The ten gigabit interface adapter

Zero-dispersion Wavelength Point where the dispersion is actually zero

INDEX

Numbers

DoS (Denial of Service), 564

DDoS attacks, 566

directed broadcasts, 566

Smurf attacks, 565

spoofing attacks, 566

SYN attacks, 565

dotted-decimal format (IP addressing), 285

DS (Digital Signals), data channels, 468

DS-0 to DS-3 data rates, 468

DSL (Digital Subscriber Lines)

modems and home networks, 32

xDSL connections, 474

ADSL, 475-476

data rates, 475

services, 475

DSSS (Direct Sequence Spread Spectrum), 175

DSU ports, Cisco 2600 series routers, 242

DTE (Data Terminal Equipment), 347-348

DUAL Finite State Machine, EIGRP, 439

DWDM (Dense Wavelength Divison Multiplex), optical networks, 143

dynamic assignments (managed switches), 234

dynamic (private) ports, 266

dynamic routing protocols, 400

administrative distance, 414

convergence, 413

defining, 413

features of, 413

load balancing, 413

metrics, 413

path determination, 413

dynamic VLAN (Virtual Local Area Networks), 367

E

E1 data rates, 469

E3 data rates, 469

EAP (Emergency Action Plans), 628-629

EAP (Extensible Authentication Protocol), 201, 580, 592

eBGP (External BGP), 499

EBS (Excess Burst Size), 483

echo requests (ICMP protocol), 520

EDGE (Enhanced Data GSM Evolution), 198

EF (Entrance Facilities), cabling standards, 69

EIA (Electronic Industries Alliance)

defining, 68

EIA/TIA 568-A standard, 69

EIA/TIA 568-B standard, 69, 80

EIA/TIA 569-B standard, 69-71

EIGRP hybrid routing protocol, 400

administrative distance, 414

DUAL Finite State Machine, 439

Neighbor Discovery Recovery, 438

Protocol Dependent Modules, 439

route configuration, 439, 444

configure terminal (conf t) command, 440-441

router eigrp command, 440, 443

show ip int brief (sh ip int brief) command, 441

show ip protocol (sh ip protocol) command, 440-442

show ip route (sh ip route) command, 441-442

show run command, 441

RTP, 439

EIR (Excess Information Rate), 483

electrostatic interference and optical networks, 128

ELFEXT (Equal Level FEXT), 97

ELTCTL (Equal Level Transverse Conversion Loss), balanced data cabling, 101

Emergency Action Plans (EAP), 628-629

EMI (Electromagnetic Interference), 78

employee alarm systems, 632

enable command, privileged EXEC mode (Router#), 343

enable secret command

routers, 344, 350

switch configuration, 369

encapsulation (data), 471-472

F

gateway addresses, 247

gateway of last resort, static routing, 408

home networks, 30

GBIC (Gigabit Interface Converters), optical networks, 152

gigabit Ethernet cables, 78

glasses (optical networks), 144

GLBA (Gramm-Leach-Bliley Act), 635

graded-index fiber (optical networks), 135

GRE (Generic Routing Encapsulation) tunneling protocol, 580

guest machines (virtualization), 605

H

half-duplex cables, interconnecting LAN auto-negotiation process, 250

hand-offs, WLAN, 174

hardware addresses. *See* **MAC addresses**

harmonics, 473

hazard communication, 633

HC (Horizontal Cross-connects), 71

HDLC (High-Level Data Link Control) protocol, 470-471

"Hello" packets, 429

hexadecimal number conversion, 280-282

HF (High-Frequency) RFID tags, 197

Hierarchical topologies, campus networks, 71

HIPAA (Health Insurance Portability and Accountability Act), 635

home networks

access, 33

AP, 30

appearance, 33

broadband modems/gateways, 30

cable modems, 30

cost, 33

data speed, 33

DSL modems, 32

hubs, 26

implementing, 33

IP addresses, 36

network adapters, 26-29

PC Card adapters, 27

routers, 29-30

switches, 26-27

troubleshooting, 33

USB network adapters, 29

wired networks

advantages/disadvantages of, 24

broadband connections, 25

defining, 24

ISP, 25

LAN, 25

routers, 25

switches, 25

wireless networks

802.11x standards, 25

advantages/disadvantages of, 25

broadband connections, 25

defining, 24

hotspots, 35

IP addresses, 36

ISP, 25

LAN, 25

range extenders, 35

routers, 25

security, 35-37

switches, 25

wireless connection, 35

Wireless-N Notebook adapters, 28

hop counts, 413

distance vector protocols, 416

RIP, 424

hopping sequences, FHSS, 175

horizontal cabling, 70-73, 85, 89

host addresses. *See* **host numbers**

host machines (virtualization), 605

host numbers (IP addresses), 22

O

P

ping command, 15

data packet inspection, 519-520

defining, 47

hubs, 231

ICMP, 274

LAN tests, 47-48

personal firewalls, 568-571

routers, 350

switches, 232

plain text, 558

PoE (Power over Ethernet)

benefits of, 385

PD, 385-387

PoE Plus, 387

PSE

endpoint PSE, 385-386

midspan (mid-point) PSE, 385-386

Resistive Power Discovery, 387

switches, 385

polarization mode dispersion, 139-140

POP (Point of Presence), 470

portable fire extinguishers, 629-630

ports

analog modem ports, Cisco 2600 series routers, 242

associations, 223

auxiliary input

Cisco 2600 series router, 242

Cisco 2800 series router, 241

bridging tables, 222

CAM, 236

COM1, 330-331

COM2, 330-331

console port (routers), 329-331

defining, 11, 43

DSU ports, Cisco 2600 series routers, 242

dynamic (private) ports, 266

Ethernet ports, Cisco 2600 series routers, 242

Fast Ethernet ports

Cisco 2800 series routers, 240

router/interconnecting LAN connections, 245

HTTP ports, 267

HTTPS ports, 267

Linux ports, nmap, 560

office LAN assembly, 44

port number assignments, 267-268

port-based VLAN, 366

registered ports, 266

router ports. *See* routers and routing, interfaces

serial ports

Cisco 2600 series routers, 242

router/interconnecting LAN connections, 246

SSH ports, 267

straight-through ports, 44

switches and, 11

switch ports, 43, 234

TCP ports, 267-268

UDP ports, 267-268

USB ports. *See* USB interfaces

well-known ports, 266

PPP (Point-to-Point Protocol), 470-472, 477, 580

PPTP (Point-to-Point Tunneling Protocol), 580

preambles and Ethernet packet frames, 17

prefix length notation, 296

Presentation layer (OSI model), 14

presentation stage (forensics examinations), 577

printers (wireless), troubleshooting, 541

private addresses, 22, 286

private ports. *See* **dynamic (private) ports**

privileged EXEC mode (Router#), 343, 349-350

enable secret command, 344

Fast Ethernet interfaces, 346

hostname command, 344

Router(config-line)# prompt, 345-346

Router(config)# prompt, 345

serial interfaces, 347-349

privileged EXEC mode (Switch#), switch configuration, 368-369

propagation delay, cabling, 97

Protocol Dependent Modules, EIGRP, 439

S

USB network adapters and home networks, 29
user EXEC mode (Router>), 336-341
Utilization/Errors Strip chart, 501
UTP (Unshielded Twisted-Pair) cables, 67, 76-78, 83
  F/UTP cables, 100
  terminating, 80
  testing, 98

V

V.44/V.34 analog modem connection standard, 473
V.92/V.90 analog modem connection standard, 473
variable length subnet masks and static routing, 405
VCSEL (Vertical Cavity Surface Emitting Lasers), optical networks, 143
verifying network connections, office LAN assembly, 44
VFL (Visual Fault Locators), troubleshooting fiber optics, 538
VIC-4FXS/DID, Cisco 2800 series routers, 241
virtualization, 604
  advantages/disadvantages of, 606
  cloud computing, 617
    CNAME, 618
    IaaS, 618
    MX Record, 618
    outsourcing, 616
    PaaS, 619
    SaaS, 619
    SLA, 618
  defining, 605
  guest machines, 605
  host machines, 605
  Hypervisors, 606
  Mac OS, 607
  VM, 606-607
  VMM, 606
  Windows 8, 607-611, 614
  Windows 10, 607-611, 614

viruses, 562, 567
VLAN (Virtual Local Area Networks), 364
  advantages of, 366
  defining, 366
  dynamic VLAN, 367
  IP VLAN interface, 370
  port-based VLAN, 366
  protocol-based VLAN, 366
  static VLAN, 367, 371-375
  switches
    configure terminal (conf t) command, 368
    configuring, 368-376
    enable secret command, 369
    hostname command, 368-369
    line console passwords, 369-371
    no shutdown command, 370
    privileged EXEC mode (Switch#), 368-369
    show configuration commands, 371
    static VLAN configuration, 371-375
    Switch(config)# prompt, 369
    Switch(config-line)# prompt, 370
  tag-based VLAN, 366, 484
VLSM (Variable Length Subnet Masks) and OSPF protocol, 429
VM (Virtual Machines), 606-607
VMM (Virtual Machine Monitors), 606
vMotion, 607
voice interface cards (VIC2-4FXO) and Cisco 2800 series routers, 241
VPN (Virtual Private Networks), 36
  Cisco VPN Client, 585-588
  IP tunnels, 579
  remote access VPN, 580
    configuring remote client connections, 582-584
    server configuration, 582
  site-to-site VPN, 580
  tunneling protocols
    GRE, 580
    L2F protocol, 581

HVAC systems, 633

MSDS, 633

SDS, 633

workstations (cabling standards), 71

worms, 562

WPA (Wi-Fi Protected Access), 201, 592

WPS (Wi-Fi Protected Setups), 35

write memory (wr m) command, static route
configuration, 410

X

X2, optical networks, 153

xDSL (Digital Subscriber Line) connections, 474

ADSL, 475-476

data rates, 475

services, 475

XenMotion, 607

XENPAK, optical networks, 153

XFP, optical networks, 153

XPAK, optical networks, 153

Y-Z

Z-Term serial communications software and
routers, 333-334

zero-dispersion wavelength, dispersion and optical
networks, 140